Introduction to Classical Civilizations
CLA101
Andrew Graham

Custom Publication for
University of Toronto Mississauga -
Dept. of Historical Studies

McGraw Hill Custom Publishing

MCGRAW-HILL RYERSON LIMITED

Toronto Montréal Boston Burr Ridge, IL Dubuque, IA Madison, WI New York San Francisco
St. Louis Bangkok Bogotá Caracas Kuala Lumpur Lisbon London Madrid Mexico City Milan
New Delhi Santiago Seoul Singapore Sydney Taipei

The West in the World, Fourth Edition: Volume I: To 1715, by Dennis Sherman and Joyce Salisbury. *ISBN 0-07-736759-6.*

Western Civilization: Sources Images and Interpretations Volume 1 To 1700, by Dennis Sherman. *ISBN 0-07-738239-0.*

Published by McGraw-Hill, a business unit of the McGraw-Hill Companies, Inc., 1221 Avenue of the Americas, New York, NY, 10020. Copyright © 2011 by the McGraw-Hill Companies, Inc. All rights reserved.

Product Development Manager, Learning Solutions: Jason Giles
Project Manager, Learning Solutions: Katherine Gaskin

Copyright © 2011 by McGraw-Hill Ryerson Limited

No part of this publication may be reproduced, stored in a retrieval system, or transmitted, in any form or by any means, electronic, mechanical, photocopying, recording, or otherwise without prior written permission from McGraw-Hill Ryerson Limited.

ISBN-10: 0-07-094512-8
ISBN-13: 978-0-07-094512-8

Printed and bound in Canada

Table of Contents

The West in the World, Fourth Edition: Volume I: To 1715,
by Dennis Sherman

        List of Primary Source Documents 1

        List of Maps 2

        List of Features 3

Chapter 1   The Roots of Western Civilization 4

Western Civilization: Sources Images and Interpretations Volume 1 To 1700,
by Dennis Sherman

Chapter 1   Civilizations of the Ancient Near East 42

The West in the World, Fourth Edition: Volume I: To 1715,
by Dennis Sherman

Chapter 2   The Contest for Excellence 62

Western Civilization: Sources Images and Interpretations Volume 1 To 1700,
by Dennis Sherman

Chapter 2   The Emergence of Greek Civilization 97

The West in the World, Fourth Edition: Volume I: To 1715,
by Dennis Sherman

Chapter 3   The Poleis Become Cosmopolitan 109

Western Civilization: Sources Images and Interpretations Volume 1 To 1700,
by Dennis Sherman

Chapter 3   Classical and Hellenistic Greece 139

The West in the World, Fourth Edition: Volume I: To 1715,
by Dennis Sherman

Chapter 4   Pride in Family and City 157

Western Civilization: Sources Images and Interpretations Volume 1 To 1700,
by Dennis Sherman

Chapter 4			The Rise of Rome 187

The West in the World, Fourth Edition: Volume I: To 1715,
by Dennis Sherman

Chapter 5			Territorial and Christian Empires 198

Western Civilization: Sources Images and Interpretations Volume 1 To 1700,
by Dennis Sherman

Chapter 5			The Roman Empire and the Rise of Christianity 238

			Glossary 252

THINKING ABOUT DOCUMENTS

LIST OF PRIMARY SOURCE DOCUMENTS

1.1 An Egyptian Nobleman Writes His Obituary 16
1.2 King Solomon Secures His Realm's Fortune 28
1.3 Cambyses Conquers Egypt 35
2.1 Theseus Founds the City of Athens 56
2.2 A Playwright Reflects on the Meaning of Life 65
2.3 Ten Thousand Greek Mercenaries Return Home 72
3.1 Alexander Restores Greek Exiles 83
3.2 Cities Celebrate Professional Women 93
3.3 Judas Maccabeus Liberates Jerusalem 97
4.1 The Power of Public Opinion 113
4.2 Hannibal Triumphs at the Battle of Cannae 122
4.3 Conspirators Assassinate Julius Caesar 132
5.1 Augustus Tallies His Accomplishments 140
5.2 Diocletian Becomes "Lord" 154
5.3 Titus Destroys Jerusalem 164
6.1 The Huns Menace Rome 182
6.2 Christians Accept Caliph Umar's Terms 201
6.3 Shahrazád Mollifies a Murderous King 208
7.1 The Visigoths Lay Down the Laws 216
7.2 Charlemagne Promotes Educational Reforms 225
7.3 A Comet Predicts Disaster 228
7.4 Feudal Relationships Grow Complex 238
8.1 Guibert of Nogent Describes His Education 253
8.2 Princess Anna Komnene Writes of Byzantium's Troubles 270

9.1 Agnolo the Fat Survives the Plague 284
9.2 Joan of Arc Is Defiant 293
9.3 A Franciscan Missionary Goes to China 299
10.1 Isabella d'Este Implores Leonardo da Vinci to Paint for Her 315
10.2 Friar Savonarola Ignites a "Bonfire of the Vanities" 319
10.3 A Courtier Describes a Suspicious King—Louis the Spider 337
11.1 Germans Rage Against Papal Exploitation 351
11.2 Marie Dentière Defends Reformation Women's Rights 356
11.3 Ignatius Loyola Argues for Education as a Solution 363
12.1 Amerigo Vespucci Describes the New World 388
12.2 Thomas Mun Praises Trade 402
13.1 Bishop Bossuet Justifies Monarchical Absolutism 419
13.2 Louis XIV Describes Monarchical Rights and Duties 422
13.3 An Ambassador Describes the Dutch Government 445
14.1 Kepler and Galileo Exchange Letters About Science 456
14.2 Isaac Newton: God in a Scientific Universe 457
14.3 Concorcet Lauds the Power of Reason 466

THINKING ABOUT GEOGRAPHY

LIST OF MAPS

1.1 Mesopotamia and Egypt, ca. 2000 B.C.E. 7
1.2 The Ancient Near East, ca. 1450 B.C.E. 21
1.3 Mediterranean Coast in the First Millennium B.C.E. 29
1.4 The Assyrian Empire, ca. 662 B.C.E. 31
1.5 The Persian Empire, ca. 500 B.C.E. 34
2.1 The World of the Greeks 43
2.2 The Greek Colonies in About 500 B.C.E. 47
2.3 The Persian Wars, 490–479 B.C.E. 59
2.4 The Peloponnesian War, 431–404 B.C.E. 66
3.1 Alexander's Empire 81
3.2 The Successor States After the Death of Alexander, ca. 240 B.C.E. 85
4.1 Rome During the Republic 114
4.2 Italy, 265 B.C.E. 115
4.3 Expansion of the Roman Republic, 264–44 B.C.E. 121
5.1 City of Rome During the Empire 144
5.2 The Silk Road, ca. 200 C.E. 145
5.3 The Roman Empire, 44 B.C.E.–284 C.E. 146
5.4 Diocletian's Division of the Empire, 304 C.E. 155
5.5 Israel at the Time of Jesus 159
5.6 The Spread of Christianity to 311 C.E. 166
6.1 Germanic Invasions, Fifth Century 181
6.2 Justinian's Conquests, 554 193
6.3 The Byzantine Empire, Eighth Century 194
6.4 The Expansion of Islam to 750 200
6.5 Islam, ca. 1000 205
7.1 Anglo-Saxon Kingdoms, ca. 700 217
7.2 England in 886 219
7.3 The Empire of Charlemagne, ca. 800 221
7.4 Partition of the Carolingian Empire, 843–Treaty of Verdun 229
7.5 Invasions of Europe, Ninth and Tenth Centuries 230
8.1 German Migration Eastward 247
8.2 Trade Routes, Twelfth and Thirteenth Centuries 249
8.3 Medieval Universities 254
8.4 Medieval France, England, and Germany, Tenth Through Fourteenth Centuries 263
8.5 Christian Expansion in Iberia 264
8.6 The Early Crusades, 1096–1192 271
8.7 The Late Crusades, 1202–1270 273
9.1 The Spread of the Black Death 283
9.2 The Great Schism, 1378–1417 288
9.3 The Hundred Years' War, 1337–1453 291
9.4 The Mongol Empire, ca. 1300 298
9.5 The Ottoman Empire, 1300–1566 301
9.6 The Rise of Moscow, 1325–1533 302
10.1 Italy in 1454 317
10.2 The Venetian Empire in the Fifteenth Century 320
10.3 France in the Fifteenth and Sixteenth Centuries 336
11.1 Europe in 1526—Habsburg-Valois Wars 345
11.2 Religions in Europe, ca. 1600 362
11.3 The Thirty Years' War, 1618–1648 370
11.4 Europe, 1648 372
12.1 Exploration and Conquest, Fifteenth and Sixteenth Centuries 386
12.2 European Expansion, ca. 1700 390
12.3 Indigenous Peoples and Empires in the Americas, ca. 1500 392
13.1 France Under Louis XIV, 1661–1715 426
13.2 Central and Eastern Europe, 1648 428
13.3 Central and Eastern Europe, 1640–1725 430
13.4 The English Civil War, 1642–1649 437
13.5 The United Provinces and the Spanish Netherlands, 1609 444

LIST OF FEATURES

THINKING ABOUT ART
Egyptian Fresco, ca. 1295–1186 B.C.E. 22
Ezekias, Suicide of Ajax, Athenian Vase, ca. 450 B.C.E. 52
Trajan's Column 119
Wall Painting from a Baker's Shop in Pompeii, ca. 70 C.E. 150
Mosaics in San Vitale, Ravenna, Italy, 548 192
Saint Matthew, from a Gospel Book, ca. 700 218
Illumination from a Book of Hours, Fifteenth Century 296
Raphael, *School of Athens*, 1510–1511 332
Festival Scene Painted on a Screen, Mexico, ca. 1650 408
Louis le Nain, *The Cart*, 1641 417
Léonard Defrance, *At the Shield of Minerva*, 1781 473

THINKING ABOUT SCIENCE & TECHNOLOGY
Finding One's Way at Sea: The Invention of Latitude and Longitude 102
Catching the Wind: The Development of Windmills 246
Destruction and Amusement: The Development and Uses of Gunpowder 346

BIOGRAPHIES
Hatshepsut and Thutmose 24
Alcibiades 67
Arsinoë II 86
Publius Terentius Afer (Terence) 125
Melania the Younger 170
Avicenna (Ibn Sina) 206
Dhuoda, Bernard, and William 233
Ramón Lull 256
Vlad III Dracula (the Impaler), King of Wallachia 304
Isabella d'Este 314
Martin Guerre 348
Maria Sibylla Merian 405
Samuel Pepys 442
Jean-Jacques Rousseau 470

GLOBAL CONNECTIONS
Nubia: The Passage from the Mediterranean to the Heart of Africa 17
Transforming Science in Asia Minor 50
China's Han Dynasty and the Silk Road 145
Yemen: Monotheism Spreads to Southern Arabia 202
The 'Abbasid Caliphate and Charlemagne 224
The Inca Empire Falls 395
The Rise and Fall of the Mughal Empire in India 432

THE WORLD & THE WEST
The Ancient World, 700 B.C.E.–400 C.E. 38
Looking Ahead to the Middle Ages, 400–1400 174

TUTANKHAMEN'S GOLDEN THRONE, ca. 1322 B.C.E.

In this image from the burial of the boy-king Tutankhamen, the king sits on his throne as his wife, Akhsenamun, anoints him with scented unguent. Both bask in the rays of the holy sun-disk that they worshiped as a god. This colorful scene vividly captures the essential character of ancient Egypt and its people: the wealth and power of the god-kings; the importance of marriage and family ties; and the deep connection of the institutions of marriage and family with religion and longing for immortality. This image also reveals the power of written words—in this case, the hieroglyphs in the background—which allow us, millennia later, to read firsthand about the past and trace the developing story of the West.

The Roots of Western Civilization

The Ancient Middle East to the Sixth Century B.C.E.

"Since time immemorial, since the seedcorn first sprouted forth . . . [powerful men] have been in charge for their own benefit. The workingman was forced to beg for his bread; the youth was forced to work for others." In 2400 B.C.E., the Sumerian ruler Uruinimgina wrote these words as he took power in a Mesopotamian city. He claimed that his reforms freed citizens from usury, burdensome controls, hunger, theft, and murder—troubles that, in varying forms, have periodically plagued civilization since it first arose in cities. With his thoughtful policies and passionate sense of justice, Uruinimgina embodied another important characteristic of Western civilization: the occasional rise to power of people who strive to correct social injustice.

In the growing cities of Mesopotamia, Egypt, and the coast of the eastern Mediterranean Sea, other ideas developed that would also form the basis of civilization in the West. Societies practicing social stratification, sophisticated religious ideas, and concepts of law emerged in the same environment that spawned the social ills Uruinimgina briefly corrected. Perhaps most important, these early peoples invented writing, which preserved their cultures in the tablets and scrolls that reveal their world to us as we explore ancient cultures. The culture of the West was born in the Fertile Crescent of what we now know as the Middle East.

By the tenth century B.C.E., some states in the Fertile Crescent were able to create large, multinational empires, introducing a new political structure in the early history of the West. The Egyptians, Assyrians, Babylonians, and finally Persians established their rule over extensive areas and developed new ways of governing, as the concept of empire entered the Western consciousness.

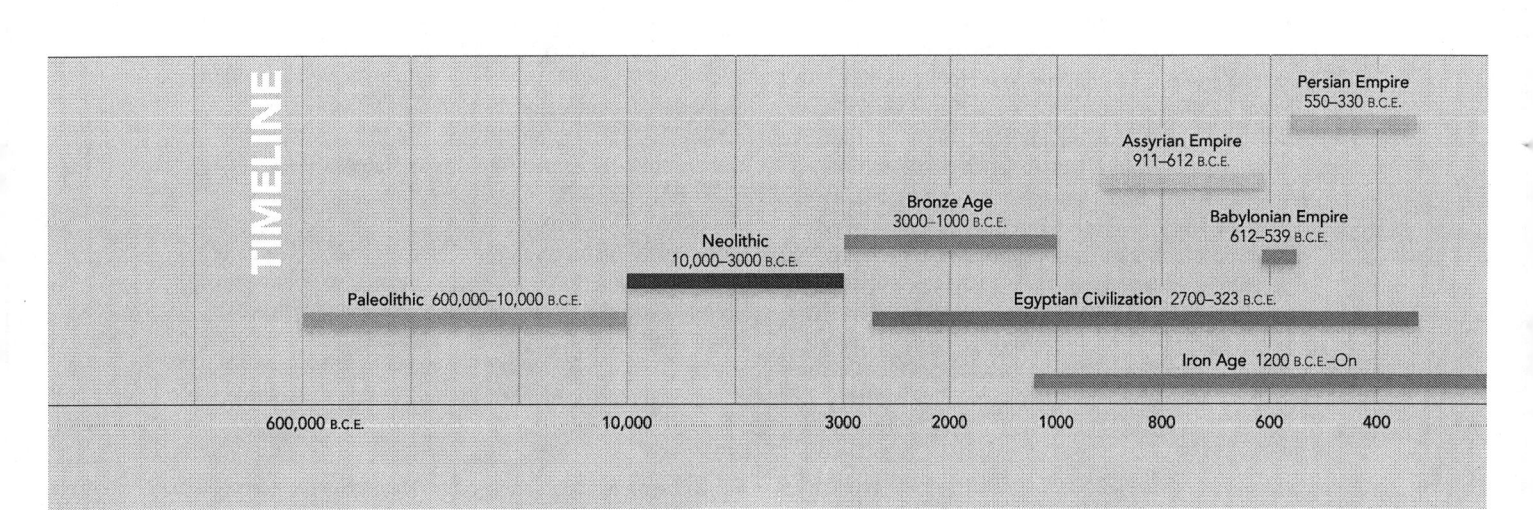

TIMELINE

- Paleolithic 600,000–10,000 B.C.E.
- Neolithic 10,000–3000 B.C.E.
- Bronze Age 3000–1000 B.C.E.
- Assyrian Empire 911–612 B.C.E.
- Persian Empire 550–330 B.C.E.
- Babylonian Empire 612–539 B.C.E.
- Egyptian Civilization 2700–323 B.C.E.
- Iron Age 1200 B.C.E.–On

600,000 B.C.E. | 10,000 | 3000 | 2000 | 1000 | 800 | 600 | 400

PREVIEW

BEFORE WESTERN CIVILIZATION
Study human prehistory through the Neolithic agricultural revolution.

STRUGGLING WITH THE FORCES OF NATURE: MESOPOTAMIA,
3000–ca. 1000 B.C.E.
Trace the history of societies of the Fertile Crescent.

RULE OF THE GOD-KING: ANCIENT EGYPT,
ca. 3100–1000 B.C.E.
Explore the rise and decline of ancient Egypt.

PEOPLES OF THE MEDITERRANEAN COAST,
ca. 1300–500 B.C.E.
Study the histories of the Phoenicians and the Hebrews.

TERROR AND BENEVOLENCE: THE GROWTH OF EMPIRES,
1200–500 B.C.E.
Examine the character and contributions of the Assyrian, Babylonian, and Persian Empires.

BEFORE WESTERN CIVILIZATION

In 2500 B.C.E., a Sumerian schoolboy wrote an essay about his struggles to learn reading and writing. He claimed in his essay that he practiced these skills in school all day, and he took his writing tablet home to his father, who praised the boy's progress. That night, the boy ate his dinner, washed his feet, and went to bed. The next day, however, he had a difficult time in school. He arrived late and was beaten for his tardiness and several other offenses, including poor handwriting. In despair, the boy invited the schoolmaster home to dinner. The father gave the teacher gifts, and the boy began having fewer problems in school.

This narrative, dating from 4,500 years ago, is perhaps most remarkable for its timeless themes. Tardy students, schools, and concerned parents are all a part of life for most of us today. Here, in the village of this young boy, we can find the roots of what we have come to call Western civilization (or "the West"). This term does not define one location but instead refers to a series of cultures that slowly evolved and spread to impact societies all over the world. Even 4,500 years ago, in the village of this Sumerian, we can identify certain characteristics that define Western civilization and that gave it an advantage—for better or worse—over competing cultures. Western civilization began in the Middle East, which enjoyed the striking advantage of having plants for agriculture and animals for domestication native to the region. Then large cities arose with attendant division of labor and social stratification based on relationships other than family. Another dramatic advantage was the development of writing, which gave schoolboys so much difficulty but allowed the preservation and transmission of advantageous developments.

Finally, one of the hallmarks of Western civilization was that it never developed in isolation. Throughout its recorded history, the peoples of the Mediterranean basin traded with other societies, and the resulting cultural diffusion strengthened all the cultures involved. For example, crops from the ancient Middle East spread westward as far as Britain as early as about 4000 B.C.E., and by the second millennium B.C.E., wheat, barley, and horses from the Middle East reached as far east as China. In fact, the trade routes from the Middle East to India and China, and west and south to Africa and Europe, have a permanence that dwarfs the accomplishments of conquerors and empire builders. These constant and fruitful interactions with other cultures perhaps gave Western civilization its greatest advantage.

> Trade

Yet, recorded history represents less than 1 percent of the time that humans have lived on the earth. Hundreds of thousands of years before this day in the life of a young, urban Sumerian, life for human beings was completely different. Before we begin the story of the development of Western civilization, we must explore the life of the first humans in the lush lands of sub-Saharan Africa.

Out of Africa: The Paleolithic Period, 600,000–10,000 B.C.E.

Human beings first appeared in sub-Saharan Africa hundreds of thousands of years ago. Archaeologists have classified the remains of these early humans into various species and subspecies, most of which were evolutionary dead ends. Modern humans belong to *Homo sapiens sapiens* ("thinking, thinking man"), a subspecies that migrated north and northeast from Africa. These earliest ancestors first appeared some 40,000 years ago and ultimately colonized the world. The first humans used tools made from materials at hand, including wood and bone, but the most useful tools were those made of stone. Initial stone tools were sharpened only roughly, but later humans crafted stones into finely finished flakes ideal for spearheads, arrowheads, and other blades. These tools have led archaeologists to name this long period of human prehistory the Old Stone Age, or the **Paleolithic.**

Throughout the Paleolithic, our ancestors were nomadic peoples living off the land as hunters and gatherers. This nomadic life involved small bands of people—about 30 to 40—who moved to follow the animals and the cycles of plant growth. A culture of hunters and gatherers prevents people from accumulating property, for whatever one owns must be portable, and that includes infants and small children. Anything extra is a burden, not a benefit. Paleolithic cultures also enjoyed a good deal of leisure time—indeed, estimates suggest that working four hours a day would usually generate enough food for a group. Of course, the ancient hunters and gatherers also faced famine if they exhausted the resources of a local area.

Our earliest human ancestors were also distinguished by their ability to use symbols to represent not only reality but also their hopes and fears. That is, the earliest humans created and appreciated what we call art. **Figure 1.1** shows a wonderful, tiny carving on mammoth tusk that was discovered in 2008 in Germany. Carbon dating places this figure between 35,000 and 40,000 years ago, making it the oldest piece of figurative sculpture in the world and demonstrating that art was one of the defining characteristics of humans. The 2.4-inch-tall carving shows a female figure that looks pregnant, and its creator seems to have designed it to be worn as a pendant. It was most likely intended as a sympathetic magic figurine to ensure fertility and perhaps safety in childbirth. This diminutive yet striking figure from the dawn of human history marks the beginning of symbolic thought expressed in sculpture, painting, and ultimately writing. These products of the human imagination serve to give us remarkably revealing windows on the past.

Paleolithic peoples developed their artistic skills over millennia, and the greatest expression of this ancient art survives in cave paintings from about 17,000 years ago. People returned seasonally to the same caves and painted new figures near, and sometimes over, earlier images. Some caves show evidence of repeated painting across an astonishing span of 10,000 years, revealing the preservation of traditions over lengths of time that are almost unimaginable today. These paintings probably coincided with the gathering of the small tribes of hunter-gatherers, and the movement of peoples and their goods shows that commerce joined art as a defining quality of early human societies.

Evidence from the late Paleolithic Age tells us that groups of humans returned seasonally to the same regions instead of wandering endlessly to new areas. As they traveled, kin groups encountered other clans and traded goods as well as stories. Archaeological evidence indicates that shells and especially stone tools were often traded in places far from their

Trade networks

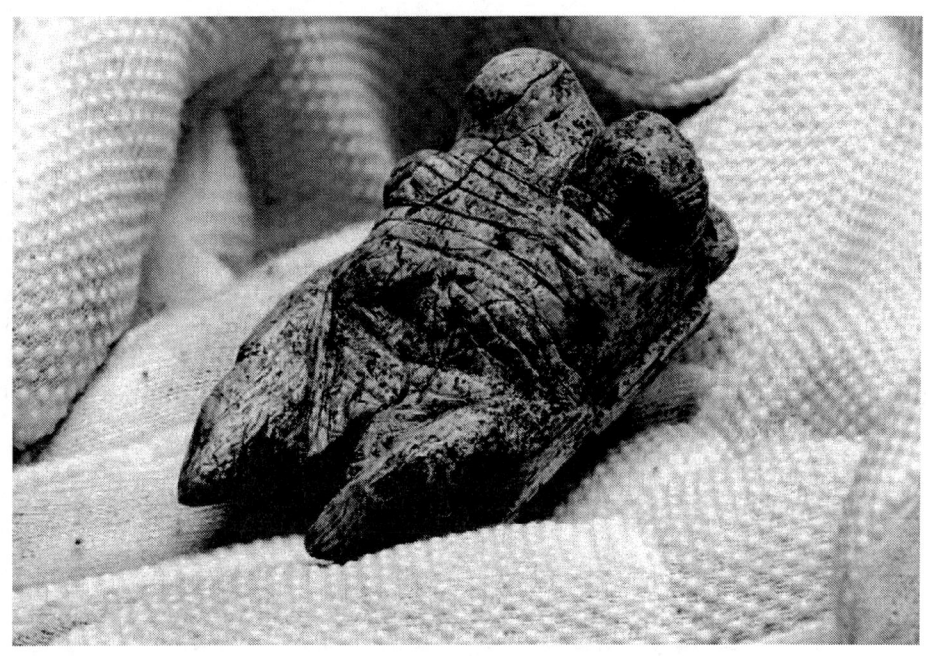

FIGURE 1.1 The World's Oldest Sculpture, ca. 33,000 B.C.E. This carving on mammoth tusk is the oldest figurative sculpture found to date. Showing a pregnant woman, it probably was a magic talisman for fertility.

original sites. For example, late Stone Age people living in what is now Scotland rowed small boats to an offshore island to bring back precious bloodstone that flaked accurately into strong tools. This bloodstone spread widely across northern Europe through trade with the original sailors. Commerce thus became established as an early human enterprise.

By the end of the Paleolithic Age (about 10,000 B.C.E.), the human population of Europe stood at about 20,000. These numbers may seem sparse by today's standards, but they suggest that *Homo sapiens sapiens* had gained a sturdy foothold on the European continent. By the late Stone Age, these early Europeans practiced agriculture and copper metallurgy, but their most enduring remains are huge stone monuments (called *megaliths*), of which Stonehenge in western England (shown in **Figure 1.2**) is probably the most famous. Stonehenge was built in stages over millennia beginning in about 7000 B.C.E., although most of the stones were erected about 3000 B.C.E. In its present form, it consists of about 160 massive rocks, some weighing up to 50 tons, which are arranged in concentric circles and semicircles. People moved the heavy stones long distances without using wheels, which were unknown in Europe at this time, and shaped many of them with only stone tools. Most scholars believe that the stones were carefully aligned to show the movements of the sun and moon. If this is so, the astonishing structure shows both a long tradition of studying the heavens and humans' impressive curiosity. Whatever the purpose of these stone structures that dot Europe, they all suggest highly organized societies that were able to marshal the labor

Stone monuments

FIGURE 1.2 Stone Age Monuments from Stonehenge, Southern England, ca. 7000–1500 B.C.E. These huge structures of stone, carefully shaped and moved long distances, testify to early human technical skill. The alignment of the stones suggests knowledge of the heavens gained from many years of observations.

needed for such complex building projects. (**Map 1.1** shows the range of the megaliths.)

However, although these early Europeans displayed some characteristics that would mark Western civilization—agriculture, a curiosity about nature, and a highly developed political structure—these great builders in stone lacked a critical component: writing. Although wisdom transmitted solely through memory can be impressive, it is also fragile, and thus engineering skills and astronomical knowledge of the earliest Europeans were lost. The real origins of Western civilization lay in the Middle East, where an agricultural revolution occurred that changed the course of human history, and where writing preserved the story of the developing West.

The Neolithic Period: The First Stirrings of Agriculture, 10,000–3000 B.C.E.

Sometime around 10,000 B.C.E., people living in what we call the Middle East learned how to plant and cultivate the grains that they and their ancestors had gathered for millennia. With this skill, humankind entered the **Neolithic** era, or the New Stone Age. Agriculture did not bring complete improvement in people's lives compared to hunting and gathering. Diets were often worse (with a reliance on fewer foods), sewage and animal wastes brought more health problems, and farming was a lot of work. People adopted this way of life because the environment changed, but once people learned how to plant crops instead of simply gathering what grew naturally, human society changed dramatically.

Just as people discovered how to control crops, they also began to domesticate animals instead of hunting them. Dogs had been domesticated as hunting partners during the Paleolithic, but around 8500 B.C.E., people first domesticated sheep as a source of food. Throughout the Middle East, some people lived off their herds as they traveled about looking for pasturage. Others lived as agriculturalists, keeping their herds near stationary villages.

`Domestic animals`

These two related developments—agriculture and animal domestication—fostered larger populations than hunting and gathering cultures, and gradually agricultural societies prevailed. In large part, the success of the Western civilization in eventually spreading throughout the world lay in its agricultural beginnings in the Middle East. Why were people in this region able to embrace agriculture so successfully? The main answer is luck—the Middle East was equipped with the necessary resources.

Of the wealth of plant species in the world—over 200,000 different varieties—humans eat only a few thousand. Of these, only a few hundred have been more or less domesticated, but almost 80 percent of the world's human diet is made up of about a dozen species (primarily cereals). The Middle East was home to the highest number of the world's prized grains, such as wheat and barley, which are easy to grow and contain the highest levels of protein. By contrast, people who independently domesticated local crops in other regions did not enjoy the same abundance.

`Middle East plants and animals`

The Middle East maintained the same advantage when it came to animals for domestication. Very few species yield to domestication; beyond the most common—dogs, sheep, goats, cows, pigs, and horses—there are only a few others—from camels to reindeer to water buffalo. Because domesticated animals provide so many benefits to humans—from food to labor—the distribution of animals fit for domestication helped determine which societies would flourish. Most of these animals were confined to Europe and Asia, and seven—including goats, sheep, and cattle—were native specifically to the Middle East. With these resources, the people of the Middle East created civilization, which quickly spread east and west (along with valuable crops and animals).

With the rise of agriculture, some small kin groups stopped wandering and instead slowly settled in permanent villages to cultivate the surrounding land. As early as 8000 B.C.E., Jericho (see **Map 1.1**) boasted about 2,000

`Population growth`

thinking about
GEOGRAPHY

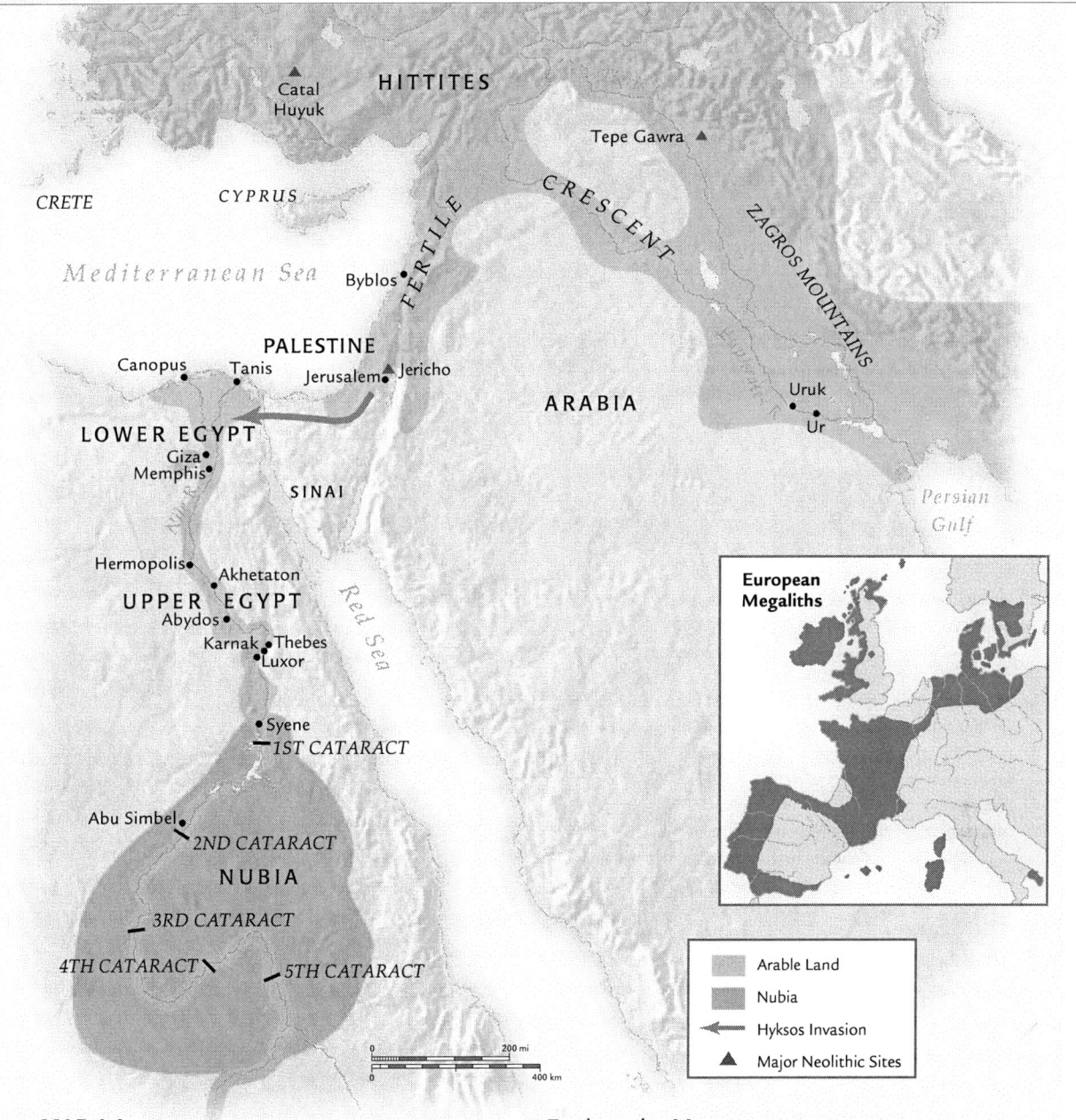

MAP 1.1

Mesopotamia and Egypt, ca. 2000 B.C.E.

This map illustrates the cradles of Western civilization in Mesopotamia (the Fertile Crescent), along the coast of the Mediterranean Sea, and in Egypt. It also identifies this region's major Neolithic sites, which may be contrasted with the locations of the European stone monuments (megaliths) in western Europe shown on the inset.

Explore the Map

1. What advantages did the locations of the rivers provide to the growing cultures?
2. How do the distances between the European megaliths (stone monuments) and Mesopotamia support the view that these cultures developed independently?
3. How did Nubia serve geographically to connect the Mediterranean world with sub-Saharan Africa?

people who lived in round huts scattered over about 12 acres. Human social forms broadened from small kin groups to include relative strangers. The schoolboy whom we met earlier had to make a point of introducing his teacher to his father. This effort would have been unheard of in the small hunting clans of the Paleolithic.

Agriculture also sparked a major change in values. Since people no longer had to carry everything they owned as they traveled, farming, animal husbandry, and fixed settlement led to the accumulation of goods, including domesticated animals. Consequently, a new social differentiation arose in agricultural villages as some people acquired more belongings than others.

The social stratification that arose in the earliest cities included slavery as part of what people thought of as the natural order of things. **Slavery** There were various ways to become a slave in ancient Middle Eastern society. Sometimes economic catastrophe caused parents to sell their children or even themselves into slavery to repay their debts, and children born to slaves were automatically enslaved. Although slavery was part of ancient societies, it was a slavery that could be fairly fluid—unlike the slavery of the early modern world, it was not a racial issue. Slaves could save money to purchase their freedom, and children born of a freewoman and a slave were free. Ancient slavery, while taken for granted, was based on an individual's bad luck or unfortunate birth, so a servile status did not hold the severe stigma it later would acquire.

The accumulation of goods also changed the nature of warfare. Although hunter-gatherers fought over territory at times, the skir- **New warfare** mishes tended to be short-lived and small scale because the individuals involved were too valuable to waste through this sort of conflict. The agricultural revolution pushed warfare to a larger scale. With the population increase that the revolution fueled, there were more people to engage in conflict and more rewards for the winners, who could gain more goods and enslave the losers. Excavations have shown that the early settlement of Jericho was surrounded by a great stone wall about three yards thick—one of the earliest human-made defensive structures. Indeed, people must have greatly feared their neighbors to invest the labor needed to build such a wall with only stone hand tools. Settlements arose throughout the Neolithic in Europe and in Asia Minor (as well as in many regions in Asia), but the mainstream in the story of the West arose farther east in a river valley where writing preserved the details of the development of even larger and more sophisticated cities.

STRUGGLING WITH THE FORCES OF NATURE: MESOPOTAMIA, 3000–ca. 1000 B.C.E.

Between 3000 and 1000 B.C.E., people began to cultivate a broad curve of land that stretched from the Persian Gulf to the shores of the Mediterranean (**Map 1.1**). This arc, the Fertile Crescent, has been called the cradle or birthplace of Western civilization. It earned this appellation in part because of its lucky possession of essential plants and animals and its central location, which placed it at a crossroads, for mingling of ideas and peoples. The **Bronze Age** ancient Greeks called this region Mesopotamia, or "land between the rivers," emphasizing the importance of the great Tigris and Euphrates rivers to the life of the area. The earliest cities in which civilization took root were located in the southern part of Mesopotamia. During the late Neolithic period, people living in this region used agriculture; sometime after 3000 B.C.E., they learned to smelt metals to make tools and weapons. By smelting, they developed a process to combine copper and tin to make a much stronger metal, bronze. At last, there was a substance that improved on stone, and archaeologists note this innovation by calling this period the Bronze Age.

Life in southern Mesopotamia was harsh but manageable. Summer temperatures reached a sweltering 120 degrees Fahrenheit, and the region received a meager average rainfall of less than 10 inches a year. Yet the slow-running Euphrates created vast marshlands that stayed muddy and wet even during the dry season. Villagers living along the slightly higher ground near the marshes poled their boats through the shallow waters as they netted abundant river fish and shot waterfowl with their bows and arrows. Domesticated cattle and sheep grazed on the rich marsh grass while agriculturalists farmed the fertile high ground, which was actually made up of islands in the marshland. The villagers used the marsh reeds as fuel and as material to make sturdy baskets, and they fashioned the swamp mud into bricks and pottery.

The Origins of Western Civilization

In about 3000 B.C.E., a climate change occurred that forced the southern Mesopotamians to alter their way of life. As they did so, they created a more complex society that we call Sumerian—the earliest civilization. Starting around 3200 B.C.E., the region became drier. The rivers no longer flooded as much of the land as before, and more and more of the marshes evaporated. When the rivers flooded, they still deposited fertile soil in the former marshlands, but the floods came at the wrong times of the year for easy agriculture. Fed by the melting snows in the Zagros Mountains (see **Map 1.1**), the Tigris flooded between April and June—a time highly inconvenient for agriculture in a region where the growing season runs from autumn to early summer. Furthermore, the floods were unpredictable; they could wash away crops still ripening in the fields or come too early to leave residual moisture in the soil for planting. Men and women had to learn how to use the river water efficiently to maintain the population that had established itself during centuries of simpler marsh life. Now people began to dig channels to irrigate the dry land and save the water for when they needed it, but these efforts were never certain because the floods were unpredictable. Mesopotamians developed an intense pessimism that was shaped by the difficult natural environment of the land between the rivers, which could bring seemingly random abundance or disaster.

To manage the complex irrigation projects and planning required to survive in this unpredictable environment, the Sumerians developed a highly organized society— **Administration** they worked hard to bring order to the chaos that seemed to surround them. Their resourcefulness paid off; by 3000 B.C.E., the valley had become a rich food-producing area. The population of Uruk, shown on **Map 1.1**, had expanded to nearly 10,000 by about 2900 B.C.E. Neighbors no longer knew each other, and everyone looked to a centralized administration to organize daily life.

Priests and priestesses provided the needed organization. In exchange, these religious leaders claimed a percentage of the land's produce. With their new wealth, they built imposing temples that dominated the skylines of cities like Uruk and Ur. **Figure 1.3** is a modern-day photograph of one of those temples, which was built about 2100 B.C.E. The temple shown here consists of levels of steps that were designed to lead the faithful up toward heaven. Known as a **ziggurat**, the structure was intended to bridge the gap between gods and humans. These huge structures were located in a temple complex that spanned several acres. A statue of a god or goddess was placed in a sacred room at the top, and after priests and priestesses conducted a ritual dedication of the statue, people believed the deity dwelled symbolically within the temple, bringing blessings to the whole community. The scale and wealth committed to the ziggurat revealed the dominant role that religion played in the Sumerians' lives.

Ziggurats also served as administrative and economic centers of cities, with storehouses and administrative rooms housed in the lower levels. They were bustling places as people came to bring goods and socialize with neighbors. Just as religion was **Economic functions** at the center of the Sumerian world, these buildings, rising like mountains out of the mud plains, served as the center of city life.

FIGURE 1.3 Ziggurat at Ur, ca. 2100 B.C.E. The great mud-brick temples known as ziggurats rose from the flat landscapes of Mesopotamia. The builder wrote that he was ordered to erect this ziggurat by his god Marduk. The structure shows both the power of religion and the skill of builders in this cradle of Western civilization.

The labor and goods of the local men and women belonged to the deity who lived in the inner room at the top of the temple. In one temple dedicated to a goddess, attendants washed, clothed, and perfumed the statue every day, and servants burned incense and played music for the statue's pleasure. Meanwhile, temple administrators organized irrigation projects and tax collection in the cities to foster the abundance that allowed the great cities to flourish and serve their patron deities. Through these centralized religious organizations, ancient loyalties to family and clan were slowly replaced by political and religious ties that linked devoted followers to the city guarded by their favored deity. This was a crucial step in creating the large political units that were to become a hallmark of Western civilization.

Life in a Sumerian City

In the shadow of the ziggurats, people lived in mud-brick houses with thick walls that insulated them from heat, cold, and noise. Women and slaves prepared the family meals, which consisted mostly of barley (in the south) or wheat (in the north). Vegetables, cheese, fish, figs, and dates supplemented the Sumerian diet. A large portion of the calories people consumed came from ale. Forty percent of all the grain grown in the region was brewed for ale by women in their homes, not only for their family's consumption but also for sale.

Although Mesopotamia offered early settlements the significant advantage of indigenous plants and animals, the area had some severe shortages. The river valleys lacked metal and stone, which were essential for tools and weapons. The earliest settlements depended on long-distance trade for these essential items, and soon the wheel was invented to move cartloads of goods more easily. Materials came from Syria, the Arabian peninsula, and even India, and Mesopotamian traders produced goods for trade. The most lucrative products were textiles. Traders transported woven wool great distances in their quest for stone, metal, and, later, luxury goods. Mesopotamian goods, animals, and even plants moved slowly as far as China as the ancient cultures of the Eurasian land embarked on mass trade. The essential trade routes that marked the whole history of Western civilization appeared at the dawn of its inception.

In the bustling urban centers, families remained the central social tie. Parents arranged marriages for their sons and daughters and bound the contract with an exchange of goods that women brought to the marriage as their dowry. The earliest written laws regulated married life in an attempt to preserve public peace through private ties. Adultery was a serious crime punished by death, but divorce was permitted. If a woman who was above reproach as a wife wished a divorce, she could keep her dowry. If, however, a wife neglected her home and acted foolishly in public, she would lose her dowry. Her husband could then insist that she remain as a servant in his house even when he remarried. The laws also recognized that men kept concubines in addition to their legal wives and provided ways for children of such informal unions to be considered legitimate. All these laws attempted to preserve the family as an economic unit and as the central social unit in a complex, changing society.

Sumerian women worked in many shops in the cities—as wine sellers, tavern keepers, and merchants. Some women were prostitutes, although in time Sumerians came to view this profession as a threat to more traditional ties. Late in Mesopotamian history, laws arose that insisted on special clothing to distinguish "respectable" women from prostitutes. Ordinary women were expected to veil their heads in public, whereas prostitutes and slaves were forced to go about their day with bare heads. At the end of Mesopotamian ascendancy, these laws were made extremely strict—any slave woman who dared to wear a veil was punished by having her ears cut off. In this society, in which people did not know one another, city residents strove mightily to distinguish social ranks. City life came with increasing emphasis on social stratification as the cornerstone of urban order.

Gods and Goddesses of the River Valley

The men and women of the Tigris-Euphrates river valley believed that all parts of the natural world were invested with will. For example, if a river flooded, the event was interpreted as an act of the gods. People also viewed intercity warfare as a battle between each city's gods. On a broader level, the Sumerians saw themselves and their deities as combatants locked in a struggle against a mysterious chaos that could destroy the world at any moment—just as sometimes the unpredictable rivers flooded and brought destruction. People viewed themselves as slaves of the gods and provided the deities with everything they needed—from sacrifices to incense to music—to try to keep order in their uncertain world. In spite of their appeasements, however, when disorder appeared in the form of natural disasters or disease, the pessimistic Sumerians were not surprised.

In addition to venerating their city's patron, Sumerians in time invested their universe with a bewildering number of demons who needed placating. Demons caused illness, and magicians or priests—rather than physicians—were called on for cures. To understand the world, priests tried to read the future in the entrails of animals (a practice known as **augury**). Magic, omens, and amulets rounded out the Mesopotamian religious world, as people struggled to try to control what seemed to be a world in which people owed everything to capricious deities.

An anonymous Sumerian poem of despair expresses the anxiety that came with this view of religious responsibility. In this poem, a once-prosperous man suffers a reversal of fortune. He laments:

> My ill luck has increased, and I do not find the right.
> I called to my god, but he did not show his face,
> I prayed to my goddess, but she did not raise her head.

The man seeks out diviners and dream priests, but no one can tell him the omission that brought about his downfall. In his despair, he can only hope that continued devotion to the gods will restore his prosperity, but his tone is not optimistic.

Neither the Sumerians nor their eventual conquerors envisioned an attractive afterlife. They believed that the spirits of the dead went to a shadowy, disagreeable place from where they might occasionally affect the living, usually for ill. Sumerians' only hope for happiness lay in the present life, and that happiness hinged on capricious deities who cared little for humans.

These beliefs prevailed in the Fertile Crescent from the fourth millennium B.C.E. up to the middle of the first millennium B.C.E., even as conquests changed the prevailing rulers. During that time, conquerors made a conscious effort to appease the local deities, and this

FIGURE 1.4 King Sargon and His Daughter, Enheduanna, ca. 2350 B.C.E. Sargon used religion to unite the people of his empire, and his daughter served as high priestess of both the Akkadian and the Sumerian goddesses. She is shown in the inset (second figure from the left) worshiping at an altar.

accommodation serves as a model for the continuing interchange of ideas that was one of the strengths of Western culture. For example, when the Akkadian ruler Sargon invaded Sumer in about 2350 B.C.E., he had to facilitate peace among the Akkadian northerners and the Sumerian southerners. The bronze head probably depicting Sargon shown in **Figure 1.4** was designed to show the power of this great king. His long beard, carefully curled, was a symbol of masculine strength, and he wears a band around his head showing his royal office.

Sargon chose religion as the key to uniting the people and appointed his daughter Enheduanna as high priestess of both the Akkadian and Sumerian goddesses. In the inset in **Figure 1.4**, the priestess (the second figure from the left) is shown wearing the elaborate clothing appropriate to her rank, surrounded by her attendants as she moves to the altar to worship. Enheduanna wrote beautiful hymns (which have survived to the present) in which she identified the Sumerian goddess Inanna with her Akkadian counterpart, Ishtar. She proved so successful in reconciling goddesses in this way that Sargon's successors continued the practice of making their daughters high priestesses, thus forging a link between the cultures of the region. As kings began to handle earthly administration, sky gods became more crucial in the heavenly hierarchy. Fearsome war gods like Marduk sometimes demanded human sacrifices in exchange for victory over invading tribes. The heavenly hierarchy grew more elaborate and demanding.

By the third millennium B.C.E., earthly society in the ancient Middle East mirrored the hierarchical heavenly one. Kingship was universally accepted as the correct political order, and castes of nobles and priests were also deemed natural. Inequality among people was seen as normal and theologically justified, and people accepted their place in this highly ordered world with kings on top and slaves on the bottom. Individuals' longings for social justice and hopes for improving their situations all took place within a frame of reality that was very different from ours—one that assumed inequality was natural.

Sometime during the second millennium B.C.E., the Sumerians began to reflect on individuals' relationships with the gods. Instead of being content with a corporate association between a city and its guardian, some men and women looked to a more personal alliance, just as the despairing poet we met earlier cried out for a divine explanation of his plight. This longing led individuals to ponder the concept of immortality, wondering whether death was avoidable. In the celebrated poem *The Epic of Gilgamesh*, the poet articulates this search for meaning in death while telling an engaging story of a Sumerian hero and his fortunes. This is an early example of an important literary genre called the epic of quest. Gilgamesh (shown in **Figure 1.5**) was a king who ruled Uruk (see **Map 1.1**) in about 2700 B.C.E. Sometime after 2000 B.C.E., stories about the by-then semimythical king were collected and written down in the epic. In one version of Gilgamesh's adventures, his best friend, Enkidu, is killed and the reality of death strikes home. Gilgamesh refuses to bury Enkidu; in his grief he is unwilling to give up his friend. When the reality of decomposition confronts the king, he travels to find the secret of immortality. At the bottom of the sea he finds a plant that will give eternal life, only to see the magic herb stolen by a snake before he can bring it back to Enkidu. Gilgamesh is left facing the reality of death and the equally important reality of the value of finding joy in the present. This pessimistic epic once again reveals the Sumerian assumption that humans are doomed to struggle endlessly in a difficult universe.

Individual longings

The carving of Gilgamesh shown in **Figure 1.5** was made in the eighth century B.C.E. and shows the enduring popularity of the Sumerian legend. Here Gilgamesh is shown with the long curled beard of a king—which looks remarkably like Sargon's in **Figure 1.4**. The captured lion illustrates his hunting prowess. These characteristics of kings—power and strength—persist through the ancient world.

FIGURE 1.5. Gilgamesh, eighth century B.C.E. *The Epic of Gilgamesh*, preserved on cuneiform tablets, is the oldest surviving epic poem, ca. 2000 B.C.E. This image of Gilgamesh holding a conquered lion reveals how visual illustrations served to remind people of their treasured literature.

The Development of Writing

Although religion dominated Mesopotamian thought, the Sumerians' real impact on the future of Western civilization derived from their more practical inventions. As Mesopotamian cities expanded and grew wealthy, the need arose for a system of keeping records that would prove more enduring and accurate than the spoken word. In response, the Sumerians developed a system of writing. Some scholars believe that writing first emerged from a system of trade tokens. For example, if a merchant wanted to verify the number of sheep someone else was supposed to deliver, he would count out tokens to represent the sheep and seal them in a clay envelope that would be broken open upon delivery. The tokens left an imprint in the clay, and in time people realized that they could omit the tokens entirely and simply mark the clay.

At first, Sumerian writing consisted of stylized pictures of the objects represented—birds, sheep, or bowls to signify food. Soon the characters became more abstract and indicated sounds as well as objects. By 2800 B.C.E., the Sumerians had developed a sophisticated writing system called **cuneiform** (named from the Latin word that means "wedge"). Scribes imprinted wedge-shaped characters into wet clay tablets, which became highly durable when dried. **Figure 1.6** shows a tablet of cuneiform script made in about 2600 B.C.E., which lists quantities of various commodities.

> Cuneiform

Scribes labored for many years to memorize the thousands of characters of cuneiform script. By 2500 B.C.E., scribal schools had been established to train the numerous clerks needed to serve the palaces and temples. Some surviving cuneiform tablets reveal that these students also studied mathematics and geometry. At first, girls attended these scribal schools, and records testify to a number of successful female scribes. Later, however, the occupation became exclusively male, but the reasons for this change have been lost. The schoolboy described at the beginning of this chapter was one of the lucky few who were trained to read and write. Anyone possessing these skills was assured a prosperous future.

Most of the Sumerian tablets that have been excavated refer to inventories, wills, contracts, payrolls, property transfers, and correspondence between monarchs. Such content reflects both the complexity of this civilization and the everyday necessity of tracking economic transactions. However, writing also let people record more abstract subject matter. *The Epic of Gilgamesh* and other myths preserved the dreams and hopes of these early civilizations, and the hymns of the priestess-poet Enheduanna attest to their spiritual longings and aesthetic sensibilities. However, beyond providing us a glimpse of this long-lost civilization, the invention of writing gave Western culture a distinct advantage over societies that depended only on human memory to recall their achievements. Writing enabled the transfer and dissemination of knowledge, which allowed people to build on previously acquired advancements instead of continually rediscovering and relearning the same material.

> Written records

Laws and Justice

Writing also fostered the emergence of another element that would remain an essential component of Western civilization: a written law code. Recording laws in writing was an attempt to establish order in the land between the rivers that seemed so susceptible to chaos. But these laws also tried to express principles of justice that outlasted the ruler who issued them. As early as 2500 B.C.E., Uruinimgina tried to reform his society by passing laws that protected the powerless while preserving the socially stratified society that all took for granted. This tradition continued throughout Mesopotamian history and formed a powerful precedent for subsequent civilizations. In about 2100 B.C.E., Ur-Nammu, king of Ur, wrote laws to preserve "the principles of truth and equity."

The most famous and complete of the ancient law codes was that of the Babylonian king Hammurabi (ca. 1792–1750 B.C.E.), who ruled the southern Mesopotamian valley. In the prologue to his law code, which is preserved in cuneiform script on a stone column, the king expressed the highest principles of justice: "I established law and justice in the language of the land and promoted the welfare of the people." Studying Hammurabi's code, which was a compilation of existing laws, opens a window into the lives of these ancient urban dwellers. It regulated everything from family life to physicians' fees to building requirements. The king seemed determined to order his society, for he introduced harsh penalties that had been absent from earlier laws. His code literally demanded an "eye for an eye"—one law stipulated that "should a man destroy another's eye, he shall lose his own." Another stated that a son who strikes his father shall have his hand cut off.

Hammurabi's code clearly expressed the strict social hierarchy that Mesopotamian society counted as natural. The laws specified different penalties for the three social orders: elites, freemen, and slaves. The elites included everyone from officials to priests and warriors. Beneath them were freemen, including artisans, merchants, professionals, and some farmers. Slaves occupied the bottom stratum, but they, too, had some rights under Hammurabi's laws—for example, they might own land and marry free persons. Many of the laws sought to protect the powerless so, as the prologue says, "that the strong may not oppress the weak."

Many laws tried to protect women and children from unfair treatment and limited the authority of husbands over their households. For example, women could practice various trades and hold public positions. Husbands could not accuse their wives of adultery without proof, for the penalty for proven adultery was harsh—the adulterous wife and her lover would be drowned. However, a woman could obtain a divorce from her husband. In spite of these protections, women still remained largely the property of their husbands. For example, a woman could be put to death for entering—without her husband—a facility that served alcoholic beverages. Furthermore, a wife's fortunes were so dependent upon her husband that he could even sell her into slavery to pay his debts.

Perhaps one of the most significant things about Hammurabi's code was that the king intended his laws to outlast his own rule. On the tablet, he inscribed: "For all future time, may the king who is in the land observe the words of justice which I have written upon my monument!" Writing, and written law in particular, gave kings and reformers like Hammurabi hope for the establishment of timeless justice and a chance for a kind of personal immortality for the king.

FIGURE 1.6 Cuneiform Script, ca. 2600 B.C.E. Sumerian writing, made with wedge-shaped indentations in wet clay, revolutionized record keeping, allowing texts to long outlast memory. This tablet records lists of trade commodities.

Indo-Europeans: New Contributions in the Story of the West

While the people in the Fertile Crescent developed many of the elements that contributed to the formation of Western civilization—agriculture, writing, and law—the emerging culture remained subject to transformation. As we have seen, one of the advantages of the ancient Middle East was its location, which permitted it to benefit from influences from the far reaches of Asia. Of course, this geographic openness also contributed to instability—ideas often came with invaders and destruction. The region north of the Black Sea and the Caucasus Mountains (see **Map 1.4**) produced peoples living on the steppes who waged war on the peoples of the Fertile Crescent and developed a culture that eventually had a profound influence on the West.

Linguists, who analyze similarities in languages, have labeled these people Indo-European because their language served as the basis for virtually all subsequent European languages (except Finnish, Hungarian, and Basque). This language family separates the Indo-Europeans from most of the original inhabitants of the Fertile Crescent, who spoke "Semitic" languages. The steady influx of Indo-European invaders (later called Celts, Latins, Greeks, or Germans) formed the dominant population of Europe. Other Indo-Europeans moved east and settled in India or traveled south into modern-day Turkey and Iran.

Indo-European languages

The Indo-Europeans were led by a warrior elite, who were buried in elaborate graves. Excavations of these graves have allowed scholars to analyze the prized possessions and weapons that were buried with these rulers, yielding many insights into this society. Some archaeologists refer to the Indo-Europeans as "battle-ax people" because of the many axes found in their burial sites. They also rode horses, which they first domesticated for riding in about 2000 B.C.E. Riding on horseback gave Indo-European warriors the deadly advantages of speed, mobility, and reach over the Stone and Bronze Age archers they encountered in their travels.

Mounted warriors

The warrior elite of the Indo-Europeans excelled in battle and moved their families with them as they journeyed and fought. They carried their belongings in heavy carts outfitted with four solid, wooden wheels. The carts were a significant departure from the Sumerian two-wheeled chariots, which proved too unstable over long distances. The heavy carts traveled best over flat surfaces, and evidence indicates that as early as 2000 B.C.E. wooden roadways were built across boglands in northern Europe to accommodate the movement of people and their goods.

Contributions

When the Indo-Europeans moved into the Fertile Crescent, they were not literate, but they preserved their values in oral traditions. Later, influenced by the literary traditions of those they conquered, Indo-Europeans developed their own written languages, and many of these tales were written down and preserved. Ideals of a warrior elite and worship of gods who lived in the sky instead of on the earth continued, as did the Indo-European language. These elements were among the Indo-European contributions to Western civilization. In turn, early in the history of the Indo-Europeans (long before they acquired a written language), they adopted some things from the Mesopotamian cradle of civilization. They acquired many of the grains and other foods that were native to Mesopotamia and spread them widely. The successful culture of the Fertile Crescent was making its impact known far outside the river valleys that spawned it.

Hittites Establish Their Empire

In about 1650 B.C.E., an Indo-European people called the Hittites established a kingdom in Asia Minor (modern Turkey) and set up their capital at Hattusas (see **Map 1.2**). For the next three hundred years, the Hittite people planted crops on the fertile lands north of their capital, irrigated their fruit groves, and mined the ore-rich mountains. Throughout this time, they interacted with their neighbors in Mesopotamia and integrated much of Mesopotamian language, literature, law, and religion into their own Indo-European heritage. The interactions were often violent as the Hittites entered into the stormy politics of the ancient world.

The Hittites introduced a new technology of warfare into the West in the form of powerful—and deadly—war chariots. The oldest reference to chariot warfare in the ancient Near East comes from about the eighteenth century B.C.E., in a text that mentions

FIGURE 1.7. War Chariot, ca. 1299 B.C.E. The Hittites' war chariot was a fearsome military innovation that launched an arms race in the ancient world. The light wheels allowed rapid deployment that overwhelmed slower infantry.

forty teams of horses at one battle. The wheels of the Hittite chariots, lighter than those for any previous vehicle, made the chariots highly maneuverable, and the axle was set forward for stability. **Figure 1.7** shows a Hittite chariot with an archer trampling a fallen enemy. The Hittites' chariot-building prowess led to an arms race of sorts, culminating in the Battle of Kadesh in 1299 B.C.E., when some five thousand chariots participated in the struggle between Egyptians and Hittites.

Fortunately for historians, the Hittites learned the art of writing from the Mesopotamians. At Hattusas archaeologists have excavated about 10,000 cuneiform tablets, which shed much light on this culture that stood at the crossroads of the Middle East for such a long time.

A king whose military and administrative skill significantly changed the Hittite fortunes came to power in about 1380 B.C.E. Suppiluliuma I (r. ca. 1380–ca. 1345) thought of himself as both avenger and conqueror, and he launched the Hittites into building an empire. Within a century, he and his successors had built the most powerful state in the region. Suppiluliuma placed his sons in control of Syrian states and gained control of the lucrative trade along the Euphrates. Inevitably, Hittite armies clashed with the culture arising to the south and west—along the river valley of the magnificent Nile River.

RULE OF THE GOD-KING: ANCIENT EGYPT,
ca. 3100–1000 B.C.E.

The food crops that proved so successful in Mesopotamia spread to Egypt, stimulating another ancient civilization that arose on the banks of a great river—the roots of Western civilization moved farther west. The Nile River in Egypt flows more than 4,000 miles, from central Africa north to the Mediterranean Sea. Just as in Mesopotamia, a climate change forced dependence on the great river. In about 6000 B.C.E. the prevailing Atlantic rains shifted, changing great grassy plains into desert and forcing people to move closer to the Nile to use its waters.

[Nile Valley]

Unlike the Tigris and Euphrates, the Nile reliably overflowed its banks every year at a time convenient for planting—flooding in June and receding by October. During this flood, the river deposited a layer of fertile black earth in time for a winter planting of cereal crops. In ancient times, the Nile also provided the Egyptians with an excellent communication and transportation system. The river flowed north, encouraging traffic in that direction, but the prevailing winds blew from north to south, helping ships to sail against the current.

Egypt was more isolated than the ancient civilizations to the northeast. The deserts to the Nile's east and west stymied most would-be invaders, and in the southern Sudan a vast marsh protected the area from encroachers. Potential invaders from the Mediterranean Sea confronted shallows that prevented ships from easily approaching the Egyptian coast. As a result, Egyptian civilization developed without the fear of conquest or the resultant blending and conflict among cultures that marked the Mesopotamian cities. By about 3100 B.C.E., a king from Upper Egypt (in the south), who according to tradition was named Menes, had consolidated his rule over the entire Egyptian land.

Prosperity and Order: The Old Kingdom, ca. 2700–2181 B.C.E.

Ancient Egyptians believed that the power of the gods was visible in the natural world—in the Nile and in the people and animals that benefited from its bounty. Consequently, they worshiped the divine spirit that was expressed through heavenly bodies, animals, and even insects. Over time, some gods were exalted over others, and deities were combined and blurred. However, through most of Egypt's history the most important deities were the sun god Re (or Amon) and the Nile spirits Isis, her husband-consort, Osiris, and their son, the falcon-god Horus. Unlike the Mesopotamians, the Egyptians were optimistic about their fortunes. They believed they were blessed by the gods, who brought such a regular and fertile flooding of the Nile, not cursed by their chaotic whims. This optimism infused Egyptian culture with extraordinary continuity—why change something that brought such blessings?

At the heart of their prosperity was the king, whom Egyptians considered the living embodiment of the deity, and this linking of political power with religion reinforced the stability of the Old Kingdom. While [Preserving order] Mesopotamians believed their kings served as priests to their gods, Egyptians believed their rulers *were* gods, who had come to earth to bring truth, justice, and order—all summarized in the word **ma'at.** In return, the populace was obligated to observe a code of correct behavior that was included in the concept of *ma'at*. In about 2450 B.C.E., a high palace official named Ptah-hotep left a series of instructions for his son, in which he urged the boy to follow the precepts of *ma'at*: "He who departs from its laws is punished. . . . Evil may win riches, but it is the strength of *ma'at* that endures long." For millennia, kings and advisors like Ptah-hotep believed strongly that the importance of proper behavior brought prosperity to the land, and such beliefs contributed to a stable society. (The funeral inscription in Document 1.1 shows

thinking about DOCUMENTS

DOCUMENT 1.1

An Egyptian Nobleman Writes His Obituary

This document from second-millennium B.C.E. Egypt records the obituary inscribed on the tomb of an Egyptian nobleman named Ameni (or Amenemhet). This excerpt reveals what he counted as his greatest deeds in his years of service during Egypt's Middle Kingdom.

First Expedition

I followed my lord when he sailed southward to overthrow his enemies among the four barbarians. I sailed southward, as the son of a count, wearer of the royal seal, and commander in chief of the troops of the Oryx nome, as a man represents his old father, according to [his] favor in the palace and his love in the court. I passed Kush, sailing southward, I advanced the boundary of the land, I brought all gifts; my praise, it reached heaven. Then his majesty returned in safety, having overthrown his enemies in Kush the vile. I returned, following him, with ready face. There was no loss among my soldiers.

Second Expedition

I sailed southward, to bring gold ore for the majesty of the King of Upper and Lower Egypt, Kheperkere (Sesostris I), living forever and ever. I sailed southward together with the hereditary prince, count, oldest son of the king, of his body, Ameni. I sailed southward, with a number, 400 of all the choicest of my troops, who returned in safety, having suffered no loss. I brought the gold exacted of me; I was praised for it in the palace, the king's-son praised god for me.

Ameni's Able Administration

I was amiable, and greatly loved, a ruler beloved of his city. Now, I passed years as ruler in the Oryx nome. All the imposts of the king's house passed through my hand. The gang-overseers of the crown possessions of the shepherds of the Oryx nome gave to me 3,000 bulls in their yokes. I was praised on account of it in the palace each year of the loan-herds. I carried all their dues to the king's house; there were no arrears against me in any office of his. The entire Oryx nome labored for me.

Ameni's Impartiality and Benevolence

There was no citizen's daughter whom I misused, there was no widow whom I oppressed, there was no [peasant] whom I repulsed, there was no shepherd whom I repelled, there was no overseer of serf-laborers whose people I took for (unpaid) imposts, there was none wretched in my community, there was none hungry in my time. When years of famine came I plowed all the fields of the Oryx nome, as far as its southern and northern boundary, preserving its people alive and furnishing its food so that there was none hungry therein. I gave to the widow as (to) her who had a husband; I did not exalt the great above the small in all that I gave. Then came great Niles, possessors of grain and all things, [but] I did not collect the arrears of the field.

SOURCE: James Henry Breasted, *Ancient Records of Egypt*, vol. 1 (Chicago: University of Chicago Press, 1906), pp. 251–253.

Analyze the Document

1. Where did the nobleman travel in the course of his service, and what does this tell you about the global connections of the ancient world?
2. What kinds of accomplishments did he most want readers of this inscription to remember about him?
3. What does this inscription reveal about the values of ancient Egypt?

---

these enduring values.) This ordered society was ruled by a god-king later called **pharaoh** (great house), a term that referred to the general institution of the monarchy as well as the ruler.

The Old Kingdom period (ca. 2700–2181 B.C.E.) saw astonishing prosperity and peace, as farming and irrigation methods provided an abundance of crops and wealth to many. Unlike the Mesopotamian valley, Egypt had ready access to mineral resources, most importantly copper, which was in great demand for tools. Egyptians refined copper ore at the site of the surface mines, and ingots of copper were transported by caravans of donkeys overland to the Nile. From there, the precious ores were manufactured or used to trade abroad. Egypt was also happily situated to capitalize on trade with Nubia, which gave access to the resources of sub-Saharan Africa. (See Global Connections on page 17.) From Nubia, Egyptians gained gold, ivory, ebony, gems, and aromatics in exchange for Egyptian cloth and manufactured goods. With the surpluses of metals and grains, Egyptians could import goods from the Middle East and beyond. In addition to textiles, Egyptians desperately needed wood to make large seagoing vessels for their trade and navy. All this industry generated prosperity for many people, and in the Old Kingdom, people used these resources to support close families.

Ptah-hotep advised his son to start a family as soon as he could afford to: "If you are prosperous you should establish a household and love your wife as is fitting. . . . Make her heart glad as long as you live." The artwork of the time suggests that many Egyptians took Ptah-hotep's advice and established

GLOBAL CONNECTIONS

Nubia: The Passage from the Mediterranean to the Heart of Africa

From the dawn of civilization, the history of the West and the history of Africa developed together through cultural interactions that unfolded along the Nubian corridor. And throughout history, diverse groups—who spoke languages different from Egyptian—mingled in ancient Nubia. At times these groups even managed to unite into large kingdoms—one of which would conquer Egypt itself. Late in ancient Egyptian history, Nubian kings even became Egyptian pharaohs.

Lush and flat, the northern Nile valley stimulated the ancient Egyptians' agriculture and settlement. But near Aswan, in the south, the land changed. Here sandstone cliffs dropped directly from the desert plateau to the riverbank, and the river churned as it descended through a succession of swift rapids. These rapids are the first of six cataracts that impeded navigation south along the great river. Early rulers of Egypt marked the First Cataract as a natural southern border of their kingdom. However, later Egyptians pushed south beyond the First Cataract into Nubia. Egyptians had strong motivation to do so: Nubia provided the only reliable route around the Sahara desert to the riches that lay deep within the interior of the African continent.

In Nubia, goods moved north to the Mediterranean and south from Egypt and Mesopotamia. From the beginning, both Nubians and northerners recognized the benefits of this trade. See **Figure 1.11** for an artistic portrayal of Nubian trade. As early as 3000 B.C.E., domestic goats and sheep that had originated in Mesopotamia showed up in Nubia. Sometime after that, Nubians began to cultivate the domestic grains from Mesopotamia along the valley of the southern Nile beyond the First Cataract.

As early as the Old Kingdom in Egypt, kings valued the goods that came through Nubia, and even the sparse records from this ancient time reveal the importance of the trade with the south. For example, the Egyptian princes who governed Aswan bore the title "Keeper of the Door of the South," and sometime around 2250 B.C.E., the pharaohs sent a prince of Aswan named Herkhuf (or Harkhuf) on three journeys into Nubia to trade and to recruit mercenary troops to fight in Egypt's armies. Herkhuf headed south on the Nile, his ships propelled against the current by the prevailing north winds. The skilled navigators he employed negotiated the roiling rapids. The proud records carved on Herkhuf's tomb do not indicate how far beyond the Second Cataract he traveled, for we cannot identify the names of the various tribes he encountered. Yet most scholars think he made it to the Third Cataract. Seven months later, Herkhuf returned from one journey with 300 donkeys laden with incense, ebony, oil, leopard skins, elephant tusks, boomerangs, and other goods. His bounty revealed that Nubia served as a trading hub for luxuries and staples far beyond the Nile. The lure of Nubia was only increased when rich gold mines were discovered there in about 1980 B.C.E.

During the Middle Kingdom under the reign of Senwosret I (ca. 1980 B.C.E.), Egyptians began to mine for gold in Nubia, and the rich mines brought Nubia into the politics as well as the trade of the north. (Indeed, "Nubia" means "gold" in Egyptian.) Egyptians began to fortify the Nile, and Nubia engaged in the wars of the north. The fall of the ancient Egyptian kingdom did not end the importance of Nubia, which remained the major passage to the heart of Africa.

Making Connections

1. What aspect of its geographic location made Nubia so important to the ancient world? What role did Nubia play in trade?
2. How did the presence of domestic animals in sub-Saharan Africa demonstrate ancient connections between this region and Mesopotamia?
3. What trade items stimulated the connections between Africa and the Mediterranean?

---

loving families during this prosperous era. **Figure 1.8** shows a limestone carving of one such family. Seneb, the man depicted in the portrait, was a dwarf who had made a successful career in the court. He headed the court's weaving mill and then became the priest of the dead for two kings. His success was acknowledged when he married a member of the royal house. Husband and wife are shown side by side, perhaps suggesting the woman's high status. In this sculpture, the couple embrace affectionately and smile with seeming self-satisfaction while they tower protectively over the children below. The two figures at the lower left are each placing a finger over their lips, the Egyptian sign for "child." Stylized portraits like these suggest the success, contentment, and prosperity of many Old Kingdom families—at least those with enough wealth to commission portraits.

scribes carved it into stone monuments. An example of hieroglyphic writing can be seen in the background of **Figure 1.10** (p. 20).

However, hieroglyphs were too cumbersome for everyday use, so scribes learned two other simplified scripts—called Hieratic and Demotic—to keep records or write literature. Whereas many of the hieroglyphs were carved into stone, everyday records were more often written on papyrus, a kind of paper made from the Nile's abundant papyrus reeds. This versatile, sturdy reed could be reused—much like recycled paper today—and in the dry desert air was very durable. Often in Egypt's history, the lucrative export of papyrus increased the royal treasury.

Scribes studied for many years to master the complicated, varied Egyptian scripts. As in Mesopotamia, there are early records of women scribes, but the occupation later became restricted to men. On one surviving papyrus fragment, a scribe praised his occupation: "Writing for him who knows it is better than all other professions. It pleases more than bread and beer, more than clothing and ointment. It is worth more than an inheritance in Egypt, than a tomb in the west."

Scribes

Pyramids and the Afterlife

Scribes furthered the prosperity of the god-kings by carefully tracking the rulers' finances as they grew rich from state monopolies and taxes on all the products created in the fertile land. Whenever they had excess income, the kings proved their greatness by building pyramids, monuments to their glory that in some cases survive today. Imhotep, the chief advisor to the Egyptian king Djoser in about 2650 B.C.E., designed and built the first pyramid at Sakkara (near Memphis, shown on **Map 1.2,** on page 21). This early pyramid, depicted in **Figure 1.9a**, is called a step pyramid. It was intended to join heaven and earth. An inscription on one pyramid explains: "A staircase to heaven is laid for [the king] so that he may mount up to heaven thereby." Unlike the ziggurats, which were made of dried clay bricks, these pyramids were built of cut stone—a remarkable building innovation.

The Old Kingdom rulers made the pyramids the great symbol of Egyptian power and longevity. An anonymous architect refined the early pyramid design and built the Great Pyramid as a burial tomb for the Fourth Dynasty ruler, Khufu (also known as Kheops), in about 2590 B.C.E. This pyramid became the model for the later Old Kingdom tombs that were built in Giza, which continue to dominate the skyline there. **Figure 1.9b** shows the pyramids at Giza, with the Great Pyramid of Khufu on the left. The pyramid of Khufu's son is in the back; it appears taller because it is on

Pyramids

FIGURE 1.8 Egyptian Family, ca. 2320–2250 B.C.E. This is the family portrait of Seneb, head of the royal weaving mill, who married a woman of the royal family. The two are shown with their children in this idealized view of Egyptian family life.

Hieroglyphs: Sacred Writing

Sometime around 3000 B.C.E., Egyptians developed a system of writing. Egyptian writing was not cuneiform, nor was it used primarily for accounting purposes. While Egyptian administrators surely had as much need for clear records as the Sumerians, they primarily used writing to forward religious and magical power. Every sign in their writing system represented a real or mythical object and was designed to express that object's power. The ancient Greeks saw these images on temples and named Egyptian script **hieroglyph,** meaning "sacred writing."

Hieroglyphs were more than a series of simple pictures. Each symbol could express one of three things: the object it portrayed, an abstract idea associated with the object, or one or more sounds of speech from the spoken Egyptian word for the object. (The technical terms for these three uses are *pictogram, ideogram,* and *phonogram.*) Because this writing had ceremonial religious use, it changed little over the centuries as higher ground. Khufu's pyramid covers about 13 acres and is made of more than two million stone blocks. Peasants labored on these pyramids before planting season during the months when the Nile was in flood. Ancient Greek historians later claimed that the Great Pyramid of Giza took twenty years to build and required the labor of 100,000 workers. Modern estimates tend to agree with these calculations. The pyramids—so visible in the ancient skyline—proclaimed the god-king's immortality and the permanence of the order he brought to the land along the Nile.

Pyramids—and later mortuary temples—were built as tombs for the god-kings or, more precisely, as houses for their departed spirits. The departed's soul was sustained in the tomb by the same food and goods that had sustained the living body. The Egyptian notion of immortality marked an important contribution to the world of ideas, for the afterlife Egyptians conceived of was dramatically different from the dark world of the Mesopotamian dead. We do not have an exact idea of how the Egyptians visualized the afterlife, but it seems to have been an improved version of this world—a heavenly Nile valley. Some poets even wrote of death as a pleasant release:

Afterlife

Death is before me today
Like a man's longing to see his home
When he has spent many years in captivity.

Upon the death of a king, or in later years a nobleman who could afford a burial, the body was embalmed. Embalmers removed the internal organs through an incision in the abdomen and placed them in a vessel filled with a salty preserving solution. The body cavity was then probably dried in a pile of natron crystals. Later in Egypt's history, embalmers used resin-soaked linen to pack the body cavity. Finally the embalmers wrapped the body in more linen with resin. The wrapped, embalmed body—the mummy—along with a box containing the internal organs, was then placed in a chamber deep within the pyramid. Stocking the tomb with an array of food, household goods, and precious jewels for the pharaoh to enjoy in the afterlife completed the burial process.

Burial rituals

Pyramids from the Old Kingdom contained no images, but later artists painted the interior walls of tombs with scenes of activities that the deceased could expect to enjoy in the afterlife, and these scenes offer us a glimpse of how Egyptians viewed the next world. **Figure 1.10** shows a happy scene that was painted on the walls of a New Kingdom tomb. In this picture, the noble family frolics on a bird-hunting trip that yields far more abundance than any real-life trip ever could. Under their boat swims a fish so fat it belongs in a fisherman's paradise. A child grips her father's leg while he catches birds with the help of his hunting falcon. His well-dressed wife stands in the background. Even the family cat enjoys an abundant afterlife, catching three

FIGURE 1.9 Pyramids, ca. 2590 B.C.E. These burial places for the royal dead had a long history in the Old Kingdom. Figure 1.9a is the earliest such structure (ca. 2680 B.C.E.), a "step pyramid" intended to join heaven and earth. Figure 1.9b shows the later, most famous pyramids at Giza, with the Great Pyramid of Khufu on the left.

KEY DATES

ANCIENT EGYPT CIVILIZATION

ca. 2700–2181 B.C.E.	Old Kingdom
2181–2140 B.C.E.	First Intermediate Period
ca. 2060–1785 B.C.E.	Middle Kingdom
ca. 1785–1575 B.C.E.	Second Intermediate Period
1570–1085 B.C.E.	New Kingdom
ca. 1504–1482 B.C.E.	Pharaoh Hatshepsut
ca. 1377–1360 B.C.E.	Pharaoh Akhenaten
ca. 1279–1213 B.C.E.	Pharaoh Ramses II

FIGURE 1.10 Egyptian Paradise, ca. 1400 B.C.E. In this tomb painting of the New Kingdom, the deceased, a court official named Nebamun, is shown with his wife and daughter on a hunting trip in the afterlife. The depiction of scenes of daily life reveals the Egyptians' joy in earthly life, as well as their expectations of a pleasant existence beyond death.

birds at once. This illustration reveals how much the Egyptian "heaven" had changed from the dark Mesopotamian netherworld.

Changing Political Fortunes, ca. 2200–1570 B.C.E.

The order and prosperity promised by the pyramids proved less enduring than the Egyptians expected. At the end of the Old Kingdom period, the climate turned against the god-kings. As drought in southern Nubia led to a series of low floods in Egypt, crops failed, and people pillaged the countryside in a desperate search for food. There was even one account of cannibalism. Under such pressure, Egypt needed a strong ruler to preserve *ma'at*, but one was not forthcoming. Near the end of the Old Kingdom, one king—Pepi II (ca. 2270–2180 B.C.E.)—reputedly ruled for more than 90 years,

Famine

which was an extraordinary feat in an age when a decade or two was considered a substantial rule and when 40 years of age was the normal life expectancy. However, the old king was unable to keep a strong rule; during his reign, authority broke down, and he outlived his heirs. After his death a succession of little-known kings with very short reigns followed—a clear indication that all was not well within Egypt. Sources indicate that one of these ephemeral rulers was a woman—Nitocris—who ruled for about two years. During these times of weak central authority, local nobles exerted power, and Egypt suffered a period of social and political instability called the First Intermediate Period (2181–2140 B.C.E.).

A text from the time articulated poignantly the widespread misery experienced during these hard years: "Everything is filthy: there is no such thing as clean linen these days. The dead are thrown into the river.... The ladies of the nobility exclaim: 'If only

thinking about GEOGRAPHY

MAP 1.2

The Ancient Near East, ca. 1450 B.C.E.

This map shows the growth of the Egyptian Empire along with the territories of its neighbors, the Hittite Empire and the Mesopotamian kingdoms.

Explore the Map

1. Compare this map with **Map 1.1.** What new territories has Egypt conquered?
2. How was Egyptian culture affected by the conquest of territories populated by peoples of different cultures?
3. How do you think the Egyptian presence in Palestine drew Egypt into the many wars of the Middle East?

---

we had something to eat!' They are forced to prostitute their daughters. They are reduced to sleeping with men who were once too badly off to take a woman."

During these difficult times, people began to hope for a more pleasant afterlife, which many began to believe was possible for more than just the royal family. In the First Intermediate Period, anyone who could afford the appropriate burial rituals and magic spells could expect to achieve immortality. Still, prosperity continued to elude the Nile valley.

In about 2060 B.C.E., Amenemhat I of Thebes finally restored peace to the crippled valley and introduced what has come to be called the Middle Kingdom period (ca. 2060–1785 B.C.E.). **Middle Kingdom** Egypt prospered once again, and one pharaoh wrote: "None was hungry in my years, none thirsted then; men dwelled in peace." During these years, the kings conquered Nubia and grew rich on the gold of that kingdom. This conquest also brought sub-Saharan Africa into closer contact with the Mediterranean world, and continued trade with Nubia integrated African goods and elements of their culture into Egypt's and into the developing Western culture in general. The funeral inscription in Document 1.1 testifies to the increased trade. Egypt's rulers also introduced impressive engineering projects that expanded Egypt's amount of irrigated land by more than 17,000 acres. The Egyptians also began engaging in lucrative trade with the peoples of the Fertile Crescent. This practice had a price, however: It drew Egypt into the volatile politics of the ancient Middle East.

In the eighteenth century B.C.E., trouble struck again. The kings at the end of the twelfth dynasty were weak, and local magnates began to claim autonomy. Without a strong central authority, the Nubians in the south revolted **Egypt conquered** and broke away from Egyptian control, taking their gold with them. In 1650 B.C.E., the Hyksos who had settled in the lowland where the Nile poured into the Mediterranean (the Delta) rose to power (see **Map 1.1**). The Hyksos brought with them a new technology of warfare. They fought with bronze weapons, chariots, and body armor against the nearly nude Egyptians, who used only javelins and light copper weapons. The Hyksos established a kingdom in the Delta and this uneasy time, the Second Intermediate Period, extended from about 1785 to 1575 B.C.E.

thinking about ART

FIGURE 1.11
Egyptian Fresco, ca. 1295–1186 B.C.E.

A fresco is a kind of mural painted on plaster. This **fresco** from Thebes shows Nubians bearing gifts (tribute) of an exotic giraffe, an animal skin draped over a man's arm, a mound of ostrich eggs, and most valuable of all, highly bred cattle, valued for their coloring. All these were brought to the Egyptian pharaoh. Egyptian artists created this fresco to show the power of their ruler, and in the process they portrayed sub-Saharan Africans realistically, with dark skin, particular hairstyles, and woven clothing that we can use as historical evidence for Nubian society.

Connecting Art & Society

1. What does the fresco suggest about the value of Nubian trade to Egypt?
2. Which of the trade items that are depicted continue to be valued today? What makes them valuable?
3. How might this image, with its accurate portrayal of Nubians, be used as historical evidence for the imperial aspirations of the Egyptians?

Political Expansion: The New Kingdom, 1570–1085 B.C.E.

In about 1570 B.C.E, the Egyptians adopted the new technology of warfare. With bronze weapons and chariots of their own, they liberated themselves from the hated Hyksos and established a new dynasty that introduced what historians call the New Kingdom (1570–1085 B.C.E.). While these kings—now officially called pharaohs—intended to restore the conservative glory of the Old Kingdom, they nevertheless remembered the lesson of the invasion from the north and no longer relied on Egypt's geographic isolation to protect their way of life. Instead, the newly militant god-kings embarked on a series of foreign wars to build an empire that would erect a territorial barrier between Egypt and any potential invaders. **Map 1.2** shows the extent of the Egyptian Empire by 1450 B.C.E.

As the Egyptian Empire expanded, it was in turn shaped by Fertile Crescent politics and culture. For example, the riches that poured into the Nile valley from foreign conquests often ended up in the hands of temple priests, who began rivaling the pharaohs in power. Slaves, captured abroad and brought to Egypt, introduced new languages, views, and religions to the valley. Not surprisingly, the lives of Egyptian soldiers, battling in foreign wars, changed for the worse. The scribe we met earlier, who praised his own occupation above all others, wrote about the grim life of a soldier of the New Kingdom: "He is called up for Syria. He may not rest. There are no clothes, no sandals. He drinks water every third day; it is smelly and tastes of salt. His body is ravaged by illness. He does not know what he is about. His body is weak, his legs fail him." As **Map 1.2** shows, the imperial expansion of Egypt encroached on the borders of the strong Hittite Empire, which soon threatened the restored New Kingdom.

Despite the challenges, the imperial pharaohs successfully built their empire and made Egypt prosperous again. However, such expansion always came with a cost. Rulers had to weigh placing resources into military expansion or into local projects. Hatshepsut's (ca. 1504–1482 B.C.E.) endeavors demonstrated this tension as she ruled the extended Egypt (see the Biography on pages 24–25). While protecting her borders, Hatshepsut concentrated her resources on domestic developments and commercial enterprises. Her inscriptions claim that she restored temples that had lain in ruins since the Second Intermediate Period, and she engaged in numerous public works, all achievements that made her popular among her people.

Hatshepsut's accomplishments were all the more remarkable since it was highly unusual for a woman to rule alone. Women in a pharaoh's family had always held the important position of consort to their brother-husbands. They joined them in being descended from gods, but the king had always been the incarnation of the principal deity. Hatshepsut used artistic representations to overcome this problem, ordering that all statues of her portray her as a man. In **Figure 1.13**, on page 25, a formal portrait, she is dressed in the traditional male royal style—bare-chested and wearing a short, stiff skirt. She even wears an artificial, ceremonial beard.

Hatshepsut's successors reversed her traditional politics and revived Egypt's imperial ambitions. The New Kingdom reached its apogee in expansion and prosperity under the reign of Amenhotep III (r. ca. 1412–ca. 1375 B.C.E.). This confident pharaoh built huge statues of himself and a spacious new temple. His luxurious lifestyle, however, took its toll on him. He died at age 38, and his mummified remains reveal a balding, overweight man with rotted teeth.

> Empire building

The Religious Experiment of Akhenaten, ca. 1377–1360 B.C.E.

During the New Kingdom, the traditional relationship between the god-king and his priests began to change. Priests of Amon became almost as powerful as the pharaohs in administering the kingdom. The priests of Osiris grew popular with wealthy people, to whom they offered the possibility of immortal life in return for money. Within this increasingly tense environment arose a reformer who tried to create a religious revolution.

Amenhotep IV (r. ca. 1377–1360 B.C.E.), the son of Amenhotep III, tried to renounce the many divine principles worshiped in all the temples of Egypt and institute worship of a single god whom he called Aten, the sun-disk. The god-king changed his name from Amenhotep (Amon is satisfied) to Akhenaten (useful to Aten, the sun-disk). Then he withdrew his support from the old temples and tried to dissolve the powerful priesthoods. Akhenaten also departed from tradition by introducing a new naturalism in art, in which he allowed himself to be portrayed realistically, protruding belly and all (see **Figure 1.12**). However, the artwork in Aten's new temples often featured portraits of Akhenaten's beautiful wife, Nefertiti, without the pharaoh, suggesting that the queen may have played a large role in planning the new cult.

> Akhenaten's religion

FIGURE 1.12 Pharaoh Akhenaten and Family, ca. 1340 B.C.E. This limestone carving shows Akhenaten, his wife, Nefertiti, and three of their daughters relaxing in a family pose that departed from the usual formal depictions of the pharaoh. They bask in the rays of Aten, the sun-disk, the new deity they worshiped.

BIOGRAPHY

Hatshepsut & Thutmose
(r. 1473–1458 B.C.E.) (ca. 1482–1450 B.C.E.)

Powerful Queen and Vengeful Son-in-Law

The Egyptian pharaoh Thutmose I had three children by his chief wife—two sons who died in their youths, and a daughter, Hatshepsut. In the complex households of the pharaohs, the succession to the throne was never clear; Thutmose I also had a son by a lesser wife. This son, Thutmose II, married his half-sister Hatshepsut and succeeded his father as pharaoh. Thutmose II apparently was sickly and died in 1504 B.C.E. after he and Hatshepsut had a daughter, Neferure. The succession again went to a son by a concubine. However, this next son, Thutmose III, was younger than 10 years old when his father died. The logical regent was his aunt/stepmother, Hatshepsut. Although it was customary for a man to rule, Hatshepsut wanted to be pharaoh, not regent. To this end, she cultivated the support of the powerful priests of Amon, and of the army, and had herself declared pharaoh. Thutmose III had to accept a position of titular co-ruler with no actual authority. Hatshepsut seems to have treated her young charge well. Contemporaries praised his extraordinary skills in reading and writing and his study of military arts. He was also healthy and a strong athlete. His remains show that he escaped even the severe dental decay that appears in many royal mummies. Thutmose III was probably married to his aunt's daughter, Neferure, to guarantee his succession.

Hatshepsut grappled with two major challenges during her reign: how to forward her political vision for Egypt and how to ensure her credibility. She approached both tasks shrewdly, ever aware of the importance of appearances as well as policy. In her political vision, she focused attention on trade and peaceful pursuits, and she turned to art and building to validate her rule. Hatshepsut commissioned portraits that showed her dressed as a male king, and she built a magnificent funerary temple intended to stand forever and proclaim her passage into the land of the gods.

While Hatshepsut focused on internal building projects, she kept the army strong, because Egypt's neighbors did not feel powerful enough to threaten the borders. The accomplishments she seemed proudest of, however, were in trade. She commissioned a great carving that recounted her successful trade mission to "Punt," an African kingdom that we can no longer exactly identify, although some historians suggest it may be near modern-day Somalia (see **Map 1.2**). In any case, this wealthy sub-Saharan kingdom had been the destination of several trade

---

Figure 1.12 shows a casual family portrait of Akhenaten, Nefertiti, and three of their daughters. Husband and wife are shown the same size. Both wear regal headdresses that suggest an unusual equality, and Akhenaten affectionately kisses one of his daughters in a remarkably informal portrayal. The sun-disk is above and shines down on both, indicating not only that the family is blessed by the sun deity, but also that they can serve to bring the blessings of the sun to their people.

A beautiful hymn to Aten has survived, perhaps written by Akhenaten himself. In the hymn, the pharaoh praises Aten as the only god: "O sole god, like whom there is no other! Thou didst create the world according to thy desire." In a development remarkable for the ancient world, Akhenaten declares this god to be universal, belonging to all peoples: "Their tongues are separate in speech, and their natures as well; Their skins are distinguished, As thou distinguishest the foreign peoples. . . . The lord of all of them, . . . The lord of every land." In the ancient world, gods were associated with individual peoples and cities, so Akhenaten's praise of a universal god is extraordinary.

Many scholars have speculated about the motives behind this dramatic religious innovation. Had Akhenaten been influenced by Israelites living in Egypt? Was his declaration of a single god a political move to reduce the power of the priests of Amon? Or was the king a sickly dreamer who merely had a strange spiritual vision? We will never know Akhenaten's motives, but his reign caused turmoil in Egypt.

The Twilight of the Egyptian Empire, 1360–ca. 1000 B.C.E.

Akhenaten was succeeded by Tutankhaton (r. 1347–1338 B.C.E.), who was only 9 years old at the time of his succession. He is shown with his wife in the chapter opener on page 2. Compare the chapter opener with **Figure 1.12**. Notice that both feature the comfortable family grouping that marked the artwork of Akhenaten's reign and that both show the sun-disk—Aten—bestowing blessings. However, the young Tutankhaton was unable to carry on the unpopular religious reforms of his father-in-law. The priests of the old cults had grown increasingly resentful of Akhenaten—whom they called "the criminal"—and within three years the young king changed his name to Tutankh*amen* as he renounced the old pharaoh's

FIGURE 1.13 Hatshepsut, ca. 1460 B.C.E.

missions during the Middle Kingdom, and all knew of the wealth that was available. The carving depicts the pharaoh meeting with the Queen of Punt—an obese and powerful woman—and bringing back many luxury items of trade. Hatshepsut's ships were filled with incense, ebony, gold, ivory, animal skins, and even live baboons, sacred to Egyptian gods. The pharaoh brought these great luxuries back to Egypt and used much of the wealth in her monumental building projects.

When Thutmose III grew to manhood, he gained control of the army and seemed ready to rule without Hatshepsut's guidance. The early death of his wife, Neferure, weakened his ties to Hatshepsut, and sources hint that the woman pharaoh was murdered (or simply deposed) in 1458 B.C.E. Late in his reign, the pharaoh Thutmose III tried to eradicate all memory of Hatshepsut. He had her temples and most of her statues destroyed and her name scraped off stone monuments. Was he angry about his long regency? Did he object to Hatshepsut's gender? Did he disapprove of her popular political agenda, or was he trying to ensure a smooth succession for his son? We can never know the answers to these questions. Fortunately for students of history, Thutmose was unable to erase all the evidence that tells of his remarkable predecessor.

Thutmose III was a great leader, although his political vision for Egypt differed markedly from that of his aunt. Specifically, he believed that Egypt should be an imperial power. During his 54-year reign, he led military expeditions and established the empire that defined Egypt during the New Kingdom. In the story of Hatshepsut and Thutmose, we see two accomplished pharaohs with conflicting visions of Egypt—one looking backward to its Old Kingdom greatness, the other looking forward to the empire building of the future. Both rules embodied major, dramatic themes in Egyptian history.

Connecting People & Society

1. In what ways does the queen's life reveal the tensions between the New Kingdom's involvement with other regions and its desire for isolation?
2. How does the queen work to rule within the constraints of her gender? How successful is this strategy?

---

religious convictions. Tutankhamen died at just 18 years of age, and the general who succeeded him as pharaoh—Harmhab—destroyed Akhenaten's temples and restored the worship of the old gods.

Egypt showed a hint of its former greatness during the reign of Ramses II (1279–1213 B.C.E.), who reestablished the imperial frontiers in Syria and restored peace under Egypt's traditional gods. After the hard-fought battle at Kadesh in 1274 B.C.E., Ramses negotiated a treaty with the Hittites that is believed to be the first recorded nonaggression pact. Ramses' success in bringing peace allowed him to free resources for huge building projects, most notably a great temple carved out of the rocky cliffs along the Nile. The tribute portrayed in **Figure 1.11** testifies to the prosperity restored during the New Kingdom.

Subsequent pharaohs, through the end of the New Kingdom in 1085 B.C.E., tried to maintain the fragile empire. However, major challengers arose to confront the god-kings. Libyans to the west and Nubians from the south invaded the Nile valley and took power for a while. Eventually, greater empires to the east and north would conquer Egypt permanently, and the center of Western civilization would move to other lands. However, the advanced culture, ordered life, and intense spirituality of the rich land of the Nile would again exert a profound impact on the early peoples of the West, as we will see in Chapter 3.

PEOPLES OF THE MEDITERRANEAN COAST,
ca. 1300–500 B.C.E.

Along the eastern coast of the Mediterranean Sea, various civilizations arose and became part of the power struggles plaguing the Middle East. Most of these Mediterranean cultures eventually were absorbed by their neighbors and disappeared. However, two of them—the Phoenicians and the Hebrews—made a lasting impact as they vigorously expanded their fortunes and furthered the worship of their gods.

The Phoenicians: Traders on the Sea

The Phoenicians were successful traders whose culture was based in the coastal cities of Sidon, Tyre, and Byblos (see **Map 1.2**). These seagoing merchants made the most of their location by engaging in prosperous trade with Egypt and the lands in the Fertile Crescent. The Phoenicians controlled forests of cedar trees that were highly prized in both Mesopotamia and Egypt. They also had an even more lucrative monopoly on purple dye made from coastal shellfish. Purple dyes were so rare that cloth of this color was expensive, so it soon became identified with royalty. Phoenician weavers dyed cloth purple and sold it throughout the Middle East and western Mediterranean for huge profits. Throughout the ancient world, nobility was demonstrated by wearing purple clothing.

Explorers from the Phoenician cities traveled widely throughout the Mediterranean Sea. By 950 B.C.E., these remarkable sailors traded as far west as Spain, and even into the Atlantic down the west coast of Africa. Like all ancient sailors, they hugged the coast as they traveled so that they could stop each night to beach the ships and sleep. To guarantee safe harbors, Phoenician traders established merchant colonies all along the north coast of Africa; by some estimates there was a colony about every 30 miles. The most important colony was Carthage, which was founded about 800 B.C.E. and would become a significant power in the Mediterranean (see Chapter 4). Through these colonies, the Phoenicians spread the culture of the ancient Middle East—from their trading expertise to their gods and goddesses—around the Mediterranean all the way to Spain.

Trading colonies

The enterprising Phoenician sailors left their mark on the Mediterranean world long after neighboring empires conquered the Phoenicians' home cities on the eastern coast. They began their early voyages in search of metals: tin, copper, iron for tools and weapons, and silver and gold for luxury items. This quest even led these intrepid sailors through the Strait of Gibraltar into the Atlantic, where they traded as far as the African coast and Britain. They were skilled at smelting metals—including the difficult-to-forge iron—and their metallurgy talents, along with the trade they fostered, stimulated growth throughout the region.

The Phoenicians' most important contribution to Western culture was their remarkable alphabet. In developing a writing system, the Phoenicians improved on the Sumerian script by creating a purely phonetic alphabet of only twenty-two letters. This system was simpler than the unwieldy cuneiform and hieroglyph that dominated the rest of the Middle East. The Phoenician alphabet spread rapidly and allowed later cultures to write without the long apprenticeships that characterized the proud scribes like the one shown at the beginning of this chapter. Through adopting a Phoenician-style alphabet, cultures of the West achieved a significant advantage over cultures whose written languages remained the exclusive province of the elite.

Phoenician alphabet

The People of the One God: Early Hebrew History, 1500–900 B.C.E.

Phoenician society in the Near East ultimately disappeared as an independent state, but not before it had performed an immense service as a transmitter of culture throughout the Mediterranean. The Phoenicians' neighbors, the Hebrews, followed an entirely different course. The Hebrews resiliently withstood both time and conquest and emerged from a difficult journey with their culture intact.

While the Sumerians and their successors in Mesopotamia developed complex civilizations based on irrigation and built ziggurats to their many deities, the seminomadic Hebrews moved their flocks from Mesopotamia into the land of Canaan, comprising much of the modern states of Israel, Lebanon, and western Syria. As they traveled, they shared many of the ancient stories of Mesopotamia, such as the tale of a great flood that destroyed the land (present in *The Epic of Gilgamesh*, described earlier) and a lost Garden of Eden. The Hebrews, perhaps seeing the Mesopotamian ziggurats from a distance, also viewed their neighbors as overly proud. The Hebrew story of the ill-fated Tower of Babel captures this theme of overweening pride.

Sometime before about 1700 B.C.E., the early leaders of the Hebrews, the patriarchs—Abraham, Isaac, and Jacob—led these seminomadic tribes that roamed the eastern Mediterranean and beyond. Jacob changed his name to Israel ("he who prevails with God"), and this name marked Jacob's followers as having a special relationship with one God. Consequently, historians refer to these tribes as the Israelites. Several clans traveled to Egypt, where Israelite texts claim they were enslaved by the Egyptians, although their status is not clear. They might simply have been employed in the labor-intensive Egyptian work projects, and their position may have changed over time to a more restrictive relationship. Some historians identify the Israelites with a group who helped build the huge projects of the Egyptian pharaoh Ramses II (r. ca. 1279–1213 B.C.E.). According to the Bible, Moses led this same group from Egypt. This Exodus (which means "journey out" in Greek) transformed them into a nation with a specific religious calling.

Patriarchs

The details of the history of the Israelites are found in the Hebrew Scriptures (later called the Old Testament by Christians). Made up of writings from oral and written traditions and dating from about 1250 to 150 B.C.E., these Scriptures record laws, wisdom, legends, literature, and the history of the ancient Israelites. The first five books (known as the Pentateuch) constitute the **Torah,** or law code, which governed the people's lives. The Bible contains some information that is historically accurate and can be generally confirmed by archaeological evidence. For example, as early as 1208 B.C.E. the pharaoh Marneptah, the son of Ramses II, erected a victory stone recording his triumphs, including the conquest of Israel: "Israel is laid waste, his seed is no more...." The Egyptian god-king would not have bothered to brag about the conquest of the Israelites if this accomplishment had not been fairly substantial, so we know that the Bible's descriptions of a strong Israelite kingdom in Palestine during the second millennium B.C.E. are well founded.

[Hebrew Scriptures]

Historians must be cautious when using the Bible as a source, because it is basically a religious book that reveals faith, not science. Archaeology and history can illuminate the events of the ancient Israelites, but these sciences can shed no light on the faith that underlies the text. Used carefully, though, the Bible is an important source of information on these early Israelites, for they made a point to record and remember their own history—they wove teachings and morality into a historical narrative. Thus, Hebrew religion was rooted in history rather than myth, and from this text we can begin to re-create the early history of this profoundly influential people.

According to the Bible, the Hebrews from Egypt eventually returned to ancient Palestine and slowly reconquered the land, uniting the other nearby Hebrew tribes in the process. During this period of settlement, between about 1200 and 1050 B.C.E., Israelites experienced a change in leadership. Instead of relying solely on tribal leaders, people turned to "judges"—charismatic leaders who helped unite the people against the threats of their neighbors. In time, the elders of the tribes felt they needed a king to lead the people, declaring, "then we shall be like other nations, with a king to govern us, to lead us out to war and fight our battles" (1 Sam. 8:20). The people insisted that Samuel, the last of the judges, anoint their first king, Saul (r. ca. 1024–ca. 1000 B.C.E.).

[Establishing a kingdom]

Saul's successor, David (r. ca. 1000–ca. 961 B.C.E.), began encouraging the tribes to settle in a fixed location, with their capital at Jerusalem. David's successor, Solomon (r. ca. 961–ca. 922 B.C.E.), brought Phoenician craftsmen to Jerusalem to build a great temple there. Now a territorial power like others in the Fertile Crescent, the Hebrews worshiped their God in the temple overlooking a majestic city. But the costs of the temple were exorbitant, causing increased taxes and the growth of an administrative structure to collect them.

Solomon was a king in the Mesopotamian style. If the biblical account is to be believed, he used marriage to forge political alliances, accumulating hundreds of wives and many hundreds more concubines, including the daughter of an Egyptian pharaoh. The biblical excerpts in Document 1.2 show Solomon's fame, long-distance trade, and the difficulties accompanying his many marriages. However, the unified kingdom of tribes barely outlasted Solomon's reign. After his death, the northern tribes—particularly angry about Solomon's taxation and administrative innovations—broke away to form the separate kingdom of Israel (**Map 1.3**). The southern state was called Judah, with its capital at Jerusalem, and at this time the southern Israelites began to be called Jews. Israel was the more prosperous of the two kingdoms and was tied more closely to Phoenicia by trade and other contacts. Judah adhered more rigorously to the old Hebrew laws. The two kingdoms often fought each other as they participated in the shifting alliances of their neighbors. Dominating all politics, however, was their commitment to their one God.

[Dividing a kingdom]

The authors of the Scriptures developed an overriding theme in Jewish history: the intimate relationship between obedience to God's laws and the unfolding of the history of the Jewish people. As these authors recorded their recollection of events, they told of periodic violations of the uncompromising covenant with God and the resulting punishments that God imposed.

A Jealous God, 1300–587 B.C.E.

When Moses led his people out of Egypt, they reportedly wandered for forty years in the wilderness of the Sinai Peninsula before returning to the land of Canaan (see **Map 1.3**). During that time, Moses bound his people to God in a special covenant, or agreement, through which the Jews would be God's "chosen people" in return for their undivided worship. The ancient Hebrews were not strictly monotheistic, for they believed in the existence of the many deities of their neighbors. For Moses' people, however, there was only one God, and this God demanded their exclusive worship. As the historian of the sixth century B.C.E. wrote in the Bible's Book of Deuteronomy, "He is the faithful God, keeping his covenant of love to a thousand generations of those who love him and keep his commands." This promise was a conditional one: God would care for his people only if they practiced his laws, and there were many laws.

[The covenant]

The core of the Hebrew legal tradition lay in the Ten Commandments that the Bible claims God gave to Moses during his exodus from Egypt, and these were supplemented by other requirements listed in the Scriptures. Adhering to these laws defined one as a Jew. While the laws bound the Jewish people together—to "love thy neighbor as thyself"—they also set the Jews apart from their neighbors. For

[Hebrew laws]

thinking about DOCUMENTS

DOCUMENT 1.2

King Solomon Secures His Realm's Fortune

These passages from the Book of Kings in the Bible show that King Solomon, like other ancient leaders, tried to secure the fortunes of his kingdom through marriages with neighboring peoples. They tell of King Solomon's fame and his relationship with women. The first passage describes the wealthy queen of Sheba (modern Yemen), and the second passage describes Solomon's many marriages.

Now when the queen of Sheba heard of the fame of Solomon concerning the name of the Lord, she came to test him with hard questions. She came to Jerusalem with a very great retinue, with camels bearing spices, and very much gold, and precious stones; and when she came to Solomon, she told him all that was on her mind. And Solomon answered all her questions; there was nothing hidden from the king which he could not explain to her. And when the queen of Sheba had seen all the wisdom of Solomon, the house that he had built, the food of his table, the seating of his officials, and the attendance of his servants, their clothing, his cupbearers, and his burnt offerings which he offered at the house of the Lord, there was no more spirit in her.

And she said to the king, "The report was true which I heard in my own land of your affairs and of your wisdom, but I did not believe the reports until I came and my own eyes had seen it; and behold, the half was not told me; your wisdom and prosperity surpass the report which I heard . . . then she gave the king a hundred and twenty talents of gold, and a very great quantity of spices, and precious stones; never again came such an abundance of spices as these which the queen of Sheba gave to King Solomon (1 Kings 10:1–7, 10).

Now King Solomon loved many foreign women: the daughter of Pharaoh, and Moabite, Ammomite, Edomite, Sidonian, and Hittite women, from the nations concerning which the Lord had said to the people of Israel, "You shall not enter into marriage with them, neither shall they with you, for surely they will turn away your heart after their gods"; Solomon clung to these in love. He had seven hundred wives, princesses, and three hundred concubines; and his wives turned away his heart. For when Solomon was old his wives turned away his heart after other gods; and his heart was not wholly true to the Lord his God, as was the heart of David his father. For Solomon went after Ashtoreth the goddess of the Sidonians and after Milcom the abomination of the Ammonites. So Solomon did what was evil in the sight of the Lord, and did not wholly follow the Lord as David his father had done. Then Solomon built a high place for Chemosh the abomination of Moab, and for Molech the abomination of the Ammonites, on the mountain east of Jerusalem. And so he did for all his foreign wives, who burned incense and sacrificed to their gods. And the Lord was angry with Solomon . . . (1 Kings 11:1–9).

SOURCE: Bible. 1 Kings 10:1–13; 1 Kings 11:1–13 (*New Oxford Annotated Bible with the Apocrypha.* New York: Oxford University Press, 1973).

Analyze the Document

1. How do the two passages, in different ways, reveal the importance of women during Solomon's reign?
2. What goods does the queen bring from Arabia? How does her gift of these materials illustrate the importance of long-distance trade to the Hebrew state?
3. What particular challenges do monotheistic Jews face in dealing with their neighbors?

KEY DATES

HEBREWS

2000–1700 B.C.E.	Patriarchs
ca. 1250 B.C.E.	Moses exodus from Egypt
ca. 1200–1050 B.C.E.	Judges
ca. 1024–ca. 1000 B.C.E.	King Saul
ca. 1000–ca. 961 B.C.E.	King David
ca. 961–ca. 922 B.C.E.	King Solomon
ca. 800 B.C.E.	Prophets
587 B.C.E.	Babylonian Captivity
515 B.C.E.	Second Temple built

example, boys were circumcised as a mark of the covenant between God and his people. In addition, Jews observed strict dietary laws that separated them from others—for example, they could eat no pork nor any animal that had been improperly slaughtered. But the fundamental commandment that allowed for no compromise with non-Jews was the injunction against worshiping the idols, or deities, of their neighbors.

Around the eighth century B.C.E., Jews were called to even higher ethical standards by a remarkable series of charismatic men—the prophets. These men, such as Amos, Micah, Hosea, Jeremiah, and Isaiah, were neither kings nor priests nor soldiers. Instead, they were common people—shepherds or tradesmen—who cared nothing for power or glory. They were brave men

Prophets

thinking about GEOGRAPHY

MAP 1.3

Mediterranean Coast in the First Millennium B.C.E.

This map shows the major kingdoms of the Mediterranean coast, together called the Land of Canaan in the Bible. The kingdoms include those of the Philistines, Hebrews, and Phoenicians.

Explore the Map

1. Look at the scale of the map. How close were these kingdoms? How might that proximity have contributed to increased warfare in the region?

2. Based on the map, why do you think there were so many battles between the Philistines and the Hebrews?

---

who urged their people to return to the covenant and traditional Hebrew law. In times of social distress, they became the conscience of Israel, and in turn they helped shape the social conscience that was to become part of Western civilization. The prophets reminded the Jews to care for the poor: "Seek justice, relieve the oppressed, Judge the fatherless, plead for the widow" (Isa. 1:17). In doing so, they emphasized the direct ethical responsibility of every individual. Unlike the other religions of the ancient Middle East, Judaism called individuals to follow their consciences to create a more ethical world. Religion was no longer a matter of rituals of the temple, but a matter of people's hearts and minds. The prophets preached a religion that would be able to withstand turmoil and political destruction, and it is fortunate that they did so, for the Hebrews would suffer much adversity, which they believed was a form of testing by their God.

According to the Bible, King Solomon had a weakness that stemmed from his polygamy. (See Document 1.2.) Not only did he violate the biblical command not to take foreign wives, but to please them he allowed the worship of other deities (especially the fertility goddess Astarte), even in the holy city of Jerusalem. Prophets claimed that it was his impiety that had divided the kingdom against itself. Later events showed a similar theme. Ahab (r. 869–850 B.C.E.), king of the northern kingdom of Israel, married a Phoenician princess, Jezebel, and erected an altar to her god Baal in order to please her. When Israel was conquered in 721 B.C.E. by the Assyrians, prophets who had predicted its downfall pointed to Ahab's breach of the covenant as the cause of the misfortune. The southern kingdom of Judah fared little better than Israel in trying to escape the aggressions of its neighbors. In 587 B.C.E., the Babylonians captured Jerusalem and destroyed Solomon's magnificent temple. Many Jews were exiled and enslaved in Babylon, and the "chosen people" were once more without a country or a religious center. From then on, there would be substantial numbers of Jews who lived outside Israel or Judah, and they later would be collectively known

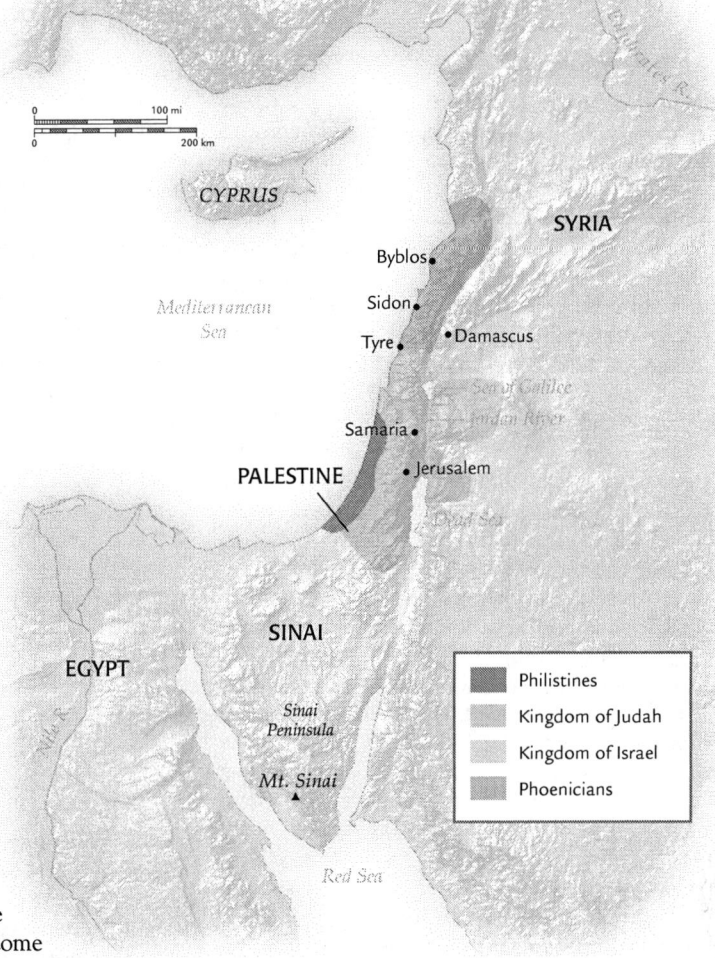

"God's punishments"

as the **Diaspora.** Instead of renouncing their God, however, the Jews reaffirmed their covenant in a different way.

Judaism in Exile

Hebrew priests in exile worried that Diaspora Jews living among non-Jews would forget the old traditions and be assimilated into the cultures of their neighbors. Therefore, they carefully compiled and edited the Scriptures to preserve their unique view of religion and history. These written accounts helped Judaism survive without a geographic center. The authors of the Scriptures arranged the history of the Jews to show that, despite hardships, God had always cared for his people. The priests believed that the destruction of the two Hebrew kingdoms had come because people either did not know the laws or had failed to obey them. As a result, Hebrew teachers emphasized the study of and strict adherence to the purity laws to keep their people separate from others even when they lived in close proximity as neighbors.

Without the temple in Jerusalem to serve as the center of worship, Jewish worship began to convene in more local establishments—synagogues and the home itself. This movement had an important impact on the status of women in Jewish culture. The emphasis on details of purity law to keep the chosen people separate reduced women's roles in formal prayer because the law stressed that anyone worshiping God had to be "clean." Women, seen as sometimes unclean because of menstrual blood or childbirth, were excluded from participating in the formal worship rituals. On the other hand, the experience of exile strengthened the family as a social and religious unit, a change that improved women's lives in other ways. For example, concubinage disappeared and women presided over the household, upholding the dietary laws and household rituals that preserved the Jewish culture wherever they lived.

In time, however, the Hebrews were able to reestablish their religious center in Jerusalem. After ruling Judah for forty-eight years, the Babylonians were, in turn, conquered by new peoples, the Persians. The Persians proved much more tolerant than the Babylonians of the varied beliefs of their subject peoples. In 538 B.C.E., the Persian king Cyrus let the Jewish exiles return to Jerusalem. The Jews built a new temple in 515 B.C.E., an event that introduced the "Second Temple" period. Again, the Jews had a temple and center of worship like other Mesopotamian peoples. However, all Jews did not return to Israel, and the question of the relationship between Diaspora Jews and the cultures in which they lived would reemerge periodically throughout history as followers of this old covenant interacted with their neighbors.

"Second Temple" period

The ancient Hebrews made a tremendous impact on the future of Western civilization. They believed that God created the world at a specific point in time, and this notion set them apart dramatically from their neighbors, such as the Egyptians, who believed in the eternity of the world. The Hebrews' view of history as a series of purposeful, morally significant events was unprecedented in the ancient world. Their concept of ethical monotheism, in which a single God of justice interacted with humans in a personal and spiritual way, offered a vision of religion that eventually dominated in the West. The many deities and demons that ruled the Mesopotamian and Egyptian worlds would in time be rendered insignificant by the God of the Hebrews, who transcended nature. The Hebrews believed that there was a profound distance between people and God, and thus individuals took more responsibility for the events of this world even as they worshiped and held in awe the deity who had made a deep and abiding covenant with the Jewish people.

Hebrew contributions

TERROR AND BENEVOLENCE: THE GROWTH OF EMPIRES, 1200–500 B.C.E.

By the second millennium B.C.E., many people could see the value of centralized control over larger territories. The Egyptians were establishing an empire, and the Hebrews had united into a kingdom. Not only did size offer the potential for larger armies, but expansion westward also secured access to valuable seaborne trade (which was making the Phoenicians wealthy) and would secure the strategically important region of Syria and Palestine. Perhaps most important, people wanted to expand their territories to acquire the metals so necessary for military and economic success. These impulses led to the growth of a new political form in the West—huge empires based on a new technology, iron.

The Age of Iron

Before the eleventh century B.C.E., ancient civilizations depended on bronze, an alloy of copper and tin. All across Europe and the Middle East, people used bronze plows to cultivate the land and employed bronze-tipped weapons to make war. While agriculture remained the most important enterprise, the economies of these civilizations were fueled by trade in copper and tin. Initially, these essential metals came largely from Asia Minor (see **Map 1.2**), Arabia, and India. Later, sources of these metals were also found in the western Mediterranean.

In about 1200 B.C.E., warfare disrupted the usual trade routes, making tin scarce. Pure copper is a soft

thinking about GEOGRAPHY

MAP 1.4

The Assyrian Empire, ca. 662 B.C.E.

This map shows the homeland of the Assyrians and their expansion as they conquered the older centers of Western civilization. Compare this map with **Maps 1.1, 1.2,** and **1.3.**

Explore the Map

1. How many cultures were included in this large empire?
2. What problems would you expect to arise in the governance of such a diverse empire?
3. How might the location of the Assyrians' homeland have facilitated their expansion?

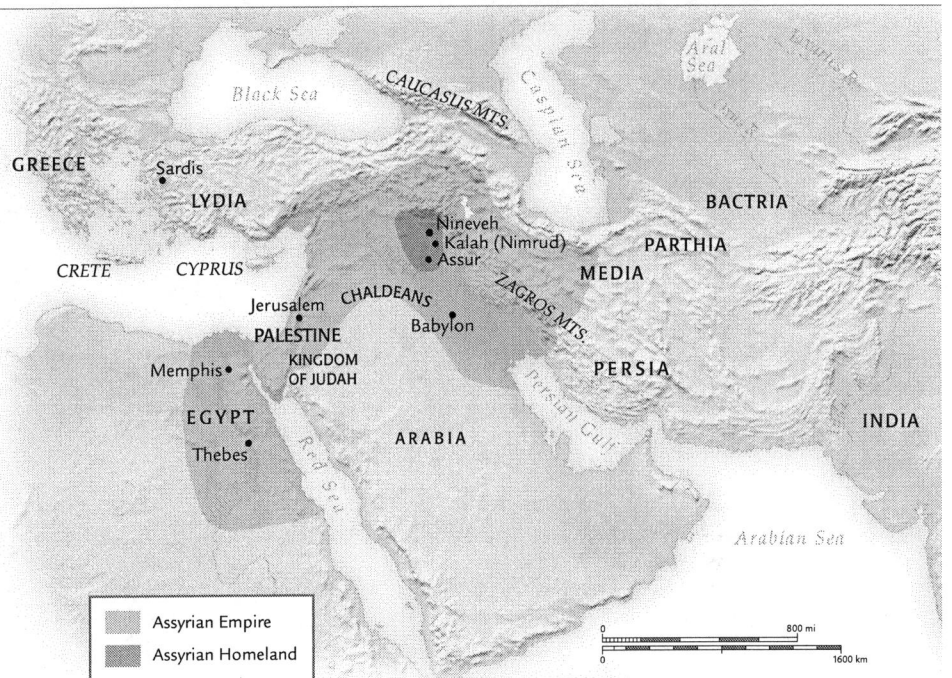

---

metal, and without the tin needed to make bronze, smiths could not produce effective tools and weapons. To overcome the tin shortage, Hittite metalworkers in Asia Minor first began to employ iron, an abundant mineral in that region. Unforged iron is not much stronger than copper. However, when it is repeatedly heated in a hot charcoal furnace, carbon molecules combine with iron molecules to form a very reliable metal known as carbon steel. Even low-carbon steel is stronger than bronze, and when it is cold hammered, the strength more than doubles. People—and particularly soldiers—gained a huge advantage by using the new metal.

Iron Age

The technology used to create the superior forged iron spread rapidly throughout the Mediterranean world, and from about 1000 B.C.E. on it was used in tools, cookware, and weapons. The use of iron spread to sub-Saharan Africa through Nubia, and ironworking became prominent throughout much of that continent, which was rich in iron ore. Soldiers wielding iron weapons easily vanquished those armed with bronze. The Age of Iron had dawned, and it dominated the world until the late nineteenth century when metalsmiths developed new ways to make iron into steel without the carbon method (Bessemer steel). Iron Age kings in Mesopotamia forged enough weapons and fielded armies so large, their extensive conquests introduced multiethnic empires that dwarfed all that had gone before.

Rule by Terror: The Assyrians, 911–612 B.C.E.

The Assyrians, a people living originally in the northern Tigris-Euphrates valley, had traded profitably with their neighbors for centuries. In the early tenth century B.C.E., they began arming themselves with iron weapons and following the one command of their god Assur: Expand the frontiers of Assyria so that Assur finally rules over all. **Map 1.4** shows the striking success of the Assyrians as they cut a swath through the civilizations of the ancient Near East.

The Assyrians' success stemmed from the skill of their armies and their willingness to engage in almost constant warfare to follow the command of Assur. Assyrian histories recounting their military campaigns were written as propaganda pieces to instill fear in their enemies. The historians accomplished their goal, and the cold-blooded details cemented the Assyrians' reputation for ruthlessness. King Sargon II's (r. 722–706 B.C.E.) description of his conquest of Babylon is one chilling example of these accounts: "I blew like the onrush of a hurricane and enveloped the city like a fog.... I did not spare his mighty warriors, young or old, but filled the city square with their corpses."

Beyond sheer brutality, the Assyrians relied on some of the most advanced military techniques that the ancient world had seen. They employed a corps of military engineers to build bridges, tunnels, and efficient siege weapons capable of penetrating strongly

FIGURE 1.14 Escaping a Battle The Assyrians were fearsome warriors. Their art frequently memorialized their accomplishments, as in the case of this image of fugitives escaping from Assyrian archers. This depiction shows an ancient technique of swimming underwater with air-filled pigskins.

fortified cities. Furthermore, they had a highly trained and well-rewarded officer corps who became the elite in Assyrian society.

The Assyrians portrayed their military achievements in their art as well as in their writings. But along with interminable portrayals of destruction and carnage, Assyrian art occasionally reveals unusual details of experience during the ninth century B.C.E. The carving shown in **Figure 1.14** depicts three men fleeing Assyrian archers as they swim the river toward the fortified town on the right. Two of the swimmers hold pigskins filled with air to breathe underwater, offering a surprising glimpse of an underwater swimming technique. This carving captures an incident that may have been particularly memorable due to the fugitives' creative escape. However, although the fugitives eluded the archers, the Assyrians conquered the town.

The Assyrians were first both to acquire such a large territory and to try to govern it cohesively. In many ways, they proved to be skilled administrators. For example, they built roads to unify their holdings, and kings appointed governors and tax collectors to serve as their representatives in the more distant territories. One of the elements that facilitated governing and trade over large areas was the Assyrians' use of Aramaic as a common language. This was a Semitic language originally spoken by the Aramaeans, successful merchants who lived in Mesopotamia in about 1100 B.C.E. Aramaic remained the official language of subsequent empires—it was even spoken by Jesus. In spite of the Assyrians' reputation for violence, the Greek historian Herodotus (ca. 484–ca. 424 B.C.E.) recalled the peaceful accomplishments of Queen Semiramis, who built "magnificent embankments to retain the river [Euphrates], which till then used to overflow and flood the whole country around Babylon."

Governing an empire

Many Assyrian rulers also appreciated the wealth of knowledge and culture that had accumulated in these lands for centuries. The great Assyrian king Ashurbanipal (669–627 B.C.E.) collected a huge library from which 20,000 clay tablets have survived. Within this collection, the king preserved the best of Mesopotamian literature, including *The Epic of Gilgamesh*. The highly educated Ashurbanipal took pride in his accomplishments: "I acquired the hidden treasure of all scribal knowledge, the signs of the heaven and the earth. . . . I have solved the laborious problems of division and multiplication. . . . I have read the artistic script of Sumer and the obscure Akkadian." This quotation offers an excellent example of how a written language served to preserve and disseminate the culture developing in the ancient Middle East.

Preserving learning

Although the Assyrians were skilled in making both war and peace, they still faced the problem that confronted all empire builders: how to keep the empire together when subject peoples resisted. The Assyrians used terror to control their far-flung territories. When individuals dissented, they were publicly tortured; when cities revolted, they were razed to serve as examples to others. To break up local loyalties, Assyrian commanders uprooted and moved entire populations. These methods worked for a while; eventually, however, they catalyzed effective opposition.

Fall of Assyrians

Ashurbanipal ruled from his capital in Nineveh—reputedly so well fortified that three chariots could ride abreast along the top of the walls surrounding the city. However, even those great walls could not save the king's successors. A coalition including Babylonians from southern Mesopotamia; Medes, an Indo-European tribe from western Iran; and Egyptians gathered against the Assyrian domination. Because the empire was so large it overextended the Assyrians' resources, and the provinces gave way quickly. Nineveh itself finally collapsed in 612 B.C.E. after a brutal two-year siege. In an ironic turn of events, the great city was defeated by the very river that had sustained it for so long—the Tigris flooded higher than normal and eroded Nineveh's defensive wall. Assyrian rule came to an ignominious end. However, the Assyrians left an enduring legacy for Western civilization: centralized empires that ruled over extended lands and different peoples.

Babylonian Rule, 612–539 B.C.E.

After vanquishing the Assyrians, the Medes left Mesopotamia and returned to their homeland near the Zagros Mountains (see **Map 1.4**). The Babylonians (also called Chaldeans, or Neo-Babylonians, to distinguish them from the earlier kingdom of Hammurabi) remained and ruled the lands of the former Assyrian Empire. The new rulers emulated the Assyrian use of terror to enforce their will on subject peoples. King Nebuchadrezzar (r. 605–561 B.C.E.) kept penalties similar to those in the Code of Hammurabi for civil crimes, but introduced extreme punishments for enemy rulers and their followers. When captured, these people were often flayed or burned alive. It was this severity that led Nebuchadrezzar to destroy Jerusalem in 587 B.C.E. and lead the Jews into captivity. This incident was the formative "Babylonian Captivity" discussed earlier that shaped much of subsequent Jewish history.

The Babylonians also continued the Assyrian passion for art and education. The king rebuilt his capital city of Babylon in such splendor that it was admired throughout the ancient world. His architects constructed huge ziggurats in praise of the Babylonian god Marduk and fortified the structures with walls more impressive than even Nineveh's had been. Under Nebuchadrezzar, Babylon blossomed into an impressive city graced by gardens, palaces, and temples.

Culture and commerce

The magnificent architecture that marked Babylon cost a fortune, and the Babylonian kings obtained these funds largely through fostering the commerce that often guided their military policies. One king, for example, besieged Tyre for thirteen years, hoping to win control over the Phoenicians' far-reaching trade. Another king established himself in Arabia in an attempt to control a new trade—in incense—that came from southern Arabia to the Mediterranean Sea.

Kings used their new wealth not only to decorate their cities, but also to foster learning. Within the cosmopolitan city, Babylonian priests excelled in astronomy and mathematics. They observed the heavens in an effort to understand the will of the gods, and in the process they charted the skies with impressive accuracy; they could predict solstices, equinoxes, and other heavenly phenomena. Their passion for predictions led them to develop another innovation with which they sought to foretell the future for individuals: astrology. By the fifth century B.C.E., Babylonian astrologers had divided the heavens into twelve signs—including the familiar Gemini, Scorpio, Virgo, and others—and began to cast horoscopes to predict people's futures based on their birth dates. The earliest surviving example of a horoscope was for a child born in 410 B.C.E. and marks the beginning of a long-standing practice.

Astronomy and mathematics

As part of their astronomical calculations, Babylonians developed advanced mathematics. Their tablets show that they regularly used multiplication, division, calculations of square and cube roots, algebra, and other operations. In addition, they based their numerical system on the number 60, working out an elaborate method of keeping time that led to the division of hours and minutes that we use today. The benefits of the Babylonians' impressive intellectual achievements were not spread widely through society. More subjects resented Babylonian rule than benefited from its accomplishments.

Rule by Tolerance: The Persian Empire, ca. 550–330 B.C.E.

In 553 B.C.E., the fortunes of the Babylonian Empire changed. The Persians, a people from east of the Zagros Mountains, overran the land of their Indo-European relatives, the Medes. Under their wise king, Cyrus the Great (r. 559–530 B.C.E.), the Persians expanded westward to establish an empire even larger than that of the Assyrians (**Map 1.5**). They quickly conquered the kingdom of Lydia in Asia Minor and then turned southeast to the Babylonian Empire. The Babylonian rulers found few supporters against the invaders even among their own people, and in 539 B.C.E. Babylon fell to the Persians virtually without a struggle.

Cyrus rejected the Assyrian policies of terror and sought to hold his vast empire together by tolerating differences among his many subject peoples. As mentioned earlier, in 538 B.C.E. he allowed the Jewish captives in Babylon to return to Jerusalem and rebuild their temple. At the same time, he appeased Babylonians by claiming he was "friend and companion" to their god Marduk. In the conquered provinces—or satrapies—Cyrus retained local officials but installed Persian governors called **satraps.** He controlled the satraps' power by appointing additional officials who were directly responsible to the king. The Persians required subject peoples to pay

Persian administration

thinking about GEOGRAPHY

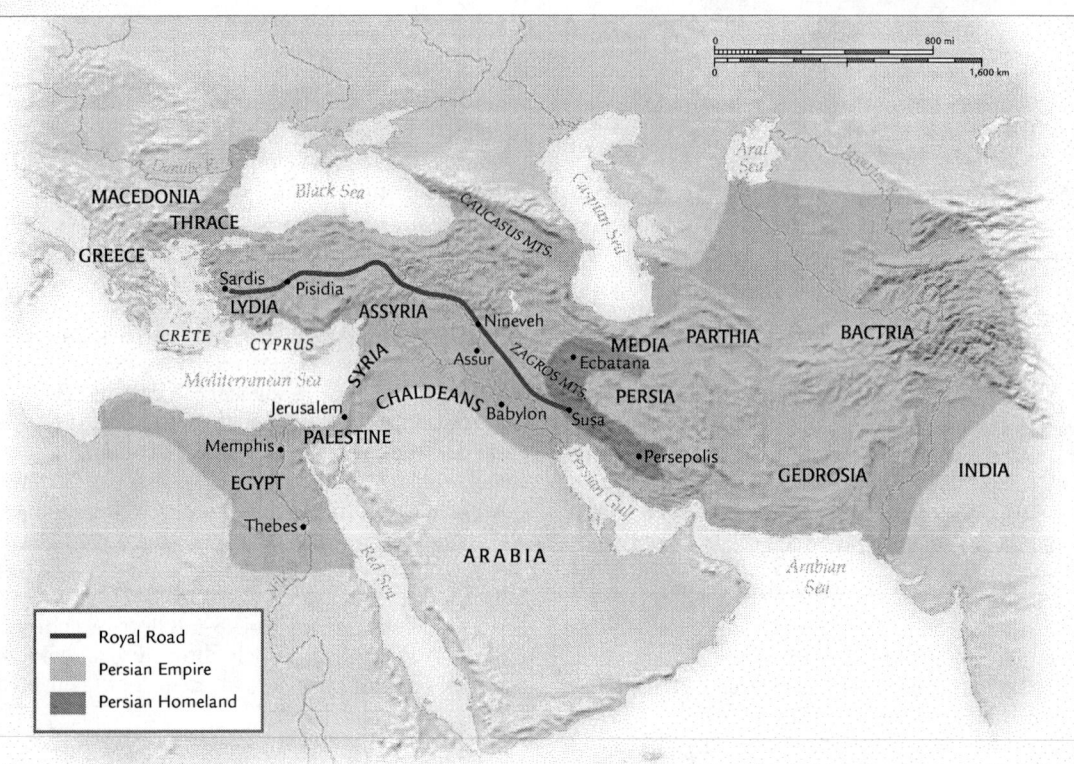

MAP 1.5

The Persian Empire, ca. 500 B.C.E.

This map illustrates the Persian Empire that replaced and greatly expanded the previous Assyrian domain and highlights the Royal Road, which spanned a large portion of the territory. It also shows the capital of the empire, Persepolis. Compare the extent of this empire with that of the Assyrians shown in **Map 1.4**.

Explore the Map

1. What problems do you think the Persians encountered due to the empire's vast expanse and diverse cultures?
2. How might the Royal Road have helped the Persian rulers to deal with the challenges of administering such a large empire?
3. Given that the Persian homeland and capital were so far east, what might the impact have been on Western culture?

---

reasonable taxes and serve in their armies, but Cyrus's system prevented local officials from abusing their power excessively. Conquered peoples could worship their own gods and follow their own customs, and under Cyrus's reign, the ancient civilizations enjoyed a long period of peace. The great king (as his subjects called him) was seen as a semidivine figure who ruled benignly from his golden throne.

After Cyrus's death in 530 B.C.E., his son Cambyses II (r. 529–522 B.C.E.) inherited the throne and continued the expansion his father had begun so effectively. The new king extended Persian control to the eastern Mediterranean by conquering Egypt and the Phoenician port cities. (See Document 1.3 for a description of Cambyses' military expansion.)

Cambyses was succeeded by Darius (r. 521–486 B.C.E.), a brilliant ruler who was able to consolidate and further organize what Cyrus and Cambyses had hastily conquered. Darius built a new capital city at Persepolis (see **Map 1.5**), moving the center of his empire east, but he also realized how important it was to facilitate travel throughout his empire. To accomplish this, he built and carefully maintained a complex system of roads, and the most famous was the Royal Road, between Susa in the east (in modern Iran) and Sardis (in modern Turkey) in the west. This impressive road, almost 1,700 miles long, fostered the economic life of the empire.

A unified empire allowed the Persians to adopt ideas that had proven successful in the civilizations

thinking about DOCUMENTS

DOCUMENT 1.3

Cambyses Conquers Egypt

This passage from the fifth-century B.C.E. Greek historian Herodotus describes the Persian king Cambyses' conquest of Egypt in 525 B.C.E. and his treatment of the pharaoh who had opposed his conquest. Cambyses was a controversial king, known for his "madness" (perhaps caused by alcoholism), yet even his reign was marked by policies that helped make the Persian Empire so successful.

After their defeat, the Egyptians fled in disorder and shut themselves up in Memphis. Cambyses called upon them to come to terms, sending a Persian herald up the river to the town in a Mytilenean vessel; but directly they saw the ship coming into the town, they rushed out from the walls in a body, smashed up the ship, tore everyone on board limb from limb, and carried the bits back inside the walls. They then stood a siege, but after a time surrendered. The neighbouring Libyans were alarmed by the fate of Egypt and gave themselves up without a battle, agreeing to pay tribute and sending presents. . . . Ten days passed, and Cambyses, wishing to see what stuff the Egyptian king Psammenitus was made of—he had been but six months on the throne—forced him with other Egyptians, to witness from a seat in the city outskirts a spectacle deliberately devised to humiliate him. . . .

[Cambyses was pleased at the young king's reactions.] They brought Psammenitus to Cambyses, at whose court he lived from that time onward. Here he was well treated; and indeed, if he had only had the sense to keep out of mischief, he might have recovered Egypt and ruled it as governor; for the Persians are in the habit of treating the sons of kings with honour, and even of restoring to their sons the thrones of those who have rebelled against them. There are many instances from which one may infer that this sort of generosity is usual in Persia. . . . Psammenitus, however, did not refrain from stirring up trouble, and paid for it. He was caught trying to raise a revolt amongst the Egyptians, and as soon as his guilt was known by Cambyses, he drank bull's blood and died on the spot. And that was the end of Psammenitus.

SOURCE: Herodotus, *The Histories*, trans. Aubrey de Sélincourt (New York: Penguin, 1996), pp. 159–160.

Analyze the Document

1. Why do you think the document emphasizes the treatment of Cambyses' enemies?
2. What persuades the Libyans to surrender? Is this strategy effective? Explain.
3. How does Herodotus expect Cambyses to treat the defeated Egyptian king? What actually happens to the king?

---

that preceded them. For example, Persians retained Aramaic as the common language of commerce, making communication easier across many cultures, and they fostered the trade routes that had brought so much wealth to the Babylonians. Persian astrologers learned from their Babylonian predecessors as well. These wise men, or magi, became celebrated for their knowledge of the heavens.

Of all the conventions the Persians borrowed from the inhabitants of their diverse empire, the adoption of coinage had the greatest long-term impact. The Lydians seem to have invented the use of coins in the seventh century B.C.E. Before this time, traders either bartered or used cumbersome bars of precious metals to purchase goods. For example, in Egypt in 1170 B.C.E., a burial vault that was priced at 5 pounds of copper might have been bought with 2½ pounds of copper, one hog, two goats, and two trees. By minting coins with precise, identifiable values, kingdoms greatly facilitated trade. The kings of Lydia were said to have grown fabulously rich after their invention, and the Persians rapidly spread the use of coins throughout their far-flung lands.

While the Persians adopted many novelties of their predecessors, they also made a unique contribution of their own: a new movement in religious thought initiated by the talented prophet Zoroaster (ca. 628–551 B.C.E.). One of the most important religious reformers of the ancient world, Zoroaster founded a new religion (later called **Zoroastrianism**) that contained the seeds of many modern belief systems. Zoroaster experienced a revelation given to him by the one god, Ahura Mazda, the Lord of Light. In this revelation, recorded in a holy book called the Avesta, Zoroaster was called to reform Persian religion by eliminating polytheism and animal sacrifice. In the tradition of Uruinimgina, Hebrew prophets, and others throughout the early history of Western civilization who called for social justice, Zoroaster also urged people to live ethical lives and to show care for others. Finally, the prophet believed that the history of the world was one of ongoing conflict between Ahura Mazda and the forces of the evil god Ahriman. Zoroaster also felt confident that Ahura Mazda would ultimately prevail over evil and that eventually the dead would be resurrected. Believers would go to paradise, while evildoers would fall into a hell of perpetual torture.

Beginning with the pious Zoroastrian Darius, the Persian kings claimed to rule the earth as Ahura Mazda's viceroys, but slowly the old nature worship returned and became incorporated into Zoroastrian beliefs. For example, people began to venerate Mithra, the ancient sun god, as an assistant to Ahura Mazda. Zoroaster's ideas had an influence that far outlasted the Persian rulers. During the Roman Empire, the worship of Mithra would be an important cult (see Chapter 5). Furthermore, followers of Zoroastrianism still exist today, and even in the ancient world many of the prophet's ideas influenced other religions as well. Over time, some believers transformed Zoroaster's monotheism into a dualistic belief in two gods, one good and one evil. Judaism—and, later, Christianity—seem to have been influenced by his vision, for Jewish texts began to write of the power of a devil and of a final struggle between good and evil. Zoroaster was the first prophet whose ideas would spread throughout a large political empire, but he would not be the last.

LOOKING BACK & MOVING FORWARD

Summary In the 3,000 years that make up the history of the ancient Middle East, many elements that characterize Western civilization emerged. Great cities sprang up, introducing commerce, excitement, diversity, and extremes of wealth and poverty that the West both values and struggles with even today. Tyranny and oppression arose, as did the laws and principles designed to hold them in check. Sophisticated religions provided vehicles for metaphysical reflection, and artists expressed those hopes and dreams in beautiful forms. Perhaps most important, writing systems evolved to let people preserve their accumulated knowledge for future generations, including ours. Finally, these early centuries established a pattern of interaction and cross-fertilization of goods and ideas that would mark Western civilization from its beginnings through today.

The great civilizations of the Nile and Tigris-Euphrates valleys—the Egyptians, Sumerians, Akkadians, Babylonians, and others—were ultimately absorbed by larger empires. Yet their contributions endured as a result of the mutual influence that always occurs when cultures mingle. The Hebrews, too, contributed much to the growing body of Western ideas and values. By 500 B.C.E., the Persian kings had united the region, creating an empire rich with the diversity of many peoples and thousands of years of history. The Persian Empire marks a culmination of the first stirrings of Western civilization in the ancient Middle East. The next developments in the story of the West would come from different peoples: the Greeks.

KEY TERMS
Paleolithic, *p. 4*
Neolithic, *p. 6*
ziggurat, *p. 9*
augury, *p. 10*
cuneiform, *p. 12*
ma'at, *p. 15*
pharaoh, *p. 16*
hieroglyph, *p. 18*
fresco, *p. 22*
Torah, *p. 26*
Diaspora, *p. 30*
satraps, *p. 33*
Zoroastrianism, *p. 35*

REVIEW, ANALYZE, & CONNECT TO TODAY

REVIEW AND ANALYZE THIS CHAPTER

Chapter 1 traces the development of Western civilization from its earliest beginnings in the cities of the ancient Middle East through the establishment of great empires. One of the significant themes throughout this chapter is the interaction among the various cultures that allowed each to assimilate and build on the innovations of the others.

1. What environmental advantages did the ancient Middle East have that permitted the growth of agriculture and cities? What disadvantages did the Middle East have? How did environmental conditions affect the various cultures?

2. Review the long-standing contributions of the Sumerians, Egyptians, Nubians, Phoenicians, and Hebrews.

3. How were the Jews able to maintain their integrity while being part of the Diaspora?

4. Review the empires—Assyrian, Babylonian, Persian—that arose in the ancient Middle East, and note the strengths and weaknesses of each.

CONNECT TO TODAY

Think about the changes in agriculture and animal husbandry discussed in this chapter.

1. How did the development of agriculture affect ancient societies? In what ways might advances in agriculture in more recent times have stimulated changes similar to those that occurred in the ancient world? Consider modern innovations such as the development of

drought-resistant grains and genetically modified foods. What other modern agricultural advances can you think of?

2. Ancient diseases moved from domesticated animals to humans, creating waves of pandemics followed by the development of immunities. What related situations do we face in our own times?

BEYOND THE CLASSROOM

BEFORE WESTERN CIVILIZATION

Diamond, Jared. *Guns, Germs, and Steel.* New York: W.W. Norton, 1997. A brilliant Pulitzer Prize–winning global analysis of the natural advantages that gave Western civilization its head start.

STRUGGLING WITH THE FORCES OF NATURE: MESOPOTAMIA, 3000–ca. 1000 B.C.E.

Binford, Lewis R. *In Pursuit of the Past.* New York: Thames & Hudson, 1988. An archaeological study of the transformation of human society.

Bryce, Trevor. *The Kingdom of the Hittites.* New York: Oxford University Press, 2006. A work that describes the rise and fall of the Hittites and includes the latest archaeology and translations of primary sources.

Crawford, Harriet. *Sumer and the Sumerians.* New York: Cambridge University Press, 1991. A summary of the historical and archaeological evidence that offers a solid survey of the field.

Hawkes, Jacquetta. *The Atlas of Early Man.* New York: St. Martin's Press, 1993. An accessible study of human thought.

Hooker, Jeremy T. *Reading the Past: Ancient Writing from Cuneiform to the Alphabet.* Berkeley: University of California Press, 1991. An exploration of the stages of the ancient scripts of past civilizations.

Postgate, Nicholas. *Early Mesopotamia: Society and Economy at the Dawn of History.* New York: Routledge, Chapman and Hall, 1992. A narrative depiction of the life of the peoples of early Mesopotamia.

Roux, Georges. *Ancient Iraq.* New York: Penguin, 1993. An excellent overview of the ancient world—from Mesopotamia to the Hellenistic conquests—that incorporates archaeological finds through 1992.

RULE OF THE GOD-KING: ANCIENT EGYPT, ca. 3100–1000 B.C.E.

Capel, A.X., and G.E. Markoe. *Mistress of the House, Mistress of Heaven: Women in Ancient Egypt.* New York: Hudson Hills Press, 1996. A beautifully illustrated study of the roles of women in ancient Egypt.

Grimal, N. *A History of Ancient Egypt.* Oxford: Oxford University Press, 1994. An insight into the essence of Egyptian culture and its relations with outsiders throughout its history.

Hornung, Erik. *History of Ancient Egypt: An Introduction.* Translated by David Lorton. Ithaca, NY: Cornell University Press, 1999. A concise and accessible summary of history that incorporates an excellent discussion of daily life in ancient times.

Tyldesley, Joyce. *Daughters of Isis: Women of Ancient Egypt.* New York: Penguin, 1995. A highly readable, illustrated account of women in Egypt.

PEOPLES OF THE MEDITERRANEAN COAST, ca. 1300–500 B.C.E.

Smith, Mark K. *Early History of God: Yahweh and the Other Deities in Ancient Israel.* San Francisco: Harper, 1990. A controversial look at the convergence and differentiation of deities toward monotheism in Israel.

Walton, John. *Ancient Near Eastern Thought and the Old Testament: Introducing the Conceptual World of the Hebrew Bible.* Grand Rapids, MI: Baker Academic, 2006. Balanced introductory look at the ideas in the Hebrew Bible, with excellent comparative dimensions.

TERROR AND BENEVOLENCE: THE GROWTH OF EMPIRES, 1200–500 B.C.E.

Curtis, J.E., and N. Tallis, eds. *Forgotten Empire: The World of Ancient Persia.* Berkeley: University of California Press, 2005. Comprehensive and scholarly view of the Persian Empire, beautifully illustrated with new archaeological finds.

Holland, Tom. *Persian Fire: The First World Empire and the Battle for the West.* New York: Anchor, 2007. Bold and engaging retelling of the Greek-Persian conflict, with a new emphasis on the Persian background.

Kuhrt, Amelie. *The Ancient Near East, ca. 3000–330 B.C.* New York: Routledge, 1997. A definitive account of ancient history, including the Israelites, that incorporates current scholarship and bib┕╌╌╌╌╌╌┙

GLOBAL CON

Adams, William Y. *to Africa.* Princeton, NJ: Princeton Universit comprehensive history of Nubia from prehistory through the nineteenth century.

THE WORLD & THE WEST

The Ancient World, 700 B.C.E.–400 C.E.

By 700 B.C.E., the roots of Western civilization had been firmly planted in the great civilizations that arose in the Fertile Crescent from Mesopotamia to Egypt. Skilled farmers cultivated diverse crops and domesticated animals. A bustling commerce connected traders from far Asia with merchants operating around the Mediterranean basin, through Egypt, and into sub-Saharan Africa. A developing sense of law and a new tradition of writing fostered growing communities, even as leaders regularly launched armies at one another in hopes of expanding their power.

Although the peoples of the Eurasian landmass did not know it, successful cultures were also developing in the extensive lands far to the west across the Atlantic ocean. While scholars are still thinking about how the Americas were settled, it is clear that humans arrived at least 20,000 years ago. Studies of blood type, teeth, and language suggest a direct link between humans in the Americas and those in northern China and northeastern Siberia. Therefore, most scholars still argue that people walked across a land bridge from Siberia to Alaska before it disappeared about 14,000 years ago under floods caused by melting glaciers. Other scholars argue that people may have migrated by boats along the coasts from Siberia down the Pacific coasts of the Americas. Whatever their origin, groups of successful hunters began to spread through this vast north-south landmass.

By 5000 B.C.E., many of the peoples of the Americas had developed maize (corn) as a domesticated crop that cannot grow on its own without human intervention. The abundance of this kind of agriculture allowed agricultural societies to spread throughout Mesoamerica. Toward the end of the second millennium B.C.E., large ceremonial centers began to appear, similar to the great centers of Egypt. Recent studies even suggest that indigenous peoples in the Amazon basin successfully began to build thriving populations in the rainforests. Certainly, there were flourishing communities from Alaska to Chile while Europe was still virtually unpopulated.

Advanced civilizations in the great river valleys of Asia—the Yellow River in China and the Indus and Ganges valleys in India—had characteristics in common with the agricultural societies in the West. They, too, cultivated crops, raised animals, and valued a bustling trade. Western civilization took a different course as Greece, and later Rome, rose to prominence and the civilization's center moved farther west.

If the agricultural roots of the West lay in the Fertile Crescent, its philosophical roots lay in Greece. This society planted the seeds for many of the West's values—from its praise of democracy and rational inquiry and its aesthetic tastes to its appreciation for individual human accomplishment. These ideas spread all the way to India with the conquests of Alexander the Great, the Macedonian military genius, in the fourth century B.C.E. However, the ideas also changed as they spread. For example, after Alexander's conquests, Greek artists began to infuse more emotion into their works, and philosophers thought less about abstract concepts of truth and justice, and more about how an individual might live a tranquil life. Indeed, when East and West met in the kingdoms that arose after Alexander's death, each transformed the other.

By the first century B.C.E., the center of Western civilization had shifted still farther west as the Romans built a powerful empire that endured for centuries. In this thriving realm, Westerners solidified their love of law, duty, and engineering (among other things). As we will see, the Roman Empire was counted among the most diverse empires of the ancient world, rivaling even the Persian Empire in its ability to bring together people from many cultures. As just one example, Roman soldiers hailing from sub-Saharan Africa helped guard Hadrian's Wall in Scotland, the northern reaches of the empire.

Of course, as these centuries unfolded, the rest of the world did not sit idle. In China, successive dynasties of rulers unified the centers of civilization along the Yellow River. Later dynasties then spread Chinese unification well beyond the Yellow River—into central Asia and south to the South China Sea. The Qin dynasty (221–207 B.C.E.) began joining culturally distinct regions into a larger Chinese society, a process that continued during the Han dynasty (206 B.C.E.–220 C.E.). Han China then spread its cultural accomplishments to neighbors in Korea, Vietnam, and central Asia and fostered the prosperous Silk Road, by which merchants in the East traded with the Roman Empire in the West.

In India, a complex society grew up in the valley of the great Indus River. Archaeologists call this culture Harappan, named after Harappa, one of its two chief cities. Scholars have not yet deciphered Harappan written records, so the details of this culture remain obscure. But thanks to archaeological remains, we do know that people living in this early society conducted long-distance trade with Mesopotamians and Egyptians.

During the second millennium B.C.E., roving bands of peoples from the north swept into India, replacing a declining Harappan society. Scholars have determined that these new arrivals, who later established the Mauryan dynasty, had connections with the West because the invaders spoke an Indo-European language similar to those that later appeared in western lands. Linguists have identified similarities between words in English, German, Greek, Latin, and Indian Sanskrit, and these commonalities testify to ancient cross-cultural contacts throughout the Eurasian landmass.

Inspired by the imperial successes of Alexander the Great in the West,

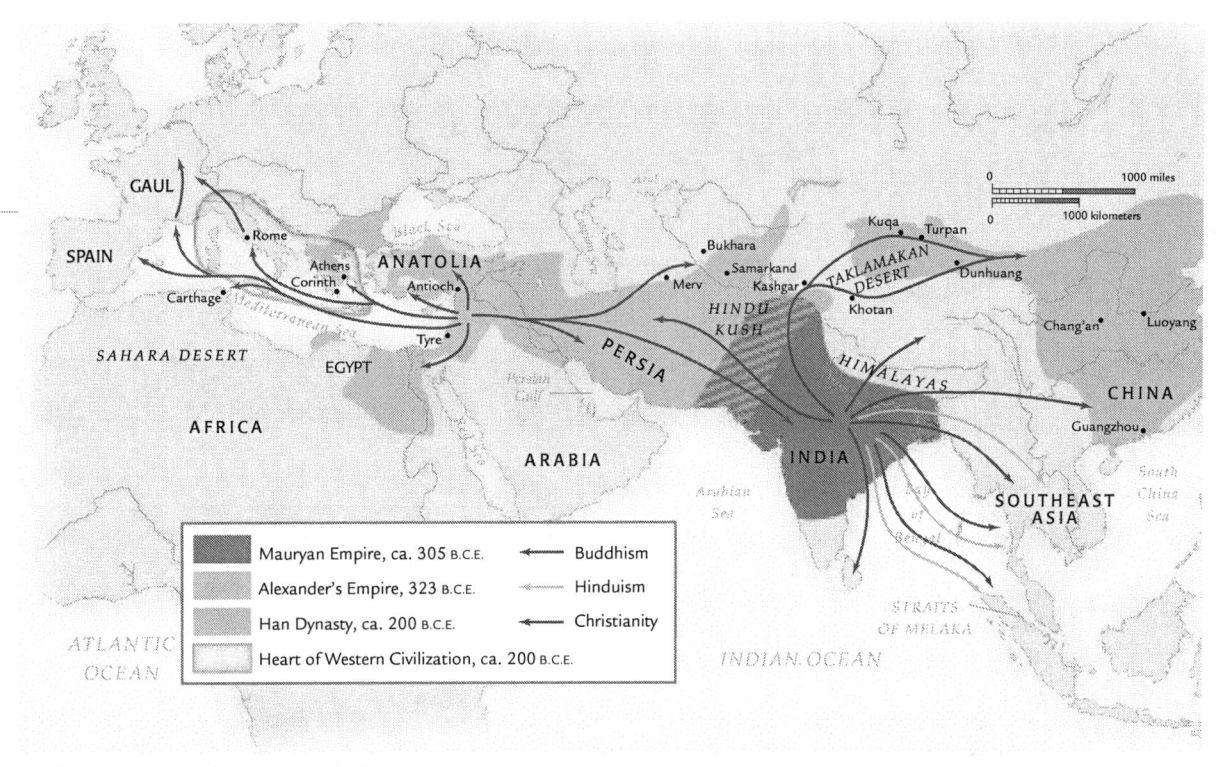

Ancient Empires and the Spread of Religion

leaders of the Mauryan dynasty unified diverse Indian peoples under one ruler in the fourth century B.C.E. When the Mauryan dynasty broke apart in the second century B.C.E., later rulers who remembered its accomplishments tried to re-create a single India. In the fourth century C.E., a new leader once again unified the northern Indian lands and established the Gupta dynasty, which endured until the end of the fifth century C.E. The idea of one India may have come initially from the West. But with the establishment of the successful Gupta dynasty, the new India served as a conduit by which goods and ideas flowed from east to west.

Thanks to such interactions, civilizations around the world flourished. The empires that expanded during the ancient world embraced and fostered profitable trade, even as rulers changed. The famous Silk Road, stretching from China to the Mediterranean, conveyed goods and peoples from realm to realm. Meanwhile, trade in India stretched northwest through the Hindu Kush mountains to Persia, east along the Silk Road, and overseas in the Indian Ocean basin, where sailors learned to predict the prevailing winds. Archaeologists working in southern India have unearthed hoards of Roman coins that offer silent testimony to the dynamic trade between east and west in the ancient world.

As always, movements of goods and peoples spurred exchanges of ideas both within and across civilizations. For example, during the ancient era, civilizations all over the Eurasian landmass experienced striking revolutions in religious thought. In China, the great philosopher Confucius (551–479 B.C.E.) urged Chinese leaders to adopt new moral and ethical principles and implored ordinary people to be kind and humane. At roughly the same time, a prince in India, Siddhartha Gautama (563–483 B.C.E.), struggled to understand and solve the problem of human suffering. Once he became "enlightened," he was called Buddha, and he initiated a movement that spread out from India during the Mauryan dynasty and influenced societies all over the world.

Westerners, too, experienced a wave of religious innovation during approximately the same time. In about the eighth century B.C.E., the ancient Hebrews were called to a higher ethical standard by prophets who maintained that worship of God belonged as much in people's hearts as in Temple rituals. Four centuries later, Socrates and his student Plato argued for a philosophy that recognized and sought transcendent moral truths.

The most influential religious transformation in the ancient West came with the life of Jesus, a Jew born in the Roman Empire. Christian apostles and missionaries traveling through the empire slowly spread Jesus' teachings even as far as India. Eventually the Roman Empire adopted Christianity as its official faith. This transformation gave the West the last attribute it acquired from the ancient world over the next millennium and beyond: The West would be equated with Judeo-Christian beliefs.

Thinking Globally

1. What empires had begun to dominate the Eurasian landmass in this period?
2. How would these empires foster global interactions?
3. What examples of the spread of cultures do you notice on the map?

Timeline

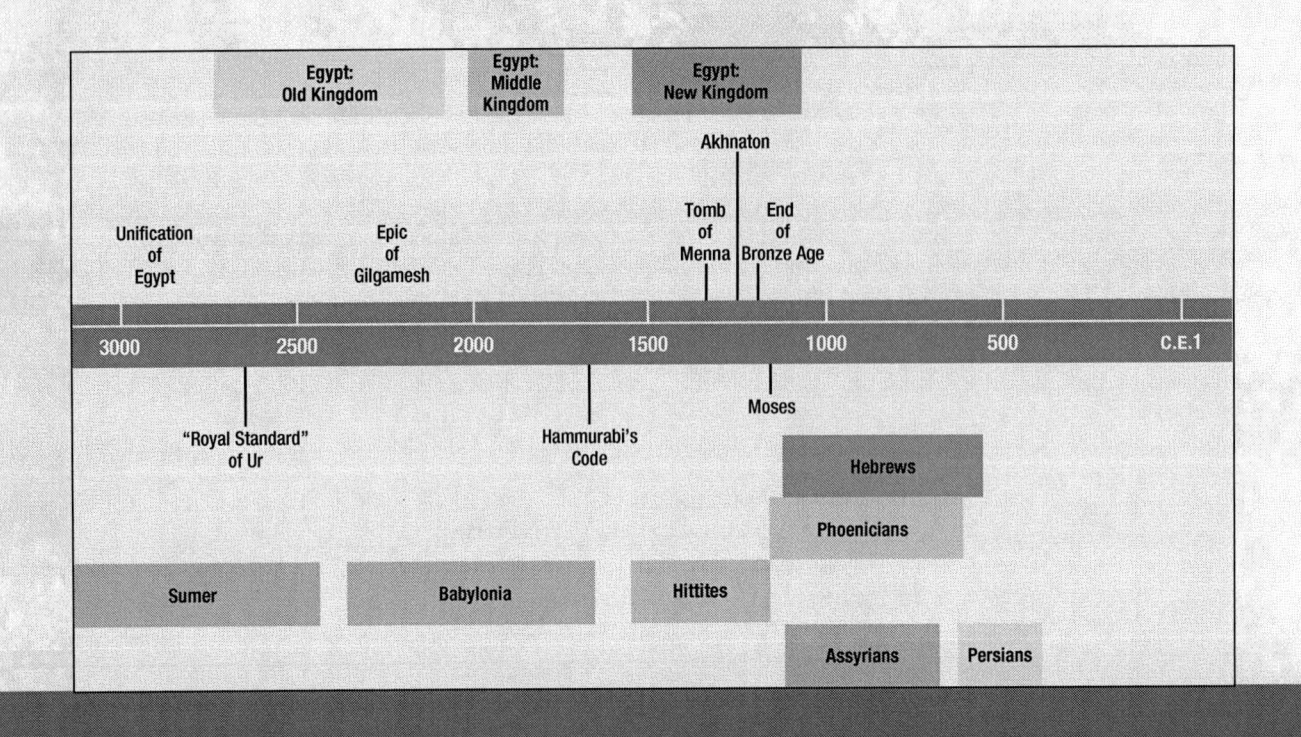

- Egypt: Old Kingdom
- Egypt: Middle Kingdom
- Egypt: New Kingdom
- Unification of Egypt
- Epic of Gilgamesh
- Akhnaton
- Tomb of Menna
- End of Bronze Age
- "Royal Standard" of Ur
- Hammurabi's Code
- Moses
- Sumer
- Babylonia
- Hittites
- Hebrews
- Phoenicians
- Assyrians
- Persians

3000 — 2500 — 2000 — 1500 — 1000 — 500 — C.E. 1

1 Civilizations of the Ancient Near East

What historians call *civilization* arose some five to six thousand years ago out of small agricultural villages in the river valleys of the ancient Near East, first in Mesopotamia near the Tigris and Euphrates rivers and shortly thereafter in Egypt around the Nile. In the delta of the Tigris-Euphrates river system, the Sumerians organized into city-states such as Ur. About 2340 B.C.E. the Sumerians were overwhelmed by the Akkadians from the north, and over the next two thousand years this area, a meeting point between Asia, Africa, and Europe, experienced great instability as in their turn the Babylonians, Hittites, Assyrians, Chaldeans, Medes, and Persians gained dominance. Egyptian civilization developed toward the end of the fourth millennium B.C.E. and is usually dated from about 3000 B.C.E., when the upper and lower Nile areas were unified under one king. Although there were some periods of change, this was a remarkably stable civilization, lasting almost three thousand years.

In many respects the Mesopotamian and Egyptian civilizations were similar. Both were dependent on rivers and the rich soil deposited by periodic floods; both had to develop and maintain organized systems of irrigation and flood control. Both eventually had powerful kings and a priestly caste. Both believed in all-powerful gods who played an active role in the world. But there were also important differences between these two civilizations. Mesopotamia was not as well protected geographically as Egypt and was thus more open to attack. Its rivers were not as navigable, nor were the floods as regular as the Nile's. Its culture and religion reflected a sense of instability and pessimism in comparison to the stability and optimism that characterized Egyptian civilization.

Between these two areas there arose a number of smaller and politically less significant states, the most important of which were the Phoenician and the Hebrew states. The Phoenicians, a mercantile people, facilitated trade, established colonies, and spread Near Eastern culture. The Hebrews developed religious and ethical ideas that would be a foundation for both Christian and Islamic civilizations.

A number of sources in this chapter deal with the origins, nature, and spread of the earliest civilizations. How should one define "civilization"? Why did civilizations arise where and when they did? What were the main characteristics of these ancient civilizations? Through what processes did civilizations spread? The rest of the documents concern each of the three main civilizations: the Mesopotamians, the Egyptians, and the Hebrews. For Mesopotamia, most of the sources center on the culture, the legal system, and the insights they provide into the nature of civilization there. Other documents focus on the position of women in Mesopotamian societies. For Egypt, what was the relation between the Nile and religion? What were some of Egypt's main economic and social characteristics? What was the significance of the pharaoh? How did the Egyptians view death and the afterlife? For the Hebrews, how did their religion, which became so important in the development of Western civilization, compare with others?

In sum, the sources in this chapter provide an introduction to the nature of civilization and its deep roots in the ancient Near East. The more direct foundations of Western civilization in ancient Greece will be examined in the next chapter.

The sources in this and all chapters are divided into three sections: Primary Sources, Visual Sources, and Secondary Sources. In this chapter, each one of these three sections begins with a guide containing suggestions on how to use the sources, focusing on the first source within the section.

For Classroom Discussion

How and why did civilization arise where and when it did in the ancient Near East? Use material from excerpts by Robert J. Braidwood, William H. McNeill, Herbert J. Muller, and the three maps.

Primary Sources

Using Primary Sources: The Laws of Hammurabi

Primary sources are briefly defined and discussed in the Preface. What follows is a more specific guide to the use of primary sources. It focuses on the first primary source in this book, the *Laws of Hammurabi*, which immediately follows as an example.

1. When reading primary sources such as the following selections from the *Laws of Hammurabi*, try to think of every line as evidence. Assume that you are a historian who knows very little about the history of Mesopotamia and that this document falls into your hands. Your job is to use this document as evidence to support some conclusions about Babylonian civilization.

   Actually, you have a head start. You already know something about the peoples of Mesopotamia from the chapter introduction, the time line, and the headnote preceding the source. You can use this information to better place the source in a historical context and to gain a sense of how the evidence in the source can be used. You also can use information from the headnote to identify the general nature of the source, where it came from, and when it was written.

2. Think of questions as you read the source. These can keep you focused on how words and lines and sections of the source might be used as evidence. A general question to keep in mind is, "What does this tell me about this civilization, about how people behaved, how they thought, what they believed?" Try reading each line as a piece of evidence to answer part of this general question. More specific questions can be derived from the "consider" points in italics just before the beginning of the document. These points indicate that the source might be particularly useful for providing evidence about the Babylonian legal system, about Babylonian social divisions, and about Babylonian politics and economics.

3. There are several ways almost any of these selections might be used as evidence. Read Article 1, the first section of the *Laws of Hammurabi*. It might be argued that the fact that a Babylonian could bring "a charge" of murder against someone,

that this charge had to be "proved," and that consequences flowed from the outcome of the process (if the accuser does not prove it he shall be put to death) constitutes evidence that the Babylonians had a formal legal system. You may further infer that this legal system was based on some principles of fairness (having to "prove" an accusation) and justice (death to those whose accusations are "not proved"). On the other hand, we must be careful not to read too much into this article—above all, not to read our own assumptions into the past. For example, this article does not tell us what constitutes proof or whether there is a jury system, although Article 3 might provide some evidence here (testimony is used and the truth of that testimony is at least open to challenge).

Read Articles 17, 18, and 19. Clearly they reveal that there were slaves within Babylonian society. They also imply that there was a problem with slaves attempting to escape, for rewards were offered to those who caught and returned slaves to their owners (Article 17) and penalties were imposed on those who hid escaped slaves (Article 19). Article 18 can be used as evidence for the existence of an organized bureaucracy of officials who kept written records ("take him to the palace in order that his record may be investigated").

Read Articles 53 and 54. They require landowners to keep dikes against water in repair (Article 53) and impose stiff penalties against those who do not (Articles 53 and 54). Together, the articles provide evidence for the existence of extensive water control systems for agriculture that required the cooperation (voluntary or imposed) of landowners and the government (by creating and enforcing these laws). Article 54 also reveals more about slavery in Babylonia, for since a landowner could be sold into slavery ("they shall sell him") we now have evidence that the source of slaves was not only external—from other societies through war, raids, or trade—but also internal.

Read Articles 141 and 142. How can the information in these articles be used to provide evidence for marriage, family life, and the relative positions of men and women in Babylonian society?

4. After working on various parts of the source, pull back and consider the source as a whole. It can be used to provide evidence for conclusions about Babylonia's system and principles of justice (the existence of laws, what the laws were, judgment and enforcement of laws, what crimes are more serious than others), its society (the importance and sources of slavery, the existence of different social classes, relations between men and women, the institution of marriage), its government (the king, the bureaucracy or core of governmental officials), and its economy (agriculture with a flood control system, a monetary system).

The Laws of Hammurabi

Much information about the peoples of Mesopotamia comes from compilations of laws, prescriptions, and decisions that were written as early as the twenty-third century B.C.E. The best known of these are the Laws of Hammurabi *(often referred to as the* Code of Hammurabi*), issued by an eighteenth-century B.C.E. Babylonian king who probably used older Sumerian and Akkadian laws. The laws refer to almost all aspects of life in Babylonia. The following selections are taken from this code, which originally had about 282 articles and included a long prologue and epilogue that traced Hammurabi's authority to the gods.*

CONSIDER: *The principles of justice reflected by these laws; the social divisions in Babylonian society disclosed in these laws; the political and economic characteristics of Babylonia revealed in this document.*

1: If a seignior[1] accused a(nother) seignior and brought a charge of murder against him, but has not proved it, his accuser shall be put to death.

SOURCE: From Pritchard, James B., *Ancient Near Eastern Texts Relating to the Old Testament,* copyright 1951 by Princeton University Press. Reprinted by permission of Princeton University Press.

[1]The word *awelum,* used here, is literally "man," but in the legal literature it seems to be used in at least three senses: (1) sometimes to indicate a man of the higher class, a noble; (2) sometimes a free man of any class, high or low; and (3) occasionally a man of any class, from king to slave. For the last I use the inclusive word "man," but for the first two, since it is seldom clear which of the two is intended in a given context, I follow the ambiguity of the original and use the rather general term "seignior," which I employ as the term is employed in Italian and Spanish, to indicate any free man of standing, and not in the strict feudal sense, although the ancient Near East did have something approximating the feudal system, and that is another reason for using "seignior."

3: If a seignior came forward with false testimony in a case, and has not proved the word which he spoke, if that case was a case involving life, that seignior shall be put to death.

4: If he came forward with (false) testimony concerning grain or money, he shall bear the penalty of that case.

6: If a seignior stole the property of church or state, that seignior shall be put to death; also the one who received the stolen goods from his hand shall be put to death.

17: If a seignior caught a fugitive male or female slave in the open and has taken him to his owner, the owner of the slave shall pay him two shekels[2] of silver.

18: If that slave will not name his owner, he shall take him to the palace in order that his record may be investigated, and they shall return him to his owner.

19: If he has kept that slave in his house (and) later the slave has been found in his possession, that seignior shall be put to death.

22: If a seignior committed robbery and has been caught, that seignior shall be put to death.

23: If the robber has not been caught, the robbed seignior shall set forth the particulars regarding his lost property in the presence of god, and the city and governor, in whose territory and district the robbery was committed, shall make good to him his lost property.

48: If a debt is outstanding against a seignior and Adad has inundated his field or a flood has ravaged (it) or through lack of water grain has not been produced in the field, he shall not make any return of grain to his creditor in that year; he shall cancel his contract-tablet and he shall pay no interest for that year.

53: If a seignior was too lazy to make [the dike of] his field strong and did not make his dike strong and a break has opened up in his dike and he has accordingly let the water ravage the farmland, the seignior in whose dike the break was opened shall make good the grain that he let get destroyed.

---

[2] A weight of about 8 g.

54: If he is not able to make good the grain, they shall sell him and his goods, and the farmers whose grain the water carried off shall divide (the proceeds).

141: If a seignior's wife, who was living in the house of the seignior, has made up her mind to leave in order that she may engage in business, thus neglecting her house (and) humiliating her husband, they shall prove it against her; and if her husband has then decided on her divorce, he may divorce her, with nothing to be given her as her divorce-settlement upon her departure. If her husband has not decided on her divorce, her husband may marry another woman, with the former woman living in the house of her husband like a maidservant.

142: If a woman so hated her husband that she has declared, "You may not have me," her record shall be investigated at her city council, and if she was careful and was not at fault, even though her husband has been going out and disparaging her greatly, that woman, without incurring any blame at all, may take her dowry and go off to her father's house.

195: If a son has struck his father, they shall cut off his hand.

196: If a seignior has destroyed the eye of a member of the aristocracy, they shall destroy his eye.

197: If he has broken a(nother) seignior's bone, they shall break his bone.

198: If he has destroyed the eye of a commoner or broken the bone of a commoner, he shall pay one mina of silver.

199: If he has destroyed the eye of a seignior's slave or broken the bone of a seignior's slave, he shall pay one-half his value.

200: If a seignior has knocked out a tooth of a seignior of his own rank, they shall knock out his tooth.

201: If he has knocked out a commoner's tooth, he shall pay one-third mina of silver.

202: If a seignior has struck the cheek of a seignior who is superior to him, he shall be beaten sixty (times) with an oxtail whip in the assembly.

209: If a seignior struck a(nother) seignior's daughter and has caused her to have a miscarriage, he shall pay ten shekels of silver for her fetus.

210: If that woman has died, they shall put his daughter to death.

211: If by a blow he has caused a commoner's daughter to have a miscarriage, he shall pay five shekels of silver.

212: If that woman has died, he shall pay one-half mina of silver.

The Epic of Gilgamesh

Insight into a people's ideas about life and death can be gained by examining their myths and their literature. The Epic of Gilgamesh, *probably written in the latter part of the third millennium (2000s) B.C.E., was the great epic poem of Mesopotamia. Its hero, Gilgamesh, ruled the Sumerian citystate of Uruk around 2700 B.C.E. The poem is about the mythical adventures this king, part god himself, has struggling with life, the gods, and death. In one adventure, Gilgamesh faces death by embarking on a search for immortality. As part of that search he descends into the Netherworld to find Utnapishtim, a human who has been granted immortality by the gods. In the following selection, Gilgamesh questions Utnapishtim, who tells him the story of the flood.*

CONSIDER: *The nature of the gods and their relations with humans; conclusions about life Mesopotamians might have come to reading or listening to this story; connections between this story and the Biblical story of Noah and the flood.*

"Oh, father Utnapishtim, you who have entered the assembly of the gods, I wish to question you concerning the living and the dead, how shall I find the life for which I am searching?"

Utnapishtim said, "There is no permanence. Do we build a house to stand for ever, do we seal a contract to hold for all time? Do brothers divide an inheritance to keep for ever, does the flood-time of rivers endure? It is only the nymph of the dragon-fly who sheds her larva and sees the sun in his glory. From the days of old there is no permanence. The sleeping and the dead, how alike they are, they are like a painted death. What is there between the master and the servant when both have fulfilled their doom? When the Annunaki,[3] the judges, come together, and Mammetun the mother of destinies, together they decree the fates of men. Life and death they allot but the day of death they do not disclose."

Then Gilgamesh said to Utnapishtim the Faraway, "I look at you now, Utnapishtim, and your appearance is no different from mine; there is nothing strange in your features. I thought I should find you like a hero prepared for battle, but you lie here taking your ease on your back. Tell me truly, how was it that you came to enter the company of the gods and to possess everlasting life?"

Utnapishtim said to Gilgamesh, "I will reveal to you a mystery, I will tell you a secret of the gods."

"You know the city Shurrupak, it stands on the banks of Euphrates? That city grew old and the gods that were in it were old. There was Anu, lord of the firmament, their father, and warrior Enlil their counsellor, Ninurta the helper, and Ennugi watcher over canals; and with them also was Ea.[4] In those days the world teemed, the people multiplied, the world bellowed like a wild bull, and the great god was aroused by the clamour. Enlil heard the clamour and he said to the gods in council, 'The uproar of mankind is intolerable and sleep is no longer possible by reason of the babel.' So the gods in their hearts were moved to let loose the deluge; but my lord Ea warned me in a dream. He whispered their words to my house of reeds, 'Reed-house, reed-house! Wall, O wall, hearken reed-house, wall reflect; O man of Shurrupak, son of Ubara-Tutu; tear down your house and build a boat, abandon possessions and look for life, despise worldly goods and save your soul alive. Tear down your house, I say, and build a boat.'

"When I had understood I said to my lord, 'Behold, what you have commanded I will honour and perform, but how shall I answer the people, the city, the elders?' Then Ea opened his mouth and said to me, his servant, 'Tell them this: I have learnt that Enlil is wrathful against me, I dare no longer walk in his land nor live in his city; I will go down to the Gulf to dwell with Ea my lord. But on you he will rain down abundance, rare fish and shy wildfowl, a rich harvest-tide. In the evening the rider of the storm will bring you wheat in torrents.'" . . .

"On the seventh day the boat was complete. . . .

"I loaded into her all that I had of gold and of living things, my family, my kin, the beasts of the field both wild and tame, and all the craftsmen . . .

"For six days and six nights the winds blew, torrent and tempest and flood overwhelmed the world, tempest and flood raged together like warring hosts. When the seventh day dawned the storm from the south subsided, the sea grew calm, the flood was stilled; I looked at the face of the world and there was silence, all mankind was turned to clay. The surface of the sea stretched as flat as a rooftop; I opened a hatch and the light fell on my face. Then I bowed low, I sat down and I wept, the tears streamed down my face, for on every side was the waste of water. I looked for land in vain, but fourteen leagues distant there appeared a mountain, and there the boat grounded; on the mountain of Nisir the boat held fast, she held fast and did not budge. . . . When the seventh day dawned I loosed a dove and let her go. She flew

---

SOURCE: N. K. Sandars, trans., *The Epic of Gilgamesh*, 2d rev. ed. (London: Penguin Books, 1972), copyright © N. K. Sandars, 1960, 1964, 1972.

[3] Gods.

[4] God of wisdom and good fortune.

away, but finding no resting-place she returned. Then I loosed a swallow, and she flew away but finding no resting-place she returned. I loosed a raven, she saw that the waters had retreated, she ate, she flew around, she cawed, and she did not come back. Then I threw everything open to the four winds, I made a sacrifice and poured out a libation on the mountain top. Seven and again seven cauldrons I set up on their stands, I heaped up wood and cane and cedar and myrtle. When the gods smelled the sweet savour, they gathered like flies over the sacrifice. Then, at last, Ishtar also came, she lifted her necklace with the jewels of heaven that once Anu had made to please her. 'O you gods here present, by the lapis lazuli round my neck I shall remember these days as I remember the jewels of my throat; these last days I shall not forget. Let all the gods gather round the sacrifice, except Enlil. He shall not approach this offering, for without reflection he brought the flood; he consigned my people to destruction.'

"When Enlil had come, when he saw the boat, he was wrath and swelled with anger at the gods, the host of heaven, 'Has any of these mortals escaped? Not one was to have survived the destruction.' Then the god of the wells and canals Ninurta opened his mouth and said to the warrior Enlil, 'Who is there of the gods that can devise without Ea? It is Ea alone who knows all things.' Then Ea opened his mouth and spoke to warrior Enlil, 'Wisest of gods, hero Enlil, how could you so senselessly bring down the flood?' . . .

"Then Enlil went up into the boat, he took me by the hand and my wife and made us enter the boat and kneel down on either side, he standing between us. He touched our foreheads to bless us saying, 'In time past Utnapishtim was a mortal man; henceforth he and his wife shall live in the distance at the mouth of the rivers.' Thus it was that the gods took me and placed me here to live in the distance, at the mouth of the rivers."

Hymn to the Nile

Most of the earliest civilizations were located in major river valleys. The Nile River provided the Egyptians with a strip of fertile land in an area otherwise relatively arid and hostile to large long-term settlement. Moreover, its predictable annual flooding ensured the continued fertility of the land and enabled the Egyptians to irrigate the crops that supported this long-lasting civilization. Understandably, the Nile became a focus for Egyptian religious beliefs and one of the Egyptians' chief deities. In the following selection from a hymn to the Nile, probably originating in an early period in Egyptian history, the Nile is praised for its power and deeds that have enabled the Egyptians to live in a relatively ordered, prosperous world.

CONSIDER: *The Egyptian view of the proper relationship between themselves and this deity; the Egyptian perception of this deity and its characteristics; the information this document provides concerning Egyptian economic, social, and political life.*

When he[5] is sluggish noses clog,
Everyone is poor;
As the sacred loaves are pared,
A million perish among men.
When he plunders, the whole land rages,
Great and small roar;
People change according to his coming,
When Khnum has fashioned him.
When he floods, earth rejoices,
Every belly jubilates,
Every jawbone takes on laughter,
Every tooth is bared.

Food provider, bounty maker,
Who creates all that is good!
Lord of awe, sweetly fragrant,
Gracious when he comes.
Who makes herbage for the herds,
Gives sacrifice for every god.
Dwelling in the netherworld,
He controls both sky and earth.
Conqueror of the Two Lands,
He fills the stores,
Makes bulge the barns,
Gives bounty to the poor.

When you overflow, O Hapy,[6]
Sacrifice is made for you;
Oxen are slaughtered for you,
A great oblation is made to you.
Fowl is fattened for you,
Desert game snared for you,
As one repays your bounty.

One offers to all the gods
Of that which Hapy has provided,
Choice incense, oxen, goats,
And birds in holocaust.

SOURCE: Miriam Lichtheim, *Ancient Egyptian Literature,* 3 vols., pp. 199, 206, 208–209. Copyright © 1973–1980 Regents of the University of California.

[5]The Nile.
[6]The Nile.

Hymn to the Pharaoh

The history of Egypt and the institution of kingship have been traced back to the end of the fourth millennium B.C.E., when Upper and Lower Egypt were unified apparently under one great conquering king. The Egyptian king, or pharaoh, was considered both a god and the absolute ruler of his country. These beliefs are reflected in laudatory hymns addressed to pharaohs. The following selection is from one of those hymns, dating from the reign of Sesostris III, who ruled from about 1880 to 1840 B.C.E.

CONSIDER: *The Egyptian perception of the pharaoh; what deeds or powers of the pharaoh seemed most important to the Egyptians; similarities and differences between the Egyptian perceptions of the pharaoh and of the Nile.*

How [the gods] rejoice:
   you have strengthened their offerings!
How your [people] rejoice:
   you have made their frontiers!
How your forbears rejoice:
   you have enriched their portions!
How Egypt rejoices in your strength:
   you have protected its customs!
How the people rejoice in your guidance:
   your might has won increase [for them]!
How the Two Shores rejoice in your dreadedness:
   You have enlarged their holdings!
How the youths whom you levied rejoice:
   you have made them prosper!
How your elders rejoice:
   you have made them youthful!
How the Two Lands rejoice in your power:
   you have protected their walls!

The Old Testament—Genesis and Exodus

Squeezed between the larger kingdoms of Mesopotamia and Egypt were a number of small states. For the development of Western civilization, the most important of these states was in Palestine, where the Hebrews formed Israel and Judah. Although their roots extend further into the past, the Hebrews were originally led out of northeastern Egypt toward Palestine by Moses near the end of the second millennium B.C.E. The power of the Hebrew nation reached its height during the tenth and ninth centuries B.C.E., but the nation's importance rests primarily in the religion developed by the Hebrews. Judaism differed in many ways from other Near Eastern religions, particularly in its monotheism, its contractual nature, and its ethical mandates. These characteristics of Judaism are illustrated in the following selections from Genesis and Exodus.

CONSIDER: *The relationship between God and people illustrated in these selections; how these Hebrew beliefs compare with Egyptian beliefs; as a set of laws, how these selections compare with Hammurabi's Code.*

12: The LORD had said to Abram, "Leave your country, your people and your father's household and go to the land I will show you.

"I will make you into a great nation and I will bless you;
I will make your name great, and you will be a blessing.
I will bless those who bless you, and whoever curses you I will curse;
and all peoples on earth will be blessed through you."

19: In the third month after the Israelites left Egypt—on the very day—they came to the Desert of Sinai. After they set out from Rephidim, they entered the Desert of Sinai, and Israel camped there in the desert in front of the mountain.

Then Moses went up to God, and the LORD called to him from the mountain and said, "This is what you are to say to the house of Jacob and what you are to tell the people of Israel: 'You yourselves have seen what I did to Egypt, and how I carried you on eagles' wings and brought you to myself. Now if you obey me fully and keep my covenant, then out of all nations you will be my treasured possession. Although the whole earth is mine, you will be for me a kingdom of priests and a holy nation.' These are the words you are to speak to the Israelites."

So Moses went back and summoned the elders of the people and set before them all the words the LORD had commanded him to speak. The people all responded together, "We will do everything the LORD has said." So Moses brought their answer back to the LORD.

20: And God spoke all these words:

"I am the LORD your God, who brought you out of Egypt,
   out of the land of slavery.
"You shall have no other gods before me.
"You shall not make for yourself an idol in the form of
   anything in heaven above or on the earth beneath or in
   the waters below. You shall not bow down to them or
   worship them; for I, the LORD your God, am a jealous
   God, punishing the children for the sin of the fathers to
   the third and fourth generation of those who hate me,
   but showing love to a thousand generations of those
   who love me and keep my commandments.

SOURCE: Miriam Lichtheim, *Ancient Egyptian Literature*, vol. I, pp. 199, 206, 208–209. Copyright © 1973–1980 Regents of the University of California.

SOURCE: Scripture taken from the *Holy Bible, New International Version*®. NIV®. Copyright© 1973, 1978, 1984 by International Bible Society. Used by permission of Zondervan Publishing House. All rights reserved.

"You shall not misuse the name of the LORD your God, for the LORD will not hold anyone guiltless who misuses his name.

"Remember the Sabbath day by keeping it holy. Six days you shall labor and do all your work, but the seventh day is a Sabbath to the LORD your God. On it you shall not do any work, neither you, nor your son or daughter, nor your manservant or maidservant, nor your animals, nor the alien within your gates. For in six days the LORD made the heavens and the earth, the sea, and all that is in them, but he rested on the seventh day. Therefore the LORD blessed the Sabbath day and made it holy.

"Honor your father and your mother, so that you may live long in the land the LORD your God is giving you.

"You shall not murder.

"You shall not commit adultery.

"You shall not steal.

"You shall not give false testimony against your neighbor.

"You shall not covet your neighbor's house. You shall not covet your neighbor's wife, or his manservant or maidservant, his ox or donkey, or anything that belongs to your neighbor."

When the people saw the thunder and lightning and heard the trumpet and saw the mountain in smoke, they trembled with fear. They stayed at a distance and said to Moses, "Speak to us yourself and we will listen. But do not have God speak to us or we will die."

Moses said to the people, "Do not be afraid. God has come to test you, so that the fear of God will be with you to keep you from sinning."

The Aton Hymn and Psalm 104: The Egyptians and the Hebrews

Several characteristics made the Hebrews unique in the ancient Near East. However, many civilizations have certain similarities, including their religious beliefs and practices. Moreover, Hebrews were connected to and influenced by the Egyptians in many ways. Geographically, Palestine served as a buffer zone between Egypt and the large kingdoms of Mesopotamia. Historically, the formative ordeal of Moses and the Exodus stemmed from Egypt. Less apparent but of great importance were connections between Hebrew and Egyptian religious concepts and forms of expression. The following comparison of selections from the Egyptian Aton Hymn, composed in the fourteenth century B.C.E. during the rule of Akhenaten, who attempted to change some traditional religious views, and Psalm 104 from the Old Testament, written six or seven centuries later, illustrates striking parallels between the two documents.

CONSIDER: *How the similarities between these two excerpts might be explained.*

THE ATON HYMN	PSALM 104
When thou settest in the western horizon,	Thou makest darkness and it is night,
The land is in darkness like death . . .	Wherein all the beasts of the forest creep forth.
Every lion comes forth from his den;	The young lions roar after their prey.
All creeping things, they sting.	The sun ariseth, they get them away . . .
At daybreak, when thou arisest in the horizon . . .	Man goeth forth unto his work,
Thou drivest away the darkness . . .	And to his labor until the evening.
Men awake and stand upon their feet . . .	O Jahweh, how manifold are thy works!
All the world, they do their labor.	In wisdom has thou made them all;
How manifold are thy works!	The earth is full of thy riches.
They are hidden from man's sight.	
O sole god, like whom there is no other,	
Thou hast made the earth according to thy desire.	

Visual Sources

Using Visual Sources: The "Royal Standard" of Ur

Visual sources are briefly defined and discussed in the Preface. What follows is a more specific guide to the use of visual sources, focusing on our first visual source, *The "Royal Standard" of Ur*, which immediately follows as an example (figures 1.1 and 1.2).

1. Try to look at visual sources as if they were written, primary documents. As with primary documents, assume that you are a historian who knows very

little about the history of Sumer and discovers this visual source, *The "Royal Standard" of Ur*. Your goal is to try to "read" it as evidence to support some conclusions about Sumerian civilization.

Without some guidance, "reading" a visual source as historical evidence is more difficult than using a written source. The reproduction makes the details harder to see and most people are not used to looking at a picture in this analytical way. Therefore, in the first paragraph of the headnote to *The "Royal Standard" of Ur*, there is a description that puts into words what appears in the visual source. In the second paragraph, there is an analysis of the evidence drawn from the photo. Here, as with most visual sources, it is useful to go back and forth between the photo and the written description and analysis that accompany the photo.

2. As with primary documents, think of questions as you look at the visual source and as you read the written guide to it. The general question to keep in mind is, What does this tell me about this civilization, about how people behaved, how they thought, or what they believed? Other questions are suggested in the "consider" points, such as what information the artist might have been attempting to convey to the viewer.

3. Here the first panel shows the Sumerians at war. The headnote alerts us to "read" this three-line panel from bottom to top, for that is how the Sumerian artist intended it to be viewed. With the aid of the headnote we can see the chariot charging the enemy, then the infantry, and finally the captives being led to the victorious king.

The second panel shows the Sumerians at peace. Again reading from bottom to top, we can see this society organizing in preparation for a banquet and then the banquet itself.

The second paragraph suggests some of the ways the information derived from *The "Royal Standard" of Ur* can be used as historical evidence that Ur in Sumer was a well-organized society with centralized political control, a society that at least by 2700 B.C.E. had mastered the use of various domesticated animals, tools, and instruments.

4. Now pull back and consider the source as a whole. Why might the artist have chosen to depict these scenes? What might be made of the lack of individualized differences in the figures? In what ways might a similar sort of decoration be made today and what might such a set of scenes depict?

Sumer: The "Royal Standard" of Ur

This piece of art—made of shell, lapis lazuli, and red stone inlaid on the sides of a wooden box and found in a grave dating around 2700 B.C.E.—illustrates two aspects of Sumerian life: war and peace. In the bottom line of the first panel, reading from left to right, a wooden chariot charges the enemy and knocks him over. In the second line the infantry, with protective cloaks, helmets, and short spears, captures and leads off the enemy. In the third line soldiers on the right lead captives to the king in the center. The king, who has just alighted from his attended chariot on the left, towers over the rest. In the second panel the fruits of victory or of peace are enjoyed, at least by the court. In the bottom and middle lines produce, manufactured goods, and livestock are brought to a banquet by bearers and menials. In the top line the king on the left and his soldiers drink wine while attended by servants and serenaded by a harpist and female singer on the right.

Clearly, this offers evidence for what historians consider a civilized society. Agricultural products are shown. Various animals have been domesticated for specialized purposes.

Important inventions such as the wheel are in use. Leisure activities have been cultivated, as revealed by the harp, the rather formal banquet, and the existence of this piece of art itself (which may have been a box for a lyre). The society has been organized and displays some discipline, as indicated by the use of chariots, the infantry, the porters, the musicians, the servants, and the banquet itself. Finally, the king represents centralized political authority that is directly tied to military prowess. Note that the sole female figure here is the singer.

CONSIDER: *Why there is a lack of individual differences in the people portrayed in this picture; bases for social distinction in Sumerian society revealed in this scene; things or scenes missing from this that you might have expected to find; reasons the artist chose to portray these particular scenes and to include only the things you see here.*

Egyptian Wall Paintings from the Tomb of Menna

This wall painting from the tomb of an Egyptian scribe, Menna, dating from the late fifteenth century B.C.E., illustrates the basis of Egyptian economic life (figure 1.3). This pictorial record of a harvest should be read from bottom to top. In the bottom row,

SOURCE: Reprinted in *The Burden of Egypt* by John A. Wilson, by permission of The Chicago Press. Copyright © 1951, p. 227.

FIGURE 1.1 Royal Standard of Ur, "War" Side, from the Sumerian Royal Graves of Ur, Early Dynastic Period, 2750 B.C.E. (Mosaic). (© The British Museum, London, UK/Bridgeman Art Library)

FIGURE 1.2 Royal Standard of Ur, "Peace" Side, from the Sumerian Royal Graves of Ur, Early Dynastic Period, 2750 B.C.E. (Mosaic). (© The British Museum, London, UK/Bridgeman Art Library.)

from left to right, commoners are harvesting wheat with sickles. The wheat is then carried in rope baskets past two girls fighting over remaining bits of wheat and past two laborers (one of whom is playing a flute) who are taking a break under a date tree, to where the wheat is being threshed and raked out by laborers. In the second row, from right to left, oxen tread on the wheat, separating the kernels from the husks, and laborers remove the chaff by scooping up the wheat and allowing it to fall in the wind. The grain is then brought to the supervising scribe, Menna, standing in a kiosk. Menna is aided by subordinate recording scribes. In the top row, from left to right, the fields are being measured by ropes as a basis for assessing taxes. In the center Menna watches as subordinates line up and whip those who have apparently failed to pay their taxes or adequately perform their duties. Finally, the grain is stacked for shipment and carried off in a boat.

The harvest seems plentiful, and Egyptian society is tightly organized around it—from the gathering, processing, and shipping of the wheat to the assessing of taxes and enforcement of laws. Menna's authority is denoted by his size, by his placement in a kiosk, and by the symbols of power placed in his hand and immediately around him. The importance of writing in early societies is also demonstrated: Menna and his immediate

FIGURE 1.3 (© Elliott Erwitt/Magnum Photos)

subordinates are in an authoritative position in part because they can write, a skill connected here to the ability of the central authority to organize the economy and exact taxes. Finally, this wall painting reveals part of the nature of Egyptian religious beliefs. The scene is painted on the inside of a tomb. Thus the paintings were not for the living public, as the tombs were not to be visited, but for the dead or the world of the dead. This implies a belief that there were strong connections between this world, what one did in it, and the afterlife.

CONSIDER: *The evidence for the existence of a civilized society here; the similarities and differences between this and The "Royal Standard" of Ur.*

The Environment and the Rise of Civilization in the Ancient Near East

These three maps relate weather, vegetation, agricultural sites, and civilizations in the ancient Near East. Map 1.1 shows the average annual rainfall in modern times (although weather patterns may have changed

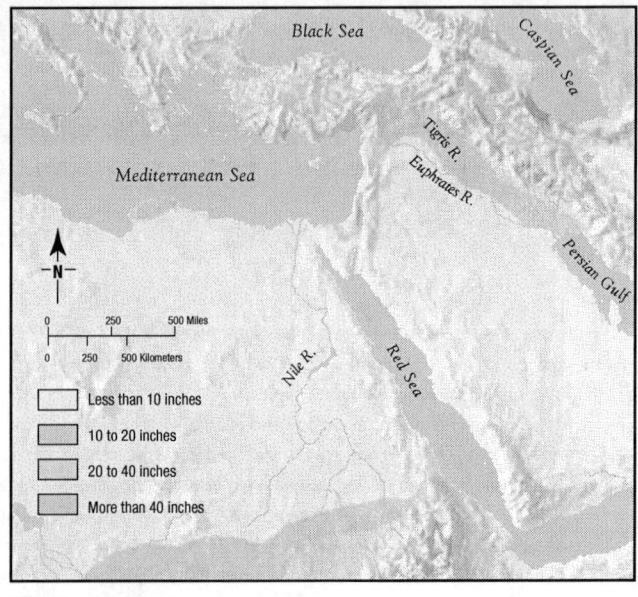

MAP 1.1 Rainfall

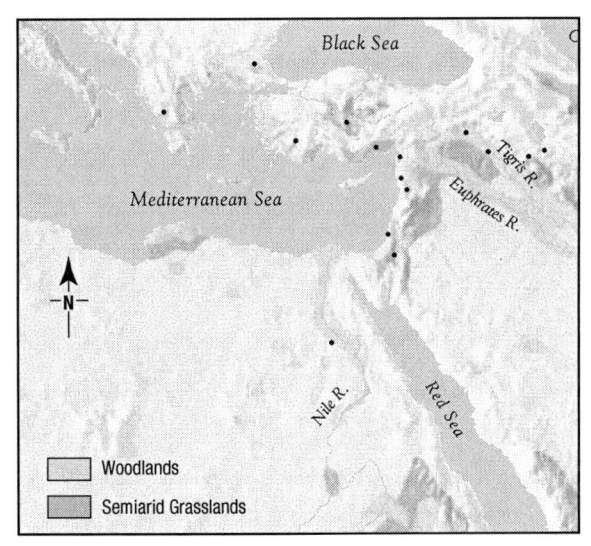

MAP 1.2 Vegetation and Agricultural Sites

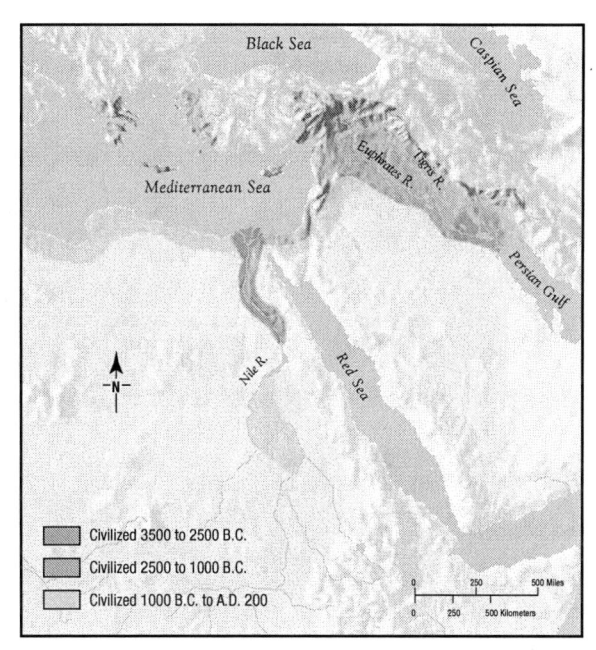

MAP 1.3 Civilization

over the last five thousand years, it is likely that they have not changed greatly). Map 1.2 shows some of the vegetation patterns and a number of the earliest agricultural sites that have been discovered in the same area. Map 1.3 shows patterns of civilization in this part of the world.

Together, these maps indicate a tendancy for early agriculture sites to locate in areas of substantial rainfall and subtropical woodland, both appropriate for cereal farming. These areas often eventually supported the development of civilizations. Yet the earliest civilizations generally do not fall in these areas, but rather in areas of low rainfall that have a narrow strip of subtropical woodland along riverbanks. The rivers could compensate for the lack of rain, but low rainfall presented the challenge of developing irrigation systems along with corresponding social and political organizations. This is what happened in the earliest civilizations of Mesopotamia and Egypt.

Secondary Sources

Using Secondary Sources: The Agricultural Revolution

Secondary sources are briefly defined and discussed in the Preface. What follows is a more specific guide to the use of secondary sources, focusing on our first secondary source, *The Agricultural Revolution*, which immediately follows as an example.

1. Try to read a secondary source like *The Agricultural Revolution* by Robert J. Braidwood not as historical evidence (as you would for a primary source), but as a set of conclusions—an interpretation of the evidence from primary sources—by a scholar (usually a historian). Your job is to try to understand what the writer's interpretation is, evaluate whether any arguments or evidence the writer presents seems to support it adequately, and decide in what ways you agree or disagree with that interpretation.

2. Try to think of questions as you read a secondary source. This process can keep you alert to why the author selects and presents only certain information and what conclusions the author is trying to convey to the reader. Perhaps the two most important questions to keep in mind are, What question is this author trying to answer? and What does all of what the author has written add up to? For each secondary source, guidance for these two questions and related questions is provided in the headnote to the source and in the "consider" points.

Here the headnote to this secondary source tells us that the author, Robert J. Braidwood, is trying to interpret the agricultural revolution, particularly its spread and significance. The "consider" section alerts us to more specific aspects of what the author is trying to convince us of, such as his interpretation for the causes of the agricultural revolution and his rejection of alternative explanations (environmental determinism) for the agricultural revolution presented by other scholars.

3. Try reading and summarizing in a few words what Braidwood is trying to say or argue in each paragraph. What conclusion is he reaching?

One could summarize the first paragraph by saying that Braidwood is trying to convince us that the agricultural revolution was an extremely important achievement of our species. He also defines the agricultural revolution ("the domestication of plants and animals" and "the achievement of an effective food-producing technology") and suggests why it was so important (the "subsequent developments" that "followed swiftly"—urban societies and later industrial civilization).

In the second paragraph Braidwood concludes that the agricultural revolution was caused ("the origin") by cultural evolution ("the record of culture"). He argues that the several independent inventions ("multiple occurrence") of agriculture support ("suggests that") his conclusion.

In the third paragraph Braidwood presents a contrary interpretation for the causes of the agricultural revolution ("environmental determinism"). He then presents an argument showing why he believes this opposing interpretation is wrong (what did and did not happen in reaction to climate change).

In the following three paragraphs Braidwood presents his interpretation and the arguments to support it in greater detail. In a few words, try to summarize what he is saying in each paragraph.

In the final paragraph, he, like many other authors, again tries to convince the reader that the topic he is writing about (the agricultural revolution) is important or of great significance. How does he do this?

4. Finally, pull back and consider a secondary source as a whole. Try to formulate the author's arguments and conclusions in a nutshell.

Here you might say that Braidwood argues two things. First, the agricultural revolution was extremely important for human history because it directly led to the creation of urban civilizations. Second, the causes for the agricultural revolution were cultural differentiation and specialization (or the record of culture), not environmental determinism (circumstances).

CONSIDER: *How geographic and climatic factors help explain the rise of civilization in Mesopotamia and Egypt; how geographic and climatic factors facilitated the growth of settlements in some areas but not the blossoming of those settlements into large, organized societies.*

The Agricultural Revolution
Robert J. Braidwood

Human beings populated parts of the earth for thousands of years before the first civilizations rose five or six thousand years ago in the ancient Near East. The causes for this relatively rapid transformation in the condition of human beings have been interpreted in a variety of ways. However, most historians and anthropologists point to the agricultural revolution of the Neolithic Age, in which—through the domestication of plants and animals—human beings became food producers rather than hunters and food gatherers, as the central development in this transformation to civilization. In the following selection, Robert J. Braidwood, an archaeologist and anthropologist, analyzes the agricultural revolution, its spread, and its significance.

CONSIDER: *The origins or causes of the agricultural revolution; Braidwood's rejection of environmental determinism and his acceptance of cultural differentiation and specialization; connections between agriculture and the beginnings of cities.*

Tool-making was initiated by pre-*sapiens* man. The first comparable achievement of our species was the agricultural revolution. No doubt a small human population could have persisted on the sustenance secured by the hunting and food-gathering technology that had been handed down and slowly improved upon over the 500 to 1,000 millennia of pre-human and pre-*sapiens* experience. With the domestication of plants and animals, however, vast new dimensions for cultural evolution

SOURCE: From *Hunters, Farmers, and Civilizations: Old World Archaeology* by C. C. Lamberg Karlovsky. Copyright © 1979 by W. H. Freeman and Company. Reprinted with permission.

suddenly became possible. The achievement of an effective food-producing technology did not, perhaps, predetermine subsequent developments, but they followed swiftly: the first urban societies in a few thousand years and contemporary industrial civilization in less than 10,000 years.

The first successful experiment in food production took place in southwestern Asia, on the hilly flanks of the "fertile crescent." Later experiments in agriculture occurred (possibly independently) in China and (certainly independently) in the New World. The multiple occurrence of the agricultural revolution suggests that it was a highly probable outcome of the prior cultural evolution of mankind and a peculiar combination of environmental circumstances. It is in the record of culture, therefore, that the origin of agriculture must be sought.

Not long ago the proponents of environmental determinism argued that the agricultural revolution was a response to the great changes in climate which accompanied the retreat of the last glaciation about 10,000 years ago. However, the climate had altered in equally dramatic fashion on other occasions in the past 75,000 years, and the potentially domesticable plants and animals were surely available to the bands of food-gatherers who lived in southwestern Asia and similar habitats in various parts of the globe. Moreover, recent studies have revealed that the climate did not change radically where farming began in the hills that flank the fertile crescent. Environmental determinists have also argued from the "theory of propinquity" that the isolation of men along with appropriate plants and animals in desert oases started the process of domestication.

In my opinion there is no need to complicate the story with extraneous "causes." The food-producing revolution seems to have occurred as the culmination of the ever increasing cultural differentiation and specialization of human communities. Around 8000 B.C.E. the inhabitants of the hills around the fertile crescent had come to know their habitat so well that they were beginning to domesticate the plants and animals they had been collecting and hunting. At slightly later times human cultures reached the corresponding level in Central America and perhaps in the Andes, in southeastern Asia and in China. From these "nuclear" zones cultural diffusion spread the new way of life to the rest of the world.

As the agricultural revolution began to spread, the trend toward ever increasing specialization of the intensified food-collecting way of life began to reverse itself. The new techniques were capable of wide application, given suitable adaptation, in diverse environments. Archeological remains at Hassuna, a site near the Tigris River somewhat later than Jarmo, show that the people were exchanging ideas on the manufacture of pottery and of flint and obsidian projectile points with people in the region of the Amouq in Syro-Cilicia. The basic elements of the food-producing complex—wheat, barley, sheep, goats and probably cattle—in this period moved west beyond the bounds of their native habitat to occupy the whole eastern end of the Mediterranean. They also traveled as far east as Anau, east of the Caspian Sea. Localized cultural differences still existed, but people were adopting and adapting more and more cultural traits from other areas. Eventually the new way of life traveled to the Aegean and beyond into Europe, moving slowly up such great river valley systems as the Dnieper, the Danube and the Rhone, as well as along the coasts. The intensified food-gatherers of Europe accepted the new way of life, but, as V. Gordon Childe has pointed out, they "were not slavish imitators: they adapted the gifts from the East . . . into a new and organic whole capable of developing on its own original lines." Among other things, the Europeans appear to have domesticated rye and oats that were first imported to the European continent as weed plants contaminating the seed of wheat and barley. In the comparable diffusion of agriculture from Central America, some of the peoples to the north appear to have rejected the new ways, at least temporarily.

By about 5000 B.C.E. the village-farming way of life seems to have been fingering down the valleys toward the alluvial bottom lands of the Tigris and Euphrates. Robert M. Adams believes that there may have been people living in the lowlands who were expert in collecting food from the rivers. They would have taken up the idea of farming from people who came down from the higher areas. In the bottom lands a very different climate, seasonal flooding of the land and small-scale irrigation led agriculture through a significant new technological transformation. By about 4000 B.C.E. the people of southern Mesopotamia had achieved such increases in productivity that their farms were beginning to support an urban civilization. The ancient site at Ubaid is typical of this period.

Thus in 3,000 or 4,000 years the life of man had changed more radically than in all of the preceding 250,000 years. Before the agricultural revolution most men must have spent their waking moments seeking their next meal, except when they could gorge following a great kill. As man learned to produce food, instead of gathering, hunting or collecting it, and to store it in the grain bin and on the hoof, he was compelled as well as enabled to settle in larger communities. With human energy released for a whole spectrum of new activities, there came the development of specialized nonagricultural crafts. It is no accident that such innovations as the discovery of the basic mechanical principles, weaving, the plow, the wheel and metallurgy soon appeared.

The Process of Civilization
William H. McNeill

Historians have long been interested in how civilizations first arose and developed. Central to this question is how early civilizations influenced each other. In the following excerpt from an article, "A Short History of Humanity" (2000), noted historian William H. McNeill stresses the importance of networks of communication—especially by sea—in the process of civilization.

CONSIDER: *How McNeill defines "civilization"; why communication and transportation were so important in the process of civilization.*

Civilizations brought strangers together and separated classes of people living side by side into distinct semiautonomous groupings. Priests and rulers, warriors and artisans, merchants and travelers, masters and servants lived very differently from one another, yet all depended on exchanges of goods and services, regulated by customary rules on the one hand and, on the other, by demographic and material limits on supply and demand.

As compared to primary communities, urban-based civilizations were (and still are) tumultuous and unstable social structures, but they were also more powerful, coordinating the actions of larger numbers of persons partly by obedience to deliberate commands, and partly by negotiated, more or less voluntary, exchanges of goods and services. Larger numbers working together, whether willingly or unwillingly, deliberately or inadvertently, had the same effect that cooperation within larger bands of more or less undifferentiated individuals had had at the beginning of human history, In other words, civilized forms of society exerted power over the natural environs and over much larger human numbers than more homogeneous societies were able to do. Ever since the first civilizations arose, civilized social complexity therefore tended to spread, until in our own time almost all humankind is caught up in a single global system, exchanging messages furiously fast and upsetting traditional ways of life almost everywhere....

An appropriately imaginative historian can hope to discern major landmarks in the civilizing process by focusing on breakthroughs in communication and transport that altered the range and flow of messages among human populations, and thereby accelerated the propagation of novelties far and wide that met human wishes or wants better than before....

When people first learned to use paddles and sails to propel rafts and boats, possibilities for long-range encounters opened up along the coasts of easily navigable seas. Almost certainly parts of Southeast Asia (and especially the offshore islands of Indonesia) were the principal sites of this breakthrough. A vague horizon for seafaring is established by the fact that people who reached Australia some 40,000 years ago (and perhaps even earlier than that) must have used some sort of flotation device to get there. But wooden rafts and ships seldom leave archaeological traces; and since melting glaciers subsequently raised sea levels substantially, early coastal settlements in Southeast Asia and everywhere else have been inundated.

Still, it seems clear that at an early time sailing vessels began to exploit the reversible monsoon winds to sail to and fro in Southeast Asia and along the shores of the Indian Ocean. Such seafaring was well developed by the time Sumerian records offer a glimpse of the sea network that connected the land of Sumer at the head of the Persian Gulf with Indus and Egyptian societies—and with a wider world of seagoing peoples beyond.

Sumerian cities, in fact, arose where this sea network connected up with a newer network of caravan portage. Donkeys, the first important caravan animal, were domesticated about seven thousand years ago; but since caravan management was almost as complicated as seafaring it presumably took a while for overland portage to become significant. But when local peoples learned that letting caravans pass for a negotiated protection fee assured a better supply of exotic and desirable items than plundering them did, overland portage across relatively long distances began to connect diverse populations more insistently than before. And it is surely not an accident that it was in Sumer, where an already ancient seagoing network intermeshed with a newly accessible hinterland, that the first cities arose between 4000 and 3000 B.C.E. Goods and ideas moved along these communications networks and, where they converged, the Sumerians were in an optimal position to pick and choose, elaborating and improving upon skills and knowledge coming from far and near.

Sumerian achievements, such as writing, metallurgy, wheeled vehicles, and an impressive religion, spread outward along the same networks. For example, on distant northern steppes Indo-European herdsmen accepted the Sumerian pantheon of seven high gods—sky, earth, thunderstorm, sun, moon, fresh water, and salt water. And, with subsequent adjustments, their Aryan, Greek, Latin, Celtic, German, and Slavic descendants carried this pagan pantheon with them into India and across Europe.

SOURCE: William H. McNeill, "A Short History of Humanity," *The New York Review of Books*, June 29, 2000, pp. 9–11 as excerpted.

Similarly, wheeled vehicles, in the form of twowheeled chariots, reached China by 1400 B.C.E. and helped to consolidate the power of the Shang dynasty. But of all Sumerian innovations, their resort to writing was perhaps the most significant since it added a new dimension to information storage and retrieval. Being more capacious, enduring, and reliable than human memory, written records allowed priests and rulers to collect and disburse indefinitely large quantities of material goods according to deliberate rules. As a result, government became more powerful; commands became more enforcible, even at a distance; and coordinated effort among thousands and eventually millions of persons became routine.

Freedom in the Ancient World: Civilization in Sumer

Herbert J. Muller

Historians generally see the development of cities as a sign of transformation into a civilized state and indeed an essential component of being civilized. Some of the earliest cities were formed by the Sumerians in the valley of the Tigris and Euphrates rivers, where settlers had already developed irrigation systems. In the following selection Herbert J. Muller analyzes the social, political, and religious significance of cities and irrigation systems for the Sumerians, and focuses particularly on the problems that civilization brought.

CONSIDER: *Why cities and irrigation systems require new systems of legal and political control; why Muller believes that the increased wealth and opportunity created by civilization was not an unmitigated benefit to the Sumerians; how political, economic, and social decisions made by the Sumerians were reflected in their religion.*

We must now consider the problems that came with civilization—problems due not so much to the sinful nature of man as to the nature of the city. "Friendship lasts a day" ran a Sumerian proverb; "kinship endures forever." The heterogeneous city was no longer held together by the bonds of kinship. Even the family was unstable. "For his pleasure: marriage," ran another proverb; "on his thinking it over: divorce." Hence the Sumerians could no longer depend on the informal controls of custom or common understanding that had sufficed to maintain order in the village. They had to supplement custom by political controls, a system of laws, backed by both force and moral persuasion. In this sense the city created the problem of evil. Here, not in Eden, occurred the Fall.

More specifically, the rise of civilization forced the social question that is still with us. By their great drainage and irrigation system the Sumerians were able to produce an increasing surplus of material wealth. The question is: Who was to possess and enjoy this wealth? The answer in Sumer was to be the invariable one: Chiefly a privileged few. The god who in theory owned it all in fact required the services of priestly bailiffs, and before long these were doing more than their share in assisting him to enjoy it, at the expense of the many menials beneath them. Class divisions grew more pronounced in the divine household, as in the city at large. The skilled artisans of Sumer, whose work in metals and gems has hardly ever been surpassed, became a proletariat, unable to afford their own products. "The valet always wears dirty clothes" noted the Sumerian scribe. Other proverbs dwelt on the troubles of the poor:

The poor man is better dead than alive;
If he has bread, he has no salt,
If he has salt, he has no bread.

The poor have not always been with us. As a class, they came with civilization. There was also the new type of the slave: victors in war had discovered that it was even more profitable to domesticate human captives than other types of animals. And outside its walls the city created still another type of man—the peasant. The villager had been preliterate, on a cultural par with his fellows; the peasant was illiterate, aware of the writing he did not know, aware of his dependence on the powers of the city, and liable to exploitation by them. Altogether, the urban revolution produced the anomaly that would become more glaring with the Industrial Revolution. As the collective wealth increased, many men were worse off, and many more felt worse off, than the neolithic villager had been.

Similarly the great irrigation system posed a political problem: Who would control the organization it required, exercise the power it gave? The answer was the same—a privileged few. As the temple estate grew into a city, the priesthood needed more secular help, especially in time of war. Sumerian legend retained memories of some sort of democratic assembly in the early cities, but it emphasized that after the Flood "kingship descended from heaven." The gods had sent kings to maintain order and to assure the proper service of them upon which the city's welfare depended. This was not a pure heavenly boon, judging by the Sumerian myth of a Golden Age before the Flood: an Eden of peace and plenty in which there was no snake, scorpion, hyena,

---

SOURCE: Excerpts from *Freedom in the Ancient World* by Herbert J. Muller. Copyright © 1961 by Harper & Row, Publishers, Inc. Reprinted by permission of HarperCollins Publishers, Inc.

lion, wild dog, wolf—"There was no fear, no terror. Man had no rival." At any rate, the divinely appointed king ruled as an absolute monarch, and might be a terror. With him descended a plague of locusts—the tax collectors. Again civilization meant an anomaly: as the collective achieved much more effective freedom, many individuals enjoyed less freedom than prehistoric villagers had.

In Sumer these problems were aggravated by a profounder paradox. All along, we have seen, man had come to depend more and more on supernatural means of power as he extended his own power over nature. Now, with the most triumphant demonstration of his creative powers, he became convinced of his utter dependence upon the gods, his utter powerlessness without them. The monumental architecture of the Sumerians exemplifies this crowning paradox. The ziggurat, which inspired the Hebrew myth of the Tower of Babel, was by no means the symbol of human presumption that Jehovah mistook it for—it was a symbol of abject subservience. Sumerian myth taught that man had been created simply to be the slave of the gods; he did all the dirty work, that they might rest and freely enjoy. They got the credit for all the highest achievements of the Sumerians. They also got the prime benefits, since the works of the city were dedicated to the promotion of their welfare, not man's welfare.

The Intellectual Adventure of Ancient Man

Henri Frankfort and H. A. Frankfort

One of the most difficult tasks of the historian is to understand ancient peoples' assumptions and attitudes about the world and their place in it. It is much easier to gather political or social information about ancient peoples, for this is often recorded in a manner understandable to us. To come to conclusions about how individuals perceived the world when those perceptions may have been quite different from our own requires a subtler use of evidence and imaginative interpretation. In the following selection Henri Frankfort, an archaeologist and cultural historian, and H. A. Frankfort attempt to describe one of the most fundamental differences in outlook between ancient and modern peoples: the ancients' perception of the physical world not as made up of inanimate things or natural forces (each one of which modern peoples refer to as "it") but as living, dynamic, individual beings (each one of which the ancients referred to as "thou").

SOURCE: Reprinted from *The Intellectual Adventure of Ancient Man*, by Henri Frankfort and H. A. Frankfort, by permission of The University of Chicago Press. Copyright © 1946, pp. 4–6.

CONSIDER: *The religious implications of this distinction of attitudes between modern and ancient peoples; the evidence that might be used to support or attack this interpretation; the role these attitudes might play in explaining the nature of science in the ancient world.*

The ancients, like the modern savages, saw man always as part of society, and society as imbedded in nature and dependent upon cosmic forces. For them nature and man did not stand in opposition and did not, therefore, have to be apprehended by different modes of cognition. We shall see, in fact, in the course of this book, that natural phenomena were regularly conceived in terms of human experience and that human experience was conceived in terms of cosmic events. We touch here upon a distinction between the ancients and us which is of the utmost significance for our inquiry.

The fundamental difference between the attitudes of modern and ancient man as regards the surrounding world is this: for modern, scientific man the phenomenal world is primarily an "It"; for ancient—and also for primitive—man it is a "Thou." . . .

The world appears to primitive man neither inanimate nor empty but redundant with life; and life has individuality, in man and beast and plant, and in every phenomenon which confronts man—the thunderclap, the sudden shadow, the eerie and unknown clearing in the wood, the stone which suddenly hurts him when he stumbles while on a hunting trip. Any phenomenon may at any time face him, not as "It," but as "Thou." In this confrontation, "Thou" reveals its individuality, its qualities, its will. "Thou" is not contemplated with intellectual detachment; it is experienced as life confronting life, involving every faculty of man in a reciprocal relationship. Thoughts, no less than acts and feelings, are subordinated to this experience. . . .

The whole man confronts a living "Thou" in nature; and the whole man—emotional and imaginative as well as intellectual—gives expression to the experience. All experience of "Thou" is highly individual; and early man does, in fact, view happenings as individual events. An account of such events and also their explanation can be conceived only as action and necessarily take the form of a story. In other words, the ancients told myths instead of presenting an analysis or conclusions. We would explain, for instance, that certain atmospheric changes broke a drought and brought about rain. The Babylonians observed the same facts but experienced them as the intervention of the gigantic bird Imdugud which came to their rescue. It covered the sky with the black storm clouds of its wings and devoured the Bull of Heaven, whose hot breath had scorched the crops.

Daily Life in Ancient Egypt: The Afterlife

Lionel Casson

Conceptions about the afterlife can reveal much about a civilization, for these conceptions often reflect the moods, struggles, problems, and attitudes of a people. The Egyptians were greatly concerned with the afterlife, as indicated by their construction of large, elaborate pyramid-tombs. In the following selection, Lionel Casson analyzes the Egyptians' attitudes toward death and the afterlife, noting broad changes in those attitudes.

CONSIDER: *Exactly how the Egyptian view of the afterlife reflects the nature of the Egyptians; evidence for change after 1200 B.C.E.; how Sinuhe's account reflects a great concern with the afterlife.*

The Egyptians, as we have several times observed, were by nature buoyant, optimistic, and confident, and their view of the afterlife reflects this: throughout most of their history they conceived of it as something to be enjoyed, certainly not to be looked on with foreboding. Being at the same time pragmatic and material minded, they indulged in no fancies about its being a better world. As they saw it, death meant a continuation of one's life on earth, a continuation that, with the appropriate precautions of proper burial, prayer, and ritual, would include only the best parts of life on earth—nothing to fear, but on the other hand, nothing to want to hurry out of this world for. This attitude lasted from Old Kingdom times right up to the end of the Nineteenth Dynasty, about 1200 B.C.E., when change becomes noticeable. Pictures and texts in tombs from this time on no longer concern themselves with life on earth. The pictures cease portraying the deceased serenely contemplating the bustling life on his estates, and concentrate morbidly on the making of the mummy, the funeral, the judgment before Osiris, the demons the dead will see, and other aspects of death. The texts give up autobiography in favor of magical recipes for getting along in the life beyond the grave. This shift of emphasis is one of the distinctive features that mark Egypt's descent toward the religion-haunted, superstitious, ritualistic nation it was to become by the time Herodotus and other Greek and Roman authors wrote down their impressions.

But the shift did not occur until the very end of the period we are concerned with. Throughout most of the New Kingdom the Egyptians prepared for their entry into the next world with calm and confidence. It was an occupation that absorbed a man's time and resources for most of his life, since no one was able to rest easy until he was assured that the place of his final repose and its furnishings were ready. In *The Story of Sinuhe*, a Middle Kingdom tale of an official who went into exile but in his old age was recalled by the pharaoh in time to end his days happily in the fatherland, Sinuhe recounts the crowning joy of his homecoming:

> There was constructed for me a pyramid-tomb of stone in the midst of the pyramid-tombs. The stonemasons who hew a pyramid-tomb took over its ground-area. The outline-draftsmen designed in it; the chief sculptors carved in it; and the overseers of works who are in the necropolis made it their concern. Its necessary materials were made from all the outfittings which are placed at a tombshaft. Mortuary priests were given to me. There was made for me a necropolis garden, with fields in it formerly (extending) as far as the town, like that which is done for a chief courtier. My statue was overlaid with gold, and its skirt was of fine gold. It was his majesty who had it made.

Women of Egypt and the Ancient Near East

Barbara S. Lesko

In the early Egyptian and Mesopotamian civilizations, women had greater access to valued political, religious, and economic positions than in civilizations that followed. What explains the changes that would make societies in the Near East more dominated by men and more oppressive to women? Barbara S. Lesko, an Egyptologist, addresses this question in the following excerpt. Here her focus is on the centuries toward the end of the third millennium and the beginning of the second millennium.

CONSIDER: *What three factors explain the decline of women's status and freedoms; how Egypt and early Sumer differed from later societies such as Assyria; other possible explanations for the decline of women's status and freedoms.*

SOURCE: Lionel Casson, "Daily Life in Ancient Egypt," *American Heritage*, pp. 107–108. Reprinted by permission of *American Heritage* magazine, a division of Forbes Inc., 1975.

SOURCE: Barbara S. Lesko, "Women of Egypt and the Ancient Near East," in Renate Bridenthal, Claudia Koonz, and Susan Stuard, *Becoming Visible: Women in European History,* 2d ed. (Boston: Houghton Mifflin Co., 1987), p. 74.

What was the real cause of the rise of patriarchy, which became increasingly oppressive to women in the Near East after Sumerian civilization waned? Several reasons suggest themselves. The first is militarism. In an early agrarian society like Egypt where internal disputes were effectively handled by the strong, centralized government, where wars usually took place beyond the borders, where no standing army existed during the first 1500 years of recorded history, and where invasion seldom affected the country, women continually shared the burdens, full rights, and obligations of citizens. However, in the newer societies, founded by the sons of ever-vigilant and suspicious desert nomads, where warfare between cities was frequent and invasion by outside hostile forces familiar, militarism developed, excluding women and rendering them dependents. Second, where commercialism held sway at the same time—as in Assyria—the worst examples of patriarchy were found. Commerce based on private initiative first appears on a well developed scale in the Old Babylonian period where the first concerted effort by men to control women for financial gain is also documented. This is seen not only in the laws of Hammurabi but in institutions like that of the cloistered *Naditu* women. Coupled with virulent militarism, as in Assyria, the rise of commercialism had a devastating effect on women's rights. In Egypt large scale commerce long remained a virtual monopoly of the state, so its impact on society remained less significant.

We might further point out that, even during the somewhat militaristic Egyptian empire of the New Kingdom, women's status and freedoms did not diminish significantly. This introduces a third factor: confidence. A supremely confident nation can afford tolerance. Egypt had confidence in its gods, in the eternity of life, and in the bounty of its land. Sumer, in its early formative years, shared these advantages too. Not so the subsequent societies. It is the threatened male and the threatened society—like Assyria, surrounded on three sides by deadly enemies, and weak impoverished Israel—which created such a restricted role for their women.

A History of the Jews

Paul Johnson

A major task of the historian is to delineate what distinguished a people, an era, or a development from others. In analyzing the Jews, most historians emphasize that the Jewish religion was monotheistic, recognizing only one god, and that major elements of Judaism would later be directly related to and incorporated into two other major religions founded in that area of the world: Christianity and Islam. In the following selection, Paul Johnson goes beyond the monotheism of the Jewish religion to focus on the ways the Jews were unique as ancient writers.

CONSIDER: *Whether Johnson's interpretation is supported by the primary documents on religion in the ancient Near East; why these two characteristics of ancient Jewish literature are so important; how this interpretation of ancient Jewish literature compares with Frankfort's interpretation of ancient peoples' mentality.*

The Jews had two unique characteristics as ancient writers. They were the first to create consequential, substantial and interpretative history. It has been argued that they learned the art of history from the Hittites, another historically minded people, but it is obvious that they were fascinated by their past from very early times. They knew they were a special people who had not simply evolved from an unrecorded past but had been brought into existence, for certain definite purposes, by a specific series of divine acts. They saw it as their collective business to determine, record, comment and reflect upon these acts. No other people has ever shown, particularly at that remote time, so strong a compulsion to explore their origins. The Bible gives constant examples of the probing historical spirit: why, for instance, was there a heap of stones before the city gate at Ai? What was the meaning of the twelve stones at Gilgal? This passion for aetiology, the quest for explanations, broadened into a more general habit of seeing the present and future in terms of the past. The Jews wanted to know about themselves and their destiny. They wanted to know about God and his intentions and wishes. Since God, in their theology, was the sole cause of all events—as Amos put it, 'Does evil befall a city unless Yahweh wills it?'—and thus the author of history, and since they were the chosen actors in his vast dramas, the record and study of historical events was the key to the understanding of both God and man.

Hence the Jews were above all historians, and the Bible is essentially a historical work from start to finish. . . .

Ancient Jewish history is both intensely divine and intensely humanist. History was made by God, operating independently or through man. The Jews were not interested and did not believe in impersonal forces. They were less curious about the physics of creation than any other literate race of antiquity. They turned their back on nature and discounted its manifestations except in so far as they reflected the divine-human drama. The notion of

SOURCE: Excerpt from *A History of the Jews* by Paul Johnson. Copyright © 1987 by Paul Johnson. Reprinted by permission of HarperCollins Publishers, Inc. and George Weidenfeld & Nicolson, Limited.

vast geographical or economic forces determining history was quite alien to them. There is much natural description in the Bible, some of astonishing beauty, but it is stage-scenery for the historical play, a mere backdrop for the characters. The Bible is vibrant because it is entirely about living creatures; and since God, though living, cannot be described or even imagined, the attention is directed relentlessly on man and woman.

Hence the second unique characteristic of ancient Jewish literature: the verbal presentation of the human personality in all its range and complexity. The Jews were the first race to find words to express the deepest human emotions, especially the feelings produced by bodily or mental suffering, anxiety, spiritual despair and desolation, and the remedies for these evils produced by human ingenuity—hope, resolution, confidence in divine assistance, the consciousness of innocence, of righteousness, penitence, sorrow and humility.

CHAPTER QUESTIONS

1. What characteristics of the societies discussed in this chapter fit with what we usually consider as "civilized"?

2. How would you explain the rise of these civilizations and particularly the similarities between them?

3. Evaluate the relative importance of geographic, economic, and other factors in explaining the differing natures of these early civilizations.

4. Drawing from both primary and secondary documents, describe some of the most likely of ancient peoples' assumptions and attitudes about the world, about their societies, and about women. How might some of these assumptions and attitudes differ in the various societies of the ancient Near East?

ATHENA *PARTHENOS*, REPRODUCTION IN NASHVILLE, TN, 2002

Athena *Parthenos*, a magnificent cult statue of the Greek goddess Athena, was unveiled in the temple known as the Parthenon, in Athens, in about 438 B.C.E. Built by the famous sculptor Phideas, the 41-foot-tall statue was made with skin of ivory and dressed in more than a ton of gold. In Phideas's interpretation, Athena held a 6-foot-high *Nike* (victory) statue in her hand. As Athenians looked with pride and awe at their patron goddess, who splendidly portrayed wisdom, wealth, and victory, they recognized their city at the height of its power. The original statue was destroyed after a millennium but was long remembered as a paragon of beauty. This carefully researched reproduction, completed in Nashville, Tennessee, in 2002, is the largest indoor statue in the West. The re-creation reveals our debt to the glory that was Greece.

The Contest for Excellence

Greece, 2000–338 B.C.E.

"It is the greatest good every day to discuss virtue . . . for life without enquiry is not worth living for a man. . . ." The Greek philosopher Socrates reputedly spoke these words, and they have become a famous articulation of the value of the spirit of inquiry. But the society that produced Socrates was also one that spawned an often-violent competition among men and among cities. Violence even swept up Socrates' voice of rationalism, for his memorable words were spoken at his trial as his neighbors accused him of undermining their way of life. Yet the philosopher/stonemason claimed he would rather die than give up challenging his neighbors to think about everything from truth and beauty to life and death. Because he refused to be silent, he was condemned to die. Fortunately his call for rational inquiry did not die with him but flourished in the contentious city-states of Greece, ultimately to become a fundamental characteristic of Western civilization.

The Greeks grappled with other challenges in addition to new philosophical approaches. Two brilliant Aegean civilizations, the Minoans and the Mycenaeans, rose and fell. In city-states such as Athens and Sparta, Greek citizens battled powerful neighbors such as the Persians, fought over spheres of influence, and invented unprecedented forms of participatory government. The individualistic Greeks also created magnificent works of art that set the standard of beauty for millennia and literature that inspires readers even in modern times. Ancient Greeks believed that in a heroic search for excellence, a man could accomplish anything. In some cases, they were almost right. However, in their quest for excellence—whether in war or peace—they also planted the seeds of their own downfall by valuing competition over cooperation.

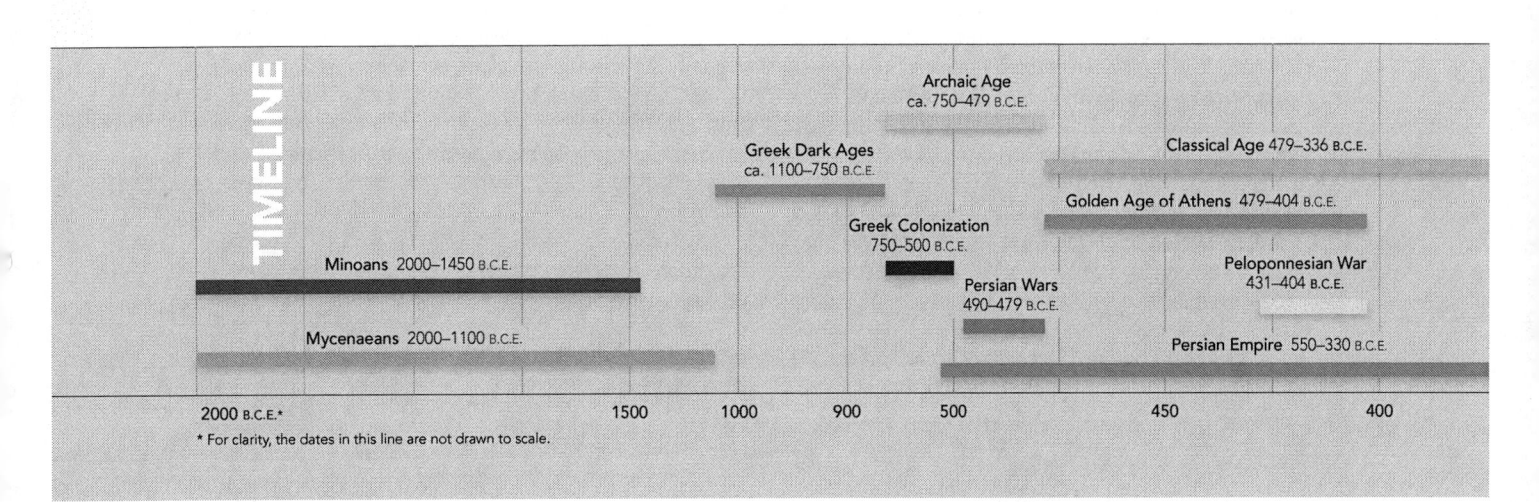

TIMELINE

- Minoans 2000–1450 B.C.E.
- Mycenaeans 2000–1100 B.C.E.
- Greek Dark Ages ca. 1100–750 B.C.E.
- Archaic Age ca. 750–479 B.C.E.
- Greek Colonization 750–500 B.C.E.
- Persian Wars 490–479 B.C.E.
- Classical Age 479–336 B.C.E.
- Golden Age of Athens 479–404 B.C.E.
- Peloponnesian War 431–404 B.C.E.
- Persian Empire 550–330 B.C.E.

2000 B.C.E.* — 1500 — 1000 — 900 — 500 — 450 — 400

* For clarity, the dates in this line are not drawn to scale.

PREVIEW

THE RISE AND FALL OF ANCIENT HEROES,
2000–800 B.C.E.
Learn about the height and decline of the Mycenaean and Minoan civilizations.

EMERGING FROM THE DARK: HEROIC BELIEFS AND VALUES
Understand Greek religion, values, and scientific inquiry.

LIFE IN THE GREEK POLEIS
Study daily life, the Olympic Games, political structure, and the Persian Wars.

GREECE ENTERS ITS CLASSICAL AGE,
479–336 B.C.E.
Examine the height of the Athenian Empire and its culture, including art, architecture, and drama.

DESTRUCTION, DISILLUSION, AND A SEARCH FOR MEANING
Study the Peloponnesian War; Greek philosophy, drama, and medicine; and the decline of the poleis.

THE RISE AND FALL OF ANCIENT HEROES,
2000–800 B.C.E.

Ancient Greek men and boys gathered in the household hall in the evenings to enjoy songs of heroic deeds recited by skilled performers. (Literary texts also show that women and girls listened from the seclusion of their own rooms.) For centuries, poets recited accounts that later were gathered together to form the epic poem the *Iliad*. This work, by the eighth-century poet Homer, told of 50 days in the 10-year war between the Greeks and the Trojans, a people living on the coast of Asia Minor. The *Iliad* was also a story of the Greek mythic hero Achilles, whose prowess in battle overcame great odds. Despite his successes, Achilles was subject to outbursts of monumental anger—a trait that, as Homer wrote, "brought the Greeks so much suffering." The leader of the Greeks, King Agamemnon, provoked a quarrel with Achilles. When exerting his right to take the booty seized in war, he took Briseis, a woman who first had been allotted to Achilles. In protest, the wrathful warrior sat in his tent and refused to fight while many of his compatriots died under the Trojan onslaught. As one Greek leader in the story said, "Now look at Achilles. He is a brave man, yet who but he will profit by that bravery?"

Modern historians understandably have questioned the accuracy of certain details in Homer's epics, but the ancient Greeks saw these poems differently. For centuries, people believed that the epics portrayed Achilles' actions accurately. Indeed, many aspiring heroes strove to emulate the mythical soldier whose mere presence or absence on the battlefield could change the course of the war. By reading or listening to these accounts of a lost age, young men learned about heroism and about the destructiveness of human weakness. The tension between heroic aspirations and dangerous individual pride became a prominent theme throughout the history of the ancient Greeks as they built their civilization on a rocky peninsula in the Aegean Sea.

The Greek Peninsula

The Greek peninsula is dominated by striking mountain ranges. Lacking large rivers that would have provided natural communication links, the ancient Greek civilization consisted of separate communities scattered throughout the peninsula and the numerous Aegean islands. The mountain ranges protected the Greeks from large-scale invasions, but the rocky soil made agriculture difficult. The Greeks had to grow their wheat and barley on the scarce lowland, and in time they came to depend on imports for the grain they needed. The Greek historian Herodotus summed up the difficulties of agriculture when he wrote, "Greece has always poverty as her companion." As **Map 2.1** indicates, most places in Greece enjoyed a close proximity to the sea, which allowed overseas trade to become an essential part of ancient Greek society. This orientation toward the sea stimulated the many cultural contacts that marked the development of Western civilization (as discussed in Chapter 1). In fact, the earliest advanced civilization that arose in this region originated on an island that lay at the heart of the eastern Mediterranean.

The Minoans,
2000–1450 B.C.E.

By 2000 B.C.E., the islanders living on Crete boasted the wealthiest, most advanced civilization in the Mediterranean. They were not Greek—nor Indo-European—but were probably a Semitic people related to those living in the eastern and southern Mediterranean. At the height of its economic and political power, Crete consisted of a number of principalities, each dominated by a great palace. Knossos (see **Map 2.1**) is the best excavated and thus the most well known of the palaces. Early Greek historians identify the ruler of Crete as King Minos, and thus modern excavators named Minoan society after this legendary king. Minoan prosperity permitted the growth of a relatively large, peaceful population. During the golden age of this culture, the population of Crete reached an impressive 250,000, with 40,000 living in Knossos alone.

thinking about GEOGRAPHY

MAP 2.1

The World of the Greeks

This map shows the Greek peninsula with the surrounding seas. Notice the locations of Asia Minor and the islands of Crete and the Cyclades. Locate the important cities of Troy (in Asia Minor), Athens, and Sparta.

Explore the Map

1. How would sea travelers best proceed from the Greek mainland to Asia Minor and back? What does this route suggest about the importance of the islands in the Aegean Sea?
2. Where is Troy? What does its location at the entrance of the Hellespont (the narrow strait that allows access to the Black Sea and the interior of Asia) indicate about its strategic importance?
3. How did the location of Crete allow the island's people to control the trade in the region?

By trading with the peoples of the Fertile Crescent, the Minoans learned much of the best of early Western civilization. They learned to make bronze from the Sumerians, and their foundries produced a steady stream of valuable bronze tools and weapons. Minoan ships were the best made in the region. With their heavy construction and high front prows, these vessels cut effortlessly through rough seas and proved reliable in conditions that the islanders' shore-hugging contemporaries deemed impossible.

Centers of economic as well as political power, Minoan palaces comprised vast mazes of storerooms, workrooms, and living quarters. These structures were markedly different from the huge buildings in Sumeria and Egypt, where architects of pyramids

Economic power

and ziggurats valued symmetry. Minoan architects preferred to build palace rooms of different sizes that wandered without any apparent design. The Greeks later called these palaces labyrinths. Kings controlling the trade through which wealth poured into Crete stashed goods away in the huge palace storerooms. One room in the palace at Knossos contained clay jars for olive oil that totaled a remarkable capacity of 60,000 gallons.

Like many maritime civilizations, the Minoans learned much from their encounters with other peoples. For example, their artwork reveals the influence of Egyptian colors and styles. The Minoans also learned writing from the Sumerians, and their script (called Linear A) was also a pictographic script written on clay tablets. As in Sumer, archaeologists have excavated clay tablets in Crete that seem to have been used for accounting and for tracking the movement of merchandise. So far, the symbols of Linear A have not been translated, so to learn about Minoan society, we must rely on archaeological remains, including their riveting artwork.

The Minoans decorated their palaces with magnificent frescoes, created by mixing paint with plaster and crafting the image as part of the wall. These paintings portrayed many of the everyday objects and activities that Minoans held dear, including religious rituals. Many statuettes from Crete showing goddesses holding snakes suggest that the predominant Minoan deity was a fertility goddess. The fresco in **Figure 2.1** shows a ritual in which men and women performed gymnastic activities with a wild bull. In this painting, one woman grabs the bull's horns to prepare to vault over it, while a man is already at the apex of his leap. Another woman waits to guide the jumper's descent. Some scholars suggest that this dangerous event may have been a religious ritual that culminated with the sacrifice of the bull and an opulent banquet at which men and women feasted on the meat and celebrated the goddess's generosity in bringing abundance to the society.

`Religious ritual`

In the centuries after the Minoans, the ancient Greeks often told their history in the form of myths that recounted heroic acts from the Greek past. Some of these myths recalled the eventual destruction of Minoan society. In their myths, Greeks remembered a time when Greece owed tribute to Crete, including young people to be sacrificed to the Minotaur—a

`Minoan destruction`

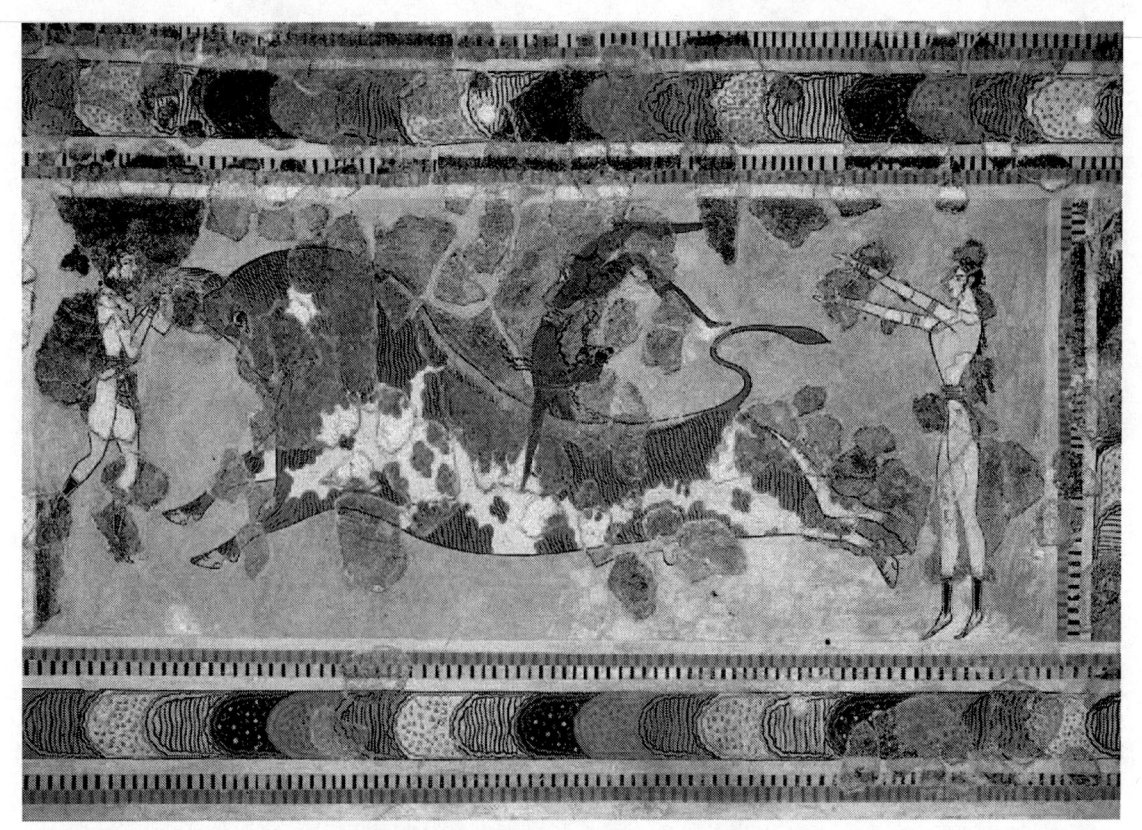

FIGURE 2.1 Minoan Acrobats, ca. 1500 B.C.E. This fresco from Knossos, Crete, depicts what was probably a religious ritual in which women (shown with pale skin) and a man leap over a charging bull.

creature that was half human and half bull. The king of Knossos may have worn the head of a bull on ceremonial occasions, and perhaps it was this tradition that gave rise to the legend of the Minotaur. One mythical Greek hero, Theseus, joined the sacrificial group, killed the Minotaur, and escaped the palace labyrinth by following a thread he had unraveled as he entered. (See Document 2.1, page 56, for more on the myth of Theseus.) This myth may hold a core of truth, for archaeological evidence shows that Minoan society was toppled by invaders. The great Minoan palaces apparently were burned by invaders who destroyed the unfortified cities. A man named Theseus may not have killed a minotaur, but it seems that Greeks killed the king of Crete.

Historians have looked further for the cause of the Minoans' downfall. Some suggest that a natural disaster contributed to their decline. In about 1450 B.C.E., a volcanic explosion on the nearby island of Thera (today known as Santorini) caused a tidal wave that may have destroyed the Minoans' protective fleet. However, this explanation is uncertain because other scholars question the date of the eruption, placing it two centuries earlier than the burning of Crete. Whatever the cause, the center of Aegean civilization passed to the earliest Greeks, whom we call the Mycenaeans.

Mycenaean Civilization: The First Greeks, 2000–1100 B.C.E.

Sometime after 2000 B.C.E., Indo-European Greek-speaking people settled on the mountainous Greek peninsula. By 1600 B.C.E., they were increasingly influenced by the Minoans and had developed a wealthy, hierarchic society centered in the city of Mycenae (see **Map 2.1**). Excavations of their shaft graves have yielded golden crowns and masks and, as with other Indo-European burials, many weapons, perhaps confirming ancient writers' characterizations of these people as the "war-mad Greeks." Yet, these early Greeks were also traders, and much of their wealth came from the growing commerce in the Aegean. As the Mycenaeans traded with wealthy Minoans, they learned much from them, evidenced by the strong Minoan influences in Mycenaean artwork. Mycenaean Greeks even learned to write from the Minoans, and their script is called Linear B for its similarity to the Minoan script. Because Linear B recorded an early form of the spoken Greek language, linguists have been able to translate Mycenaean tablets.

After Minoan society was destroyed in about 1450 B.C.E., the Mycenaeans took over as the commercial masters of the Mediterranean. As their wealth increased, so did the complexity of their governing system, which had a hierarchy of kings, nobles, and slaves. Powerful kings built palaces of stone so large that later Greeks thought they must have been constructed by giants. Unlike Minoan palaces, these structures were walled, indicating to archaeologists that there was a great deal of warfare, necessitating defensive fortifications. This conclusion is reinforced by written sources claiming that the kings surrounded themselves with soldiers.

Mycenaean states were not self-sufficient. Like the civilizations of the ancient Middle East, they depended on trade for many essentials. For example, there was little copper and no tin on the peninsula, so they had to trade for ore to make bronze weapons and tools. The vast expanse of Mycenaean trade is clear. Mycenaean pottery has been found on the coast of Italy, and after the destruction of Crete, Mycenaean pottery replaced Minoan pottery in Egypt, Syria, Palestine, and Cyprus. These pottery remnants testify to the beginnings of the trade that linked the fortunes of the ancient Greeks intimately with those of their neighbors. *Trade*

In about 1200 B.C.E., violence and a wide-ranging movement of peoples disrupted the eastern Mediterranean. A scarcity of sources does not allow historians to detail the exact causes of the upheaval, but we can see the effects on kingdoms and individuals. The Egyptian Empire was besieged and lost territory as Syria and cities all along the coast confronted invaders. A letter from the king of the island of Cyprus urged the king of a city in Syria to hold firm against invaders: "You have written to me: enemy ships have been seen at sea. . . . Where are your troops and chariots? . . . Await the enemy steadfastly." Archaeological evidence shows towns sacked and burned throughout the region during these times of trouble. The important trade in copper from Cyprus was interrupted, and as we saw in Chapter 1, this violent era stimulated the dawning of the Iron Age. *Violence and disruption*

The Mycenaeans were surely involved in these invasions that disrupted the ancient civilizations. According to later Greek myths, part of this violence included the Mycenaean invasion of Troy (see **Map 2.1**) in about 1250 B.C.E. The Trojan War became the basis of Homer's influential epics. Greek mythology attributes the conflict to a rivalry over a beautiful Greek woman, Helen, who was seduced by the Trojan prince Paris. Less-romantic historians believe the war stemmed primarily from the intensifying economic competition and growing violence in the eastern Mediterranean. Either way, the fighting was relentless and devastating—Homer claimed that the Greeks besieged Troy for ten years. At the end of this ordeal, Troy was destroyed (demonstrated by evidence from archaeological excavations).

Sometime after 1200 B.C.E., Mycenaean civilization itself dissolved. Later Greeks attributed this downfall to the Trojan War, which supposedly kept the Mycenaean leaders and soldiers away from home for so long. Archaeological evidence, however, shows that during and shortly after the Trojan War, the highly structured life on the Greek mainland broke down. Amid crop failures due to drought and internal instability, more Greek invaders from the north (later called Dorian Greeks) moved into the peninsula, especially the southern part, the Peloponnese. Population dropped dramatically. Excavations in one region reveal thirteen villages during the Mycenaean period; by 1100 B.C.E. only three remained. We do not know exactly what happened, but the flourishing Bronze Age Mycenaean society came to such a complete end that even the valuable art of writing was lost. All the great Mycenaean centers except Athens were destroyed. Life on the Greek mainland now consisted of a smattering of small villages, where people survived largely through subsistence farming.

From Dark Ages to Colonies

The period after the fall of Mycenae is called the Dark Ages (which extend from about 1100 B.C.E. to about 750 B.C.E.), because with the loss of writing, we have no texts that illuminate life during this time. For three centuries, life went on in the small villages, and people told tales that preserved their values. At the end of the Dark Ages, in about 800 B.C.E., Homer brilliantly recast some of these oral tales. The details he included offer glimpses into life during the previous three centuries. For example, Homer's descriptions of the cremation of the dead, which had not been practiced in Mycenaean civilization, suggest that cremation was developed after the fall of the early Greeks. As tantalizing as these bits of literary evidence are, most of our information for this period nevertheless must come from archaeology.

Excavations show that during these years, bronze gave way to iron as the primary metal used in weapons and tools. Archaeological findings also reveal that near the end of the Dark Ages, trade of wine, olive oil, and other goods began to flourish again all over the Mediterranean. By tracing the movement of Greek goods through the remnants of pottery and other artifacts excavated around the Mediterranean, archaeologists have discovered that Greek culture spread through the many colonies Greeks established in the region. At first, Greeks fled the disasters on the peninsula by settling on the numerous islands of the Aegean and the coast of Asia Minor (called Ionia) (see Global Connections on page 50). Later, colonists may have left the peninsula to escape overpopulation and seek new land and prosperity. Some aristocrats in Greek cities used the founding of

Founding colonies

new colonies as a way to diffuse social unrest by sending the dissatisfied elsewhere. **Map 2.2** shows the extent of the Greek colonies along the coast of the Mediterranean Sea. They were rivaled in number only by the Phoenicians, the master colonists we met in Chapter 1. Greek colonies were very different from modern colonial efforts because Greeks in the new settlements arranged themselves in cities that were just as independent as the mother city. The ties to the original cities were ones of emotion, not of colonial control.

For a time, Greeks in the new colonies remained independent from the other civilizations around them—the neighboring Phoenicians and the Babylonian and Persian Empires. However, while trading with their neighbors, the Greeks participated in the growth of Western civilization by adopting much that had gone before. For example, they derived their systems of weight from Babylonia and Phoenicia and adopted the practice of making coins from the Lydians (see Chapter 1). Societies transform acquired innovations, and the Greeks were no exception. For their coins, they minted silver (instead of the Lydian white gold) and usually placed secular images on them—sometimes illustrating their exports, like grapes or fish, and sometimes using emblems of civic pride. However, when describing Greek use of others' inventions, the Greek philosopher Plato (428–348 B.C.E.) characteristically gave the Greeks undue praise, boasting, "Whatever the Greeks have acquired from foreigners, they have in the end turned into something finer."

EMERGING FROM THE DARK: HEROIC BELIEFS AND VALUES

Through their trade with the Phoenicians, the Greeks acquired and adapted the Phoenician alphabet, and writing reemerged among the Greeks around 800 B.C.E. Once more Greek society was illuminated for historians. The Greeks did not use writing only for trade and contractual agreements—the Phoenician alphabet was simpler than other scripts, so it lent itself to a wider use. Talented Greeks used writing to record and transmit powerful and inspiring poetry that had been preserved for centuries only through human memory, and the ideas of the ancient Greeks once more came to light; the Dark Ages were over.

Heroic Values Preserved

The earliest of this Greek literature preserved a series of values that define what historians call a heroic society, in which individuals seek fame through great deeds and advocate values such as honor, reputation, and prowess.

thinking about GEOGRAPHY

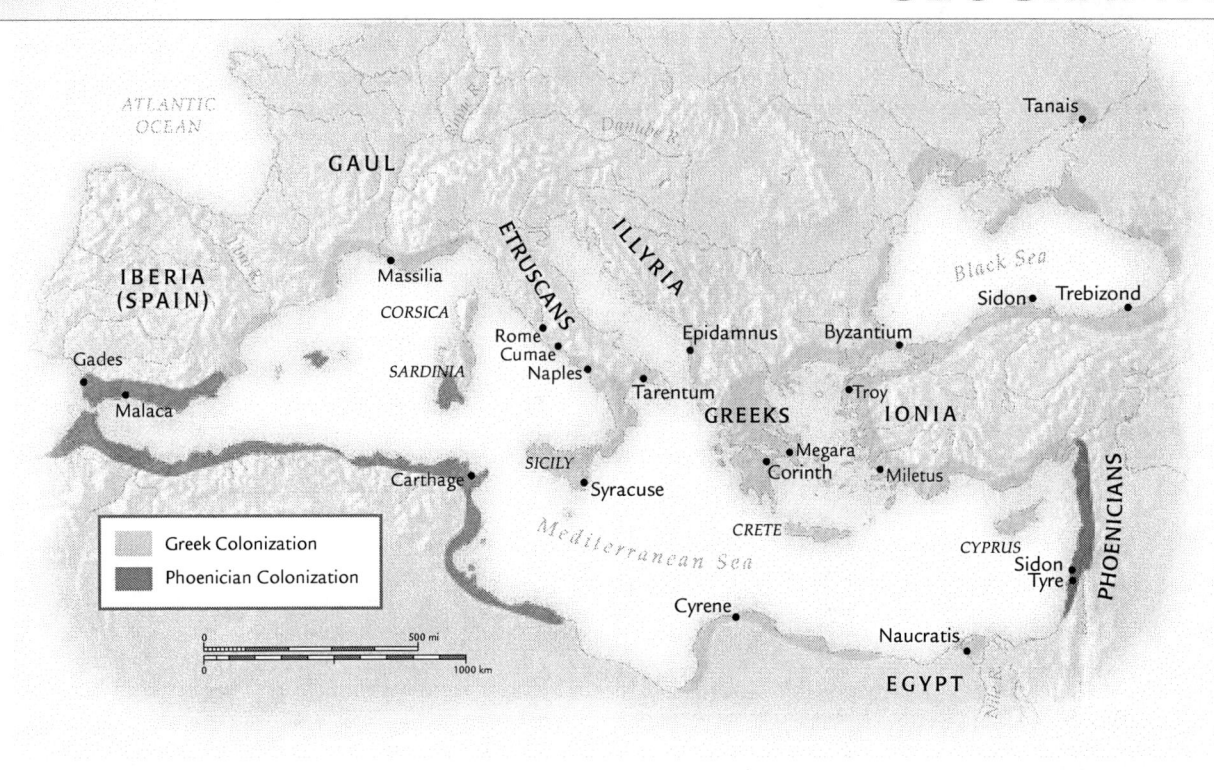

MAP 2.2

The Greek Colonies in About 500 B.C.E.

This map shows the locations of the Greek and Phoenician colonies. Because ancient ships could not navigate at night, these colonies provided essential stopping points for long-distance trade.

Explore the Map

1. What spheres of influence are implied by the locations for the respective colonies?
2. Based on the map, in what regions would the Greeks most likely come in conflict with other powers?
3. How did the fall of Troy allow for Greek colonization around the Black Sea?

As we saw in the opening account of Achilles, the most influential Greek poet was Homer, who historians believe lived in the early eighth century B.C.E. Homer's two greatest epics were the *Iliad*, the tale of Achilles' heroic wrath, and the *Odyssey*, the story of the Greek warrior Odysseus's ten-year travels to return home from Troy. The *Iliad* became a seminal text for later ancient Greeks—schoolchildren and adults never tired of this tale of heroic deeds that captured details from Homer's times and preserved many Mycenaean values.

Homer

The highest virtue for Homer (and subsequent Greeks) was **arête**—manliness, courage, and excellence. Arête was best revealed in a "contest," whether sporting, warfare, or activities extending into many other areas of life and recreation. The ancient Greeks believed that striving for individual supremacy enhanced one's family honor, and the hero's name would live in poetic memory. Such beliefs and values helped fuel the greatness of ancient Greece. However, this striving for excellence—for heroism—was not always beneficial. At times it created a self-centered competitiveness that caused much suffering—just as Achilles' heroic-scale rage was said to have caused his companions' deaths. Harboring such intense competitive spirit, Greeks also held a deep disregard for all cultures other than their own (and they even had disdain for neighboring Greeks from different cities). Greeks distinguished themselves from "barbarians"

In literature, too, poets praised human accomplishments. Hesiod, an early Greek poet who wrote around 750 B.C.E., left almost as important a mark as Homer. His *Works and Days* describes farm life, wisdom, and values near the end of the Greek Dark Ages. Like social critics who had come before him, Hesiod complained of the powerful who cheat and exploit the poor and strive only for riches. Deploring the selfish "age of iron" in which he lived, Hesiod lamented the loss of what he believed were more virtuous heroic ages of "gold" and "bronze." He was no doubt wrong in assuming that the leaders of the Mycenaean age were less corrupt than those in his time, but his vision reveals the desire to imagine better times.

Hesiod lived in poverty—cheated out of his inheritance by a greedy brother and corrupt officials—yet he still articulated the ideals of heroic individualism. However, he clearly saw that the pursuit of excellence was a two-sided coin. At the end of *Works and Days*, he wrote of two kinds of "strife." One was good—a healthy spirit of competitiveness that Hesiod believed made people work and achieve their best. The other kind of strife, however, was bad and led to some people exploiting others, as happened in Hesiod's own life. This tension within heroic values marked Greek life and values and even their gods and goddesses.

The Family of the Gods

The ancient Greek historian Herodotus (482–425 B.C.E.) claimed that Homer and Hesiod powerfully shaped subsequent Greek religious beliefs. As Herodotus observed, these early poets "gave the gods their epithets, divided out offices and functions among them and described their appearance." The poems of Homer's and Hesiod's day were indeed populated by an extended family of gods and goddesses, loosely ruled by Zeus and his wife, Hera. This family included ten other main deities, among them Aphrodite, goddess of love; Athena, goddess of wisdom and war; Poseidon, god of the sea; Apollo, god of music, divination, and healing; and Demeter, goddess of fertility. These gods lived on Mount Olympus and periodically interfered in human affairs.

The Greek gods and goddesses resembled humans so much that one Greek critic from the sixth century B.C.E. observed that "Homer and Hesiod ascribed to the gods everything that among men is a shame and disgrace: theft, adultery, and deceiving one another." It is true that the gods shared human flaws, but they also shared admirable human qualities. Like the Greeks themselves, they loved beauty, banquets, processions, athletic competitions, music, and theater. The Greeks therefore infused all these activities with a feeling of worship. Religious rituals, for example, had an intensely festive air, and ancient Greek

FIGURE 2.2 Perfecting the Human Form, ca. 530 B.C.E.
Greek artists glorified humanity by carving monumental, realistic life-size statues. Sculptors revealed their interest in the human form by depicting the males—called *kouros* (pl. *kouroi*), a word that is Greek for "boy"—without clothing. The females—called *kore* (pl. *korai*), the Greek word for "girl"—are always portrayed modestly clothed. Yet the female humanity is indicated by a smile on the female's face, referred to as the *archaic smile*.

who "spoke other languages" and felt it demeaned them to work alongside such foreigners. Individuals adhering to "heroic" values brought a combination of good and bad results, and the best of the Greeks from Homer on recognized this ambiguity.

Visual artists in the archaic age also glorified humanity in their increasingly realistic portrayal of the human figure. **Figures 2.2a and b** show two typical sculptures from the sixth century B.C.E. Both portray adolescent youths, called **kouros** (male) and **kore** (female). Such figures begin an aesthetic that will dominate ancient Greece—the male body is portrayed nude as the ideal of human perfection and beauty; the female is modestly clothed.

writings characterize religious activities as "sacrificing and having a good time."

As with the ancient religions of the Middle East, proper worship for the Greeks involved sacrificing a portion of human production to the gods. In contrast to the Mesopotamians, Greeks sacrificed things of relatively little value—the fat-wrapped thigh bones or internal organs of sacrificial animals—while keeping the best parts for themselves. Families, magistrates, and citizen assemblies were primarily responsible for observing proper respect for the gods. As a result, unlike in Egypt and Mesopotamia, powerful religious institutions never developed in ancient Greek society. Each temple had a priest or priestess, but their duties were usually part-time activities requiring little training.

The real religious professionals were oracles—people who interpreted divine will. Among these, the Delphic oracle, a woman who reputedly could enter into a trance and receive cryptic messages from Apollo, was the most famous. **Figure 2.3** shows the Delphic oracle sitting on a tripod under which vapors emerge from the earth, sending her into a trance. The latest scientific speculation suggests that the vapors were ethane, a gas that can be used as an anesthetic. The oracle consults a bowl in which float herbs or animal entrails to help stimulate her vision so that she might advise the man (here, Theseus's father) seeking advice.

> Oracles

Oracle messages were received in the form of ambiguous riddles and had to be interpreted by humans, so a central role for human agency remained in Greek religion. Perhaps the most famous inquiry at Delphi was made by King Croesus of Lydia in about 546 B.C.E. Croesus was worried about the Persian king Cyrus, who was threatening his kingdom (see Chapter 1), and asked the oracle whether he should wage war against Persia. The priests of Delphi returned with the answer: If Croesus were to make war on the Persians, he would destroy a mighty empire. Croesus was elated, but he had misinterpreted the oracle: The mighty empire that fell was that of Croesus as Cyrus defeated the Lydians. Messages from oracles needed to be interpreted very carefully, indeed.

Just as they envisioned their gods with all the qualities and foibles of humans, the Greeks embraced all facets of human behavior, even the irrational. To Homer's list of Olympians, subsequent Greeks added the worship of Dionysus, the god of wine and fertility. Men worshiped this god during lavish banquets, but the cult had special appeal to women. During worship of Dionysus, women temporarily escaped their domestic confinement and engaged in drinking, ecstatic dancing, and sometimes sexual license as part of the ritual.

> Worship of Dionysus

FIGURE 2.3 Foretelling the Future, ca. fifth century B.C.E. This pottery depicts the famous Delphic oracle sitting on a tripod where vapors from the earth sent her into a trance. Here she is shown recovered from her trance and reading the future in the bowl she holds.

Greek religious thought marked a significant departure from the forms of worship of the ancient Middle East. In Greece, the gods were so much like humans that worshiping them encouraged people to aspire to the greatest in human accomplishments and to acknowledge the worst in human frailties. It was this view, for instance, that caused them to count Achilles as a flawed, yet powerful, hero. The Greeks did add a cautionary warning in their praise of humanity. If people exhibited excessive pride or arrogance as they tried to become godlike (called **hubris**), the gods would destroy them. Yet they still had a great deal of room to celebrate human accomplishments. As Greek thinkers placed humans rather than gods at the center of their understanding of the world, and as they studied reality from a human perspective, they began to transform the Mesopotamian view that had contributed so much to Western civilization. Humans were no longer impotent before a chaotic world ruled by arbitrary deities; instead, they were encouraged to understand and master their world.

> Impact of religious ideas

Studying the Material World

The Greeks had great confidence in their ability to learn everything about the world. They rejected many earlier explanations and began an objective, almost scientific, approach to comprehending nature. This special search for knowledge was termed

GLOBAL CONNECTIONS

Transforming Science in Asia Minor

In 585 B.C.E., Asia Minor—the turbulent crossroads where Eastern empires met Western Greeks—once again became embroiled in warfare. Lydians (in Asia Minor) and Medes (Persians) had skirmished over land and power for five years, when suddenly, amid a battle, the sun darkened. Frightened by this apparent message from the gods, the two armies laid down their weapons and negotiated peace. Not far away, the Ionian Greeks interpreted the darkening sun differently. One of their own, the esteemed teacher Thales of Miletus (ca. 642–ca. 548 B.C.E.), had predicted this solar eclipse well in advance of that day. Based on his studies of the heavens, he knew eclipses were natural occurrences, not messages of divine anger. This kind of thinking gave birth to a new, rational approach to understanding previously mysterious events.

How did this new view of natural occurrences appear in Ionia on the coast of Asia Minor? (See **Map 2.1** for the locations of Lydia and Ionia.) Miletus was a cosmopolitan city on the coast of the Aegean Sea (see **Maps 2.1 and 2.2**). In this bustling urban center, travelers from the New Babylonian Empire, Egypt, and Greece mingled and shared ideas. By the seventh century B.C.E., these Ionian Greeks had already learned much from their Asian neighbors. For example, they were using the Phoenician alphabet, a Babylonian system of weights, and Phrygian structures of music, called modes. Soon they would also begin using coins invented by the Lydians. But as Thales' knowledge of eclipses demonstrated, these practical tools were only a few of the important ideas that spread from the East to Greece.

Thales himself probably came from a distinguished family of mixed Greek and Phoenician background. He took an interest in everything from Greek myths to Babylonian science, and his unconventional, cross-cultural background proved fertile soil for sprouting new ideas. Fortunately for him, he had access to the sophisticated learning of the Babylonians.

The Babylonian king Nebuchadrezzar (r. 605–561 B.C.E.), though he destroyed Jerusalem in 587 B.C.E. and led the Jews into the Babylonian Captivity, was also a builder. He made Babylon the greatest city in the world. Covering 2,100 acres—far more than the 135 acres of the typical Sumerian city—Babylon amazed the Ionian Greeks who visited the city to trade or simply tour. They returned home with captivating stories of grand palaces and temples aglow with brightly colored glazed bricks. These architectural wonders only underscored the considerable skill of the Babylonian engineers.

The greatest Babylonian accomplishments, however, came in the fields of astronomy and mathematics. For thousands of years, Mesopotamians had studied the night sky, and Babylonians perfected this art. Starting in 747 B.C.E., Babylonian court astronomers kept monthly tables on which they recorded all planetary movements together with reports of earthly affairs. These efforts gave birth to the pseudoscience of astrology, through which Babylonians tried to understand the effect of heavenly objects on earthly events. Their observations set the stage for astronomical science in the Greek world and beyond.

The Babylonians also made great strides in mathematics. Using their base-60 number system, Babylonian mathematicians pioneered detailed calculations such as square and cube roots, as well as many other impressive reckonings. To demonstrate the complexity of solving mathematical problems using a base-60 system, **Figure 2.4** shows a calculation to obtain the square of 147 (or 147 times 147). Using our number system, multiplying 147 by itself is fairly simple and yields the result of 21,609. In the cuneiform calculation shown in the figure, the number 147 is indicated as 2,27, and squaring gives the answer of 6,0,9. The location of these digits refers to a position of a number on a complex chart containing six columns, each of which had ten numbers. Only specialists had access to such charts.

The difficulties of these early mathematics makes Thales' ability to apply their principles even more impressive. He purportedly mastered mathematics and geometry so thoroughly that he could determine the height of a pyramid by measuring the length of its shadow at the time of day when the length of a person's shadow equaled his or her height. Thales' skill made him a much-sought-after teacher who could explain the Babylonians' arcane mathematical wisdom to ordinary people and extend that learning to a new generation.

In 539 B.C.E., the Persians finally conquered Asia Minor. One of Thales' students, Pythagoras, fled the violence in Ionia to settle in Croton in southern Italy. There he continued his studies of mathematics and geometry, spreading the mix of Asian and Greek science farther west. His work would leave a lasting influence on Western science.

Making Connections

1. Why was Ionia well placed to serve as a crossroads between East and West?

2. How did Thales help make mathematics and astronomy relevant to the Greeks?

3. How difficult would it have been to use Babylonian mathematics? Can you figure the system out?

4. How did this fruitful combination of Eastern and Western science influence our science today?

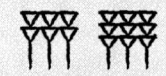

FIGURE 2.4 147 squared = 21,609. Babylonian: 2,27 squared is 6,0,9.

philosophy (love of wisdom) and would become the Greeks' most important intellectual invention. The earliest known scholar of this kind was Thales of Miletus (ca. 624–ca. 548 B.C.E.). The location of Miletus on the Ionian coast (see **Map 2.2**, on page 47) shows how Greek culture and its tremendous influence had moved beyond the Greek mainland itself.

Thales reputedly studied Egyptian and Babylonian astronomy and geometry and brought this knowledge to practical use by measuring pyramids, based on the length of their shadows, and predicting a solar eclipse. (See Global Connections on page 50.) Departing from most of his Egyptian and Mesopotamian predecessors, Thales believed in an orderly cosmos that was accessible to human reason. This formed the heart of much subsequent Greek (and Western) inquiry. He sought a single primal element that would explain a cosmic unity and believed that element was water. Although Thales' conclusion was wrong, his assumption of an orderly universe accessible to human inquiry was pivotal to the future of Western thought.

<mark>Thales and Democritus</mark>

Thales was followed by others who continued the rational approach to the natural world. Democritus (ca. 460–ca. 370 B.C.E.), for example, posited an infinite universe of tiny atoms with spaces between them. Although his ideas were not widely supported in ancient Greece, they were proven by early-twentieth-century physicists.

Pythagoras (ca. 582–507 B.C.E.), who fled from Ionia to Italy, made even greater discoveries in the fields of mathematics and astronomy. He believed that order in the universe was based on numbers (not water), and that mathematics was the key to understanding reality. Pythagoras is credited with being the first to suggest that the number 13 is unlucky, but his mathematics extended far beyond such attempts to quantify fortune. He developed the Pythagorean Theorem, the geometrical statement that the square of the hypotenuse of a right triangle is equal to the sum of the squares of the other two sides. He went on to explore additional theories of proportion that have contributed to much modern mathematics. Pythagoras was also among the first to claim that the earth and other heavenly bodies were spherical and that they rotated on their axes. The mathematician was so respected that his followers later developed a religious cult in his name.

<mark>Pythagoras</mark>

These philosophers, in a dramatic way, changed the direction of thinking about the world. They rejected the mythopoeic approach to understanding the world and made the first attempts to understand and explain the world in a scientific and philosophical way. Because they had little experimental equipment and no prior knowledge to draw upon, their ideas were not necessarily accurate by our standards, but we would not be who we are without them.

Men like Thales, Democritus, and Pythagoras operated on an abstract level of almost pure science. Yet the Greeks also practiced an applied technology, with results that continue to astound us. The sixth-century B.C.E. engineer Eupalinus, for example, constructed a 3,000-foot-long tunnel through a mountain in order to bring water from a spring into a city. To accomplish this feat, he used only hand tools, and he had to work in the dark because he lacked a light source. Most extraordinary, he dug from both sides of the mountain—and the two parts of the tunnel met in the middle with only a slight adjustment needed. Pythagoras was on Eupalinus's island of Samos at about the time the tunnel was dug, so some scholars speculate that the mathematician helped in the process. Others have suggested that Eupalinus used a system of mirrors to line up the halves of the tunnel and illuminate the interior as he excavated. However he managed this feat, he counts among the most accomplished Greeks who applied reason to practical matters.

<mark>Practical applications</mark>

While modern scholars admire these early Greek thinkers, many contemporaries looked with suspicion on those who studied the world while seemingly ignoring the gods. Even though the Greeks worshiped humanlike gods and goddesses, they still revered them, and accusations of impiety always hovered on the borders of scientific inquiry. In 432 B.C.E., the democratic assembly of Athens made it a crime to "deny the gods, or disseminate teachings about the things that take place in the heavens." This law was precipitated by the teachings of Anaxagoras (ca. 500–ca. 428 B.C.E.), who claimed that the sun was a white-hot stone instead of a god. Even in the field of rational inquiry, in which the Greeks made such impressive strides, the ambiguities that marked this dynamic society are evident. The same culture that produced impressive thinkers like Anaxagoras and Socrates (whom we met at the beginning of this chapter) sometimes recoiled from the results of their studies. Nevertheless, Greek intellectual accomplishments formed one of their central contributions to Western civilization.

<mark>Fears of "impiety"</mark>

LIFE IN THE GREEK POLEIS

As we saw in Chapter 1, ancient societies had taken for granted a natural order of society that placed kings and priests in charge, and the Mycenaean Greeks had shared this view. With the brisk trade that comes so naturally to sea peoples, however, a new prosperity based on commercial expansion emerged, creating

thinking about ART

FIGURE 2.5
Ezekias, Suicide of Ajax, Athenian Vase, ca. 450 B.C.E.

The famous vase painter Ezekias has portrayed a significant moment in the Trojan War. After the death of Achilles, the hero Ajax expected to be named to lead the army. Instead, the Greeks chose Odysseus. In his humiliation, Ajax commits suicide. The artist shows him preparing for his death, burying the hilt of his sword in the earth so that he can fall on his sword. On the right, the artist shows the all-important hoplite weaponry: the great shield with the head of the mythological monster Gorgon emblazoned on the front, the helmet, and the long spear. Yet, in this contest for excellence the pride of the individual was more important than the strength of the army, and the artist shows this in the vase.

Connecting Art & Society

1. Would the Greeks have considered this act heroic or cowardly?
2. Is Ajax showing the same kind of individualistic pride as Achilles did in the incident described at the beginning of this chapter, when he refused to fight?
3. What would our society think of this act?

---

an urban middle class of merchants and artisans who owed no loyalty to aristocratic landowners.

By 700 B.C.E., changes in warfare brought about in part by the growth of Greek trade also made aristocratic warriors less important. First, the growing commercial classes became wealthier, and at the same time the increased trade brought down the price of metals. Now more men could afford to arm themselves and go to war. New armies of infantrymen (called **hoplites**) dominated the art of making war. Common citizens armed with swords, shields, and long thrusting spears formed a **phalanx**—a tight formation about eight men deep and as wide as the number of troops available. As long as these soldiers stayed tightly pressed together, they were virtually impenetrable. Elite warriors once could rely on their own heroism and on their monopoly of horses and cavalry to ensure victory on the battlefield. Now that a hoplite phalanx could withstand cavalry charges, the aristocracy no longer maintained a privileged position; they needed the support of citizen armies. This dependence further weakened aristocratic rule. Figure 2.5 shows the tension between the traditional values of heroic pride on the one hand and the needs of the phalanx-dependent hoplite army on the other hand. Even as the artist immortalized the hero's prideful suicide, he also highlighted the hoplite weaponry that made the phalanx invincible.

The Invention of Politics

Between 650 and 550 B.C.E., civil war broke out in many cities as the lower classes rose to overthrow the aristocracy. This violence led to the rule of men who became rulers by physical force. Although kingship had a long-standing tradition in the West, this was a new form of authority—based on power, not hereditary right. The Greeks called such rulers *tyrants* to distinguish them from more traditional kings. At first the term had no pejorative connotation—one could easily be a kind tyrant, and indeed some were sincere reformers seeking to end aristocratic exploitation. For example, some tyrants gained popular support by such reforms as freeing slaves, eliminating debts, redistributing land. Later, however, as these rulers relied on force to hold power, the term *tyrant* acquired the negative meaning it holds today. Tyrants often favored the commercial classes to try to hold on to power, but such alliances proved insubstantial. In some city-states, tyrants were replaced by various forms of participatory governments.

Greek citizens—especially those who controlled the lucrative trade and fought in the successful phalanxes—thus began to take charge of the political life of their cities. A Greek city-state was called a **polis** (pl. *poleis*). It was a small but autonomous political unit that generated intense loyalty from its citizens, who conducted their political, social, and religious activities in its heart. The poleis frequently included a fortified high ground—called an *acropolis*, the most famous of which is in Athens. They also had a central place of assembly and market, called the **agora** (pl. *agorae*). Surrounding villages began to consolidate and share a political identity, and the word *polis* came to mean the city-state itself and its surrounding countryside. Each city-state was an independent governing entity, but in the view of its residents, a polis was also a state of mind. Unlike in Mesopotamia, Egypt, and Mycenae, polis inhabitants did not think of themselves as subjects of a king or as owing obedience to a priesthood. Instead, they were "citizens" who were actively responsible for guiding their poleis. Aristotle (384–322 B.C.E.) even characterized humans by their participation in politics (the word *politics* is derived from the word *polis*), arguing that "man is a political animal" (although a more accurate translation is "man is an animal of the polis").

Although Greece's rocky terrain separated the land into many small city-states, they shared certain characteristics. They all developed self-government by male citizens, with variations as to the exact form. For example, Corinth and many other small poleis had an **oligarchy** (rule by a few), whereas Athens developed an early form of democracy that was strikingly new in the West and in the world. All the states relied on hoplite armies, and all used slavery to run their small-scale industries and farming. In all the city-states as well, Greek men who fought together in the hoplite armies gathered daily in the agorae to discuss matters of life and politics.

The Heart of the Polis

The heart of the polis was the household, which consisted of a male citizen, his wife and children, and their slaves. This configuration formed the basis for both the rural and urban economies. In the villages outside the walls of the city itself, household members herded sheep and goats, worked in the vineyards and olive groves, and struggled to plant crops in the rocky ground. Olive trees yielded abundant fruit, but harvesting required a good deal of labor.

Olive harvesting was well worth the effort, however, for the olives and their precious oil brought much wealth into some of the city-states. Athens's economy in particular depended upon its olive oil exports. A well-known story about the philosopher Thales illustrates the economic importance of olives to the Greeks. His neighbors mocked him, saying, "If you are smart, why aren't you rich?" In response, he purchased the use of all the local olive presses cheaply during the off season. Then, when everyone was trying to press their olives after the harvest, they had to buy the use of the presses from Thales. He made a fortune and silenced his neighbors. As his final retort, Thales pointed out that philosophers could easily become rich, but they loved the life of the mind more than money.

In addition to olive harvesting, craftsmanship and trade completed the polis economy. Artisans in the polis labored at their crafts or sold their merchandise in the open market during the mornings. After a large afternoon meal, they napped and then either returned to their shops or (more likely) went to the gymnasium to exercise and talk with other citizens. The gymnasium grew in part out of the Greek belief in cultivating perfection in all things; thus a skilled artisan or philosopher also needed to cultivate his physical prowess as part of his pursuit of excellence. The gymnasium proved an enduring feature of life in the Mediterranean city-states. This was a highly public life for male citizens; work, exercise, and talk were all central activities of the masculine life.

Men's and women's roles

In most city-states, women's lives were more restricted than men's—at least in the ideal. Wealthy, upper-class women were married at puberty and were supposed to stay indoors. A text from the early fourth century B.C.E. describes how a husband educated his 15-year-old wife on domestic responsibilities. He told her that men belonged outdoors: "For a man to remain indoors . . . is a thing discreditable." Women, on the other hand, should stay inside, teaching female slaves necessary skills, managing the goods brought into the household, and presiding over the spinning and weaving. When men entertained their peers at dinner parties or visited, "respectable" women stayed home and out of sight along with their female slaves and children. (As we will see, life for women in Sparta marked an exception to this pattern.)

Of course, real life seldom measures up to the extremes of the ideal. Even in Athens, many women were visible in the marketplace: Slaves went to the fountains to carry water, prostitutes offered their services, and priestesses served in more than forty religious cults of the city. Between these extremes, there were many women of the poorer classes who sold their wares—cloth or garden produce—in market stalls as they worked hard to supplement the family income.

In addition to having defined gender roles, Greek society depended heavily on slave labor; virtually every household had a few slaves. In the earliest years of the poleis, just as elsewhere in the ancient Middle East, slaves were either captives of war or debtors. By the sixth century B.C.E., debt slavery had been virtually banned throughout the Greek world, but slavery itself remained a central institution. However, in many ways slaves' lives resembled those of their owners. Numerous slaves worked alongside free men and women in almost every occupation. (There were even slave policemen in Athens.) Slaves frequently lived in their own residences, worked in a trade, and earned their own money. Sometimes called "pay-bringers," they owed their owners a portion of their income but could retain some of the money they earned. With this revenue, some slaves in turn bought slaves for themselves or purchased their own freedom. Many Greek cities even had benefit clubs that lent slaves

Slave labor

enough money to buy their freedom and repay the loan later. Numerous bright, ambitious slaves gained their freedom and became quite prosperous.

All slaves did not enjoy this relatively easy life. Some slaves had brutal masters and suffered all forms of abuse; in Athens, some slaves who tried to flee their condition bore the brand of a runaway on their foreheads. Slaves who lived under the worst conditions were those who had the misfortune to work in the silver mines, an essential source of income for Athens. In these mines, they were fed just enough to stay strong and were beaten regularly to keep them working in the mines that produced immense wealth for free Greeks. For the most part, however, slavery was treated as a simple fact of life—an essential tool for getting necessary work done.

Fears and Attachments in Greek Emotional Life

The extreme separation of men and women seems to have contributed to a wide range of insecurities and emotional attachments in Greek society. Many Greek writers expressed a great suspicion of women. As one poet, Semonides of Amorgos, wrote: "God made the mind of women a thing apart." The strict segregation of men and women through their lives may have contributed to misunderstandings. Men with little experience with women believed that virtuous women were scarce. Many husbands feared that their wives would escape their seclusion and take lovers, and thereby raise questions about the paternity of their children. These fears permeate many writings by Greek men.

Perhaps as part of their overall praise of masculinity, many ancient Greeks accepted bisexuality, at least among wealthy urban dwellers. The ideal of such a relationship took the form of a mentoring arrangement between a well-connected older man and a "beardless youth" (although school-aged, free-born boys were protected from such liaisons). As the pair matured, the elder man would marry and take up his family responsibilities, and the younger would serve as a mentor to a new youth. Such relationships were seen as a natural part of a world in which men often feared female sexuality, spent all their time together, exercised nude in the gymnasia, and praised the male body as the ideal of beauty. Indeed, many Greeks believed that the male-male relationship offered the highest possibility for love and that such ties usually brought out the best in each partner, making both braver and nobler.

We have fewer examples of women engaging in homosexual behavior, probably because their lives were conducted in privacy and were not recorded in as many historical documents. However, one sixth-century B.C.E. poet, Sappho from the island of Lesbos, expressed passionate love for the young women in her social circle. Her poetry has since been both highly respected for its beauty and severely criticized for its content. The philosopher Plato admired Sappho so much that he referred to her as a goddess of poetry, but some Greek playwrights dismissed and ridiculed her as an ugly woman who could not attract a man. Nevertheless, Sappho's poetry was so influential that the word *Lesbian*, meaning a resident of Sappho's island of Lesbos, has become synonymous with female homosexuality.

Not all women were confined to the home. While respectable women stayed carefully indoors, some women—slaves or foreigners—who had no economic resources or family ties became prostitutes and courtesans who shared men's public lives at dinners and drinking parties. Prostitutes were even registered and taxed in many Greek city-states and thereby became a legitimate part of social and economic life. Men and prostitutes drank freely together from the wine bowls abundantly filled at banquets. These bowls were decorated inside and out with appropriate themes. **Figure 2.6** shows a prostitute dressed in loose, seductive clothing who holds a wine bowl in each hand as she plays a Greek drinking game in which the participant twirls the drinking vessel until the dregs go flying. Such exuberant images not only portrayed scenes from the parties but also were intended to spur people on to greater abandon. Women in ancient Greece, particularly Athens, were thus placed in the peculiar situation of being invisible if they were "respectable," and mingling with and influencing powerful men only if they were not.

All the city-states shared many of these elements of urban life, from work to pleasure. However, each polis had its own distinctive character, as citizens structured their political lives to suit themselves. The two best-documented Greek cities were Athens and Sparta, and yet most of the cities did not match the extremes in art and austerity that marked these two influential states.

Athens: City of Democracy

Theseus, whose father was portrayed consulting the Delphic oracle in **Figure 2.3**, founded Athens. Document 2.1 relates the city's founding myth and suggests that participatory democracy was at the heart of its origins. The reality of a developing democratic form of government was more complicated. By 700 B.C.E., Athenian aristocrats had established a form of government that allowed them to run and control the growing city. Three (and later nine) administrators—called *archons*—were elected by an assembly of male

FIGURE 2.6 A Drinking Game, ca. fifth century B.C.E. This pottery cup shows a courtesan swirling a wine bowl until the dregs fly out. It reminds us that although respectable women stayed home, prostitutes were a regular part of Athenian social life.

citizens (the *Ecclesia*) and ran the business of the city. They served for only one year, and after their tenure they permanently entered a council called the Areopagus (eventually numbering 300 men), which held the real power because it was composed of senior men who could not be removed from office. This government, in which the wealthy effectively controlled power, proved unable to respond to changing economic fortunes, which had profound political consequences.

By about 600 B.C.E., the weaknesses in the Athenian economy had become apparent. Small farmers could not produce enough to feed the growing population, and many fell into debt and even slavery by offering themselves as security in exchange for food. At about the same time, the hoplite armies caused the aristocracy to lose its monopoly over the military. A social crisis was in the making, but it was resolved by a far-sighted Athenian aristocrat, Solon, who was elected as sole archon in 594 B.C.E. Like so many men in the West who periodically tried to alleviate social ills, Solon introduced reforms intended to appease these lower classes while keeping aristocrats in power.

> Solon's reforms

Solon first addressed the alarming debt crisis by introducing reforms—called the Shaking Off of Burdens—that canceled (or limited) existing debts and banned debt slavery altogether. Solon also introduced some agricultural reforms, striking at the economic heart of the problem. He ordered that no agricultural product could be exported except olive oil, thus stimulating the cultivation of the valuable olives that would become the basis of Athens's prosperity. He also standardized the weights used by the Athenians, making it easier for them to trade with other poleis. With the economic reforms in place, Solon turned to the political structures that had proved inadequate to prevent civil strife.

Solon did not try to eliminate the old families from power; instead, he paved the way for men growing wealthy from the export trade to participate in government. He first divided up all citizens into four groups based on wealth (instead of birth), and only members of the top two groups were eligible to become archons (and subsequently members of the Areopagus). While this preserved some privilege of rank, it nevertheless appeased the newly wealthy, who were now permitted to aspire to the highest offices. Solon then revitalized the assembly of citizens, and to further weaken the power of the Areopagus, he created a Council of 400 to set the agenda for the Ecclesia. To round out the reforms, Solon tried to ensure justice for everyone by establishing a special people's court of appeal intended to offer protection against the abuse of power by archons.

> Increased democracy

Solon's reforms were balanced and attempted to provide a compromise among the contentious social groups in Athens. However, his attempts to placate the various factions were unsuccessful because each party tried to gain more privileges. During the resulting civil strife, Athens turned to tyranny, bringing Peisistratus to power in 560 B.C.E. He ruled (between periods of exile) until 527 B.C.E., when his son Hippias tried to continue the rule. He was to be the last of Athens's tyrants. He fell to a coalition of aristocrats and Greeks from other city-states hoping to gain some political advantage for themselves. The period of tyranny broke the power of the aristocrats and paved the way for full democracy.

> Tyranny

The people rallied to Cleisthenes, a nobleman who stood for popular interests. In 508 B.C.E., Athens adopted the Constitution of Cleisthenes, which refined Solon's reforms and brought a remarkable degree of direct democracy to the city. Cleisthenes kept Solon's basic structure, but his major innovation (which has earned him the credit for establishing democracy in Athens) was to redistrict the city in a way that old alliances of geography and clan were broken and could no longer control the city offices. Everyone was divided up into ten tribal units, and this was how they were represented in the Assembly. Furthermore, Solon's old Council of 400 was increased to 500—each tribal unit could select 50 members by lot. By breaking the old alliance system, Cleisthenes

thinking about DOCUMENTS

DOCUMENT 2.1

Theseus Founds the City of Athens

The famous ancient biographer Plutarch (46–120 C.E.) related Athens's founding myth, in which the hero Theseus defeated the Minotaur of Crete and returned to establish a city that would be unlike any that had gone before.

After the death of Ægeus, Theseus conceived a great and important design. He gathered together all the inhabitants of Attica and made them citizens of one city, whereas before they had lived dispersed, so as to be hard to assemble together for the common weal, and at times even fighting with one another.

He visited all the villages and tribes, and won their consent, the poor and lower classes gladly accepting his proposals, while he gained over the more powerful by promising that the new constitution should not include a king, but that it should be a pure commonwealth, with himself merely acting as general of its army and guardian of its laws, while in other respects it would allow perfect freedom and equality to every one. By these arguments he convinced some of them, and the rest knowing his power and courage chose rather to be persuaded than forced into compliance.

He therefore destroyed the prytanea, the senate house, and the magistracy of each individual township, built one common prytaneum and senate house for them all on the site of the present acropolis, called the city Athens, and instituted the Panathenaic festival common to all of them. He also instituted a festival for the resident aliens, on the sixteenth of the month, Hecatombaion, which is still kept up. And having, according to his promise, laid down his sovereign power, he arranged the new constitution under the auspices of the gods. . . .

Wishing still further to increase the number of his citizens, he invited all strangers to come and share equal privileges, and they say that the worlds now used, "Come hither all ye peoples," was the proclamation then used by Theseus, establishing as it were a commonwealth of all nations. But he did not permit his state to fall into the disorder which this influx of all kinds of people would probably have produced, but divided the people into three classes, of Eupatridæ or nobles, Geomori or farmers, Demiurgi or artisans.

To the Eupatridæ he assigned the care of religious rites, the supply of magistrates for the city, and the interpretation of the laws and customs sacred or profane; yet he placed them on an equality with the other citizens, thinking that the nobles would always excel in dignity, the farmers in usefulness, and the artisans in numbers. Aristotle tells us that he was the first who inclined to democracy, and gave up the title of king; and Homer seems to confirm this view by speaking of the people of the Athenians alone of all the states mentioned in his catalogue of ships.

SOURCE: Plutarch, "Life of Theseus," in *The Great Events by Famous Historians*, vol. I, ed. Rossiter Johnson (The National Alumni, 1905), pp. 50–51.

Analyze the Document

1. What was unusual about Theseus's vision for the city?
2. How might this myth have influenced the development of Athenian democracy?
3. Might the myth have been created after Athens had adopted a democratic constitution?

---

secured a remarkable form of direct democracy for Athens with provisions to curb the power of any group that might become too strong.

Although the Ecclesia offered a new level of participation to the men of the ancient world and a model of representation that has been praised since, it was not a perfect democracy. It still represented only about 20 percent of the population of Athens, for it excluded women and slaves. Also excluded were the *metics*, resident foreigners who lived and worked in Athens in manufacturing and commerce and who represented nearly one-third of the free population of Athens. Furthermore, recent scholarship shows that only a minority of the qualified citizens could attend the assembly at any given time—only about 6,000 can fit into the meeting place, a small sloping hillside. It seems that when the meeting place was full, no one else could enter and a quorum was declared. Thus, probably many of the same people (those living nearby) attended the Ecclesia regularly.

Assessing democracy

However, other parts of the Athenian government made sure the principle of egalitarian democracy prevailed. The Council of 500 was chosen annually by lot from male citizens over age 30, and citizens could not repeat tenure. Choosing representatives by lot (instead of by election or other device) removed much of the influence of wealth and personal power from the political process. The Council set the agenda for the Ecclesia, preparing forms of legislation for the assembly's action. Its influence was enormous, but the full governing power remained in the direct democracy of the Ecclesia. These practices assumed that all citizens could fulfill the duties of government, and this egalitarian assumption is astonishing for the ancient world (and perhaps for the modern one as well). The great leader of Athens Pericles, in a famous funeral oration preserved (or paraphrased) by the historian Thucydides, rightly observed: "Our constitution is called a democracy because it is in the hands not of the few but of the many."

The people did recognize that sometimes individuals could threaten the rule of the many, and to protect the democracy, Cleisthenes instituted an unusual procedure early in the sixth century B.C.E.: ostracism. Once a year, Athenians could vote for the man they considered most dangerous to the state by inscribing his name on a scrap of pottery (called an *ostracon*). If a man received 6,000 votes, he was sent into exile for ten years. **Figure 2.7** shows examples of these pottery shards. The scrap on the lower left votes to exile a man named Hippocrates, while the other three cast votes for "Themistocles, son of Neocles." It appears that Themistocles was well on his way to exile! Although Athenian democracy was not perfect, it was an extraordinary new chapter in the history of the West, and one that has held long-standing appeal.

> Ostracism

Sparta: Model Military State

Sparta's development led to the emergence of a state thoroughly different from Athens, with a markedly different set of values. Whereas Athenians were creative, artistic, and eloquent, Spartans were militaristic, strict, and sparing of words (our word *laconic* comes from the Greek word for "Spartans" or the region they inhabited). The nature of their state was shaped by an early solution to their land hunger. Instead of sending out colonists or negotiating partnerships with the peoples in their vicinity (as the Athenians had done), the Spartans conquered their neighboring districts and enslaved the local populations. The slaves, called **helots,** were treated harshly. As one Spartan poet observed, they were like "donkeys worn down by intolerable labor." Sparta's helots greatly outnumbered free citizens and always seemed to threaten rebellion. To keep the helots in slavery, the Spartans virtually enslaved themselves in a military state of perpetual watchfulness. They consoled themselves by observing that at least they had chosen their harsh life, whereas their helots had not.

The Spartan constitution—reputedly introduced by the semilegendary Lycurgus in about 600 B.C.E.—reflected their deep conservatism and made a minimal concession to democracy. Authority was carefully kept in the hands of the elders. In this oligarchy, citizen representation was firmly guided by age and experience, and many outsiders admired Sparta's "mixed constitution," which seemed to balance democracy with oligarchy.

Life in Sparta was harsh, although it was much admired by many Greeks who appreciated the Spartans' powers of self-denial. At birth, each child was examined by elders, and if deemed physically deficient, the child would be exposed—left outdoors to die. At the age of 7, boys were turned over to the state and spent the next thirteen years in training to learn military skills, endurance, and loyalty to the polis. At 20, young men entered the army and lived the next ten years in barracks. They could marry but could visit their wives only by eluding the barracks guards. At 30, men became full citizens and could live at home. Nevertheless, they were expected to take all meals in the military dining hall, where food was sparse and plain.

> Spartan life

While their men lived isolated in the barracks, Spartan women had far more freedom than Greek women of other city-states. Because men concentrated on their military activities, women handled most of the household arrangements and had wide economic powers. They attended contests to cheer the brave and mock the losers, but they were not simply spectators. Women, too, trained in athletic endurance, and the fierceness of Spartan women was said to match that of their men. The Greek biographer Plutarch (46?–120? C.E.) recorded a series of quotations that were supposedly the words of Spartan women. The most famous is from a woman who tells her son to come back from war either with his shield (victorious) or on it (dead). Such resolve made the armies of Sparta the best in Greece, and though the Spartans created no works of art, they probably would have said that their own lives were masterpiece enough.

FIGURE 2.7 Pottery Voting Ballots Once a year, Athenians were able to vote for someone whom they believed should be exiled for ten years. They inscribed his name on pottery scraps called *ostraca*, such as the ones shown here. That Greek word is the source of the English word *ostracize*, meaning "to ban from the group."

The Love of the Contest: Olympic Games

Athens and Sparta were only two examples of the many varieties of city-states that developed with fierce independence on the Greek mainland and in the colonies throughout the Mediterranean. But, although there was much rivalry among the poleis, they still shared a certain sense of identity. They spoke the same language, worshiped the same gods, cherished Homer's poetry, and had a passionate love for individual competition. They recognized these affinities, calling themselves *Hellenes* (the Romans later called them "Greek" after a Greek colony), and they considered all Hellenes to be better than other peoples. Their love of contest caused Hellenes to gather at many local competitions that included drama as well as sport. The largest and most famous of these events was a religious festival dedicated to Zeus, and Hellenes even stopped their almost interminable warfare to come together and compete.

The first pan-Hellenic Olympic Games were held in 776 B.C.E. At first, the event consisted only of a footrace, but soon the games expanded to include boxing, wrestling, chariot racing, and the grueling pentathlon, which consisted of long jumping, discus and javelin throwing, wrestling, and the 200-meter sprint. Olympic victors brought glory to their home cities and were richly rewarded there with honor and free meals.

[Olympic Games]

The Olympics were so popular that they served as an inspiration to many artists. The athletes shown in **Figure 2.8** demonstrate the perfection that people expected from their athletic heroes. The scene portrays several of the contests: the footrace, the javelin throw, and, in the center of the relief, the most difficult event, wrestling. The athletes tense all their muscles as they begin the contest that virtually defined Greek life. Critics, such as the playwright Euripides (485–406 B.C.E.), chided Greeks for their adulation of athletes. "We ought rather to crown the good man and the wise man," he scolded. Nevertheless, spectators flocked to the games.

Olympic planners prohibited women from attending the contest, although they could purchase a chariot and horses with which men would compete in their names. One woman defied the convention and dressed as a trainer so that she could watch her son compete. After he won, she jumped over a fence in her excitement and accidentally revealed her gender. Olympic officials promptly passed a law requiring all future trainers to attend the games in the nude to prevent further disguises.

[Women at Olympics]

Some women conducted games of their own separately from the men's. These games, dedicated to Zeus's wife, Hera, involved footraces run by unmarried women of various ages. Women judged and sponsored the games and awarded the fastest competitors crowns of olive branches. However, these winners did not receive the high level of acclaim or wealth accorded to male victors, who brought prestige to their cities and fame for themselves through their athletic prowess. Although the Olympic Games offered a safe outlet for the Greeks' love of competition, Greek history was shaped by more devastating strife in which city-states tried to outdo each other on the battlefields.

The Persian Wars, 490–479 B.C.E.

Greek colonists who settled in Asia Minor built their city-states in lands that the Persian Empire had claimed by 500 B.C.E. As we saw in Chapter 1, the

FIGURE 2.8 The Olympic Games, late sixth century B.C.E. As part of their ongoing contest for excellence, the Greeks developed the Olympic Games in honor of Zeus. Here, athletes participate in the footrace, wrestling, and the javelin throw.

thinking about GEOGRAPHY

2.3(a) The first invasion—490 B.C.E.

2.3(b) The second invasion—480 B.C.E.

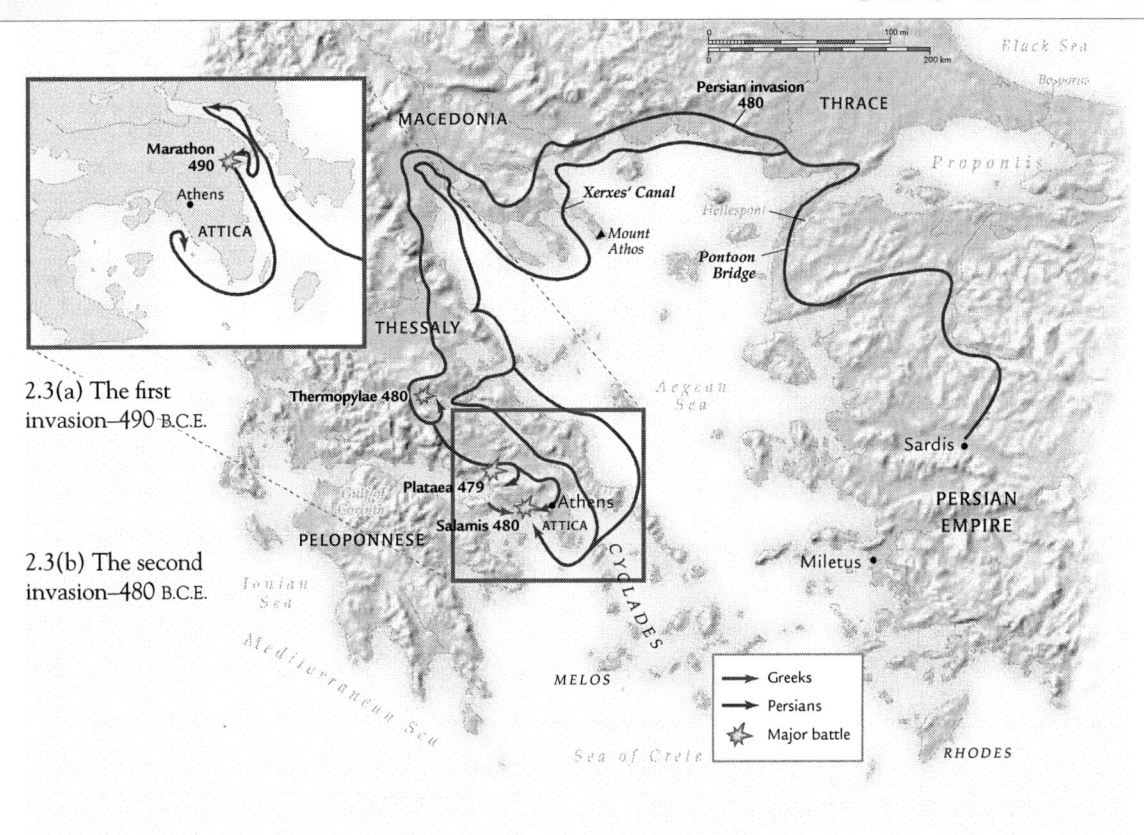

MAP 2.3A & B

The Persian Wars, 490–479 B.C.E.

This map shows the routes of invasions and the major battles of the wars between Persia and the Greek poleis. Map 2.3a traces the first invasion by sea in 490 B.C.E., and Map 2.3b illustrates the routes of the second invasion, during which armies marched by land, supported by accompanying ships.

Explore the Map

1. What might have been the particular advantages and disadvantages posed by the land and sea routes?
2. How did the topography of Greece, with its narrow passes, serve as a disadvantage to the more numerous Persian forces?
3. Why did the Persian land route require engineering marvels such as the Pontoon Bridge and Xerxes' canal? How might these have served as models for future military expeditions?

Persians were tolerant of the various subject peoples within their territories, so they did not object to the growing spirit of independence that accompanied the prosperity of these successful commercial cities. However, open revolt was another matter.

In 499 B.C.E., the Greek tyrant ruling in the city of Miletus (**Map 2.3**) offended the Persian rulers. Hoping to avoid retribution, he staged a revolt against Persian rule and asked for help from his compatriots on the Greek mainland. Sparta refused, but Athens sent twenty ships—enough only to anger the Persians

Causes of war

but not to save Miletus. The Greek city was sacked, and the Persians turned their attention to the Greek peninsula. They planned an invasion in part to punish Athens for its involvement in the Miletus uprising.

Any forces seeking to invade the Greek mainland had to negotiate the mountainous terrain and the narrow passes that afforded the only access to the interior. Furthermore, an invading land army had to be supplied by a shore-hugging fleet that backed up the infantry while navigating the narrow straits of the Aegean shoreline. In 490 B.C.E., the Persian king

Darius I (r. 522–486 B.C.E.), therefore, sailed across the Aegean and landed near Athens. **Map 2.3a** depicts the route of the invading Persian army and the battle site located on the plain of Marathon.

Battle of Marathon At the Battle of Marathon, the Athenians and their allies were far outmatched by the numerous Persians. The worried Athenians asked their Spartan compatriots for reinforcements, but the Spartans replied that they had to complete their religious festival first—then it would be too late to repel the Persians. Athens and its allies had to stand alone. In spite of being outnumbered, the Athenians decided to march from Athens to meet the Persians near their landing site on the plain of Marathon. Confident of an easy victory, the Persians launched their attack. Things did not go as expected for the Persians, however. The Athenian general, Miltiades, developed a clever strategy that helped the Greeks outwit the lightly armed Persians. Weakening the center of their line and strengthening the two wings, the Athenians outflanked the advancing Persian force and inflicted severe damage. The Greeks also made a running advance, a novelty that surprised and confused their enemy. Athenian innovation and energy won the day, bringing a decisive and stunning victory to the Greeks. According to the texts, 6,400 Persians perished in the battle, compared with only 192 Athenians. This unexpected victory of the polis over the huge empire of Persia earned Athens great prestige, and the Athenian victory also inspired confidence in the newly emerging democracy itself.

One of the heroes of Marathon was a fast runner, Philippides, who ran approximately 150 miles in two days to request the help of the Spartans. However, he is more remembered for a probably untrue story that claims he ran to Athens to deliver the news of victory to the polis and then died on the spot from his exertions. Modern-day races are called *marathons* in commemoration of Philippides' legendary 26-mile run from the plain of Marathon to Athens.

A second invasion Athens had fended off the invaders, but the humiliated Persians were determined to try again. Ten years after the disaster at Marathon, Darius's successor, Xerxes (r. 486–465 B.C.E.), plotted a full-scale invasion of the Greek mainland. Xerxes brought the best of ancient engineering to the invasion to try to avoid the disaster of the first war. To move a large infantry force, he built a pontoon bridge across the Hellespont and marched 180,000 soldiers to Greece. Even more impressive, he ordered his men to build a canal a mile and a quarter long through a peninsula in northern Greece so that his fleet could supply the ground force. Historians have debated for decades about whether the canal existed, but recently, scientists from Britain and Greece proved conclusively that the canal was built. It spanned about 100 feet at the surface, just wide enough for two war galleys to pass. It was an astonishing engineering feat and showed Xerxes' determination. (Both the bridge and the canal are shown on **Map 2.3b**.)

As the Persians invaded, several Greek city-states in the north surrendered quickly to the Persian Great King. Meanwhile, Athens had readied its own fleet, assuming that the best way to withstand the Persians was to control the Aegean and therefore the supply routes to troops on the march. Athens also secured the participation of Sparta and its allies to aid in the battle.

Thermopylae For the Persian army, the gateway to the south lay through the pass at Thermopylae (see **Map 2.3b**). Yet the narrow pass, held by a small coalition of Greeks led by Spartans, turned the Persians' greater numbers into a liability. The Greeks held the pass for days against repeated assaults by the best Persian forces. In the end, however, they were betrayed by a Greek who expected to enrich himself by aiding the attackers. The traitor led the Persians around the defended pass, where they could fight the Greeks from the rear. Only the Spartans stayed to fight to the death. Defending themselves from front and back, the Spartans fought fiercely in a long-remembered feat of bravery, and all died with sword in hand. An inscription placed on their graves immortalized their heroic stand: "Tell them the news in Sparta, passer by. That here, obedient to their words, we lie."

The Persians' success at Thermopylae opened a route for them to march south to Athens itself. The outmatched Athenians consulted the Delphic oracle (shown in **Figure 2.3**), who told them to trust in wooden walls. The Athenian leader, Themistocles, persuaded the people that the oracle meant the wooden "walls" of their ships, not the walls of Athens, so the Athenians scattered, taking refuge in their fleet and abandoning the polis for nearby islands. Many horrified Greeks were close enough to watch as the Persians plundered Athens and burned the temples on the Acropolis as an act of revenge for their previous losses. Yet, as in Marathon, the tide again turned against the mighty Persians, this time in the bay of Salamis (see **Map 2.3b**).

Greek naval victory Artemisia, queen of Caria in Persia and commander of a squadron of Xerxes' fleet, immediately saw that the Persians would lose their advantage in numbers fighting in a narrow bay and strongly advised the Persian king against it. Her military wisdom proved well founded; the swift Greek vessels rallied and crushed almost the entire Persian fleet. Artemisia managed to escape through her remarkable strategy and bravery. Xerxes withdrew from the melee after sending his children home to safety on Artemisia's ship. The despondent emperor, watching Artemesia's success and the destruction of the rest of his fleet, lamented: "My men have become women, and my women men." The next year, the Spartans led a coalition that defeated the remnants of the Persian army at Plataea (see **Map 2.3b**). The individualistic, dispersed Greeks had triumphed once more over the vast, unified Persian Empire.

Herodotus: The Father of History

In a famous work called simply *The History*, the Greek historian Herodotus recorded the great deeds of the Persian Wars with a combination of a broad perspective and an attention to detail. This monumental work—some 600 pages long—was so pathbreaking that he is universally considered the father of Western history. With his first sentence, Herodotus placed himself within the Greek heroic tradition, claiming to have written in order "that the deeds of men may not be forgotten, and that the great and noble actions of the Greeks and Asiatics may not lose their fame." While immortalizing these warriors, Herodotus did not take the traditional approach of converting heroic deeds into godlike myths. Instead, he drew from oral traditions acquired during his extensive travels—the things he had "seen and been told"—and wrote what he intended to be a total picture of the known world. This was an account not simply of a war but of a heroic-scale conflict between two types of societies, the poleis and the Asian empire—or, for Herodotus, between freedom and despotism.

Herodotus did much for the discipline of history by striving to record historical events as accurately as possible and separating fact from fable, but his efforts marked only a beginning in the quest for historical objectivity. He clearly shared the Greeks' belief that their culture was far superior to that of the "barbarians," and these preconceptions biased his conclusions.

Although Herodotus wrote a lively, fascinating history, as we will see, he was wrong in identifying the Persians as the Greeks' worst enemies. Just as a Greek had betrayed the Spartans at Thermopylae, the Greeks themselves would one day bring about their own downfall. But for the time being, they gloried in their astounding victory over Persia, the great power of Asia.

GREECE ENTERS ITS CLASSICAL AGE, 479–336 B.C.E.

Victory over the mighty Persian Empire launched the Greeks into a vigorous, creative period that later historians and art critics admired so much they named it the classical age. This period was marked by stunning accomplishments in art, architecture, literature, philosophy, and representative democracy in Athens. This same age that saw such impressive artistic innovations ended as the contest for excellence among the city-states plunged them into devastating wars. At the beginning of the period, however, Athens, which took the lead in guarding Greece from Persian incursions, began to flex its muscles.

Athens Builds an Empire, 477–431 B.C.E.

The Greeks' defeat of the Persians, though sweet, presented the fiercely independent poleis with a new dilemma. The Persian Empire was still powerful. How would the Greek city-states work together to remain vigilant in the face of this threat, and who would lead them? The most effective defense of Greece lay in controlling the Aegean, and the Athenians possessed the strongest fleet.

In 477 B.C.E., most maritime poleis on the coasts and the islands of the Aegean finally decided to form a defensive league. Each member of the league contributed money to maintain a large fleet for the defense of them all. The island of Delos (near modern Mykonos) is small and rocky, only about 2 miles long and less than a mile wide, but its importance was disproportionate to its size (see **Map 2.1,** on page 43). Its location was perfect; as the halfway point between mainland Greece and Ionia, it capitalized on the trade through the Aegean. Furthermore, it was reputed to be the birthplace of Apollo, so its sanctuary to that god brought pilgrims (and wealth) from all over the Greek world. Even Homer mentioned Delos as a religious center for Ionian Greeks. Because people thought the sanctuary was sacred and protected by the god, the alliance decided to establish their treasury on Delos. The coalition was thus called the **Delian League**. Theoretically, all league members were entitled to an equal voice in decision making, but Athens was the strongest member and began to dominate league policy.

As early as the 470s B.C.E., some members took offense at Athens's prominent role and sought to withdraw from the arrangement. But the Athenians swiftly made the situation clear: This was not a league of independent states after all, but an Athenian empire with subject cities. In 454 B.C.E., the Athenians dropped any pretense of the member states' autonomy and moved the league's treasury from Delos to Athens. It is hard to imagine how deeply the Athenian actions horrified the Greek world, but consider that it was a sacrilege to raid the shrine that had been safe under Apollo's protection for centuries. It is also hard to grasp how vast were the stores of money on Delos. The Athenians would use this wealth to rebuild the Acropolis and to fund Athens's Golden Age, which included dressing the cult statue of Athena in astonishing amounts of gold (see the chapter-opening photo on page 40).

One critic of Athenian policy complained that, because the smaller Aegean states depended on seaborne imports and exports for their survival, they did not dare to defy the Athenian "rulers of the sea." Nevertheless, the Athenian Empire did succeed in protecting the mainland from further Persian assaults and conferred other benefits: The poleis of the Aegean and Asia Minor were free to trade safely under the protection of the Greek ships. They received peace in exchange for autonomy.

During the Persian Wars, the Athenian military commanders had understandably acquired a good deal of power. Officials called **strategoi** (sing. *strategos*) were elected as commanders of the tribal army units, and during Athens's imperial age, a particularly strong strategos came to wield considerable power for a time. The political architect of Athens's Golden Age was the statesman Pericles (495–429 B.C.E.), who was elected strategos every year from 443 B.C.E. to his death in 429 B.C.E. He so dominated Athenian affairs that many compared him to a tyrant, yet this powerful aristocrat eloquently championed democracy in the assembly of Athens and encouraged democratic principles within the states of the league. However, he did not permit independent action by subject states. Thus, Pericles supported Athens's removal of the league treasury. As he pointed out, it was only right that Athenians enjoy the money, given that they had led the victory over Persia in the first place and their city had been burned in the process. Pericles followed up this argument by playing an instrumental role in plans for spending the money.

> Pericles

Pericles' closest companion and most influential advisor was the talented courtesan Aspasia, who headed an establishment that boasted the most cultured young courtesans in Athens, and in the mid-440s B.C.E., she became Pericles' mistress. Despite her status with Pericles, Aspasia drew intense criticism for her "undue" influence over Athens's great leader. For example, the Athenians suspected her of persuading Pericles to involve Athens in military alliances advantageous to her native city of Miletus. Rumors also circulated that she helped write the orator's speeches. The ever-loyal Pericles ignored all these complaints, however, and maintained his close relationship with Aspasia until his death.

Pericles forwarded democracy within Athens by trying to ensure that even poor citizens could participate fully in Athenian politics and culture. His most significant contribution was to pay the people who served as jurors or on the Council of 500. Now all male citizens—not just the rich—could

> Pericles' democracy

participate in the democracy. Equally important, he used much of the treasury to employ citizens on a project designed to beautify the public spaces of Athens. He organized armies of talented artists and artisans and paid thousands of workers to participate in the project. Finally, he put about 20,000 Athenians on the municipal payroll, a move that stimulated widespread involvement in the democratic proceedings of the city.

Artistic Athens

Pericles' leadership made Athens the political and cultural jewel of Greece. At the heart of the reconstruction program lay a plan to rebuild the Acropolis, which the Persians had destroyed. The restored Acropolis consisted of several temples and related buildings. As they designed the buildings, architects drew from the best of Greek tradition to make a political as well as an artistic statement. Design came first: Greek temples had always been constructed of *post and lintel* form, in which columns supported the roof. By 600 B.C.E., Greeks had developed "orders" of architecture to describe the various designs of the columns (and buildings), and these orders have influenced architecture down to the modern day. There were three orders of classic Greek buildings—Doric, Ionic, and Corinthian. **Doric,** the oldest order, developed on the Greek mainline, has a simple capital on top of a fluted column. The **Ionic** order, developed in Ionia on the eastern Mediterranean (see **Map 2.2**), features taller, more slender columns topped with elegant scroll shapes. The **Corinthian** order was a later development (probably from the fifth century B.C.E.) and was not used on the Acropolis, but its columns, topped with an acanthus-leaf capital, were extremely popular in later architecture. **Figure 2.9** shows a sketch of the major elements of these three

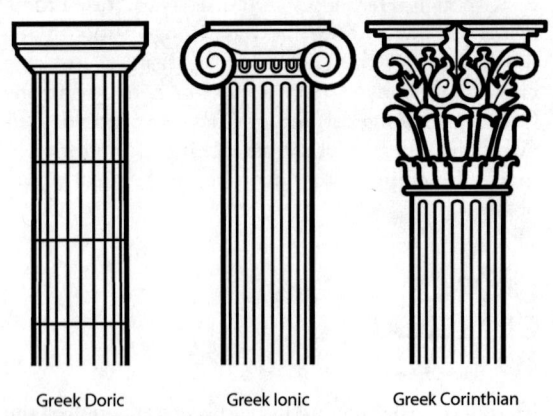

Greek Doric   Greek Ionic   Greek Corinthian

FIGURE 2.9 Architectural Orders The magnificent Greek architects developed *orders*, conventional architectural styles most readily identified by the tops of the columns. The Doric, Ionic, and Corinthian orders are shown here. The Greeks' orders have influenced architecture into modern times.

FIGURE 2.10 Acropolis of Athens, 448–432 B.C.E. After raiding the treasury of Delos, Athenians rebuilt their Acropolis with temples to the deities. The greatest temple was the Parthenon, featured here, which continues to be a model of architectural perfection.

orders that make them recognizable. The architects of the buildings on the Acropolis used both Doric and Ionic columns in the temples, as you can see in **Figure 2.10.** Specifically, the Doric style was featured on the magnificent Parthenon, and the Ionic on the Temple of Athena Nike.

In effect, these structures were nothing less than a political statement. Indeed, visitors to the Acropolis could see the empire's might in the majestic columns, which proclaimed Athenian control over the mainland to the Ionian coast. Although people would forget that political statement over time, the architectural elements would constantly be duplicated.

Builders designed all the temples with extraordinary care, constructing them according to principles of mathematical proportion, which the Greeks (following in the footsteps of Pythagoras) believed underlay the beauty of the universe. At the same time, the architects knew that human beings cannot visually perceive absolute, mathematical perfection, so they compensated by creating an optical illusion, curving some of the temples' lines to make them appear straight to the human eye. In other words, Greek architects used practical means to strive for abstract perfection. In this longing, the buildings of the Acropolis mirrored the Greeks' pursuit of excellence.

The largest temple in the Acropolis was the Parthenon (shown in the center in **Figure 2.10**), located on the highest point and dedicated to Athena, the patron goddess of the city. The temple had a magnificent statue of the goddess (now lost) created by Phidias, the greatest sculptor of the day, whose reputation for excellence continues today. The reproduction of this statue is on page 40.

The Athenians adorned the Parthenon with many sculptures and statues of both gods and humans. (Today, few statues remain in Athens—most are in museums elsewhere.) These statues, which all bear a strong resemblance to one another, echo the Greek belief that gods and humans had much in common.

Figures 2.11 and **2.12**, photos of sculptures from the Parthenon, depict both gods and ordinary Athenians. The gods and goddess in **Figure 2.11** are seated, waiting for the procession of the Athenians to begin. They are shown posed and dressed as Athenian citizens. At the same time, the Athenian youths in **Figure 2.12** who ride in the procession are as beautifully formed and as serenely confident as gods. By blurring humanity and divinity in their visual arts in this way, the Greeks explored the highest potential of humanity in their artwork. Their sculpture represented an idealized humanity, not real people.

simple staging. Men played both male and female parts, and all actors wore stylized masks. The themes of these plays centered on weighty matters such as religion, politics, and the deep dilemmas that arose as people grappled with their fates. During Athens's Golden Age, playwrights reminded the Athenians that, even at the height of their power, they faced complex moral problems.

One of Athens's most accomplished playwrights was Aeschylus (ca. 525–456 B.C.E.), who had fought at the Battle of Marathon. His earliest play, *The Persians*, added thoughtful nuance to the celebrations that the Athenians had enjoyed after their victory. Instead of simply praising Athenian success, Aeschylus studied Persian loss, attributing it to Xerxes' hubris at trying to upset the established international order. This also subtly warned the Athenians not to let their own arrogant pride bring about their own destruction.

<blockquote>Aeschylus and Sophocles</blockquote>

The most revered playwright of this period, however, was Sophocles (ca. 496–406 B.C.E.), who is best known for *The Theban Plays*, a great series about the mythological figure Oedipus and his family. All Athenians would have known the story of Oedipus, an ill-fated man whose family was told by a soothsayer at his birth that he was doomed to kill his father and marry his mother. The family exposed the baby to die, but he was rescued by a shepherd and raised as a prince in a faraway land. When he was grown, a soothsayer in his new land repeated the prediction, and when Oedipus fled to avoid killing the man he believed was his father, he returned to his original home, where he unintentionally fulfilled the prophecy. In Sophocles' hands, the play became a study in the range of human emotions measured by how man responds to tragic fates. As Document 2.2 shows, Oedipus moves from pride in his own position as king to deep agony and humility as he discovers the horrifying truth of his life. The play concludes with a reminder to all spectators not to feel complacent in their own lives.

DESTRUCTION, DISILLUSION, AND A SEARCH FOR MEANING

Sadly for the Athenians, they failed to heed Sophocles' warnings about pride and impiety. Their era of prosperity came to a violent end with the onset of the Peloponnesian War, a long, destructive conflict between Athens and Sparta and their respective allies. Like the Persian Wars, this new contest generated its own historian. Thucydides (460–400 B.C.E.), an even more objective historian than Herodotus, wrote: "I began my history at the very outbreak of the war, in

<blockquote>Thucydides</blockquote>

FIGURE 2.11 Gods on the Parthenon, ca. 440 B.C.E. Every four years, Athenians staged a major festival, the Panathenaic procession. The frieze along the Parthenon's inner colonnade memorializes the event. In this detail, the humanlike gods are shown reclining and enjoying their tribute.

FIGURE 2.12 Athenians on the Parthenon, ca. 440 B.C.E. The human riders in this detail from the frieze along the Parthenon's inner colonnade look godlike as they take part in the Panathenaic procession. The artist, Phidias, carved the horses' legs in deeper relief to cast shadows on the lower part of the frieze and thereby to increase the optical illusion of movement.

Greek Theater: Exploring Complex Moral Problems

In addition to their architecture and sculpture, the Athenians' theatrical achievements set new standards for Greek culture. Greek theater grew as part of the religious celebration of Dionysus, held in the late spring. Every year, Athens's leaders chose eight playwrights to present serious and comic plays at the festival in a competition as fierce as the Olympics. The plays were performed in open-air theaters with

thinking about DOCUMENTS

DOCUMENT 2.2

A Playwright Reflects on the Meaning of Life

The tragic playwright Sophocles wrote Oedipus the King *in about 429 B.C.E. at the beginning of the Peloponnesian War and at the height of Athenian power. The two passages included here express two Greek views of life. In the first, Oedipus has just learned of his adoptive father, Polybus's, death, which seemed to make a lie of the prophecy that Oedipus would kill his father and marry his mother. Oedipus's wife, Jocasta, urges him to the heroic values of fearlessness and boldness. The final speech, given by the chorus, reminds all of Athens never to be prideful and complacent. Notice the contrast between these two speeches.*

Oedipus: It was sickness, then [that killed Polybus]?

Messenger: Yes, and his many years.

Oedipus: Ah! Why should a man respect the Pythian hearth, or give heed to the birds that jangle above his head? They prophesied that I should kill Polybus, kill my own father; but he is dead and buried, and I am here—I never touched him, never, unless he died of grief for my departure, and thus, in a sense, through me. No. Polybus has packed the oracles off with him underground. They are empty words.

Jocasta: Had I not told you so?

Oedipus: You had; it was my faint heart that betrayed me.

Jocasta: From now on never think of those things again.

Oedipus: And yet—must I not fear my mother's bed?

Jocasta: Why should anyone in this world be afraid? Since Fate rules us and nothing can be foreseen? A man should live only for the present day. Have no more fear of sleeping with your mother: How many men, in dreams, have lain with their mothers! No reasonable man is troubled by such things.

. . . .

Chorus: Men of Thebes: look upon Oedipus. This is the king who solved the famous riddle and towered up, most powerful of men. No mortal eyes but looked on him with envy. Yet in the end ruin swept over him. Let every man in mankind's frailty consider his last day; and let none presume on his good fortune until he find life, at his death, a memory without pain.

SOURCE: Dudley Fitts and Robert Fitzgerald, *The Oedipus Rex of Sophocles: An English Version* (New York: Harcourt Brace, 1977) in Lamm, *The Humanities in Western Culture* (New York: McGraw-Hill, 2003), p. 13.

Analyze the Document

1. Which of the two speeches—by Jocasta or the chorus—better represents the Greek heroic ideal? Why?
2. What are Jocasta's and Oedipus's views on prophecies and auguries? Why do you think the playwright included these skeptical opinions?
3. How do you think the Athenian audience would have reacted to Sophocles' warning against pride just as Athens was beginning a war against Sparta?

---

the belief that it was going to be a great war. . . . My belief was based on the fact that the two sides were at the very height of their power and preparedness. . . ." Historians today share his desire for intellectual analysis of the facts but might come to different conclusions about the results. In any case, as a result of Thucydides' *History of the Peloponnesian War*, we now have the earliest, most carefully detailed record of a war—and of the destruction of a way of life.

The Peloponnesian War, 431–404 B.C.E.

To counter growing Athenian power, Sparta gathered together allies—the Peloponnesian League—to challenge the power of the Athenian Empire. While the flash point of the conflict was a dispute between two poleis, Thucydides recorded the Spartan viewpoint: "What made war inevitable was the growth of Athenian power and the fear which this caused in Sparta." At its core, this was a war to preserve the independence of each city-state and the unique brand of competitiveness among all the poleis. Athens had grown too strong, and the contest too uneven. Sparta felt compelled to take action when Athens increased its imperial ambitions.

The actual fighting proved awkward and difficult, for Athens and Sparta each had differing strengths and military styles. Athens was surrounded by long walls that extended to the shore (see inset in **Map 2.4**). Therefore, as long as the Athenian navy controlled the sea, Athens could not be successfully besieged. Thus Athens preferred to conduct battle with its navy and harried Spartan and allied territories from the sea. Sparta, on the other hand, put its trust in its formidable infantry. Bolstering their individual strengths, Athens's allies surrounded the Aegean Sea, while Sparta's allies were largely land based, as **Map 2.4** shows. As the Spartans marched across the isthmus near Megara to burn Athens's crops and fields, Athenians watched safely from behind their walls and supplied their needs with their massive fleet. However, there were bloody clashes as young Athenians tried to stop the Spartans, who were ravaging

thinking about GEOGRAPHY

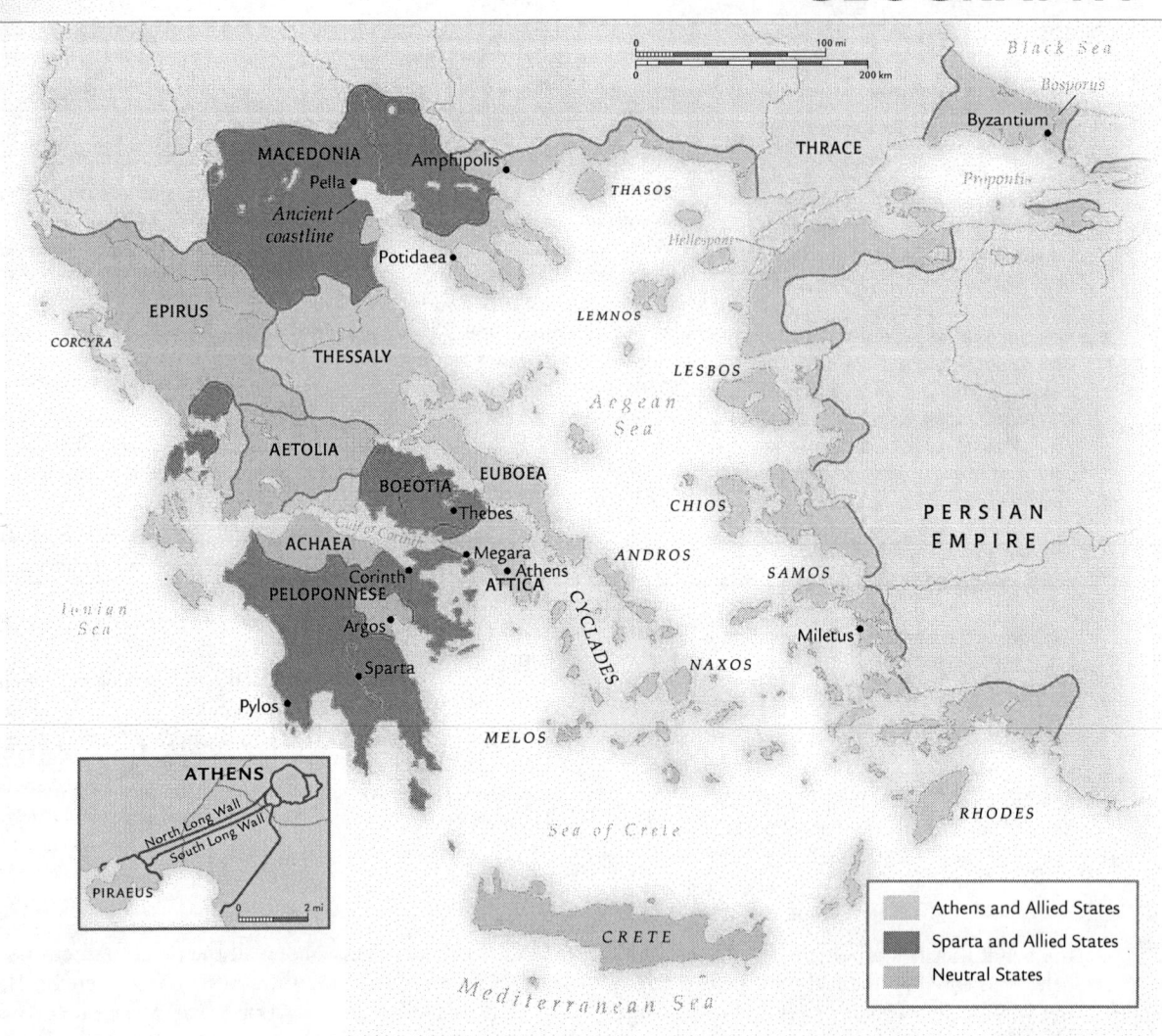

MAP 2.4

The Peloponnesian War, 431–404 B.C.E.

This map shows Athens and Sparta and their allies during the Peloponnesian War. The inset illustrates the "long walls" that joined Athens to the sea at its port of Piraeus.

Explore the Map

1. What evidence for the importance of Athens's fleet can you draw from the map?
2. Which city-state's allies were closest to Persia? Given the proximity of these allies, which side might Persia be disposed to support in this war? Why?

---

the countryside, and Athenians suffered inside the city, which was overcrowded with refugees. Under these conditions, plague struck the city in 430–429 B.C.E. Even Pericles succumbed, along with about one-quarter of the population. Athenian leadership fell to lesser men, whom contemporaries denounced as selfish and impulsive (such as Alcibiades, featured in the Biography on page 67).

The realities of war caused Athenian ethics to deteriorate further with the city-state's shameful

BIOGRAPHY

Alcibiades
(ca. 450–404 B.C.E.)

Alcibiades was born to a well-placed family in Athens, but his father died when the boy was only about three. The child was then raised in the house of Pericles, the talented leader of Athens, who was his mother's cousin. Tall, handsome, wealthy, charming, and a skilled orator (in spite of a lisp), Alcibiades had all the advantages of a privileged Athenian youth. The philosopher Socrates took a personal interest in the promising young man and spent a great deal of time teaching him. Alcibiades was perfectly positioned to succeed Pericles as a leader in Athens. However, he lacked his foster father's integrity and his teacher's sense of virtue. Instead, he seems to have been overly proud and impulsive and placed his own interests above those of his polis.

The outbreak of the Peloponnesian War in 431 B.C.E. gave the young man the opportunity to win the admiration of his countrymen. At one point in the war, Alcibiades shared a tent with Socrates, who saved his life during a skirmish but allowed the youth to take credit for heroism. Alcibiades' political career was launched on the battlefield, where Athenian men traditionally proved their manhood.

Alcibiades married a well-born woman, Hipparete, with whom he had a son. Hipparete quickly learned of Alcibiades' character flaws and licentiousness and tried to divorce him. Family ties and political expedience were against her, however, and she was forced to remain a dutiful wife. She chose to ignore her husband's philandering, while he built his reputation in public life.

When the war against Sparta subsided temporarily after 421 B.C.E., Alcibiades turned to other means to buttress his fame. In 416 B.C.E., he entered seven four-horse teams in the chariot races of the Olympics and won the top prizes. Except for one Greek king, no one had ever before spent so much money on the races, and no one had won so much. Yet Alcibiades saw war as the real path to glory. He maneuvered to revive the conflict with Sparta and urged Athens to request a deputation from Sicily, which wanted Athens's assistance against Syracuse. Alcibiades saw in this alliance an opportunity to win riches and land, and he persuaded the Athenians to send a large expedition to Sicily.

Before the expedition could depart, however, the Athenians were shocked by a display of impiety that seemed to bring a bad omen. The statues of Hermes that adorned the city had been smashed and mutilated. During an investigation into this desecration, which struck at the very heart of Athenian pride, the citizens heard testimony that implicated Alcibiades himself. In addition, one of his own slaves accused Alcibiades of ridiculing the sacred "mysteries" of Demeter by drunkenly mocking the goddess's religious rituals at a dinner party. The charge seems to have been true and shows the tension between those Athenians who had little fear of the gods and those who found impiety terrifying.

As the proceedings against Alcibiades dragged on, the summer sailing season began to wane. The Athenian expedition left for Sicily with Alcibiades in the lead. However, the fleet had not even reached Sicily when Alcibiades was recalled to answer the mounting charges against him. The Sicilian expedition ended in disaster, but Alcibiades was not there to see it.

Instead of returning to Athens, Alcibiades fled to Sparta, offering advice and leadership to his traditional enemy. He impressed the Spartans with his obvious talents and with his seeming ability to live with no luxuries. He stayed in Sparta for two years, helping his newfound allies plot against Athens.

Alcibiades' luck evaporated when he reputedly seduced the Spartan king's wife. To escape the king's ire, he fled to Persia, the enemy of both Sparta and Athens. The Persians, too, were impressed with Alcibiades' talents. He negotiated an alliance with the Persians that would prove damaging to Sparta and then returned triumphant to Athens. When war broke out again between Sparta and Athens, Alcibiades was given command of the Athenian fleet and the opportunity to assume the kind of power that Pericles had held. However, the Spartan commander Lysander won a spectacular victory. The loss was not Alcibiades' fault, but the Athenians blamed him and he was again forced to flee. In 404 B.C.E., the Spartans and Persians arranged the assassination of Alcibiades. In an ironic twist, the heroic opportunist who chose personal glory over allegiance to his polis died at the hands of his former partners in treachery.

Hero, Military Genius, and Traitor

Connecting People & Society

1. How did Alcibiades' life illustrate the concept of the drive for excellence and personal greatness at any expense?
2. How might Alcibiades' relationship to Socrates have contributed to the philosopher's condemnation?

treatment of Melos, an island that sought neutrality in 416 B.C.E. in the conflict between Athens and Sparta. Athens argued that its superior strength gave it the right to force Melos into serving as its ally. Maintaining that they had the right to make their own choices, the Melians held their ground. The furious Athenians struck back, killing every last man on Melos and enslaving the women and children. Dismayed by this atrocity, Thucydides observed that the ravages of war had reduced "men's characters to a level with their fortunes." By this he meant that, under the relentless pressure of war, the Athenians had sacrificed their ideals of justice in favor of expediency.

<small>Melos destroyed</small>

A significant event in the war came when Alcibiades, one of the new leaders of Athens, persuaded residents of the polis to meddle in a dispute between two Greek city-states in Sicily. Alcibiades saw this involvement as a way to gain glory for himself, and perhaps as a ploy by which Athens could extend its control outside the Aegean Sea. It may have worked, for if Athens could control the sea trade between Greece and Italy (the Ionian Sea), Sparta's commercial allies would have been ruined. However, the venture ended in disaster: Athens lost as many as 200 ships and 40,000 men. Its fleet severely weakened, Athens could no longer rule the Aegean, and its reluctant "allies" began to fall away. Although eight years would elapse between the Sicilian disaster and Athens's final defeat, the city-state could not recover enough to prevail. The Peloponnesian League's fleet, partially financed by a Persia eager to help weaken Athens, destroyed the remnants of the Athenian fleet. Cut off from the trade that would have let them survive a siege, the Athenians were forced to surrender in 404 B.C.E. Their defeat would have profound political and philosophic ramifications.

<small>Athens loses</small>

Philosophical Musings: Athens Contemplates Defeat

During the devastating war, some Athenians started asking themselves sobering questions about justice and the meaning of life. The answers they came up with led them down new pathways of thought—pathways that would permanently alter the direction of Western philosophy. Athenian politicians like Alcibiades and the architects of the Melos atrocity had promulgated the principle of moral relativism—whatever was good for them was right. At the time, some philosophers in Athens shared this belief. These Sophists (or "wise ones") doubted the existence of universal truths and, instead, taught their followers how to influence public opinion and how to forward their own fortunes. Rather than seeking truth, the Sophists argued that "man is the measure of all things" and that people should therefore act in accordance with their own needs and desires—exactly what Alcibiades had done during the Peloponnesian conflict.

Socrates (ca. 470–399 B.C.E.), the first great philosopher of the West, developed his ideas as a reaction against the Sophists' moral relativism. Supposedly, the Delphic oracle had reported that there was "no man wiser than Socrates." After this revelation, the philosopher spent the rest of his life roaming the streets of Athens, questioning his fellow citizens in an effort to find someone wiser than he. His questions took the form of dialogues that forced people to examine their beliefs critically and confront the logical consequences of their ideas. Socrates came to the conclusion that, indeed, he was the wisest man because he alone understood that he knew nothing, and that wisdom lies in the endless search for knowledge. Athenians came to know the rather homely man, whose father worked as a stonemason and whose mother was a midwife. Socrates, who saw himself as giving birth to ideas, claimed to have followed his mother's occupation more closely than his father's.

<small>Socrates</small>

Socrates left no writings, so we know of his ideas only from the words of one of his students, Plato. According to these texts, Socrates expressed the idea that there were absolutes of truth and justice and excellence, and that a dormant knowledge of these absolutes rested within all people. In these inquiries, Socrates departed not only from the Sophists but from the early philosophers like Thales who wanted to know the nature of the world—Socrates wanted to explore the nature of right action. The method he employed was that of questioning and refuting students' answers, and with this method—now called the **Socratic method**—he brought students to see the truth.

Socrates called himself a gadfly for his efforts to goad other Athenians into examining their opinions—but gadflies that sting painfully are seldom appreciated. Socrates began his inquiries in the dynamic period before the Peloponnesian War, but in the times of disillusionment after the war, Athenian jurors were suspicious of anyone who seemed to oppose the democracy—even by pointing out humankind's inadequacies. Socrates was brought to trial and accused of impiety and corruption of the young. The latter charge was no doubt forwarded by the reprehensible behavior of Alcibiades, who had been Socrates' student, but the former charge had no basis. Socrates was found guilty, even though he shrewdly refuted the charges during his trial. His friends urged him to stop questioning others and to simply flee, to which he replied with the famous words that began this chapter: "Life without enquiry is not worth living." He received the death penalty and drank a cup of the deadly poison hemlock.

Socrates' ideas, however, did not die with him but lived on in his students. Plato, his best-known follower, wrote many dialogues in which he seems to have preserved his teacher's ideas, although historians are uncertain where Socrates' teachings end and Plato's begin. Plato believed that truth and justice existed only as ideal models, or forms, but that humans could apprehend those realities only to a limited degree. Real people, he argued, lived in the imperfect world of the senses, a world that revealed only shadows of reality. This was his answer to the relativist Sophists, who saw the imperfect world as the true measure of right and wrong. For Plato, the goal of philosophical inquiry was to find the abstract and perfect "right" that was so elusive in this world. He established a school in Athens called the Academy to educate young Greek men in the tenets of virtue, for he believed that only through long training in philosophy could one learn to understand the ideal forms that exist outside the human world.

Plato was disillusioned with the democracy that had killed his teacher, Socrates, and admired Sparta's rigorous way of life. This political affinity shaped what is perhaps Plato's best-known work, *The Republic*, in which he outlined the ideal form of government. Instead of encouraging democracy, he explained, states should be ruled autocratically by philosopher-kings. In this way, the world might exhibit almost perfect justice. In some respects, this work expresses an articulate disillusionment with the failure of Athenian democracy to conduct a long war with honor or to tolerate a decent man pointing out citizens' shortcomings.

Plato's perfect state was never founded, but his ideas nevertheless had an enduring impact on Western civilization. Subsequent philosophers would confront his theory of ideal forms as they created other philosophic systems. His call for introspection and an awareness of self as the way to true knowledge would also have profound intellectual and religious implications.

Plato's ideas were not accepted universally in the Greek world. The career of his student Aristotle is one example. The son of a physician, Aristotle studied at Plato's Academy and then spent another twenty years refining his thinking, debating his ideas, and writing. As much as Aristotle valued his teacher, he departed from Plato's theory of "perfect forms" and declared that ideas cannot exist outside their physical manifestations. Therefore, he concluded, to study anything—from plants to poetics to politics—one had to observe and study actual entities. Through his practical observations, Aristotle divided knowledge into categories, which remained the organizing principle of learning for over a thousand years. He said there were three categories of knowledge: ethics, or the principles of social life; natural history, the study of nature; and metaphysics, the study of the primary laws of the universe. He approached these studies through logic, which, in his hands, became a primary tool of philosophy and science. Aristotle's approach represented a major departure from the perspective of Plato, who argued that one should think about ideals instead of studying the imperfect nature of this world.

Aristotle also departed from his teacher on the subject of politics. As was his custom, the philosopher studied the different kinds of governments—monarchies, aristocracies, and republics—and discussed how each style could degenerate into corruption. He thought the ideal state was a small polis with a mixed constitution and a powerful middle class to prevent extremes. Aristotle recoiled from extremes in all aspects of life and argued for a balance—in his famous phrase, a "golden mean"—that would bring happiness. The philosopher extended his idea of moderation to the realm of ethics, arguing that the lack of excess would yield virtue.

Tragedy and Comedy: Innovations in Greek Theater

Athens's disillusioning war with Sparta had prompted philosophers to explore challenging questions of justice and virtue. Athenian theater, too, underwent change during the conflict. The playwright Euripides (485–406 B.C.E.) wrote tragedies in which people grappled with anguish on a heroic scale. In these plays, he expressed an intense pessimism and the lack of a divine moral order that marked Athens after the Peloponnesian War. In *Women of Troy*, written in the year of Alcibiades' expedition against Sicily, Euripides explored the pain of a small group of captured Trojan women. Though set in the era of the war immortalized by Homer, *Women of Troy* also had a strong contemporary message. In part, it represented a criticism of Athens's treatment of Melos and of the enslavement of Greek women and children. When a character in *Women of Troy* mused, "Strange how intolerable the indignity of slavery is to those born free," Euripides was really asking the Athenians to reflect on their own actions. In foretelling destruction to the Greeks who abused the women of Troy, Euripides predicted the eventual downfall of Athens.

Tragedy was not the only way to challenge contemporary society; talented playwrights also used comedy. As Greeks laughed at the crudest of sexual jokes and bathroom humor, they criticized public figures and conquered their own anxieties. These plays appeal less to modern audiences than do the Greek tragedies, for in their intense fascination with human nature, Greeks embraced even our basest inclinations. The comedies of this era also reveal much about Greek perceptions of the human body; just as their character flaws became the subject of tragedies, their bodies were often the focus of comedies.

The vase in **Figure 2.13** portrays a typical scene from Greek comedy. In this rendering, each actor sports a long, artificial phallus hanging well below his tunic, and padded buttocks to increase the comic effect. The actors also wear highly stylized masks. In the window is a man wearing a woman's mask. The scene portrays Zeus trying to seduce the woman in the window, and the extreme costuming highlights the bawdy and disrespectful subject matter. Although we often find such graphic portrayals tasteless at best, Greek society was surrounded with them, and we cannot fully understand the Greeks without recognizing the way they accepted their humanity in its fullest sense.

Aristophanes

While people laughed at these comic portrayals, the greatest of the comic playwrights also used humor for serious purposes. Aristophanes (455–385 B.C.E.), for example, used costumes and crude humor to deliver biting political satire. This esteemed Athenian playwright delivered a ruthless criticism of contemporary Athens. Like many citizens, Aristophanes longed for peace. In 411 B.C.E.—at the height of the Peloponnesian War—he wrote *Lysistrata*, a hilarious antiwar play in which the women of Athens force their men to make peace by refusing to have sexual intercourse with them until they comply. With *Lysistrata*, Aristophanes reminded people that life and sex are more important than death and war.

FIGURE 2.13 Greek Comedy, fourth century B.C.E. This urn depicts a scene from a comedy with all the typical features: artificial phallus, stylized masks, and simple staging. Bawdy comedies reveal the Greeks' love of everything human, even tasteless jokes.

Hippocrates and Medicine

While philosophers and playwrights mulled over abstract notions of life and human nature, Greek physicians turned to a practical study of the human body, influencing subsequent opinions of medicine. Previous ancient societies had made a number of strides in medical knowledge—the Babylonians and Assyrians kept catalogs of healing herbs, and the Egyptians were famed for medical treatments such as setting fractures, amputating limbs, and even opening skulls to relieve pressure on head injuries. However, most of the medical knowledge that influenced the West for centuries came from the Greeks, whose systematic treatises really began to separate medicine from the supernatural. Hippocrates (ca. 460–ca. 377 B.C.E.), considered the father of modern Western medicine, supposedly claimed that "every disease has a natural cause, and without natural causes nothing ever happens." With this statement Hippocrates rejected the ancient belief that spirits were responsible for human ailments.

KEY DATES

GREEK HISTORY AND CULTURE

ca. 1250 B.C.E.	Trojan War
ca. 750 B.C.E.	Homer composes *Iliad* and *Odyssey*
490 B.C.E.	First Persian invasion repelled
495–429 B.C.E.	Pericles leads Athens, builds Acropolis temples
480–479 B.C.E.	Second Persian invasion repelled
431–404 B.C.E.	Peloponnesian War—Athens vs. Sparta
399 B.C.E.	Death of Socrates
399–347 B.C.E.	Plato flourishes
322 B.C.E.	Death of Aristotle

Hippocrates was a highly respected physician and gave his name to a body of medical writing known as the *Hippocratic Collection,* compiled between the fifth and third centuries B.C.E. The *Collection* established medicine on a rational basis devoid of supernatural explanations of disease—a major innovation in Western culture. Consistent with other Greek thinkers from Thucydides to Aristotle, Hippocrates also emphasized careful observation. This body of writings contains more than four hundred short observations about health and disease—for example, "People who are excessively overweight are far more apt to die suddenly than those of average weight," or "Extremes in diet must be avoided." Overall, this new approach to medicine put human beings, rather than the gods, at the center of study. The human-centered outlook of Greek medicine culminated in a long-standing idea expressed in the Hippocratic Oath. Modern physicians still take this oath, in which they vow first to do no harm to their patients.

Though Athens suffered some dark days of war and disillusionment, this difficult era also witnessed the rise of geniuses who used the hard times as a backdrop for exploring the complex nature of humanity. Greek philosophers, playwrights, and physicians created brilliant works and conceived of ideas that transcended their time despite the turmoil of the age.

The Aftermath of War, 404–338 B.C.E.

As a condition of its surrender at the end of the Peloponnesian War, Athens agreed to break down its defensive walls and reduce its fleet to only twelve ships. These harsh measures not only ended the Athenian Empire but also erased any possibility for a politically united Greece. The Spartans left a garrison in Athens and sent the rest of their troops home to their barrack state to guard their slaves. Sparta's subsequent attempts to assemble a political coalition foundered on its high-handed and inept foreign policy. Sparta's major allies, especially Corinth, opposed the Peloponnesian peace treaty, accusing Sparta of grabbing all the tribute and objecting to what they saw as lenience toward Athens. The generous treaty also stipulated that the Greek states in Asia Minor be given to Persia as the price for Persia's aid to Sparta, further eroding Greek unity.

All these postwar developments heightened competition among the poleis in the years after Athens's loss. For example, Corinth and Thebes fought wars to earn control of other Greek city-states, while Sparta ineptly struggled to preserve some leadership. Persia remained involved in Greek affairs, shrewdly offering money to one side and then another so that the Greeks would continue to fight one another. In this way, Persia kept the poleis from marshaling their strength against their longtime imperial enemy.

Power struggles

These wars among the poleis only aggravated serious weaknesses within each city. Democracy in Athens as a political form, for example, had been deeply threatened by the long, devastating war, especially since decisions made by the citizens led to failure. Antidemocratic feelings expressed in the works of Plato erupted as Athens fell. As Thucydides had noted, democracy was not safe during turbulent times. As the war came to an end in 404 B.C.E., Sparta imposed an oligarchy of 30 men over Athens, a brutal tyranny that tried to stamp out the vestiges of democracy. Fifteen hundred democratic leaders were killed in the coup, and 5,000 more were exiled. This oligarchy lasted only eight months before democracy was restored, but the revived government had only a shadow of its former vigor. Fed by an involved citizenry, democracy had flourished in Athens. Now, without its empire and large fleet, fewer citizens became wealthy, and political involvement waned.

Traditional participatory government in all the poleis unraveled further with innovations in military tactics. Under skillful generals, lightly armed javelin throwers, slingers, and archers began to defeat the heavily armed citizen hoplite armies that had once been the glory of Greece. Moreover, in the century following the Peloponnesian War, more and more Greeks served as mercenaries. See Document 2.3 for a famous account of Greek mercenaries fighting in Persia. These paid soldiers, owing allegiance to no city, added further disruption to an already unstable time, finally breaking the link between the poleis and the citizen-soldiers who defended them. In this period of growing unrest, every major Greek polis endured at least one war or revolution every ten years.

The nascent collective power of the Greek city-states also deteriorated during the postwar era. None of the poleis had succeeded in forging a lasting Hellenic coalition. The sovereignty of each city remained the defining idea in Greek politics. With this principle as a backdrop, individualism and loyalty to one's own city overrode any notions of a larger civic discipline. This competitive attitude had fueled the greatest of the Greeks' accomplishments in the arts, athletics, and politics, but it also gave rise to men like Alcibiades, who could not see beyond their own self-interests. In the midst of the troubled fourth century B.C.E., many Greeks feared that Persia would return to conquer a weakened Greece. As we will see in the next chapter, they should have worried about the "backward" people to the north instead.

thinking about DOCUMENTS

DOCUMENT 2.3

Ten Thousand Greek Mercenaries Return Home

After the Peloponnesian War ended (404 B.C.E.), many Greek soldiers served as mercenaries in the Persian armies. This account written by the Greek historian Xenophon (ca. 434–ca. 355 B.C.E.), who traveled with the expedition, tells of a famous incident in which some mercenaries struggled to return home to Greece.

It was thought necessary to march away as fast as possible, before the enemy's force should be reassembled, and get possession of the pass.

Collecting their baggage at once, therefore, they set forward through a deep snow, taking with them several guides, and, having the same day passed the height on which Tiribazus had intended to attack them, they encamped. Hence they proceeded three days' journey through a desert tract of country, a distance of fifteen parasangs, to the river Euphrates, and passed it without being wet higher than the middle. The sources of the river were said not to be far off. From hence they advanced three days' march, through much snow and a level plain, a distance of fifteen parasang; the third day's march was extremely troublesome, as the north wind blew full in their faces, completely parching up everything and benumbing the men. One of the augurs, in consequence, advised that they should sacrifice to the wind, and a sacrifice was accordingly offered, when the vehemence of the wind appeared to everyone manifestly to abate. The depth of the snow was a fathom, so that many of the baggage cattle and slaves perished, with about a third of the soldiers.

They continued to burn fires through the whole night, for there was plenty of wood at the place of encampment. But those who came up late could get no wood; those, therefore, who had arrived before and had kindled fires would not admit the late comers to the fire unless they gave them a share of the corn or other provisions that they had brought. Thus they shared with each other what they respectively had. In the places where the fires were made, as the snow melted, there were formed large pits that reached down to the ground, and here there was accordingly opportunity to measure the depth of the snow.

From hence they marched through snow the whole of the following day, and many of the men contracted the *bulimia*. Xenophon, who commanded in the rear, finding in his way such of the men as had fallen down with it, knew not what disease it was. But as one of these acquainted with it told him that they were evidently affected with bulimia, and that they would get up if they had something to eat, he went round among the baggage and wherever he saw anything eatable he gave it out, and sent such as were able to run to distribute it among those diseased, who, as soon as they had eaten, rose up and continued their march. . . . Some of the enemy too, who had collected themselves into a body, pursued our rear, and seized any of the baggage-cattle that were unable to proceed, fighting with one another for the possession of them. Such of the soldiers also as had lost their sight from the effects of the snow, or had their toes mortified by the cold, were left behind. It was found to be a relief to the eyes against the snow, if the soldiers kept something black before them on the march, and to the feet, if they kept constantly in motion, and allowed themselves no rest, and if they took off their shoes in the night. But as to such as slept with their shoes on, the straps worked into their feet, and the soles were frozen about them, for when their old shoes had failed them, shoes of raw hides had been made by the men themselves from the newly skinned oxen.

From such unavoidable sufferings some of the soldiers were left behind, who, seeing a piece of ground of a black appearance, from the snow having disappeared there, conjectured that it must have melted, and it had in fact melted in the spot from the effect of a fountain, which was sending up vapor in a wooded hollow close at hand. Turning aside thither, they sat down and refused to proceed farther. Xenophon, who was with the rear-guard, as soon as he heard this tried to prevail on them by every art and means not to be left behind, telling them, at the same time, that the enemy were collected and pursuing them in great numbers. At last he grew angry, and they told him to kill them, as they were quite unable to go forward. He then thought it the best course to strike a terror, if possible, into the enemy that were behind, lest they should fall upon the exhausted soldiers [so he urged the tired Greeks to rise and make noise to frighten the Persians following them].

SOURCE: *The Great Events by Famous Historians,* vol. II, ed. Rossiter Johnson (The National Alumni, 1905), pp. 70–71.

Analyze the Document

1. What kinds of hardships do the Greeks face, and what do we learn about ancient travel?
2. What is the Greek view of augurs and sacrifices? How does this perspective contrast with the ideas of Jocasta in Document 2.2?
3. Why do you think this account became so inspiring and influential to future Greek armies?

LOOKING BACK & MOVING FORWARD

Summary Small city-states nestled in the mountains of the Greek peninsula rerouted the course of Western civilization. These fiercely independent cities developed participatory forms of government that encouraged men to take active roles in all aspects of their cities. Through their vigorous involvement in the life of their poleis, the men of ancient Greece created magnificent works of art, theater, and architecture that came to define Western aesthetics. These men also developed a rational approach to inquiry that has enriched Westerners' understanding of life, history, philosophy, and medicine even in modern times.

But the pride in individual accomplishment that catalyzed such extraordinary accomplishments also contained the seeds of Greece's own political destruction. The future leadership of the eastern Mediterranean would come from a people who could set aside their heroic individualism to support a larger unity. However, this influx of new ideas did not erase the legacy of Greek achievement. The newcomers would ultimately spread the accomplishments of this complex culture as far east as India as they forged a new empire.

KEY TERMS

arête, p. 47
kouros, p. 48
kore, p. 48
hubris, p. 49
hoplites, p. 52
phalanx, p. 52
polis, p. 52
agora, p. 52
oligarchy, p. 53
helots, p. 57
strategoi, p. 62
Doric order, p. 62
Ionic order, p. 62
Corinthian order, p. 62
Socratic method, p. 68

REVIEW, ANALYZE, & CONNECT TO TODAY

REVIEW THE PREVIOUS CHAPTER

Chapter 1—"The Roots of Western Civilization"—described the growth and development of the civilizations of Mesopotamia, Egypt, and the eastern Mediterranean coast, highlighting their contributions to the future of Western civilization. It also described the growth of empires in that region.

1. Review the growth of empires in the ancient Middle East and contrast that process with the political development of Greece.
2. Review the characteristics of Phoenician society discussed in Chapter 1. Consider what qualities the Phoenicians had in common with the early Greeks that might have led both peoples to be such successful colonizers.

ANALYZE THIS CHAPTER

Chapter 2—"The Contest for Excellence"—looks at the rise and fall of the civilizations in the Aegean region culminating in the growth of classic Greek civilization. It describes life in ancient Greece, the political fortunes of the city-states, and the dramatic accomplishments in culture and science that influenced the future.

1. Review the causes of the decline of the Minoans, the Mycenaeans, and the Athenian Empire.
2. Review the economic life of the Greek city-states, and consider the impact of geography on their economic choices. Also consider how the Greek economy influenced political decisions.
3. Compare and contrast Athens and Sparta and their political and social systems. Why did Spartan women play a more meaningful role in society than did Athenian women?
4. Consider the Greeks' views on religion and review how these views influenced their approach to other aspects of their lives, like science and medicine.
5. Review Greek accomplishments in the arts, sciences, and political life, and consider why they would be so influential on future societies.

CONNECT TO TODAY

Think about the tensions in the ancient Greek world between individualism and society, as discussed in this chapter.

1. In what ways do societies today have to struggle with the same issues? Give some examples.
2. The trial of Socrates has remained a reference point for discussions of freedom of speech and thought. How do you think his trial might apply to contemporary issues such as hate speech and political postings on Internet sites such as Facebook and YouTube? For what other present-day issues is Socrates' trial relevant?

BEYOND THE CLASSROOM

Morris, Ian, and B.B. Powell. *The Greeks: History, Culture, and Society.* Upper Saddle River, NJ: Prentice Hall, 2005. A comprehensive and up-to-date work that integrates art, architecture, literature, and political history.

THE RISE AND FALL OF ANCIENT HEROES, 2000–800 B.C.E.

Burkert, Walter. *Greek Religion.* Cambridge, MA: Harvard University Press, 1985. A masterful reconstruction of Greek festival activities that addresses the problem of rituals of animal sacrifice.

Fitton, J. Lesley. *The Discovery of the Greek Bronze Age.* Cambridge, MA: Harvard University Press, 1996. An informed and elegantly written account of the history of archaeological investigations.

Graves, Robert. *The Greek Myths: Complete Edition.* New York: Viking Penguin, 1993. An in-depth study of the major Greek myths.

Larson, Jennifer. *Greek Heroine Cults.* Madison: University of Wisconsin Press, 1995. A solid study of an unusual and little explored phenomenon: women venerated as heroes.

LIFE IN THE GREEK POLEIS

Cartledge, Paul. *The Spartans: The World of Warrior Heroes of Ancient Greece.* New York: Vintage, 2004. A detailed description of Spartan life, arguing that the Spartans contributed discipline and self-sacrifice to the ideals of Western civilization.

Dodds, Eric R. *The Greeks and the Irrational.* Berkeley: University of California Press, 1968. A classic study of human experience through the Greek mind.

Dover, Kenneth J. *Greek Homosexuality.* Cambridge, MA: Harvard University Press, 1978. A description of homosexual behavior and sentiment in Greek art and literature between the eighth and second centuries B.C.E.

Fantham, E., H.P. Foley, N.B. Hampen, S.B. Pomeroy, and H.A. Shapiro. *Women in the Classical World.* New York: Oxford University Press, 1995. A readable, illustrated, chronological survey of Greek and Roman women's lives, focusing on vivid cultural and social history.

Garland, Robert. *Daily Life of the Ancient Greeks.* Westport, CT: Greenwood Press, 2008. An exploration of the daily lives of ordinary people, illuminating every aspect of ancient Greece life.

Miller, Stephen G. *Arete: Greek Sports from Ancient Sources,* enl. ed. Berkeley: University of California Press, 2004. A study of all aspects of ancient sports, including male and female athletes and athletic festivals.

Sealey, R. *Athenian Democracy.* University Park: Pennsylvania State University Press, 1987. An interpretation of Athenian constitutional history.

GREECE ENTERS ITS CLASSICAL AGE, 479–336 B.C.E.

Herodotus. *The History of Herodotus,* trans. D. Grene. Chicago: University of Chicago Press, 1987. The primary source for the Persian Wars by the acknowledged father of history.

McGregor, Malcolm F. *The Athenians and Their Empire.* Vancouver: University of British Columbia Press, 1987. The standard brief history of the Athenian Empire.

Pedley, John Griffiths. *Greek Art and Archaeology.* New York: H.N. Abrams, 1993. A study of the architecture, sculpture, pottery, and wall paintings of ancient Greece.

Wood, Ellen M. *Peasant-Citizen and Slave: The Foundations of Athenian Democracy.* New York: Routledge, Chapman and Hall, 1988. Controversial piece disputing two modern myths—that of the idle mob and that of slavery—as the basis of Athenian democracy.

DESTRUCTION, DISILLUSION, AND A SEARCH FOR MEANING

Lindberg, David C. *The Beginnings of Western Science: The European Scientific Tradition in Philosophical, Religious, and Institutional Context, 600 B.C. to A.D. 1450.* Chicago: University of Chicago Press, 1992. An accessible and comprehensive study showing scientific advances and offering the benefits of a broad historical view.

Roochnik, David. *Retrieving the Ancients: An Introduction to Greek Philosophy.* Oxford: Wiley-Blackwell, 2004. Highly accessible narrative surveying Greek thought—a perfect introduction to the subject.

Sutton, D. *Self and Society in Aristophanes.* Washington, DC: University Press of America, 1980. A sophisticated analysis of the portrayal of Greek society in the plays of Aristophanes.

Thucydides. *The Peloponnesian War,* trans. J.H. Finley. New York: The Modern Library, 1951. The great primary source on the Peloponnesian War, which forms the starting point for any study.

Timeline

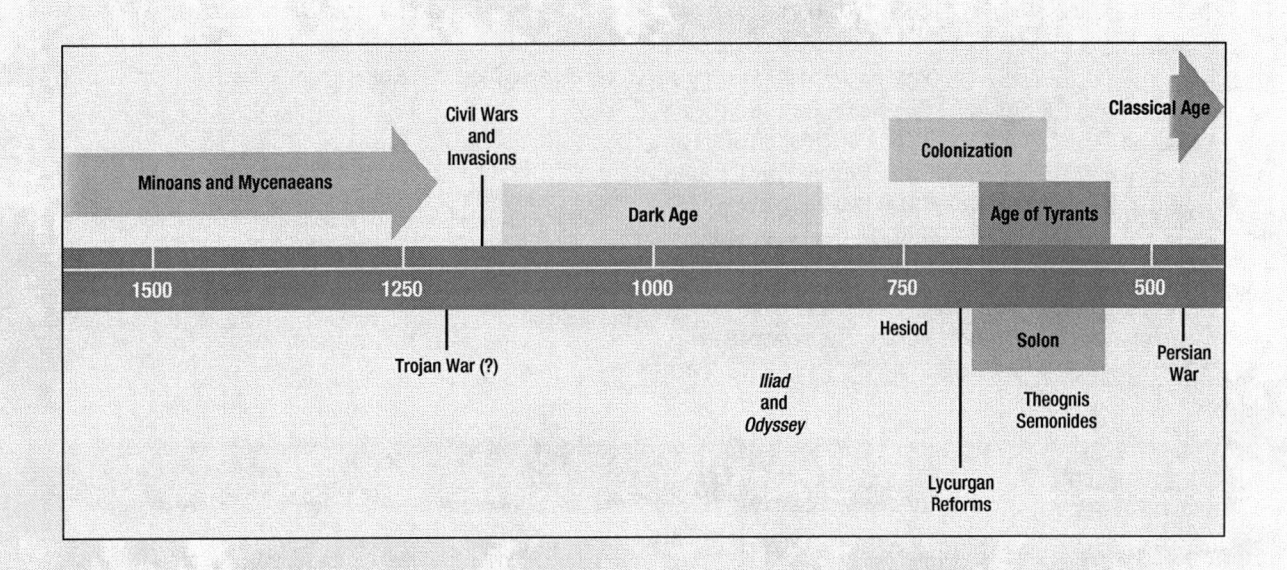

- **Minoans and Mycenaeans** (1500–)
- **Civil Wars and Invasions** (~1250)
- **Dark Age** (~1150–750)
- **Colonization** (~750–)
- **Age of Tyrants**
- **Classical Age**

Timeline markers: 1500 — 1250 — 1000 — 750 — 500

Events:
- Trojan War (?) ~1250
- *Iliad* and *Odyssey*
- Hesiod
- Lycurgan Reforms
- Solon
- Theognis, Semonides
- Persian War

2 The Emergence of Greek Civilization

Although Western civilization was born in the ancient Near East, we can more easily recognize our own roots in Greek civilization. Before reaching its apex during the fifth and fourth centuries B.C.E., Greek civilization has a long developmental history. During the third and second millennia, the Minoans on the island of Crete developed a sophisticated maritime civilization that would have strong connections to mainland Greece. During the second millennium, the Mycenaean Greeks, a militaristic people, rose to prominence on the Greek mainland. Both of these Bronze Age peoples fell to a series of upheavals between about 1400 and 1000 B.C.E. After three centuries of cultural decline, the Greeks reemerged and entered into a period of vigorous growth. Commerce expanded and the Greeks colonized lands from the Black Sea to the western Mediterranean. At the same time the city-states entered into a period of political evolution and cultural development.

Two city-states in particular became prominent toward the end of this period: Sparta and Athens. Each represents an extreme of developments other city-states would also experience. The Spartans developed a tightly organized, militaristic, land-based state, dominating the Peloponnesian Peninsula. Athens developed a relatively open, democratic, maritime state, dominating Attica and supporting commercial and cultural expansion. During the first decades of the fifth century B.C.E., these rivals managed to ally in face of the greater Persian threat; thereafter, they were competitors in struggles that involved most of the Greek world.

The selections in this chapter address five major questions. First, how do we explain the end of the Bronze Age civilizations of the Mycenaeans and Minoans and the decline into the succeeding "Dark Age"? Interpretations ranging from invasions to civil wars are examined. Second, what is the historical significance of the Homeric epics? What historical information about Mycenaean times and the

Dark Age do the Homeric epics provide? What was their significance for the Greeks and for Greek culture in general? Third, how did the Greek city-state evolve in the period between 800 and 500 B.C.E.? The focus here is on early Sparta and early Athens. Some of the social divisions reflected by political changes are also explored here. Fourth, what was the significance of Greek colonization between about 750 and 550 B.C.E.? How was colonization related to Greek economy and society? What role did colonization play in the spread of Greek civilization? Finally, what was the nature of Greek societies and ideals in this early period?

The sources in this chapter take us to the end of the sixth century B.C.E. At that point the Classical Age, which will be examined in the next chapter, began.

For Classroom Discussion

What distinguished Greek civilization from others, particularly those of the ancient Near East? Use the selections by Sarah Pomeroy and Finley Hooper.

Primary Sources

The Iliad

Homer

Homer's The Iliad, a work of literature and an important cultural, religious, and social source on Greek civilization, is one of our few historical documents from the early period of Greek history. Most likely orally composed or assembled during the ninth or eighth century B.C.E., it refers to the great war between the Greeks of the Mycenaean Age and the Trojans (occupants of a city in Asia Minor near the mouth of the Hellespont), probably fought in the thirteenth century B.C.E. The social and political conditions described in The Iliad are a mixture of traditions during Mycenaean times and typical practices during the ensuing "Dark Age." The following selection refers to a shield being forged by Hephaistos, the Greek god of metalworking. The shield is decorated with scenes of two cities. In the first city, which is at peace, a trial is taking place. Around the second one, which is being besieged, are signs of a prosperous economy.

CONSIDER: *The political characteristics of these cities; the basis upon which this trial will be decided; the economic characteristics of the second city.*

On it he wrought in all their beauty two cities of mortal
   men. And there were marriages in one, and festivals.
They were leading the brides along the city from their
   maiden chambers under the flaring of torches, and
   the loud bride song was arising.
The young men followed the circles of the dance, and
   among them the flutes and lyres kept up their
   clamour as in the meantime the women standing
   each at the door of her court admired them.

SOURCE: Reprinted from Homer, *The Iliad,* trans. by Richmond Lattimore, by permission of The University of Chicago Press. Copyright © 1977, pp. 388–390.

The people were assembled in the market place, where
   a quarrel had arisen, and two men were disputing
   over the blood price for a man who had been killed.
   One man promised full restitution in a public
   statement, but the other refused and would accept
   nothing.
Both then made for an arbitrator, to have a decision;
   and people were speaking up on either side, to help
   both men.
But the heralds kept the people in hand, as meanwhile
   the elders were in session on benches of polished
   stone in the sacred circle and held in their hands the
   staves of the heralds who lift their voices.
The two men rushed before these, and took turns
   speaking their cases, and between them lay on the
   ground two talents of gold, to be given to that judge
   who in this case spoke the straightest opinion.
But around the other city were lying two forces of
   armed men shining in their war gear. For one side
   counsel was divided whether to storm and sack, or
   share between both sides the property and all the
   possessions the lovely citadel held hard within it.
But the city's people were not giving way, and armed for
   an ambush.
Their beloved wives and their little children stood on
   the rampart to hold it, and with them the men with
   age upon them, but meanwhile the others went out.
   And Ares led them, and Pallas Athene.
These were gold, both, and golden raiment upon them,
   and they were beautiful and huge in their armour,
   being divinities, and conspicuous from afar, but the
   people around them were smaller.
These, when they were come to the place that was set
   for their ambush, in a river, where there was a
   watering place for all animals, there they sat down in
   place shrouding themselves in the bright bronze.

But apart from these were sitting two men to watch for the rest of them and waiting until they could see the sheep and the shambling cattle, who appeared presently, and two herdsmen went along with them playing happily on pipes, and took no thought of the treachery.

Those others saw them, and made a rush, and quickly thereafter cut off on both sides the herds of cattle and the beautiful flocks of shining sheep, and killed the shepherds upon them. . . .

He made upon it a soft field, the pride of the tilled land, wide and triple-ploughed, with many ploughmen upon it who wheeled their teams at the turn and drove them in either direction. . . .

He made on it the precinct of a king, where the labourers were reaping, with the sharp reaping hooks in their hands. Of the cut swathes some fell along the lines of reaping, one after another, while the sheaf-binders caught up others and tied them with bind-ropes.

There were three sheaf-binders who stood by, and behind them were children picking up the cut swathes, and filled their arms with them and carried and gave them always; and by them the king in silence and holding his staff stood near the line of the reapers, happily.

And apart and under a tree the heralds made a feast ready and trimmed a great ox they had slaughtered. Meanwhile the women scattered, for the workman to eat, abundant white barley.

He made on it a great vineyard heavy with clusters, lovely in gold, but grapes upon it were darkened and the vines themselves stood out through poles of silver. About them he made a field-ditch of dark metal, and drove all around this a fence of tin; and there was only one path to the vineyard, and along it ran the grape-bearers for the vineyard's stripping.

Young girls and young men, in all their light-hearted innocence, carried the kind, sweet fruit away in their woven baskets, and in their midst a youth with a singing lyre played charmingly upon it for them, and sang the beautiful song for Linos in a light voice, and they followed him, and with singing and whistling and light dance-steps of their feet kept time to the music.

Works and Days

Hesiod

While the Homeric epics reflected many of the heroic values of the early Greeks, most Greeks faced the everyday realities of work. One of the earliest sources that describes these concerns with work and wealth was written by the Greek poet Hesiod,

SOURCE: Hugh G. Evelyn-White, trans., *Hesiod, the Homeric Hymns and Homerica.* New York: The Macmillan Co., 1914, pp. 25–31.

who lived in the eighth century B.C.E. In Works and Days, *he includes thoughts about his own life and labor in the fields as well as fables and allegories. In the following excerpt, Hesiod discusses the importance of hard work and how wealth should be gained.*

CONSIDER: *The values Hesiod supports; the problems within Greek society that concern Hesiod; how, according to Hesiod, wealth is best obtained and guarded.*

Both gods and men are angry with a man who lives idle, for in nature he is like the stingless drones who waste the labour of the bees, eating without working; but let it be your care to order your work properly, that in the right season your barns may be full of victual. Through work men grow rich in flocks and substance, and working they are much better loved by the immortals. Work is no disgrace: it is idleness which is a disgrace. But if you work, the idle will soon envy you as you grow rich, for fame and renown attend on wealth. And whatever be your lot, work is best for you, if you turn your misguided mind away from other men's property to your work and attend to your livelihood as I bid you. An evil shame is the needy man's companion, shame which both greatly harms and prospers men: shame is with poverty, but confidence with wealth.

Wealth should not be seized: god-given wealth is much better; for if a man take great wealth violently and perforce, or if he steal it through his tongue, as often happens when gain deceives men's sense and dishonour tramples down honour, the gods soon blot him out and make that man's house low, and wealth attends him only for a little time. . . . He who adds to what he has, will keep off bright-eyed hunger; for if you add only a little to a little and do this often, soon that little will become great. What a man has by him at home does not trouble him: it is better to have your stuff at home, for whatever is abroad may mean loss. It is a good thing to draw on what you have; but it grieves your heart to need something and not to have it, and I bid you mark this. Take your fill when the cask is first opened and when it is nearly spent, but midways be sparing: it is poor saving when you come to the lees.

Let the wage promised to a friend be fixed; even with your brother smile—and get a witness; for trust and mistrust, alike ruin men.

Do not let a flaunting woman coax and cozen and deceive you: she is after your barn. The man who trusts womankind trusts deceivers.

There should be an only son, to feed his father's house, for so wealth will increase in the home; but if you leave a second son you should die old. Yet Zeus can easily give great wealth to a greater number. More hands mean more work and more increase.

If your heart within you desires wealth, do these things and work with work upon work.

A Colonization Agreement

From about 750 to 550 B.C.E. Greeks from the mainland, the Aegean islands, and Asia Minor founded colonies throughout the Mediterranean region and as far east as the shores of the Black Sea. Historians speculate that this was one way for the Greeks to solve various social, political, and economic pressures, particularly resulting from population growth. In any case, the spread of colonies facilitated the growth of Greek commerce and laid the foundations for long-lasting Greek cultural influence throughout the Classical world. The following is a colonization agreement made around 630 B.C.E. by settlers sailing from Thera, an Aegean island, to Cyrene in North Africa.

CONSIDER: *The evidence for a sense of urgency or necessity in gaining support for this expedition; the kind of penalties considered legitimate and effective to enforce the will of the Assembly.*

OATH (AGREEMENT?) OF THE FOUNDERS

It was resolved by the Assembly [at Thera]. Since Apollo spontaneously ordered Battus and the Theraeans to colonize Cyrene, the Theraeans are determined to send to Libya Battus as leader and king; and the Theraeans shall sail as his companions. They shall sail on equal terms from each household, one son from each. Men in the prime of youth are to be enlisted from all the districts. Of the other Theraeans any free man may sail if he wishes. If the colonists occupy the settlement, men from the same households who later land in Libya shall share in citizenship, shall be eligible for office, and shall be allotted unoccupied land. But if they fail to occupy the settlement and if the people of Thera are unable to help them and if for five years they are beset by privation, then they may without fear leave the land [and return] to Thera, [receive back] their property and be citizens. He who refuses to sail when the city sends him shall be liable to the death penalty and his property shall be confiscated. Any father who gives refuge or asylum (?) to his son or any brother who [does the same] for his brothers shall suffer the same penalty as the person refusing to sail.

Poem on Women

Semonides of Amorgos

There are few sources in this early period of Greek history that tell us about Greek attitudes toward women. Most of the sources available were written by men, usually mentioning women only in passing. However there is evidence that misogyny was a common theme in early Greek literature. The following selection is an example of this theme. The selection is an excerpt from a poem about women by Semonides of Amorgos, who lived on the island of Amorgos during the seventh century. The poem emphasizes how different females are from men, describing nine negative types of women and one positive type.

CONSIDER: *What this indicates about Greek men's attitudes toward women; the ways in which the good woman differs from the bad woman according to Semonides.*

In the beginning the god made the female mind separately. One he made from a long-bristled sow. In her house everything lies in disorder, smeared with mud, and rolls about the floor; and she herself unwashed, in clothes unlaundered, sits by the dungheap and grows fat.

Another he made from a wicked vixen; a woman who knows everything. No bad thing and no better kind of thing is lost on her; for she often calls a good thing bad and a bad thing good. Her attitude is never the same.

Another he made from a bitch, vicious, own daughter of her mother, who wants to hear everything and know everything. She peers everywhere and strays everywhere, always yapping, even if she sees no human being. A man cannot stop her by threatening, nor by losing his temper and knocking out her teeth with a stone, nor with honeyed words, not even if she is sitting with friends, but ceaselessly she keeps up a barking you can do nothing with.

Another is from a bee; the man who gets her is fortunate, for on her alone blame does not settle. She causes his property to grow and increase, and she grows old with a husband whom she loves and who loves her, the mother of a handsome and reputable family. She stands out among all women, and a godlike beauty plays about her. She takes no pleasure in sitting among women in places where they tell stories about love. Women like her are the best and most sensible whom Zeus bestows on men.

Zeus has contrived that all these tribes of women are with men and remain with them. Yes, this is the worst plague Zeus has made—women; if they seem to be some use to him who has them, it is to him especially that they prove a plague. The man who lives with a woman never goes through all his day in cheerfulness; he will not be quick to push out of his house Starvation, a housemate who is an enemy, a god who is against us. Just when a man most

---

SOURCE: *The Ancient World to A.D. 300*, 2d ed., edited by Paul J. Alexander. Copyright © 1963 by Macmillan Publishing Co., Inc. Reprinted by permission.

SOURCE: Hugh Lloyd-Jones, *Females of the Species: Semonides on Women* (Park Ridge, N.J.: Noyes Press, 1975), pp. 30, 32, 34, 38.

wishes to enjoy himself at home, through the dispensation of a god or the kindness of a man, she finds a way of finding fault with him and lifts her crest for battle. Yes, where there is a woman, men cannot even give hearty entertainment to a guest who has come to the house; and the very woman who seems most respectable is the one who turns out guilty of the worst atrocity; because while her husband is not looking . . . and the neighbours get pleasure in seeing how he too is mistaken. Each man will take care to praise his own wife and find fault with the other's; we do not realise that the fate of all of us is alike. Yes, this is the greatest plague that Zeus has made, and he has bound us to them with a fetter that cannot be broken. Because of this some have gone to Hades fighting for a woman. . . .

Aristocrats and Tyrants

Theognis of Megara

Between the seventh and fifth centuries B.C.E. there was a trend in most city-states away from aristocratic political and social dominance. Often part of that trend involved the rise of tyrants who professed to be leaders of the lower classes and who succeeded, if only temporarily, against the aristocrats. The rise of tyrants was particularly common during the sixth century and the results were painful to aristocrats. This is illustrated in the following selection from the bitter poems of Theognis of Megara, a sixth-century aristocrat who lost his property and was exiled upon the rise of a tyrant in his state.

CONSIDER: *How Theognis compares commoners and aristocrats; how a commoner might respond to Theognis; how a tyrant might respond to Theognis.*

Our commonwealth preserves its former frame,
Our common people are no more the same:
They that in skins and hides were rudely dress'd
Nor dreamt of law, nor sought to be redress'd
By rules of right, but in the days of old
Flock'd to the town, like cattle to the fold,
Are now the brave and wise; and we, the rest,
(Their betters nominally, once the best)
Degenerate, debasèd, timid, mean!
Who can endure to witness such a scene?
Their easy courtesies, the ready smile,
Prompt to deride, to flatter, and beguile!
Their utter disregard of right or wrong,
Or truth or honour!—Out of such a throng
(For any difficulties, any need,
For any bold design or manly deed)

Never imagine you can choose a just
Or steady friend, or faithful in his trust.
    But change your habits! Let them go their way!
Be condescending, affable, and gay! . . .
Court not a tyrant's favour, nor combine
To further his iniquitous design;
But, if your faith is pledg'd, though late and loth,
If covenants have pass'd between you both,
Never assassinate him! keep your oath!
But should he still misuse his lawless power
To trample on the people, and devour,
Depose or overturn him; anyhow!
Your oath permits it, and the gods allow. . . .
    Yet much I fear the faction and the strife,
Throughout our Grecian cities, raging rife,
And their wild councils. But do thou defend
This town of ours, our founder and our friend! . . .

Early Athens

Solon

Between the eighth and fifth centuries B.C.E. Athenian society became more complex. This affected Athens' political structure, which evolved from monarchical and aristocratic forms to more democratic institutions. A central struggle throughout this period took place between the wealthy aristocracy and the poorer classes. In the late seventh and early sixth centuries this struggle threatened to break out into civil war. In 594 Solon, a poet and wealthy aristocrat of recognized integrity, was called on to mediate and effect decisions to end this struggle. In the following document Aristotle quotes Solon and describes how Solon managed to find just solutions that recognized the issues on both sides without completely satisfying anyone.

CONSIDER: *The principal social divisions within Athenian society according to Solon; Solon's justifications for his decisions; the political and social significance of Solon's decisions.*

The truth of this view of Solon's policy is established alike by the common consent of all, and by the mention which he has himself made of it in his poems. Thus:—

I gave to the mass of the people such rank as befitted
    their need,
I took not away their honour, and I granted naught to
    their greed;
But those who were rich in power, who in wealth were
    glorious and great,
I bethought me that naught should befall them unworthy
    their splendour and state;

SOURCE: George Howe and Gustave A. Harrer, eds., *Greek Literature in Translation*, J. H. Frere, trans., rev. ed., Preston H. Epps, ed. (New York: Harper and Brothers, 1948), pp. 139–140. Reprinted by permission of the Estates of George Howe and Gustave A. Harrer.

SOURCE: Aristotle, *The Athenian Constitution*, trans. F. G. Kenyon (London: George Bell and Sons, 1891), pp. 18–20.

And I stood with my shield outstretched, and both were
    safe in its sight,
And I would not that either should triumph, when the
    triumph was not with right.

Again he declares how the mass of the people ought to be treated:—

But thus will the people best the voice of their leaders obey,
When neither too slack is the rein, nor violence holdeth
    the sway:
For satiety breedeth a child, the presumption that
    spurns control,
When riches too great are poured upon men of
    unbalanced soul.

And again elsewhere he speaks about the persons who wished to redistribute the land:—

So they came in search of plunder, and their cravings
    knew no bound,
Every one among them deeming endless wealth would
    here be found,
And that I with glozing[1] smoothness hid a cruel mind
    within.
Fondly then and vainly dreamt they; now they raise an
    angry din,
And they glare askance in anger, and the light within
    their eyes
Burns with hostile flames upon me. Yet therein no
    justice lies.
All I promised, fully wrought I with the gods at hand to
    cheer,
Naught beyond of folly ventured. Never to my soul
    was dear
With a tyrant's force to govern, nor to see the good
    and base
Side by side in equal portion share the rich home of
    our race.

Once more he speaks of the destitution of the poorer classes and of those who before were in servitude, but were released owing to the Seisachtheia[2]:—

Wherefore I freed the racked and tortured crowd
From all the evils that beset their lot,
Thou, when slow time brings justice in its train,
O mighty mother of the Olympian gods,
Dark Earth, thou best canst witness, from whose breast
I swept the pillars[3] broad-cast planted there,
And made thee free, who hadst been slave of yore.
And many a man whom fraud or law had sold
Far from his god-built land, and outcast slave,
I brought again to Athens; yea, and some,
Exiles from home through debt's oppressive load,
Speaking no more the dear Athenian tongue,
But wandering far and wide, I brought again;
And those that here in vilest slavery
Crouched 'neath a master's frown, I set them free.
Thus might and right were yoked in harmony,
Since by the force of law I won my ends
And kept my promise. Equal laws I gave
To evil and to good, with even hand
Drawing straight justice for the lot of each.
But had another held the goad as I,
One in whose heart was guile and greediness,
He had not kept the people back from strife.
For had I granted, now what pleased the one,
Then what their foes devised within their hearts,
Of many a man this state had been bereft.
Therefore I took me strength from every side
And turned at bay like wolf among the hounds.

And again he reviles both parties for their grumblings in the times that followed:—

Nay, if one must lay blame where blame is due,
Wer't not for me, the people ne'er had set
Their eyes upon these blessings e'en in dreams:—
But greater men, the men of wealthier life,
Should praise me and should court me as their friend.

For had any other man, he says, received this exalted
    post,—
He had not kept the people back, nor ceased
Till he had robbed the richness of the milk.
But I stood forth, a landmark in the midst,
And barred the foes from battle.

Constitution of the Lacedaemonians

Xenophon

Sparta was one of the most powerful and well-known Greek city-states. Located on the Peloponnesian Peninsula, it developed a reputation during the seventh and sixth centuries B.C.E. for being conservative, disciplined, inward-looking, and devoted to military pursuits and strength. Much of this reputation derived from events during the middle of the seventh century when the helots, formerly the neighboring Messenians who had been conquered by the Spartans and subjected to serfdom, revolted against the far outnumbered Spartans. With great difficulty the revolt was put down, but from that point on the Spartans committed themselves to preserving their dominance at all costs. Various constitutional reforms were instituted to ensure Spartan unity and military strength. Traditionally, these reforms

---

[1] Explaining away.

[2] "Shaking off of burdens"—Solon's reform of the law of debt.

[3] These were the pillars set up on mortgaged lands, to record the fact of the encumbrance.

SOURCE: Francis R. B. Godolphin, ed., *The Greek Historians*, vol. II, trans. Henry G. Dakyns (New York: Random House, 1942), pp. 658–661, 666–669. Reprinted by permission.

were attributed to a perhaps legendary lawgiver, Lycurgus. Direct primary sources for these reforms are thin. The best evidence we have comes from Xenophon (c. 434–c. 355), an Athenian admirer of Sparta who wrote some two centuries after these occurrences. The following is a selection from his Constitution of the Lacedaemonians.

CONSIDER: Xenophon's explanation for the extraordinary power and prestige of Sparta; the nature and purposes of Sparta's education system; how Sparta differed from other Greek city-states.

I recall the astonishment with which I first noted the unique position of Sparta among the states of Hellas, the relatively sparse population, and at the same time the extraordinary power and prestige of the community. I was puzzled to account for the fact. It was only when I came to consider the peculiar institutions of the Spartans that my wonderment ceased. Or rather, it is transferred to the legislator who gave them those laws, obedience to which has been the secret of their prosperity. This legislator, Lycurgus, I admire, and hold him to have been one of the wisest of mankind. . . .

He insisted on the training of the body as incumbent no less on the female than the male; and in pursuit of the same idea instituted rival contests in running and feats of strength for women as for men. His belief was that where both parents were strong their progeny would be found to be more vigorous. . . .

Marriage, as he ordained it, must only take place in the prime of bodily vigour, this too being, as he believed, a condition conducive to the production of healthy offspring. . . .

But when we turn to Lycurgus, instead of leaving it to each member of the state privately to appoint a slave to be his son's tutor, he set over the young Spartans a public guardian, the Paidonomos, to give him his proper title, with complete authority over them. . . .

Instead of softening their feet with shoe or sandal, his rule was to make them hardy through going barefoot. This habit, if practised, would, as he believed, enable them to scale heights more easily and clamber down precipices with less danger. . . .

Instead of making them effeminate with a variety of clothes, his rule was to habituate them to a single garment the whole year through, thinking that so they would be better prepared to withstand the variations of heat and cold.

Again, as regards food, according to his regulation the prefect, or head of the flock, must see that his messmates gathered to the club meal, with such moderate food as to avoid that heaviness which is engendered by repletion, and yet not to remain altogether unacquainted with the pains of penurious living. His belief was that by such training in boyhood they would be better able when occasion demanded to continue toiling on an empty stomach. . . .

On the other hand, in order to guard against a too great pinch of starvation, though he did not actually allow the boys to help themselves without further trouble to what they needed more, he did give them permission to steal this thing or that in the effort to alleviate their hunger. . . .

It is obvious, I say, that the whole of this education was intended to make the boys craftier and more inventive in getting in supplies, while at the same time it cultivated their warlike instincts. . . .

Furthermore, and in order that the boys should not want a ruler, even in case the guardian himself were absent, he gave to any citizen who chanced to be present authority to lay upon them injunctions for their good, and to chastise them for any trespass committed. . . .

We all know that in the generality of states every one devotes his full energy to the business of making money: one man as a tiller of the soil, another as a mariner, a third as a merchant, whilst others depend on various arts to earn a living. But at Sparta Lycurgus forbade his freeborn citizens to have anything whatsoever to do with the concerns of moneymaking. As freeman, he enjoined upon them to regard as their concern exclusively those activities upon which the foundations of civic liberty are based. . . .

In Sparta, on the contrary, the stronger a man is the more readily does he bow before constituted authority. And indeed, they pride themselves on their humility, and on a prompt obedience, running, or at any rate not crawling with laggard step, at the word of command. Such an example of eager discipline, they are persuaded, set by themselves, will not fail to be followed by the rest.

Accordingly the ephors[4] are competent to punish whomsoever they choose: they have power to exact fines on the spur of the moment; they have power to depose magistrates in mid career, nay, actually to imprison and bring them to trial on the capital charge. Entrusted with these vast powers, they do not, as do the rest of states, allow the magistrates elected to exercise authority as they like, right through the year of office; but, in the style rather of despotic monarchs, or presidents of the games, at the first symptom of an offence against the law they inflict chastisement without warning and without hesitation. . . .

And yet another point may well excite our admiration for Lycurgus largely. It had not escaped his observation that communities exist where those who are willing to make virtue their study and delight fail somehow in ability to add to the glory of their fatherland. That lesson the legislator laid to heart, and in Sparta he enforced, as a matter of public duty, the practice of every virtue by every citizen. And so it is that, just as man differs from man in some excellence, according as he cultivates or neglects to cultivate it, this city of Sparta, with good reason, outshines all other states in virtue; since she, and she alone, has made the attainment of a high standard of noble living a public duty.

---

[4]Elected magistrates.

Visual Sources

Trade, Culture, and Colonization

This scene (figure 2.1) is from the inside of a Laconian cup dating from about 560 B.C.E. It shows King Arcesilas II of the Greek North African colony of Cyrene (a Dorian Greek colony originally founded by Thera around 630 B.C.E.) supervising the weighing and loading of a shipment of what is probably silphium, a medicinal plant exported from the area. On the left Arcesilas is sitting on the deck of a ship underneath a canopy, apparently arguing with his steward. On the right workers carry on the silphium and call out the weight while below workers fill the hold with it. Around are animals of the area: a lizard, a monkey, and birds.

This cup reflects the importance of trade for the Greeks and the role Greek colonies played in this trade. It also indicates a growing interconnectedness based on the Mediterranean—a familiarity with the shoreland areas in which Greeks had settled and contact with the cultures and environment they found there, as might be surmised by the use of a North African plant for medicinal purposes in the Greek homeland and by the large number of cups similar to these that were being exported from Laconia. The words on the cup provide evidence for the spread of literacy among Greeks.

CONSIDER: Connections between this cup and the colonization agreement; how this cup can be used as evidence for the importance of commerce and colonization in the Greek world.

FIGURE 2.1 (© Bibliothèque Nationale, Paris, France, Archives Charmet/The Bridgeman Art Library)

Migration and Colonization

These two maps reveal a number of relationships between history and geography in the Greek world. Map 2.1 shows some of the dialects of the Greeks; the arrows indicate some of the probable directions of Greek migrations as traced by these dialects in the aftermath of the Dorian invasions between the thirteenth and tenth centuries B.C.E. Map 2.2 shows the extent of Greek settlement around the Mediterranean and Black seas between 750 and 550 B.C.E. in comparison with the previously colonized or colonizing areas originating from Phoenicia and the relatively stable Etruscans in northern Italy. This map also distinguishes the Ionian, Dorian, and Aeolian origins of some of those Greek colonies.

Comparison of these two maps shows that there is a trend for colonies to be located near, or be logical geographic extensions of, the earlier migrations of Greeks. For example, as Dorians spread south and southeast to Thera, Crete, and Rhodes, so would future colonies extend further south, such as those in North Africa (Cyrenaica), and southeast, to, for

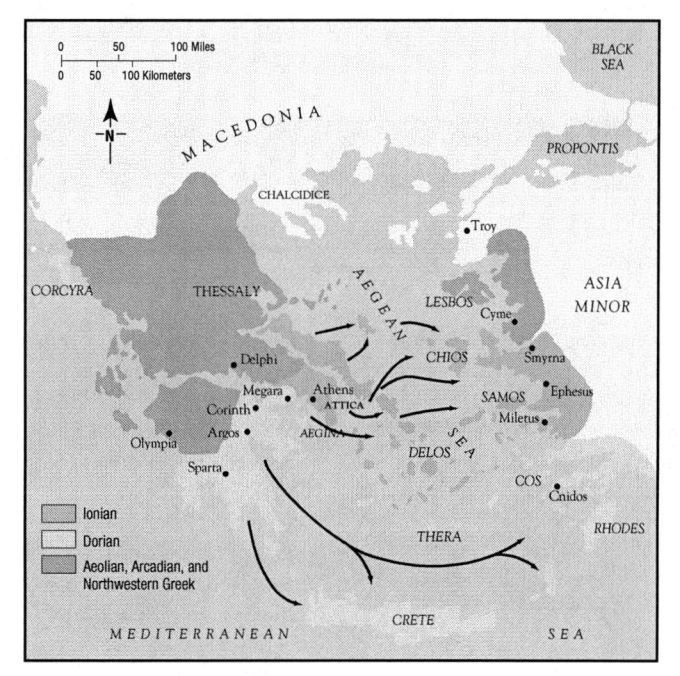

MAP 2.1 Dialects

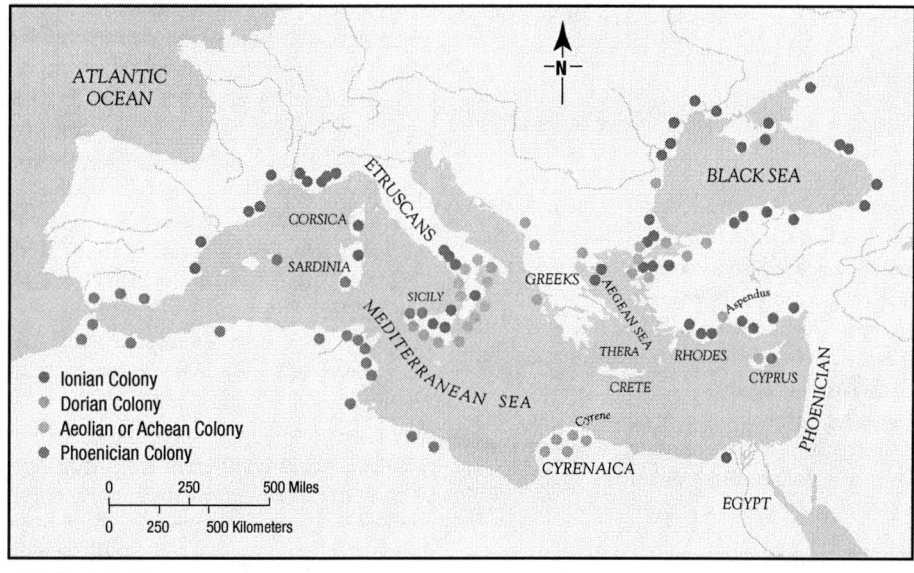

MAP 2.2 Colonies

example, Aspendus. Generally, the Ionians were the most mobile in face of the Dorian invasions and fled across the islands of the Aegean to the east and to the coast of Asia Minor. They were the most prolific colonizers in number and extent, stretching from Spain in the West to the extremes of the Black Sea in the North and East. Although colonies became independent city-states, some of the history of migrations and colonization affected future military alliances. For example, Greeks of the Ionic dialect tended to support each other in the Persian and Peloponnesian wars.

The extent of Greek colonization suggests the importance of colonies for diffusing culture throughout the Mediterranean. Greeks often came into contact (at times through war) with the competing Phoenicians as well as with the established Etruscans and later the Romans in the western Mediterranean. All this helps explain how Greek and Greco-Roman civilization came to dominate most of the Mediterranean basin even when the Greeks were no longer a great military-political force and their colonies were no longer independent.

CONSIDER: How the history and geography of Greek migrations and colonization helped diffuse culture in the ancient world; how a geographic analysis of dialects can shed light on the history of a civilization.

Secondary Sources

The End of the Mycenaean World
Frank J. Frost

The highly developed Bronze Age civilizations of the Minoans and Mycenaeans seem to have collapsed suddenly between the thirteenth and twelfth centuries B.C.E. Indeed, the collapse was so complete that few records remain. This has forced historians and archaeologists to offer rather speculative interpretations for the fall. Some of these interpretations are evaluated in the following selection by Frank Frost.

CONSIDER: *The problems with the Dorian invasion interpretation; why Frost supports the civil wars interpretation.*

> The return of the Greeks from Troy after such a long time caused many changes; in general, there was civil strife in the cities, and exiles from these founded other cities.... And eighty years after the War, the Dorians occupied the Peloponnesus with the Sons of Heracles.
>
> Thucydides 1.12

Thus the historian Thucydides described the end of the Mycenaean world, but his brief words do little to describe the true picture: nearly every Mycenaean citadel and settlement destroyed or abandoned, an almost complete end to overseas trade, and the disappearance of a sophisticated town economy. There followed a 300-year period that may with every justification be called the "Dark Ages" of Greece.

Anyone interested in a given society must also be concerned with the reasons for the disintegration of that society. There is still disagreement about the end of the Mycenaean world: epic tradition and archaeology combined can only hint at the great disturbances that seem to have overtaken the entire eastern Mediterranean in the twelfth century B.C.E. For many years, scholars were content to assume that the great palaces were destroyed and the surrounding lands taken over by the Dorians led by the descendants of Heracles, as tradition suggested. There can be no doubt that the Dorians occupied lands once ruled by the Mycenaeans, because in classical times, the people of these areas spoke Doric and related dialects and were proud of their tribal heritage. The difficulty comes from analyzing the archaeological evidence, which indicates only that the old society had broken down. There was no replacement of Mycenaean hardware with Dorian counterparts.

Today many scholars concentrate on the first part of Thucydides' statement, which focuses attention on internal strife. There is widespread literary tradition to support this theory because even before the war, Thebes had been destroyed by returning exiles. Furthermore, all the heroes who returned from Troy found unrest at home. Agamemnon was butchered in his bathtub; Odysseus survived only by the skin of his teeth through a bloody massacre of his rivals. In city after city new dynasties had taken over, and refugees filled the eastern Mediterranean. In 1191 B.C.E., Rameses III repelled a great invasion of "sea peoples" from the coasts of Egypt, and it is often assumed that these marauders were a product of the contemporary disturbances in Greece. We are told by tradition that only Nestor returned to safety and prosperity at Pylos. Unfortunately, the archaeological record challenges tradition at this point, showing that the palace at Pylos was one of the first to be destroyed and its destruction was awful and complete.

Civil war, therefore, may have been responsible for the destruction of many citadels, for depopulation and abandonment of other sites, and finally, for a breakdown in

SOURCE: From Frank J. Frost, *Greek Society*, 3d ed., pp. 11–13. Copyright © 1987 DC Heath and Company.

the Mycenaean economy. Such an elaborate social and economic structure must always depend for survival on relatively peaceful conditions: the crops must be sown and harvested at the right times, goods must exchange hands, ships must arrive at their destinations, taxes must be paid, and clerks must keep records. A generation of war can easily upset the delicate balance of such an economy. Once foreign trade ends, domestic prosperity begins to decline. Towns become isolated, driving artisans and merchants who have no more markets back to the soil as farmers—for farmers at least eat during hard times.

Greek Realities: The Homeric Epics
Finley Hooper

While the Homeric epics are significant in themselves as literature, they are doubly important for the historian. First, they supply us with much information about Greece during the late Bronze Age and the Dark Age, periods we would otherwise know little about. Second, since the epics were of tremendous educational, religious, and cultural significance to the Greeks for centuries after the Dark Age, they provide insight into Greek civilization during the Classical and Hellenistic ages. In the following selections Finley Hooper explains the importance of the Iliad *and the* Odyssey.

CONSIDER: *How Hooper compares the Homeric epics and the Bible; the ways in which it is useful to think of the epics as religious documents.*

The Homeric epics were as important to ancient Greek society as the Bible is to our own. Perhaps more so, for the *Iliad* and the *Odyssey* were the primers of Greek education. They still are. To the credit of the Greeks, their children have always learned to read and write by examples from the very best in native literature. A child may not go far with his schooling, but if he learns to read and write he knows Homer. When Socrates made his famous appeal to a large jury in Athens in 399 B.C.E. he quoted from the *Iliad*. Here at least was common ground.

Homer's writings did not comprise scripture in the sense that they were the "revealed word of God." Yet, as in the Bible, there were woven into these epics three persistent themes of human interest: the nature of the supernatural, the intervention of the supernatural in human events, and acute observations about the behavior of men toward one another.

The epics describe the province of each of the twelve Olympian gods. Nearly all of them were named in the Linear B tablets. Homer writes about the same deities as the Mycenaeans had actually worshipped. Yet the tablets mention other gods and not all of them have been clearly identified. Perhaps some of these represent the cruder aspects of religious practices, snake cults and fertility rites which Homer ignores. When the poet limited the number of gods to be given preference, he introduced order and a degree of sophistication into a highly confusing, often interchangeable, list of deities.

In the remote past, sticks and stones had been considered divine, but Homer spoke for an age when supernatural powers were personified as men and women, larger than life, living forever on special food. They acted according to the same passions and prejudices of men, even as the Hebrew Yahweh who walked and talked in the cool of the evening, and described himself as a jealous God.

The nature of God is not a matter which historians need to decide for others, but the various ways in which men have conceived of the divine is a matter of historical interest. It may be observed that although a few Greek philosophers spoke of a single creative principle, the overwhelming majority of the Greeks throughout ancient times accounted for events according to the wishes of these anthropomorphic gods which Homer describes....

Homer's epics do not offer an evolutionary development toward a higher concept of God, nor any single set of answers to life's major questions. As such, these "teachings" gave the religion common to all the Greeks a totally undogmatic character. The gods of course aided men and they must be worshipped, flattered, and obeyed. The welfare of the state could depend on this. To deny the gods was dangerous, even unpatriotic. But there was no creed or set of tenets to which a man must subscribe. Although the Greeks often quarreled over the physical control of their shrines, they never fought a religious war over faith. Ironically, the adherents of the later higher religions have suffered the embarrassment of bloodshed in the name of sacred books. Homer's writings actually united the Greeks by reconciling them to the common dilemma of human existence.

Social Values and Ethics in the "Dark Age" of Greece
Sarah B. Pomeroy et al.

The Homeric epics exemplify a theme that runs throughout Greek history: the image of the good man. This image characterized Greek visions of the Mycenaeans as well as Greek ideals expressed in various cultural productions. In the following selection, Sarah B. Pomeroy, in collaboration with others, analyzes the social values and ethics that made up the essence of the "good man" during the "Dark Age" of Greece.

SOURCE: Reprinted from *Greek Realities* by Finley Hooper, by permission of the Wayne State University Press. Copyright © 1967, pp. 58–60.

SOURCE: Sarah B. Pomeroy et al., *Ancient Greece: A Political, Social, and Cultural History* (New York: Oxford University Press, 1999), pp. 60–61.

CONSIDER: *What the key components of the "good man" were; the ways these values reflect a warrior society; how this analysis compares with Hooper's interpretation.*

In all societies, the notions of good and bad, right and wrong, are largely determined by their own peculiar conditions of life. The codes of behavior for Homeric males center around war. The Greek adjective *agathos* ("good") when used of men in Homer, is almost always restricted to the qualities of bravery and skill in fighting and athletics. The opposite word, *kakos* ("bad"), means cowardly, or unskilled and useless in battle. In a society in which every ablebodied man fights to defend his community, all men are under constraint to behave bravely. The leaders are expected to be especially valiant, and in addition, to excel in public speaking and counsel.

Other traditional rules of conduct dictate that a "good man" should honor the gods, keep promises and oaths, and be loyal to friends and fellow warriors. He should exhibit self-control, be hospitable, and respect women and elders. Pity should be shown to beggars and suppliant strangers. It is proper to show pity even toward captured warriors and to refrain from defiling the corpses of the enemy. These gentler qualities are desirable, but they are not required; the sole criterion for being called agathos is good warriorship.

A warrior society is forced to breed into its future warriors a savage joy in the grim "works of Ares," a lust to annihilate the enemy. At the end of a poignant family scene in the *Iliad*, the Trojan hero Hector lifts up his baby son and prays to the gods that he may grow up to be a better warrior than his father and "bring back the bloody spoils of a dead enemy and make his mother's heart glad" (*Iliad* 6.479–481). Homeric Greeks are not only fierce in war but also savage in victory: they loot and burn captured villages, slaughter the male survivors including infants, and rape and enslave the women and girls.

A strong competitive spirit was an important part of the Greek male ethos. Homeric characters constantly compare themselves, or are compared with, one another. Men are driven to win and to be called *aristos* ("best"). One man is said to be "best of the Achaeans in bowmanship," while another "surpassed all the young men in running," or in spear throwing, or chariot racing, or speaking. This type of extracompetititve society is called agonistic, from the Greek word *agōn* ("contest," "struggle"). The instinct to compete and win permeates the society. A poor farmer is roused to work hard when he sees his neighbor getting rich, says Hesiod (c. 700); and "potter resents potter and carpenter resents carpenter, and beggar is jealous of beggar and poet of poet" (*Works and Days* 20–26).

The sole object of competing and striving is to win *timē* ("honor" and "respect"). *Timē* is always public recognition of one's skills and achievements. It always involves some visible mark of respect: the seat of honor and an extra share of meat at a feast, or an additional share of booty, or valuable prizes and gifts, including land. To modern readers, Homeric warrior-chiefs may appear overly greedy for material things, but their purpose in acquiring and possessing many animals and precious objects was mainly to increase their fame and glory. Not to be honored when honor is due, or worse, to be dishonored, are unbearable insults. Thus, when Agamemnon in the *Iliad* grievously dishonored Achilles by taking back the captive girl Briseis, a "prize of honor" awarded to Achilles by the army, a great quarrel arose between them that led to disaster for all the Greeks.

Adherence to the competitive ethic (summed up in the motto "always be the best and be preeminent over the others") spurred men on to accomplish great things and kept the quality of leadership high. On the other hand, the relentless pursuit of personal and family honor and obsession with avenging dishonor could cause enormous political instability. For better or worse, the Homeric codes of male behavior would endure throughout antiquity, and later generations of Greek writers would continue to look to the *Iliad* and *Odyssey* for models of right and wrong conduct.

CHAPTER QUESTIONS

1. How should the historical usefulness of the various primary documents, particularly those that are usually considered pieces of literature, be evaluated? What problems might arise for historians who rely on literary documents for their interpretations of early Greek civilization?

2. In what ways do the primary documents support interpretations of various ideals, such as the "good man," as particularly Greek?

3. Considering historical, geographic, and cultural factors, in what ways did the Greeks differ from the earlier civilizations of the ancient Near East? How would you explain some of these differences?

OLD MARKET WOMAN, third or second century B.C.E.
In the great cosmopolitan cities of the Hellenistic world, many people lived in poverty and struggled all their lives just to survive. Artists began to portray these people in realistic images that were much less heroic than those favored by earlier Greek artists. Change was afoot in the Greek world.

The Poleis Become Cosmopolitan 3

The Hellenistic World, 336–150 B.C.E.

Alexander "conducted himself as he did out of a desire to subject all the races in the world to one rule and one form of government making all mankind a single people." The Greek biographer Plutarch (46–119 C.E.) wrote these words four hundred years after the death of the Macedonian king Alexander the Great (356–323 B.C.E.). In his description of Alexander, Plutarch attributed high ideals to the young conqueror that Alexander himself may not have held. However, the biographer's glowing portrayal captured the reality of Alexander's conquests, whereby he joined the great civilizations of the ancient Middle East and classical Greece in a way that transformed them both.

This new world that began in 336 B.C.E. with Alexander's conquest of Persia was described as "Hellenistic" (meaning "Greek-like") by nineteenth-century historians. During this time, the ideal Greek poleis changed from scattered, independent city-states into large, multiethnic urban centers—what the Greeks called "world cities," or cosmopolitan sites—firmly anchored within substantial kingdoms. Greek colonists achieved high status in the new cities springing up far from the Greek mainland, making the Greek language and culture the ruling ideal from Egypt to India. In this Hellenistic age, classical Greek culture was in turn altered through the influences of the subject peoples, and the new world left the old world of the Greek mainland behind. Society, economy, and politics all played out on a larger scale, and kings, rather than citizens, now ruled. Royal patronage stimulated intellectual and cultural achievement among the privileged classes, while ordinary people struggled to find their place in a new world.

The Hellenistic culture continued even as these kingdoms were conquered by Rome, the next power to rise in the West. In this chapter, we will see the origins and characteristics of this cosmopolitan culture that endured for so long.

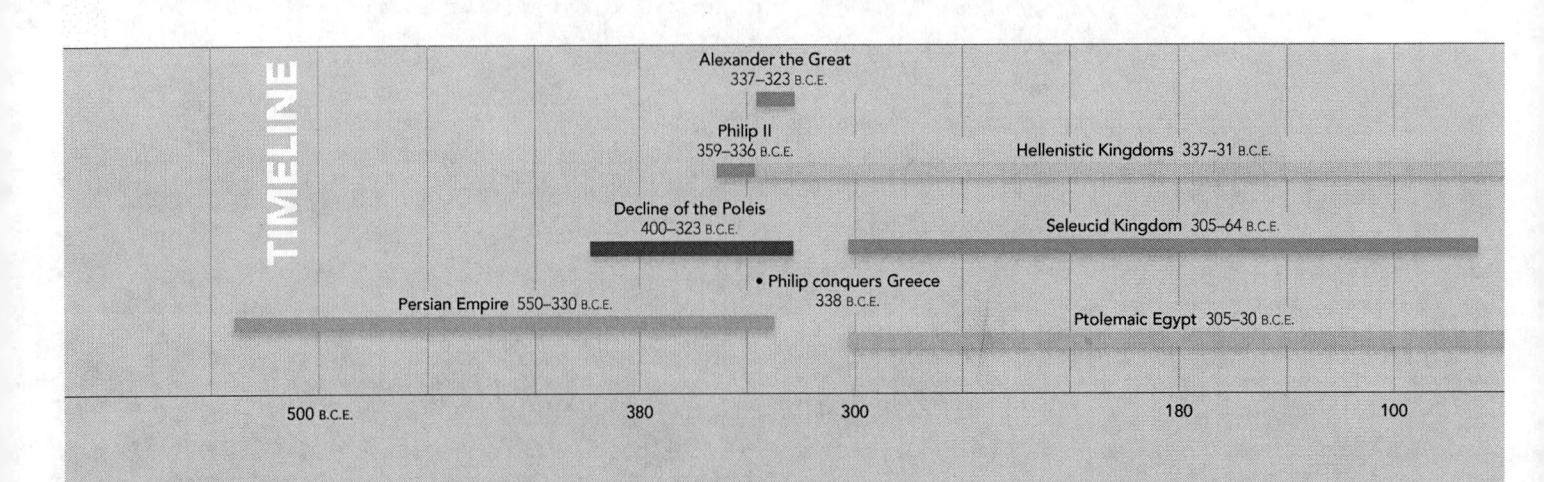

TIMELINE

- Alexander the Great 337–323 B.C.E.
- Philip II 359–336 B.C.E.
- Hellenistic Kingdoms 337–31 B.C.E.
- Decline of the Poleis 400–323 B.C.E.
- Seleucid Kingdom 305–64 B.C.E.
- Persian Empire 550–330 B.C.E.
- Philip conquers Greece 338 B.C.E.
- Ptolemaic Egypt 305–30 B.C.E.

500 B.C.E. — 380 — 300 — 180 — 100

PREVIEW

THE CONQUEST OF THE POLEIS
Learn how Macedonia conquered Greece and how Alexander conquered the Persian Empire.

THE SUCCESSOR KINGDOMS,
323–ca. 100 B.C.E.
Study the Hellenistic kingdoms that emerged after the death of Alexander.

EAST MEETS WEST IN THE SUCCESSOR KINGDOMS
Explore the economy, culture, and military of the Hellenistic kingdoms.

THE SEARCH FOR TRUTH: HELLENISTIC THOUGHT, RELIGION, AND SCIENCE
Understand Hellenistic theater, philosophy, religion, and science.

THE CONQUEST OF THE POLEIS

In 220 B.C.E., an Egyptian father appealed to the Greek king to help him resolve a domestic dispute. He claimed that his daughter, Nice, had abandoned him in his old age. According to the father, Nice had promised to get a job and pay him a pension out of her wages every month. To his dismay, she instead became involved with a comic actor and neglected her filial duties. The father implored the king, Ptolemy IV, to force Nice to care for him, pleading, "I beg you O king, not to suffer me to be wronged by my daughter and Dionysus the comedian who has corrupted her."

This request—one of many sent to the king during this period—reveals several interesting points about Mediterranean life in the Hellenistic era. For example, it suggests that women worked and earned money instead of staying carefully guarded within the home. It also shows a loosening of the tight family ties that had marked the Greek poleis and the ancient Middle East civilizations—a father could no longer exert authority over his rebellious daughter and could no longer count on his children to care for him in his old age. Finally, it indicates people's view of their king as the highest authority in redressing personal problems. These were dramatic changes, and to trace their origins, we must look to Macedonia, a province on the northeast border of Greece. There, in a land traditionally ruled by strong monarchs, a king arose who would redefine life in the ancient world.

Tribal Macedonia

Although Macedonia was inhabited by Greek-speaking people, it had not developed the poleis that marked Greek civilization on the peninsula. Instead, it had retained a tribal structure in which aristocrats selected a king and served in his army bound by ties of loyalty and kinship. The southern Greek poleis—populated by self-described "civilized" Greeks—had disdain for the Macedonians, whom they saw as backward because they did not embrace the political life of the city-states.

The Macedonian territory consisted of two distinct parts: the coastal plain to the south and east, and the mountainous interior. The plain offered fertile land for farming and lush pastures in which fine warhorses grazed along with sheep and oxen. The level land of the coastline bordered two bays that afforded access to the Aegean Sea. The Macedonian interior, by contrast, was mountainous and remote and posed the same problems for rulers that the Greek landscape presented. Kings struggled to exert even a little authority over the fierce tribes in the hills. Yet, concealed within the mountains were precious reserves of timber and metals, including abundant veins of gold and silver in the more remote locations. *[Geography]*

For centuries, the weak Macedonian kings failed to take full advantage of such treasures, in large part because they could not control the remote tribes. Repeated invasions of Macedonia by its neighbors to the north only added to the problem. Throughout this turbulent period, the southern Greeks thought of Macedonia only as an area to exploit for its natural resources. The Greeks neither helped nor feared their beleaguered relatives to the north and instead focused on keeping their old enemy, Persia, at bay. Nevertheless, eventually a Macedonian king arose who not only succeeded in marshaling the resources of his land but also rerouted the direction of Greek history. *[Uniting the tribes]*

This great king, Philip II (r. 359–336 B.C.E.), had participated in some of the many wars that disrupted Greece during the fourth century B.C.E. (see Chapter 2) and, as a result, had been held hostage as a young man in the Greek city-state of Thebes for three years. During his captivity, he learned much about the strengths and weaknesses of Greek politics and warfare. When he returned to Macedonia, he used his new knowledge to educate his people. As his son Alexander later reminded the Macedonians: "Philip took you over when you were helpless vagabonds mostly clothed in skins, feeding a few animals on the mountains. . . . He gave you cloaks to wear instead of skins, he brought you down from the mountains to the plains. . . . He made you city dwellers and established the order that comes from good laws and customs."

Philip II: Military Genius

The pride of the Macedonian army was the cavalry, led by the king himself and made up of his nobles, known as "companions." Yet Philip showed his military genius in the way he reorganized the supporting forces. The shrewd monarch changed the traditional Greek phalanx, already threatened by a new fighting style that favored lightly armed—and therefore more mobile—foot soldiers. Philip strengthened the phalanx by arming his soldiers with pikes 13 feet long or longer instead of the standard 9-foot weapons. Then he instructed the infantry to arrange themselves in a more open formation, which let them take full advantage of the longer pikes. Philip also hired lightly armed, mobile mercenaries who could augment the Macedonian phalanx with arrows, javelins, and slings.

In battle, the long Macedonian pikes kept opponents at a distance, while the cavalry made the decisive difference in almost every battle. **Military innovations** The mounted warriors surrounded the enemy and struck at their flank, leaving the lightly armed mercenaries to move in to deliver the final blow. This strategy, which combined traditional heavily armed foot soldiers with the mobility of cavalry and light troops, would prove virtually invincible.

Philip also developed weapons for besieging walled cities. During the Peloponnesian War, even mighty Sparta's only strategy against the sturdy walls of Athens had been to starve the inhabitants to death—a slow and uncertain method. Philip is credited with using a torsion catapult that twisted launching ropes to gain more force than the older models that used counterweights could exert. With this new device, his forces could fire rocks at city walls with deadly force. Although Philip is credited with developing these siege weapons, his son would be the one to successfully use them against many fortified cities.

With his forces reorganized and equipped with the latest weapons, Philip readied himself to expand his kingdom. First, he consolidated his own highlands and the lands to the north and east. These conquests allowed him to exploit the gold and silver mines in the hills, which yielded the riches he needed to finance his campaigns. With his northern flank secure and his treasury full, the conqueror then turned his attention to the warring Greek cities to the south.

Philip dreamed of uniting the Greek city-states under his leadership. Some southern Greeks shared this dream, looking to the Macedonian king to save them from their own intercity violence. **Greek responses** Isocrates (436–338 B.C.E.), an Athenian orator and educator, made eloquent speeches in which he supported Philip's expansionist aims. Expressing a prevalent disillusionment with democracy, Isocrates argued that the Greeks were incapable of forming a cohesive union without a leader like Philip. In his view, this form of participatory governance had become so corrupt that "violence is regarded as democracy, lawlessness as liberty, impudence of speech as equality." Isocrates believed that only Philip could unify the Greeks and empower them to face Asia as one people finally to vanquish their ancient enemy, Persia.

Isocrates' words were compelling. But Athens had another great orator who opposed Philip and who proved more convincing than Isocrates. Demosthenes (384–322 B.C.E.) argued brilliantly for a position that rejected union under a tyrant like Philip in order to preserve Athens's traditional freedom and the self-government of the polis. As we saw in Chapter 2, the classic polis had eroded in the aftermath of the Peloponnesian War, but the orator was looking backward to a more golden age of democracy. Historians have characterized Demosthenes as everything from a stubborn, old-fashioned orator to the last champion of the lost cause of Athenian freedom. Ultimately, however, the spirited debate about Philip became moot. The question of freedom was answered not in the marketplace of Athens but on the battlefield.

In 338 B.C.E., Philip and his armies marched south toward the peninsula, where they confronted a Greek coalition led by Athens and Thebes, longtime rivals who at last joined in **Greece conquered** cooperation. The belated cooperation among the Greeks came too late. At the Battle of Chaeronea near Thebes, the powerful left wing of Philip's phalanx enveloped the approaching Greeks. The Macedonian cavalry, led by Philip's talented son, Alexander, slaughtered the surrounded Greeks. The victory paved the way for Philip to take control of the Greek city-states (except Sparta).

Philip proved a lenient conqueror; he charged the Greeks no tribute, but instead united them in a league under his command, so they were technically allies with Macedonia. No longer allowed to wage war against one another, the poleis joined the combined army of Greeks and Macedonians. Isocrates' hope was fulfilled, and the Greeks reluctantly renounced internal warfare. Now they prepared to follow Philip to attack the Persian Empire, which extended far beyond the borders of the Persian homeland into Asia.

Death of the King

Philip's brilliance on the battlefield exceeded his judgment in domestic matters. In the tradition of Macedonian kings, Philip had taken at least six wives. The most important was Olympias, daughter of the king of Epirus (which was southwest of Macedonia and bordered the Greek city-states) and mother of Alexander. According to Plutarch, who drew from earlier sources, Olympias and Alexander were highly insulted when Philip, in his forties, took a young bride, Cleopatra. At the wedding, Cleopatra's uncle made a toast implying that he hoped Philip would disinherit Alexander.

Political and personal resentments came to a head in 336 B.C.E. at the wedding of Alexander's sister, also named Cleopatra. On the morning of the festivities, members of the court attended the theater. Philip was escorted by his son, the bridegroom, and his bodyguards. As the little group separated to enter the theater, Pausanias, one of Philip's jilted companions, saw his opportunity. He stepped in and mortally stabbed the king. Pursued by the guards, Pausanias ran outside but tripped and fell. A guard drew his sword and killed him on the spot.

> **Philip murdered**

Alexander, suspecting a conspiracy behind the assassination, vigorously investigated the murder. He tried and executed the diviner who had predicted good omens for the day, and he put to death anyone who he thought had even a remote claim to the Macedonian throne. Later, even Philip's wife Cleopatra and their infant child were killed, an act that finally eliminated Alexander's rivals. Because of insufficient evidence, historians have never ascertained the full reasons for Philip's assassination. Some ancient sources accused Olympias of organizing the murder; others blame a conspiracy of nobles; still others consider the killing the solitary act of a jealous courtier. Whatever the cause, Alexander was now king.

Alexander's Conquests

The brilliant king was dead, but Philip's son, Alexander, would make an even greater mark on the world than his father had. Alexander (r. 337–323 B.C.E.) was born in 356 B.C.E. and raised by his parents expressly to rule. Philip diligently taught the young boy the arts of Macedonian warfare, including horsemanship, an essential skill for service in the cavalry. Philip and Olympias also encouraged Alexander's intellectual development. They appreciated the accomplishments of the classical Greeks and hired the revered philosopher Aristotle (384–322 B.C.E.) to tutor their promising heir. We cannot know the exact influence of the philosopher on his young student, but Aristotle certainly imparted a love of Greek culture and literature to Alexander. Moreover, he may well have cultivated Alexander's curiosity about the world, which would fuel the young man's later urge to explore. However, Alexander seems to have rejected Aristotle's prejudice against non-Greek "barbarians." Philip's son imagined a world much wider than that of Aristotle's ideal, small city-state.

As soon as Alexander ascended the Macedonian throne, he needed to be recognized as the legitimate king, so he consolidated his rule in the region with a decisive ruthlessness that marked all his subsequent campaigns. For example, when the Greeks revolted after hearing false rumors of Alexander's death, the king promptly marched south, sacked the city of Thebes, and slaughtered or enslaved the inhabitants. With the Greeks subdued, he then turned to implementing Philip's planned war against the Persian Empire. In 334 B.C.E., Alexander advanced into Asia Minor with a large army of hoplites and cavalry. He was joined by Callisthenes, Aristotle's nephew, who later wrote the history of Alexander's campaigns. Although this text has been lost, it served as a pro-Macedonian, but carefully detailed source for Alexander's early campaigns, and subsequent chroniclers who had access to the work have passed elements of it on to us.

> **Military exploits**

After several decisive victories in Asia Minor, Alexander engaged the full power of Persia at the Battle of Issus (**Map 3.1**), where he matched with Persian forces and Greek mercenaries led by the Persian Great King Darius III. Through skillful deployment and swift action, Alexander's armies defeated a force more than twice as large as their own. Darius fled the battle, leaving his mother, wife, and children. The young king captured Darius's family but treated them with respect and courtesy. In this way, he showed his belief that savagery should be reserved for the battlefield.

Before driving deeper into Asia, Alexander turned south along the Phoenician coast, shrewdly recognizing the problem of the superior Persian fleet, which was reinforced by Phoenician vessels. He captured the great coastal cities of Sidon, Tyre, and finally Gaza, thus rendering the fleet useless without ever engaging it. The brilliant young strategist also perfected the art of siege warfare, improving on Philip's catapults and adding siege towers erected next to the defensive walls that allowed attackers to penetrate the fortresses. As the proud cities fell one by one, Alexander gained a reputation for brutal warfare but generosity to subject peoples. Subsequent cities surrendered quickly and joined the rapidly growing Macedonian Empire.

KEY DATES

POLITICAL EVENTS

359–336 B.C.E.	Philip II rules Macedonia
338 B.C.E.	Philip conquers Greece
337–323 B.C.E.	Alexander rules
333 B.C.E.	Battle of Issus
332 B.C.E.	Alexander conquers Egypt
331 B.C.E.	Battle of Gaugamela
330 B.C.E.	Alexander destroys Persepolis
323 B.C.E.	Successor kingdoms established
ca. 166–164 B.C.E.	Maccabean Revolt

thinking about GEOGRAPHY

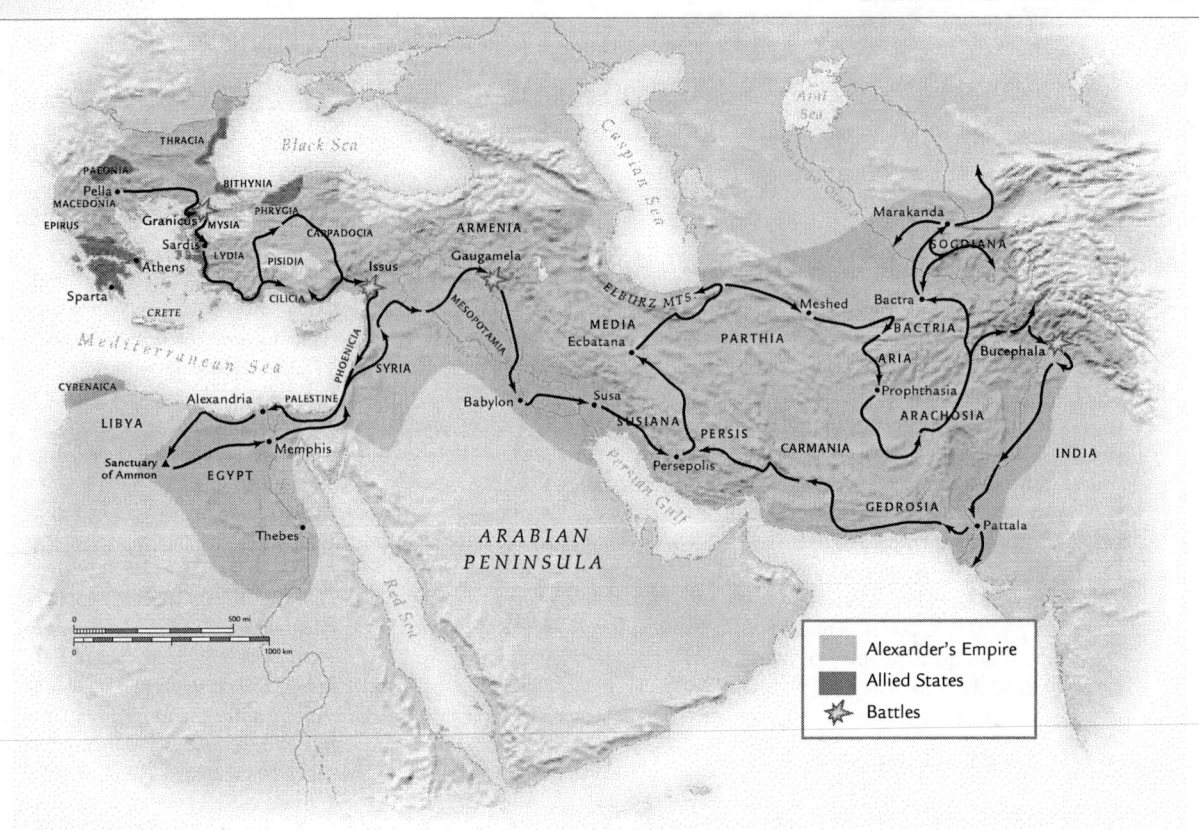

MAP 3.1

Alexander's Empire

This map shows the vast territory Alexander conquered, the route he took, and the major battle sites. Using the scale on the map, calculate the distance Alexander traveled. Consider the difficulties of supplying an army over this distance.

Explore the Map

1. Compare this map with **Map 1.5,** of the Persian Empire. What additional lands did Alexander conquer?

2. Based on the map and what you have learned from the text, what effects might Alexander's expansion have on the old Persian Empire?

3. What effects might his conquests have on Egypt?

After conquering Gaza, Alexander swept into Egypt virtually unopposed in 332 B.C.E. The Egyptian priests declared Alexander the incarnation of their god Amon, treating him as pharaoh. Now the god-king of Egypt, the young Macedonian founded a new city, Alexandria, on the Delta. This development brought Egypt more fully into Mediterranean economy and culture than it had ever been before, as the new northern, coastal capital encouraged trade and attracted colonists from elsewhere—a cosmopolitan center was founded in Egypt. With his western flank thus secured, Alexander once again headed for Asia to revive his pursuit of the Persian Great King, Darius.

After crossing the Euphrates and Tigris rivers, Alexander encountered Darius at Gaugamela in 331 B.C.E. The Persian ruler had fitted chariots with sharp scythes to cut down the Macedonian infantry, and his forces far outnumbered Alexander's army—by about 250,000 to 47,000 (although these figures are certainly exaggerated). Despite the Persian strength, Alexander's superior strategy vanquished the Persian warriors yet again. He forced the Persians to turn to confront his wheeling formation and thus opened fatal gaps in the long Persian line. His cavalry set upon the trapped Persian infantry. In the ensuing slaughter, a reputed 50,000 Persians died. Alexander entered Babylon and was welcomed as a liberator. He then turned southeast to Persepolis, the Persian capital. Despite fierce resistance, in 330 B.C.E. Alexander captured the city and plundered it ruthlessly, acquiring enough wealth to fund his future military ambitions. Then he burned it to the ground. Alexander never met Darius on the battlefield again, for the Persian king was assassinated by one of his own guards. After this, no one could doubt that the mighty Persian Empire had a new master—Alexander, who was crowned Great King.

Alexander thought of himself as a powerful, semidivine Greek hero; he claimed descent from Achilles through his mother and from Heracles (whom we remember by the Roman name Hercules) through his father. The shrewd conqueror was also a skilled propagandist, and his identification with ancient heroes helped consolidate his authority in the minds of Greeks raised on the stories of Homer. **Figure 3.1** *The Greek hero* shows a portion of a beautifully carved sarcophagus from the city of Sidon, on the Phoenician coast of the Mediterranean. The local royalty buried here had commissioned a scene of Alexander's victory over Darius to grace the side of the coffin, recognizing the moment that the Sidonian king changed his allegiance from Persia to Macedonia. Alexander sits astride a rearing horse at the left, while the defeated Persians fall before him. The conqueror wears a lion skin on his head, in a typical portrayal of Heracles. It is highly unlikely that Alexander fought in anything other than the traditional Macedonian armor, but the artistic license reveals the popular view of Alexander as a true Greek hero.

Alexander himself identified most strongly with the hero Achilles. According to Plutarch, Alexander slept with a copy of Homer's *Iliad*, edited by Aristotle, under his pillow and "esteemed it a perfect portable treasure of all military virtue and knowledge." Through Alexander, then, the heroic values of the Greek world endured and spread, and as Plutarch maintained, "thanks to Alexander, Homer was read in Asia. . . ."

The war against Persia had finally ended, but the young conqueror was still not satisfied. Having studied world geography as documented by the ancient Greeks, Alexander yearned to push his conquests to the edge of the known world. He mistakenly believed that this enticing frontier lay just beyond the Indus River in India. *India* A last major battle against an Indian king eliminated opposition in northern India, and Alexander made plans to press farther into the subcontinent. However, his Macedonian troops had had enough and refused to go on. Alexander wept in his tent for days at the mutiny of his beloved troops, but he finally conceded and turned back. However, instead of returning along the northern route, he led his troops south to explore the barren lands at the edge of the Arabian Sea (see **Map 3.1**). His exhausted, parched army finally reached the prosperous lands of Mesopotamia. Yet their relief was marred by an ironic tragedy: Alexander, seriously weakened by ever-growing alcohol abuse, caught a fever and died in Babylon in 323 B.C.E. He was just 32 years old. Others would have to rule the lands conquered by Alexander the Great.

A Young Ruler's Legacy

Was Plutarch right in thinking that Alexander wanted to make "all mankind a single people"? This ideal, which marked a radical departure from traditional Greek attitudes, has provoked intense historical debate virtually from the time of Alexander's life to the present. The Macedonian conqueror implemented several policies that some have interpreted as his desire to rule over a unified rather than a conquered people. One such policy, and certainly the most influential, was his founding of cities. In all his conquered territories, Alexander established an array of new cities. He intended these urban centers in part to recreate the Greek city life that he and his father had so admired. To this end, the conqueror helped settle numerous Greek and Macedonian

FIGURE 3.1 Alexander in Battle, fourth century B.C.E
This magnificent marble sarcophagus (burial casket) found in Sidon (present-day Lebanon) shows a victorious Alexander defeating the Persians at the Battle of Issus. Originally painted in brilliant colors, the coffin reveals the tremendous influence of classic Greek art.

thinking about DOCUMENTS

DOCUMENT 3.1

Alexander Restores Greek Exiles

In 324 B.C.E., Alexander issued a proclamation that all Greek exiles should be allowed to return to their homes, even though many had been gone for generations. This policy pleased the exiles, but it also offended many residents who resented Alexander's high-handed interference in their affairs—in stark contrast to Philip's promise to give the Greeks a measure of autonomy. The Sicilian historian Diodorus describes the decree and its reception. Alexander died less than a year after this decree, and his successors rescinded it.

A short time before his death, Alexander decided to restore all the exiles in the Greek cities, partly for the sake of gaining fame and partly wishing to secure many devoted personal followers in each city to counter the revolutionary movements and seditions of the Greeks. Therefore, the Olympic games being at hand, he sent Nicanor of Strageira to Greece, giving him a decree about the restoration, which he ordered him to have proclaimed by the victorious herald to the crowds at the festival. Nicanor carried out his instructions, and the herald received and read the following message: "King Alexander to the exiles from the Greek cities. We have not been the cause of your exile, but, save for those of you who are under a curse, we shall be the cause of your return to your own native cities. We have written to Antipater about this to the end that if any cities are not willing to restore you, he may constrain them." When the herald had announced this, the crowd showed its approval with loud applause; for those at the festival welcomed the favour of the king with cries of joy, and repaid his good deed with praises. All the exiles had come together at the festival, being more than twenty thousand in number.

Now people in general welcomed the restoration of the exiles as a good thing, but the Aetolians and the Athenians took offence at the action and were angry. The reason for this was that the Aetolians had exiled the Oeniadae from their native city and expected the punishment appropriate to their wrongdoing; for the king himself had threatened that no sons of the Oeniadae, but he himself would punish them. Likewise, the Athenians who had distributed [the island of] Samos in allotments to their citizens, were by no means willing to abandon that island.

SOURCE: R.M. Greer, trans., *Diodorus of Sicily* 18.8, vol. 8 of Loeb Classical Library (Cambridge, MA: Harvard University Press, 1969).

Analyze the Document

1. Why was the problem of displaced Greeks so significant during this period? (Consider this in the light of Document 2.3.)
2. Why do you think Alexander made the announcement at the Olympic Games?
3. What were Alexander's motives according to Diodorus?
4. Who supported and opposed the decree?
5. Why do you think the decree was rescinded?

---

colonists in the new cities. Hundreds of thousands of Greeks emigrated to the newly claimed lands in Asia, taking privileged positions. We will see that as they introduced their culture into Asia, these colonists inevitably influenced and were changed by the subject peoples. These culturally rich cities rank among Alexander's most enduring legacies.

The movement of Greeks to cities far into Asia raised questions about exiles' continued ties with their cities of origin, and Alexander's royal power raised questions about the traditional autonomy of the Greek poleis. Document 3.1 reproduces an edict issued by Alexander near the end of his life that intended to address these lingering issues.

Meanwhile, in Asia, Alexander strongly supported the intermarriage of Greeks and Macedonians with Asians. He himself married the daughter of Darius and Roxane, the daughter of an Asian tribal king who ruled near modern-day Afghanistan. Alexander also presided over the weddings of hundreds of his generals to highborn Persian women. As Plutarch said, he "joined together the greatest and most powerful

Intercultural marriages

peoples into one community by wedlock." Ten thousand more of Alexander's soldiers also married Asian women. Alexander might well have imagined that the offspring of these marriages would help seal the union of the two populations.

Finally, Alexander had a constant need for additional soldiers to support his campaigns, and he obtained these men from the conquered peoples. He accepted both Persian soldiers and commanders into his companies. Preparing for the future, he also chose about 30,000 Asian boys whom he slated to learn the Greek language and the Macedonian fighting style. These boys would become the next generation of soldiers to fight for the king in a combined army.

Alexander's cultural blending disturbed those upper-crust Greeks and Macedonians who saw themselves as conquerors rather than as equals among the subject peoples. Indeed, while in Persia, Alexander adopted Persian robes and courtly ceremonies, including having his subjects prostrate themselves on the ground in his presence. Without a doubt, this ritual helped Persians accept their new king—but it also

Resentments

offended the proud Macedonians. Alexander's inclusion of Asians in the military elite only intensified Macedonian resentment. At one point, an outcry arose among Alexander's soldiers when the king apparently sought to replace some of them with Asians. Alexander squelched these objections decisively, executing 13 leaders and suggesting that the rest of them go home so that he could lead the Asian troops to victory. The Macedonians backed down, pleading for their king's forgiveness. Alexander resolved the incident with a lavish banquet of reconciliation, at which Asians and Macedonians drank together and Alexander prayed for harmony (sometimes mistranslated as "brotherhood") between them.

Alexander died too soon for historians to be certain of his exact plans for ruling his vast, multiethnic empire. For all we know, he might well have intended that Greeks and Macedonians would remain a ruling elite. The cities and colonies guaranteed a continued Greek presence, as did the invaders' weddings to local women. The conqueror's inclusive army might have been simply a practical means of ensuring a large enough force to fulfill his ambitions. Whatever his intentions, Alexander created a fertile combination by joining the cultures of the ancient Middle East and classical Greece.

Alexander's legacy included more than his political conquests—which in some regions hardly outlasted the young king himself. The memory of his accomplishments has endured in an embellished way far beyond even his most impressive victories. For example, Plutarch's interpretation of Alexander's desire for a blending of peoples made this notion a foundational characteristic of Western culture, regardless of whether the king truly held this ideal. Moreover, a highly imaginative version of Alexander's accomplishments, titled *The Alexander Romance*, was translated into twenty-four languages and found its way from Iran to China to Malaysia. The idea of a great empire ruled by one king may have exerted an influence as far as the Han dynasty in China. It certainly shaped Mediterranean thinking, where would-be conquerors reverently visited Alexander's tomb in the spectacular Egyptian city of Alexandria that he founded.

Alexander's memory

THE SUCCESSOR KINGDOMS, 323–ca. 100 B.C.E.

Admirers across the world may have romanticized Alexander's supposed dream of a unified kingdom. In reality, however, brutal politics sullied the picture soon after the Great King's death. Legends preserve the probably false tale that as Alexander lay dying, he told his comrades that the kingdom should go "to the strongest." Even if Alexander never said this, the story reflects the reality of the violent fighting that broke out among the Macedonian generals shortly after the king died. Alexander's wife, Roxane, was pregnant when he succumbed, and presumably the empire should have gone to his infant son, Alexander IV. But within thirteen years of Alexander's death, both Roxane and her young son had been murdered. Moreover, the Macedonian generals had carved up the great empire into new, smaller kingdoms that became the successors to Alexander's conquests. **Map 3.2** shows the successor kingdoms.

Egypt Under the Ptolemies

Upon Alexander's death, one of his cavalry "companions," Ptolemy, moved toward Egypt with his own loyal troops to take control of that wealthy region. Ptolemy diverted the king's corpse, which was being returned to Macedonia for burial, and took it to Alexandria, where he erected an imposing tomb for Alexander. It seems that Ptolemy believed the presence of the conqueror's remains would help legitimize his own rule. Fending off attempts by Alexander's other generals to snatch the rich land of the Nile, Ptolemy and his successors ruled as the god-kings of Egypt for the next three hundred years.

The **Ptolemies** inherited a land with a long tradition of obedience to authority. Accordingly, the new kings wisely struck a bargain with the Egyptian priests, promising to fulfill the traditional duty of the pharaohs to care for the temples (and the priests) in exchange for protection of their legitimacy. Through most of their history, the Ptolemies lived in luxury in Alexandria, conducting official business in Greek while Egyptian peasants continued to obey the age-old dictates of the Nile, the priests, and the tax collectors. Life away from the court under the new order changed very little, which made it easier for the new dynasty to rule. The parallel practicing of both Egyptian and Greek ways continued throughout most of the Ptolemaic rule. In fact, the majority of these Greek kings rarely carried out traditional ritual functions, and some were probably not even formally crowned. For their part, the priests honored the Ptolemies while still governing in the traditional way.

Continuity of life

However, in one significant way the Hellenistic rulers departed from their Egyptian predecessors—their queens took a more prominent role. Many of the Ptolemaic rulers engaged in brother-sister marriages as the ancient Egyptians had done, but many women were able to exert considerable power. Hellenistic queens derived much of their authority from controlling substantial wealth and spending it on public works (and on hiring large armies). The height of the

Hellenistic queens

thinking about GEOGRAPHY

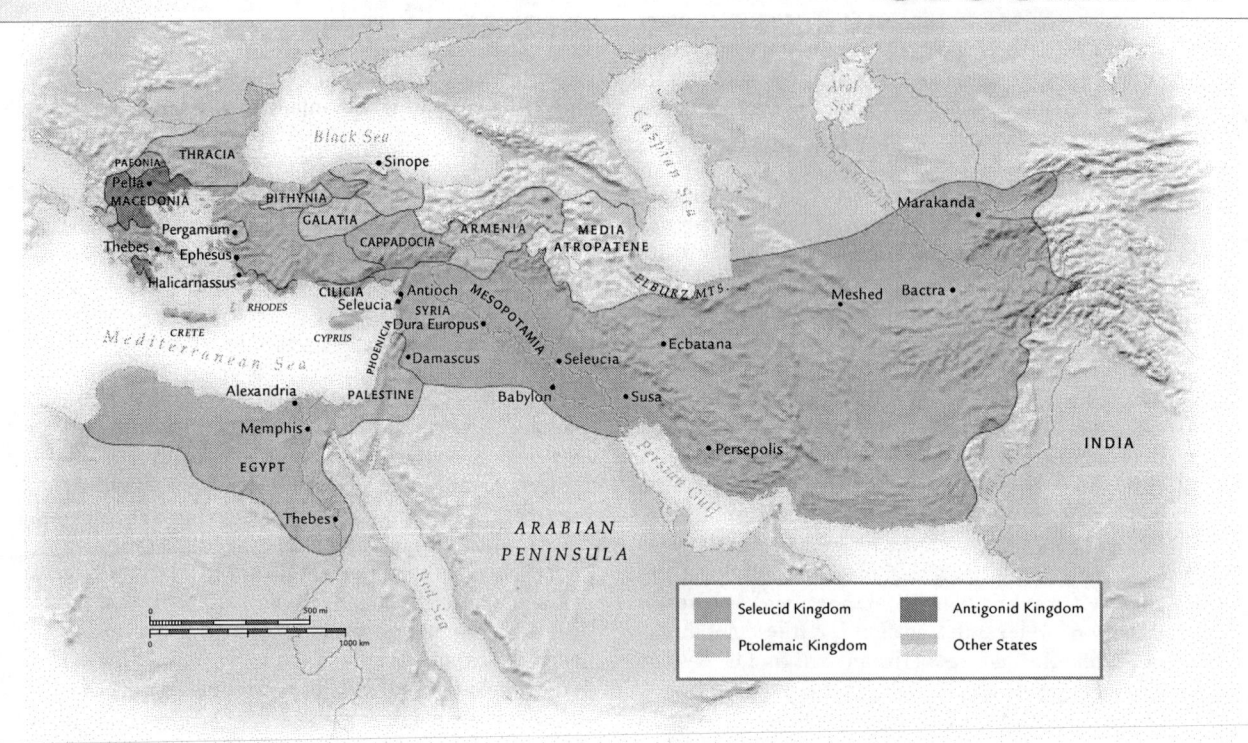

MAP 3.2

The Successor States After the Death of Alexander, ca. 240 B.C.E.

This map shows the breakup of Alexander's empire into three states and illustrates the relative sizes of the successor kingdoms.

Explore the Map

1. Based on your analysis of previous maps, as well as the information in the text, what were the historical and geographic reasons for the differing sizes of the successor kingdoms?
2. How might the movement of the Egyptian capital from Thebes to Alexandria have affected Egypt?

Hellenistic queens of Egypt came with the last one—Cleopatra VII—who challenged the growing power of Rome (discussed in Chapter 4).

Under the Ptolemies, the port city of Alexandria became the premier city of the Hellenistic world. It was a dynamic cosmopolitan city that by the end of the first century B.C.E. boasted almost one million inhabitants. Alexandria was a bustling port city where the main enterprise was the pursuit of wealth. The harbors were busy and the markets thronging, and international banks grew up to serve the people. To make sure ships could enter the port safely, Hellenistic scientists built a huge lighthouse on an island (Pharos) outside the harbor. The structure was 440 feet high, and the light from the lantern at the top was intensified by a system of reflectors. Ships approaching the harbor were guided by the beam of the lantern. This lighthouse came to be regarded as one of the seven wonders of the ancient world.

For all its commercial value, Alexandria under the Ptolemies also became an intellectual and cultural center. The rulers established a world-famous museum (the word *museum* means "temple to the muses," the Greek goddesses who served as inspiration to creativity). At the museum, scholars from around the Mediterranean and Asia gathered to study texts and discuss ideas. The Greek rulers founded a great library as part of this museum and ambitiously designed it to stand as the West's first complete collection of published works. Well established by 280 B.C.E., the library boasted more than 700,000 volumes just one century later, making it the largest collection the ancient world had seen.

BIOGRAPHY

Arsinoë II
(315–ca. 270 B.C.E.)

Brilliant and Ruthless Queen of Egypt

The Hellenistic dynasties created by the successor states to Alexander's empire (see **Map 3.2**) set new precedents for the ancient world by bringing strong women to power. These queens of all three dynasties (Seleucid, Antigonid, and Ptolemaic) derived their power from two main things: their descent from the original founders of the dynasties and their great wealth. Many of these women strongly influenced the great events of the day. The story of Arsinoë II, queen of Egypt, reveals the violent world of Hellenistic politics and shows the fierce will for power that both men and women leaders often needed to rule effectively.

Arsinoë was the daughter of the first Ptolemy, Alexander's successor who took over Egypt. Like most Hellenistic princesses, she was well educated and raised to rule. She was married at age 15 to the king of Thrace, Lysimachus, an old companion-in-arms of Ptolemy. Lysimachus renounced his first wife in favor of the young, and very beautiful, Arsinoë. By the time Arsinoë was 30, she had borne three sons and had begun to plan for their (and her) future. To position her sons to inherit the throne, she accused Lysimachus's son by his first wife of treason and perhaps had him poisoned.

Yet despite Arsinoë's plans, her family became ensnared in one of the seemingly endless Hellenistic wars of power. First, Seleucus marched from Asia to Thrace to conquer Lysimachus. Amid the combat, Arsinoë's husband (now almost 80 years old) died. Then as Arsinoë fled with her children to Greece, her half-brother Ceraunus seized control of her old realm. Ceraunus well understood the benefits of legitimacy that Arsinoë's bloodline could provide, and the advantages of her great wealth. He offered to marry her and make her children his heirs. She agreed, but he betrayed her, killing her two youngest children in order to secure the kingdom for his own progeny. She and her eldest son managed to escape to Egypt to seek the protection of her brother, Ptolemy II.

Safe in Egypt, Arsinoë moved to rebuild her power. Not content to be simply sister to the king, she had Ptolemy's wife exiled and married him herself to assure herself the title of queen. From then on, she and her brother were known as "sibling-lovers" (*philadelphus*). If we are to believe the poets of the period, the couple genuinely loved each other. One poet wrote, "No more splendid wife than she ever clasped in bridal chamber her bridegroom, loving him from her heart, her brother and her lord." Satisfied with her newly secured position as the head of Egypt's ruling family, Arsinoë ignored her husband's many mistresses, although purportedly she quickly killed any political rivals who tried to reduce her authority.

The sibling marriage not only gave Arsinoë the power she craved but also helped consolidate the power of the dynasty by bringing the Ptolemies closer to traditional Egyptian practices; sometimes Egyptian pharaohs had married their sisters. However, the Greek Macedonians decried the practice as incest and forbade it. In marrying each other, Arsinoë and Ptolemy reclaimed an older form of legitimacy that had shaped the Egyptian ruling families. Artistic portrayals of Queen Arsinoë depict this movement toward traditional Egyptian practices. **Figure 3.2a** shows her in the traditional Macedonian fashion, crowned only by the slim band that

---

Eventually, however, the Ptolemies encountered both internal and external pressure to change. Under the reign of Ptolemy V (r. ca. 205–ca. 183 B.C.E.), a boy not yet in his teens, priests began demanding that the young king be more involved in religious rituals. The boy-king's problems only worsened when sub-Saharan Nubians (see Global Connections, Chapter 1), detecting his weakness, clamored for their own pharaoh. In addition, the armies of Alexander's successor in Asia were threatening Egypt's borders. Pressured on all sides, Ptolemy offered concessions to the powerful priests in return for their support in rallying the Egyptians to his cause. The young ruler reduced taxes on the peasants and increased payments to the priests. In return for his cooperation, the priests brought Ptolemy to Memphis, the traditional capital of the pharaohs, where they placed the great double crown of Egypt—the sign of royalty—on his head. Finally, they ordered that Ptolemy V be worshiped in every Egyptian shrine. To make good on this policy, they demanded that scribes write all the accomplishments of Ptolemy V "on a slab of hard stone, in the writing of the words of god, the writing of documents and the letters of the Northerners, and set it up in all the temples. . . ."

Figure 3.3 shows the **Rosetta Stone**, the tablet that resulted from this decree, which was unearthed in 1799. Demonstrating the presence of both Greeks and Egyptians in the kingdom of the Ptolemies, the stone records Ptolemy's deeds in three written versions: the sacred hieroglyphics at the top, Egyptian cursive administrative script at the center, and Greek ("the letters of the Northerners") at the bottom.

FIGURE 3.2a Arsinoë

FIGURE 3.2b Arsinoë

marked their rulers. **Figure 3.2b,** on the other hand, shows Arsinoë wearing the traditional headdress of the Egyptian rulers. The Macedonian queen had become an Egyptian one. During the next centuries, the Ptolemies in Egypt followed the precedent set by Arsinoë and Ptolemy. They preserved much of their Macedonian ways while adopting enough Egyptian traditions to let them rule the ancient country effectively. Historians have argued over how much political influence Arsinoë wielded. However, we should perhaps believe the ancient historian Memnon, when he wrote, "Arsinoë was one to get her own way."

In addition, in a decree after her death, Ptolemy wrote that he followed the "policy of his ancestors and of his sister in his zeal for the freedom of the Greeks." Arsinoë's zeal for freedom stemmed more from her hostility to the Seleucid rulers (who had driven her from her lands in Thrace) than from any abstract ideals of independence. The queen wanted to be sure her Egyptian dynasty would be free from intrusion from the successors of Alexander coming from the north, so she even traveled to the front to survey the defenses. Furthermore, she and Ptolemy knew that their safety in Egypt would hinge on sea power, so they expanded the Egyptian fleet significantly.

Even while securing the independence of Egypt, the Ptolemies did not forget the Greek love of learning that marked all the successor kingdoms. As their greatest accomplishment, they constructed an immense library in Alexandria, which served as the center of learning in the Mediterranean world for almost the next thousand years.

Egyptian priests followed Ptolemy's lead in worshiping Arsinoë as a goddess, and following her death in about 270 B.C.E., Ptolemy issued edicts and built shrines to stimulate her cult. Poets described Arsinoë as a special patron of sailors, claiming, "She will give fair voyages and will smooth the sea even in midwinter in answer to prayer." The veneration of Queen Arsinoë by Egyptians and Greeks alike ensured that the cultural blending that emerged during her lifetime continued long after her death.

Connecting People & Society

1. How did the reign of Arsinoë II contribute to the blending of Greek and Egyptian culture that marked the Ptolemaic dynasty?

2. How do the portrayals of the queen in art reflect the transformation of the Macedonian kingship?

In the hieroglyphic section the king's name is enclosed in circles, which supposedly protected his name and, because the names of pharaohs had always been so encircled, also signaled to all who saw it that Ptolemy was indeed the rightful god-king. Equally significant, the Rosetta Stone provided the key that finally let nineteenth-century scholars decipher hieroglyphic writing. Without the stone, the meaning embedded in the great carvings of the ancient Egyptians might still remain a mystery.

The Seleucids Rule Asia

In the violent political jockeying that broke out after the death of Alexander, one of Ptolemy's lieutenants, Seleucus, entered Babylon in 311 B.C.E. and captured the imperial treasure there. With this money, Seleucus laid claim to the old heartland of the Persian Empire. Yet the extensive eastern lands that Alexander had conquered eluded his grasp. As early as 310 B.C.E. Seleucus gave northwest India back to its native rulers in return for five hundred war elephants, and by the third century B.C.E., eastern Asia Minor had fallen away. Nevertheless, Seleucus founded a long-standing kingdom that continued the Hellenizing process begun by Alexander.

Like Alexander, the **Seleucids** founded cities and populated them with imported Greek and Macedonian bureaucrats and colonists. Seleucia, about fifty miles north of Babylon, was established as the new capital of the kingdom, and Dura Europus, near the midpoint of the Euphrates River, was another important center. Their locations reveal that the Seleucid

Commercial cities

FIGURE 3.3 Rosetta Stone, 197 B.C.E. Greek-speaking Macedonian rulers had to communicate with Egyptians. Fortunately, the Macedonians wrote an edict in Greek and translated it into two Egyptian scripts on this famous stone. This translation provided the key to scholars' ability to read Egyptian hieroglyphs.

kings recognized the crucial role of eastern trade in the prosperity of their kingdom. These cities controlled the trade routes through the Tigris-Euphrates valley and the caravan trails that crossed the desert from Damascus and, along with Antioch, became vital political and economic centers within the former Persian lands (see **Map 3.2**).

While the Ptolemies could depend on an established Egyptian priesthood to facilitate their control of their kingdom, the Seleucids had no such ready-made institution. Instead, they relied in part on Macedonian and Greek colonists to secure their hold on their Asian lands. After Alexander's death, the Seleucids settled at least 20,000 Macedonian colonists in Syria and Asia Minor. This number was supplemented by others from Macedonia who came looking for riches and privileges.

<u>Seleucid colonists</u>

The Macedonian settlers viewed themselves as world conquerors and expected to maintain their high-status positions in the new lands. The Seleucid kings, who saw the colonists as the backbone of their armies, granted them considerable farmlands. Some charters from this time show that certain colonists were exempt from paying taxes and even received free food until their first crops could be harvested. These colonists did not expect to work the land themselves; instead, resident dependent laborers farmed the land for their foreign conquerors. Again, as in Egypt, the resident peasantry served their Greek-speaking masters. Not surprisingly, the Seleucid kings gained a loyal following among the elite with these allocations of land.

Although Greek sovereignty faded quickly in the easternmost edges of the Seleucid lands, evidence remains of the impact of the Greek presence there. To illustrate, consider the great king of northern India Aśoka (r. ca. 268–ca. 233 B.C.E.). Aśoka is perhaps most remembered for spreading the ideals of Buddhism through inscriptions on stones. Like the Rosetta Stone, these Rock Edicts testify to the Hellenic presence in India, because Aśoka's sayings were preserved both in the Indian language of Prakrit and in Greek. In wise phrases such as "Let them neither praise themselves nor disparage their neighbors, for that is vain," the ideas of Buddhism met the language of Hellenism in the farthest lands of Alexander.

Antigonids in Greece

The Seleucid kings concentrated on ruling the western portions of their Asian provinces, ever watchful for opportunities to gain advantage over the Ptolemies or the Macedonian leaders who now ruled in Macedonia and Greece. These kings, known as the **Antigonids,** were descended from Antigonus the One-Eyed (382–ca. 301 B.C.E.), a general who had joined in the struggle for succession after Alexander's death. Antigonus failed to score a decisive military victory, however, and died on the battlefield at the venerable age of 80, still trying to win control of the entire Macedonian Empire. Nevertheless, his descendants eventually took power in Macedonia and Greece and introduced the Antigonid dynasty.

In the short run, Alexander's conquests profoundly affected Macedonian society and economy. At first, wealth poured from the east into the young king's homeland. Indeed, near the end of his life, Alexander sent home one shipment of booty that proved so large that 110 warships were needed to escort the merchant vessels on their return journey. Numismatic evidence also confirms the volume of wealth that initially flowed into Macedonia, for its mint churned out about 13 million silver coins immediately after Alexander's reign. Much of this coinage came into wide circulation, for officials used it to pay troops and provide stipends for veterans' widows and orphans. Yet the money did not profoundly alter Macedonian society. By the reign of Antigonus's

<u>Life in Macedonia</u>

great-grandson, Demetrius II (r. 239–229 B.C.E.), life in Macedonia had changed little from even as far back as Philip II's time. The army still consisted mainly of Macedonian nobles, who fought as companions to their king. Invaders from the north still threatened; indeed, in the 280s B.C.E. the Gauls, a tribe on the Macedonians' northern border, launched an attack that cost Macedonia dearly. To make matters worse, the Greeks to the south, who had never really accepted Macedonian rule, kept revolting.

The Greek city-states experienced more change than Macedonia did, for the traditional democracy of Athens and the other poleis had evaporated. The poleis relaxed their notions of citizenship, so many immigrants and freed slaves became citizens, but at the same time people had less attachment to their cities. Many jobs—from soldier to athlete—became the province of specialists, not citizens, and thus international professionals replaced the native competitors who brought glory and wealth to their cities. Furthermore, the new economy of the Hellenistic world widened the gulf between rich and poor, and the disparity undermined participatory government: Rich Greeks took over governance and frequently forgot that they had any responsibility to the poor.

Changes in Greece

Despite these tensions, outright revolution never materialized. The relentless warfare plaguing the poleis simply proved too distracting. In addition, Greeks from all walks of life continued emigrating to the other Hellenistic kingdoms in search of a better life, and this exodus helped ease population pressures at home. Bureaucrats and scientists headed for the Greek colonies to take advantage of the tempting opportunities there—for example, a talented mathematician, Apollonius, first worked in Alexandria, Egypt, and then was lured to the Seleucid kingdom in the east. The poleis, which in the old days had claimed people's loyalty, had given way to cosmopolitan cities. Now individuals sought to enhance their own fortunes in a wider world.

EAST MEETS WEST IN THE SUCCESSOR KINGDOMS

The vast breadth of the Hellenistic kingdoms stimulated the West's economy to new heights. Trade rhythms quickened, and merchants raked in unprecedented wealth. Under Alexander and his successors in the various kingdoms, Greek became the universal language of business. Now traders could exchange goods across large distances without confronting confusing language barriers. The Greeks also advanced credit, a business practice that let merchants ply their trade without having to transport unwieldy quantities of hard currency.

FIGURE 3.4 Hellenistic Coins Standardized currency facilitated trade among all the Hellenistic kingdoms and serves as fine historical evidence. Coin (a) is an eight-drachma coin of Ptolemy II of Egypt (r. ca. 284–ca. 247 B.C.E.). Coin (b) is a silver coin of King Orophernes (2nd century B.C.E.) from Cappadocia in the Seleucid kingdom.

Money in the New Cosmopolitan Economies

The Hellenistic kings standardized currency as well, another boon for trade. There were two weights of coins in the Hellenistic world: One was based on Alexander's standard, in which one drachma contained 4.3 grams of silver. The Ptolemies in Egypt abided by a different standard, using only 3.5 grams of silver in the drachma. Despite the dual standards, the consistency of both helped merchants buy and sell with ease throughout the extensive region. **Figure 3.4** shows two coins from this era. The gold coin from Egypt in **Figure 3.4a** is worth eight drachmas. It shows Ptolemy II with his wife Arsinoë II (featured in the Biography) on the front and Ptolemy's parents, Ptolemy I and Berenice, on the reverse. By showing two generations of royalty, the coin is proclaiming a dynastic succession that was traditionally important in Egypt. The silver coin in **Figure 3.4b** is a "tetradrachma," from Cappadocia in Asia Minor (modern Turkey). It shows King Orophernes, with the Greek goddess Athena on the reverse. These coins show that the Hellenistic kingdoms had much in common. Both coins show the monarchs in the style of Macedonian rulers, wearing the simple diadem that since Philip II's time had marked Macedonian kingship, and both are based on the drachma. They also graphically represent both the wealth that the Macedonian conquests generated and

Coinage and trade

the spread of Greek cultural influence throughout the region as trade intensified.

Goods moved briskly through the Hellenistic kingdoms, reshaping old patterns of trade and consumption. Athens initially benefited from the widespread demand for Greek goods like pottery and weapons, but a century after the death of Alexander, Alexandria had replaced Athens as the commercial capital of the eastern Mediterranean. The small islands of Rhodes and Delos also rose to prominence because of their advantageous locations along the routes that connected the north and southeast areas of the Mediterranean with Greece and Italy.

Heightened trade led to new approaches to agriculture as people rushed to develop and sell novel delicacies. As one example, Greek farmers began planting their precious olive trees and grapevines in the eastern kingdoms, permanently altering the ecosystems in those regions. In turn, eastern spices transformed cooking on the Greek mainland and in Egypt. Agricultural crossbreeding also became common, though it failed in some cases—even seeds imported from Rhodes to cross with Egypt's bitter cabbage could not sweeten that pungent vegetable of the Nile valley.

While commerce made countless merchants rich, the individual kingdoms also benefited—mainly by taking control of economic activity. In Egypt, where pharaohs traditionally controlled much trade and industry—a system called a command economy—the Ptolemies increased their controls to funnel the riches of the Nile valley into the royal treasury. They converted the most successful industries into royal monopolies, controlling such essentials as sesame oil, salt, perfumes, and incense. Their most successful venture, however, was the beer industry, which had been a royal monopoly since the Old Kingdom. The Ptolemies insisted that the millions of gallons of beer consumed each year in Egypt be manufactured in the royal breweries, though many women doubtless continued to brew the beverage for household consumption as they had always done.

[Command economies]

Kings also levied taxes on imports and exports, such as grain, papyrus, cosmetics, timber, metals, and horses. These policies required a complex administrative system, which in turn led to the proliferation of Greek-speaking bureaucrats. Equally important, the kings used their new riches not only to live lavishly, but also to fund the expensive wars that ravaged the Hellenistic world.

Armies of the Hellenistic World

One of the most famous statues of the Hellenistic world, shown in **Figure 3.5**, is the Nike of Samothrace—called Winged Victory because Nike was the Greek goddess of victory—and it is a perfect

FIGURE 3.5 Statue of Nike (Winged Victory), ca. 190 B.C.E. This 8-foot-tall marble sculpture shows the goddess Nike descending through the wind to celebrate a victory at sea. The blowing draperies mark the Hellenistic style of flowing movement.

symbol of the war-dominated Hellenistic age. Originally part of a sculptural group that included a war galley, Nike strides confidently into the wind, certain of victory. However, the battles of the Hellenistic world seemed to bring endless suffering more often than clear victory.

The Macedonian kings thought of themselves as conquerors and derived their legitimacy in large part from their military successes. Like Alexander, whom they strove to emulate, these monarchs fully expected to participate in the hardships of battle and the dangers of combat. Consequently, they regularly made war on one another in hopes of gaining land or power. The ideal of conquest thus persisted after Alexander's death. However, the scale of warfare had broadened.

This broadening occurred partly because of the larger territories in dispute. Some boundaries now far surpassed the dimensions of the earlier Greek poleis. To cover these daunting distances, monarchs accumulated vast armies. Philip had conquered Greece with a force of about 30,000 men, and Alexander had increased the [Mercenary armies] numbers significantly as he moved east. Alexander's force in India may have exceeded 100,000—exceptional for ancient armies. The Hellenistic kings, however, regularly fielded armies of between 60,000 and 80,000 troops. These large armies consisted no longer primarily of citizen-soldiers but of mercenaries—who were loyal only to their paymaster and who switched sides with impunity. Tellingly, Hellenistic theater often featured mercenary soldiers who returned home with lots of money to spend and a newly cynical outlook.

The Macedonian armies were also influenced by their contact with the far eastern provinces. For example, in these distant lands they encountered war elephants for the first time. Just as horses had offered mounted warriors advantages of mobility and reach over foot soldiers, soldiers mounted on elephants had an even greater military advantage. Furthermore, elephants participated in the fray, trampling men and using their trunks as weapons. As mentioned previously, the earliest Seleucids had exchanged territory in India for the prized elephants, and these formidable animals eventually became part of the Hellenistic armory. The Seleucids tried to breed elephants in Syria but had to keep trading with India for more elephants when their efforts failed. To retain their advantage, the Seleucid kings cut off the Ptolemies' trade in Asian elephants, forcing the Egyptians to rely on the smaller, less effective African breed. The Greek historian Polybius (ca. 200–ca. 118 B.C.E.) described a confrontation between the two classes of pachyderms: The African elephants, "unable to stand the smell and trumpeting of the Indian elephants and terrified, I suppose, also by their great size and strength, . . . at once turn tail and take to flight." As impressive as the Asian elephants were, foot soldiers learned to dodge the beasts and stab or hamstring them. However, the massive animals remained a valuable tool for moving heavy siege engines to walled cities and attacking fortified positions.

Large, wealthy, and well-equipped armies now routinely toppled defensive walls, and kings followed Alexander's ruthless model of wiping out any city that showed even a hint of defiance. Mercenaries, too, cared little for civilians, and historical sources describe soldiers drunkenly looting private homes after a conquest. The countryside also suffered from the warfare, and peasants repeatedly petitioned kings to ease their burdens. Peasants faced increased taxes levied to fund expensive wars and then frequently confronted violence from marauding mercenaries. To an unprecedented level, civilians became casualties in wars waged between kings.

The incessant warfare also changed the nature of slavery in the Greek world. As we have seen, during the classical Greek period—as throughout the ancient world—slavery was taken for granted. Every household had one or two domestic slaves, and most manufacturing and other labor was done by slaves. Alexander's immediate successors generally avoided mass enslavement of prisoners, but traditionally it was customary to enslave losers in battle. Therefore, by the late third century B.C.E., prisoners began to be enslaved in huge numbers. This changed the scale of the institution of slavery and, ultimately, the treatment of the slaves themselves. By 167 B.C.E., the island of Delos in the Aegean Sea housed a huge slave market. Claiming that 10,000 slaves could arrive and be sold in a day on Delos, the Greek historian Strabo quoted a contemporary saying about the slave markets that suggested how quickly the slave-traders sold their human cargo: "Merchant, put in, unload—all's sold." Although these large numbers are surely an exaggeration, they testify to the huge increase in numbers of slaves that began to be moved around the eastern Mediterranean. Wealthy households now could have hundreds of slaves, and others worked in gangs in agriculture and mining. This new scale of slavery further dehumanized those who had been taken, and slaves joined civilians as a population suffering under the new kingdoms.

A True Cultural Blending?

Whether or not Alexander had envisioned a complete uniting of east and west, in reality a full blending of peoples never occurred in the lands he conquered. The Hellenistic kingdoms in Egypt and Asia consisted of local native populations ruled by a Greek/Macedonian elite who made up less than 10 percent of the population. However, this elite was not limited to people of direct Macedonian descent; it also included those who acquired Greek language and culture through formal or informal education. Alexander's conquests opened opportunities for people from many ethnic backgrounds to join the elite—a development that inevitably transfigured Greek culture itself.

The intermingling of East and West intensified with the movement of travelers, which the common use of the Greek language and the size of the kingdoms facilitated. Travelers included merchants and mercenaries and diplomats seeking political and economic advantages or opportunities to spy. Perhaps most instrumental in blending cultures were the artists and artisans who journeyed widely in search of patrons and prizes.

In this new, cosmopolitan world, even women traveled with a freedom unheard of in the classical Greek poleis. Female musicians, writers, and artists embarked on quests for honors and literary awards. One inscription on a commemorative stone recalls

"Aristodama, daughter of Amyntas of Smyrna, an epic poetess, who came to the city and gave several readings of her own poems." The citizens were so pleased with this poet's work that they granted her citizenship. During such readings, authors shared experiences from one part of the world with the people of another, enhancing the diversity that marked this vibrant time.

Such diversity showed up vividly in the art of the period. For example, classical Greek artists had sometimes depicted black Africans in their works. In the Hellenistic age such portrayals grew more frequent. **Figure 3.6** exemplifies the cultural blending that occurred in the visual arts of this period. This bronze figure was cast in the Greek style, yet *Diverse art* it shows a youth from sub-Saharan Africa, possibly Nubia, which partook in continued close interaction with Egypt (discussed in Global Connections in Chapter 1). The subject's pose suggests that he may have once held a lyre, a traditional Greek (not African) musical instrument. The young man might well have been a slave, given that the Hellenistic kingdoms traded heavily in slaves of all ethnic backgrounds. Or he might have been one of the many traveling performers who earned a living by entertaining newly wealthy, cosmopolitan audiences.

All travelers left some evidence of their visits in the farthest reaches of the Hellenistic world. In the third century B.C.E., for example, the Greek philosopher Clearchus discovered a Greek-style city, complete with a gymnasium at the center, on the northern frontier of modern Afghanistan. In the gymnasium, Clearchus erected a column inscribed with 140 moral maxims taken from a similar pillar near the shrine of Apollo at Delphi. Like the Rock Edicts of Aśoka, the pillar of Clearchus preserves in stone the mingling of ideas at the fringes of the Hellenistic world.

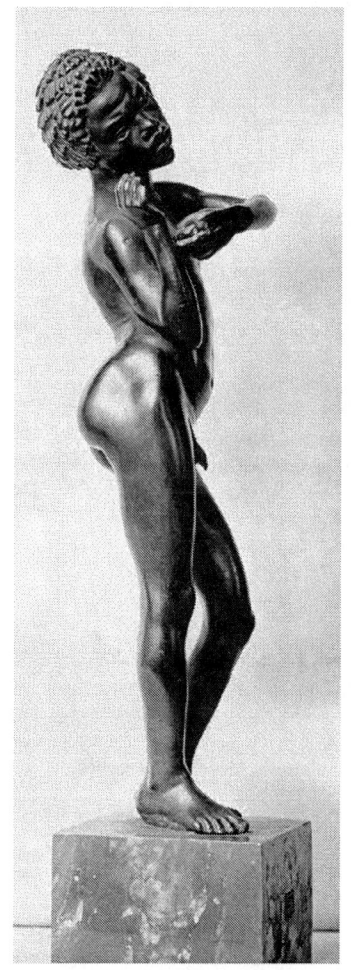

FIGURE 3.6 African Musician, second century B.C.E. The Hellenistic kingdoms were characterized by a movement of peoples and a resulting cultural blending, exemplified by this African musician playing a Greek musical instrument.

Struggles and Successes: Life in the Cosmopolitan Cities

The new cities founded by Alexander and his successors were in many ways artificial structures—they did not grow up in response to local manufacturing or commercial needs. Instead, they were simply created by rulers as showcases of their wealth and power. Expensive to maintain, these cities burdened local peasants with extra taxes and produced little wealth of their own. However, they played a crucial role as cultural and administrative centers, and they became a distinctive feature of Hellenistic life. Modeled on the Greek city-states, these cities still differed markedly from the poleis in several important ways, including the opportunities for women.

The travelers and the diversity of the cities helped break down the tight family life and female seclusion that had marked traditional Greek cities. Women were more free to move about in public. Furthermore, many texts indicate that Hellenistic women had more independence of *Women* action than their Greek counterparts. For example, a marriage contract explicitly insists that a couple will make joint decisions: "We shall live together in whatever place seems best to Leptines and Heraclides, deciding together." These new opportunities for independence made possible the situation at the opening of this chapter, when the young working woman ran off with her lover.

The Hellenistic cities also differed from their Greek counterparts in that they owed allegiance to larger political entities, the kingdoms. Now Greek monarchies had *Cities and kings*

thinking about DOCUMENTS

DOCUMENT 3.2

Cities Celebrate Professional Women

Throughout the Hellenistic age, there is evidence of women whose public service brought them to the attention of their communities. The following three inscriptions commemorate women who served as a physician, a public official, and a musician. Notice that the inscription for the public official indicates that she was the first woman to serve, so this reflects a change from previous practice.

1. Physician and Midwife: Phanostrate of Athens, fourth century [B.C.E.] Funeral inscription

Phanostrate . . . , the wife of Melitos, midwife and doctor, lies here. In life she caused no one pain, in death she is regretted by all.

2. Public Servant: Phile of Priene, first century [B.C.E.] Public inscription

Phile daughter of Apollonius and wife of Thessalus, the son of Polydectes, having held the office of stephanephoros, the first woman [to do so], constructed at her own expense the reservoir for water and the city aqueduct.

3. Harpist: Polygnota of Thebes, Delphi, 86 [B.C.E.] Public inscription

Since Polygnota, daughter of Sokrates, a harpist from Thebes, was staying at Delphi at the time the Pythian games were to be held, but because of the present war, the games were not held, on that same day she performed without charge and contributed her services for the day; and having been asked by the magistrates and the citizens, she played for three days and earned great distinction in a manner worthy of the god and of the Theban people and of our city, and we rewarded her also with five hundred drachmas; with good fortune, the city shall praise Polygnota, daughter of Sokrates, a Theban for her reverent attitude toward the god and her piety and her conduct with regard to her manner of life and art; and there shall be given by our city to her and to her descendants the status of a proxenos, priority in consulting the oracle, priority of trial, inviolability, exemption from taxes, a front seat at the contests which the city holds, and the right to own land and a house. . . .

SOURCES:

1. *Inscriptiones Graecae* 2.3(2), 6873, in *The Ancient World: Readings in Social and Cultural History*, ed. D. Brendan Nagle (Englewood Cliffs, NJ: Prentice Hall, 1995), p. 174.
2. *Die Inschriften von Priene*, 208, in *Women in the Classical World*, ed. Elaine Fantham et al. (New York: Oxford University Press, 1994), p. 156.
3. *Sylloge Inscriptionum Graecarum* (3) 738, in ed. D. Brendan Nagle, p. 174.

Analyze the Document

1. What are the contributions of each woman, and how do their communities recognize their contributions (money, acclaim, and so on)?
2. What evidence do you see for the continued importance of families in the Hellenistic world?
3. What aspects of Hellenistic cities allow women to become prominent?

---

replaced Greek city-states as the influential political form in the developing history of the West. The relationship between the Hellenistic kings and the new cities derived from both Macedonian and Greek traditions. For example, during and after Alexander's reign, monarchs advocated democracy within the cities they founded. Cities were governed by magistrates and councils, and popular assemblies handled internal affairs. In return, the kings demanded tribute and special taxes during times of war. However, these taxes were not onerous, and a king might even exempt a city from taxation. In response, many cities introduced a civic religious cult honoring their kings. As one example, to show this dual allegiance to both their king and city, citizens of the city of Cos had to swear the following oath: "I will abide by the established democracy . . . and the ancestral laws of Cos, . . . and I will also abide by the friendship and alliance with King Ptolemy."

These cities flourished under the patronage of their kings, but they also struggled with all the problems **[Urban problems]** endemic in any urban area. To feed the townspeople, city officials often had to import supplies from distant sources. Following Hellenistic ideas of a command economy, these urban leaders set grain prices and sometimes subsidized food to keep the costs manageable. They also regulated millers and bakers to prevent them from making large profits from cheap grain. Finally, the cities suffered the unavoidable problems of what to do about sewerage and water drainage; the largest urban centers had drainpipes under the streets for these purposes. Gangs of slaves owned by the city maintained the drainage system and cleared the streets.

City leaders gave little attention to public safety. They hired a few night watchmen to guard some public spaces, but for the most part, they considered safety a personal matter. Consequently, people mingling in the crowded markets or venturing out at night were often victims of robberies, or worse. Danger lurked everywhere, but especially in the many fires that broke out from residents' use of open flames to cook and heat their wooden homes. Despite the perils of fire, crime, and lack of sanitation, however, cities still offered the best hope of success for enterprising people.

The greatest of the new cities—Alexandria, Antioch, Seleucia—drew people from around the world. No longer connected to the original Greek city-states, such newcomers felt little obligation to participate in democratic politics or to profess loyalty to a clan or polis. Greeks, Phoenicians, Jews, Babylonians, Arabs, and others gathered in the cosmopolitan centers to make their fortunes. As the most ambitious among them took Greek names, the old divisions between Greek and "barbarian" blurred. Traditional family ties dissolved, too, as we saw in the story that opened this chapter.

City dwellers improved their lot in several ways, some of them advancing through successful military activities. The Greek Scopas, for example, unable to find work in his home city, "turned his hopes toward Alexandria," where he got a job in the army. *New opportunities* Within three years, Scopas had risen to command the armies of Ptolemy V. Women, too, had opportunities to participate in the public sphere. Document 3.2 offers examples of women who were remembered for their contributions to their cities.

Though cities opened up new opportunities, they also spawned miseries. Many poor people were forced to continue working well into their old age; indeed, the elderly market woman shown at the beginning of the chapter would have been a common sight in the Hellenistic period. The father in the chapter's opening story looked to his king to spare him an impoverished old age. His pleas probably went unheard, however; cities and their royal patrons tended to ignore the mounting problems of poverty. Slums cropped up, becoming just as characteristic of Hellenistic cities as the palaces of the wealthy and the libraries of the wise.

In some cities, destitute people designed institutions to help themselves. Artisans' guilds, for example, offered a sense of social connection to people bewildered by the large, anonymous cosmopolitan cities. Some people organized burial clubs, in which members contributed money to ensure themselves a decent interment at the end of lives that had little material security. Historical evidence suggests that some rich city dwellers worried about the possibility of social revolution. As one illustration of this fear, the citizens of a city in Crete were required to include the following statement in their oath of citizenship: "I will not initiate a redistribution of land or of houses or a cancellation of debts."

Patronage, Planning, and Passion: Hellenistic Art

The monarchs who were becoming fabulously wealthy did not spend much money on the urban poor. What did they do with the mounds of coins that filled their coffers? In part, they spent fortunes as patrons of the arts, commissioning magnificent pieces that continue to be treasured today. However, not all critics have admired the products of the Hellenistic artists. For example, early in the first century C.E., the prolific Roman commentator Pliny the Elder (23–79 C.E.) energetically discussed Greek art. A passionate admirer of classical Athenian art, Pliny claimed that after the accomplishments of Lysippus (ca. 380–ca. 318 B.C.E.), "art stopped." His dismissal of the Hellenistic world's artistic contributions has since been shared by many observers who admire the idealized poses of classical Greek works. But art did not stop with Lysippus; it merely changed as its center migrated from Athens to the great cosmopolitan centers of the East.

Classical Greek artists had been supported by public funding by democratic poleis. By contrast, Hellenistic artists received their funding from wealthy kings seeking to build and decorate their new cities. Royal *Royal patrons* patronage began with monarchs who wanted their newly established cities to reflect the highest ideals of Greek aesthetics. At the same time, this policy served the political agenda of promoting Greek culture. These rulers hired architects to design cities conducive to traditional Greek life, with its outdoor markets and meeting places, and employed artists to decorate the public spaces. Pergamum (see **Map 3.2**) posed a special challenge to architects: Its center was perched on a high hill, so city planners had to take the steep slopes into account in designing the city. In the end, they arranged the royal palaces at the top of the hill—visibly proclaiming the king's ascendancy—and the markets at the bottom. The layout of this magnificent city is typical of many Hellenistic urban centers.

Citizens in Pergamum shopped in the colonnaded building shown at the lower left corner of **Figure 3.7**. Higher up the hill was an altar to Zeus and higher still, a temple to Athena that served as the entrance to the library. The heights were dominated by the royal palaces and barracks. (The temple shown at the center of the hilltop was built later by Roman conquerors.) On the left side of the model, there are theater seats built into the hillside, where some 10,000 spectators could gather to watch the latest dramatic productions. The city preserved the gracious outdoor life of the classical Greek cities, yet was dominated by the majesty and power of the new kings.

After cities were designed, kings commissioned sculptors to decorate the great public buildings, especially temples. Throughout the Hellenistic period, sculptors also found a *Sculpture* market in the newly wealthy, who hired these artists to create works of beauty to decorate their homes. Hellenistic sculpture built on classical models in the skill with which artists depicted the human form and in the themes that harked back to the age of Greek heroes and the Trojan War. Still, Hellenistic artists departed from the classical style in significant ways. Classical Greek sculptors sought to portray the ideal—that is, they depicted scenes and subjects that were above the tumult and passion of this world. By contrast, Hellenistic artists faced passion and emotion head-on. Their works exhibit a striking expressiveness, violence, and sense of movement, along with contorted poses that demonstrate these artists' talents for capturing human emotion in marble.

Hellenistic artists also portrayed themes that the classical artists in Athens would have considered undignified or even demeaning. These themes included realistic portrayals of everyday life. For example, classical artists, in their search for ideal beauty instead of imperfect reality, would have ignored subjects such as the market woman shown at the beginning of the chapter. The boxer in **Figure 3.8** also exemplifies the contrast to the Olympic heroism that we saw in Chapter 2. Here the artist shows his knowledge of Greek idealism in the perfectly crafted hair and musculature of the bronze figure. Yet this boxer is tired, not heroic. He rests his taped hands on his knees and his shoulders sag in exhaustion, or perhaps defeat. The marks of his contest show clearly on his face—his cheek bleeds, his nose is broken, and his ear is deformed from too many blows. Many art critics, like Pliny, who mourned the "death of art," have condemned Hellenistic artists for not striving to portray perfection. Nonetheless, they had remarkable courage in showing the flawed reality of cosmopolitan life.

Resistance to Hellenism: Judaism, 323–76 B.C.E.

Much of Hellenistic art and life in the cosmopolitan cities reflected a deep and, in many ways, successful blending of classical Greek culture with that of the ancient Middle East and Egypt. Yet Alexander's desire to make "all mankind a single people" did not appeal to everyone in the Hellenistic world. Throughout their history, Jews had worked to preserve their distinctive identity, and this desire came directly into conflict with spreading Hellenism (ancient Greek culture). Although Judea remained an independent political unit under Alexander and the Ptolemies, the successor kingdoms offered opportunities for Jews from Palestine to trade and settle throughout the Hellenistic world. In the new multiethnic areas, urban Jews struggled to clarify and sustain their sense of identity. The most pious among them lived together in Jewish quarters where they could observe the old laws and maintain a sense of separate community. Alexandria and Antioch had substantial Jewish quarters, and most large cities had a strong Jewish presence.

Some Jews compromised with Hellenism, learning Greek and taking advantage of the opportunities available to those who at least had the appearance of Hellenism. As they learned to speak and write in Greek and studied the classical texts, some of their

<u>Hellenized Jews</u>

FIGURE 3.7 Restored Model of Pergamum Hellenistic rulers built great new cities such as Pergamum in what today is the country of Turkey. The city spread over a high hill, from the royal palace at the top to markets at the bottom. A new style of life developed in the royal cities.

FIGURE 3.8 Seated Boxer, second century B.C.E. This bronze sculpture reveals much about the Hellenistic world. Hellenistic peoples still praised the Greek sports contests, but they recognized and documented emotions other than the joy of victory. This boxer, for example, appears to be dejected, tired, and bruised.

traditional beliefs changed, especially where they sought to reconcile Judaism with Hellenism. Sometime in the third century B.C.E., the Hebrew Scriptures were translated into Greek, in the influential document known as the **Septuagint**. (The name derives from the Latin word for "seventy," recalling the legendary group of 72 translators who were credited with the accomplishment.) In great cities like Alexandria, Jews gathered in synagogues to pray in a traditional fashion, but in many of these centers of worship, the Scriptures were read in Greek.

In Palestine, too, Jews and Gentiles, or non-Jews, met and mingled. Palestine had many Greek settlements, and even in Jerusalem Jews faced the question of what it meant for them to compromise with Hellenism. Jesus Ben Sirach, a Jewish scribe and teacher in Jerusalem, wrote a text called *Ecclesiasticus* (ca. 180 B.C.E.) in which he scolded believers who had turned away from the traditional Jewish Law of Moses and warned them that God would exact vengeance for their impiety. In an ironic twist, his text was translated into Greek by his grandson.

These uncertainties within the Jewish community came to a head when the Seleucid kings wrested Palestine from the Ptolemies in 200 B.C.E. The pace of Hellenization quickened after this pivotal event. Both Jewish and pagan historical sources claim that the Seleucid king Antiochus IV (r. 175–163 B.C.E.) intended to change Jewish observance in order to "combine the peoples"—that is, to Hellenize the Jews. According to an early Jewish text, even the high priest of Jerusalem supported the king and "exercised his influence in order to bring over his fellow-countrymen to the Greek ways of life." Antiochus established Greek schools in Jerusalem and went so far as to enter Jewish contestants in the Greek-style athletic games celebrated at Tyre. In 168 B.C.E., he ordered an altar to Zeus to be erected in the Temple of Jerusalem and sacrifices to be offered to the Greek god. The Roman historian Josephus (75 C.E.) later described the sacrilege: "He sacrificed swine upon the altars and bespattered the temple with their grease, thus perverting the rites of the Jews and the piety of their fathers."

Antiochus's policies proved too much for pious Jews, and in ca. 166 B.C.E., Judas Maccabeus (Judas the Hammer) led an armed revolt against the Seleucids. (See Document 3.3.) The account of the **Maccabean Revolt** is preserved in a text titled *The First Book of the Maccabees*, probably written in 140 B.C.E. by a Jew in Judea. The author articulated the goal of Antiochus clearly: "Then the king wrote to his whole kingdom that all should be one people, and that each should give up his customs." This decree of Antiochus is reminiscent of Plutarch's praise of Alexander quoted at the beginning of this chapter, and it confirms the differing, intensely felt opinions that people often have about cultural blending.

In the end, the Maccabeans prevailed. In 164 B.C.E. the Jewish priests rededicated the Temple, and the Jews celebrated the restoration of their separate identity. The historian of *First Maccabees* wrote that "Judas and his brothers and all the assembly of Israel determined that every year at that season the days of the dedication of the altar should be observed with gladness and joy for eight days." This declaration instituted the feast of Hanukkah, which Jews continue to celebrate today.

The Maccabean revolutionaries established a new theocratic state of Judea, which the Seleucids were too busy with war on their eastern borders to challenge. The reinvigorated Jewish state continued its conquests of neighboring states, including Greek cities in Galilee, and by 76 B.C.E. the Jews had established a kingdom almost as extensive as

thinking about DOCUMENTS

DOCUMENT 3.3

Judas Maccabeus Liberates Jerusalem

In the first century C.E., the Jewish historian Josephus wrote a history of the Jews in which he described the revolt of Judas Maccabeus against the Hellenistic king Antiochus in ca. 166 B.C.E. As part of his desire to bring together his diverse peoples, Antiochus erected an altar to Zeus in the Temple at Jerusalem.

[Judas Maccabeus] overthrew the idol altar and cried out, "If," said he, "anyone be zealous for the laws of his country and for the worship of God, let him follow me"; and when he had said this he made haste into the desert with his sons, and left all his substance in the village. Many others did the same also, and fled with their children and wives into the desert and dwelt in caves; but when the King's generals heard this, they took all the forces they then had in the citadel at Jerusalem, and pursued the Jews into the desert; and when they had overtaken them, they in the first place endeavored to persuade them to repent, and to choose what was most for their advantage and not put them to the necessity of using them according to the law of war; but when they would not comply with their persuasions, but continued to be of a different mind, they fought against them on the Sabbath day, and they burned them as they were in the caves, without resistance, and without so much as stopping up the entrances of the caves. And they avoided to defend themselves on that day because they were not willing to break in upon the honor they owed the Sabbath, even in such distresses; for our law requires that we rest upon that day.

There were about a thousand, with their wives and children, who were smothered and died in these caves; but many of those that escaped joined themselves to Mattathias and appointed him to be their ruler, who taught them to fight even on the Sabbath day, and told them that unless they would do so they would become their own enemies by observing the law [so rigorously] while their adversaries would still assault them on this day, and they would not then defend themselves; and that nothing could then hinder but they must all perish without fighting. This speech persuaded them, and this rule continues among us to this day, that if there be a necessity we may fight on Sabbath days.

SOURCE: Josephus, "The Jewish Wars," in *The Great Events by Famous Historians*, vol. II, ed. Rossiter Johnson (The National Alumni, 1905), p. 247.

Analyze the Document

1. What religious motivations undergirded this war?
2. How did the Maccabees compromise their own religious beliefs to fight the war?
3. How did this conflict resemble modern controversies regarding fighting during Ramadan or Christmas?

---

that of Solomon (r. 970–931 B.C.E.) (see Chapter 1). Though they had revolted to preserve their cultural and religious purity, the new rulers proved intolerant of their Gentile subjects, forcing many to convert and insisting that non-Jewish infant boys be circumcised. These practices worsened the instability already plaguing the region.

THE SEARCH FOR TRUTH: HELLENISTIC THOUGHT, RELIGION, AND SCIENCE

Hellenistic rulers from Alexander on consciously spread Greek ideas and learning. To do this, they vigorously supported education, which they saw as key to the preservation of Greek ideals and the training ground for new Hellenized civil servants. Within these educated circles occurred most of the intellectual and cultural blending that created the brilliance of Hellenistic art as well as the struggles of cultural identity. However, these communities of the educated also proved a fertile ground for intellectual inquiry in which great minds eagerly sought truth about the world, religion, and the meaning of life.

A Life of Learning

Great speculations, however, began first in the schoolrooms. Families who wanted their boys to succeed invested heavily in education. At the age of 7, boys attended privately funded schools and practiced Greek and writing. The parchment samples of their

KEY DATES: INTELLECTUAL LIFE

ca. 400–ca. 325 B.C.E.	Diogenes advocates Cynicism
ca. 342–ca. 292 B.C.E.	Life of playwright Menander
ca. 335–ca. 280 B.C.E.	Life of physician Herophilus
ca. 312 B.C.E.	Zeno founds Stoicism
ca. 310–ca. 230 B.C.E.	Life of Aristarchus, who posited heliocentric universe
ca. 306 B.C.E.	Epicurus founds school of philosophy
ca. 300 B.C.E.	Euclid publishes *Elements* on mathematics
ca. 220 B.C.E.	Archimedes advances engineering

assignments reveal a strong anti-"barbarian" prejudice in which the culture of all non-Greeks was dismissed. Thus, even early schooling aimed to inculcate Greek values among non-Greek peoples. This indoctrination was reinforced by an emphasis on Homer's works as the primary literary texts.

At 14, boys expanded their education to include literary exercises, geography, and advanced studies of Homer. Successful students then continued their studies in the gymnasium, the heart of Hellenistic education and culture. Most cities boasted splendid gymnasia as their central educational institutions. Often the most beautiful building in the city, the gymnasium sported a running track, an area for discus and javelin throwing, a wrestling pit, and baths, lecture halls, and libraries. Here Greek-speaking boys of all ethnic backgrounds gathered, exercised naked, and finished an education that allowed them to enter the Greek ruling class.

Hellenistic kings cultivated education just as they served as patrons of the arts. They competed fiercely to hire sought-after tutors for their families and schools and to purchase texts for their libraries. The best texts were copied by hand on Egyptian papyrus or carefully prepared animal hide called parchment. (The word *parchment* derives from *Pergamena charta*, or "Pergamum paper," which refers to where the best-quality parchment was made.) Texts were prepared in scrolls rather than bound in books and were designed to be unrolled and read aloud.

This advocacy of education yielded diverse results. Many scholars produced nothing more than rather shallow literary criticism; others created literature that captured the superficial values of much of Hellenistic life; and some created highly sophisticated philosophy and science. The range of these works, however, contributed important threads to the tapestry of Western civilization.

Theater and Literature

The tragedies and comedies of classical Greek theater had illuminated profound public and heroic themes ranging from fate and responsibility to politics and ethics. Theater proved extremely popular in the Hellenistic cities as well. Though some cosmopolitan playwrights wrote tragedies, few of these works have survived. We do have many comedies from this era, which contrast so starkly with the classic Greek examples of this genre that this body of work is called New Comedy. Hellenistic plays were almost devoid of political satire and focused instead on the plights of individuals.

The best-known playwright of New Comedy is Menander (ca. 342–ca. 292 B.C.E.), whose works often centered on young men who fell in love with women who were unattainable for some reason. Most of these plots ended happily with the couples overcoming all obstacles. In general, New Comedy characters were preoccupied with making money or indulging themselves in other ways. **New comedies** This focus on individual concerns reflected the realities of cosmopolitan life—ruled by powerful and distant kings, individuals had limited personal power. Menander and the other playwrights of the age shed light on this impotence by focusing on the personal rather than on larger questions of good and evil.

A new genre of escapist literature—the Hellenistic novel—also emerged in this environment. The themes in these novels echo those of the plays: Very young men and women fall in love (usually at first sight), but circumstances separate them. They must endure hardships **Hellenistic novels** and surmount obstacles before they can be reunited. Surprisingly, most of these novels portray young women as resourceful and outspoken individuals. For example, a remarkable heroine in the novel *Ninos* dresses in gender-ambiguous clothing and leads a band of Assyrians to capture a fortified city. Although wounded, she makes a brave escape while elephants trample her soldiers.

Both the New Comedy and the Hellenistic novel sought to provide an escape from the realities of cosmopolitan life. Yet they also reflected new ideals in this society that often looked to the personal rather than to the polis for meaning. For example, unlike the writings of classical Greece, Hellenistic texts expressed an ideal of affection within marriage. The philosopher Antipater of Tarsus wrote, "The man who has had no experience of a married woman and children has not tasted true and noble happiness." The literature of the day also revealed an increased freedom of Hellenistic women to choose their partners. While families still arranged most marriages, some women (and men) began to follow their hearts in choosing a spouse. Woman also gained more freedom in divorce laws. Like men, they could seek divorce if their husbands committed adultery. One marriage contract from as early as 311 B.C.E. included clauses forbidding the husband to "insult" his wife with another woman. Taken together, all these themes expressed a new emphasis on love within the family.

Cynics, Epicureans, and Stoics: Cosmopolitan Philosophy

Like their literary counterparts, Hellenistic philosophers also narrowed the focus of their inquiry. Most of them no longer tackled the lofty questions of truth and justice that had preoccupied Socrates and Plato. Instead, they considered how an individual could achieve happiness in an age in which vast, impersonal kingdoms produced the kind of pain and weariness embodied by the market woman pictured at the beginning of the chapter.

The sensibilities of the Hellenistic age had been first foreshadowed by Diogenes (ca. 400–ca. 325 B.C.E.), an early proponent of the philosophic school called **Cynicism**. Diogenes was disgusted with the hypocrisy and materialism emerging around him in the transformed life of Athens as traditional polis life deteriorated. Diogenes and his followers believed that the only way for people to live happily in a fundamentally evil world was to involve themselves as little as possible in that world. The Cynics therefore claimed that the more people rejected the goods and connections of this world—property, marriage, religion, luxury—the more they would achieve spiritual happiness.

To demonstrate his rejection of all material things, Diogenes reputedly lived in a large tub. The carving in **Figure 3.9** shows him in the tub, oblivious to the lavish villa behind him. He is talking to Alexander the Great, enacting a likely apocryphal story in which Alexander offers the famous philosopher anything in the world. Diogenes simply asks Alexander to "stand out of my light and let me see the sun." The dog perched on top of the tub symbolizes Cynicism. (The word *cynic* derives from the Greek word *kunos*, which means "of a dog," or "doglike," because Cynics supposedly lived as simply and as filthily as dogs.)

Although Plato had dismissed Diogenes as "Socrates gone mad," Cynicism became popular during the Hellenistic period as people searched for meaning in their personal lives, rather than justice for their polis. Some men and women chose to live an ascetic life of the mind instead of involving themselves in the day-to-day activities of the Hellenistic cities. However, most found it difficult to reject material goods completely.

Other Hellenistic philosophies offered more practical solutions to the question of where to find personal happiness in an impersonal world. Epicurus (ca. 342–ca. 270 B.C.E.), for example, founded a school of philosophy that built on Democritus's (460–370 B.C.E.) theory of a universe made of atoms (described in Chapter 2). Envisioning a purposeless world of randomly colliding atoms, Epicurus proclaimed that happiness came from seeking pleasure while being free from pain in both body and mind. From a practical standpoint, this search for happiness involved pursuing pleasures that did not bring pain. Activities such as overeating or overdrinking, which ended in pain, should thus be avoided. In Epicurus's view, the ideal life was one of moderation, which consisted of being surrounded by friends and free of the burdens of the public sphere. His circle of followers included women and slaves. The Roman **Epicurean** Lucretius Carus (ca. 99–ca. 55 B.C.E.) articulated Epicurus's ideal: "This is the greatest joy of all: to stand aloof in a quiet citadel, stoutly fortified by the teaching of the wise, and to gaze down from that elevation on others wandering aimlessly in a vain search for the way of life." Of course, this "greatest joy" required money with which to purchase the pain-free pleasures that Epicurus advocated. His was not a philosophy that everyone could afford.

While Epicurus honed his philosophy in his private garden, the public marketplace of Athens gave rise to a third great Hellenistic philosophy: **Stoicism**. Named after *stoa*, the covered walkways surrounding the marketplace, the school of Stoicism was founded by Zeno (ca. 335–ca. 261 B.C.E.). Zeno exemplified the cosmopolitan citizen of the Hellenistic world, for he was born in Cyprus of non-Greek ancestry and spent most of his life in Athens.

At age 22, Zeno was a follower of Crates the Cynic, but later he abandoned his early connection to Cynicism, arguing that people could possess material goods as long as they were not emotionally attached to them. Indeed, the Stoic philosophers advocated indifference to external things. While this attitude paralleled Epicurus's desire to avoid pain, Zeno and

FIGURE 3.9 Diogenes and Alexander Diogenes argued that people should live a simple life, much like the dog shown sitting on the barrel in which the great philosopher lived. The artist included in this scene Alexander the Great, who reputedly admired the simple lifestyle that was so rare in the Hellenistic kingdoms.

the Stoics did not frame their philosophy in terms of the materialism of an atomic universe. Instead, they argued for the existence of a Universal Reason or God that governed the universe. As they explained, seeds of the Universal Reason lay within each individual, so everyone was linked in a universal brotherhood. In quasi-religious terms, this belief validated Alexander's supposed goal of unifying diverse peoples.

The Stoics' belief in a Universal Reason led them to explain the apparent turbulence of the world differently than the Epicureans. Stoics did not believe in random events but instead posited a rational world with laws and structures—an idea that would have a long history in the West. While individuals could not control this universe, they could control their own responses to the apparent vagaries of the world. Followers were implored to pursue virtue in a way that kept them in harmony with rational nature, not fighting it. The ideal Stoic renounced passions (including anger) even while enduring the pain and suffering that inevitably accompany life. Through self-control, Stoics might achieve the tranquillity that Epicureans and Cynics desired.

Cynicism, Epicureanism, and Stoicism had many things in common. Arising in settings where individuals felt unable to influence their world, they all emphasized control of the self and personal tranquility. Whereas the classical Greeks had found meaning through participation in the public life of their poleis, Hellenistic philosophers claimed that individuals could find contentment through some form of withdrawal from the turbulent life of the impersonal cosmopolitan cities. Moreover, all three philosophies appealed primarily to people with some measure of wealth. The indifferent, pain-free life of both the Epicureans and the Stoics required money, and the self-denial of the Cynics seldom appealed to really destitute people.

New Religions of Hope

For most ordinary people, the philosophies of the Hellenistic age had little relevance. These people looked instead to new religious ideas for a sense of meaning and hope. During this period, the gods and goddesses of the poleis gave way to deities that had international appeal and that were accessible to ordinary individuals—two features that marked a dramatic departure from previous religions of the West. Furthermore, the new religions offered hope in an afterlife that provided an escape from the alienation of the Hellenistic world. The international component paved the way for a blending of religious ideas—syncretism—and individuals felt a deeply passionate spiritual connection to their deities. The most popular new cults were known as **mystery religions** because initiates swore not to reveal the insights they received during the highest ceremonies. The historical roots of these cults stretched back to early Greece, Egypt, and Syria, but they acquired a new relevance throughout the Hellenistic era.

Mystery cults included worship of fertility goddesses like Demeter and Cybele, and a revitalized cult of Dionysus. However, the most popular was that of the Egyptian goddess Isis, who achieved a remarkable universality. Inscription stones offering her prayers claim that Isis ruled the world and credited her with inventing writing and cultivation of grain, ruling the heavenly bodies, and even transcending fate itself—the overarching destiny that even the old Homeric gods could not escape. Isis reputedly declared: "I am she who is called Lawgiver.... I conquer Fate. Fate heeds me." In other inscriptions, worshipers claimed that Isis was the same goddess that other peoples called by different names: "In your person alone you are all the other goddesses named by the peoples."

Figure 3.10, a marble relief from Athens, demonstrates religious syncretism in action. The piece was carved in the classical technique showing an apparently traditional Greek family worshiping at an altar. At the right of the altar, standing before the veil of mystery, is the Egyptian goddess Isis, depicted in traditional Greek style. The god seated at the right resembles Zeus, but he is Isis's brother/husband Osiris, the traditional Egyptian consort of the goddess-queen. This figure shows the syncretic nature of the new Hellenistic religions, in which patron deities of particular cities acquired international appeal. In their worship of these mysteries, the people of the Hellenistic kingdoms may have almost achieved Alexander's rumored ideal of universalism.

Men and women who wanted to experience the mysteries of these new religions believed that they had been summoned by a dream or other supernatural call. They took part in a purification ritual and an elaborate public celebration, including a procession filled with music and, sometimes, ecstatic dance in which people acted as if possessed by the goddess or god. Finally, the procession left the public spaces and entered the sacred space of the deity, where the initiate experienced a profound connection with the god or goddess. Many mysteries involved sacred meals through which people became godlike by eating the flesh of the deity. Such believers emerged from this experience expecting to participate in an afterlife. Here lay the heart of the new religious impulses: the hope for another, better world after death. The mystery religions would continue to draw converts for centuries, and perhaps paved the way for Christianity—the most successful mystery religion of all.

Hellenistic Science

The philosophic and religious longings of the Hellenistic world bred longstanding consequences for the future. People living in later large, impersonal cities turned to the philosophies of indifference and religions of hope. Equally impressive were the improvements on classical Greek science and technology that emerged in the Hellenistic learning centers. This flourish of intellectual activity was fostered in part by the generous royal patronage that made Alexandria and Pergamum scholastic centers, and in part by the creative blending of ideas from old centers of learning.

One scholar who benefited from the new Hellenistic world of learning was Herophilus (ca. 335–ca. 280 B.C.E.), who traveled to Alexandria from the Seleucid lands near the Black Sea to study medicine. The first physician to break the strong Greek taboo against cutting open a corpse, Herophilus performed dissections that led him to spectacular discoveries about human anatomy. (His curiosity even reputedly led him to perform vivisections on convicted criminals to learn about the motion of living organs.) His careful studies yielded pathbreaking knowledge: He was the first to recognize the brain as the seat of intelligence and to describe accurately the female anatomy, including the ovaries and fallopian tubes. However, all physicians were not as willing as Herophilus to treat the human body as an object of scientific study. Even in intellectually advanced Alexandria, dissection became unpopular, and subsequent physicians focused on techniques of clinical treatment rather than on anatomy. However, they made major strides in pharmacology, carefully studying the influence of drugs and toxins on the body.

[Medical advances]

In spite of these noteworthy advances, the most important achievements of the Hellenistic scientists occurred in the field of mathematics. Euclid (335–270 B.C.E.), who studied in Alexandria, is considered one of the most accomplished mathematicians of all time. In his most famous work, *Elements* (ca. 300 B.C.E.), Euclid presented a geometry based on increasingly complex axioms and postulates. When Euclid's patron, King Ptolemy, asked the mathematician whether there was an easier way to learn geometry than by struggling through these proofs, Euclid replied that there was no "royal road" (or shortcut) to understanding geometry. Euclid's work became the standard text on the subject, and, even today, students find his intricate proofs both challenging and vexing.

[Mathematics and astronomy]

Euclid's mathematical work laid the foundation for Hellenistic astronomy. Eratosthenes of Cyrene (ca. 275–ca. 195 B.C.E.), for example, used Euclid's theorems to calculate the circumference of the earth with remarkable accuracy—he erred only by about 200 miles. Aristarchus of Samos (ca. 310–ca. 230 B.C.E.) posited a heliocentric, or sun-centered, universe (against prevailing Greek tradition) and attempted to use Euclidean geometry to calculate the size and distance of the moon and sun. Although Aristarchus's contemporaries rejected his work, he and other astronomers introduced a striking change into the study of the heavens: They eliminated superstition and instead approached their work with mathematics.

Many Greek thinkers combined theoretical science with practical applications. One of the most influential in this regard was Hipparchus of Nicaea (160–125 B.C.E.). A brilliant mathematician, Hipparchus invented trigonometry—the mathematics of measuring angles—and applied these insights to measuring the heavens and the earth. His accomplishments demonstrated once again the benefits of cultural blending, for he introduced into Greece the Babylonian mathematical convention of measuring the circle in terms of 360 degrees (see Global Connections, Chapter 1), the method by which we

FIGURE 3.10 Isis and Osiris, later second century B.C.E. This sculpture is a votive relief, a carving that would have been placed in a temple and dedicated to fulfill a vow to a deity. Commissioned in Athens, it shows a family worshiping the Egyptian deities Isis and Osiris, who both look remarkably Greek in this rendering. The work illustrates the blending of religions that occurred in the Hellenistic world.

thinking about SCIENCE & TECHNOLOGY

Finding One's Way at Sea: The Invention of Latitude and Longitude

Long before the invention of global positioning system (GPS) devices, ancient mariners faced a nearly impossible task: finding their way when out of sight of land. To avoid disaster, sailors needed to be able to determine where they were in a vast ocean without any landmarks to guide them. But someone would first have to map and measure the earth before sailors would have the essential tools for calculating their location.

Hipparchus of Nicaea developed trigonometry, the mathematics of measuring angles, in the second century B.C.E. He used trigonometry to create an imaginary grid of latitude and longitude lines on the globe of the world (see **Figure 3.11**). Latitude (horizontal) lines measure the angle from the equator, and longitude (vertical) lines measure the angle from the prime meridian. All places on the earth have an address of sorts that we can express by their position on this grid, and because mathematics measures a circle in "degrees," we use this designation for the globe's address. Sicily, for example, is about 37 degrees north latitude and 14 degrees east longitude. This "address" is the same on Hipparchus's chart and in the GPS instruments we use today. Thus, with trigonometry's invention, early sailors got the tools to compute their position on the global grid.

Yet mapping the earth and having the means to calculate one's position was just a first step. Mariners still had to determine their location on the global grid *while sailing on a vast, featureless*

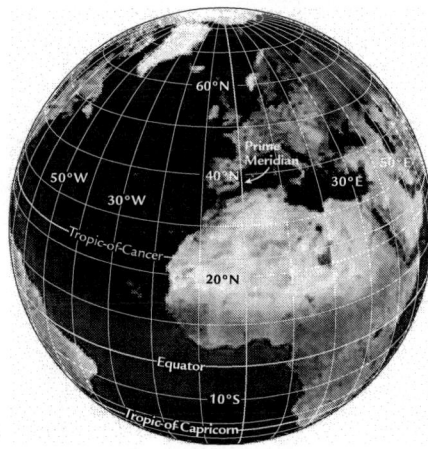

FIGURE 3.11 Global Map Divided by Latitude and Longitude Lines

ocean. Calculating latitude was relatively easy, for that required only measuring the angle between the horizontal and a fixed location in the sky—either Polaris or the sun. Longitude was far more difficult to measure, because as the earth rotates during a 24-hour day, the positions of Polaris and the sun move across the sky. One therefore has to know the exact time of day to calculate longitude. (For example, at the equator, a one-minute error in time causes about a 17-mile error in computing one's east-west position.)

Precise measurements of longitude while at sea would have to wait until the eighteenth century, when sophisticated clocks were invented that could compensate for the rough movements, caused by wind and waves, that had thrown off the accuracy of older clocks. Only then, with an accurate measure of the time of day, could a mariner calculate an exact reading of his longitude, just as we can do with our GPS devices.

Follow the development of navigation through the book. See, for example, the astrolabe in Figure 6.14 and the exploration of the world in Chapter 12.

Connecting Science & Society

1. How did Hipparchus's invention of trigonometry aid ancient sailors? What is the connection between measuring angles and finding one's way at sea?

2. What does the invention of latitude and longitude suggest about the relationships among science, people's practical needs, and inventions? What inventions (of new products or new processes) in your own lifetime show these relationships in action?

---

continue to measure the globe. Among Hipparchus's other practical applications were measuring the length of the lunar month within an error of one second, a stunning achievement, and being the first to use the ideas of latitude and longitude consistently to measure the earth. The map in Thinking About Science and Technology illustrates this significant application of trigonometry to empirical observation.

Another beneficiary of Greek mathematics was Archimedes (ca. 287–ca. 212 B.C.E.), often considered the greatest inventor of antiquity. Like so many cosmopolitan scholars, Archimedes, who was born in Syracuse, traveled to Alexandria to study. He later returned to Syracuse, where he worked on both abstract and practical problems. He built further on Euclid's geometry, applying the theorems to cones and spheres. In the process, he became the first to determine the value of pi—essential in calculating the area of a circle. He also applied geometry to the study of levers, proving that no weight was too heavy to move. He reportedly coined the optimistic declaration "Give me a place to stand, a long enough lever, and I will move the earth."

Archimedes did more than advance theoretical mathematics: He also had a creative, practical streak. For example, he invented the compound pulley, a

Archimedes

valuable device for moving heavy weights. His real challenge, however, came at the end of his life. As we will see in Chapter 4, Syracuse, the city of Archimedes' birth, was besieged by Rome, a rising power in the Mediterranean. Throughout the siege, Syracuse used both offensive and defensive weapons that Archimedes had invented. Yet the great man's inventions could not save the Sicilian city. The Romans ultimately prevailed, and in 212 B.C.E. Archimedes was struck down by a Roman soldier as he was drawing a figure in the sand.

Archimedes serves as an apt symbol for the Hellenistic world that produced him. He was educated with the best of Greek learning and combined it with the rich diversity of Asia and the Mediterranean lands—a blending that gave Western civilization dramatic impetus. The Hellenistic scientist died at the hands of a new people—the Romans—who embraced the practical applications of men like Archimedes and who next took up the torch of Western culture.

LOOKING BACK & MOVING FORWARD

Summary The Macedonian kings Philip and Alexander permanently transformed the life of the polis that had marked the glory of Greece. Their conquests of Greece, and then Egypt and the Asian portion of the Persian Empire, created a unique blend of these ancient civilizations. By establishing a ruling elite of Greeks and Macedonians in cities from the Mediterranean to India, Alexander and his successors spread key elements of Greek civilization. Yet they also reshaped the culture of the polis. Political and cultural centers moved from the Greek city-states to bustling cosmopolitan areas, where people from all over the Hellenistic world mingled. Some benefited greatly from the new opportunities for personal enrichment that cosmopolitan life offered; many more sank to unprecedented levels of poverty. Some peoples embraced the cultural blending; others rejected it.

Though the armies of the Hellenistic kings competed endlessly for land and power, kings still had the resources to support culture and learning. Scientists, artisans, and scholars of this complex age made impressive advances. However, a new force was gathering momentum in the West, one that would profoundly impact the fate of Hellenistic civilizations.

KEY TERMS

Ptolemies, *p. 84*
Rosetta Stone, *p. 86*
Seleucids, *p. 87*
Antigonids, *p. 88*
Septuagint, *p. 96*
Maccabean Revolt, *p. 96*
Cynicism, *p. 99*
Epicurean, *p. 99*
Stoicism, *p. 99*
mystery religions, *p. 100*

REVIEW, ANALYZE, & CONNECT TO TODAY

REVIEW THE PREVIOUS CHAPTERS

In Chapter 1—"The Roots of Western Civilization"—we explored the beginnings of city life in Mesopotamia. Chapter 2—"The Contest for Excellence"—looked at the life, culture, and political fortunes of the classical Greek city-states.

1. Contrast the culture of classical Athens with artistic and philosophic ideas of the Hellenistic world, and consider what contributed to the transformation in ideas.

2. Review the urban experiences of Mesopotamia and Greece, and compare and contrast them with those of people in the cosmopolitan cities of the Hellenistic world. What do you think are the most significant differences, and what elements of urban life remained constant?

3. Chapter 1 summarized the early history of the Jews. Consider how their past contributed to the Maccabean Revolt under the Seleucids.

ANALYZE THIS CHAPTER

Chapter 3—"The Poleis Become Cosmopolitan"—describes the conquest of Greece by Macedonia and traces the spread of Greek culture as far east as India, as vibrant new monarchies combined Greek culture with the diversity of many other peoples to create the Hellenistic world.

1. What contributed to the conquest of the Greek city-states by Macedonia? Consider both the weaknesses of the poleis and the strengths of Macedonia.

2. What elements of Hellenic culture were most transformed, and in what ways were the cultures of the Persian Empire changed by contact with Greek culture?
3. Describe the changes in economics and warfare that were introduced in the Hellenistic world.
4. How did the opportunities for women change under the Hellenistic monarchies?

CONNECT TO TODAY

Think about some of the major issues the Hellenistic kingdoms faced—for example, cultural diversity, urban problems, and people's struggles to find meaning.

1. Does the United States, as a society, share some of these problems today? If so, how have the American people responded?
2. Do religious struggles such as those experienced by the Jews in Hellenistic times have parallels in the contemporary world? If so, how have countries responded?

BEYOND THE CLASSROOM

THE CONQUEST OF THE POLEIS

Borza, Eugene N. *In the Shadow of Olympus: The Emergence of Macedon.* Princeton, NJ: Princeton University Press, 1992. A chronological survey seeking to trace the emergence of Macedonia as a major force in the political affairs of the fourth-century B.C.E. Balkans.

Cartledge, Paul. *Alexander the Great.* Woodstock, NY: Overlook Hardcover, 2004. A riveting narrative of the life of Alexander that argues he was more concerned with his own glory than with a spread of Hellenism.

Harding, Philip. *From the End of the Peloponnesian Wars to the Battle of Ipsus.* New York: Cambridge University Press, 1985. A sophisticated analysis of the late Greek world before its conversion into the Hellenistic world by Alexander's conquest.

Worthington, Ian. *Philip II of Macedonia.* New Haven, CT: Yale University Press, 2008. Detailed biographical account, nicely illustrated with maps, offering a compelling argument that Philip is to be credited with the military innovations that Alexander put so effectively to use.

THE SUCCESSOR KINGDOMS, 323–ca.100 B.C.E.

Chaniotis, Angelos. *War in the Hellenistic World: A Social and Cultural History.* Hoboken, NJ: Wiley-Blackwell, 2005. Excellent discussion of military history and the ways almost-constant warfare shaped the Hellenistic world.

Grant, M. *From Alexander to Cleopatra: The Hellenistic World.* New York: Scribner, 1982. A general survey of the Hellenistic world.

Green, Peter. *From Alexander to Actium.* Berkeley: University of California Press, 1990. A complex analysis of the Hellenistic world's politics, literature, art, philosophy, and science.

EAST MEETS WEST IN THE SUCCESSOR KINGDOMS

Bartlett, John. *Jews in the Hellenistic and Roman Cities.* London: Routledge, 2002. A collection of essays offering a wide-ranging analysis of Jews in the classical world.

Billows, Richard A. *Kings and Colonists: Aspects of Macedonian Imperialism.* New York: E.J. Brill, 1995. An in-depth study of the problems of Macedonian imperial rule.

Cohen, Getzel M. *The Hellenistic Settlements in Europe, the Islands and Asia Minor.* Berkeley: University of California Press, 1995. A good general history of Hellenistic settlement—its founders, early history, and organization.

Dmitriev, Sviatoslav. *City Government in Hellenistic and Roman Asia Minor.* Oxford: Oxford University Press, 2005. An examination of city governments in the Hellenistic world and of the social and administrative transformation of Greek society.

Laks, Andre, and Malcolm Schofield. *Justice and Generosity: Studies in Hellenistic Social and Political Philosophy.* New York: Cambridge University Press, 1995. A comprehensive guide to the social and political philosophies in a period of increasing interest to classicists, philosophers, and cultural and intellectual historians.

Stewart, Andrew. *Faces of Power: Alexander's Image and Hellenistic Politics.* Berkeley: University of California Press, 1993. A remarkable look at art as a legitimate source of historical evidence.

THE SEARCH FOR TRUTH: HELLENISTIC THOUGHT, RELIGION, AND SCIENCE

Clauss, James. *Companion to Hellenistic Literature.* Malden, MA: Blackwell, 2009. Essays exploring the social and intellectual context of literature from the Hellenistic period.

Hicks, R.D., trans. *Diogenes Laertius: Lives of the Eminent Philosophers*. Cambridge: Loeb Classical Library, 1922. An excellent primary source on the giants of speculative thought in Greece.

Martin, Luther H. *Hellenistic Religions: An Introduction*. New York: Oxford University Press, 1987. A well-written survey of Hellenistic religions, their characteristic forms and expressions, differences and relationships, and their place in the Hellenistic system of thought.

Pollitt, J.J. *Art in the Hellenistic Age*. New York: Cambridge University Press, 1986. An accessible and well-illustrated look at Hellenistic art as an expression of cultural experience and aspirations of the Hellenistic age.

Sharples, R.W. *Stoics, Epicureans and Sceptics*. New York: Routledge, 1996. A readable account of the principal doctrines of these Hellenistic philosophies.

Timeline

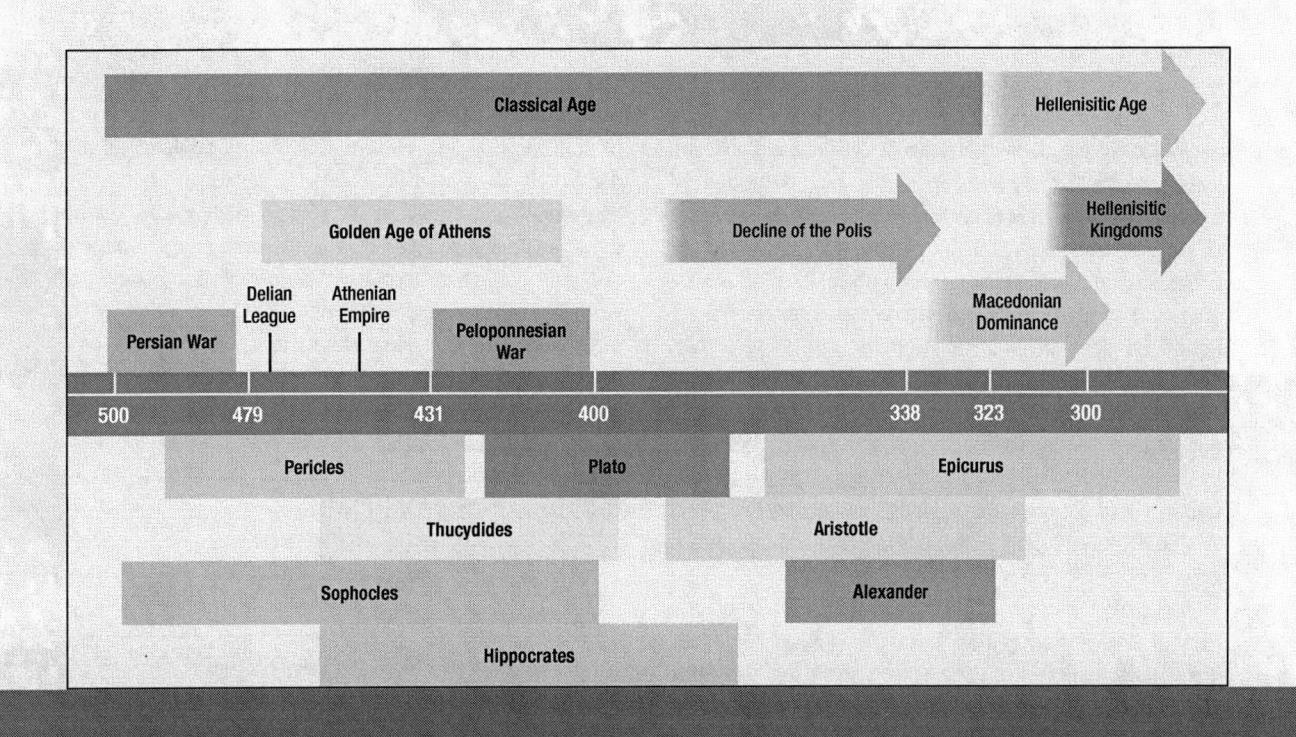

Period/Event	Dates
Classical Age	500–323
Hellenistic Age	323–31
Golden Age of Athens	
Decline of the Polis	
Hellenistic Kingdoms	
Persian War	500–479
Delian League	
Athenian Empire	
Peloponnesian War	431–400
Macedonian Dominance	338–323
Pericles	
Plato	
Epicurus	
Thucydides	
Aristotle	
Sophocles	
Alexander	
Hippocrates	

3 Classical and Hellenistic Greece

During the fifth and fourth centuries B.C.E. Greek civilization reached its apex. Historians have been fascinated with this period of Greek history for several reasons. First, Classical Greece is considered the most direct foundation of Western civilization, more so than the civilizations of the ancient Near East that preceded it. Second, many Greeks took a rationalistic and naturalistic approach to almost all fundamental questions; thus they developed scientific explanations for the world around them and applied reason to questions of politics, ethics, history, and philosophy. Third, the Greeks explored and experienced the range of human emotions, above all in their literature and in the triumphant and tragic wars they fought. Fourth, they produced stunning aesthetic creations, particularly in their sculpture, architecture, and drama. Fifth, Greeks strongly believed in the dignity and power of human beings and in balance and control as a human ideal. Sixth, the Greeks experienced and experimented with a large variety of political forms. In short, we often recognize ourselves and our own concerns when we study Classical Greece.

This chapter surveys Greek civilization as it evolved from the Classical Age (500–323 B.C.E.) to the Hellenistic Age (323–31 B.C.E.). Three overlapping topics are discussed. The first concerns the nature of the polis, of central importance to the ancient Greeks. Greeks perceived the polis as the appropriate political and geographic context for the good life, as well as the center of social, economic, religious, and cultural life. How should it be ruled? How strong was the obligation to one's own polis compared with an allegiance to the Greek world as a whole? What was the proper balance between the individual and the state? To explore these questions, it is useful to look at divisions between rival poleis of different political and social forms, as exemplified by the Peloponnesian War. It is also helpful to examine Greek ideas about the political nature of humans and in particular Greek ideas about democracy—one of the many forms of government experimented with by the Greeks. And finally, the student of Greek civilization can learn a great deal by investigating the tension between the individual and his or her obligation as a citizen of the polis.

The second topic is the nature of Greek thought. Historians have traditionally been impressed by the "modernity" of Greek thought. This is particularly the case with the scientific and rationalistic nature of Greek thought and the Greek tendency to generalize and abstract their ideas without resort to religious or supernatural assumptions. A number of questions are examined to demonstrate these traits. What was the nature of scientific thought for the Greeks? How did they apply such thought to medicine, history, and politics? What methodological differences were within this rationalistic thought? In what ways did they tend to abstract and generalize their ideas? What was the role of irrational thought and belief in the supernatural among large portions of Greek society?

The third topic questions the validity of the traditional view of Greece during the Classical and Hellenistic ages. We usually think of the Greeks, and especially the Athenians, as being balanced, democratic, just, individualistic, rational, naturalistic, liberal, and open. Their great fault, supposedly, was in their inability to unify politically: thus the fratricidal tragedy of the Peloponnesian War, the decline of the fourth century B.C.E., the conquest of the Macedonians, the shift of a center of gravity away from the polis to the eastern Hellenistic kingdoms, and the end of the Classical Age. How true is this perception? To address this question it is necessary to examine a number of related questions: What were Greek ideals during the Classical Age, particularly in Athens, the epitome of Greek culture at its height? What was the position of women in Greek society? What was the significance of slavery for Greece? How democratic were the Greeks, and how did their greatest thinkers evaluate this democracy? How can the "decline" of the fourth century be explained, and indeed should it be considered a "decline" or simply a change?

For Classroom Discussion

Debate the relative merits of Athens and Sparta. Use the description of Sparta by Xenophon in Chapter 2, the eulogy delivered by Pericles and reported by Thucydides, and the selections by Finley Hooper and Anthony Andrews.

Primary Sources

The History of the Peloponnesian War: The Historical Method

Thucydides

The first of the great historians lived in Greece during the Classical Age. They provide us with the most useful material we have to trace events of the period. The greatest of these was Thucydides (c. 471–c. 400), a high-ranking and wealthy Athenian who was a general early in the war and who was later banished from Athens for twenty years for losing a campaign against the Spartans. In The History of the Peloponnesian War Thucydides traces the origins of the war, its course, and its consequences for the participants and for the Greek world in general. In the following selection Thucydides outlines his approach and method as a historian and analyzes the origins of the conflict, distinguishing the immediate from the underlying causes.

SOURCE: From Francis R. B. Godolphin, ed., *The Greek Historians*, vol. I (New York: Random House, 1942), pp. 576–577. Reprinted by permission.

CONSIDER: *Thucydides' assumptions and reasoning; what modern historians might point to as evidence for questionable practices of historical writing or a lack of a scientific approach; how Thucydides distinguishes the "immediate" from the "real" causes of the Peloponnesian War.*

Yet any one who upon the grounds which I have given arrives at some such conclusion as my own about those ancient times, would not be far wrong. He must not be misled by the exaggerated fancies of the poets, or by the tales of chroniclers who seek to please the ear rather than to speak the truth. Their accounts cannot be tested by him; and most of the facts in the lapse of ages have passed into the region of romance. At such a distance of time he must make up his mind to be satisfied with conclusions resting upon the clearest evidence which can be had. And, though men will always judge any war in which they are actually fighting to be the greatest at the time, but, after it is over, revert to their admiration of some other which has preceded, still the Peloponnesian, if estimated by the actual facts, will certainly prove to have been the greatest ever known.

As to the speeches which were made either before or during the war, it was hard for me, and for others who reported them to me, to recollect the exact words. I have therefore put into the mouth of each speaker the sentiments proper to the occasion, expressed as I thought he would be likely to express them, while at the same time I endeavoured, as nearly as I could, to give the general purport of what was actually said. Of the events of the war I have not ventured to speak from any chance information, nor according to any notion of my own; I have described nothing but what I either saw myself, or learned from others of whom I made the most careful and particular enquiry. The task was a laborious one, because eye-witnesses of the same occurrences gave different accounts of them, as they remembered or were interested in the actions of one side or the other. And very likely the strictly historical character of my narrative may be disappointing to the ear. But if he who desires to have before his eyes a true picture of the events which have happened, and of the like events which may be expected to happen hereafter in the order of human things, shall pronounce what I have written to be useful, then I shall be satisfied. My history is an everlasting possession, not a prize composition which is heard and forgotten.

The greatest achievement of former times was the Persian War; yet even this was speedily decided in two battles by sea and two by land. But the Peloponnesian War was a protracted struggle, and attended by calamities such as Hellas had never known within a like period of time. Never were so many cities captured and depopulated—some by barbarians, others by Hellenes themselves fighting against one another; and several of them after their capture were repeopled by strangers. Never were exile and slaughter more frequent, whether in the war or brought about by civil strife. And rumours, of which the like had often been current before, but rarely verified by fact, now appeared to be well grounded. There are earthquakes unparalleled in their extent and fury, and eclipses of the sun more numerous than are recorded to have happened in any former age; there were also in some places great droughts causing famines, and lastly the plague which did immense harm and destroyed numbers of the people. All these calamities fell upon Hellas simultaneously with the war, which began when the Athenians and Peloponnesians violated the thirty years' truce concluded by them after the recapture of Euboea. Why they broke it and what were the grounds of quarrel I will first set forth, that in time to come no man may be at a loss to know what was the origin of this great war. The real though unavowed cause I believe to have been the growth of the Athenian power, which terrified the Lacedaemonians and forced them into war; but the reasons publicly alleged on either side were as follows.

The History of the Peloponnesian War: Athens During the Golden Age
Thucydides

The most famous "speech" presented by Thucydides in his History of the Peloponnesian War *is a eulogy delivered by the Athenian leader Pericles (c. 490–429 B.C.E.) during the winter of 431–430 B.C.E. for the Athenians killed during the first campaigns. In it Pericles compares the life and institutions of Athens with those of the enemy, Sparta. He explains to his fellow Athenians what made Athens so great. This funeral oration provides a superb idealized description of the Athenian city-state at its height.*

CONSIDER: *The reliability of this report of Pericles' speech, especially considering Thucydides' description of his methods in the previous document; the description of Athens, its institutions, and its people in this document; how Pericles compares Athens and Sparta and how a Spartan leader might reply; how Pericles defines the proper balance between Athenians' freedom as individuals and their commitments as citizens.*

"I will speak first of our ancestors, for it is right and becoming that now, when we are lamenting the dead, a tribute should be paid to their memory. There has never been a time when they did not inhabit this land, which by their valour they have handed down from generation to generation, and we have received from them a free state. But if they were worthy of praise, still more were our fathers, who added to their inheritance, and after many a struggle transmitted to us their sons this great empire. And we ourselves assembled here to-day, who are still most of us in the vigour of life, have chiefly done the work of improvement, and have richly endowed our city with all things, so that she is sufficient for herself both in peace and war. Of the military exploits by which our various possessions were acquired, or of the energy with which we or our fathers drove back the tide of war, Hellenic or barbarian, I will not speak; for the tale would be long and is familiar to you. But before I praise the dead, I should like to point out by what principles of action we rose to power, and under what institutions and through what manner of life our empire became great. For I conceive that such thoughts are not unsuited to the occasion, and that this numerous assembly of citizens and strangers may profitably listen to them.

"Our form of government does not enter into rivalry with the institutions of others. We do not copy our neighbours, but are an example to them. It is true that

---

SOURCE: From Francis R. B. Godolphin, ed., *The Greek Historians*, vol. I (New York: Random House, 1942), pp. 648–651. Reprinted by permission.

we are called a democracy, for the administration is in the hands of the many and not of the few. But while the law secures equal justice to all alike in their private disputes, the claim of excellence is also recognised; and when a citizen is in any way distinguished, he is preferred to the public service, not as a matter of privilege, but as the reward of merit. Neither is poverty a bar, but a man may benefit his country whatever be the obscurity of his condition. There is no exclusiveness in our public life, and in our private intercourse we are not suspicious of one another, nor angry with our neighbour if he does what he likes; we do not put on sour looks at him which, though harmless, are not pleasant. While we are thus unconstrained in our private intercourse, a spirit of reverence pervades our public acts; we are prevented from doing wrong by respect for authority and for the laws, having an especial regard to those which are ordained for the protection of the injured as well as to those unwritten laws which bring upon the transgressor of them the reprobation of the general sentiment.

"And we have not forgotten to provide for our weary spirits many relaxations from toil; we have regular games and sacrifices throughout the year; at home the style of our life is refined; and the delight which we daily feel in all these things helps to banish melancholy. Because of the greatness of our city the fruits of the whole earth flow in upon us; so that we enjoy the goods of other countries as freely as of our own.

"Then, again, our military training is in many respects superior to that of our adversaries. Our city is thrown open to the world, and we never expel a foreigner or prevent him from seeing or learning anything of which the secret if revealed to an enemy might profit him. We rely not upon management or trickery, but upon our own hearts and hands. And in the matter of education, whereas they from early youth are always undergoing laborious exercises which are to make them brave, we live at ease, and yet are equally ready to face the perils which they face. And here is the proof. The Lacedaemonians come into Attica not by themselves, but with their whole confederacy following; we go alone into a neighbour's country; and although our opponents are fighting for their homes and we are on a foreign soil, we have seldom any difficulty in overcoming them. Our enemies have never yet felt our united strength; the care of a navy divides our attention, and on land we are obliged to send our own citizens everywhere. But they, if they meet and defeat a part of our army, are as proud as if they had routed us all, and when defeated they pretend to have been vanquished by us all.

"If then we prefer to meet danger with a light heart but without laborious training, and with a courage which is gained by habit and not enforced by law, are we not greatly the gainers? Since we do not anticipate the pain, although, when the hour comes, we can be as brave as those who never allow themselves to rest; and thus too our city is equally admirable in peace and in war.

"For we are lovers of the beautiful, yet with economy, and we cultivate the mind without loss of manliness. Wealth we employ, not for talk and ostentation, but when there is a real use for it. To avow poverty with us is no disgrace; the true disgrace is in doing nothing to avoid it. An Athenian citizen does not neglect the state because he takes care of his own household; and even those of us who are engaged in business have a very fair idea of politics. We alone regard a man who takes no interest in public affairs, not as a harmless, but as a useless character; and if few of us are originators, we are all sound judges of a policy. The great impediment to action is, in our opinion, not discussion, but the want of that knowledge which is gained by discussion preparatory to action. For we have a peculiar power of thinking before we act and of acting too, whereas other men are courageous from ignorance but hesitate upon reflection. And they are surely to be esteemed the bravest spirits who, having the clearest sense both of the pains and pleasures of life, do not on that account shrink from danger. In doing good, again, we are unlike others; we make our friends by conferring, not by receiving favours. Now he who confers a favour is the firmer friend, because he would fain by kindness keep alive the memory of an obligation; but the recipient is colder in his feelings, because he knows that in requiting another's generosity he will not be winning gratitude but only paying a debt. We alone do good to our neighbours not upon a calculation of interest, but in the confidence of freedom and in a frank and fearless spirit.

"To sum up: I say that Athens is the school of Hellas, and that the individual Athenian in his own person seems to have the power of adapting himself to the most varied forms of action with the utmost versatility and grace."

Antigone

Sophocles

Much of our information about Greece comes from dramas, which played such an important educational, religious, and cultural role in Greek life. Sophocles (c. 496–406 B.C.E.), an Athenian of aristocratic birth and an important public official, was one of the greatest dramatists of the Classical Age. In Antigone, *which was first staged in 441, he focused on the conflicts between social obligations and individual convictions, between political and moral conscience. The first excerpt is a speech by Creon, King of Thebes, to his counselors. He refers*

SOURCE: *Sophocles: Three Tragedies,* trans. H. D. F. Kitto (© Oxford University Press, London, 1962), pp. 8–9, 16–17, by permission of Oxford University Press.

to the recent strife in Thebes between the two sons of the tragically fallen King Oedipus. One of the sons, Polyneices, gathered Greek enemies of Thebes and attacked the city, which was defended by the other son, Eteocles. Both were killed in battle, and thus Creon, the brother of Oedipus, assumed the throne. A struggle arose between the strongwilled Antigone, Polyneices' sister, who felt compelled by dictates of blood and religion to give her brother a proper burial, and Creon, who felt that as ruler he had to uphold the authority of the state and punish rebellion. Here Creon justifies his decision to bury Eteocles honorably but to leave Polyneices unburied. In the second excerpt, Antigone justifies her burial of Polyneices and her disobeying the laws of the state.

CONSIDER: *The attitudes and ideals revealed in this selection; Creon's view of the duties of the ruler and how these duties conflict with obligations of conscience and religion; how Antigone replies to Creon; how the relation between the individual and the state presented in this document compares with the same relation presented in Pericles' funeral oration.*

CREON. My lords: for what concerns the state, the gods
Who tossed it on the angry surge of strife
Have righted it again; and therefore you
By royal edict I have summoned here,
Chosen from all our number. I know well
How you revered the throne of Laius;
And then, when Oedipus maintained our state,
And when he perished, round his sons you rallied,
Still firm and steadfast in your loyalty.
Since they have fallen by a double doom
Upon a single day, two brothers each
Killing the other with polluted sword,
I now possess the throne and royal power
By right of nearest kinship with the dead.

There is no art that teaches us to know
The temper, mind or spirit of any man
Until he has been proved by government
And lawgiving. A man who rules a state
And will not ever steer the wisest course,
But is afraid, and says not what he thinks,
That man is worthless; and if any holds
A friend of more account than his own city,
I scorn him; for if I should see destruction
Threatening the safety of my citizens,
I would not hold my peace, nor would I count
That man my friend who was my country's foe,
Zeus be my witness. For be sure of this:
It is the city that protects us all;
She bears us through the storm; only when she
Rides safe and sound can we make loyal friends.

This I believe, and thus will I maintain
Our city's greatness.—Now, conformably,
Of Oedipus' two sons I have proclaimed
This edict: he who in his country's cause
Fought gloriously and so laid down his life,
Shall be entombed and graced with every rite
That men can pay to those who die with honour;
But for his brother, him called Polyneices,
Who came from exile to lay waste his land,
To burn the temples of his native gods,
To drink his kindred blood, and to enslave
The rest, I have proclaimed to Thebes that none
Shall give him funeral honours or lament him,
But leave him there unburied, to be devoured
By dogs and birds, mangled most hideously.
Such is my will; never shall I allow
The villain to win more honour than the upright;
But any who show love to this our city
In life and death alike shall win my praise.

CREON. You: tell me briefly—I want no long speech:
Did you not know that this had been forbidden?
ANTIGONE. Of course I knew. There was a proclamation.
CREON. And so you dared to disobey the law?
ANTIGONE. It was not Zeus who published this decree,
Nor have the Powers who rule among the dead
Imposed such laws as this upon mankind;
Nor could I think that a decree of yours—
A man—could override the laws of Heaven
Unwritten and unchanging. Not of today
Or yesterday is their authority;
They are eternal; no man saw their birth.
Was I to stand before the gods' tribunal
For disobeying *them*, because I feared
A man? I knew that I should have to die,
Even without your edict; if I die
Before my time, why then, I count it gain;
To one who lives as I do, ringed about
With countless miseries, why, death is welcome.
For me to meet this doom is little grief;
But when my mother's son lay dead, had I
Neglected him and left him there unburied,
That would have caused me grief; this causes none.
And if you think it folly, then perhaps
I am accused of folly by the fool.

The Republic

Plato

Various city-states in Classical Greece, and particularly Athens, have been admired for their democratic institutions and practices. Yet Plato (c. 427–347 B.C.E.), the greatest

SOURCE: M. J. Knight, ed., and B. Jowett, trans., *A Selection of Passages from Plato for English Readers* (Oxford, England: The Clarendon Press, 1895), pp. 80–82.

political theorist of the time, was a harsh critic of democracy. An aristocratic Athenian who grew up during the Peloponnesian War, Plato became embittered by the trial and death of his teacher, Socrates, in 399. After an extended absence from Athens, Plato returned in 386 and founded a school, the Academy, where he hoped to train philosopher-statesmen in accordance with his ideals as expounded in The Republic. In the following selection from that work, Plato employs the dialogue form to examine democracy and its perils. This represents more than abstract thoughts, for at the time that it was written, there was a rivalry between democratic forms of government, best represented by Athens, and more structured authoritarian forms, represented by Sparta.

CONSIDER: *The strengths and weaknesses of Plato's argument; how Plato's view of (Athenian) democracy compares with the view of Pericles.*

And then democracy comes into being after the poor have conquered their opponents, slaughtering some and banishing some, while to the remainder they give an equal share of freedom and power; and this is the form of government in which the magistrates are commonly elected by lot.

Yes, he said, that is the nature of democracy, whether the revolution has been effected by arms, or whether fear has caused the opposite party to withdraw.

And now what is their manner of life, and what sort of a government have they? For as the government is, such will be the man.

Clearly, he said.

In the first place, are they not free; and is not the city full of freedom and frankness—a man may say and do what he likes?

'Tis said so, he replied.

And where freedom is, the individual is clearly able to order for himself his own life as he pleases?

Clearly.

Then in this kind of State there will be the greatest variety of human natures?

There will.

This, then, seems likely to be the fairest of States, being like an embroidered robe which is spangled with every sort of flower. And just as women and children think a variety of colours to be of all things most charming, so there are many men to whom this State, which is spangled with the manners and characters of mankind, will appear to be the fairest of States.

Yes.

Yes, my good Sir, and there will be no better in which to look for a government.

Why?

Because of the liberty which reigns there—they have a complete assortment of constitutions; and he who has a mind to establish a State, as we have been doing, must go to a democracy as he would to a bazaar at which they sell them, and pick out the one that suits him; then, when he has made his choice, he may found his State.

He will be sure to have patterns enough.

And there being no necessity, I said, for you to govern in this State, even if you have the capacity, or to be governed, unless you like, or to go to war when the rest go to war, or to be at peace when others are at peace, unless you are so disposed—there being no necessity also, because some law forbids you to hold office or be a dicast, that you should not hold office or be a dicast, if you have a fancy—is not this a way of life which for the moment is supremely delightful?

For the moment, yes.

And is not their humanity to the condemned in some cases quite charming? Have you not observed how, in a democracy, many persons, although they have been sentenced to death or exile, just stay where they are and walk about the world—the gentleman parades like a hero, and nobody sees or cares?

Yes, he replied, many and many a one.

See too, I said, the forgiving spirit of democracy, and the "don't care" about trifles, and the disregard which she shows of all the fine principles which we solemnly laid down at the foundation of the city—as when we said that, except in the case of some rarely gifted nature, there never will be a good man who has not from his childhood been used to play amid things of beauty and make of them a joy and a study—how grandly does she trample all these fine notions of ours under her feet, never giving a thought to the pursuits which make a statesman, and promoting to honour any one who professes to be the people's friend.

Yes, she is of a noble spirit.

These and other kindred characteristics are proper to democracy, which is a charming form of government, full of variety and disorder, and dispensing a sort of equality to equals and unequals alike.

We know her well.

Politics

Aristotle

Aristotle (384–322 B.C.E.), a student of Plato, the tutor of Alexander the Great, and the founder of the Lyceum (a school rivaling Plato's Academy), had a different approach to

SOURCE: Aristotle, *Politics*, trans. Benjamin Jowett (Oxford, England: The Clarendon Press, 1905), pp. 25–28, 239–241.

politics. Aristotle emphasized the collection and classification of facts, as in the biological and physical sciences. Although Aristotle believed that democracy was a deterioration of a more balanced, high-minded polis, his approach was more descriptive and thus seems less condemning of democracy than Plato's. This is reflected in the following selections from Politics. In the first passage Aristotle examines the political and social nature of humans, revealing the typically Greek assumption that it is part of human nature to be organized into a polis. In the second passage Aristotle analyzes democracy.

CONSIDER: *How the arguments of Aristotle and Plato compare in style and form; how Aristotle's description of democracy compares with Pericles' description of Athenian institutions; the characteristics of democracy listed by Aristotle that are generally not practiced today.*

Every state is a community of some kind, and every community is established with a view of some good; for mankind always act in order to obtain that which they think good. But, if all communities aim at some good, the state or political community, which is the highest of all, and which embraces all the rest, aims, and in a greater degree than any other, at the highest good. . . .

For governments differ in kind, as will be evident to any one who considers the matter according to the method which has hitherto guided us. As in other departments of science, so in politics, the compound should always be resolved into the simple elements or least parts of the whole. We must therefore look at the elements of which the state is composed, in order that we may see in what they differ from one another, and whether any scientific distinction can be drawn between the different kinds of rule.

He who thus considers things in their first growth and origin, whether a state or anything else, will obtain the clearest view of them. In the first place (1) there must be a union of those who cannot exist without each other; for example, of male and female, that the race may continue; and this is a union which is formed, not of deliberate purpose, but because, in common with other animals and with plants, mankind have a natural desire to leave behind them an image of themselves. And (2) there must be a union of natural ruler and subject, that both may be preserved. For he who can foresee with his mind is by nature intended to be lord and master, and he who can work with his body is a subject, and by nature a slave; hence master and slave have the same interest. Nature, however, has distinguished between the female and the slave For she is not niggardly, like the smith who fashions the Delphian knife for many uses; she makes each thing for a single use, and every instrument is best made when intended for one and not for many uses. But among barbarians no distinction is made between women and slaves, because there is no natural ruler among them: they are a community of slaves, male and female. Wherefore the poets say,—

"It is meet that Hellenes should rule over barbarians;" as if they thought that the barbarian and the slave were by nature one.

Out of these two relationships between man and woman, master and slave, the family first arises. . . .

The family is the association by nature for the supply of men's everyday wants, and the members of it are called by Charondas "companions of the cupboard" and by Epimenides the Cretan, "companions of the manger." But when several families are united, and the association aims at something more than the supply of daily needs, then comes into existence the village. And the most natural form of the village appears to be that of a colony from the family, composed of the children and grandchildren, who are said to be "suckled with the same milk." And this is the reason why Hellenic states were originally governed by kings; because the Hellenes were under royal rule before they came together, as the barbarians still are. Every family is ruled by the eldest, and therefore in the colonies of the family the kingly form of government prevailed because they were of the same blood. . . .

When several villages are united in a single community, perfect and large enough to be nearly or quite self-sufficing, the state comes into existence, originating in the bare needs of life, and continuing in existence for the sake of a good life. And therefore, if the earlier forms of society are natural, so is the state, for it is the end of them, and the [completed] nature is the end. For what each thing is when fully developed, we call its nature, whether we are speaking of a man, a horse, or a family. Besides, the final cause and end of a thing is the best, and to be self-sufficing is the end and the best.

Hence it is evident that the state is a creation of nature, and that man is by nature a political animal. And he who by nature and not by mere accident is without a state, is either above humanity, or below it. . . .

The basis of a democratic state is liberty; which, according to the common opinion of men, can only be enjoyed in such a state—this they affirm to be the great end of every democracy. One principle of liberty is for all to rule and be ruled in turn, and indeed democratic justice is the application of numerical not proportionate equality; whence it follows that the majority must be supreme, and that whatever the majority approve must be the end and the just. Every citizen, it is said, must have equality, and therefore in a democracy the poor have more power than the rich, because there are more of them, and the will of the majority is supreme. This, then, is one note of liberty which all democrats affirm to be the principle of their state. Another is that a man should live as he likes. This, they say, is the privilege of a freeman; and, on the other hand, not to live as a man likes is the mark of a slave. This is the second characteristic of democracy, whence has arisen the claim of men to be ruled by none, if possible, or, if this is impossible, to rule and be ruled in turns; and so it coincides with the freedom based upon equality.

Such being our foundation and such the nature of democracy, its characteristics are as follows:—the election of officers by all out of all; and that all should rule over each, and each in his turn over all; that the appointment to all offices, or to all but those which require experience and skill, should be made by lot; that no property qualification should be required for offices, or only a very low one; that no one should hold the same office twice, or not often, except in the case of military offices; that the tenure of all offices, or of as many as possible, should be brief; that all men should sit in judgment, or that judges selected out of all should judge in all matters, or in most, or in the greatest and most important—such as the scrutiny of accounts, the constitution, and private contracts; that the assembly should be supreme over all causes, or at any rate over the most important, and the magistrates over none or only over a very few. Of all institutions, a council is the most democratic when there is not the means of paying all the citizens, but when they are paid even this is robbed of its power; for the people then draw all cases to themselves, as I said in the previous discussion. The next characteristic of democracy is payment for services; assembly, law-courts, magistrates, everybody receives pay, when it is to be had; or when it is not to be had for all, then it is given to the law-courts and to the stated assemblies, to the council and to the magistrates, or at least to any of them who are compelled to have their meals together. And whereas oligarchy is characterized by birth, wealth, and education, the notes of democracy appear to be the opposite of these—low birth, poverty, mean employment. Another note is that no magistracy is perpetual, but if any such have survived some ancient change in the constitution it should be stripped of its power, and the holders should be elected by lot and no longer by vote. These are points common to all democracies; but democracy and demos in their truest form are based upon the recognized principle of democratic justice, that all should count equally; for equality implies that the rich should have no more share in the government than the poor, and should not be the only rulers, but that all should rule equally according to their numbers. And in this way men think that they will secure equality and freedom in their state.

Household Management
Xenophon

Public life in Greece was dominated by men. Everyday life for women, even upper-class women in Athens, rarely extended beyond the bounds of the household. An image of this life for women, from a man's point of view, is provided by the Athenian historian and essayist Xenophon (c. 434–355 B.C.E.). In this excerpt from Oeconomicus (Household Management), Ischomachus and Socrates discuss marriage, women, and domestic life.

CONSIDER: *How women are perceived; the relationship of husband and wife; the differing roles of men and women.*

"Here's another thing I'd like to ask you," said I. "Did you train your wife yourself or did she already know how to run a house when you got her from her father and mother?"

"What could she have known, Socrates," said he, "when I took her from her family? She wasn't yet fifteen. Until then she had been under careful supervision and meant to see, hear, and ask as little as possible. Don't you think it was already a lot that she should have known how to make a cloak of the wool she was given and how to dole out spinning to the servants? She had been taught to moderate her appetites, which, to my mind, is basic for both men's and women's education."

"So, apart from that," I asked, "it was you, Ischomachus, who had to train and teach her her household duties?"

"Yes," said Ischomachus, "but not before sacrificing to the gods.... And she solemnly swore before heaven that she would behave as I wanted, and it was clear that she would neglect none of my lessons."

"Tell me what you taught her first...."

"Well, Socrates, as soon as I had tamed her and she was relaxed enough to talk, I asked her the following question: 'Tell me, my dear,' said I, 'do you understand why I married you and why your parents gave you to me? You know as well as I do that neither of us would have had trouble finding someone else to share our beds. But, after thinking about it carefully, it was you I chose and me your parents chose as the best partners we could find for our home and children. Now, if God sends us children, we shall think about how best to raise them, for we share an interest in securing the best allies and support for our old age. For the moment we only share our home....'"

"My wife answered, 'But how can I help? What am I capable of doing? It is on you that everything depends. My duty, my mother said, is to be well behaved.'"

SOURCE: Excerpts from *Not in God's Image: Women in History from Greeks to the Victorians* by Julia O'Faolain and Lauro Martines. Copyright © 1973 by Julia O'Faolain and Lauro Martines. Reprinted by permission of HarperCollins Publishers, Inc.

"'Oh, by Zeus,' said I, 'my father said the same to me. But the best behavior in a man and woman is that which will keep up their property and increase it as far as may be done by honest and legal means.'"

"'. . . And do you see some way,' asked my wife, 'in which I can help in this?'"

"'. . . it seems to me that God adapted women's nature to indoor and man's to outdoor work. . . . As Nature has entrusted woman with guarding the household supplies, and a timid nature is no disadvantage in such a job, it has endowed woman with more fear than man. . . . It is more proper for a woman to stay in the house than out of doors and less so for a man to be indoors instead of out. If anyone goes against the nature given him by God and leaves his appointed post . . . he will be punished. . . . You must stay indoors and send out the servants whose work is outside and supervise those who work indoors, receive what is brought in, give out what is to be spent, plan ahead what should be stored and ensure that provisions for a year are not used up in a month. When the wool is brought in, you must see to it that clothes are made from it for whoever needs them and see to it that the corn is still edible. . . . Many of your duties will give you pleasure: for instance, if you teach spinning and weaving to a slave who did not know how to do this when you got her, you double her usefulness to yourself, or if you make a good housekeeper of one who didn't know how to do anything. . . .' Then I took her around the family living rooms, which are pleasantly decorated, cool in summer and warm in winter. I pointed out how the whole house faces south so as to enjoy the winter sun. . . . I showed her the women's quarters which are separated from the men's by a bolted door to prevent anything being improperly removed and also to ensure that the slaves should not have children without our permission. For good slaves are usually even more devoted once they have a family; but good-fornothings, once they begin to cohabit, have extra chances to get up to mischief."

Medicine and Magic

Hippocrates

By the fifth century B.C.E. the Greeks had developed a scientific approach to knowledge. One of the many subjects reflecting this development was medicine. Hippocrates of Cos (c. 460–377 B.C.E.) founded a medical school that stressed careful observation and natural causes for disease. This method involved abandoning many religious or supernatural assumptions about diseases and rejecting various forms of divine healing. In the following selection attributed to Hippocrates, or at least his school, this approach is applied to the "sacred disease," the common term for epilepsy.

CONSIDER: *How scientific the assumptions in this document are; the points that might be rejected or applauded by modern doctors.*

I do not believe that the "Sacred Disease" is any more divine or sacred than any other disease but, on the contrary, has specific characteristics and a definite cause. Nevertheless, because it is completely different from other diseases, it has been regarded as a divine visitation by those who, being only human, view it with ignorance and astonishment. This theory of divine origin, though supported by the difficulty of understanding the malady, is weakened by the simplicity of the cure consisting merely of ritual purification and incantation. If remarkable features in a malady were evidence of divine visitation, then there would be many "sacred diseases." Quotidian, tertian and quartan fevers are among other diseases no less remarkable and portentous and yet no one regards them as having a divine origin. I do not believe that these diseases have any less claim to be caused by a god than the so-called "sacred" disease but they are not the objects of popular wonder. Again, no less remarkably, I have seen men go mad and become delirious for no obvious reason and do many strange things. I have seen many cases of people groaning and shouting in their sleep, some who choke; others jump from their bed and run outside and remain out of their mind till they wake, when they are as healthy and sane as they were before, although perhaps rather pale and weak. These things are not isolated events but frequent occurrences. There are many other remarkable afflictions of various sorts, but it would take too long to describe them in detail.

It is my opinion that those who first called this disease "sacred" were the sort of people we now call witch-doctors, faith-healers, quacks and charlatans. These are exactly the people who pretend to be very pious and to be particularly wise. By invoking a divine element they were able to screen their own failure to give suitable treatment and so called this a "sacred" malady to conceal their ignorance of its nature. . . .

They also employ other pretexts so that, if the patient be cured, their reputation for cleverness is enhanced while, if he dies, they can excuse themselves by explaining that the gods are to blame while they themselves did nothing wrong; that they did not prescribe the taking of any medicine whether liquid or solid, nor any baths which might have been responsible. . . .

It seems, then, that those who attempt to cure disease by this sort of treatment do not really consider the maladies thus treated of sacred or of divine origin. If the

---

SOURCE: From Hippocrates, *The Medical Works of Hippocrates,* trans. John Chadwick and W. N. Mann, 1950. Courtesy of Charles C. Thomas, Publisher, Springfield, Illinois, and Basil Blackwell, Publisher, Oxford, England.

disease can be cured by purification and similar treatment then what is to prevent its being brought on by like devices? The man who can get rid of a disease by his magic could equally well bring it on; again there is nothing divine about this but a human element is involved. By such claims and trickery, these practitioners pretend a deeper knowledge than is given to others; with their prescriptions of "sanctifications" and "purifications," their patter about divine visitation and possession by devils, they seek to deceive. And yet I believe that all these professions of piety are really more like impiety and a denial of the existence of the gods, and all their religion and talk of divine visitation is an impious fraud which I shall proceed to expose....

I believe that this disease is not in the least more divine than any other but has the same nature as other diseases and a similar cause. Moreover, it can be cured no less than other diseases so long as it has not become inveterate and too powerful for the drugs which are given.

Like other diseases it is hereditary. If a phlegmatic child is born of a phlegmatic parent, a bilious child of a bilious parent, a consumptive child of a consumptive parent and a splenetic child of a splenetic parent, why should the children of a father or mother who is afflicted with this disease not suffer similarly? The seed comes from all parts of the body; it is healthy when it comes from healthy parts, diseased when it comes from diseased parts. Another important proof that this disease is no more divine than any other lies in the fact that the phlegmatic are constitutionally liable to it while the bilious escape. If its origin were divine, all types would be affected alike without this particular distinction.

Individual Happiness

Epicurus

The Hellenistic Age's greater concern for individual happiness distinguished it from the preceding Classical Age. This concern is reflected in the teachings of Epicurus (342–268 B.C.E.), who founded a school in Athens and was a very influential Hellenistic philosopher. The following selection presents an excerpt from a letter to a student, in which Epicurus describes what he means by pleasure, and a section from his Fragments, *in which he also focuses on individual happiness but broadens his comments to justice and injustice.*

CONSIDER: *Whether this document supports the common association of Epicureanism with indulgence in luxury or sensual pleasures; how this document reflects differences between the Classical and Hellenistic ages.*

SOURCE: From *Epicurus: The Extant Remains,* trans. Cyril Bailey (1926), pp. 89–91, 95–97, 103, by permission of Oxford University Press.

When, therefore, we maintain that pleasure is the end, we do not mean the pleasures of profligates and those that consist in sensuality, as is supposed by some who are either ignorant or disagree with us or do not understand, but freedom from pain in the body and from trouble in the mind. For it is not continuous drinkings and revellings, not the satisfaction of lusts, nor the enjoyment of fish and other luxuries of the wealthy table, which produce a pleasant life, but sober reasoning, searching out the motives for all choice and avoidance, and banishing mere opinions, to which are due the greatest disturbance of the spirit.

Of all this the beginning and the greatest good is prudence. Wherefore prudence is a more precious thing even than philosophy: for from prudence are sprung all the other virtues, and it teaches us that it is not possible to live pleasantly without living prudently and honourably and justly (nor, again, to live a life of prudence, honour, and justice without living pleasantly). For the virtues are by nature bound up with the pleasant life, and the pleasant life is inseparable from them.

II. Death is nothing to us: for that which is dissolved is without sensation; and that which lacks sensation is nothing to us.

VIII. No pleasure is a bad thing in itself: but the means which produce some pleasures bring with them disturbances many times greater than the pleasures.

IX. If every pleasure could be intensified so that it lasted and influenced the whole organism or the most essential parts of our nature, pleasures would never differ from one another.

X. If the things that produce the pleasures of profligates could dispel the fears of the mind about the phenomena of the sky and death and its pains, and also teach the limits of desires (and of pains), we should never have cause to blame them: for they would be filling themselves full with pleasures from every source and never have pain of body or mind, which is the evil of life.

XII. A man cannot dispel his fear about the most important matters if he does not know what is the nature of the universe but suspects the truth of some mythical story. So that without natural science it is not possible to attain our pleasures unalloyed.

XXXIII. Justice never is anything in itself, but in the dealings of men with one another in any place whatever and at any time it is a kind of compact not to harm or be harmed.

XXXIV. Injustice is not an evil in itself, but only in consequence of the fear which attaches to the apprehension of being unable to escape those appointed to punish such actions.

Visual Sources

Education

Most of the few pictorial representations of Greek life that have survived are on pottery. What is portrayed on this early fifth-century B.C.E. cup (figure 3.1) is stylized. The intention is to show an aspect of everyday life that would be recognized by the viewers—the education of Greek boys. On the left a boy is being taught to play the lyre; on the right a boy is being taught to read. The figure on the far right is probably a slave chaperon, who served as a guard and an aid in moral upbringing. On the other side of the cup (not shown) students are learning another musical instrument and writing. Since there were no state schools, instruction was limited to those who could afford a private teacher.

CONSIDER: *The connections between the scenes depicted on this cup and Pericles' description of Athenian society.*

The Women's Quarters

According to Greek social ideals, women spent most of their lives indoors at home. While the majority of Greek women were not wealthy enough to live without working, elite women might approach the ideal. The scene on this fifth-century jar used by women to fetch water from a well or communal fountain (figure 3.2) depicts the activities that form part of this ideal. Here women have gathered to share cultural activities. In the center a woman sits reading aloud from a scroll. In front of her stands another woman holding a chest of scrolls. On each side, women listen to the recitation. The perfume flask on the upper left emphasizes that this is a scene from a wealthy woman's quarters.

CONSIDER: *What this reveals about social life for upper-class Greek women.*

The Dying Niobide: The Classical Balance

The Dying Niobide (c. 440), an example of the Classical style, mixes realism and idealism (figure 3.3). The human body is depicted more or less as it appears to the human eye. Suffering shows in the mouth, perhaps fear in the eyes. Yet it is difficult to say that this is a real individual. The body is not that of a real woman but of an ideal—the artist's vision of the perfect female body. This vision fits a broader Greek cultural ideal of the human form: It reflects a balance between the private statement and the public expression, between the individual and the community, which characterized Greeks during the Classical Age. The subject is also a lesson for the viewer. It shows the mythical story of an innocent woman being killed by the gods because of her

FIGURE 3.1 (© Bildarchiv Preussischer Kulturbesitz/Art Resource, NY)

FIGURE 3.2 (© The British Museum)

FIGURE 3.3 (© Erich Lessing/Art Resource, NY)

FIGURE 3.4 (Image copyright © The Metropolitan Museum of Art/Art Resource, NY)

mother's excess pride. Still, the Classical balance dominates, for while there is some action, it is not overly dramatic, not shocking. On the whole it invites the viewer to observe and contemplate as well as to enjoy.

CONSIDER: *How* The Dying Niobide *relates to the emotional and philosophical conflicts illustrated by the selection from* Antigone.

The Old Market Woman: Hellenistic Individualism

The Old Market Woman (second century B.C.E.) exemplifies the Hellenistic style (figure 3.4). Gone is the mixture of realism and idealism that characterized the Classical style. Instead, individualism and emotionalism are emphasized. A realistic individual is shown. She is far from ideal in almost every detail, from her facial lines to the basket she carries. One can empathize with the pains of old age and the situation of this individual, straining under an everyday task. No reference is made to a well-known myth or a heroic trait. This statue reflects the greater concern for the individual, the focus on the material aspects of life, and the technical brilliance of the Hellenistic Age.

CONSIDER: *The emotions, ideals, and experiences of the viewer being appealed to by the sculptors of this and the preceding statue.*

Geography and Political Configurations in Greece

Map 3.1 shows Athens and the surrounding areas during the fifth century B.C.E. Like many other Greek city-states, Athens was located near the sea on a cultivated plain surrounded by mountains. The city was walled and surrounded an easily defensible high point (the acropolis). The Athenians extended the walls to protect their access to their port at Piraeus. The surrounding mountains facilitated the Athenian defense of their lands while discouraging regular communication by land with other Greek city-states. The smallness of the Athenian plain and its easy access to the sea encouraged maritime commerce, especially to obtain foods the Athenians could not grow themselves. A large number of the other Greek city-states were actually inhabited islands and port

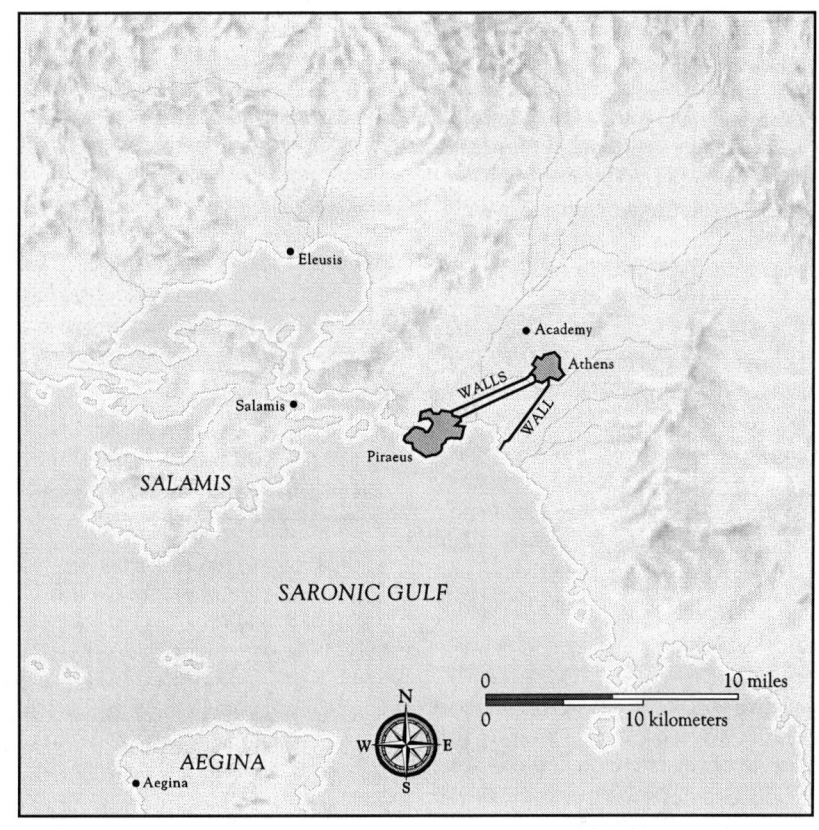

MAP 3.1 Athens in the Fifth Century B.C.E

cities lacking natural geographic protection and thus were vulnerable to attack from the sea. Athens took advantage of its own protected location and its neighbors' vulnerability to become a significant naval power.

CONSIDER: *How geography can help explain some aspects of the city-states, of the wars against Persia and between Athens and Sparta, and of the dominance over Greece achieved by Philip and Alexander.*

Secondary Sources

Goddesses, Whores, Wives, and Slaves: Women and Work in Athens

Sarah B. Pomeroy

The traditional image of Greek society is based primarily on what men did and thought. In recent decades historians have focused on the roles women played in Greek society and how those roles differed from men's roles. In the following excerpt from her well-known study of women in Greece and Rome, Sarah B. Pomeroy analyzes the economic roles played by women in Athens during the Classical Age. Here she emphasizes the effect of urban living on their lives.

CONSIDER: *How the position of women differed from that of men in Athens; the possible effects of urbanization on women; the kind of work women engaged in and how it was valued.*

By the late fifth century B.C.E., owing to the need for the safety afforded by city walls, urban living replaced farming for many Athenians. Thus, when one compares Sparta to Athens, it is necessary to remember that the former never comprised more than a settlement of villages, while Athens was one of the largest Greek cities. The effect of urbanization upon women was to have their activities moved indoors, and to make their labor less visible and hence less valued.

SOURCE: From *Goddesses, Whores, Wives, and Slaves* by Sarah B. Pomeroy. Copyright © 1975 by Sarah B. Pomeroy. Reprinted by permission of Schocken Books, Pantheon Books, a division of Random House, Inc.

Urban living created a strong demarcation between the activities of men of the upper and lower classes, as well as between those of men and women. Men were free to engage in politics, intellectual and military training, athletics, and the sort of business approved for gentlemen. Some tasks were regarded as banausic and demeaning, befitting slaves rather than citizens. Naturally, a male citizen who needed income was unable to maintain the ideal and was forced to labor in banausic employment. Women of the upper class, excluded from the activities of the males, supervised and—when they wished—pursued many of the same tasks deemed appropriate to slaves. Since the work was despised, so was the worker. Women's work was productive, but because it was the same as slaves' work, it was not highly valued in the ideology of Classical Athens. The intimacy of the discussions between heroines and choruses of female slaves in tragedy and the depictions of mistress and slave on tombstones imply a bond between slave and free, for they spent much time together and their lives were not dissimilar.

Women of all social classes worked mainly indoors or near the house in order to guard it. They concerned themselves with the care of young children, the nursing of sick slaves, the fabrication of clothing, and the preparation of food. The preparation of ordinary food was considered exclusively women's work.

Transporting water in a pitcher balanced on the head was a female occupation. Because fetching water involved social mingling, gossip at the fountain, and possible flirtations, slave girls were usually sent on this errand.

Women did not go to market for food, and even now they do not do so in rural villages in Greece. The feeling that purchase or exchange was a financial transaction too complex for women, as well as the wish to protect women from the eyes of strangers and from intimate dealings with shopkeepers, contributed to classifying marketing as a man's occupation.

Wealthier women were distinguished by exercising a managerial role, rather than performing all the domestic work themselves.

Poorer women, even citizens, went out to work, most of them pursuing occupations that were an extension of women's work in the home. Women were employed as washerwomen, as woolworkers, and in other clothing industries. They also worked as vendors, selling food or what they had spun or woven at home. Some women sold garlands they had braided. Women were also employed as nurses of children and midwives.

The Greeks: Slavery
Anthony Andrews

It has long been known that the Greeks, like other ancient peoples, practiced slavery. But focusing only on the glories of Greece sometimes leads one to forget how much slavery existed at that time and the role slavery played in supporting the Greek style of life. A historian who takes this into account is Anthony Andrews, a professor at Oxford University who has written a major text on the Greeks. In the following selection he examines Greek assumptions about slavery and the relations between slaves and masters in the Greek world.

CONSIDER: *How this analysis undermines an image of Athens as an open, democratic, and just society; what distinctions might be made between slavery in different times and societies—such as between slavery in Athens and in eighteenth-century America.*

In the broadest terms, slavery was basic to Greek civilisation in the sense that, to abolish it and substitute free labour, if it had occurred to anyone to try this on, would have dislocated the whole society and done away with the leisure of the upper classes of Athens and Sparta. The ordinary Athenian had a very deeply ingrained feeling that it was impossible for a free man to work directly for another as his master. While it is true that free men, as well as slaves, engaged in most forms of trade and industry, the withdrawal of slaves from these tasks would have entailed a most uncomfortable reorganisation of labour and property....

No easy generalisation is possible about the relations between slave and master in the Greek world, since the slave's view, as usual, is not known. In the close quarters of Greek domestic life, no distance could be preserved like that which English middle-class families used to keep between themselves and their servants—and the Greek was unlikely to refrain from talking under any circumstances. The closer relation of nurse and child, tutor and pupil, easily ripened into affection, nor need we doubt stories of the loyal slave saving his master's life on the battlefield, and the like. But at its best the relationship was bound to have unhappy elements, as that when a slave was punished it was with physical blows of the kind that a free man had the right to resent....

The domestic slave who was on good terms with his master stood some chance of liberation, and the slave "living apart" and practising his trade might hope to earn enough to buy his release. Manumission was by no means uncommon, though the practice and the formalities differed a good deal from place to place. The master often retained the right to certain services for a fixed period, or for his own lifetime. Some of those "living apart"

SOURCE: Anthony Andrews, *The Greeks* (New York: Random House, 1967), pp. 133, 138–139, 142.

prospered conspicuously, giving rise to disgruntled oligarchic comment that slaves in the streets of Athens might be better dressed than free men....

But the domestic slave with a bad master was in poor case, with little hope of redress, and the prospects were altogether bleaker for those who were hired out to the mines and other work—and we are not given even a distorted reflection of their feelings. But, after the Spartans had fortified their post outside Athens in 413, Thucydides tells us that over 20,000 slaves deserted to the enemy, the bulk of them "craftsmen" (the word would cover any sort of skilled labour and need not be confined to the miners of Laurium, though no doubt many of the deserters were from there). We do not know what promises the invaders had held out to them, still less what eventually became of them, but the suggestion is clear that the life of even a skilled slave was one which he was ready to fly from on a very uncertain prospect....

In the generation of Socrates, when everything was questioned, the justice of slavery was questioned also. Isolated voices were heard to say that all men were equally men, and that slavery was against nature. The defence of Aristotle, that some were naturally slaves, incapable of full human reason and needing the will of a master to complete their own, rings hollow to us, quite apart from the accident that "naturally free" Greeks might be enslaved by the chances of war. But this was a world in which slavery, in some form or other, was universal, and no nation could remember a time when it had not been so. It is not surprising that there was no clamour for emancipation. It has been convincingly argued that the margin over bare subsistence in Greece was so small that the surplus which was needed to give leisure to the minority could only be achieved with artificially cheap labour. If that is right, there was not much alternative for Greece. For Athens, it had come, by the opening of the sixth century, to a choice between reducing citizens to slavery or extensive import of chattel slaves from abroad. Only a greatly improved technology, something like an industrial revolution, could effectively have altered these conditions.

The Ancient Greeks: Decline of the Polis

M. I. Finley

Typically, the fourth century B.C.E. is seen as a period of decline, at least for the Greek polis. This decline and the reasons for it have long fascinated historians. Some point to the disillusionment following the Peloponnesian War, others to the inability of Greek city-states to control wars among themselves and ally in the face of the threat from Macedonia. In the following selection M. I. Finley, a leading historian of ancient times from Cambridge University, deals with this issue from a different point of view: The Greek polis could flourish only under unusual circumstances and only for a short period of time.

CONSIDER: *Additional factors that could explain the "decline" of the polis; what policies or developments might have delayed the decline of the polis; whether the fate of Greek civilization was tied to that of the polis.*

All this movement, like the constant *stasis*, marked a failing of the community, and therefore of the *polis*. The more the *polis* had to hire its armed forces, the more citizens it could no longer satisfy economically, and that meant above all with land, so that they went elsewhere in order to live; the more it failed to maintain some sort of equilibrium between the few and the many, the more the cities were populated by outsiders, whether free migrants from abroad or emancipated slaves (who can be called metaphorically free migrants from within)—the less meaningful, the less real was the community. "Decline" is a tricky and dangerous word to use in this context: it has biological overtones which are inappropriate, and it evokes a continuous downhill movement in all aspects of civilization which is demonstrably false. Yet there is no escaping the evidence: the fourth century was the time when the Greek *polis* declined, unevenly, with bursts of recovery and heroic moments of struggle to save itself, to become, after Alexander, a sham *polis* in which the preservation of many external forms of *polis* life could not conceal that henceforth the Greeks lived, in Clemenceau's words, "in the sweet peace of decadence, accepting all sorts of servitudes as they came."...

Even fourth-century Athens was not free from signs of the general decline. Contemporary political commentators themselves made much of the fact that whereas right through the fifth century political leaders were, and were expected to be, military leaders at the same time, so that among the ten generals were regularly found the outstanding political figures (elected to the office because of their political importance, not the other way round), in the fourth century the two sides of public activity, the civil and the military, were separated. The generals were now professional soldiers, most of them quite outside politics or political influence, who often served foreign powers as mercenary commanders as well as serving their own *polis*. There are a number of reasons for the shift, among which the

---

SOURCE: From *The Ancient Greeks* by M. I. Finley. Copyright © 1963 by M. I. Finley. Copyright renewed © 1991 by Paul O'Higgens and Charles Richard Watten. Used by permission of Viking Penguin, a division of Penguin Books USA, Inc.

inadequate finances of the state rank high, but, whatever the explanation, the break was a bad thing for the *polis*, a cleavage in the responsibility of the members to their community which weakened the sense of community without producing visibly better generalship. In the navy the signs took a different form. A heavy share of the costs still fell on the richest 1200 men and the navy continued to perform well, but there was more evasion of responsibility, more need than before to compel the contributions and to pursue the defaulters at law. The crews themselves were often conscripted; voluntary enlistment could no longer provide the necessary complements. No doubt that was primarily because the treasury was too depleted to provide regular pay for long periods, just as the unwillingness of some to contribute their allotted share of the expenses resulted from an unsatisfactory system of distributing the burden, rather than from lack of patriotism. Wherever the responsibility lay, however, the result was again a partial breakdown in the *polis*.

There is no need to exaggerate: Athens nearly carried it off, and the end came because Macedon, or at least Alexander, was simply too powerful. But Macedon did exist, and so did Persia and Carthage, and later Rome. The *polis* was developed in such a world, not in a vacuum or in Cloud-Cuckoo-Land, and it grew on poor Greek soil. Was it really a viable form of political organization? Were its decline and disappearance the result of factors which could have been remedied, or of an accident—the power of Macedon—or of inherent structural weaknesses? These questions have exercised philosophers and historians ever since the late fifth century (and it is noteworthy how the problem was being posed long before the *polis* could be thought of as on its way out in any literal sense). Plato wished to rescue it by placing all authority in the hands of morally perfect philosophers. Others blame the *demos* and their misleaders, the demagogues, for every ill. Still others, especially in the past century or so, insist on the stupid failure to unite in a national state. For all their disparity, these solutions all have one thing in common: they all propose to rescue the *polis* by destroying it, by replacing it, in its root sense of a community which is at the same time a self-governing state, by something else. The *polis*, one concludes, was a brilliant conception, but one which required so rare a combination of material and institutional circumstances that it could never be realized; that it could be approximated only for a very brief period of time; that it had a past, a fleeting present, and no future. In that fleeting moment its members succeeded in capturing and recording, as man has not often done in his history, the greatness of which the human mind and spirit are capable.

Alexander the Great
Richard Stoneman

If one argues that there were great individuals who changed the course of history, Alexander (356–323 B.C.E.) seems to have had the right characteristics. In his short career he led the Greeks in a stunning conquest of the Persian Empire. For most historians his death in 323 marks a convenient dividing line between the Classical and Hellenistic ages. It used to be common for historians, like W. W. Tarn, to laud Alexander's greatness in deeds as well as in dreams. But as exemplified by the following selection, most historians now reject this older view. Here Richard Stoneman evaluates Alexander's personality, plans, and accomplishments.

CONSIDER: *The connections between Alexander's accomplishments and his purposes; how Alexander, often thought of as a hero, might be criticized; why Alexander's empire did not last long.*

Alexander's career was the motive force for the spread of Hellenism throughout the western Mediterranean and the Near East, and his achievement thus provided the matrix in which the Roman Empire, Christianity and other important aspects of western civilisation could take root. . . . [However] such grandiose prospects were far from Alexander's imagining and . . . his own aims and ambitions were very different. It is time to draw some of the threads together and to bring those aims and ambitions face-to-face with his actual legacy.

On the assumption, current today among most scholars, that [Alexander's "Last Plans"] . . . represent genuine plans of Alexander, we can deduce that Alexander's megalomania was increasing. He had come to believe, in some degree, his own propaganda, that made him a son of the god Ammon and possibly divine himself. Buttressed by this sublime form of self-confidence (and he had never, at any stage of his career, been short of confidence), he had become increasingly ruthless in executing his purposes. Disloyalty was instantly punished, but corruption and peculation were treated with casualness as long as the perpetrator's loyalty was not in doubt. Opportunistic and flexible, Alexander had been as quick to lose his conquests in India as he had been to gain them, abandoning them when they no longer threatened his immediate position. Babylon and Iran had become the heartland of his empire, but what kind of empire was that to be?

Administration was never to his taste, and Augustus' observation that Alexander had done surprisingly little to set in order the vast empire he had gained is a telling

SOURCE: Richard Stoneman, *Alexander the Great* (New York: Routledge, 1997), pp. 92–94.

one. The king's state of mind seems to have been a strange one in his last months; besides his megalomania, he was perhaps already ill with the disease that killed him and suffering from a consequent *accidie*. The only activity he could conceive of that was worthy of his self-image was further conquest. Preparations were already far advanced for the invasion of Arabia, and it is not unreasonable to believe that he had plans to conquer the west—Italy and Carthage, and perhaps beyond. Italians and Carthaginians plainly believed it.

In hindsight it may seem inevitable that an empire based purely on rapid military conquest could not be held together. It was Alexander's pleasure to have his satraps loyal to him; he was not interested in imposing a uniform style of government on his empire, and the Greek lands were virtually forgotten. It was inevitable that such an empire would collapse once his own strong personality was removed. In addition, the fact that he did nothing to appoint a successor strengthened this inevitability....

But it was a world that spoke Greek. In addition, all the successor kings revered the memory of Alexander as their founder. All minted coins with his image....

If we turn now from Macedon to the wider world, we can see that, although it was far from Alexander's intention to mingle cultures for any kind of altruistic or philosophical motive, it was an end result of his actions that the cultures did mix. This happened at different rates, and in different degrees, in different parts of the empire. Greece, with its strong cultural traditions, was essentially unaffected by the empire. The city-states continued their own way under Macedonian overlordship, though they had to get used to honouring "Royal Friends." The same is largely true of the Greek cities of Asia Minor, which were able to continue as "independent cities" under the relatively weak rule of Antigonus and then Lysimachus. Some of the cities prospered remarkably, notably Pergamon which developed a literary and artistic culture to rival that of Alexandria itself. When the last Attalid king of Pergamon bequeathed his kingdom to Rome, the fate of the rest of Asia Minor was also sealed.

Greek Realities

Finley Hooper

Most historians stress the intellectual and scientific accomplishments of the Greeks, above all their extraordinary use of reason. In recent years historians have been pointing to the less rational and individualistic aspects of the Greeks. Finley

SOURCE: Reprinted from *Greek Realities* by Finley Hooper, by permission of the Wayne State University Press. Copyright © 1967, pp. 1–3.

Hooper exemplifies this trend in the following selection by focusing on the context of the supernatural and the demand to conform that typified everyday life for most Greeks.

CONSIDER: *Ways the primary documents support or refute Hooper's argument; considering this interpretation along with that of Andrews, whether it is a mistake to view the Greeks as democratic; the context Hooper is using for making his evaluation.*

For the most part, this history of the Greek people from the earliest times to the late fourth century B.C.E. is about a few men whose talents made all the others remembered. That would be true, in part, of any people. In ancient times, the sources of information about the average man and his life were very limited, yet one of the realities of Greek history is the wide disparity in outlook between the creative minority which held the spotlight and the far more numerous goatherders, beekeepers, olive growers, fishermen, seers, and sometimes charlatans, who along with other nameless folk made up the greater part of the population.

Romantic glorifications of Greece create the impression that the Greeks sought rational solutions and were imaginative and intellectually curious as a people. Actually, far from being devoted to the risks of rationality, the vast majority of the Greeks sought always the safe haven of superstition and the comfort of magic charms. Only a relatively few thinkers offered a wondrous variety of ideas in their tireless quest for truth. To study various opinions, each of which appears to have some element of truth, is not a risk everyone should take and by no means did all the ancient Greeks take it. Yet enough did, so as to enable a whole people to be associated with the beginnings of philosophy, including the objectivity of scientific inquiry.

The Greeks who belonged to the creative minority were no more like everybody else than such folk ever have been....

They were restless, talkative, critical and sometimes tiresome. Yet their lives as much as their works reveal Greece, for better or for worse, in the way it really was. After Homer, lyric poets went wandering from place to place, in exile from their native cities; before the time of Aristotle, Socrates was executed. If the Greeks invented intellectualism, they were also the first to suppress it. They were, in brief, a people who showed others both how to succeed and how to fail at the things which men might try.

As has often been said, the first democratic society known to man originated in Greece. For this expression of human freedom the Greeks have deservedly received everlasting credit. Yet it is also true that democratic governments were never adopted by a majority of Greek states, and those established were bitterly contested from within and without. In Athens where democracy had its best chance, the government was always threatened by the schemes of oligarchical clubs which sought by any means possible to subvert it. Ironically, Athenian democracy actually failed because of the mistakes of those whom it benefited most, rather than through the machinations of men waiting in the wings to take over. Then, as now, beneath the surface of events there persisted the tension between the material benefits to be obtained through state intervention and the more dynamic vitality which prevails where individuals are left more free to serve and, as it happens, to exploit one another.

A historian must be careful in drawing parallels. The number of individuals in a Greek democracy whose freedom was at stake would be considerably fewer than nowadays. The history of ancient Greece came before the time when all men were created equal. Even the brilliant Aristotle accepted at face value the evidence that certain individuals were endowed with superior qualities. He saw no reason why all men should be treated alike before the law. In fact, he allowed that certain extraordinary persons might be above the law altogether. Some men seemed born to rule and others to serve. There was no common ground between them.

The egalitarian concept that every human being has been endowed by his creator with certain inalienable rights was not a part of the Greek democratic tradition. Pericles, the great Athenian statesman, said that the Athenians considered debate a necessary prelude to any wise action. At the same time, he had a narrow view as to who should do the debating. At Athens, women, foreigners and slaves were all excluded from political life. The actual citizenry was therefore a distinct minority of those living in the city.

In other Greek cities, political power continued to be vested in a small clique (an oligarchy) or in the hands of one man, and often with beneficial results. Various answers to the same political and social problems were proposed and because there were differences there were conflicts. Those who sought to reduce the conflicts also sought to curb the differences, the very same which gave Greek society its exciting vitality. Here we have one of the ironies of human history. Amid bitter often arrogant quarrelsomeness, the Greeks created a civilization which has been much admired. Yet, the price of it has been largely ignored. Hard choices are rarely popular. The Greeks provide the agonizing lesson that men do struggle with one another and in doing so are actually better off than when they live in collective submission to a single idea.

CHAPTER QUESTIONS

1. Evaluate the role of democracy in explaining the rise to greatness of Athens as well as the nature of Athenian society during the Classical Age.

2. Many of the documents have dealt with the nature of the city-state, emphasizing some of the tensions and changes the Greeks experienced. Basing your answers on the information and arguments presented in these sources, what do you think were the advantages and disadvantages for the Greeks of being organized into such relatively small, independent units?

3. On the one hand, the sources have focused on various admired characteristics of Greek civilization, such as their art, drama, democracy, political thought, science, and philosophy. On the other hand, the documents reveal certain criticized qualities of Greek civilization, such as the instability of the polis, the relatively common occurrence of war, the nonegalitarian attitudes of the Greeks, the negative attitude toward women, and the support of slavery. Considering this, do you think that the Greeks have been overly romanticized or appropriately admired? Why?

ORATOR ADDRESSING THE ROMAN PEOPLE

Romans lived public lives in which men were encouraged to serve their city in public office. This calling required rhetorical skills to gain the support of Roman crowds, who gathered in the Forum to listen to speeches and shout for their favorite speakers. Since the crowds were so large, orators had to rely on broad gestures to sway masses outside the range of the human voice. Rome grew great served by men such as Aulus Metellus, the orator depicted here in a life-size bronze statue from the first century B.C.E.

Pride in Family and City

Rome from Its Origins Through the Republic, 753–44 B.C.E.

"No country has ever been greater or purer than ours or richer in good citizens and noble deeds; . . . nowhere have thrift and plain living been for so long held in such esteem." The Roman historian Livy (59 B.C.E.–17 C.E.) wrote a long history of Rome, in which he wanted to show how the heroic citizens of a small city-state became the masters of the world. He attributed their success to their upright character. At the same time Greek civilization was flourishing, a people had settled in the center of Italy, on the hills surrounding what would become the city of Rome. They were a serious, hardworking people who placed loyalty to family and city above all else. In time, this small group conquered the Italian peninsula, forging a coalition of peoples that enjoyed the benefits of peace and prosperity while relentlessly expanding through military conquest.

After overthrowing the monarchy, Rome developed a republican form of government, in which rich and poor citizens alike participated in a highly public legislative process. Within the city, men worked, relaxed, and talked in public spaces while noble women directed the household. Both nonnoble men and women worked in many areas of the city and contributed to an increasingly prosperous urban life.

Roman experience conquering and ruling the tribes of Italy prepared Roman armies to face foes farther afield. As Rome became a great power in the Mediterranean, it came into conflict with Carthage in North Africa. The two powers fought three wars—the Punic Wars—which destroyed Carthage. Rome was then drawn into wars in the eastern Mediterranean, in Greece, and into Asia Minor. These wars transformed Roman identity as Rome became a world power, in which an orator speaking in the Forum could hardly address the problems of the far-flung lands, and the republican form of government was no longer effective. Conquests funneled untold wealth and numerous slaves into Rome, and contact with Hellenistic civilization brought new culture, ideas, and values—causing Livy to lament the decline of "plain living" that he believed had made the Romans great.

At the end of this period, the stresses would prove too great, and the Roman Republic would end in civil war and murder. Yet despite its troubled demise, the Republic left a lasting legacy. Throughout the Mediterranean world, everyone knew of the proud city and its old families who had established laws, technology, and a way of life that exerted a continuing influence.

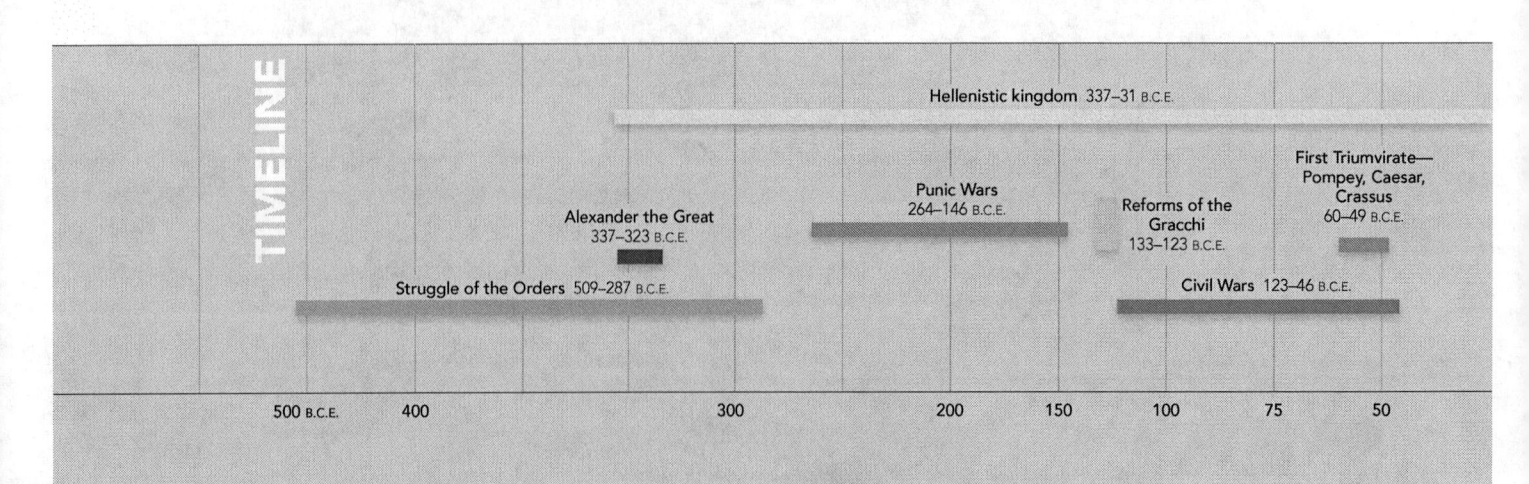

TIMELINE

- Struggle of the Orders 509–287 B.C.E.
- Alexander the Great 337–323 B.C.E.
- Hellenistic kingdom 337–31 B.C.E.
- Punic Wars 264–146 B.C.E.
- Reforms of the Gracchi 133–123 B.C.E.
- Civil Wars 123–46 B.C.E.
- First Triumvirate—Pompey, Caesar, Crassus 60–49 B.C.E.

500 B.C.E. — 400 — 300 — 200 — 150 — 100 — 75 — 50

PREVIEW

THE RISE OF ROME,
753–265 B.C.E.
Learn about the founding, development, and expansion of the Roman Republic.

FAMILY LIFE AND CITY LIFE
Study the values and daily life of the Romans.

EXPANSION AND TRANSFORMATION,
265–133 B.C.E.
Trace the expansion of the Republic and examine how this growth changed Rome.

THE HELLENIZING OF THE REPUBLIC
Analyze how expansion transformed Roman culture in engineering, architecture, and literature.

THE TWILIGHT OF THE REPUBLIC,
133–44 B.C.E.
Study the forces and events that led to the end of the republican form of government.

THE RISE OF ROME,
753–265 B.C.E.

On a warm spring day in 458 B.C.E., a Roman farmer was plowing the land adjacent to his small, round hut when the Senate recognized an imminent threat from a nearby tribe. In the face of such emergencies, the Roman Senate could offer one man supreme power for the duration of the crisis, giving him the title "dictator." The Senate offered the dictatorship to the farmer, Cincinnatus. He accepted the task and successfully led his armies to defeat the invaders. His grateful fellow villagers asked him to continue his leadership after the crisis, but he refused, preferring to return to his plow. Throughout the next centuries, this story of the strong, unassuming farmer Cincinnatus was told and retold by conservative Romans who looked back to the "ways of the fathers," *mos maiorum*, for models of virtue. (The American city Cincinnati was so named to honor George Washington—another savior farmer-general.) Romans preserved stories like this to remember their heroes and transmit their values to their families. Though they exist on the border between history and legend, these stories offer a glimpse of the origins of the greatness that would become Rome.

A Great City Is Founded

The historian Livy did not mind mixing history with myth, for he said: "There is no reason to object when antiquity draws no hard line between the human and the supernatural; it adds dignity to the past." Romans regularly remembered their history in terms of legends. Perhaps the most beloved of these stories told Romans how their city was founded. Like the story of Cincinnatus, the tale of the birth of Rome is filled with drama, conflict, heroes, and values. The tale begins with Aeneas, a Trojan hero who escaped from the destruction of his city after the Trojan War (described in Chapter 2). A royal female descendant of Aeneas decided to dedicate her life to serving the gods. She became pregnant by the god Mars and bore twin boys, Romulus and Remus. The princess's uncle did not believe in the miraculous conception, nor did he want her sons to threaten his rule, so he threw the infant boys in the Tiber River. Soon a shepherd found them being suckled by a wolf and raised them as his own sons. Many years later, after the boys had grown up, Romulus killed his brother during a quarrel and became the first king of the newly founded city of Rome. The traditional date of the founding of the city is 753 B.C.E., and archaeological evidence confirms the existence of a settlement there by this time.

Figure 4.1 shows a well-known statue from the fifth century B.C.E. that depicts the two brothers, Romulus and Remus, being suckled by the wolf that saved them. The age of the original statue—which was only of the nursing wolf—reveals how much the Romans treasured this myth of their city's founding. The twins were added about 2,000 years later, during the Renaissance, showing the continued attraction of the myth. Images like this helped Romans remember and carry on their valued traditions from generation to generation. Reflecting this sense of destiny and heroic action, Livy concluded that "with reason did gods and men choose this site for our city—all its advantages make it of all places in the world the best for a city destined to grow great."

FIGURE 4.1 Wolf of Rome, fifth century B.C.E. The Romans often looked back to their founding myth, in which a wolf nursed the brothers Romulus and Remus. This Roman statue celebrates that myth, though the nursing infants were a Renaissance addition. In ancient Rome, a live wolf was kept on the Capitoline Hill to remind Romans always to venerate their ancestors' history and ways.

Rome was located on hills overlooking a fertile, low-lying plain and the Tiber River, which afforded access to the Mediterranean Sea and to the inland regions. The geography of the surrounding Italian peninsula offered a number of advantages that would ultimately favor the growth of the young city. In contrast to Greece, whose mountainous terrain discouraged political unification, the large plains along Italy's western and eastern shores fostered trade, communication, and agriculture. The Apennine mountain range that marches down through the peninsula also creates abundant rainfall on the western plain. Therefore, Rome's fields were better situated for large-scale agriculture than had been possible for the Greek city-states. In addition, calm, accessible harbors along the western coast opened avenues for trade throughout the Mediterranean, which was further enhanced by Italy's central location in that important sea.

The initial settlers of Rome, like many of the other tribes in the region, were Indo-Europeans, those ubiquitous migrants from near the Black Sea whom we first saw in Chapter 1. They farmed, living in round huts and plowing their land. Cato the Elder (234–149 B.C.E.), a Roman political leader known for expressing traditional Roman values, summarized the Romans' pride in this way of life: "From farmers come the bravest men and sturdiest soldiers." Yet Rome also grew stronger through absorbing some of the culture and ways of its particularly talented neighbors. Greek colonies were well established in southern Italy and Sicily; Phoenician colonies prospered along the coast of North Africa. Most influential, however, were the Romans' immediate neighbors to the north, the Etruscans.

The Etruscan Influence

The Etruscans had appeared in Italy by 800 B.C.E., and for millennia historians argued about the origin of these peoples who did not speak an Indo-European language. Did they come from northern Europe, Italy, or North Africa? Modern DNA testing has confirmed the ancient historian Herodotus's claim that they arrived from Lydia in Asia Minor. The DNA evidence demonstrates that not only did the people come from modern Turkey, but they also brought their own cattle, setting that breed apart from the indigenous Italian cattle. The Etruscans settled the land and prospered. They traded all over the Mediterranean, importing luxury items and enjoying a good life.

Scholars have not yet deciphered all the Etruscan writings, so our best source of information about their daily life is their surviving artwork. **Figure 4.2** shows an Etruscan sarcophagus, or stone coffin, adorned by

FIGURE 4.2 Etruscan Sarcophagus, ca. 520 B.C.E. This sarcophagus (stone burial casket) was designed to hold cremated remains. The decoration celebrates the couple's life. They are shown reclining at dinner, an activity in which the wife and husband shared equal status.

a carving of a married couple. The couple recline together as they would have at dinner, and their poses suggest much affection between them. Indeed, women's active participation in this society surprised many of the Etruscans' contemporaries. The famous Greek philosopher Aristotle (384–322 B.C.E.), writing centuries later, described with some shock how even respectable Etruscan women joined in banquets with men.

Etruscan kings ruled Rome for a time, and the Romans learned a good deal from their civilization; indeed, much that we define as Roman was in fact Etruscan. For example, the Romans adopted Etruscan engineering and used their newfound skills to drain their lowland marsh, which formed the center of the growing city of Rome, and to build the great sewers that drained water from the city. They also adopted Etruscan architectural features—among them, the arch and vault construction—and modeled their temples on those of the Etruscans. Inside the temples, Romans learned to rely on divination—interpreting the will of the gods in the entrails of sacrificial animals—from Etruscan priests. Romans also adopted the toga, the white woolen robe worn by citizens, as well as the *fasces*, a bundle of rods surrounding an ax that was the powerful emblem of Roman authority.

Finally, the Romans acquired the Etruscan alphabet and began using it to write in their own Latin language. Note the statue of the orator shown at the beginning of this chapter. This perfect model of Roman life has his Roman name written in Etruscan letters on the bottom of his Etruscan-style toga. The Italian region of Tuscany is named after this early people who exerted an enduring influence on the growing culture of Rome.

The Roman Monarchy, ca. 753–509 B.C.E.

Like other ancient civilizations, the early Romans were ruled by kings, but to work out the details of the monarchy, historians have to struggle with combinations of history and legend. Romulus (ca. 753–ca. 715 B.C.E.) was the first king, and more unverifiable legends claim he was followed by four more monarchs. By the seventh century B.C.E., it seems, Rome was ruled by an Etruscan dynasty that governed for almost a century, from about 616 to about 509 B.C.E.

By the end of the sixth century B.C.E., the Roman aristocracy had come to chafe against the Etruscan kings' authority. Roman tradition holds that rebellion against the Etruscans erupted in response to the violation of Lucretia, a virtuous Roman matron. According to Livy, Sextus, son of the Etruscan king Tarquin the Proud, raped Lucretia at knifepoint. Her husband, Collatinus, told her not to blame herself, but after extracting her husband's promise to exact vengeance, she committed suicide. She was remembered as a chaste, heroic woman who chose death over dishonor. After her death, Romans rallied around the leadership of an Etruscan nobleman—Brutus—who joined Collatinus in a revolt that toppled the monarchy. The story of Lucretia illuminates the values of bravery and chastity held by early Roman men and women, but it also became a symbol of Romans' revulsion against kings, which would be a continuing theme throughout their history.

Overthrow of Etruscans

The legend accurately concluded that the Etruscan monarchy was overthrown, but the historical reality was more complex. All Romans did not support the overthrow of the monarchy—many in the lower classes relied on the monarchy to control the power of the noble families (the **patricians**), and some patricians who were related to kings also supported the monarchy. With these competing social forces, simply overthrowing a monarchy would not resolve social issues. However, just as the Greek poleis had overthrown their own kings and replaced them with oligarchies of nobles during their early history, the situation was repeated in Rome. The erection of a stable governmental form would require time and struggle.

Governing an Emerging Republic, 509–287 B.C.E.

With the overthrow of the Etruscan monarchy, the Romans established a republic, a Latin word that meant "public matter" (often rendered "public realm" or "commonwealth" in English), which they distinguished from the "private realm" of the Etruscan kings. For Romans, this meant that power rested with the people assembled together and that magistrates served the state. This influential vision of government was in striking contrast to that of the Hellenistic kings, who generally viewed their kingdoms as their own property, their spoils of war, their private realm.

In practice, the Republic consisted of three parts—consuls, the Senate, and the assemblies. Executive authority rested with two male **consuls** who were elected annually by an Assembly of Centuries organized by army groupings of 100 men, or "centuries." The consuls were advised by a body of elder statesmen, the **Senate**. Finally, adult male citizens met in **assemblies,** outdoor public gatherings in which the participants voted—by group, not as individuals—on issues that had previously been presented to them by leading statesmen. Beyond this governmental structure, the Roman people were separated by two general social distinctions into groups called patricians and plebeians. The patricians, old families who composed about 6 percent of the population, were recognized as socially and legally superior to everyone else. The **plebeians,** who made up the majority of the population, were the Republic's working people; their numbers, however, did not include slaves. Although the republican system seemed to offer a balance of power, in reality authority rested with the patricians, who sat in the Senate, and with the wealthy men who dominated the Assembly of Centuries.

Perhaps not surprisingly given that so few dominated the many, some individual patricians found ways to enrich themselves and their families. Many abused their power and oppressed the commoners in their charge, even enslaving many because of debts they incurred. By the fifth century B.C.E., social relations between patrician and plebeian had deteriorated enough that a social revolution occurred, which historians have called the **Struggle of the Orders.** Two main issues fueled this controversy: First, the poor wanted guarantees against the abuses of the powerful, and second, the wealthy plebeians wanted a role in government. This struggle was not a civil war, but instead a series of political reforms forced on the aristocracy from about 509 to 287 B.C.E.

Struggle of the Orders

Plebeians began their revolution by establishing themselves as a political alternative to the patricians. They withdrew from the city, held their own assemblies, established their own temple to counter the patrician cults, and even elected their own leaders, called **tribunes,** who were to represent plebeian interests. Tribunes could veto unfavorable laws and represent plebeians in law courts, for example. Patricians also had a practical reason to listen to the voice of the people through their tribunes, because they needed the plebeians to fight in the infantry. Just as Greek citizens forced concessions from aristocrats who needed armies, Roman citizen-soldiers threatened to refuse military service unless some of their demands were met. This was an effective threat; slowly, plebeians gained in political skill and, through the pressure of their tribunes, extracted meaningful concessions.

Plebeians won a number of important rights: First they gained a written law code that could be consistently enforced. Between 451 and 449 B.C.E., the laws were written down and displayed in a form called the **Twelve Tables.** Subsequent Romans looked back proudly to this accomplishment, which established a Roman commitment to law that became one of Rome's most enduring contributions to Western culture. To mark the importance of the establishment of written law, Roman children continued to memorize the Twelve Tables for up to four centuries later. Plebeians also won the right to hold sacred and political offices. Although, in practice, offices more readily went to the wealthy, upward mobility was possible. Perhaps the greatest concession the plebeians eventually won was the right to marry patricians. This removed birth as the most serious impediment to the rise of talented and wealthy plebeians.

The plebeian struggle for representation culminated in 287 B.C.E., when the Tribal Assembly became the principal legislative body. **Figure 4.3** shows this new republican structure. This group was named because the assembly was organized in "tribes" or regions, urban and rural, where plebeians lived. Laws passed by the Tribal Assembly did not need Senate approval, but bound everyone—rich or poor. The resulting society in Rome contained three main social classes: patricians, wealthy plebeians—later called **equestrians** (or knights) because they could afford to be in the cavalry—and the poorer plebeians. Money and connections dominated Roman politics as patricians and equestrians fought to increase their power. In spite of these problems, Polybius believed the people retained important powers, as Document 4.1 describes.

Governing the Republic

As **Figure 4.3** shows, the Roman constitution was complex, but logical. All citizens participated in the two Assemblies that elected the magistrates who served the state. Roman men with money and influence could move through the *cursus honorum*, the career path of a successful public official. A man would be elected to each office for one year, and then (through the late Republic) automatically become a member of the Senate—that venerable institution which by now had no actual constitutional power but a great deal of influence. The Roman system probably worked in part because most of the political life took place within a more informal system.

Informal Governance: Patrons and Clients

From the earliest years of the Republic, Romans relied on semiformal ties to smooth social and even political intercourse. Powerful members of society, called patrons, surrounded themselves with less powerful people—clients—in a relationship based on informal yet profoundly important ties. Patrons provided clients with what they called "kindnesses," such as food, occasional financial support, and help in legal disputes. Clients consisted of people from all walks of life: aristocratic youths who looked to powerful patrons for help in their careers (or hoped to be remembered in a rich patron's will), businessmen who wanted to use a patron's political influence to profit in their enterprises, poets who needed money, or freed slaves who remained attached to their former owners. Because Rome remained overwhelmingly an agricultural society, the largest group of clients was small farmers, who depended on their patrons to help them survive in a land that was becoming dominated by powerful aristocratic landowners. Clients owed their patrons duties, such as financial and political support.

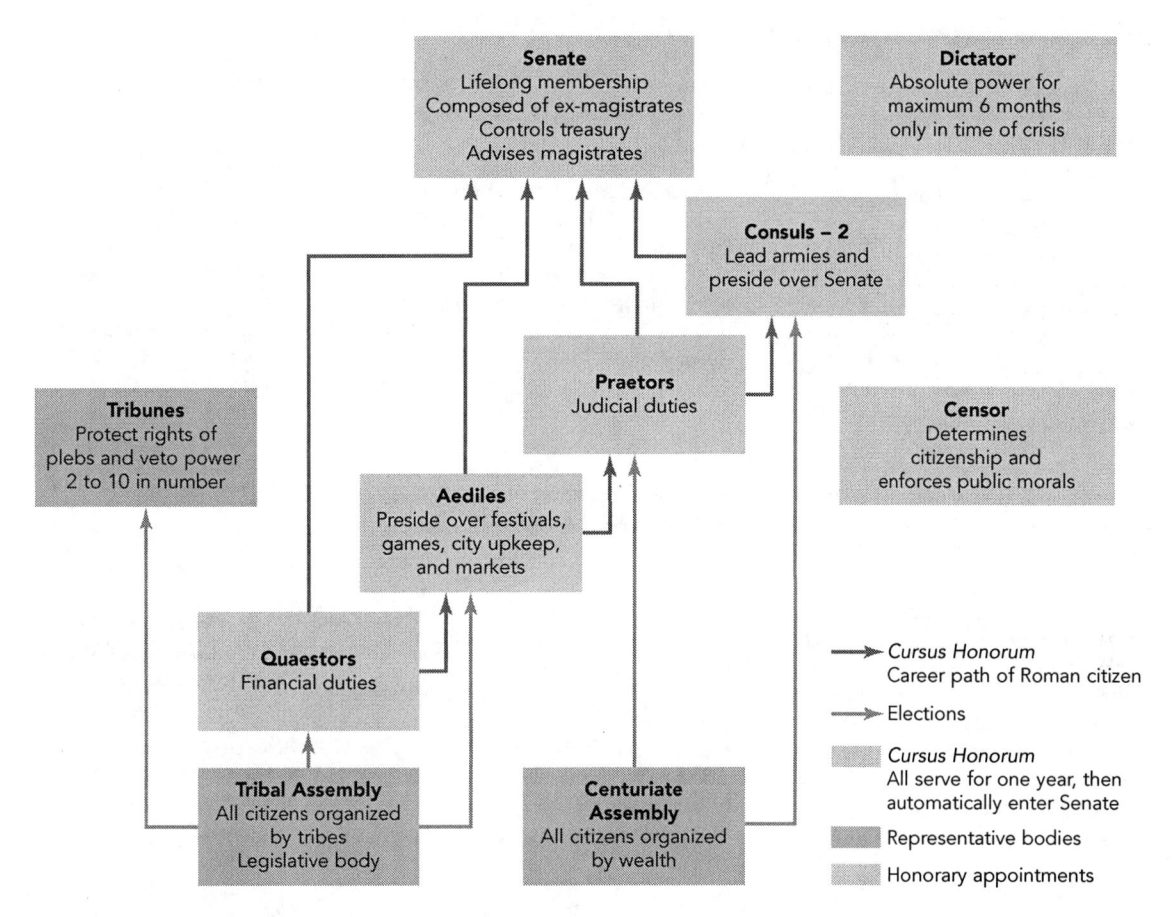

```
                          Senate                              Dictator
                   Lifelong membership                  Absolute power for
                  Composed of ex-magistrates            maximum 6 months
                     Controls treasury                  only in time of crisis
                     Advises magistrates

                                              Consuls – 2
                                            Lead armies and
                                           preside over Senate

                                    Praetors
                                  Judicial duties                    Censor
                                                                  Determines
    Tribunes                                                    citizenship and
 Protect rights of                                             enforces public morals
plebs and veto power         Aediles
  2 to 10 in number      Preside over festivals,
                         games, city upkeep,
                           and markets

          Quaestors                                      ──▶ Cursus Honorum
        Financial duties                                     Career path of Roman citizen

                                                         ──▶ Elections

                                                             Cursus Honorum
     Tribal Assembly              Centuriate                 All serve for one year, then
  All citizens organized          Assembly                   automatically enter Senate
        by tribes            All citizens organized          Representative bodies
     Legislative body             by wealth
                                                             Honorary appointments
```

FIGURE 4.3 The Roman Republic The Republic had a complex political structure that still influences governments today. This chart illustrates both the representative bodies and the positions the Roman assemblies elected. It also shows the *cursus honorum*, that is, the expected political path of a Roman man as he rose in public office.

Many clients gathered at their patrons' doors every morning as the cock crowed—failure to appear would jeopardize one's tie of clientage. This mixed crowd numbering in the tens to hundreds received ritual gifts, ensuring that the poorest would eat and the richest were remembered, and everyone was invited into the patron's home to greet him. The patron was supposed to exert a moral authority over his clients, helping them to be good citizens. As the Roman poet Horace (65–8 B.C.E.) wrote, "A wealthy patron governs you as a good mother might do and requires of you more wisdom and virtue than he possesses himself."

Clients' role

In the public world of Mediterranean society, clients provided patrons visible proof of their authority. After the morning greeting, clients accompanied their patron to the center of the city, where the day's business took place. A patrician surrounded by hundreds of clients was a man to be reckoned with. Political life of the Republic was conducted in the **Forum**, a large gathering area surrounded by temples and other public buildings. The Forum included the Senate chamber, the people's assembly, and a speaker's platform—called the Rostra—where politicians addressed the Roman people. **Map 4.1** shows the City of Rome with its important public spaces, including the Rostra and the Senate chamber. Clients would cheer their patron, shout down his opponents, and offer their votes to his agenda. An aristocrat who abandoned this public life that gave him stature and dignity was described sadly: "He will have no more entourage, no escort for his sedan chair, no visitors in his antechamber."

The Struggle of the Orders created a republic in which rich and poor both had a voice. In fact, it was a system dominated by wealth and an aristocracy that used its influence in the Senate and the Forum to preserve traditional privileges. However, the wealthy never forgot they needed the support of the Roman clients who gathered at their doors in the morning, shouted their support in the Forum, and manned Rome's armies.

Dominating the Italian Peninsula

As the Republic gathered strength, territorial wars between Rome and its neighbors broke out almost

thinking about DOCUMENTS

DOCUMENT 4.1

The Power of Public Opinion

The Greek historian Polybius (ca. 200–ca. 118 B.C.E.) was a great admirer of the Roman constitution, which he described in his Histories. *He thought the republican constitution would ensure a stable government. After he described the roles of the Senate and all the officers of the state, he turned to the more informal power of the people of Rome.*

After this one would naturally be inclined to ask what part is left for the people in the constitution, when the Senate has these various functions, especially the control of the receipts and expenditure of the exchequer; and when the Consuls, again, have absolute power over the details of military preparation, and an absolute authority in the field? There is, however, a part left for the people, and it is a most important one. For the people is the sole fountain of honour and of punishment; and it is by these two things and these alone that dynasties and constitutions and, in a word, human society are held together: for where the distinction between them is not sharply drawn both in theory and practice, there no undertaking can be properly administered,—as indeed we might expect when good and bad are held in exactly the same honour. The people then are the only court to decide matters of life and death; and even in cases where the penalty is money, if the sum to be assessed is sufficiently serious, and especially when the accused have held the higher magistracies. . . .

Again, it is the people who bestow offices on the deserving, which are the most honourable rewards of virtue. It has also the absolute power of passing or repealing laws; and most important of all, it is the people who deliberate on the question of peace or war. And when provisional terms are made for alliance, suspension of hostilities, or treaties, it is the people who ratify them or the reverse. These considerations again would lead one to say that the chief power in the state was the people's, and that the constitution was a democracy.

SOURCE: Polybius, *The Histories of Polybius* (London: Macmillan, 1889), in eds. Brian Tierney and Joan W. Scott, *Western Societies: A Documentary History*, vol. I, 2nd ed. (New York: McGraw-Hill, 2000), pp. 102–103 (page citations are to second edition).

Analyze the Document

1. What powers does Polybius describe as belonging to the Senate and consuls?
2. What powers does he attribute to the people? Do you think he's right that these powers are substantial?

---

annually. What led Rome into these repeated struggles? Romans themselves claimed that they responded only to acts of aggression, so their expansion was self-defensive. The reality, however, was more complicated. Rome felt a continual land hunger and was ever eager to acquire land to establish colonies of its plebeians. Roman leaders also had a hunger for glory and plunder that would let them acquire and reward clients—victorious generals were well placed to dominate Rome's political life. Thus, farmers often had to drop their plows, as Cincinnatus did, to fight.

By the beginning of the fourth century B.C.E., Rome was increasingly involved in wars in the Italian peninsula. From an early period, Romans identified themselves with fellow Latin tribes as they fought together against surrounding hillside tribes. By the early Republic, this alliance was known as the Latin League. Under Rome's leadership, the Latin League successfully defended its borders during the fifth and fourth centuries B.C.E. However, Rome's allies became increasingly resentful of Rome's leadership and revolted in 340 B.C.E. Two years later, Rome decisively defeated the rebellious allies and dissolved the League. Here, however, Rome showed its genius for administration. Instead of crushing the rebellious states, Rome extended varying degrees of citizenship to the Latins. Some received the rights of full Roman citizenship, while others became partial citizens who could earn full citizenship by moving to Rome. This benign policy allowed Rome with its allies to confront and conquer other peoples of the peninsula.

As **Map 4.2** shows, Rome acquired territories to the south and north. This was not a time of endless victories, however. In 390 B.C.E., the Gauls of northern Italy (a Celtic tribe) sacked much of the city before being bribed to leave with a large tribute payment, but it would be another eight hundred years before a foreign army once more set foot in the city. However, their invasion had weakened the Etruscan cities of the north, so by 295 B.C.E., Roman armies controlled the north of the peninsula. By the middle of the third century B.C.E., Rome dominated most of the Italian peninsula.

The Romans' successful expansion in part stemmed from their renowned courage and tenacity in battle. Most of their success, however, came from their generosity in victory. Although in **Map 4.2** it looks as if Rome had "united" Italy, in fact, the peninsula remained a patchwork of diverse states allied to Rome by separate treaties. These treaties were varied, but all were generous to conquered peoples. Romans allowed all the tribes to retain full autonomy in their own

thinking about GEOGRAPHY

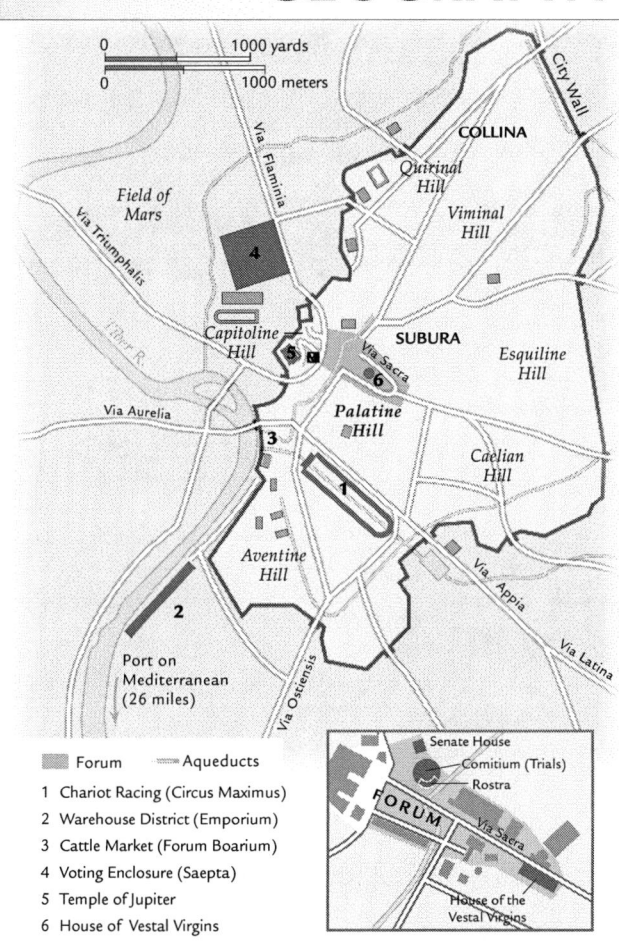

MAP 4.1

Rome During the Republic

This map shows the city of Rome during the late Republic. The inset pinpoints the locations of the important features of the Forum.

Explore the Map

1. Which elements in the Forum and at the center of the city show how political life and religious institutions dominated life in Rome?
2. What were the political implications of the fact that the famous slum district, the Subura, was located so near the Forum and the Palatine Hill, where the wealthiest Romans lived?

---

territories and to elect their own officials, keep their own laws, and collect their own taxes. These peoples were required to supply troops for Rome's armies and to avoid pursuing independent foreign policy. Many of the conquered peoples did have to give up some territory for Rome to use as colonies to feed their land hunger, but the colonies served to help Rome watch over and control its ever-widening borders of influence. As a result of Rome's leadership, the conquered territories at times enjoyed more peace and freedom than they ever had. Rome's sensible policy toward the territories bought the loyalty of many states and created a relatively cohesive unit that would fuel further imperial expansion.

FAMILY LIFE AND CITY LIFE

The great Roman orator Cicero (106–43 B.C.E.) wrote that the Romans were like other peoples except in their religious fervor: "In reverence for the gods, we are far superior." Perhaps more than other ancient civilizations, the Romans saw the world as infused with spirits; in their view, almost every space was governed by some divinity. Rome itself was guarded by three deities that protected the state—Jupiter, Juno, and Minerva—but there were gods for even smaller spaces. There were goddesses for the countryside, for the hills, and for the valleys. There were three gods to guard entrances—one for the door, another for the hinges, and a third for the lintel, the door's upper supporting beam. The remaining spaces within the home were equally inhabited by spirits that demanded worship and sacrifice.

A Pious, Practical People

Formal worship of the many gods and goddesses took place at the temples, where priests presided over sacrifices and divination officials looked for favorable omens in the entrails of sacrificial animals. The Vestal Virgins, six priestesses who presided over the temple of Vesta, goddess of the hearth, kept the sacred fire of the state hearth burning. (See the major Temple of Jupiter and the House of the Vestal Virgins in **Map 4.1**.)

According to the Roman people, their success hinged on proper worship, which meant offering sacrifices. Sacrifices could be as small as a drop of wine or a honeycake, or as large as an ox, but the Romans believed their destiny was deeply tied to their proper observation of religious rituals. When Rome was sacked by the Gauls in 390 B.C.E., Livy reported, one Roman general supposedly said, "All things went well when we obeyed the gods, but badly when we disobeyed them."

In addition to piety, Romans valued moral seriousness. These hardworking men and women prized duty to family, clients, patrons, and the Republic itself. They rejected the individualism of the Greeks and would have found the idea of Achilles sulking in his tent while his compatriots died incomprehensible.

thinking about GEOGRAPHY

Legend:
- Territory of Roman Citizens
- Roman Territorial Conquests
- Carthaginian Territories
- Greek Territories

Map labels: Po R., Adriatic Sea, UMBRIA 290, ETRURIA 280, CORSICA, Rome, Ostia, LATIUM, SAMNIUM 290, Lateria, APULIA 312, CAMPANIA, Beneventum, Naples, Tarentum, BRURRIUM 272, Tyrrhenian Sea, SARDINIA, Mediterranean Sea, Palermo, Messana, Rhegium, Ionian Sea, SICILY, Syracuse, Carthage

MAP 4.2

Italy, 265 B.C.E.

This map shows the tribes of the Italian peninsula who were conquered by the Romans, the dates of the conquests, and the nearby Carthaginian territories.

Explore the Map

1. How would the location of the Tiber River yield advantages for Rome's developing trade?
2. How would Rome's expansion in the western Mediterranean begin to intrude on Carthaginian holdings?
3. Why would Messana's location (where Rome and Carthage would first clash) be strategically important?

These serious men and women, who stressed collective responsibility and obedience to both secular and religious authority, would one day rule the entire Mediterranean world.

Loyalty to the Family

Roman religion, duty, and loyalty began in the family. A father, in theory, had complete authority over everyone in his household, including his wife, children, slaves, and even ex-slaves. The father served as guardian of the family's well-being and shared with his wife the responsibility for venerating the household gods. In addition to recognizing all the spirits who guarded the home, families worshiped their ancestors, whom they considered the original source of their prosperity. The best families displayed busts of their important ancestors in niches in the home. **Figure 4.4** shows a Roman man holding the busts of his forefathers, revealing the piety and ancestor worship so vital to Romans at that time.

Marriages in early Rome were arranged, to make politically advantageous alliances between families and ensure the continuation of the family through children. A woman could be given **Marriage patterns** in marriage in two ways. Her family of origin might transfer her to her husband's control, in which case she became part of his family and participated in the worship of his ancestors. Or she might remain under her father's "hand," never becoming a full part of her husband's family. In this case, the woman's family of origin kept more political and financial control of her resources. **Figure 4.5** shows a modest, serious Roman couple with their child. They do not touch, and they stand together looking into the distance. The couple in this gravestone contrasts strikingly with the affectionate Etruscan couple shown in **Figure 4.2** and suggests that Romans considered marriage a serious duty.

Despite the authority of husbands, women still played an important role in the family. They instilled the values of Rome in their children and raised them to be responsible and obedient citizens. Historical evidence such as letters indicate that mothers exerted as much stern authority as fathers and therefore wielded some political power through their sons.

The Challenges of Childhood

Birth in a Roman home always involved great risk to the newborn. When a child was born, the midwife inspected it, even before the umbilical cord was cut, to judge whether it was physically perfect. If it was not, she would likely cut the cord too closely, thus killing the child. A healthy newborn was placed at the father's feet. If he accepted the infant, picking

FIGURE 4.4 Roman Patrician, first century C.E. The conservative Romans took great pride in their ancestors, whose lives, they believed, gave legitimacy to their descendants. Romans venerated busts of their ancestors, as this statue of a Roman holding two busts of his forebears shows.

up a boy or acknowledging a girl, then the child was raised. If he did not, the baby would be "exposed"—placed outside to die or to be taken in and raised as a slave. Roman law required the father to raise one daughter, but he could choose to raise all his daughters, as many families did. However, it is impossible to know how many children were exposed and how many died as a result. In one chilling letter, a soldier matter-of-factly instructs his pregnant wife to keep the child if it is a boy and to expose it if it is a girl. We can only conclude that the practice of exposure was not considered extraordinary.

When the child was accepted, however, he or she received endless attention. Influential physicians like Soranus and Galen (second century C.E.) detailed explicit instructions on how to raise an infant, and all the child-rearing advice focused on molding the baby to be shapely, disciplined, and obedient. Newborns were tightly bound in strips of cloth for two months to ensure that their limbs would grow straight. Once a day they were unwrapped to be bathed in a tepid bath. Parents would then stretch, massage, and shape the screaming babies before tightly wrapping them again. Noble children were usually breast-fed by a wet nurse (a slave woman who had recently had a child), and many physicians recommended that children begin to drink sweet wine at 6 months. Infant mortality was high despite the recommendations of physicians and the attentions of loving parents—fewer than half of the newborns raised reached puberty.

Child-rearing practices

At the age of 6 or 7, children were put in the care of tutors, and their formal education began. Patrician children of both genders were expected to receive an education so as to transmit Roman culture to the next generations. Girls also learned to spin and weave wool, activities that consumed much of their time in their adult years.

By age 12, boys had graduated to higher schooling, learning literature, arithmetic, geometry, music, astronomy, and logic. This general education prepared boys for public life—the honorable and expected course for a wealthy boy. If a boy was talented, at age 16 he began an advanced study of rhetoric. This skill would help him later to speak persuasively to the crowds that had so much influence on the political life of the Republic.

Life in the City

By the late Republic (ca. 50 B.C.E.), the population of Rome had reached an astounding 1,000,000. The richest lived on the hills (shown on **Map 4.1**), aloof from the bustle of the crowds and the smells of the lower city. They surrounded themselves with elegance and beauty and often decorated their houses with wall paintings called frescoes.

The painting in **Figure 4.6** adorned the inner wall of a house of a wealthy Roman and shows an urban scene where attractive houses range up the hills. This view not only gives us a sense of what the ideal city looked like but also reveals the degree to which Romans praised the urban life that formed the heart of Roman culture. The decorated door at the front of the painting demonstrates how separate the noble Roman's private space was from the public space of the colonnaded temple at the top of the illustration. At this front door, clients gathered in the hopes of

FIGURE 4.5 Family Gravestone, first century B.C.E. This memorial stone of Lucius Vibius and his wife and child captures the qualities of the ideal republican Roman family: serious and modest, with no visible emotion.

being welcomed in. Even in this urban life, Romans did not forget their affection for the land—notice the potted plants near the door. The houses of the wealthy featured elaborate, well-tended pleasure gardens and fountains. Even landless renters kept potted plants on the terraces and balconies of their apartment buildings.

Below the hills, most city dwellers lived in small houses or crowded, multistoried tenements. The region of the city called Subura was the most notorious, and as **Map 4.1** shows, it was near the Forum and at the foot of the most prestigious house on the Palatine Hill. People brought water from the public fountains and heated their homes with open flames or burning charcoal. Waste ran down sewers and washed out of the city, but never with the efficiency that modern hygiene requires. Townspeople dumped garbage just outside city walls near the cemetery for the poor, where shallowly buried corpses rotted and carrion crows circled endlessly. Wealthy urban men and women carried little bouquets of fragrant flowers that they held to their noses to protect themselves from the smells of the city.

In addition to being the political center of Rome, the Forum was the economic and social center. Two rows of shops lined the large square, and merchants shouted, hawking their wares as slaves shopped for the household needs. In the afternoon, work ceased and the men headed for the baths. (Women, too, probably had public bathing time set aside for them as well, but the historical evidence for the Republic does not explicitly discuss it.) The baths served much as a

Life in the Forum

FIGURE 4.6 Urban Scene Fresco, ca. 45 B.C.E. When Mount Vesuvius erupted in 79 C.E., it buried a beautiful villa at Boscoreale, near Pompeii. Excavations have uncovered magnificent frescoes such as this urban scene that was painted on a wall to give the illusion of looking out a window at the urban spaces the Romans designed and built so well.

EXPANSION AND TRANSFORMATION, 265–133 B.C.E.

The Romans who enjoyed and contributed so much to the good life of the city represented only a part of the population. Rome's success derived primarily from its army. Over time, the army began to define the very structure of what was becoming an empire. As we saw in the example of Cincinnatus, the army of the Republic was made up of citizen-soldiers who set aside their work to fight for a season. When Rome's leaders believed they were threatened by foreign invaders, the consuls raised a red flag in the Forum. Then free householders throughout the territory—that is, tax-paying men between the ages of 17 and 46—had to report to the capitol within thirty days. From this large group, the consuls and military tribunes chose their army.

Weapons and discipline

The Romans' Victorious Army

By the early Republic, the army was organized in legions of about 4,000 men—about 40 companies of 100 men each, although the actual numbers that constituted a legion or a company varied over time. These were mostly foot soldiers fighting bare-legged in their tunics. All soldiers took an oath binding themselves to the army until death or the end of the war. The remarkable strength of this citizen army lay in its unequaled discipline. For example, commanders practiced decimation, in which one soldier in ten was killed if a unit disobeyed an order or failed badly. Traditionally, warfare in the Mediterranean was governed by informal rules that allowed surrender before either side suffered extensive losses. The Roman soldier, however, hated to return home defeated. The shame of it would prevent him from resuming his life in the city where everyone met face-to-face in the Forum.

The Roman army was an obedient, iron-willed fighting machine under the strict command of its leaders. Roman soldiers ate only wheat bread and drank only water while at war. In hot weather, they added some vinegar. Sometimes during campaigns in which the wheat ran out, the soldiers had to eat meat, but they feared the meat would "soften" them and erode their invincibility. They sneered at their opponents who slept heavily on wine and food, and this attitude probably gave them confidence in the heat of battles. The iron discipline extended to camp life, because soldiers could not rest until they had fortified their camp to make them impregnable to surprise attack. **Figure 4.7a** shows soldiers building such a camp after a long day's march.

The victorious republican soldier returned after a season of fighting with only a few gold coins in his

modern health club. People exercised or played ball, swam, took steam baths, had massages, got their body hair plucked, and socialized. Then, in the late afternoon and evening, it was time for leisure. The crowds in the Forum strolled, chatted, and gossiped. Romans always included a political dimension in this informal talk, for here politicians gained nicknames like "knock-knees" or more obscene appellations. In the course of passing on rumors and jokes, Romans helped set future political fortunes.

In the afternoon and at home, men abandoned their togas (a huge length of unbleached wool, carefully wrapped around the wearer) and wore their undergarments: usually a tunic that came down to the thighs. Men who wore sleeves or long tunics were considered effeminate. Women, on the other hand, covered themselves with long, sleeved tunics that they wore under their dresses.

As in cities today, life in the urban heart of Rome was a mixture of ease and hardship, and of excitement, fellowship, and danger. Yet this complex, vibrant center marked the ideal of the Republic: a place where citizens met and mingled in a public setting, and where political and economic dramas unfolded. Unfortunately for the Romans, this appealing way of life could not last. As Rome expanded, its spectacular military successes brought changes that undermined the Roman civic ideal.

thinking about ART

FIGURE 4.7(a)
Trajan's Column

This relief carving (a) is a detail of one of the winding panels from Trajan's Column, which was dedicated in 113 C.E. to celebrate the emperor Trajan's victories in war. The full column is shown on the right (b). Even though this column is from later than the republican period, it remains one of the important historical sources for Roman military life. The scene highlighted here depicts soldiers, dressed in battle armor (except

FIGURE 4.7(b)

their helmets), building a camp—a common daily activity for soldiers while they were on campaign.

Connecting Art & Society

1. What specific tasks are the soldiers performing?
2. Why do you think the artists included these tasks on a column celebrating a military victory?
3. How did these activities contribute to the might of the Roman army?

---

hand and the pride of victory in his heart. Through a relentless series of such victories, by 265 B.C.E. Rome had unified virtually the whole Italian peninsula (see **Map 4.2**). However, the Republic's growing wealth and power clashed with new foes outside the peninsula. These contests would transform the army, the Republic, and the Romans.

Wars of the Mediterranean

As we saw in **Map 4.2**, after Rome consolidated its hold on the Italian peninsula, it confronted Carthage, the other great power in the western Mediterranean. Carthage was founded around the same time as the city of Rome (ca. 800 B.C.E.) by a group of colonists from Phoenicia. The colony profited from its trade, prospered, and became a diverse and cosmopolitan city as great as those of the Hellenistic kingdoms. At the height of its power, the population of Phoenician Carthage probably approached 400,000, of whom no more than 100,000 were of fairly pure Phoenician heritage. In the busy shops, merchants spoke Greek and many other languages of the Mediterranean as they sold wares drawn from the farthest reaches of the Hellenistic kingdoms.

The skillful Phoenician sailors even ventured outside the Mediterranean basin, trading along the western coast of Africa. The Greek historian Herodotus (ca. 484–ca. 424 B.C.E.) described how Carthaginian merchants traded with African tribes, relying on mutual trust instead of language skills. The merchants unloaded their cargo on the African shore, summoned local tribesmen by smoke signals, and then returned to their ships. The Africans approached and laid out what they thought would be a fair amount for the goods and then withdrew without taking the goods until the Carthaginians indicated their agreement on the price. As Herodotus wrote, "They say that thus neither party is ill-used; for the Carthaginians do not take the gold until they have the worth of their merchandise, nor do the natives touch the merchandise until the Carthaginians have taken the gold." By the third century B.C.E., the wealthy, enterprising Carthaginians had gained control of many territories in the western Mediterranean (see **Map 4.2**) and confronted the growing power of the Roman Republic.

Rome's expansion and growing alliances began to encroach upon the Carthaginians, who had controlled the western Mediterranean for so long, and it was only a matter of time before tensions came to a head. Rome's clash with Carthage began over who would control the Sicilian city of Messana, an area that the Romans saw as strategically vital to the security of southern Italy because it was on the straits between the island and the mainland (see **Map 4.2**). Carthage, for its part, resented the idea of Rome as a presence in Sicily. In 264 B.C.E., both sides sent troops in an effort to conquer the disputed island. This confrontation began the first of three hostile encounters between Rome and Carthage, called the Punic Wars. *Punic* meant "Phoenician," by which the Romans recalled the origins of the Carthaginians.

> **First Punic War**

But to broaden their military efforts beyond Italy, the Romans needed ships. The city managed to raise some money and build a fleet, yet it had trouble finding admirals who had any solid seafaring experience. The Romans nevertheless demonstrated their famous tenacity and designed a new warship that would change the nature of naval battles. Before the Romans, the basic tactic at sea was ramming one ship into another, thus sinking the second. Sometimes sailors would board the opposing ship to engage the enemy, but not very often. The Romans changed this. They developed a new vessel that featured a special platform that allowed many infantrymen on board. When they approached an opposing ship, Roman soldiers could then board the enemy vessel and fight hand to hand, a style that was their specialty. In the Punic Wars, Carthaginian naval commanders did what usually brought them success—they rammed the Roman ships. Before the Carthaginian vessel could pull away, however, a platform descended and Roman troops swept across, taking the lightly manned Carthaginian ship. The Romans would then simply scuttle their own destroyed ship and seize the Carthaginian one. **Figure 4.8** shows one of these impressive warships with infantrymen poised to fight.

> **New Roman navy**

FIGURE 4.8 Roman Warship The Roman infantry was unbeatable, but when Romans challenged Carthage, they had to learn to fight at sea. Instead of ramming an opponent's ship, Romans lowered a gangplank so that their infantry, shown here, could board the enemy ship and fight by hand.

In 241 B.C.E., Rome finally won a decisive sea battle against Carthage, and the First Punic War ended with a Roman victory. The Republic received control of Sicily and a large financial indemnity from the Carthaginians. But the larger question of who would control the western Mediterranean remained unresolved. A second contest seems to have been inevitable.

The Second Punic War (218–201 B.C.E.) began in Spain, where Rome and Carthage had signed a treaty dividing the spheres of influence at the Ebro River (see **Map 4.3**). However, the treaty left one issue unresolved: Who would control the city of Saguntum, which lay south of the Ebro? Under the terms of the treaty it was in Carthaginian territory, but Rome had an alliance with Saguntum that predated the treaty. The Carthaginian general, Hannibal Barca, attacked Saguntum and in the process began the Second Punic War. This war was different from the first one, for when war was declared, the Romans had control of the sea, so Carthaginians knew victory would come only if they brought war to Rome itself.

> **Second Punic War**

The Carthaginians may have lacked a fleet, but in their general Hannibal they possessed one of the greatest military strategists in history. The confident general surprised the Romans by taking the war to Italy, moving his large Hellenistic-style army overland from Spain into the peninsula. Now Roman legions had to confront the military power of armies that included war elephants. Crossing the Alps with 30,000 to 40,000 men, 6,000 horses, and about 35 elephants was a difficult feat; many men and elephants fell and died in the dangerous passes. However, Hannibal emerged in northern Italy with enough of an army (complete with a dozen or so elephants) to shock the local population and win many victories.

Hannibal expected Rome's subject peoples to rise up in his support, and while some did, the inner

thinking about GEOGRAPHY

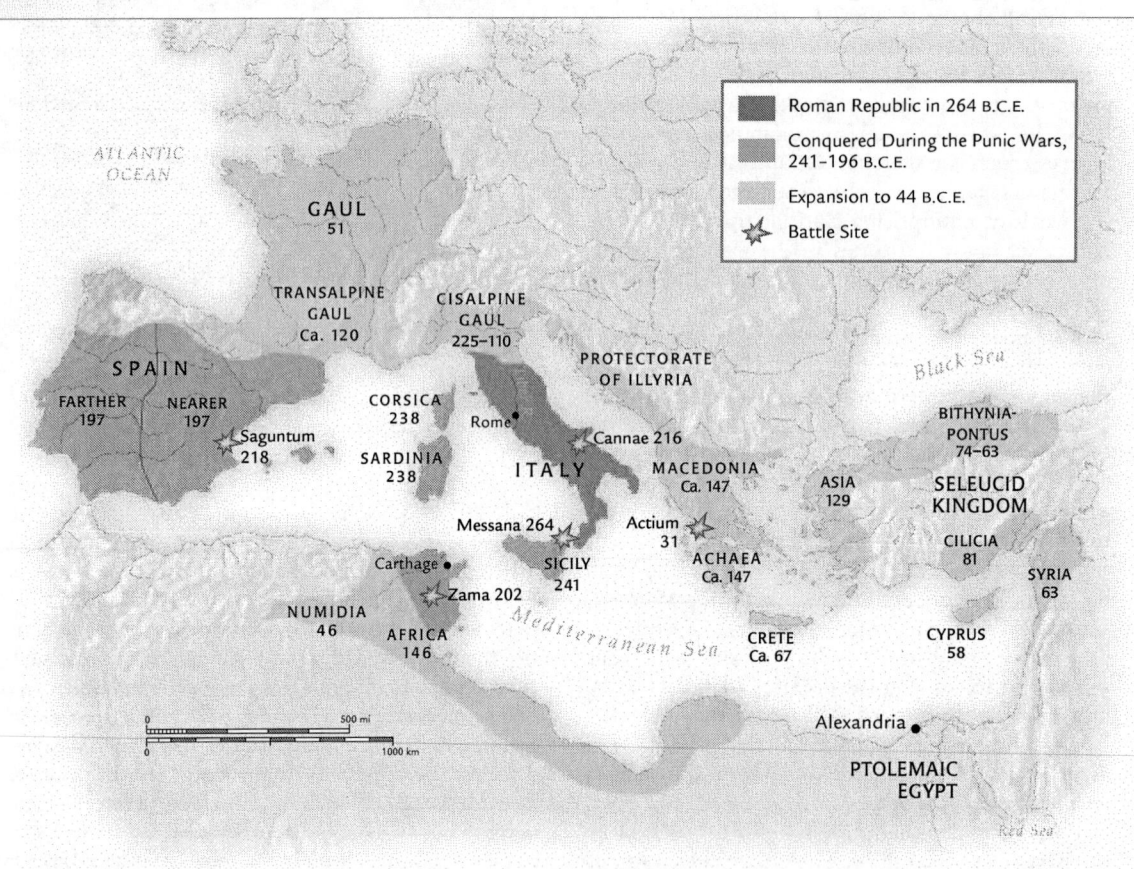

MAP 4.3

Expansion of the Roman Republic, 264–44 B.C.E.

This map shows the expansion of the Republic as it fought victorious wars against Carthage and the Macedonian and Seleucid kingdoms in the East. Notice the scale for distances.

Explore the Map

1. How hard would it have been for the Carthaginian general Hannibal to transport his army and elephants across the distances from Spain to Italy? Why?
2. Given Rome's expansion, how likely was it that the Hellenistic kingdoms of the Seleucids and Ptolemies would come into conflict with Rome?
3. How would Romans become influenced by Hellenistic culture in these conquests?

---

core of central Italy stayed loyal. The strong alliance system that Rome had built gave it a huge advantage. Nevertheless, the astonishing general handed Rome its worst defeat ever at the Battle of Cannae in 216 B.C.E., in which approximately 30,000 Romans died (see **Map 4.3**). Document 4.2 describes this significant battle and shows Hannibal's battle plan. Romans were shocked and frightened—for years Roman mothers would scare naughty children with the threat "Hannibal will get you"—and yet the Romans would not surrender. They adopted a defensive attitude of delay and refusal to fight while the Carthaginian forces marched up and down Italy for almost seventeen years—wreaking havoc along the way.

Finally, Rome produced a general who could match Hannibal's skill. Publius Cornelius Scipio (236–183 B.C.E.) had studied Carthaginian battlefield tactics and had the skill to improve on them. Scipio took Carthage's Spanish lands and then sailed to North Africa, bringing the war to Carthage. Hannibal had to leave Italy to defend his homeland, and he had to face the Romans virtually unaided. The

thinking about DOCUMENTS

DOCUMENT 4.2

Hannibal Triumphs at the Battle of Cannae

The Battle of Cannae, 216 B.C.E.

Rome
→ Advance ■ Infantry
→ Retreat   ■ Cavalry

Carthage
→ Advance ■ Infantry
→ Retreat   ■ Cavalry

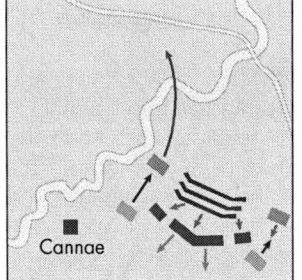

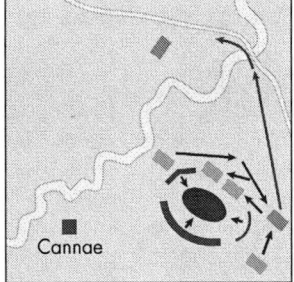

The Carthaginians, led by Hannibal, were able to inflict the single greatest defeat of the Romans in the history of their empire. By feigning retreat and convincing the Romans that they were abandoning Cannae, the Carthaginian army was able to surround the Romans and defeat them without mercy. This defeat caused great alarm to the citizens of Rome, as it left them nearly defenseless.

FIGURE 4.9 The Battle of Cannae, 216 B.C.E.

The Roman historian Florus (ca. 70–ca. 140 C.E.) wrote History of the Romans, *in which he recounted the long-remembered Battle of Cannae (216 B.C.E.), a turning point during the Second Punic War between Rome and Carthage. Military thinkers today still study Hannibal's winning battle strategy, but Florus notes Hannibal's mistake. Study* **Figure 4.9** *to understand Hannibal's winning strategy.*

The fourth and almost mortal wound of the Roman Empire was at Cannæ, an obscure village of Apulia; which, however, became famous by the greatness of the defeat, its celebrity being acquired by the slaughter of forty thousand men. Here the general, the ground, the face of heaven, the day, indeed, all nature conspired together for the destruction of the unfortunate army. For Hannibal, the most artful of generals, not content with sending pretended deserters among the Romans, who fell upon their rear as they were fighting, but having also noted the nature of the ground in those open plains, where the heat of the sun is extremely violent, the dust very great, and the wind blows constantly, and as it were statedly, from the east, drew up his army in such a position that, while the Romans were exposed to all these inconveniences, he himself, having heaven, as it were, on his side, fought with wind, dust, and sun in his favor. Two vast armies, in consequence, were slaughtered till the enemy were satiated, and till Hannibal said to his soldiers, "Put up your swords." Of the two commanders, one escaped, the other was slain; which of them showed the greater spirit is doubtful. Paulus was ashamed to survive; Varro did not despair. Of the greatness of the slaughter the following proofs may be noticed: that the Aufidus was for some time red with blood; that a bridge was made of dead bodies, by order of Hannibal, over the torrent of Vergellus, and that two *modii* of rings were sent to Carthage, and the equestrian dignity estimated by measure.

It was afterward not doubted but that Rome might have seen its last day, and that Hannibal, within five days, might have feasted in the Capitol, if—as they say that Adherbal, the Carthaginian, the son of Bomilcar, observed—"he had known as well how to use his victory as how to gain it." But at that crisis, as is generally said, either the fate of the city that was to be empress of the world, or his own want of judgment, and the influence of deities unfavorable to Carthage, carried him in a different direction. When he might have taken advantage of his victory, he chose rather to seek enjoyment from it, and, leaving Rome, to march into Campania and to Tarentum, where both he and his army soon lost their vigor, so that it was justly remarked that "Capua proved a Cannæ to Hannibal"; since the sunshine of Campania and the warm springs of Baiæ subdued—who could have believed it?—him who had been unconquered by the Alps and unshaken in the field.

SOURCE: Florus, *History of the Romans,* in *The Great Events by Famous Historians,* vol. II, ed. Rossiter Johnson (The National Alumni, 1905), pp. 186–187.

Analyze the Document

1. What are the tactics of ancient battles, and in what ways is Hannibal particularly skilled?
2. How much devastation is caused by the Battle of Cannae? Why does this destruction make the battle so traumatic to Romans?
3. Why does Hannibal not follow up with a decisive victory?

Roman control of the sea prevented the Carthaginian ally Philip V of Macedonia (of the Hellenistic Macedonian kingdom discussed in Chapter 3) from helping, and Carthaginian support in North Africa was weak. Scipio decisively defeated Hannibal at the Battle of Zama in 202 B.C.E. (see **Map 4.3**) and won the surname "Africanus" to commemorate his great victory that saved Rome. Carthage again sued for peace—giving up Spain and promising not to wage war without Rome's permission. But peace would prove temporary.

Carthage was placed in a difficult position, for Numidia, one of Rome's allies in North Africa, was encroaching on its territory. Yet Carthage could not wage war against Numidia without Rome's permission, and Rome withheld it. The Senate was led by Cato the Elder (234–149 B.C.E.), who was

Third Punic War

virulently anti-Carthaginian. Plutarch recorded his famous rousing speech in 150 B.C.E. as he tried to spur his countrymen to resume the fighting against Carthage. He reminded the Senate that Carthage was "only three days' sail from Rome," and he ended all his speeches with the phrase "Carthage must be destroyed." Cato spoke for many Romans who wanted to take on their old enemy again. The inflammatory language worked, and the Third Punic War began. After a long siege of the citadel at the top of the hill overlooking the town, Rome crushed the city of Carthage in 146 B.C.E. The Carthaginian general surrendered, and his wife, accusing him of cowardice, committed suicide by leaping with her two children into the flames of the burning city. The Roman general—another Scipio called Aemilianus—reputedly shed tears at the sight of the ruin of the great city. The once-shining city of Carthage would lie in ruins for a century until Rome itself recolonized it.

The wars against Carthage drew the Romans into battling in the eastern Mediterranean, leading to three wars against Macedonia between 215 and ca. 168 B.C.E. Romans felt drawn into the first war because the Macedonian king, Philip V (221–179 B.C.E.), had allied with Hannibal after the Roman defeat at Cannae. Following this indecisive war, Rome was again drawn into eastern affairs as some of the Greek poleis solicited Rome's help against a coalition between the Macedonian and Seleucid kings. This time Rome won decisively and Macedonia agreed to stay out of Greek affairs. The third war arose when Macedonia again tried to reassert control over Greece. As a result of this war, Rome ruthlessly divided up Macedonia and eliminated any opposition.

Macedonia and Greece

At first, Rome left the Greeks "free," but there quickly arose a difference of opinion about the meaning of this term. The Greeks believed freedom meant to do as they liked; Romans believed it meant to act as obedient Roman clients. The Roman Senate finally ran out of patience and decided to annex the Greek mainland. To set an example to the recalcitrant Greeks, a Roman commander burned the city of Corinth, enslaved its inhabitants, and brought rich plunder back to Rome. The expansion eastward had begun, and it continued with the establishment of the province of Asia in 137 B.C.E., when the last king of Pergamum died, willing his land to Rome. Money, art, and slaves now flowed from the east to Rome, and the Republic had to decide how to govern its new far-flung conquests (see **Map 4.3**).

Historians still disagree about Rome's motives for continuing the warfare. Rome often marched to protect its allies—waging what they called "just wars." At the same time, some Romans were becoming rich in these enterprises, and Roman generals saw war as the road to upward mobility. Now the path to success for an ambitious Roman lay not in impressing his fellow citizens in the Forum, but in leading victorious armies.

Rome did not always annex territories outright. Sometimes it operated through client states, leaving local rulers in place. Sometimes victorious Romans established the conquered territories as provinces—one in Africa, one in Asia, and later across the Alps in Gaul (southern France) in an area that is still called Provence. Within the provinces, people lived as they had in the past, but Rome's leaders expected these states to conform to their wishes (which at times caused friction). Governors were appointed by the Roman Senate to preserve peace and administer justice to Roman citizens. Other duties were given to private individuals, who could make fortunes performing administrative duties. For example, tax collectors received a contract to collect a certain amount of taxes, and they could legally keep some profits they squeezed from local populations. The governors were supposed to make sure tax collectors did not abuse their privilege, but, not surprisingly, many of them took full advantage of this system and extracted huge amounts of money from helpless residents. The conquests in Italy had yielded most profits from land. In the provinces, on the other hand, people made money from land, slaves, and graft. In the process, the Roman Republic itself was transformed in various ways by its military success abroad.

Administering provinces

An Influx of Slaves

In the ancient world, successful military campaigning earned a victor not just new territory and riches but also slaves. As Rome expanded, it accumulated more and more bondsmen and -women. After the Second Punic War, more than 200,000 men and women were captured as prisoners of war and brought to Italy as slaves. Numbers like these changed the nature of Roman society. Now, instead of each small householder having one to three slaves (as we saw was the pattern in

KEY DATES

EXPANSION OF ROME

340 B.C.E.	Revolt of Latin allies
264–241 B.C.E.	First Punic War
263 B.C.E.	Rome rules Italian peninsula
218–203 B.C.E.	Hannibal fights in Italy
218–201 B.C.E.	Second Punic War
215–ca. 168 B.C.E.	Wars of Macedonia
149–146 B.C.E.	Third Punic War
148–146 B.C.E.	Macedonia and Greece become provinces

ancient Greece), rich households might have hundreds of domestic slaves. By the end of the Republic, there were between two and three million slaves in Italy, an astounding 35 to 40 percent of the population.

Thousands of slaves labored in agriculture or mining, working in large anonymous gangs. However, in the cities, slaves and citizens often worked in the same occupations, and all could earn money through their labor. The most undesirable jobs—garbage collection, mining, acting, and prostitution—were generally reserved for slaves, although freed men and women, while technically citizens, were willing to do the most lucrative of these jobs. Often slaves dominated some of the higher-status jobs. After Rome's conquest of Greece (ca. 148 B.C.E.), most of the tutors and teachers to Roman children were Greek slaves. The Biography on page 125 describes the successful career of a playwright who had been a slave. Most physicians were either Greek or trained in Greece, and it was not unusual for physicians to be succeeded by their Greek slaves, whom they had trained and then freed to take their place.

Slave occupations

Perhaps not surprisingly, Romans often feared their slaves. The Stoic philosopher Seneca (4 B.C.E.–65 C.E.) wrote that "the least of your slaves holds over you the power of life or death." As the numbers of slaves increased, Romans had more and more reason to worry, and they passed laws to try to protect themselves. For example, the punishment for murdering one's master was severe—all the slaves in the household were to be executed. The Roman historian Tacitus (ca. 56–ca. 120 C.E.) recorded an incident when an ex-consul was murdered by a slave. A senator arguing that the state should enforce the harsh law and kill the whole household said: "Whom will a large number of slaves keep safe, when four hundred could not protect Pedanius Secundus? . . . In every wholesale punishment there is some injustice to individuals, which is compensated by the advantage to the state." Not only did individual instances of slave treachery crop up, but large-scale slave rebellions broke out as well.

Slave revolts

Three great slave uprisings disrupted Italy and Sicily between 135 and 71 B.C.E. The most famous was led by the gladiator Spartacus between 73 and 71 B.C.E. Spartacus escaped his master with 70 of his fellow gladiators. Many others joined them as the army of almost 70,000 slaves ravaged portions of Italy. They succeeded in defeating many of the soldiers sent after them. Some sources suggest that Spartacus even tried to take his army to Sicily to rally the slaves there but could not gather enough ships to cross the sea. Spartacus was finally killed and the rebellion crushed. Six thousand of Spartacus's followers were crucified—the brutal form of execution reserved for slaves. This revolt was suppressed, but Rome did not forget the potential for violence that simmered within the many men and women they had enslaved in their imperial expansion.

Economic Disparity and Social Unrest

Just as the expansion of Rome altered the nature of slavery, it transformed many other aspects of life in the Republic. These changes were noted sadly by many conservative Romans who watched their traditional way of life fade. One Roman (Silius Italicus) lamented the aftermath of Rome's victory in the Punic Wars: "[I]f it was fated that the Roman character should change when Carthage fell, would that Carthage was still standing." But such qualms were too late; the Republic was transmuting into something else entirely, even as some Romans mourned it.

One of the most noticeable changes came in the form of increasing disparity between rich and poor. Many of the upper classes had grown very rich indeed. Governors of provinces had the opportunity to make fortunes undreamed of in the Republic's earlier years. Other enterprising Romans made fortunes in ship-building contracts, banking, slave trading, and many other high-profit occupations. Rome had become a Hellenistic state like the successor states of Alexander the Great (see Chapter 3), with a growing distance between the rich and the poor.

While some Romans amassed great fortunes, others suffered a worsening of their economic situations. The example of Cincinnatus, who fought for only one season and then returned to his plow, was impossible to repeat when foes were far away and wars long. During the Punic Wars, military time was extended. As a result, more than 50 percent of adult males spent over seven years in the army, and some spent as long as twenty years. Throughout most of the Republic, the army was not formally paid, and this caused both some hardship and a particularly strong relationship between soldiers and their generals. By right, generals controlled all booty taken in war, and they distributed some of it to their troops. Thus generals acted as patrons to their client soldiers, who increasingly owed loyalty to their general rather than to Rome itself. Meanwhile, as soldiers stayed longer in the army, their family fields remained unplowed. Numerous farmers went bankrupt, and soldiers returned to their homes to find them sold and their wives and children turned out of the family farm.

Newly rich men and women eagerly purchased these neglected lands, and small landholders were replaced by large plantations worked by gangs of new slaves. Fields that had cultivated wheat were slowly transformed to produce olives and wine grapes, much more lucrative crops. Other great landowners in Italy grew rich on ranches that raised animals for meat, milk, or wool. Now Romans had to import their wheat from abroad, particularly North Africa.

BIOGRAPHY

Publius Terentius Afer (Terence) (ca. 190–159 B.C.E.)

A Talented Slave

During the peaceful interlude between the First and Second Punic Wars, a slave trader in Carthage purchased a young man named Terence. We have no idea how Terence came into the hands of a slave dealer; we do know he was not a prisoner of war. However, many North Africans were enslaved by the Carthaginians; Terence may have come from one such slave family. His surname, Afer, meaning "the African," suggests that he was not originally from Carthage. He was described as being "of medium stature, graceful in person, and of dark complexion," and some scholars have suggested that he was from a black sub-Saharan family. The ambiguity of Terence's background points to the cosmopolitan, highly diverse nature of the city of Carthage. It was one of the jewels of the Mediterranean—a bustling city where people mingled from all over and shared in a dynamic cultural life. Terence's early experience in the cosmopolitan city no doubt prepared him to contribute to Rome's growing interest in Hellenistic literature.

The young slave was brought to Rome and sold to a senator, M. Terentius Lucanus, who must have recognized the youth's promise. The senator had him educated as a freeman and then granted him his freedom. This is but one example of many talented slaves who were freed by their owners during the optimistic years of the Republic. Terence then pursued a literary career.

The intellectual gifts that had won Terence his freedom earned him the acceptance of an aristocratic circle of young men who were interested in literature. These educated youths were actively involved in fostering Greek literature, and such literary circles had much influence in Hellenizing Roman society.

At first, Terence was outside the guild of poets and the working playwrights. He made his artistic breakthrough when he got a chance to submit one of his plays for production to the aging but well-established poet Caecilius. Terence found out where the poet was dining and approached him as he reclined on his couch eating with friends. Because Terence was a stranger and plainly dressed, Caecilius invited him only to sit on a stool and recite from his work. After a few verses, however, the old poet was so impressed with Terence's talent that he invited him to join him on the couch and share the festive dinner. The budding playwright's career was launched.

Terence wrote six plays based on traditional Greek models, even specifying that they be performed in Greek dress. These plays show Terence's talent and understanding of both human nature and the social realities in Rome. Yet he received mixed reactions from the Romans. During his short lifetime, Terence was much criticized by other playwrights, and like so much else in Rome, these critiques were conducted publicly. Terence addressed his critics (and attacked other playwrights) in the prologues to the plays. These public debates tell us much about the openly competitive nature of the artistic world during the Republic.

Terence was accused first of plagiarism, meaning that someone else claimed to have been the first to translate Greek plays into Latin. In a prologue, Terence flatly denies "any knowledge of the play's previous Latinization." Terence was also charged with being "untraditional"—a serious insult to Romans. According to his accusers, he did not remain true to the Greek originals. Terence admitted that he combined plots and created interesting works of art rather than translations. As he put it, precise translations often turned "the best Greek plays . . . into Latin flops." These criticisms reveal a people struggling to discover a new art form and to determine the rules with which to judge it.

Terence challenged his audiences to judge his works on their own merits. Not surprisingly, many of his contemporaries appreciated his talent, for he did more than reproduce classic plays—he gave them his own stamp. For example, instead of simply relying on slapstick humor (as Plautus did), Terence developed a clever use of language to provide humor. He also used suspense as a dynamic device that would have a long history in the theater. His fame long outlasted him. Long after Terence's death, Cicero and Caesar, both known for their eloquence, praised his work as a model of elegant language. Audiences ever since have found his plays brilliant.

Unfortunately, Terence died while still in his prime. In 159 B.C.E., the 31-year-old undertook a journey to Greece, possibly to study theater or to escape the jealous rumors of his rivals. He died on the way, from either illness or shipwreck. He left a revered body of work that people still enjoy and appreciate today. Perhaps equally important, Terence exemplified the kind of upward mobility available to educated slaves during an age when Rome fell in love with Greek intellectual life.

Connecting People & Society

1. How does Terence's life demonstrate the Hellenizing of the Republic after the North African conquests?

2. What does this life reveal about the nature of Roman slavery?

3. What problems does Terence face, and what do they reveal about Roman culture?

Spurred by economic hardship, the displaced citizens flocked to the city. The population swelled with a new class of people—propertyless day laborers who were unconnected to the structures of patronage and land that had defined the early Republic. These mobs created more and more problems for the nobility because they always represented a potentially revolutionary force in the Forum. Aristocrats tried to keep them happy and harmless by subsidizing food, but this short-term solution could not solve the deeper problem of lost jobs taken by newly captured slaves and land seized by the newly rich. The situation had become volatile indeed.

[New poverty]

THE HELLENIZING OF THE REPUBLIC

As if these social tensions were not disruptive enough, new intellectual influences further modified Rome's traditional value system. As the Republican armies conquered some of the great centers of Hellenistic culture from Greece to North Africa, Romans became deeply attracted to many of the Hellenistic ways. As the Roman poet Horace (65–8 B.C.E.) observed: "Captive Greece took her Captor Captive." With the capture of slaves from Greece, Greek art, literature, and learning came to Rome, and many in the Roman aristocracy became bilingual, adding Greek to their native Latin. Rome became a Hellenized city, with extremes of wealth and poverty and a growing emphasis on individualism over obedience to the family.

Cato the Elder (234–149 B.C.E.)—the anti-Carthaginian orator—was one Roman who feared the changes that came with the increasing wealth and love of things Greek, and when he held the office of censor (see **Figure 4.3**), he tried to stem the tide of Hellenization. The office of censor had come to be an influential one. During the early Republic, censors had made lists of citizens and their property qualifications, but in time the censors became so powerful that they revised the lists of senators, deleting those whose behavior they deemed objectionable. To preserve the old values, Cato tried taxing luxury goods and charging fines to those who neglected their farms, but his efforts were in vain. Romans had added an appreciation of Greek beauty to their own practical skills, and they adopted a new love of luxury and power that seemed to erode the moral strength of old Rome. To men like Cato, the Republic was becoming unrecognizable.

[Resisting change]

Roman Engineering: Fusing Utility and Beauty

Most of the great building projects that so characterize Rome arose in the building boom during the early years of the empire, as we will see in the next chapter. However, the techniques that led to those projects were developed during the Republic and were refined by the influx of Greek ideas and artists during the wars of expansion in the third and second centuries B.C.E. During these years Rome developed a new aesthetic sense that combined its traditional love of utility with the Hellenistic ideals of beauty.

As we have seen, the Romans had learned much about engineering from the Etruscans, especially techniques for draining swamps and building conduits to move water. The early Romans had a strong practical side themselves and greatly admired feats of science and engineering. The Roman orator Cicero revealed this admiration when he traveled to Syracuse in 75 B.C.E. to visit the grave of Archimedes, the esteemed engineer we met in Chapter 3. When Cicero discovered that Archimedes' countrymen had forgotten him, he found the old engineer's grave and restored it.

[Engineering]

Rome's military success stemmed in part from the engineering achievements that supported the legions. For example, armies had to forge many rivers, and the Roman engineers invented ingenious devices to help them. General Julius Caesar (100–44 B.C.E.), in his account of one military campaign, described how he had to sink heavy timbers into the fast-moving Rhine River to build a bridge. The task was completed in ten days, and the army crossed. Engineers could build pontoon bridges even faster by floating flat-bottomed boats down the river and anchoring them at the intended crossing.

Perhaps Rome's greatest military engineering lay in the area of siege engines. Caesar described how the Romans patiently built a tall, fortified mound and tower next to a city they were besieging. As some soldiers fought from the top of the tower, they protected others who were beneath sturdy beams below. These hidden soldiers were then able to dismantle the bottom of the wall, causing it to collapse so the army could enter and take the city. Some Roman siege engines were so impressive that even Chinese sources documented them.

Engineering skills also brought many benefits to civilian life. The arch is a key example. The Greeks used post and lintel construction, which limited the variety of structures they could build. By using arches, Romans enhanced the size, range, and flexibility of their constructions. The use of the arch can most readily be seen in the aqueducts—perhaps the greatest examples of Roman civil engineering. Aqueducts brought water from rivers or springs into cities.

Romans had a huge thirst for water. The first aqueduct, the Aqua Appia, was built as early as 312 B.C.E., and it brought water through underground pipes from about 8 miles

[Aqueducts]

outside Rome. Later aqueducts used both subterranean pipes and overhead pipes mounted on arches, which allowed the engineers to adjust the height of the aqueduct to regulate the rate of the water flowing through the channel at the top. The more than 46-mile-long Claudian aqueduct, finished in 52 C.E., cost a fortune, what would be millions of dollars today. By the end of the first century C.E., nine aqueducts directed an astonishing 22,237,000 gallons of water into the city each day. (**Map 4.1** shows the locations of Rome's aqueducts.)

Rome exported these marvels of engineering to cities throughout the Mediterranean world, and some of the best-preserved aqueducts are outside Rome itself. **Figure 4.10** shows the most spectacular surviving aqueduct, the Pont du Gard outside Nîmes in southern France, which spans the River Gard and its valley. The water flows through an enclosed channel on the top, and a roadway runs over the lowest row of arches. Structures like these were marvels of Roman engineering, featuring solid design, practical application, visual appeal, and durability.

FIGURE 4.10 Pont du Gard Aqueduct, late first century B.C.E. Roman engineers built monumental aqueducts to carry water over great distances into their cities. This aqueduct in southern France brought water from springs 30 miles away to serve the city of Nîmes. The careful engineering maintains a constant decline, allowing the water to flow freely and gently.

Concrete: A New Building Material

In the late third century B.C.E., Roman architects discovered a new building material that opened even more architectural possibilities than the perfection of the arch. Masons found that mixing volcanic brick-earth with lime and water resulted in a strong, waterproof building material—concrete. With this new substance, architects could design large, heavy buildings in a variety of shapes.

Combining concrete construction with the knowledge of the arch allowed for even more flexibility than before. After they had mastered the arch, Romans built with barrel vaults, a row of arches spanning a large space. As early as 193 B.C.E., builders constructed a gigantic warehouse in Rome using this technique. Concrete and barrel vaults also made possible the design of large bathhouses, for the concrete was strong enough to withstand the heat of steam rooms. Finally, the new technology permitted the design of the oval amphitheaters that so characterized Rome.

Of course, people as religious as the Romans applied their architectural skills to their temples as well. Although most structures in Rome were made of brick or concrete covered with stucco, the growing Hellenization began to influence architectural tastes. Marble columns would soon grace the traditional buildings. In this new architecture, we can see the degree of the Greek slaves' influence on the Romans and Rome's own growing appreciation of Hellenistic art.

The fullest development of this temple construction took place early in the empire. The outstanding example of Roman religious architecture is the **Pantheon,** a temple dedicated to all the gods, shown in **Figure 4.11**. It was built in 125 C.E. on the site of a previous temple that had been constructed during the late Republic. The structure is a perfect combination of Roman and Hellenistic styles and thus embodies the transformation of republican Rome imposed by Hellenistic influences. The front of the temple has a classical rectangular porch with Corinthian columns (see **Figure 2.9,** on page 62) and a pediment, the triangular structure on top of the columns. From the front, the Pantheon resembles the Greek temples we saw in Chapter 2. Inside the temple, however, any resemblance to Hellenistic architecture disappears.

The interior of the Pantheon consists of a massive round space (visible in **Figure 4.11**) covered by a high dome, revealing the Romans' engineering skills. A heavy concrete base supports the weight of the whole, while the upper walls are constructed of a lighter mix of concrete. The center of the dome has an opening

FIGURE 4.11 The Pantheon, 125 C.E. The Romans' use of concrete permitted the construction of stunning, enduring structures such as the Pantheon, a temple devoted to all the gods. The dome's circular hole, called the *oculus* (eye), reminded visitors of the eye of Jupiter that watched them continuously.

that lets in natural light—and rain, though drainpipes beneath the ground (which still function today) took care of flooding problems.

Latin Comedy and the Great Prose Writers, 240–44 B.C.E.

In the third century B.C.E., Roman literature emerged. Written in Latin, it reflected the elements we have discussed throughout this chapter: Roman values, society, and the influence of Hellenistic culture. The earliest surviving examples of Roman literature are comic plays. Latin comedy flowered with the works of Plautus (205–185 B.C.E.) and Terence (190–159 B.C.E.), who wrote plays based on Hellenistic models but modified them for their Italian audience. Plautus and Terence wrote in verse, but unlike their Greek predecessors, they added a good deal of music, with flutes and cymbals accompanying the productions.

Like the Hellenistic plays, most comedies involved the triumph of love over obstacles. In Plautus's works particularly, the humor centered on jokes and elaborate puns within the stories and the plays were marked by slapstick, bawdy humor. For example, in one play Plautus described a confrontation in which a man threatened to beat a slave. The man said: "Whoever comes here eats my fists." The slave responded: "I do not eat at night, and I have dined; Pray give your supper to those who starve." The audience would have laughed at the play on words associating a punch with food, as well as the suggestion that the nobles were not really charitable to the starving. The plays included all types of Roman characters, from smart, scheming slaves to boastful soldiers and clever prostitutes, to many clients and patrons. Thus, Romans who watched these plays recognized and laughed at all the types of people that populated their world.

The Latin prose literature of the Republic emphasized the serious side of Roman character. The best of the prose writers were men who combined literary talent with public service—for example, Cicero and Julius Caesar.

Latin literature was shaped—indeed defined—by the writings of Cicero, whose career coincided with the decline of the Republic. His skillful oratory and strong opinions about Roman values placed him in the center of public life, but his long-standing influence derived from his prose, not his political involvement. His writings cover an extraordinary range of topics, from poetry to formal orations to deeply personal letters. From his more than nine hundred letters, we get a revealing picture of the personality of this influential man. He was deeply concerned about public affairs and political morality, writing, "our leaders ought to protect civil peace with honor and defend it even at the risk of life itself." At the same time, his letters reveal him to be vindictive, mercurial of mood, and utterly self-centered. Although scholars are ambivalent about the character of this complex man, there is no doubt about his influence. Cicero's writings defined the best use of Latin language, and his works were used as textbooks of how to construct elegant prose.

> **Cicero**

Julius Caesar's literary legacy also grew out of his active political life. As Caesar rose to power, he used literature to enhance his reputation in Rome. His accounts of his dazzling military campaigns in Gaul (across the Alps in modern France), vividly told in his *Commentaries*, intensified his popularity and have fascinated generations ever since. His Latin is clear and accessible, and his narrative vivid and exciting.

> **Caesar's writings**

By the middle of the second century B.C.E., the Roman Republic had reached a crucial threshold. Vibrant, wealthy, and victorious in war, the Republic had established political and social structures that steadily fueled its success. But in crafting their society, the Romans had unwittingly planted the seeds of their own undoing. Their much-loved precepts, established in a simpler age, would prove unsustainable in a future where Rome boldly sought to extend its reach farther than ever before.

THE TWILIGHT OF THE REPUBLIC, 133–44 B.C.E.

In the mid-second century B.C.E., Rome suffered a sudden economic downturn. The wars of expansion had brought vast riches into Rome, and this wealth drove prices up. When the wars ended, the influx of slaves and wealth subsided. Furthermore, an unfortunate grain shortage made grain prices skyrocket. This shortage worsened in 135 B.C.E. with the revolt of the slaves in Sicily. Half of Rome's grain supply came from Sicily, so the interruption of grain flow threatened to starve the masses of people who had fled to Rome when their own small farms had been taken over. To stave off disaster, two tribunes of the plebeians, Tiberius and Gaius Gracchus, proposed reforms. (The brothers were known as the Gracchi, which is the plural form of their name in Latin.)

The Reforms of the Gracchi, 133–123 B.C.E.

The Gracchi brothers came from a noble family, yet they devoted their lives to helping the Roman poor. They credited their mother, Cornelia, with giving them the education and motivation they needed to use their privilege for the good of the Roman people. The Gracchi seemed to many Romans to represent the best of republican men—devoted to a public life. Of course, many modern historians have observed that helping the poor would increase their own clients and prestige. Regardless of the motivations of the brothers, they set themselves apart from many aristocrats who no longer obeyed the rigorous demands of public service, preferring private pleasures instead. There were too few nobles willing to sacrifice their own interests for those of Rome when Tiberius became tribune of the plebeians in 133 B.C.E.

In Tiberius's view, Rome's problems came from the decline of the small farmer, which in turn prompted migrations into the city and a shift to large-scale and cash-crop agriculture. Tiberius compassionately expressed the plight of the displaced soldier-farmers: "They are styled masters of the world, and have not a clod of earth they can call their own." Tiberius recognized an additional problem with the growing landlessness—Rome did not have a pool of soldiers, for men had to meet a property qualification to enter the army. Thus, the newly poor could neither farm nor serve in the army—Rome had moved a long way from the days of the farmer-soldier Cincinnatus.

Tiberius proposed an agrarian law that would redistribute public land to landless Romans. The idea may have made a difference, but it alarmed greedy landlords. The law passed, but the Senate appropriated only a tiny sum to help Tiberius administer the law. Many senators were particularly worried when Tiberius announced he was running for reelection. Although in the distant past, tribunes had run for a second term, that had not been done for a long time, and Tiberius's opponents argued that it was illegal. In the ensuing turmoil, a riot occurred at an assembly meeting, and some senators with their followers beat Tiberius and 300 of his followers to death. With one stroke, a new element emerged in Roman political life: political murder.

Tiberius's land law continued to operate for a time, but not very effectively. In 123 B.C.E. Tiberius's brother Gaius became tribune in an effort to continue his brother's work, and he wisely appealed to a broad sector of the Roman people. He built granaries, roads, and bridges to improve the distribution of grain into the city, and these projects created jobs for many Romans. Gaius also tried to fix the price of grain to keep it affordable, and he appealed to the equestrian order by giving them more influence in the wealthy provinces. Gaius opened the new Asian provinces to equestrian tax collectors and placed equestrians in the courts that tried provincial governors accused of abusing their powers. Many senators believed these reforms were politically motivated to destroy the Senate (which had destroyed Tiberius), and it was true that cheap grain might weaken the patron-client relationship that represented the backbone of senatorial power. The Senate moved to undo his reforms as soon as Gaius was out of office, and he and some 250 supporters were murdered in 122 B.C.E.—their deaths were arranged by one of the consuls supporting the Senate.

The Gracchi's sacrifices did not solve the Republic's problems. Their careers focused Rome's attention on its worries, but the brothers had also established a new style of republican government. From their time on, a struggle unfolded in Rome between men like the Gracchi, who enjoyed popular support (*populares*), and *optimates,* who intended to save the Republic by keeping power in the Senate. The old image of a nobility surrounded by and caring for its clients became supplanted by a much more confrontational model. The Gracchi were only the first to die in this struggle, and perhaps the greatest legacy of the Gracchi was the subsequent violence that descended upon the political arena. Roman public life would not be the same again.

Populares vs. Optimates: The Eruption of Civil Wars, 123–46 B.C.E.

Even as Rome experienced violence in its political life, life in the provinces, too, seemed threatened. In North Africa, Rome's old ally Numidia caused trouble, and the Gauls threatened Italy from the north. Just as the military emerged as a primary instrument of political power, the generals, especially, had new opportunities to play a role in internal politics. The political struggle between the *populares* and the *optimates* catalyzed by the Gracchi was continued by popular generals.

The first general to come to power based on the support of the army was Gaius Marius (ca. 157–86 B.C.E.). An equestrian tribune, Marius took up the cause of the *populares*. To address the problem of the African wars and the shortage of soldiers noted by Tiberius, Marius initiated a way of enlisting new soldiers that would redefine the Roman military. He created a professional army, eliminating the previous requirement that soldiers own property. In addition, he formally put the soldiers on the payroll, making official the previous informal patron-client relationship between generals and their troops. Marius also promised them land after their term of service. In this way, he cultivated an army with many rootless and desperate men who were loyal only to him. Although Marius could not foresee the results, his policies established a dangerous pattern that continued through the rest of Roman history. With his new army at his back, the victorious general decisively defeated first the Numidians in Africa and then the Celts to the north. In his battles against Africans and Celts, Marius was accompanied by a brilliant young second-in-command, Lucius Cornelius Sulla (ca. 138–78 B.C.E.). In these wars that brought Marius so much power, Sulla felt that his brave exploits deserved some of the credit that Marius took, and he seethed with resentment.

New crises paved the way for the *optimates* to restore their own power under the aristocrat Sulla, who had learned warfare and resentment from Marius. The first threat to Rome's safety came from within Italy itself—the Italian allies who had first been conquered wanted a greater share in the prosperity that Rome's conquests were bringing. The violent fighting that took place between 90 and 88 B.C.E. finally forced Rome to give full citizenship to the Italian allies. This revolt by the Italian allies is called the "Social War" (from the Latin word *socii*, which means "allies"). The violence that devastated much of the countryside further weakened the Republic. As one of the consuls for 88 B.C.E., Sulla commanded six legions in the final stages of the Italian wars, and his successes earned him a governorship in Asia, where he was given the command to lead the armies against a second threat to Rome—Mithridates (120–63 B.C.E.), a king in Asia Minor who was threatening Rome's borders. However, fearing Sulla's growing strength, the assembly called Marius out of retirement and tried to give him control of Sulla's army. Perhaps Sulla's most dramatic moment came when he marched his army directly into Rome to confront Marius. The hostilities between the two generals made a permanent mark on the city, changing the peaceful Forum into a war zone. After defeating Mithridates, Sulla returned to Rome in 83 B.C.E. to take up the cause of the *optimates*.

Sulla assumed the long-dormant office of dictator (see **Figure 4.3**) but violated tradition by making the term unlimited. He also repealed laws that favored equestrians, and he killed off his political opponents. He buttressed the power of the Senate by passing laws to guarantee it, instead of allowing the tradition of Senate leadership to suffice. The venerable Roman constitutional system was becoming changed, and power politics began to fill the vacuum.

With the wars of Marius and Sulla, a new question confronted Roman politicians: how to protect the citizens from people seeking power and personal gain. Clearly, the old system of checks and balances no longer worked. The next group of popular leaders bypassed most of the formal structures and made a private alliance to share power. Modern historians have called this agreement the First **Triumvirate,** or the rule by three men. A contemporary called it a "three-headed monster."

The First Triumvirate (60–49 B.C.E.) was made up of three men who appealed to various sectors of Roman society. Pompey, beloved of the *optimates*, was a brilliant general who had won striking battles in the east against Sulla's old enemy, Mithridates, and Mediterranean pirates. Julius Caesar was probably an even more talented general and brilliant orator, who won wars in Gaul and Britain and had the support of the

KEY DATES

RISE AND FALL OF THE REPUBLIC

509 B.C.E.	Defeat of Etruscan monarchy
509–287 B.C.E.	Struggle of the Orders
451 B.C.E.	Twelve Tables published
133–123 B.C.E.	Reforms of the Gracchi
90–88 B.C.E.	Social Wars—Rome vs. Italian allies
60–49 B.C.E.	First Triumvirate
49–ca. 46 B.C.E.	Civil war—Caesar vs. Pompey
44 B.C.E.	Julius Caesar murdered

populares. The third man was Crassus, a fabulously rich leader of the business community who had also led armies (including defeating the rebel slave Spartacus). In keeping with tradition in Roman society, the political alliance was sealed by marriage between Pompey and Caesar's daughter, Julia. Instead of bringing peace, however, the triumvirate simply became an arena in which the three powerful figures jockeyed for control.

Events soon came to a head. Crassus perished leading armies to confront a new threat in Rome's eastern frontier. Julia died in childbirth, along with her infant. With her death, little remained to hold Caesar and Pompey together. *Optimates* in the Senate co-opted Pompey in their desire to weaken the popular Caesar, and they declared Pompey sole consul in Rome. Pompey accepted this command from the Senate, breaking his agreement with Caesar, ensuring retribution from the popular general. Caesar defied the Senate, which had forbidden him to bring his army into Italy, and in 49 B.C.E. marched across the Rubicon River into Italy. There was no retreating from this defiant act—a new civil war had erupted.

Julius Caesar, 100–44 B.C.E.

Julius Caesar came from one of the oldest noble families of Rome. As with the Gracchi, his family associated itself with the *populares*. In the civil wars to come, Caesar enjoyed a high degree of support from the plebeians, but before he could take power, he needed the backing of an army. This he achieved in his wars of conquest in Gaul. Both his military successes and his captivating literary accounts of them won him broad popularity. According to the ancient writers, this accomplished general was tall with a fair complexion and piercing black eyes. The bust of Caesar shown in **Figure 4.12** reveals his memorable strength of character. Clearly a brilliant man in all fields, he enthralls historians today much as he fascinated his contemporaries.

The civil war between Caesar and Pompey that began in 49 B.C.E. was not limited to Italy; battles broke out throughout the Roman world. Caesar's and Pompey's armies clashed in Greece, North Africa, and Spain. After losing a decisive battle in Greece in 48 B.C.E., Pompey fled to Egypt, where he was assassinated. When Caesar followed Pompey to Egypt, he became involved with Queen Cleopatra VII (r. 51–30 B.C.E.) (also discussed in Chapter 5), who was engaged in a dynastic struggle with her brother. Caesar supported her claims with his army, spent the winter with her, and fathered her child; then he left in the spring to continue the wars that consolidated his victory over Pompey's supporters. In 46 B.C.E., Caesar returned to Rome.

<mark>Civil war</mark>

FIGURE 4.12 Julius Caesar One of the most controversial figures from the late Republic was Julius Caesar. As was customary with old patrician families, his family commissioned this bust after his death so that they and others would remember his deeds.

Cleopatra joined Caesar in Rome as he took up a task harder than winning the civil war: governing the Republic. The new leader faced two major challenges. First, he had to untangle the economic problems that had plagued the Republic since before the Gracchi attempted reform. Second, Rome needed a form of government that would restore stability to the factions that had burdened the city with so much violence.

Caesar applied his genius for organization to these practical tasks. He reformed the grain dole and established an ambitious program of public works to create jobs for the unemployed. To help displaced peasants, he launched a program of colonization all around the Mediterranean. Caesar's policies extended widely. With the help of an Egyptian astronomer who had accompanied Cleopatra to Rome, Caesar even reformed the calendar. The new "Julian calendar" introduced the solar year of 365 days and added an extra day every four years (the prototype of the "leap year"). With modifications made in 1582, the Julian calendar has remained in use throughout the West.

thinking about DOCUMENTS

DOCUMENT 4.3

Conspirators Assassinate Julius Caesar

The ancient biographer Plutarch (46–120 C.E.) carefully chronicled the lives and deaths of ancient heroes, and his account of the assassination of Julius Caesar remains an important one. As Julius Caesar, the dictator for life, walked to the Senate building, he was surrounded by conspirators who stabbed him to death. After the murder, chaos reigned.

When Cæsar entered the house, the senate rose to do him honor. Some of Brutus' accomplices came up behind his chair, and others before it, pretending to intercede, along with Metillius Cimber, for the recall of his brother from exile. They continued their instances till he came to his seat. When he was seated he gave them a positive denial; and as they continued their importunities with an air of compulsion, he grew angry. Cimber, then, with both hands, pulled his gown off his neck, which was the signal for the attack. Casca gave him the first blow. It was a stroke upon the neck with his sword, but the wound was not dangerous; for in the beginning of so tremendous an enterprise he was probably in some disorder. Cæsar therefore turned upon him and laid hold of his sword. At the same time they both cried out, the one in Latin, "Villain! Casca! what dost thou mean?" and the other in Greek, to his brother, "Brother, help!"

After such a beginning, those who knew nothing of the conspiracy were seized with consternation and horror, insomuch that they durst neither fly nor assist, nor even utter a word. All the conspirators now drew their swords, and surrounded him in such a manner that, whatever way he turned, he saw nothing but steel gleaming in his face, and met nothing but wounds. Like some savage beast attacked by the hunters, he found every hand lifted against him, for they all agreed to have a share in the sacrifice and a taste of his blood. Therefore Brutus himself gave him a stroke in the groin. Some say he opposed the rest, and continued struggling and crying out till he perceived the sword of Brutus; then he drew his robe over his face and yielded to his fate....

Cæsar thus despatched, Brutus advanced to speak to the senate and to assign his reasons for what he had done, but they could not bear to hear him; they fled out of the house and filled the people with inexpressible horror and dismay. Some shut up their houses; others left their shops and counters. All were in motion; one was running to see the spectacle; another running back. Antony and Lepidus, Cæsar's principal friends, withdrew, and hid themselves in other people's houses. Meantime Brutus and his confederates, yet warm from the slaughter, marched in a body with their bloody swords in their hands, from the senate house to the Capitol, not like men that fled, but with an air of gayety and confidence, calling the people to liberty, and stopping to talk with every man of consequence whom they met. There were some who even joined them and mingled with their train, desirous of appearing to have had a share in the action and hoping for one in the glory....

Next day Brutus and the rest of the conspirators came down from the Capitol and addressed the people, who attended to their discourse without expressing either dislike or approbation of what was done. But by their silence it appeared that they pitied Cæsar, at the same time that they revered Brutus. The senate passed a general amnesty; and, to reconcile all parties, they decreed Cæsar divine honors and confirmed all the acts of his dictatorship; while on Brutus and his friends they bestowed governments and such honors as were suitable; so that it was generally imagined the Commonwealth was firmly established again, and all brought into the best order.

But when, upon the opening of Cæsar's will, it was found that he had left every Roman citizen a considerable legacy, and they beheld the body, as it was carried through the Forum, all mangled with wounds, the multitude could no longer be kept within bounds. They stopped the procession, and, tearing up the benches, with the doors and tables, heaped them into a pile, and burned the corpse there. Then snatching flaming brands from the pile, some ran to burn the houses of the assassins, while others ranged the city to find the conspirators themselves and tear them in pieces; but they had taken such care to secure themselves that they could not meet with one of them....

SOURCE: Plutarch, "Lives," in *The Great Events by Famous Historians*, vol. II, ed. Rossiter Johnson (The National Alumni, 1905), pp. 328–329.

Analyze the Document

1. How did the chaos and confusion after Caesar's death contribute to Rome's instability?
2. What caused the Romans first to support Brutus and then to reject him?

Despite his organizational skill, Caesar could not solve the problem of how to govern the Republic. In 48 B.C.E., he accepted the title of dictator, the venerable title Romans reserved for those who stepped in during a crisis. Unlike Cincinnatus (the Roman with whom we began this chapter), Caesar did not renounce the title when the emergency was over, but ultimately proclaimed himself dictator for life, a shocking departure from the traditional six-month tenure. He reportedly refused the title of king to avoid offending the republicans, yet he took on many of the trappings of a monarch. He wore royal regalia and established a priesthood to offer sacrifice to his "genius"—what the Romans called each person's spirit. In 44 B.C.E., Caesar had his image placed on coins—perhaps the first time a living Roman was so honored. (Some historians believe Pompey may have beat Caesar to that distinction.) Some people began to question whether the Republic of Rome was changing too radically.

Political titles

The Roman Republic Ends

The peace and order that Caesar brought to Rome pleased many, particularly the *populares* whose support had lifted Caesar to power. However, many Romans, even among his supporters, were outraged by the honors Caesar took for himself. He had shrunken the role of the *optimates*, and peace seemed to come at the price of the traditional Republic and at the expense of the old power structure. Some conspirators were simply self-serving, hoping to increase their own power. Sixty senators with various motives entered into a conspiracy to murder their leader. Even Brutus, a friend and protégé of Caesar, joined in the plot. He would be like the Brutus of early Rome who had avenged Lucretia and freed Rome from the Etruscan kings. This Brutus would save Rome from a new king—Caesar.

Conspiracy

Caesar was planning a military campaign for March 18, 44 B.C.E., so the assassins had to move quickly. On March 15, the date the Romans called the "ides," or middle of the month, they surrounded the unwary dictator as he approached the Senate meeting place. Suddenly they drew knives from the folds of their togas and plunged them into his body. He died at the foot of the statue of Pompey, his old enemy. Most of the killers seem to have genuinely believed they had done what was best for Rome. They saw themselves as "liberators" who had freed Rome from a dictator and who would restore the Republic. In 43 B.C.E., they issued the coin shown in **Figure 4.13**. The coin depicts the assassins' daggers and reads "Ides of March." On the other side of the coin is a portrait of Brutus.

Caesar's murder

FIGURE 4.13 Commemorative Coin Coins were struck to memorialize famous people and important events. Caesar's assassins produced this coin, marked with the Ides of March, the date of Caesar's murder, as well as the dagger that killed him.

This attempt to celebrate a great victory on the coin was mere propaganda. The conspirators had no real plan beyond the murder. They apparently had made no provision for control of the army, nor for ensuring peace in the city. In the end, their claim to "save the Republic" rang hollow. Document 4.3 reveals the chaos that followed the assassination. After Caesar's death, one of his friends supposedly lamented, "If Caesar for all his genius, could not find a way out, who is going to find one now?" The republican form of government so carefully forged during the Struggle of the Orders crumbled under the stress of civil wars and murder.

LOOKING BACK & MOVING FORWARD

Summary The Republic of Rome, with its emphasis on family and city, rose to great power from 509 B.C.E. to the death of Caesar in 44 B.C.E. By that year, Rome controlled much of the Mediterranean world, and a system of wealthy slave owners and a large standing army had replaced the citizen farmer-soldier who had laid the foundation for the Republic's success. Whereas the early Romans had emphasized the ties between citizens, now violent power struggles tore at the social fabric. A people who had preserved stories of serious Roman heroes began to treasure Greek models of beauty and individualism.

Julius Caesar became a central figure in Rome's transformation from republic to empire. Since Caesar's death, historians have argued about his qualities. Was he a great man who detected the inability of the republican form of government—designed to govern a city-state—to adapt to the changed circumstances of empire and social unrest? Or was he a power-hungry politician who craved control and blocked his fellow citizens from having any political involvement in the Republic? The truth no doubt falls somewhere between these extremes. One thing is certain: Despite the assassins' confident claims, Caesar's murder did not solve anything. More violence would ensue until a leader arose who could establish a new form of government that would endure even longer than the Republic.

KEY TERMS

patricians, *p. 110*
consuls, *p. 110*
Senate, *p. 110*
assemblies, *p. 110*
plebeians, *p. 110*
Struggle of the Orders, *p. 111*
tribunes, *p. 111*
Twelve Tables, *p. 111*
equestrians, *p. 111*
Forum, *p. 112*
Pantheon, *p. 127*
populares, *p. 129*
optimates, *p. 129*
Triumvirate, *p. 130*

REVIEW, ANALYZE, & CONNECT TO TODAY

REVIEW THE PREVIOUS CHAPTERS

Chapter 1—"The Roots of Western Civilization"—discussed the rise of the first empires of the West, the Assyrian and the Persian. In Chapter 3—"The Poleis Become Cosmopolitan"—we saw the rise of large Hellenistic monarchies throughout the old empires of the ancient world. Rome inherited much from these empires.

1. Review the Persians' and the Assyrians' treatment of conquered peoples and consider which most closely resembled the Romans' approach. To what degree did the Romans' treatment of their subjects contribute to their success as an imperial power?
2. Compare and contrast Roman and Greek governments.
3. In what ways do you think Rome came to resemble the great Hellenistic cities, and what problems did they share?

ANALYZE THIS CHAPTER

This chapter—"Pride in Family and City"—traces the rise of the small city of Rome to a Hellenistic power whose territory extended throughout the Mediterranean world. In the course of this expansion, the old values of Rome were transformed and new constructs were slowly and violently implemented.

1. Review these changes in early Roman life and values as the armies successfully expanded Roman influence. How did Romans struggle with their changing identity as Rome moved from city to empire?
2. Review the political structure of the Roman Republic. What were its strengths and weaknesses? How did the patron-client system contribute to the strengths and weaknesses of the political system?
3. What were the strengths of the Roman army? Consider how and why Rome expanded its territories so extensively.
4. What were Rome's contributions to the fields of art and technology?

CONNECT TO TODAY

The government of the United States looks back to the Roman Republic as its model of representative democracy.

1. Compare the power of the people in ancient Rome with that of Americans today. In which system do you think the people have exerted the most authority? Support your answer.
2. Romans found it impossible to maintain their republican form of government during their expansion. What similar stresses can you identify in world democracies today? Consider, for example, the flow of immigrants into European countries that has changed the face of traditionally homogeneous European populations, or the feeling among some U.S. citizens that the United States has grown so large, they have little say about what their legislators do in Washington, D.C. In what other ways might people feel disconnected from their government?

BEYOND THE CLASSROOM

THE RISE OF ROME, 753–265 B.C.E.

Bell, Sinclair, and Helen Nagy, eds. *New Perspectives on Etruria and Early Rome*. Madison: University of Wisconsin Press, 2009. Collection of essays exploring the latest archaeological discoveries yielding insights into early Italy; enhanced with maps and illustrations.

Garland, Lynda, and Matthew Dillon. *Ancient Rome: From the Early Republic to the Assassination of Julius Caesar*. London: Routledge, 2005. An accessible yet comprehensive summary that includes translations of documents and spotlights social and political developments during the Republic.

Meyer, J.C. *Pre-Republican Rome*. Odense, Denmark: Odense University Press, 1983. A highly illustrated archaeological look at pre-republican Rome.

Mitchell, Richard E. *Patricians and Plebeians: The Origin of the Roman State*. New York: Cornell University Press, 1990. A description of the separate patrician and plebeian systems.

FAMILY LIFE AND CITY LIFE

Aldrete, Gregory S. *Gestures and Acclamations in Ancient Rome*. Baltimore: Johns Hopkins University Press, 1999. An accessible, nicely illustrated, and fascinating discussion on the verbal and nonverbal communications between Roman crowds and their leaders.

Bradley, Keith R. *Discovering the Roman Family: Studies in Roman Social History*. New York: Oxford University Press, 1991. Essays that study the composition of the Roman family and household-central features of the Roman state.

De Albentiis, Emidio. *Secrets of Pompeii: Everyday Life in Ancient Rome*. Los Angeles: Getty Publications, 2009. A survey of how ancient Romans interacted in their public squares and marketplaces, decorated their homes, and spent their leisure time, as well as how they worshiped.

Gardner, J.F. *Women in Roman Law and Society*. Bloomington: Indiana University Press, 1986. An interesting look at the ways in which the practice of law affected women in various aspects of their lives.

Orlin, Eric M. *Temples, Religion and Politics in the Roman Republic*. New York: E.J. Brill U.S.A., 1996. An exploration into the relationship between the individual and the community.

Robinson, O.F. *Ancient Rome: City Planning and Administration*. New York: Routledge, 1994. A remarkable study of the level of organization, laws, and local governmental arrangements made to allow a large population to live together in the ancient world.

EXPANSION AND TRANSFORMATION, 265–133 B.C.E.

Bagnall, Nigel. *The Punic Wars*. London: Hutchinson, 1990. A detailed, chronological study of the different campaigns, studying them strategically, operationally, and tactically.

Goldsworthy, Adrian. *The Complete Roman Army*. New York: Thames & Hudson, 2003. A wonderfully comprehensive study of the development of the army from its days as a citizen's militia to the highly professional army that was the wonder of the Mediterranean world.

Mayor, Adrienne. *Greek Fire, Poison Arrows, and Scorpion Bombs: Biological and Chemical Warfare in the Ancient World*. Woodstock, NY: Overlook TP, 2008. A fascinating look at ancient weapons of mass destruction.

Ostenberg, Ida. *Staging the World: Spoils, Captives, and Representations in the Roman Triumphal Procession*. Oxford: Oxford University Press, 2009. Study of how Rome presented and perceived the defeated on parade, discussing what was displayed, how it was paraded, and observers' responses.

THE HELLENIZING OF THE REPUBLIC

Ogilvie, R.M. *Roman Literature and Society*. Harmondsworth, England: Penguin, 1980. A brief introduction to and fresh opinion of major Latin writers.

Rawson, Elizabeth. *Intellectual Life in the Late Roman Republic*. Baltimore: Johns Hopkins University Press, 1985. A summary intending to capture the full range of intellectual activity in the Republic.

THE TWILIGHT OF THE REPUBLIC, 133–44 B.C.E.

Lacey, W.K. *Cicero and the Fall of the Republic*. New York: Barnes and Noble, 1978. An in-depth study of all aspects of the man—speaker, author, philosopher—that shows how elements of Cicero's character developed over time in reaction to the social conditions of his age.

Langguth, A.J. *A Noise of War: Caesar, Octavian and the Struggle for Rome*. New York: Simon & Schuster, 1994. A chronologically organized focus on the personalities of these influential men.

Meier, Christian. *Caesar*. New York: Basic Books, 1997. A fine study that places Caesar, a remarkable individual, within his cultural context and encourages us to consider the relationship between the man and his times.

Shotter, David. *The Fall of the Roman Republic*. New York: Routledge, 1994. A brief survey of the elements surrounding the fall of the Roman Republic—a good introductory survey.

Timeline

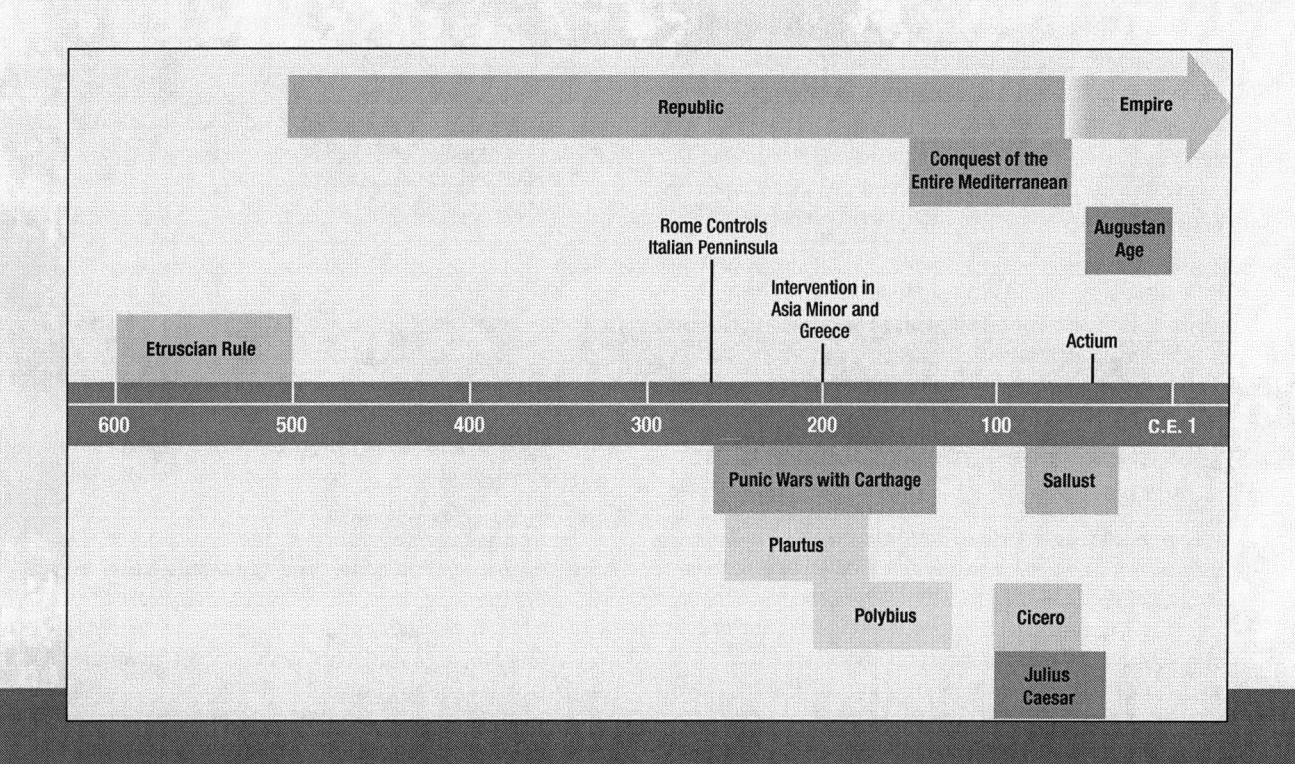

- Etruscian Rule
- Republic
- Rome Controls Italian Penninsula
- Intervention in Asia Minor and Greece
- Conquest of the Entire Mediterranean
- Actium
- Augustan Age
- Empire
- Punic Wars with Carthage
- Plautus
- Polybius
- Sallust
- Cicero
- Julius Caesar

(600 — 500 — 400 — 300 — 200 — 100 — C.E. 1)

4 The Rise of Rome

Roman civilization arose during the middle of the first millennium B.C.E. After the Romans gained independence from the ruling Etruscans in 509 B.C.E., they slowly established control over the Italian peninsula, the western Mediterranean, the whole Mediterranean basin, and large parts of Europe. Although Rome retained its republican form of government until the first century B.C.E., there was considerable political turmoil and struggle, often reflecting tensions between the lower and middle classes and the ruling elites. Eventually, the Republic was unable to support these and other tensions. After a century of "slow revolution," Augustus took command in 27 B.C.E., making Rome an empire in all but name. By the time the Republic was transformed into the Empire, the combination of Roman political control and Greek culture had provided considerable unity to the Mediterranean basin. This Greco-Roman civilization enjoyed full maturity following the triumph of Augustus.

The Republic's most stunning accomplishments were military, political, and administrative. Rome was in the long run consistently successful in its wars, each time extending its rule. One reason for this success was her ability to develop political, administrative, and legal policies to manage newly won territories—something at which the Greeks were much less successful. During the late Republic and particularly during the Empire, these accomplishments were facilitated and symbolized by great architectural achievements—the roads, aqueducts, public facilities, and monuments that helped hold Roman lands together. Culturally, the Romans borrowed freely from the Greeks, acknowledging Greek superiority but nevertheless adding their own style to what they borrowed.

This chapter deals with two main issues. First, what was the structure of the Roman state? This involves an examination of the Roman constitution. Second, what was the nature of Roman society during the Republic? To get at this issue, a number of documents focus on the life and education of the aristocracy, the importance of Roman religious practices, the position of women, the use of slaves, and the place of Greek culture in Roman life. The sources in this chapter should provide a background for developments during the Empire, which will be covered in the next chapter.

> **For Classroom Discussion**
>
> *How do we explain the "success" of Rome, particularly the rise of Rome during the Republic? Use the analysis of the Roman constitution by Polybius, the account by Cicero, and Sallust's* The Conspiracy of Catiline.

Primary Sources

Histories: The Roman Constitution
Polybius

One of the Romans' greatest achievements was the development of political institutions that, despite problems, accommodated Rome's needs. Probably the best general description of these institutions during the Republic is provided by Polybius (c. 205–123 B.C.E.), a Greek politician and one of the greatest historians of the ancient world. He spent sixteen years in Rome, where he was in a position to observe the functioning of the Roman state and examine relevant documents. Part of his stated purpose in examining Rome's institutions was to explain why Rome had been so successful, particularly in comparison with his own Greek world. Some of his conclusions are presented in the following selection in which he describes the balanced nature of the Roman constitution.

CONSIDER: *The relative powers of the consuls, the Senate, and the people; the most important functions of the Roman government according to Polybius; the potential dangers or sources of instability in such a constitution.*

As for the Roman constitution, it had three elements, each of them possessing sovereign powers: and their respective share of power in the whole state had been regulated with such a scrupulous regard to equality and equilibrium, that no one could say for certain, not even a native, whether the constitution as a whole were an aristocracy or democracy or despotism. And no wonder: for if we confine our observation to the power of the Consuls we should be inclined to regard it as despotic; if on that of the Senate, as aristocratic; and if finally one looks at the power possessed by the people it would seem a clear case of democracy. What the exact powers of these several parts were, and still, with slight modifications, are, I will now state.

The Consuls, before leading out the legions, remain in Rome and are supreme masters of the administration. All other magistrates, except the Tribunes, are under them and take their orders. They introduce foreign ambassadors to the Senate; bring matters requiring deliberation before it; and see to the execution of its decrees. If, again, there are any matters of state which require the authorisation of the people, it is their business to see to them, to summon the popular meetings, to bring the proposals before them, and to carry out the decrees of the majority. In the preparations for war also, and in a word in the entire administration of a campaign, they have all but absolute power. It is competent to them to impose on the allies such levies as they think good, to appoint the Military Tribunes, to make up the roll for soldiers and select those that are suitable. Besides they have absolute power of inflicting punishment on all who are under their command while on active service: and they have authority to expend as much of the public money as they choose, being accompanied by a quaestor[1] who is entirely at their orders. A survey of these powers would in fact justify our describing the constitution as despotic,—a clear case of royal government. Nor will it affect the truth of my description, if any of the institutions I have described are changed in our time, or in that of our posterity: and the same remarks apply to what follows.

The Senate has first of all the control of the treasury, and regulates the receipts and disbursements alike. For the Quaestors cannot issue any public money for the various departments of the state without a decree of the Senate, except for the service of the Consuls. The Senate controls also what is by far the largest and most important expenditure, that, namely, which is made by

---

SOURCE: Polybius, *Histories,* vol. I, trans. Evelyn S. Shuckburgh (New York: Macmillan and Co., 1889), pp. 468–471.

[1] Official responsible for finance and administration.

the censors[2] every *lustrum*[3] for the repair or construction of public buildings; this money cannot be obtained by the censors except by the grant of the Senate. Similarly all crimes committed in Italy requiring a public investigation, such as treason, conspiracy, poisoning, or wilful murder, are in the hands of the Senate. Besides, if any individual or state among the Italian allies requires a controversy to be settled, a penalty to be assessed, help or protection to be afforded,—all this is the province of the Senate. Or again, outside Italy, if it is necessary to send an embassy to reconcile warring communities, or to remind them of their duty, or sometimes to impose requisitions upon them, or to receive their submission, or finally to proclaim war against them,—this too is the business of the Senate. In like manner the reception to be given to foreign ambassadors in Rome, and the answers to be returned to them, are decided by the senate. With such business the people have nothing to do. Consequently, if one were staying at Rome when the Consuls were not in town, one would imagine the constitution to be a complete aristocracy: and this has been the idea entertained by many Greeks, and by many kings as well, from the fact that nearly all the business they had with Rome was settled by the Senate.

After this one would naturally be inclined to ask what part is left for the people in the constitution, when the Senate has these various functions, especially the control of the receipts and expenditure of the exchequer; and when the Consuls, again, have absolute power over the details of military preparation, and an absolute authority in the field? There is, however, a part left the people, and it is a most important one. For the people is the sole fountain of honour and of punishment; and it is by these two things and these alone that dynasties and constitutions and, in a word, human society are held together: for where the distinction between them is not sharply drawn both in theory and practice, there no undertaking can be properly administered,—as indeed we might expect when good and bad are held in exactly the same honour. The people then are the only court to decide matters of life and death; and even in cases where the penalty is money, if the sum to be assessed is sufficiently serious, and especially when the accused have held the higher magistracies. And in regard to this arrangement there is one point deserving especial commendation and record. Men who are on trial for their lives at Rome, while sentence is in process of being voted,—if even only one of the tribes whose votes are needed to ratify the sentence has not voted,—have the privilege at Rome of openly departing and condemning themselves to a voluntary exile. Such men are safe at Naples or Praeneste or at Tibur, and at other towns with which this arrangement has been duly ratified on oath.

Again, it is the people who bestow offices on the deserving, which are the most honourable rewards of virtue. It has also the absolute power of passing or repealing laws; and, most important of all, it is the people who deliberate on the question of peace or war. And when provisional terms are made for alliance, suspension of hostilities, or treaties, it is the people who ratify them or the reverse.

These considerations again would lead one to say that the chief power in the state was the people's, and that the constitution was a democracy.

Such, then, is the distribution of power between the several parts of the state.

The Education of a Roman Gentleman

Cicero

Roman society during the last century of the Republic was turbulent and mobile. One way to rise in this society was through education and talent. Marcus Tullius Cicero (106–43 B.C.E.) rose in this way. Born into a moderately wealthy but nonaristocratic family, he became an extremely successful orator in the law courts, rose to the position of consul in 63 B.C.E., and became one of the most prolific, influential, and admired authors of Roman times. Cicero attributed part of his success to the excellent education he received. This is described in the following excerpt from one of his numerous letters.

CONSIDER: *The nature of this process of education; the importance of Greek culture for Cicero's education; Cicero's social and political environment.*

I daily spent the remainder of my time in reading, writing, and private declamation, I cannot say that I much relished my confinement to these preparatory exercises. The next year Quintus Varius was condemned, and banished by his own law; and I, that I might acquire a competent knowledge of the principles of jurisprudence, then attached myself to Quintus Scævola, the son of Publius, who, though he did not choose to undertake the charge of a pupil, yet, by freely giving his advice to those who consulted him, answered every purpose of instruction to

---

[2]Officials responsible for supervising the public census and public behavior and morals.

[3]A ceremonial purification of the Roman population after the census every five years.

SOURCE: From J. S. Watson, trans., *Cicero on Oratory and Orators* (London: Henry G. Bohn, 1855), pp. 495–499.

such as took the trouble to apply to him. In the succeeding year, in which Sylla and Pompey were consuls, as Sulpicius, who was elected a tribune of the people, had occasion to speak in public almost every day, I had opportunity to acquaint myself thoroughly with his manner of speaking. At this time Philo, a philosopher of the first name in the Academy, with many of the principal Athenians, having deserted their native home, and fled to Rome, from the fury of Mithridates, I immediately became his scholar, and was exceedingly taken with his philosophy; and, besides the pleasure I received from the great variety and sublimity of his matter, I was still more inclined to confine my attention to that study; because there was reason to apprehend that our laws and judicial proceedings would be wholly overturned by the continuance of the public disorders. In the same year Sulpicius lost his life; and Quintus Catulus, Marcus Antonius, and Caius Julius, three orators who were partly contemporary with each other, were most inhumanly put to death. Then also I attended the lectures of Molo the Rhodian, who was newly come to Rome, and was both an excellent pleader, and an able teacher of the art. . . .

The three following years the city was free from the tumult of arms. . . . I pursued my studies of every kind, day and night, with unremitting application. I lodged and boarded at my own house (where he lately died) Diodotus the Stoic; whom I employed as my preceptor in various other parts of learning, but particularly in logic, which may be considered as a close and contracted species of eloquence; and without which, you yourself have declared it impossible to acquire that full and perfect eloquence, which they suppose to be an open and dilated kind of logic. Yet with all my attention to Diodotus, and the various arts he was master of, I never suffered even a single day to escape me, without some exercise of the oratorical kind. I constantly declaimed in private with Marcus Piso, Quintus Pompeius, or some other of my acquaintance; pretty often in Latin, but much oftener in Greek; because the Greek furnishes a greater variety of ornaments, and an opportunity of imitating and introducing them into the Latin; and because the Greek masters, who were far the best, could not correct and improve us, unless we declaimed in that language. This time was distinguished by a violent struggle to restore the liberty of the republic; the barbarous slaughter of the three orators, Scævola, Carbo, and Antistius; the return of Cotta, Curio, Crassus, Pompey, and the Lentuli; the re-establishment of the laws and courts of judicature, and the entire restoration of the commonwealth; but we lost Pomponius, Censorinus, and Murena, from the roll of orators. I now began, for the first time, to undertake the management of causes, both private and public; not, as most did, with a view to learn my profession, but to make a trial of the abilities which I had taken so much pains to acquire. I had then a second opportunity of attending the instructions of Molo, who came to Rome while Sylla was dictator, to solicit the payment of what was due to his countrymen for their services in the Mithridatic war. My defence of Sextus Roscius, which was the first cause I pleaded, met with such a favourable reception, that, from that moment, I was looked upon as an advocate of the first class, and equal to the greatest and most important causes; and after this I pleaded many others, which I precomposed with all the care and accuracy I was master of. . . .

[A]fter I had been two years at the bar, and acquired some reputation in the forum, I left Rome. When I came to Athens, I spent six months with Antiochus, the principal and most judicious philosopher of the old Academy; and under this able master, I renewed those philosophical studies which I had laboriously cultivated and improved from my earliest youth. At the same time, however, I continued my *rhetorical exercises* under Demetrius the Syrian, an experienced and reputable master of the art of speaking. After leaving Athens, I traversed every part of Asia, where I was voluntarily attended by the principal orators of the country, with whom I renewed my rhetorical exercises. The chief of them was Menippus of Stratonica, the most eloquent of all the Asiatics; and if to be neither tedious nor impertinent is the characteristic of an Attic orator, he may be justly ranked in that class. Dionysius also of Magnesia, Æschylus of Cnidos, and Xenocles of Adramyttium, who were esteemed the first rhetoricians of Asia, were continually with me. Not contented with these, I went to Rhodes, and applied myself again to Molo, whom I had heard before at Rome; and who was both an experienced pleader and a fine writer, and particularly judicious in remarking the faults of his scholars, as well as in his method of teaching and improving them. His principal trouble with me was to restrain the luxuriancy of a juvenile imagination, always ready to overflow its banks, within its due and proper channel. Thus, after an excursion of two years, I returned to Italy, not only much improved, but almost changed into a new man. The vehemence of my voice and action was considerably abated; the excessive ardour of my language was corrected; my lungs were strengthened; and my whole constitution confirmed and settled.

Eulogy for a Roman Wife
Quintus Lucretius Vespillo

Romans of high social rank usually married for political and economic reasons, but that did not mean affection and love were absent from such alliances. The following is an excerpt

---

SOURCE: Dana C. Munro, ed., *A Source Book of Roman History* (Boston: D.C. Heath, 1904), pp. 201–204.

from a funeral eulogy composed in about 8 B.C.E. by ex-Consul Quintus Lucretius Vespillo for his wife Turia. In it, Vespillo discusses their life together and the qualities that made Turia such a good woman.

CONSIDER: *What this reveals about the proper role of Roman wives; the qualities that made Turia an admired and powerful figure.*

Before the day fixed for our marriage, you were suddenly left an orphan, by the murder of your parents in the solitude of the country. . . .

Through your efforts chiefly, their death did not remain unavenged. . . .

In our day, marriages of such long duration, not dissolved by divorce, but terminated by death alone, are indeed rare. For our union was prolonged in unclouded happiness for forty-one years. Would that it had been my lot to put an end to this our good fortune and that I as the older—which was more just—had yielded to fate.

Why recall your inestimable qualities, your modesty, deference, affability, your amiable disposition, your faithful attendance to the household duties, your enlightened religion, your unassuming elegance, the modest simplicity and refinement of your manners? Need I speak of your attachment to your kindred, your affection for your family—when you respected my mother as you did your own parents and cared for her tomb as you did for that of your own mother and father,—you who share countless other virtues with Roman ladies most jealous of their fair name? These qualities which I claim for you are your own, equalled or excelled by but few; for the experience of men teaches us how rare they are.

With common prudence we have preserved all the patrimony which you received from your parents. Intrusting it all to me, you were not troubled with the care of increasing it; thus did we share the task of administering it, that I undertook to protect your fortune, and you to guard mine. . . .

You gave proof of your generosity not only towards several of your kin, but especially in your filial devotion. . . . You brought up in your own home, in the enjoyment of mutual benefits, some young girls of your kinship. And that these might attain to a station in life worthy of our family, you provided them with dowries. . . .

I owe you no less a debt than Caesar Augustus [27 B.C.E.–C.E. 14, emperor of Rome] himself, for this my return from exile to my native land. For unless you had prepared the way for my safety, even Caesar's promises of assistance had been of no avail. So I owe no less a debt to your loyal devotion than to the clemency of Caesar. . . .

When all the world was again at peace and the Republic reestablished, peaceful and happy days followed. We longed for children, which an envious fate denied us. Had Fortune smiled on us in this, what had been lacking to complete our happiness? But an adverse destiny put an end to our hopes. . . . Disconsolate to see me without children . . . you wished to put an end to my chagrin by proposing to me a divorce, offering to yield the place to another spouse more fertile, with the only intention of searching for and providing for me a spouse worthy of our mutual affection, whose children you assured me you would have treated as your own. . . .

I will admit that I was so irritated and shocked by such a proposition that I had difficulty in restraining my anger and remaining master of myself. You spoke of divorce before the decree of fate [death] had forced us to separate, and I could not comprehend how you could conceive of any reason why you, still living, should not be my wife, you who during my exile had always remained most faithful and loyal . . .

Menaechmi: Roman Slavery

Plautus

It should not be overlooked that the Romans, like other peoples in the ancient world, were supported by slaves. Indeed, slaves were a familiar component of everyday life for the Romans during the Republic. Some notion of the Roman treatment and perception of slaves can be gained from the following extract from Menaechmi *by Plautus (c. 254–184 B.C.E.), a Roman who wrote numerous comedies, often adapted from Greek originals. Here, Messenio, a slave, soliloquizes.*

CONSIDER: *What distinguished the "good" from the "bad" slave; the "right" way to treat a servant; the presence or absence of a sense of guilt or injustice about the institution of slavery.*

Mess. (*to himself*). This is the proof of a good servant, who takes care of his master's business, looks after it, arranges it, thinks about it, in the absence of his master diligently to attend to the affairs of his master, as much so as if he himself were present, or *even* better. It is proper that his back[4] should be of more consequence than his appetite, his legs than his stomach, whose heart is rightly placed. Let him bear in mind, those who are good for nothing, what reward is given them by their masters—lazy, worthless fellows. Stripes, fetters, the mill, weariness, hunger, sharp cold; these are the rewards of idleness. This evil do I terribly stand in awe of.

SOURCE: H. T. Riley, *The Comedies of Plautus,* vol. I (London: G. Bell and Sons, Ltd., 1852), pp. 364–365.

[4] *That his back*—Ver. 970. For the purpose of keeping his back intact from the whip, and his feet from the fetters.

Wherefore 'tis sure that to be good is better than to be bad. Much more readily do I submit to words, stripes I do detest; and I eat what is ground much more readily than supply it *ground* by myself.[5] Therefore do I obey the command of my master, carefully and diligently do I observe it; and in such manner do I pay obedience, as I think is for the interest of my back. And that *course* does profit me. Let others be just as they take it to be their interest; I shall be just as I ought to be. If I adhere to that, I shall avoid faultiness; so that I am in readiness for my master on all occasions, I shall not be much afraid. *The time is near, when, for these deeds of mine, my master will give his reward.*

The Conspiracy of Catiline: Decline of the Republic

Sallust

The Roman Republic came to an end during the second half of the first century B.C.E. *after a long period of conflict and civil war. Many saw this period as one of moral, social, and political decline from the more glorious and virtuous days of the Republic. Sallust (86–36* B.C.E.*) was both a participant and an observer in this period. He became a tribune of the people in 52* B.C.E. *and a close supporter of Julius Caesar in the following years. Later in his life he devoted himself more to historical writing. In the following selection he describes his own sense of disgust and disillusionment with the recent course of events.*

CONSIDER: *The main developments that disturbed Sallust; how Sallust compared characteristics of his own times with characteristics of the early Republic; the reliability of this account.*

My earliest inclinations led me, like many other young men, to throw myself wholeheartedly into politics. There I found many things against me. Self-restraint, integrity, and virtue were disregarded; unscrupulous conduct, bribery, and profit-seeking were rife. And although, being a stranger to the vices I saw practised on every hand, I looked on them with scorn, I was led astray by ambition and, with a young man's weakness, could not tear myself away. However much I tried to dissociate myself from the prevailing corruption, my craving for advancement exposed me to the same odium and slander as all my rivals.

After suffering manifold perils and hardships, peace of mind at last returned to me, and I decided that I must bid farewell to politics for good. But I had no intention of wasting my precious leisure in idleness and sloth, or of devoting my time to agriculture or hunting—tasks fit only for slaves. I had formerly been interested in history, and some work which I began in that field had been interrupted by my misguided political ambitions. I therefore took this up again, and decided to write accounts of some episodes in Roman history that seemed particularly worthy of record—a task for which I felt myself the better qualified inasmuch as I was unprejudiced by the hopes and fears of the party man....

Thus by hard work and just dealing the power of the state increased. Mighty kings were vanquished, savage tribes and huge nations were brought to their knees; and when Carthage, Rome's rival in her quest for empire, had been annihilated,[6] every land and sea lay open to her. It was then that fortune turned unkind and confounded all her enterprises. To the men who had so easily endured toil and peril, anxiety and adversity, the leisure and riches which are generally regarded as so desirable proved a burden and a curse. Growing love of money, and the lust for power which followed it, engendered every kind of evil. Avarice destroyed honour, integrity, and every other virtue, and instead taught men to be proud and cruel, to neglect religion, and to hold nothing too sacred to sell. Ambition tempted many to be false, to have one thought hidden in their hearts, another ready on their tongues, to become a man's friend or enemy not because they judged him worthy or unworthy but because they thought it would pay them, and to put on the semblance of virtues that they had not. At first these vices grew slowly and sometimes met with punishment; later on, when the disease had spread like a plague, Rome changed: her government, once so just and admirable, became harsh and unendurable....

As soon as wealth came to be a mark of distinction and an easy way to renown, military commands and political power, virtue began to decline. Poverty was now looked on as a disgrace and a blameless life as a sign of ill nature. Riches made the younger generation a prey to luxury, avarice, and pride. Squandering with one hand what they grabbed with the other, they set small value on their own property while they coveted that of others. Honour and modesty, all laws divine and human, were alike disregarded in a spirit of recklessness and intemperance.

---

[5] *Ground by myself*—Ver. 979. He alludes to the custom of sending refractory slaves to the "pistrinum," where the corn was ground by a handmill, which entailed extreme labour on those grinding. He says that he would rather that others should grind the corn for him, than that he should grind it for others.

SOURCE: Sallust, *The Conspiracy of Catiline*, trans. S. A. Hanford (London: Penguin Books Ltd., 1963), pp. 174–178. Copyright © 1963. Reprinted by permission of Penguin Books Ltd.

[6] In 146 B.C.E.

To one familiar with mansions and villas reared aloft on such a scale that they look like so many towns, it is instructive to visit the temples built by our godfearing ancestors. In those days piety was the ornament of shrines; glory, of men's dwellings. When they conquered a foe, they took nothing from him save his power to harm. But their base successors stuck at no crime to rob subject peoples of all that those brave conquerors had left them, as though oppression were the only possible method of ruling an empire. I need not remind you of some enterprises that no one but an eyewitness will believe—how private citizens have often levelled mountains and paved seas for their building operations. Such men, it seems to me, have treated their wealth as a mere plaything: instead of making honourable use of it, they have shamefully misused it on the first wasteful project that occurred to them. Equally strong was their passion for fornication, guzzling, and other forms of sensuality. Men prostituted themselves like women, and women sold their chastity to every comer. To please their palates they ransacked land and sea. They went to bed before they needed sleep, and instead of waiting until they felt hungry, thirsty, cold, or tired, they forestalled their bodies' needs by self-indulgence. Such practices incited young men who had run through their property to have recourse to crime. Because their vicious natures found it hard to forgo sensual pleasures, they resorted more and more recklessly to every means of getting and spending.

Visual Sources

Evidence from Coins

Historians can generally use coins for dating and for determining changes in dynasties and regimes. For ancient times, deposits of coins are often the best evidence for the presence of a people in a particular area. They can indicate the geographic area and quantity of trade relations. By analyzing changing patterns of deposits of coins, growing trade rivalries and changes of commercial, political, or military dominance can be discovered.

The designs and representations on coins often reveal much about a society. On this Roman coin from about 137 B.C.E. (figure 4.1), a citizen is pictured dropping a ballot into a voting urn. This reveals something about the type of political system present in Rome at the time and indicates that Romans were particularly proud of that system. In fact, Roman citizenship and voting rights were highly valued and part of what facilitated Rome's expansion. Yet too much should not be assumed: This scene could denote a limited oligarchy as much as a democracy or anything between. The writing on the coin is evidence of some level of literacy.

CONSIDER: *How modern American coins might reveal characteristics of American society to future historians.*

The Geographic and Cultural Environment

Map 4.1 shows some of the peoples and civilizations that occupied Italy and its immediately surrounding territory during the fifth century B.C.E. In the process of Rome's formation and expansion, the Romans came into direct and extended contact with these peoples. Before Rome became a dominant power, the Etruscans, Carthaginians (descendants of the Phoenicians), and Greeks had already established strong, literate, sophisticated civilizations. Understandably, then, as Rome expanded the Romans drew from and even copied many of the institutions and practices of these civilizations, particularly the closer Etruscans and Greeks. Other peoples, such as the Samnites, constituted a barrier to Roman expansion that the Romans overcame during the fifth, fourth, and third centuries B.C.E., usually by force of arms. Rome's geographic and cultural environment, therefore, played an important role in the development of the Roman Republic.

CONSIDER: *How the experience gained during the early years of the Roman Republic laid the foundations for later Roman imperialism.*

FIGURE 4.1 (© Snark/Art Resource, NY)

MAP 4.1 Italy, Fifth Century B.C.E.

Secondary Sources

The Ancient City: Religious Practices

Fustel de Coulanges

Ancient Rome is usually described in political, military, and cultural terms. The Romans themselves are typically described as practical, rational, disciplined, and secular. Yet like the Greeks, they were also very religious. This is emphasized in the following selection from The Ancient City, *which has become a minor classic. Here Fustel de Coulanges, a nineteenth-century French historian, shows how central religious beliefs were to the Roman's everyday life.*

CONSIDER: *How the Romans related to the gods; what the author means in arguing that the Roman patrician was a priest.*

We must inquire what place religion occupied in the life of a Roman. His house was for him what a temple is for us. He finds there his worship and his gods. His fire is a god; the walls, the doors, the threshold are gods; the boundary marks which surround his field are also gods. The tomb is an altar, and his ancestors are divine beings.

Each one of his daily actions is a rite; his whole day belongs to his religion. Morning and evening he invokes his fire, his Penates,[7] and his ancestors; in leaving and entering his house he addresses a prayer to them. Every meal is a religious act, which he shares with his domestic divinities. Birth, initiation, the taking of the toga, marriage, and the anniversaries of all these events, are the solemn acts of his worship.

He leaves his house, and can hardly take a step without meeting some sacred object—either a chapel, or a place formerly struck by lightning, or a tomb; sometimes he must step back and pronounce a prayer; sometimes he must turn his eyes and cover his face, to avoid the sight of some ill-boding object.

Every day he sacrifices in his house, every month in his cury, several months a year with his gens or his tribe. Above all these gods, he must offer worship to those of the city. There are in Rome more gods than citizens.

He offers sacrifices to thank the gods; he offers them, and by far the greater number, to appease their wrath. One day he figures in a procession, dancing after a certain ancient rhythm, to the sound of the sacred flute. Another day he conducts chariots, in which lie statues of the divinities. Another time it is a *lectisternium:* a table is set in a street, and loaded with provisions; upon beds lie statues of the gods, and every Roman passes bowing, with a crown upon his head, and a branch of laurel in his hand.

There is a festival for seed-time, one for the harvest, and one for the pruning of the vines. Before corn has reached the ear, the Roman has offered more than ten sacrifices, and invoked some ten divinities for the success of his harvest. He has, above all, a multitude of festivals for the dead, because he is afraid of them.

He never leaves his own house without looking to see if any bird of bad augury appears. There are words which he dares not pronounce for his life. If he experiences some desire, he inscribes his wish upon a tablet which he places at the feet of the statue of a divinity.

At every moment he consults the gods, and wishes to know their will. He finds all his resolutions in the entrails of victims, in the flight of birds, in the warning of the lightning. The announcement of a shower of blood, or of an ox that has spoken, troubles him and makes him tremble. He will be tranquil only after an expiatory ceremony shall restore him to peace with the gods.

He steps out of his house always with the right foot first. He has his hair cut only during the full moon. He carries amulets upon his person. He covers the walls of his house with magic inscriptions against fire. He knows of formulas for avoiding sickness, and of others for curing it; but he must repeat them twenty-seven times, and spit in a certain fashion at each repetition.

He does not deliberate in the senate if the victims have not given favorable signs. He leaves the assembly of the people if he hears the cry of a mouse. He renounces the best laid plans if he perceives a bad presage, or if an ill-omened word has struck his ear. He is brave in battle, but on condition that the auspices assure him the victory.

This Roman whom we present here is not the man of the people, the feeble-minded man whom misery and ignorance have made superstitious. We are speaking of the patrician, the noble, powerful, and rich man. This patrician is, by turns, warrior, magistrate, consul, farmer, merchant; but everywhere and always he is a priest, and his thoughts are fixed upon the gods. Patriotism, love of glory, and love of gold, whatever power these may have over his soul, the fear of the gods still governs everything.

SOURCE: Numa Denis Fustel de Coulanges, *The Ancient City,* trans. Williard Small (Boston: Lee and Shepard, Publishers, 1874), pp. 281–283.

[7] Gods of the household.

Life and Leisure: The Roman Aristocrat

J. P. V. D. Balsdon

Although it is appropriate to concentrate on the major events and the important accomplishments of the Romans, at times this leads one to forget that the Romans were real people with everyday lives. The religious aspects of their lives are brought out in the selection by Fustel de Coulanges. In the following selection J. P. V. D. Balsdon of Oxford focuses on the occupations, alternatives, and patterns of life open to a typical Roman aristocrat.

CONSIDER: *The occupations most appropriate for a Roman aristocrat and the limitations he had to face; connections between this description and Cicero's life and education as revealed in the document by Cicero; any connections between this picture of Roman life and the image presented by Fustel de Coulanges.*

By upper-class standards public service was the noblest activity of man—the life of the barrister, the soldier, the administrator and the politician; for normally the senator's life embraced all those four activities. Rhetoric was a main constituent of his education and at an early age he put his learning into practice by pleading at the Bar. He climbed the ladder of a senatorial career, absent from Rome sometimes for considerable periods in which he served as an army officer or governed a province. If he committed no indiscretion, he was a life-member of the Senate—if he held the consulship, an important elder statesman from then onwards. In the Empire he might be one of the Emperor's privy counsellors.

This was not a career in which, except in the last centuries of the Republic, great fortunes were to be made. The senator therefore needed to be a wealthy man, in particular to own considerable landed property. To this he escaped when he could, particularly if he came of a good family, for the Roman aristocrat was a countryman at heart, interested in farming well, happy in the saddle, fond of hunting. He would have been shocked by the parvenu Sallust's description of farming and hunting as "occupations fit for a slave"; and other Romans no doubt were shocked too, for in the case of the farmer (and perhaps only of the farmer) the notion of work had a wide romantic fascination. Everyone liked to be reminded of Cincinnatus in the fifth century B.C.E., of how, when they sent for him to be dictator, they found him ploughing and how, once the business of saving Rome as dictator was accomplished, he returned happily to his farm. When Scipio Africanus found himself driven from public life, he worked on the land with his own hands.

If an aristocrat's means were not sufficient to support him in a life of public service, he might turn to business, banking, trading, tax-farming, the activities of the "Equestrian order." In this way distinguished families sometimes disappeared from politics for a generation or more and then, their wealth restored, they returned. There was nothing disgraceful about being a business man, as long as you were rich and successful enough, in which case you were likely to invest largely in land and to become one of the land-owning gentry. Equestrians, whether business men or rich country residents, were fathers of senators often and sometimes sons, frequently close personal friends, Atticus of Cicero for instance.

A man who avoided or deserted "the sweat and toil" of a public career in favour of industrious seclusion—"a shady life" (*vita umbratilis*)—could excuse himself and indeed (like Cicero and Sallust when, elbowed out of an influential position in public life, they became writers) found it desirable to excuse himself. If he became a writer, then he made it clear that he wrote as an educationalist, employing his seclusion to teach valuable lessons to his readers, particularly his young readers, a purpose which nobody disparaged. But if his retirement was the retirement of self-indulgence (*desidia*), like the later life of L. Lucullus, an obsession with fantastically expensive landscape gardening and extravagant fish ponds, he was a traitor to serious and responsible standards of living (*gravitas*) and won the contempt—however envious—of all but his like-minded friends. There was no secure happiness in such a life, as serious men like Lucretius, Horace and Seneca knew.

Roman Women

Gillian Clark

Until recently most historians presented an image of Roman life that mentioned women only in passing. This void about the experience of Roman women is being filled by new scholarship, much of it written by feminist historians. In the following selection Gillian Clark analyzes the position and experience of women during the late Republic and age of Augustus, emphasizing the political, legal, and social restraints on women.

CONSIDER: *Ways in which women might influence public life despite restraints placed on them; what the characteristics of the good woman were; how one might evaluate whether*

SOURCE: From "Life and Leisure," by J. P. V. D. Balsdon in *The Romans*, ed. by J. P. V. D. Balsdon, pp. 270–272, © 1965 by Basic Books, Inc., Publisher, New York. Reprinted with permission.

SOURCE: Gillian Clark, "Roman Women," *Greece and Rome,* 28 (1981), 206–207, 209–210.

Roman women were happy; how this description of Roman women compares with Balsdon's description of aristocratic Roman men.

Women did not vote, did not serve as *iudices*,[8] were not senators or magistrates or holders of major priesthoods. They did not, as a rule, speak in the courts.... As a rule, women took no part in public life, except on the rare occasions when they were angry enough to demonstrate, which was startling and shocking....

Women might, then, have considerable influence and interests outside their homes and families, but they were acting from within their families to affect a social system managed by men: their influence was not to be publicly acknowledged. Why were women excluded from public life? The division between arms-bearers and child-bearers was doubtless one historical cause, but the reasons publicly given were different. Women were alleged to be fragile and fickle, and therefore in need of protection; if they were not kept in their proper place they would (fragility and fickleness notwithstanding) take over. As the elder Cato ... said ...

"Our ancestors decided that women should not handle anything, even a private matter, without the advice of a guardian; that they should always be in the power of fathers, brothers, husbands.... Call to mind all those laws on women by which your ancestors restrained their licence and made them subject to men: you can only just keep them under by using the whole range of laws. If you let them niggle away at one law after another until they have worked it out of your grasp, until at last you let them make themselves equal to men, do you suppose that you'll be able to stand them? If once they get equality, they'll be on top." ...

A social system which restricted women to domestic life, and prevailing attitudes which assumed their inferiority, must seem to us oppressive. I know of no evidence that it seemed so at the time. The legal and social constraints detailed above may have frustrated the abilities of many women and caused much ordinary human unhappiness. But there evidently were, also, many ordinarily happy families where knowledge of real live women took precedence over the theories, and women themselves enjoyed home, children, and friends. There were some women who enjoyed the political game, and who found an emotional life outside their necessary marriages. And there were certainly women who found satisfaction in living up to the standards of the time. They were, as they should be, chaste, dutiful, submissive, and domestic; they took pride in the family of their birth and the family they had produced; and probably their resolution to maintain these standards gave them the support which women in all ages have found in religious faith. But the religious feelings of Roman women, as opposed to the acts of worship in which they might take part, are something of which we know very little....

The son of Murdia, in the age of Augustus, made her a public eulogy ... [which] may make the best epitaph for the women who did not make the history books.

"What is said in praise of all good women is the same, and straightforward. There is no need of elaborate phrases to tell of natural good qualities and of trust maintained. It is enough that all alike have the same reward: a good reputation. It is hard to find new things to praise in a woman, for their lives lack incident. We must look for what they have in common, lest something be left out to spoil the example they offer us. My beloved mother, then, deserves all the more praise, for in modesty, integrity, chastity, submission, woolwork, industry, and trustworthiness she was just like other women."

CHAPTER QUESTIONS

1. Describe the circumstances, options, and everyday life of a Roman aristocrat during the first century B.C.E. as revealed in the documents in this chapter.

2. In what ways did Greeks, Greek culture, and Greek history affect Roman civilization?

3. Describe the similarities and differences between Greek and Roman civilizations. What were some of the main strengths and weaknesses of each?

---

[8] Judges.

THE GEM OF AUGUSTUS (GEMMA AUGUSTEA), SARDONYX CAMEO, ca. 14 C.E.
This beautiful cameo was carved to praise a new order in Rome. At the top, Augustus is holding the staff of emperor while he is crowned as a god by other deities. At the left, his heir, Tiberius, descends from a chariot that he has ridden in triumph to celebrate his military victory in Germany. In the lower level, the army raises a trophy of victory while watched by defeated Germans. This piece shows how Rome had been transformed: No longer a republic, Rome was now led by a living god whose family expected to succeed him, and the greatness of the empire depended on soldiers and far-flung conquests.

Territorial and Christian Empires

5

The Roman Empire, 31 B.C.E.–410 C.E.

"... [T]he newborn babe shall end that age of iron, [and] bid a golden dawn upon the broad world...." With these words, the Roman poet Virgil foretold the birth of a child who would save the world from the civil wars plaguing the late Roman Republic. For many Romans, that child arrived in the person of Caesar Augustus, a talented leader whose political and economic policies introduced almost two hundred years of internal peace. But this *Pax Romana* was no cure-all. The Romans still faced the challenges of unifying a multiethnic empire while ensuring a succession of capable emperors. They also struggled to preserve their concept of private morality, and they grappled with the complexity of people's political involvement under an imperial system. In the third century C.E., economic and political hardship nearly wiped out the empire, as soldiers created military emperors who battled each other, often leaving Rome's borders at risk. In the fourth century, the reforms of two great rulers—Diocletian and Constantine—temporarily held Rome's extensive dominions together.

Meanwhile, another child born in the time of Caesar Augustus inspired a new creed that seemed to offer salvation. Followers of Jesus grew steadily in numbers through the first centuries C.E. At first, the empire ignored them and occasionally persecuted them, but it later adopted Christianity as its own. This fusion of Roman and Christian ideas created a new Christian empire that many ancient Romans believed fulfilled the promise of the child Virgil praised. Both empires—Roman and Christian—contributed a great deal to the continuing development of the West.

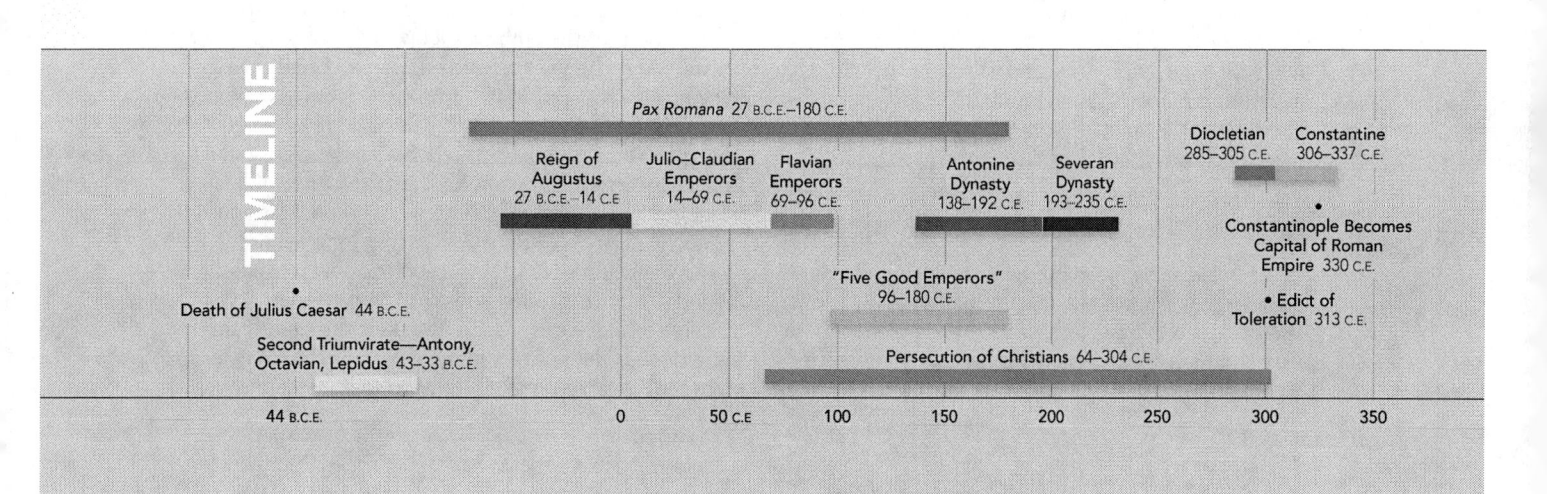

TIMELINE

- Death of Julius Caesar 44 B.C.E.
- Second Triumvirate—Antony, Octavian, Lepidus 43–33 B.C.E.
- Reign of Augustus 27 B.C.E.–14 C.E.
- *Pax Romana* 27 B.C.E.–180 C.E.
- Julio–Claudian Emperors 14–69 C.E.
- Flavian Emperors 69–96 C.E.
- "Five Good Emperors" 96–180 C.E.
- Antonine Dynasty 138–192 C.E.
- Severan Dynasty 193–235 C.E.
- Persecution of Christians 64–304 C.E.
- Diocletian 285–305 C.E.
- Constantine 306–337 C.E.
- Edict of Toleration 313 C.E.
- Constantinople Becomes Capital of Roman Empire 330 C.E.

44 B.C.E.　　0　　50 C.E.　　100　　150　　200　　250　　300　　350

PREVIEW

THE *PAX ROMANA*,
27 B.C.E. to 180 C.E.
Learn about the governance of Augustus's new empire: its successes and challenges.

LIFE DURING THE PEACE OF ROME
Study daily life from medicine and population problems to games in the arena.

CRISIS AND TRANSFORMATION,
192–ca. 400 C.E.
Understand how Diocletian transformed the empire in order to save it.

THE LONGING FOR RELIGIOUS FULFILLMENT
Explore Roman and Jewish religious ideas and the beginnings of Christianity.

FROM CHRISTIAN PERSECUTION TO THE CITY OF GOD,
64–410 C.E.
Learn how Christianity developed from a persecuted faith to the religion of the empire.

THE HOLY LIFE
Understand how early Christians changed the culture of Rome.

FIGURE 5.1 Cleopatra VII, ca. 30 B.C.E. This bust portrays the famous Egyptian queen who bore Julius Caesar a child and seduced Mark Antony. Although Cleopatra was a Hellenistic ruler, the sculptor portrayed her face in the Roman manner.

THE *PAX ROMANA*,
27 B.C.E.–180 C.E.

On the eve of their wedding, a young Roman couple, Vespillo and Turia, paused during the celebration to reflect on a sad memory. Turia's parents had perished in the civil war that had elevated Julius Caesar to power, but the troubled times were not over for the young couple. During new civil wars, Turia had to sell her jewelry to help her husband escape the political strife in the city and even had to beg for a pardon for Vespillo. Finally, the wars were over, and the couple "enjoyed quiet and happy days" through forty-one years of marriage, although sadly they produced no children. They were representative of many Romans who struggled through the violence after Julius Caesar's death finally to enjoy a long ***Pax Romana,*** or Roman Peace, that was introduced by his successor.

Augustus Takes Power

In 43 B.C.E., three powerful men emerged who established a new triumvirate to rule the Republic. Unlike the first, the Senate legitimized this Second Triumvirate, which ruled from 43 to 33 B.C.E. and seemed to offer a way to bring peace to the turbulent land. Marc Antony, who managed Caesar's vast fortune, was a strong general who seemed to challenge senatorial power. To balance his power, the Senate turned to Julius Caesar's grandnephew and adopted son, Octavian—a remarkably talented 19-year-old who played on popular sympathy for the murdered dictator by calling himself Caesar. The young Octavian offered respect to the Senate as he jockeyed for position against Marc Antony. The two brought into their partnership one of Julius Caesar's loyal governors and generals, Lepidus. At first, the three men controlled various parts of the empire: Octavian based his power in Italy and the provinces to the west; Lepidus held North Africa; and Marc Antony governed Egypt, Greece, and the provinces to the east. However, like the First Triumvirate, the second soon deteriorated into a power struggle among the three rulers. Octavian forced Lepidus into retirement in 36 B.C.E., and he and Antony vied for sole control of the empire.

As was traditional in Rome, politics was intimately bound up with family and with the women who, through childbearing, held the key to future family alliances. Not surprisingly, the political struggles between Octavian and Antony were to some degree played out in the bedroom. Having lost Julius Caesar, Cleopatra sought to continue her ruling dynasty through a new alliance with a new ruler of Rome. **Figure 5.1** is a portrait bust of Queen Cleopatra showing her regal bearing and her fairly ordinary looks. She seduced Antony with the wit and charm that had so impressed the ancient biographers and bore him twins. Antony, however, was not yet committed to an alliance with Egypt's ruling house. Octavian's popularity in Rome was too high for Antony to risk offending the Roman people. Rumors already circulated in Rome's Forum that Antony wanted to move the Roman capital to Alexandria, so Antony had to negotiate a marriage that would be more acceptable to the public.

Antony and Octavian finally negotiated a peace that was to be secured by Antony's marriage to Octavian's sister, the young, beautiful Octavia. Octavia soon became pregnant, so the two families had the opportunity to seal their agreement permanently. But Antony left Octavia and traveled to Egypt. It is uncertain whether he decided that a strong political ally like Cleopatra afforded better security against Octavian than marriage to his rival's sister, or whether he was driven by the Egyptian queen's allure. In either case, the alliance bound through marriage dissolved. Octavian and Antony resumed their battle over who would rule all of Rome.

[Civil war]

The war between the two leaders finally came to a head in 31 B.C.E., when Antony and Cleopatra, surrounded by Octavian's forces, risked all on a sea battle near the city of Actium, off the western coast of Greece. During this famous battle, Cleopatra and Antony proved less determined than Octavian, for Cleopatra's squadron left for Egypt in the course of the battle, and Antony followed her. They abandoned their navy and about twenty legions of their troops. Octavian's navy destroyed the Egyptian fleet, and his land forces quickly occupied Egypt.

Antony committed suicide, and Octavian personally inspected his corpse to be sure his rival was dead. Cleopatra refused to be taken prisoner and, according to legend, ordered her servant to bring her a poisonous snake. She committed suicide by its bite. Although robbed of an imprisoned Egyptian queen, Octavian stood as sole ruler of Rome. With Cleopatra's death in 31 B.C.E., the last Macedonian kingdom fell, ending the Hellenistic age that had begun with the empire of Alexander the Great. Now the new empire of Rome dominated the Mediterranean world.

A New Form of Governing

Unlike his uncle, Julius Caesar, Octavian successfully established a form of government that let him rule without offending the traditions of conservative Romans. This delicate balance between his leadership style and the old ways earned him widespread popularity. On January 1, 27 B.C.E., the young general appeared before the Senate and claimed that he had brought peace and was thus returning the rule of the state to the Senate and the people of Rome. Octavian acted in the spirit of Cincinnatus (see Chapter 4), the general who gave up rule to return to his plow, and the tradition-loving Romans appreciated his gesture. The Senate showed its gratitude by giving him the title Augustus, a name that implied majesty and holiness. It is by this informal title that his people addressed him and historians remember him. Augustus, however, modestly referred to himself as the *princeps*—that is, the "first citizen." The government he established was in turn called the **principate,** after the first citizen upon whom everyone depended.

[The principate]

The principate transformed the republican form of government, and historians roughly date the beginning of the Roman Empire from 27 B.C.E.—the date of Augustus's famous renunciation and acceptance of power. Under this new imperial form, the traditional representatives of government—the Senate and the Roman people—continued to exist and appoint the traditional magistrates to carry out their public business. The Senate continued to make disbursements from the traditional treasury and, in fact, slowly increased its power as it began to take over elections from the popular assemblies. The Senate also maintained control over some of the provinces—the older ones that did not require so many soldiers to guard the borders. In these ways, Augustus avoided offending the senators as Julius Caesar had done.

[Governmental structure]

However, the vast extent of the empire and the increased complication of public affairs required a special magistrate—the princeps—to coordinate the administration of the empire and, more importantly, to control the army. By 70 C.E., the princeps was more often called emperor, a title with which troops had customarily hailed their generals. Building further on military precedent, Augustus established an imperial legion in Rome as his personal bodyguard. Known as the **praetorian guard,** this new body was named after the headquarters of the legion, or the *praetorium*. Roman generals had always had their own elite bodyguard, but because of its close association with the emperor, the praetorian guard, led by the praetorian prefect, became a powerful force on its own. The guard was unquestionably loyal to Augustus and worked to avert civil war such as the strife that had torn apart the Republic, but after his death a new political force had been created in Rome.

With these efforts, Augustus created a new structure on the remnants of the traditional Republic. Document 5.1 relates in Augustus's own words how

thinking about DOCUMENTS

DOCUMENT 5.1

Augustus Tallies His Accomplishments

Shortly before he died in 14 C.E., Augustus left a number of state papers with the Vestal Virgins, including an account of his accomplishments that he wanted inscribed on bronze pillars to be installed in front of his mausoleum. Excerpts of this document give us a glimpse into this early period of the principate, which set the stage for subsequent imperial success.

3. I waged many wars throughout the whole world by land and by sea, both civil and foreign, and when victorious I spared all citizens who sought pardon. Foreign peoples who could safely be pardoned I preferred to spare rather than to extirpate. About 500,000 Roman citizens were under military oath to me. Of these, when their terms of service were ended, I settled in colonies or sent back to their own municipalities a little more than 300,000, and to all of these I allotted lands or granted money as rewards for military service. I captured 600 ships, exclusive of those which were of smaller class than triremes.

4. Twice I celebrated ovations, three times curule triumphs, and I was acclaimed *imperator* twenty-nine times. When the senate decreed additional triumphs to me, I declined them on four occasions....

5. The dictatorship offered to me in the consulship of Marcus Marcellus and Lucius Arruntius by the people and by the senate, both in my absence and in my presence, I refused to accept. In the midst of a critical scarcity of grain I did not decline the supervision of the grain supply, which I so administered that within a few days I freed the whole people from imminent panic and danger by my expenditures and efforts. The consulship, too, which was offered to me at that time as an annual office for life, I refused to accept.

6. In the consulship of Marcus Vinicius and Quintus Lucretius, and again in that of Publius Lentulus and Gnaeus Lentulus, and a third time in that of Paullus Fabius Maximus and Quintus Tubero, though the Roman senate and people unitedly agreed that I should be elected sole guardian of the laws and morals with supreme authority, I refused to accept any office offered me which was contrary to the traditions of our ancestors. The measures which the senate desired at that time to be taken by me I carried out by virtue of the tribunician power. In this power I five times voluntarily requested and was given a colleague by the senate....

15. To the Roman plebs I paid 300 sesterces apiece in accordance with the will of my father; and in my fifth consulship I gave each 400 sesterces in my own name out of the spoils of war; and a second time in my tenth consulship I paid out of my own patrimony a largess of 400 sesterces to every individual.... These largesses of mine reached never less than 250,000 persons.

17. Four times I came to the assistance of the treasury with my own money, transferring to those in charge of the treasury 150,000,000 sesterces. And in the consulship of Marcus Lepidus and Lucius Arruntius I transferred out of my own patrimony 170,000,000 sesterces to the soldiers' bonus fund, which was established on my advice for the purpose of providing bonuses for soldiers who had completed twenty or more years of service....

22. I gave a gladiatorial show three times in my own name, and five times in the names of my sons or grandsons; at these shows about 10,000 fought. Twice I presented to the people in my own name an exhibition of athletes invited from all parts of the world, and a third time in the name of my grandson. I presented games in my own name four times, and in addition twenty-three times in the place of other magistrates.... Twenty-six times I provided for the people, in my own name or in the names of my sons or grandsons, hunting spectacles of African wild beasts in the circus or in the Forum or in the amphitheaters; in these exhibitions about 3,500 animals were killed....

34. In my sixth and seventh consulships, after I had put an end to the civil wars, having attained supreme power by universal consent, I transferred the state from my own power to the control of the Roman senate and people. For this service of mine I received the title of Augustus by decree of the senate, and the doorposts of my house were publicly decked with laurels, the civic crown was affixed over my doorway, and a golden shield was set up in the Julian senate house, which, as the inscription on this shield testifies, the Roman senate and people gave me in recognition of my valor, clemency, justice, and devotion. After that time I excelled all in authority, but I possessed no more power than the others who were my colleagues in each magistracy.

35. When I held my thirteenth consulship, the senate, the equestrian order, and the entire Roman people gave me the title of "father of the country" and decreed that this title should be inscribed in the vestibule of my house, in the Julian senate house, and in the Augustan Forum on the pedestal of the chariot which was set up in my honor by decree of the senate. At the time I write this document I was in my seventy-sixth year.

SOURCE: Naphtali Lewis and Meyer Reinhold, *Roman Civilization: Sourcebook II: The Empire* (New York: Harper Torchbooks, 1966), pp. 10, 11, 14, 16, 19.

Analyze the Document

1. Why was Augustus so popular with the Roman people?
2. Which offices did he accept and which did he refuse? How did this help him avoid Julius Caesar's fate?
3. Notice the blurring of private and public funds. How do you think that blending contributed to Rome's stability and Augustus's office?

he balanced traditional offices with new demands. The document shows how he used his enormous personal wealth to balance the national treasury, to rebuild Rome, and to fund gladiator shows and other popular spectacles. In 2 B.C.E., the Senate awarded Augustus the title Father of the Fatherland. In a culture that depended on the father to guard his family's prosperity and honor, perhaps no other title could convey greater respect.

Of course, all these titles and honors, though significant, had little to do with the day-to-day practical problems of managing a large empire. Like any good father, Augustus ran the empire as one would run a household. He kept authority for himself, but the everyday business was handled by freedmen and slaves in his household. Although Rome itself remained governed largely by the traditional forms, Augustus made dramatic changes in governing the provinces.

Administering an empire

Augustus kept about half of the provinces—including wealthy Egypt—under his direct control, sending out representatives to govern there in his name. He began to create a foreign service drawn from the equestrian class (wealthy, upwardly mobile nonnobles), whose advancement depended upon their performance. This reform eliminated some of the worst provincial abuses that had gone on during the late Republic—for example, Augustus began eliminating private tax collectors. To keep the peace on the borders, Augustus stationed troops permanently in the provinces; the empire began to maintain fixed borders with military camps along the frontiers. Document 5.1 includes Augustus's own assessment of his accomplishments.

For all these reforms, even by ancient standards, the empire was astonishingly undermanaged—a few thousand individuals controlled some 50 million people. The genius of the system lay in a combination of limited goals on top—maintain peace, collect taxes, and prevent power from accumulating—with actual power exerted at the local level. Through its relative simplicity, the principate established by Augustus continued to function efficiently even during years of remarkably decadent rulers. The Roman people recognized Augustus's accomplishments by according him a level of respect almost suiting a god, and this veneration would dramatically shape the future of the principate.

Figure 5.2 reveals the Romans' love of this strong, wise leader. This famous statue—named for the villa of Augustus's wife, Livia, where the sculpture stood—captures the people's hopes for Augustus. In the statue, Augustus holds his right arm up in the fashion of a traditional republican orator. Compare this sculpture with the image at the beginning of Chapter 4, on page 106.

FIGURE 5.2 Augustus of Prima Porta, ca. 20 B.C.E. This idealized portrait of Augustus shows the first Roman emperor as a divine guardian of Rome.

The sculptor's interpretation of Augustus shows that the Republic had been transformed. Instead of a toga, Augustus wears the armor of a soldier, and in his left hand he holds the staff of an emperor, traditionally the commander of the army and now the leader of the state. He is also shown as more than a mortal hero. His bare feet indicate that he is a hero, perhaps even semidivine. The cupid astride the dolphin refers to the claim that Augustus's family was descended from the goddess Venus, mother of Cupid. The symbols on Augustus's breastplate—a victorious general and a generous Mother Earth—promise divine aid and prosperity. Although Augustus refused to let himself be portrayed explicitly as a god, these associations left no doubt about his near-divine status. Augustus allowed altars in his name to be erected in the provinces, but he refused to allow Romans to worship their "first citizen." His formal deification would come after his death.

This image of Augustus as a divine being was reinforced in the great literature produced under his patronage. Virgil's famous epic, the *Aeneid* (ca. 29–19 B.C.E.), is a mythological tale of the wandering of the Trojan hero Aeneas, who founded the city of Rome. However, in spite of the book's echoes of Homer, Aeneas was a kind of hero different from Achilles, and in this portrayal, Virgil was able to show that the virtues of the past could work in the new age of the principate. Aeneas refuses to yield to his weaknesses or his passions and is rewarded with a vision of the future in which his descendants will extend Rome's rule "to the ends of the earth." In his epic, Virgil promises:

> ... *yours will be the rulership of nations. Remember Roman, these will be your arts: to teach the ways of peace to those you conquer, to spare defeated peoples, tame the proud.*

The *Aeneid* did for Rome what Homer had done for classical Greece: It defined the Roman Empire and its values for subsequent generations, and in the process it contributed to the deification of Augustus. It was also a fine example of Augustus's talent for propaganda.

What Virgil did for Roman literature, Livy (59 B.C.E.–17 C.E.) did for the empire's recorded history. In his long, detailed work, *The History of Rome* (ca. 26 B.C.E.–15 C.E.), Livy recounted the development of his city from the earliest times to the principate, and he included many speeches that brought the past to life. Like Virgil, Livy emphasized Roman religion and morality, looking nostalgically back to republican values. And again like Virgil, the historian recognized that the future lay with the new imperial form of government. His history strongly influenced subsequent ancient historians and has remained a central source of information today.

The system established by Augustus was not perfect, but Augustus lived for so long that the principate became tradition. The Roman historian Tacitus (56–120 C.E.) wrote that by Augustus's death in 14 C.E., no one left alive could remember any other way to govern. For the next two centuries his successors ruled with the benefits of the imperial system that Augustus had established. But they also inherited major problems he left unresolved—Who should succeed the "first citizen"? How should one best govern such a large empire, and how would rulers handle such power?

Challenges to the Principate, 69–193 C.E.

Augustus's long tenure as emperor postponed the problem of imperial succession, but this weakness in the principate showed up soon after his death. The next four emperors all ascended the throne based on their ties to Augustus's family, and this succession showed how flimsy the concept of "first citizen" really was. An imperial dynasty had been established, and it did not matter that the rulers lacked the moral stature of Augustus or traditional republican virtues. During the Republic, leaders regularly confronted the Roman people in the Forum and yielded to the pressure of scorn or applause. However, the new rulers of the empire experienced no such corrective public scrutiny, and the successors of Augustus immediately proved that power corrupted. The historian Suetonius (69–130 C.E.) recorded the popular scandalous rumors that circulated about the decline of Augustus's successor, his stepson Tiberius (r. 14–37), shown celebrating his victory over the Germans in the chapter-opening art on page 136: "No longer feeling himself under public scrutiny, he rapidly succumbed to all the vicious passions which he had for a long time tried, not very successfully, to disguise." Tiberius "made himself a private sporting house where sexual extravagances were practiced for his secret pleasure," and in his isolation, Suetonius claimed, his paranoia grew. He even executed people for insulting his stepfather's memory if they carried a coin bearing Augustus's image into a lavatory or brothel. The Roman people believed that such excesses continued throughout the dynasty of Augustus's heirs.

One of the heirs in this dynasty was Caligula (r. 37–41), an irrational—if not insane—ruler who wanted to be worshiped as a god. The praetorian guard took matters into its own hands and assassinated Caligula. The guard then found Claudius, a retiring, neglected relative of Augustus, hiding in the palace and promptly declared him emperor. Claudius (r. 41–54) was regarded by many Romans as an imbecile subject to the whims of his wives, but the power of the connection to the family of Augustus prevailed to solidify his rule. The cameo in **Figure 5.3** is a beautiful piece of propaganda as well as art. It shows Claudius and his wife, Agrippina the Younger, in the foreground superimposed on Germanicus—Caligula's father—and his wife, Agrippina the Elder (the Younger's mother). The superimposition on the cameo emphasizes the family connections that gave Claudius the right to rule as "first citizen," and the horns of plenty on the front allude to the prosperity this dynasty promised to bring to the Romans. However, in contrast to the calm portrayal on the cameo, the dynasty only brought more family feuds.

FIGURE 5.3 Claudius and Agrippina the Younger This cameo gem depicts the emperor Claudius with his wife, Agrippina. In the background are his ancestors Germanicus and Agrippina the Elder. The design includes horns of plenty, symbolizing the prosperity the emperors were to bring to Rome.

Suetonius's history of those years tells of a series of murders within the family as members vied for the power of the princeps. Nero (r. 54–68) marked the most excessive of the murderers, for he killed many of his family members, mostly using his favorite means, poison. He even killed his mother, although it was not easy. He poisoned her three times, but she had taken a preventive antidote. Nero then tried to arrange for the ceiling of her room to collapse on her and for her boat to sink. When all these techniques failed, he simply sent an assassin to kill her and make it appear that she had committed suicide.

Nero was so despised that even his personal guard deserted him, and to avoid being captured and publicly executed, Nero commanded his slave to slit his throat, saying, "How ugly and vulgar my life has become!" It is not surprising that there were no more members of Augustus's family left to claim the succession, and the armies and the praetorian guard fought a bloody civil war to see which family would succeed to the imperial throne. Fortunately for Rome, Vespasian took power in 69 C.E. and restored some order to the empire, but even so fine an emperor could not ensure that his son would be equally competent. Each subsequent dynasty would eventually end through the weakness or corruption of one of the rulers, and the flaws in the succession policy were repeatedly highlighted. The assassination of Vespasian's murderous son Domitian (r. 81–96) introduced a new period, that of the "Five Good Emperors" (96–180). These rulers increasingly centralized their power at the expense of the Senate, but they ruled with a long-remembered

> A new dynasty

integrity. From Nerva (r. 96–98) to Marcus Aurelius (r. 161–180), these emperors established a tone of modest simplicity and adherence to republican values.

Marcus Aurelius represented the highest expression of a ruler whose political life was shaped by moral philosophy. He was highly educated in law, poetry, and philosophy, but the latter was his greatest love. When he was only 11, he adopted the coarse dress and sparse life of Stoic philosophers (discussed in Chapter 3), and when he became emperor, he continued to act based on the self-containment embodied in Stoic principles. His ideas have been preserved in a collection of his contemplative notes, called his *Meditations* (171–ca. 180). Within these notes he wrote a caution that should have been followed by all who rose to great power: When one is seduced by fame and flattery, one should remember how flatterers are frequently wrong on other occasions, so one should remain humble. Unfortunately, too many emperors did not share Marcus's wise self-containment.

Through these years, the City of Rome was transformed from a center of republican power to a glorification of imperial power. As **Map 5.1** shows, the entertainment centers—baths, games—offered by the emperors began to dominate the city, and temples to divine emperors sprang up.

Throughout the reigns of emperors good and bad, the borders had to be guarded. Armies fought in the east and as far away as Britain. Centuries of Roman military presence along the frontiers had brought Roman-style cities and agriculture—indeed, Roman civilization—to the edges of the empire. This long-term presence of Rome in lands far from Italy served to add Roman culture to the growing Western civilization in the north of Europe as well as the Mediterranean.

> Provincial defense

However, holding such extensive lands caused many of these soldier-emperors to be away from Rome for extended periods. Hadrian (r. 117–138) spent twelve of his twenty-one ruling years traveling around the provinces, establishing fortifications and checking on provincial administration. However, it was one thing to establish definite borders and quite another to hold them. The Stoic emperor Marcus Aurelius spent the better part of thirteen years in fierce campaigns to keep the border tribes out of the empire and he died while on campaign. His death brought an end to the era of the "good emperors," caused once again by a decadent son.

The long rule by good emperors may have been more the result of biological accident than anything else: Four of the emperors had no sons, so each of them adopted as his successor a man he thought best able to rule. However, Marcus Aurelius fathered a son, Commodus (r. 180–192), who unfortunately brought the age of the Five Good Emperors and the *Pax Romana* to an ignoble end through his cruel reign. Commodus

thinking about GEOGRAPHY

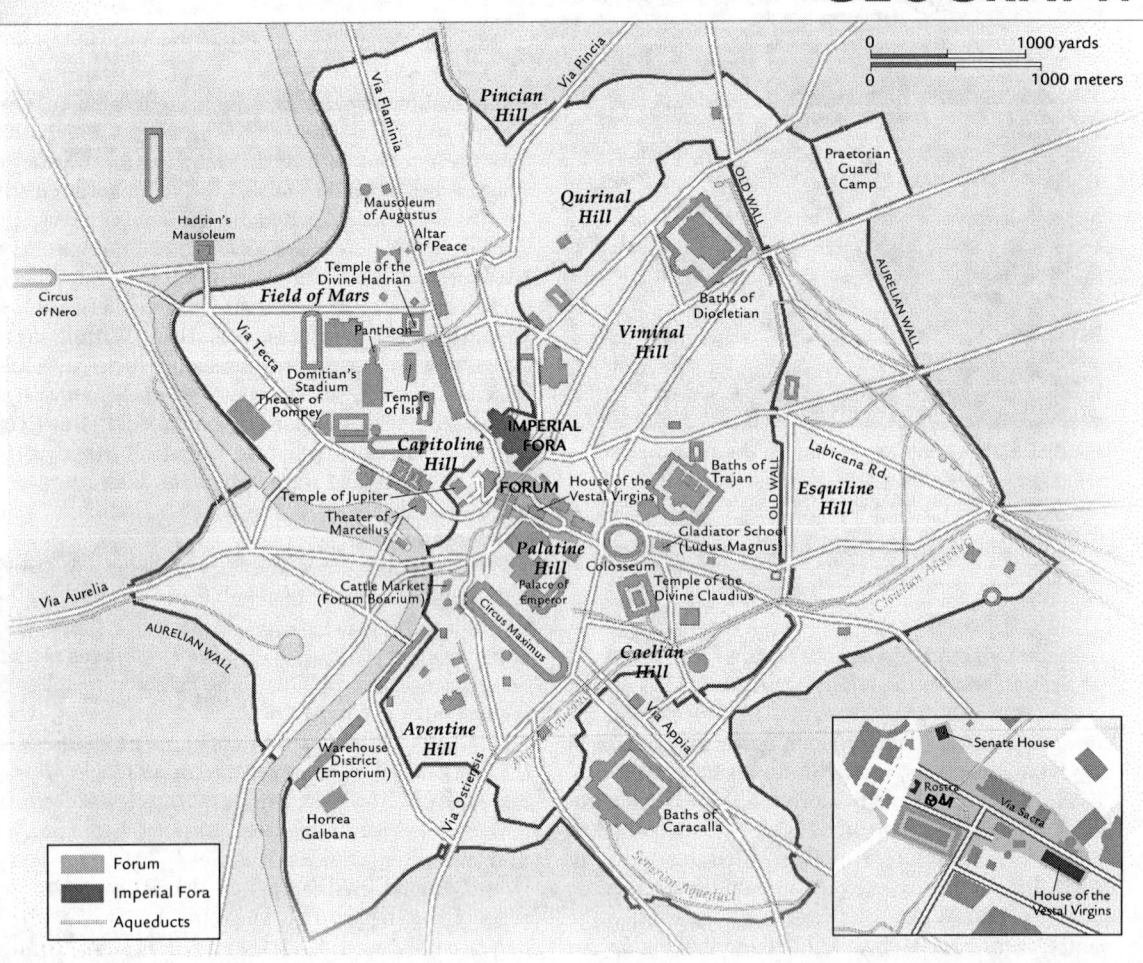

MAP 5.1

City of Rome During the Empire

This map shows the city of Rome during the empire and identifies the new buildings constructed by the emperors. Compare this map with **Map 4.1**, of Rome during the Republic. Notice how monuments of imperial power and establishments for entertainment dominated the city during the empire.

Explore the Map

1. What new buildings dominated the city? What were their functions? What do these buildings reveal about the cultural focus of the Roman people under the empire?

2. Where were the new fora (plural of *forum*) built by the emperors? Where was the imperial palace? In what ways do these features demonstrate how the emperors displaced old republican centers of power?

---

seems to have been a simpleminded man who loved the games. He even shocked Rome by fighting in the arena as a gladiator. With Commodus's murder (he was strangled by his wrestling partner), peace ended in Rome in a fresh outbreak of civil war.

A Vibrant, Far-Flung Empire

One must credit the genius of Augustus's political system and the steadfastness of the Roman administrators for the empire's ability to flourish even during

China's Han Dynasty and the Silk Road

In 206 B.C.E, while the Roman Republic was expanding, a strong Chinese military commander, Liu Bang, brought order to warring factions in China. Liu established the Han dynasty (named after his native land), which would endure for more than four hundred years. The Han emperors developed a centralized authority supported by a large bureaucracy, and they built an extensive network of roads and canals to facilitate communication throughout the realm. The emperors also knew the value of educated royal servants. Thus, in 124 B.C.E, Emperor Han Wudi established an imperial university. This university incorporated Confucianism as the basis for its curriculum, so the Confucian tradition took root in China. Like the Romans in the West, the Han emperors developed an influential body of law, written first on bamboo and silk. Their legal system became the most comprehensive and best organized in the world.

The centralized, ordered rule of the Hans facilitated trade. It also led to the development of the "Silk Road," which linked China and the West in significant ways. Luxury items moved from China and India to Mesopotamia and the Mediterranean basin. Incoming goods arrived through a complex series of trades. Roman sailors used the prevailing monsoon winds to sail their ships from Red Sea ports to the mouth of the Indus River in India at Barygaza. There, they traded their goods—mostly gold and silver—for Indian spices and silks. The Indian merchants took their share of the merchandise and proceeded to trade with the Han merchants.

Chinese traders shipped spices—ginger, cinnamon, cloves, and others—that Westerners craved both as flavorings and as medicines. However, the most prized commodity was Chinese silk, which gave its name to the trade route. By the first century C.E., Romans were willing to pay premium prices for the prized fiber. The Chinese knew how to feed silkworms on mulberry leaves and harvest the cocoons before the moths chewed through the precious silk strands. The silk traveled west in bales—as either woven cloth or raw yarn—and went to processing centers, most of them in Syria. There workers ungummed the rolls and unwound the fiber before weaving the fabric that sold for top prices throughout the Roman Empire. For hundreds of years, the trade flourished, bringing West and East into close contact. This contact sparked the exchange of ideas as well as goods. Unfortunately, it also spread diseases that dramatically reduced populations in China as well as in the Roman Empire.

Despite the thriving trade, the later Han emperors proved unable to maintain the centralization and prosperity that had marked the early centuries of their reign. In the face of social and economic tensions, as well as epidemic diseases, disloyal generals grabbed more and more power. By 200 C.E., the Han dynasty had collapsed and the empire lay in pieces. The trade along the Silk Road suffered too, but stories of the prosperous East continued to capture the imaginations of Westerners.

Making Connections

1. What did the Han emperors do to facilitate long-distance trade with the West?
2. What trade items flowed along the Silk Road?
3. What impact did this trade have on the Roman Empire?

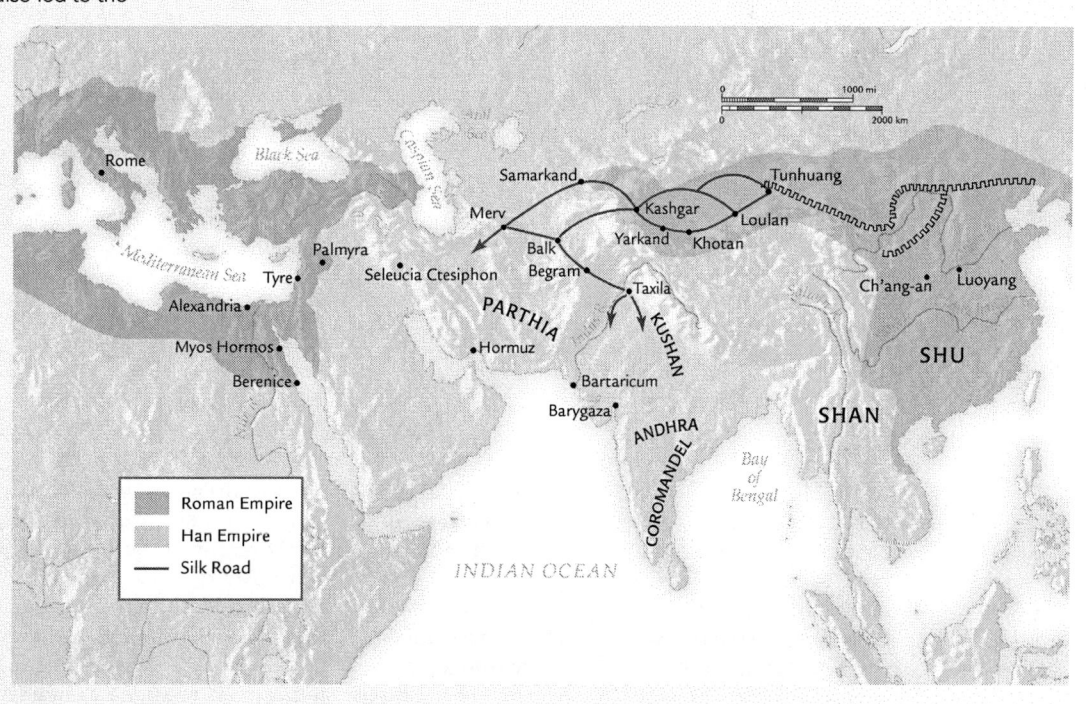

GLOBAL CONNECTIONS

MAP 5.2 The Silk Road, ca. 200 C.E.

thinking about GEOGRAPHY

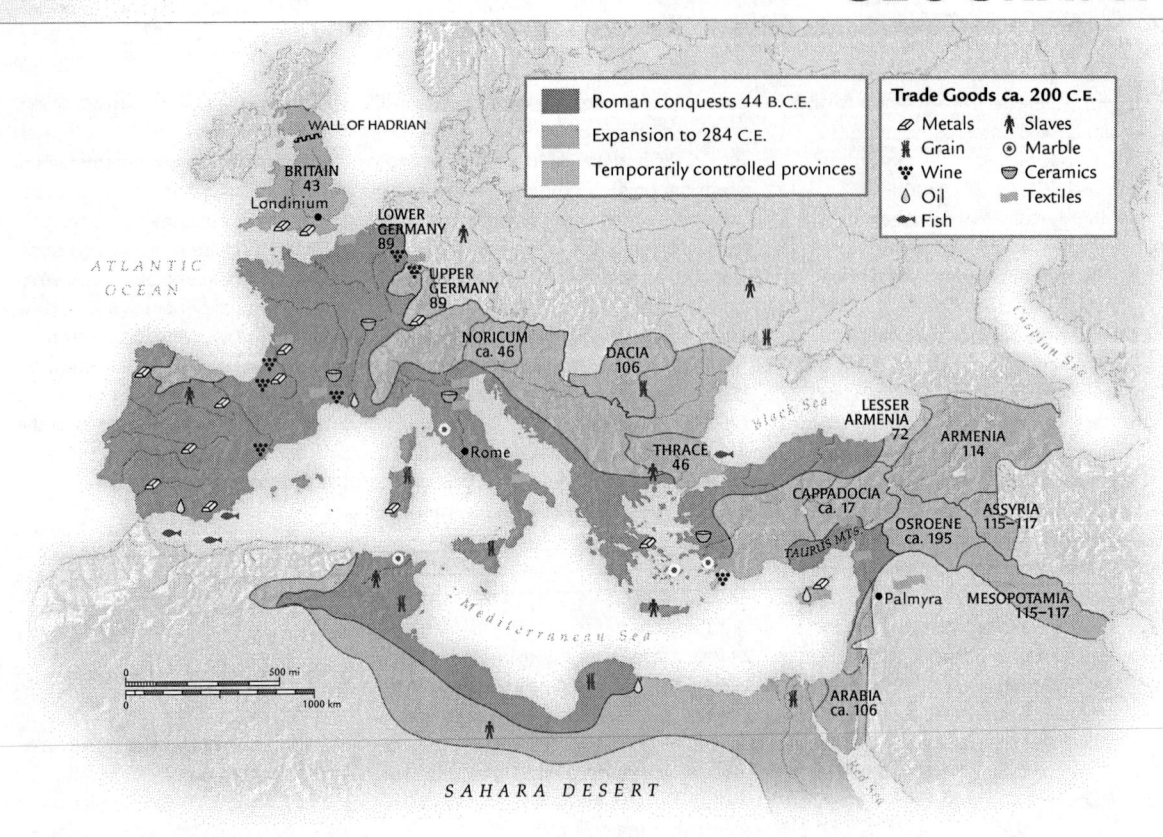

MAP 5.3

The Roman Empire, 44 B.C.E.–284 C.E.

This map shows the greatest extent of the Roman Empire. Notice how much of this territory was acquired during the Republic, before Augustus's rule. The key also shows the major trade goods from the various parts of the empire.

Explore the Map

1. How long did it take for a rapid message to go from Rome to the farthest reaches of the empire? (The most rapid travel time was about 90 miles a day; average travel was 20 miles a day.) What difficulties did such vast distances create?

2. Which territories brought the most essential or expensive trade goods?

3. Which territories might the empire have first abandoned when under pressure? Why?

---

years of imperial decadence. In our age of rapid communication and many levels of administrators and financial managers, it is difficult to imagine how hard it must have been to govern, with a small bureaucracy, an area as large as the Roman Empire. **Map 5.3** shows the extent of the empire through 284 C.E. Although this map looks impressive, it still requires some imagination to understand the meaning of these distances in the third century. For example, in good sailing weather, it took three weeks to sail from one end of the Mediterranean Sea to the other, and travel overland was even harder. Hauling goods by wagon train with escorts armed against bandits took so much time and manpower that it was cheaper to send a load of grain all the way across the Mediterranean than to send it 75 miles overland. Information moved almost as slowly as goods. What could hold the empire together against the centrifugal force of these distances?

The empire found a partial answer in Romanization. From the time of the Republic, Romans had established colonies for military veterans in the provinces, and such colonial expansion continued under the empire. Furthermore, to boost the strength of his army, Augustus recruited auxiliary troops from the noncitizen population all over the empire. After serving twenty-four years, these veterans were awarded with citizenship and land in the colonies. These auxiliary troops also served to spread Roman culture. Colonies became the cities that grew up in Britain, North Africa, Germany, and the East, bringing Roman culture to the most distant corners of the empire. The cities boasted all the amenities that Romans had come to expect: theaters, baths, a colosseum, roads, and townhouses. These urban communities had so much in common that they seemed to erase the huge distances that separated them.

Colonies

In these scattered, Romanized centers, local officials ruled. Town councils, for example, collected taxes and maintained public works, such as water systems and food markets. To collect taxes, officials maintained census figures on both the human population and agricultural produce and reported all to their superiors in Rome. This combination of local rule, Romanization, and some accountability to the central authority helped hold the fabric of the huge empire together.

Provincial administration

The provinces depended not only on the administrative skills of local officials but also on their philanthropy. In the best tradition of ancient Rome, men and women used their private resources for the public good. Inscriptions recalling private contributions survive in towns and cities all over the empire and reveal how essential such charity was to the maintenance of the Roman Peace. One woman in central Italy bequeathed one million coins in her will for the town to use to provide monthly child-assistance payments for all children until boys reached 16 years of age and girls 14. In another instance, the governor of the Asian city of Troy observed that the city was "ill-supplied with baths and that the inhabitants drew muddy water from their wells." The governor persuaded Emperor Hadrian to contribute three million coins to build an aqueduct, but when costs rose to seven million the governor paid for the difference from his own pocket. Philanthropists ensured that Roman life prospered all over the empire by contributing funds for baths, libraries, poor relief, and even public banquets.

The empire also remained unified through the marvels of Roman engineering. Fifty thousand miles of roads supplemented the great rivers as primary means of transportation. As is true today, the upkeep of roads posed a constant challenge and expense, and the empire used public and private means to fund them. The government collected tolls on goods in transit to fund road maintenance, but the toll payments seldom generated enough income. When in need, the empire turned to traditional philanthropy to make up the difference, asking local individuals and businesses to sponsor the upkeep of a particular portion of the road and erecting stones acknowledging their contribution. Such stones remain today in silent testimony to the philanthropy and organization that helped tie together the vast imperial lands.

Roman authorities also established a transportation system that provided travelers with horses and carriages and that monitored the movement of heavy goods. Regulations established maximum loads but were frequently ignored by inspectors, who often took bribes. With these elaborate networks of roads, lightly burdened travelers could cover an astonishing 90 miles a day—an extraordinary feat in ancient times.

Roads and transportation

During the early centuries of the empire, goods moved over great distances not only along the road network, for there was also a great deal of shipping. For the first time in the ancient world, the Roman navy kept the Mediterranean Sea relatively free of pirates, so shipping flourished. The sea had become a virtual Roman lake, and the Romans confidently called it Mare Nostrum (our sea) to show the degree to which the Mediterranean world was united under Rome.

The peace and unity of the empire allowed merchants to increase trade with the farthest reaches of Asia. The fabulous Silk Road brought spices and silks from as far away as China and only whetted the appetite of wealthy Romans for exotic goods from the East. Global Connections on page 145 discusses the Chinese empire that also profited from trade between the West and East.

Finally, the movement of people and armies also held the empire together. The Roman Empire boasted a remarkably multiethnic and multicultural population. Many educated provincials, for example, spoke at least three languages: Greek, Latin, and a local dialect. The imperial lands included a bewildering array of climates and geological features as well. **Figure 5.4** shows the 80-mile-long wall of Hadrian, the northern outpost of the empire in Britain built in the early second century. Here, Roman forts dotted the wall at 1-mile intervals. Roman soldiers peered into the damp fog, on alert against the fierce northern

Imperial diversity

FIGURE 5.4 Hadrian's Wall This photo shows the remains of the wall that marked the northern boundary of the Roman Empire on the British Isles. Ancient writers described the mist that hung on the wall through which soldiers watched for invaders from the wild north.

tribes who threatened to swarm across the imperial boundary. By contrast, **Figure 5.5** shows the forum of the ruins of Dougga, a Roman city in North Africa. You can see in the background the desert that marked the southern border of the empire. Beyond the great groves of olive trees that, together with abundant fields of grain, produced much of the agricultural wealth of North Africa, Roman legions stood watch against the Bedouin tribesmen who came galloping out of the desert to menace the edge of the empire.

With this remarkable diversity came the constant movement of people. Merchants traveled with their goods, and just as in the Hellenistic world, enterprising people moved about to seek their fortunes. Furthermore, to defend the empire's 6,000 miles of border, Roman authorities moved approximately 300,000 soldiers to wherever they were needed. The armies usually did not patrol their own regions. A garrison of black sub-Saharan Africans, for example, was stationed in the foggy north along Hadrian's Wall, and Germans from the north patrolled the desert. At the height of the *Pax Romana*, this flexible system seemed to ensure peace within Rome's borders.

As we will see, in time the centrifugal forces began to work against the ability of such a far-flung empire to hold together. The expense and difficulties of long-distance trade caused more and more provinces to produce their goods locally. Outside the empire itself, more tribes wanted to enter and share Rome's prosperity, and the borders would become all too permeable. But for the first two hundred years of the empire, it seemed as if the promise of a glorious new age had been fulfilled.

LIFE DURING THE PEACE OF ROME

Just as Augustus wanted to return politics to the traditional morality of the Roman Republic, he also tried to revive the old morality in the private lives of Rome's citizens. However, the new wealth that poured into the pockets of well-placed Romans made the old morality seem quaint and antiquated.

A New Decadence

Although the growing separation between rich and poor that began under the Republic continued through the empire, those getting more wealthy began to flaunt their riches. Silks and embroidery replaced the rough wool of republican virtue, and satirists wrote

FIGURE 5.5 Roman Ruins The southern boundary of Rome was marked by a desert. These Roman ruins in the city of Dougga in modern Tunisia show how Roman culture extended to the dry southern lands.

scathingly of women sporting makeup, high heels, elaborate hairstyles, and lots of jewelry. Men, too, indulged in similar excesses to ensure their appearance reflected their wealth and status. Augustus and subsequent moralists would fight a losing battle against such decadent displays.

The new wealth from trade and peace extended beyond Rome itself to people living in other growing urban areas. **Figure 5.6** is a painting from the wall of a baker's shop in the city of Pompeii (about 150 miles south of Rome, near Naples). Pompeii was a prosperous city that was buried in 79 C.E. under the ash of a violently erupting volcano, Mount Vesuvius. The rain of ash froze the city and its people in time, allowing modern excavators to see individuals engaged in many activities of daily life. The image in **Figure 5.6** offers insights into the Italian peninsula's urban life, in which both men and women participated and grew wealthy in commerce.

The Problem with Population

During the Republic, marriage and family ties were central values of the Roman people, and Augustus used his power to support those values. The princeps promoted legislation that assessed penalties on people who remained unmarried and instituted strong laws against adultery. These laws, though intended to strengthen the family, fell far short of their mark. Morality is singularly hard to legislate, and the Roman historian Tacitus observed that many people simply ignored the laws. Augustus himself experienced this phenomenon firsthand: Unable to control his own daughter's behavior (which he perceived as inappropriate), he ended up exiling her.

At heart, however, the laws were probably as much about children as about morality. The future of Rome, like the succession of the emperor, depended on offspring to carry on the family and other cultural traditions. Yet, throughout the empire, Romans had a particularly hard time reproducing. Augustus even promoted a law that exempted women from male guardianship if they bore three children (four children for a freed slave). These numbers are a far cry from those in earlier times; Cornelia, mother of the Gracchi, earned praise for bearing 12 children! Fecundity in the empire certainly had plummeted to alarmingly low levels.

Birthrates

This phenomenon had cultural as well as physical causes. Wealthy Roman men and women often wanted few children, so as to preserve their inheritance intact. Yet, Augustus's law specifically tried to influence women. This law is particularly interesting in its assumptions: It recognized women's desire for freedom, and it assumed that women controlled their own fecundity. The former assumption may have been accurate, but the latter was only partially so. Sometimes women used birth-control methods based on herbs, spermicidal drugs, or douches. The texts also refer to abortion, although drugs strong enough to abort a fetus often endangered the life of the mother.

thinking about ART

FIGURE 5.6
Wall Painting from a Baker's Shop in Pompeii, ca. 70 C.E.

This painting is from a baker's shop in the city of Pompeii, which was destroyed by the volcano Vesuvius in 70 C.E. Pompeii's preservation of small elements of Roman daily life makes it an important source of information about the past. The painting shows a prosperous, middle-class couple; the woman holds writing implements—a stylus and wax tablet—and the man holds a scroll (equivalent to an ancient book) with a label that identifies its contents. Notice how realistically the couple is portrayed.

Connecting Art & Society

1. Why might the couple have chosen to have themselves portrayed so realistically? What does the image indicate about what the couple valued?
2. What does this image suggest about the importance of literacy to a prosperous urban economy?
3. What does the image suggest about the woman's role in business, and in urban economy more generally?

The causes of Roman infertility lay in a full complex of medical misunderstandings combined with cultural practices.

Sexual and Medical Misunderstandings

Despite the scandalized commentary lamenting the sexual excess of "loose" women and decadent emperors, Romans in fact were very circumspect about sex. Medical wisdom warned men against the fatiguing effects of sexual activity, which they thought deprived the body of vital spirit. Roman physicians believed semen was made of brain fluid, and urged men to conserve it carefully.

By contrast, physicians did not believe that sexual intercourse weakened females. Indeed, medical advice for women focused on helping them to bear as many children as possible. Yet, medical misinformation actually contributed to Rome's falling birthrate. Physicians concluded, incorrectly, that women were most fertile soon after their menstrual periods, so they recommended reserving intercourse for that time. Furthermore, some doctors thought that women had to have intercourse before puberty in order to mature correctly. Medical misunderstanding about women's bodies and children's health care contributed to a low birthrate. These factors combined with other cultural issues—the desire to restrict children to keep from reducing inheritances, for example—help explain why Rome had so much trouble maintaining its population.

Despite the confusion regarding human reproduction, Roman medicine proved highly influential for the next 1,500 years. In particular, the physician Galen (131–201) popularized views that have prevailed even into modern times. Galen used some modern scientific techniques—for example, he performed vivisections on pigs to see the process of digestion—but his conclusions were strongly rooted in the classical world. He embraced the notion of moderation that was so central to ancient thought (recall Aristotle's "golden mean," discussed in Chapter 2) and therefore saw disease as the result of an imbalance, or excess. Galen believed that good health resulted from a balance among the four "humors,"

Galen

or bodily fluids—blood, bile, urine, and phlegm. He argued that each of these humors had its own properties—warm, cold, dry, and moist—and when a person was out of balance—that is, when one humor dominated—the cure was to restore an appropriate equilibrium. For example, if a person was feverish and flushed, he or she was considered to have an excess of blood. An application of blood-sucking leeches or the initiation of bleeding would reduce the blood and restore the balance. These ideas may not have improved people's health, but they formed the subsequent basis for medical treatment.

The Games

Families may have formed the basis of Roman society, but as we saw in Chapter 4, during the Republic, men forged critical ties in the world of civic affairs centered in the Roman Forum. Under the empire this focus changed; real power moved from the Forum to the emperor's household. Yet the Roman people still needed a public place to gather and express their collective will. Over time, they began satisfying this need at the great games and spectacles held in the amphitheaters across the empire. During the late Republic, wealthy men who craved the admiration of the people, and politicians who sought the loyalty of the crowd, spent fortunes producing chariot races in the Circus Maximus and hunts and gladiator games. After the time of Augustus, the emperors had a virtual monopoly on providing entertainment in Rome, although in the provinces others could produce spectacles. These games always had a religious significance to the Roman people, ritualizing Roman power and authority.

Figure 5.7 shows the Roman Colosseum, built by Emperor Vespasian (r. 69–79) as a gift to his subjects. **Map 5.1** shows its location within the city. This structure was the largest of its kind in the Roman world and held about 50,000 people. The photograph on the right (see **Figure 5.7**) shows what remains of the interior, including subterranean passages that held animals and prisoners. The photograph on the left shows the exterior, which dominated the skyline of Rome. Men and women flocked to the arena in the mornings to watch men hunt exotic animals that had been transported to Rome from the farthest reaches of the empire. Augustus proudly claimed to have provided a total of 3,500 animals in these hunts; other emperors were equally lavish in their displays.

From Forum to arena

The crowds then witnessed the public executions of criminals who were either set aflame or put in the path of deadly wild animals. Through such rituals, Rome displayed its power over its enemies. **Figure 5.8** shows a criminal being attacked by a leopard in the arena. This horrifying scene suggests that it was not easy to make animals attack humans; the victims had to be immobilized and the animals goaded into aggression. The very existence of the mosaic, however, which was displayed in a private home, reveals the Romans' pride in the empire's dominance over its perceived enemies. As we will see, these enemies would eventually include Christians.

Afternoons at the Colosseum were reserved for the main event, the gladiator contests. Gladiators were condemned criminals who were trained in the gladiator school near the Colosseum (see **Map 5.1**). They then received the right to live a while longer by fighting against each other in the arena. In time, the gladiatorial ranks were increased by slaves who were specifically bought and trained for this purpose. Gladiators armed with weapons were paired to fight until one was killed, and the winner won the right to live until his next fight. At first, gladiator contests were part of funeral rites, and the death blood of the losers was seen as an offering to the recently departed. Later, however, emperors sponsored contests featuring hundreds of gladiators. At the end of a gladiator contest,

Gladiators

FIGURE 5.7 The Colosseum This magnificent building was inaugurated in 80 C.E. The concrete foundations were 25 feet deep to support the structure of concrete and marble. More than 50,000 spectators entered through numbered gates to their seats.

FIGURE 5.8 Condemned to the Beasts, ca. second century C.E. During the mid-afternoon at the games in the amphitheaters, criminals sentenced to death were attacked by beasts. This mosaic from a private home was designed to celebrate Rome's victory over its enemies.

the man who had been overpowered was supposed to bare his throat unflinchingly to the killing blade of the victor. Not all defeated gladiators were killed; those who had fought with extreme bravery and showed a willingness to die could be freed by the emperor's clemency.

It is easy to judge these activities as wanton displays of brutality. Yet, from the Roman perspective, these rituals actually exemplified and perpetuated Roman virtue. In the arenas, private honor and public good intersected: The private generosity that funded the games served the community's need for ritual, and the emperor's sponsorship strengthened the community's loyalty to its leaders. Finally, individuals learned to face death bravely by watching people die; as the historian Livy (59 B.C.E.–17 C.E.) wrote: "There was no better schooling against pain and death." Nevertheless, all these demonstrations of Roman largesse, prowess, and courage could not stave off the threats to the empire that came at the end of the *Pax Romana*.

CRISIS AND TRANSFORMATION, 192–ca. 400 C.E.

The violence that accompanied the assassination of Marcus Aurelius's decadent son Commodus in 192 transformed Augustus's principate. The armies had grown strong under the military policy of the Five Good Emperors, so armies even beyond the praetorian guard became the king makers. Septimius Severus (r. 193–211) was a new kind of emperor—a North African general who came to power because of his army's support. A military man to the core, he also embodied the multicultural elements of the empire. He spoke Latin with a North African accent and seemed to feel more at home among provincials than among the old, wealthy families of Rome.

The Military Monarchy

Septimius transformed the political base for Roman rule. Under the principate as established by Augustus, the empire was ruled by a partnership between the emperor and the Senate; Septimius and his successors ruled with the support of the army, creating a military dictatorship. [Severan dynasty] Septimius enlarged the army until it contained several legions more than the army of Augustus. He also raised soldiers' pay, ensuring their loyalty. Septimius militarized the civil government as well, by making extensive use of generals in positions of power. With these changes, the route to high office lay through the emperor's army instead of the *cursus honorum* (described in **Figure 4.3**). Rome had changed indeed.

Septimius established a dynasty (the Severan) that uneasily held power until 235. His son Caracalla (r. 211–217) was ruthless and was murdered while on campaign. Strong women in the Severan family—Julia Maesa, Caracalla's aunt, and her two daughters—managed to ensure that two more incompetent boys took the throne, but both Elagabalus (r. 218–222) and Alexander (r. 222–235) were murdered.

In the fifty years that followed Alexander's death, Rome was beset with chaos. During this period, legions in various parts of the empire put forth their own claimants to the throne. This era of conflict—from 235 to 285—was dominated by what has come to be called "barrack-room emperors," men who had little allegiance to the ancient values of the city of Rome. From 235 to 285, the number of claimants to the throne exploded. In one nine-year period, the emperor Gallienus fought off as many as 18 challengers. A unit whose general became emperor increased its own status, so armies fought for the throne.

While armies were busy trying to create emperors, Rome's borders were threatened on all fronts. In the north, Germanic tribes (discussed more fully in Chapter 6) began to penetrate across the Rhine and Danube defenses. Soldiers and resources had to be moved north to try to stem the tide. Meanwhile in the east, Rome seemed so weakened that Zenobia, a powerful queen of Palmyra (a city in Syria), declared [Border wars] independence from Rome and led armies against the legions. Emperor Aurelian (r. 270–275) crushed Palmyra after two wars and brought Queen Zenobia in chains to Rome. The resourceful queen ended up living out her life in an extravagant villa near Tivoli in

Italy, but her city was destroyed. Rome was not as successful in other eastern campaigns, as the Persian Empire encroached on Rome's eastern provinces. A Persian rock inscription celebrates a Persian victory and indicates the stress on the empire during these dark days: "We attacked the Roman Empire and annihilated . . . a Roman force of 60,000."

This whole military era demonstrates the centrifugal force that had marked Rome's growth from the beginning. Emperors were created in barracks far from Rome, and territories on the edges of the empire were slipping from centralized control. As if these internal and external pressures were not enough, a severe economic downturn loomed.

Ravaged by Recession, Inflation, and Plague

At the height of the empire, certain families accumulated astonishing wealth. Even though they gave some of it back to the public in the form of monuments or games, they still lived lavishly. Not only did they buy jewels and fine silks, but they gave banquets featuring exotic (and expensive) imported foods. One menu from a Roman cookbook recommends rare dishes from the far reaches of the empire: sow's udders stuffed with salted sea urchins, Jericho dates, boiled ostrich, roast parrot, boiled flamingo, and African sweet cakes.

This kind of luxury spending seriously damaged an already weakening economy for two reasons: It drained hard currency from the West and transferred it to the Far East, which supplied many of the luxuries; and it kept money from circulating, thus limiting the avenues for the growth of a prosperous middle class. As the poor in Rome received more and more food subsidies, the city had to spend more money on imported grain, further reducing the treasury. With the increase in imports from the East, the western centers of the empire began to suffer a shortage of hard currency, as money flowed to the great eastern centers that supplied most of the imports. As we will see, this shifting of wealth to the East had profound ramifications for the governing of the empire.

There was a further inherent weakness in the imperial economy: When territorial expansion stopped, there was little to bring new wealth into the empire. Instead, a growing bureaucracy, increased military expenses, and costly military rivalries served to drain money. The economy stagnated while expenses increased.

Emperors throughout the centuries tried to address the problem of a shortage of hard currency by debasing the coinage, which meant that plenty of money still circulated, but it was not worth as much as it had been before. Gold coins virtually disappeared from circulation, and by the mid-third century the silver content of coins had dropped to a negligible 1 percent. Not surprisingly, inflation struck. The price of grain climbed so much that a measure that cost two coins in 200 C.E. cost 330 coins just a century later. Inflation always hits the poor hardest, and many people turned to banditry out of desperation. The resulting fear and unrest further rocked life in the empire.

To worsen matters, plague from China spread through the empire along with the luxury goods that came along the Silk Road. (See Global Connections, page 145.) Just as in China, the disease caused intense suffering and depleted the already low Roman population. Labor became as scarce as hard currency. The Roman government turned to the tribes outside its borders to replenish its armies. Mercenaries crossed the borders to fight for Rome, and the legions of Rome increasingly came to resemble the "barbarians" from the outside. Structures like Hadrian's Wall no longer clearly separated the "civilized" from the "uncivilized."

All the problems of the late second and third centuries demonstrated that the Roman Peace was over. The borders between Roman and non-Roman had dissolved, and hungry, restless residents agitated within the empire. Medical knowledge was helpless in the face of pandemics like the mid-third-century plague, and Roman families could no longer populate the empire. The empire seemed to teeter on the brink of collapse.

The Reforms of Diocletian, 285–305 C.E.

Considering the many disasters facing the empire in the mid-third century, it is a wonder that the empire did not fall then. In fact, it was the dramatic measures of Diocletian, an autocratic new emperor, that helped Rome avert ultimate disaster—at least for the time being. Diocletian (r. 285–305) was a general who rose from the ranks to wear the imperial purple. Not content to be called emperor, he assumed the title "lord" and demanded that his subjects worship him as a living god. (See Document 5.2.) The change in title marked the formal end of the principate founded by Augustus—from then on, emperors were no longer "first citizens." Diocletian had a shrewd, practical side and used his considerable administrative talents to address the problems plaguing the empire. The new Roman lord was up to the task and stopped the decline.

Turning to the problems of communication, administration, and succession, Diocletian organized the government into a **tetrarchy,** or rule by four men. Diocletian ruled in the wealthier eastern region of the empire, while assigning his partner, Maximian, to

thinking about DOCUMENTS

DOCUMENT 5.2

Diocletian Becomes "Lord"

The Roman historian Aurelius Victor in the middle of the fourth century wrote a brief work titled Lives of the Emperors *in which he described the transformation of Diocletian from a "first citizen" like Augustus to a more aloof, godlike figure.*

By decision of the generals and [military] tribunes, Valerius Diocletian, commander of the palace guards, was chosen emperor because of his wisdom. A mighty man he was, and the following were characteristics of his: he was the first to wear a cloak embroidered in gold and to covet shoes of silk and purple decorated with a great number of gems. Though this went beyond what befitted a citizen and was characteristic of an arrogant and lavish spirit, it was nevertheless of small consequence in comparison with the rest. Indeed, he was the first after Caligula and Domitian to allow himself to be publicly called "lord," and to be named "god," and to be rendered homage as such. . . . But Diocletian's faults were counterbalanced by good qualities; for even if he took the title of "lord," he did act [toward the Romans] as a father.

SOURCE: Aurelius Victor, *Lives of the Emperors*, in *Roman Civilization: Sourcebook II: The Empire*, eds. Naphtali Lewis and Meyer Reinhold (New York: Harper Torchbooks, 1966), p. 456.

Analyze the Document

1. How did Diocletian present himself to the Roman public?
2. What innovations does Aurelius Victor describe? Did this historian approve of Diocletian's actions?
3. Contrast this view of leadership with that of Augustus shown in Document 5.1. Why do you think the Romans were prepared to accept such a kinglike demeanor in Diocletian?

---

rule in the West. To address the issue of succession, each of these "augusti" adopted a "caesar" who would succeed him. In the Roman tradition dating back to Octavian, each caesar married his augustus's daughter, sealing the alliance through family bonds. **Figure 5.9** depicts the ideals behind the tetrarchy. The four emperors—all military men—rest their hands on their swords. They also embrace one another. The overall arrangement of their figures conveys the concept of a unified rule by four men. **Map 5.4** shows the territorial division of the tetrarchy.

Diocletian then turned his administrative talents to problems other than succession. He recognized that the military that had created so many emperors from the time of Septimius Severus onward was a threat to political stability. He brought the army under control in part by reversing Septimius's policy of uniting civil and military offices. He separated the two so that provincial governors could not command armies, thus making it harder for generals to aspire to the purple. To address the problem of incursions along the imperial frontiers, Diocletian rearranged the armies. Instead of placing his greatest martial strength along the borders, he stationed mobile legions deep inside the empire. That way, they could move quickly to meet a threat rather than just react as outsiders encroached. The Germanic tribes on the northern borders were particularly eager to enter the empire, looking for wealth. Diocletian recruited many of these Germans to serve in this new army, further diluting its traditional Roman character even as he made it more effective.

Military reforms

FIGURE 5.9 Tetrarchs, ca. 305 C.E. Diocletian's division of the Roman Empire's administration among four men might have seemed to some to fragment it. This statue from Venice shows the four tetrarchs embracing and thus strongly linked as one, assuring the viewer that the empire still stood united.

thinking about GEOGRAPHY

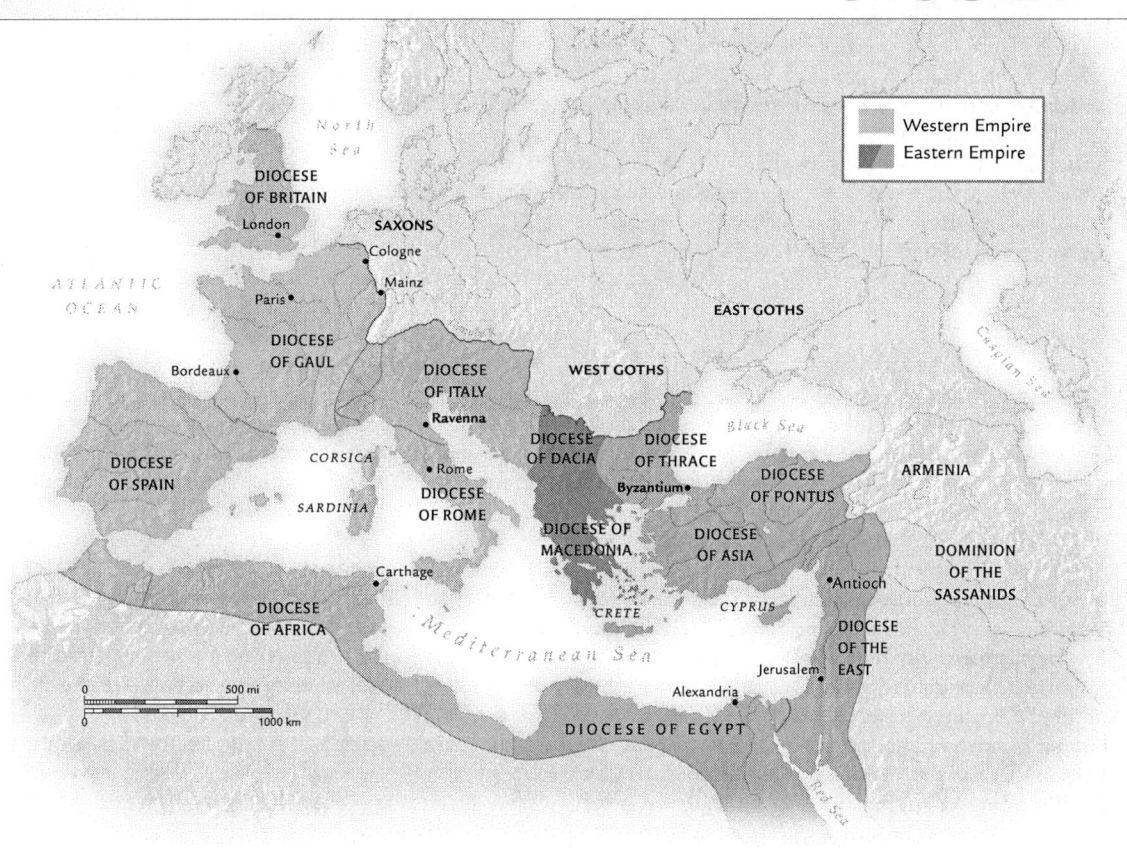

MAP 5.4

Diocletian's Division of the Empire, 304 C.E.

This map shows Diocletian's administrative reform of the empire and its division into four parts that would be governed by a tetrarchy (four men). Notice the primary division into east and west, with each unit ruled by an augustus.

Explore the Map

1. What geographic advantage led Diocletian to take the eastern portion of the empire?
2. Ravenna and Byzantium became the two new capitals of the empire, replacing Rome. What advantages did each city's location offer for trade and defense?

Finally, Diocletian turned to the severe economic problems troubling the empire. In the same way Augustus had tried to improve morality by decree, Diocletian issued economic edicts. He addressed the rampant inflation by freezing prices and wages, but these policies simply led merchants to withdraw goods from the open market to participate in informal black market exchanges. The emperor also raised taxes to pay for an expanding army, but he reformed the tax system so that it was partially based on payment in goods instead of in the inflated, scarce coins. This kind of authoritarian approach could not solve the empire's most deep-seated economic troubles, but it kept the economy from collapsing altogether.

The last problem that Diocletian addressed was the simple shortage of people to perform the tasks needed to keep the empire running. Again, he sought solutions in decrees. He identified "essential" occupations—ranging from soldier to farmer, baker,

Economic reforms

and tax collector—and froze people in these jobs. Furthermore, he made these occupations hereditary. His decrees had a serious unintended consequence: They weakened the willingness of well-off locals to contribute to the public works and the games that had so defined imperial life. Instead, great estates became more self-contained, pulling away from the central authority and maintaining their own mercenary armies. People increasingly complained about the tax collectors and the central government that seemed to ask more and more of its citizens while providing less and less.

The Capital Moves East

Diocletian's attempts to stabilize the succession barely outlasted him. He and his co-augustus stepped down in 305 as planned, leaving the empire to be ruled by their two caesars, but Diocletian's hopes for a smooth transition proved overly optimistic. There were years of intrigue and civil war as several rulers fought for the throne. Finally, one of the caesars was succeeded by an ambitious son, Constantine (r. 306–337), who defeated his rivals to assume sole control of the empire. The new emperor finally disbanded the powerful praetorian guards, who had backed his rival. Beyond that, he kept Diocletian's economic and military reforms but put his own unique stamp on the empire.

In 330, Constantine made a momentous decision for the future of the empire: He built a new urban center on the site of the old Greek city of Byzantium. Later the city would be called Constantinople, after its founder, and become a second capital to the empire, eclipsing Rome itself in power and grandeur. Rome was no longer a practical site for the capital of the empire because it was too far from the center of the military actions on the borders, and the conservative old Roman nobility made it very difficult for emperors to implement vigorous new ideas. Constantine could not have chosen a better site for a new capital city, which he called his "new Rome." It was easily defended and located along the rich eastern trade routes. Since Diocletian, when emperors ruled autocratically based in cities away from Rome, the great Roman Senate that had governed in concert with Augustus had shrunk to no more than a city council. The Roman Empire seemed to have little to do with Rome anymore and bore scant resemblance to the principate created by Augustus.

Constantinople

As the capital moved east, the western provinces came under increasing pressure from the Germanic tribes outside the empire. Great estates in the provinces—called *latifundia*—became more self-sufficient, needing nothing from the central authority. After the death of Constantine in 337, emperors reacted to Germanic invaders by inviting some tribes into the empire to settle and become allies. The borders had already proved permeable, and with the continued population decline within the empire, there seemed to be enough space for everyone. This influx, however, carried the seeds of the empire's eventual disintegration. The Visigoths (more fully described in Chapter 6) were one of the tribes the Romans invited across the border to settle. However, the Romans treated them abysmally, giving them land they could not farm, raping their women, and forcing them to sell their children into slavery in return for food. The warlike tribe went on a rampage.

In 378, Romans under Emperor Valens (r. 364–378) confronted Gothic troops, and the resulting battle marked a change in military tactics. The Goths were heavily outnumbered by the heavy Roman infantry that had always seemed invincible. The Romans pushed the Goths back to their circled wagons, and defeat seemed imminent. Just then, Gothic cavalry dashed from the hills, smashing the Roman line. The infantry was no match for mobile cavalry, and the Roman army was destroyed. Emperor Valens was killed on the field. This battle dispelled the aura of invincibility that had surrounded the Roman legions for centuries and demonstrated the military importance of cavalry. It seemed that military might now lay in the hands of the "barbarians" rapidly pouring through the borders.

Even Rome itself was no longer the center of the empire, for by the fourth century, the emperors in the West had made Milan their capital. Then, in 402, Emperor Honorius fled from the invading Visigoths to create a new capital in Ravenna, behind defensible marshes. Ravenna was safe, but Rome was not, and in 410, the Visigoths plundered the "eternal city," Rome itself. Masses of panicked Romans (like Melania in the Biography on page 170) fled to Africa and the East.

It seemed that an era had passed and that the empire had finally fallen—but the end had not come quite yet. The Visigoths left Italy and settled in Spain as allies of the empire, just as many other tribes had done in other provinces. An emperor remained in the west, ruling from Italy, and a co-ruler continued to govern in the east, from Constantinople. But by 410 the western region had disintegrated so much that there seemed to be no point in referring to a Roman Empire in the West at all.

Twilight of the empire

For the last few centuries, historians have spent a great deal of thought (and paper) exploring what has come to be known as the "fall" of the Roman Empire that began in the turmoil of the third century. Historians point to dwindling population, economic problems, reliance on slave labor, civil warfare, and moral decay as the causes of the decline. All of these factors contributed to the transformation of the old Roman world, but perhaps more important than

Rome's "fall"

anything else was the great influx of peoples from the north who invaded the empire. These invasions (which we will explore in more detail in Chapter 6) caused the breakup of the huge empire that had dominated the Mediterranean world since the time of Augustus. The territorial empire was ending, but throughout these years of power and turmoil a religion arose that would give a new source of unity to the Mediterranean world.

THE LONGING FOR RELIGIOUS FULFILLMENT

As we saw in Chapter 4, the Romans were a deeply religious people who carefully linked their deities to cherished spaces. As the empire controlled more and more land, its subjects seemed increasingly distanced from their traditional gods. In part, worship of the emperor served as a unifying religious cult. By the middle of the third century, some twenty festival days honored deified emperors or their families each year. However, for all the reverence given to the emperors, a spiritual dissatisfaction still gnawed at the Roman people. Many Romans seemed to long for a closer relationship to a truly transcendent divinity, and Romans expressed this longing through a rise in various philosophic and religious movements.

We can see this attempt to bring the gods a little closer to earth in the increasing numbers of spells and charms that Roman men and women purchased. People tried everything from healing and love charms to curses placed on chariot racers. Prophets, magicians, and charlatans also proliferated. One late-second-century writer described a man who made a fortune by pretending to prophesy through a giant serpent that he wrapped around himself. However, all the religious movements of the Roman world were not as superficial as magical curses and false prophets.

Stoicism and Platonism

The Hellenistic philosophies (Chapter 3) all continued to offer religious satisfaction to some educated Romans. The great Roman Stoic Seneca (ca. 4 B.C.E.–65 C.E.) wrote that by focusing on their own ethical behavior, people could locate the divinity that dwells within each person. As mentioned earlier, the Stoic emperor Marcus Aurelius used this philosophy to bring meaning to the challenges of his life. Like the reflective emperor, many people found in Stoicism ethical principles to help guide their lives, and Stoicism exerted an important influence on both Christianity and Western ideas in general.

The most influential philosophical system, however, came with a new form of Platonism, **Neoplatonism,** that emerged during the late empire. In the third century, these Neoplatonists created a complex system that offered an explanation for the link between the divine and the human.

Like Stoics, Neoplatonists believed that each person contained a spark of divinity that longed to join the divinity that had created it. Through study, contemplation, and proper living, people could cultivate that bit of divinity within themselves and thereby reduce the distance between the human and the divine.

> Neoplatonism

These philosophies, though intriguing, had limited appeal. Just as they had in the earlier Hellenistic kingdoms, they attracted people with leisure, education, and a respectable income. Most people instead tried to satisfy their spiritual desires through one or more of the mystery cults that gained popularity in the second century.

Mystery Cults

The mystery cults that had become popular during the Hellenistic world (Chapter 3) had an even stronger appeal in the difficult times of the late empire. These cults had always offered hope to individuals seeking meaning in their lives and ecstatic celebrations that seemed to transport individuals outside themselves into the world of the gods. Some cults claimed to offer a universality lacking in many of the Roman deities, and many offered hopes of a better afterlife to people disenchanted with their current existence.

The ancient Greek cult of Dionysus is one example of a cult that promised all these things. In this popular worship, men and women celebrated the mysteries of the god of wine and rebirth by drinking, engaging in sex acts, and ritually eating the raw flesh of beasts. **Figure 5.10** shows a painting discovered in Pompeii that probably depicts the worship of Dionysus. The young woman on the left is being whipped, probably to bring about an ecstatic state. The woman on the right dances in naked ecstasy with a cymbal while the woman before her prepares to hand her the staff marking her entrance into the mysteries. Such ceremonies appealed to people's need to feel personally connected with the divine.

> Cult of Dionysus

The cult of Isis, the Egyptian goddess of fertility, enjoyed remarkable popularity throughout the empire. Septimius Severus and his wife portrayed themselves as Isis and her consort, Serapis. As we saw in Chapter 1, the ancient Egyptians called Isis's husband Osiris, but in the Hellenistic period, when many of the Egyptian deities were assimilated into the Greek pantheon, Osiris began to be called Serapis. As the noted Greek biographer Plutarch (ca. 46–ca. 120 C.E.) explained, "Serapis received this name at the time when he changed his nature. For this reason

> Cult of Isis

FIGURE 5.10 Mystery Religions, first century C.E. This fresco is from the Villa of the Mysteries near Pompeii, a site that was preserved by its burial in volcanic ash from the eruption of Mount Vesuvius. The image shows women participating in a sacred ritual, probably for the god Bacchus.

Serapis is a god of all peoples in common." In his new form as Serapis, the old god Osiris left his traditional home of the Nile and brought protection to wide areas of the empire. Thus, Serapis was an appropriate incarnation for Septimius, a North African emperor who wanted to combine imperial worship with that of a popular mystery religion to try to overcome Rome's lack of a single, unifying religion.

While some cults, like that of Serapis, strove for universal appeal, the worship of other deities was not intended to be for everyone. Instead, initiates prided themselves on participating in an exclusive and difficult worship. For example, some men and women celebrated the mystery of the Great Mother, the female goddess who brought fertility and comfort. In frenzied rituals, celebrants flogged themselves until their blood flowed, and some men castrated themselves as an ultimate sacrifice to the goddess. In another example, imperial soldiers felt particularly drawn to the mysteries of Mithraism, whose followers were exclusively men, and the religion's emphasis on self-discipline and courage made it very popular with the armies of Rome. These soldiers gathered in special buildings, ritualistically ate bread and water, and awaited salvation.

These different mysteries practiced throughout the Roman world reflected the multicultural nature of the empire. People were willing to partake in mysteries of any origin, whether Egyptian, Syrian, or Persian. All these practices emphasized the irrational at the expense of the rational, in contrast to the Stoic or Platonist approaches. But in the ancient world, people did not feel compelled to choose only one path to spiritual fulfillment. The famous second-century author Apuleius, for example, was a magician, a Platonist, and an initiate into the mysteries of Isis.

The Four Faces of Judaism

Although Palestine had struggled for religious purity while under the Hellenistic kings, the Jews under Roman rule were not exempt from the religious angst

thinking about GEOGRAPHY

MAP 5.5

Israel at the Time of Jesus

This map shows the kingdom of Herod under the rule of Rome. It also illustrates how this kingdom reunited Judah and Israel and at the same time how much smaller it was than the old empire of King David.

Explore the Map

1. Where do the trade route lines go? What diverse influences did Judaism experience from the countless travelers who passed through the small kingdom?
2. Where were the major sites of Jesus' ministry? How close together were they? (Consult the scale.) How might these distances have contributed to the ministry?

---

that swept the empire. At the time of Julius Caesar, the kingdom of Judah had been ruled by descendants of Judas Maccabes (see Chapter 3), but the kingdom was swept into the turmoil of Rome's civil wars following the death of Julius Caesar. Finally, Herod, a member of a prominent family in Hebron, south of Jerusalem, rose to power and, with the support of Octavian, was made king of Judea and subject to Rome by the Senate of Rome. **Map 5.5** shows the kingdom of Herod and illustrates its central location in the trade of the Middle East. Herod was unpopular with the Jews, and during this kingdom, controversies grew. The struggles of four main Jewish groups shaped the religious and political future of this region and beyond.

The **Sadducees** largely comprised members of priestly families. They emphasized Jewish worship at the Temple in Jerusalem, which they saw as the cult center of the Israelites. (In Chapter 3 we saw that the Temple had been rebuilt in the sixth century B.C.E., and this structure—which had been further rebuilt in 19 B.C.E.—is known as the Second Temple.) The Sadducees were religious conservatives who rejected any "new" ideas that they did not find in the Torah—the first five books of the Bible.

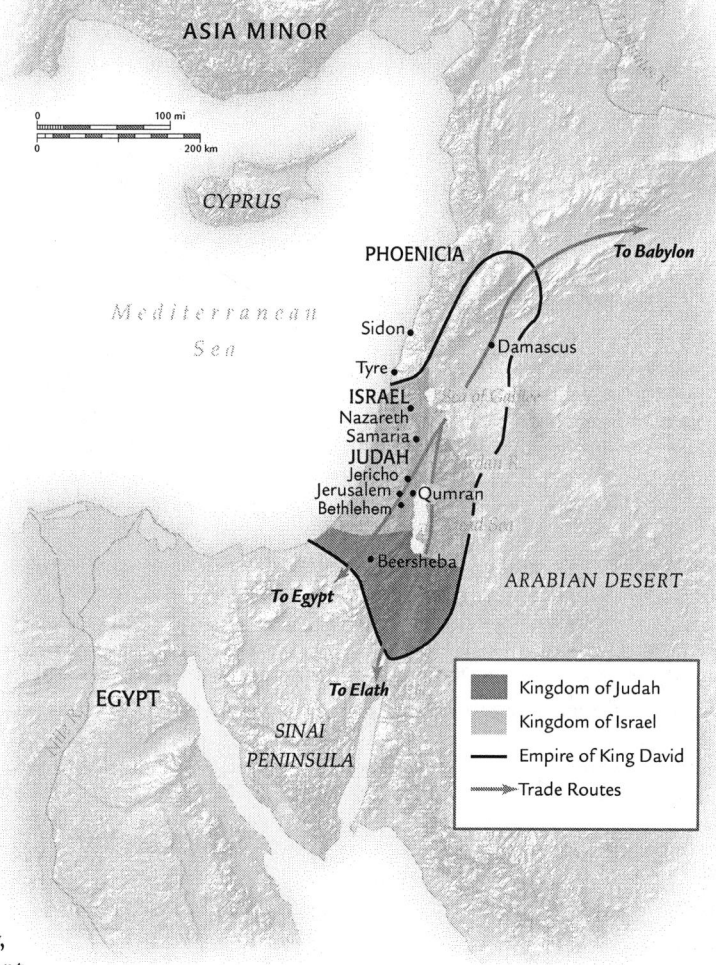

Sadducees and Pharisees

These innovations included the ideas of angels and resurrection of the dead, both of which began to win more adherents. The Sadducees were also willing to compromise with the Hellenized world and the Roman rulers as long as the Temple cult remained secure. However, the Sadducees would not continue as a viable force after Titus destroyed the Temple in 70 C.E.

The **Pharisees,** on the other hand, emphasized Jewish purity laws. They refused all compromise with the Hellenized world and adhered strictly to dietary rules and rituals to reinforce their separateness from all non-Jews. However, the Pharisees did accept new ideas such as the resurrection of the just and the existence of angels. For Pharisees, Judaism centered not on public worship in the Temple but on the private observances of Jews all over the Roman world. The Pharisees also supported sayings and interpretations of Jewish scholars, such as the influential Hillel the Elder (ca. 30 B.C.E.–ca. 10 C.E.), that later became part of the Jewish tradition. It was the work of the Pharisees that would ultimately lead to the expanded writings that updated the practice of the Torah.

Although the Pharisees believed strongly in separating themselves from the surrounding non-Jewish world, they avoided political revolution. Another group in Palestine, the **Zealots**, took a different approach. This group looked back to the successful revolt of the Maccabees against Seleucid rule and urged political revolt against Roman rule as a way to restore Israel to an independent state. Not surprisingly, clashes between the Zealots and Roman troops broke out throughout the early first century C.E.

Despite their differences, all these groups were struggling in some way with the same question that had plagued Jews since the first Hellenistic conquest: how to maintain a separate identity within the Roman world. A fourth group, the **Essenes**, tried to avoid the problem altogether by withdrawing from the social world. The Essenes moved to separate communities and attempted to live pure lives, seemingly alienating themselves from the Temple cult. The Essenes have drawn much scholarly attention because they probably authored one of the most exciting archaeological finds in biblical history, the Dead Sea Scrolls.

In 1947, a shepherd boy discovered a deep cave containing ancient pottery jars holding hundreds of scrolls of texts dating from as early as 250 B.C.E. The scrolls include such valuable works as the oldest version of portions of the Hebrew Bible and other documents revealing the historical context of the biblical texts. Most of the works are severely damaged and have been reconstructed from hundreds of tiny fragments, which leaves lots of room for differing interpretations. Although many of the texts have been studied since the 1950s, there is still no scholarly consensus surrounding these precious scrolls.

Most scholars believe these texts were produced by the Essenes in their mountain retreat in Qumran (see **Map 5.5**)—a desert community fifteen miles from Jerusalem, near the Dead Sea—and hidden in the cave during the turbulent times when Rome was exerting its dominance in the region. All the writings were completed before 68 C.E., when the Romans destroyed the settlement at Qumran. Some scholars believe the writings came from a large library of various Hebrew documents, and thus they may reveal the origins of the many strains of Judaism, perhaps even the early Jesus movement. It is certain that continued analysis of these texts will shed a good deal of light on these early centuries that were so fertile to spiritual impulses.

In this time of spiritual longing, many Jews believed that a savior—a Messiah—would come to liberate them. Some believed that he would be a political figure who would liberate the Jews from foreign domination, and people like the Zealots were poised to fight for this political leader. Others, however, expected a spiritual savior—a Chosen One who would bring a kingdom of righteousness to earth. The Essenes may have withdrawn to the desert community to wait for the spiritual Messiah—their "Teacher of Righteousness." It was into this volatile religious time that Jesus of Nazareth was born.

The Jesus Movement

During the reign of Augustus (r. 27 B.C.E.–14 C.E.), at the beginning of the empire, a child named Jesus was born in about 4 B.C.E., possibly in Bethlehem (about 10 miles southeast of Jerusalem, shown on **Map 5.5**). This event dramatically influenced the empire by the fourth century. Thus, we must return to the time of Augustus to trace the fortunes of a small religious sect in Judea that would ultimately conquer Rome itself.

The information we have on Jesus' life and teachings is drawn largely from the Gospels of the New Testament of the Bible, which were written sometime after his death, probably by people who never knew him. (Estimates on the time of the composition of the Gospels range from thirty to ninety years after Jesus' death.) The Gospels offer little information about the first thirty years of Jesus' life. They do tell us that he was the son of a woman named Mary and a carpenter named Joseph and that he excelled in his religious studies, for he confounded the priests of the Temple with his knowledge of matters of faith.

According to the limited historical information available, Jesus drew from the rich religious environment in the Jewish lands. Like the Pharisees, he appealed to the poor, and many of his sayings resembled those of Hillel the Elder. His teachings also had some qualities in common with those of the Essenes, who had written of a coming Teacher of Righteousness. Unlike the Zealots, Jesus spoke of a heavenly kingdom rather than a violent revolution and attracted a large following of those who longed for a better life. Jesus began his ministry after being baptized by John the Baptist, and the Gospels tell the story of his activities after this defining event in some detail. For many, Jesus was the awaited Messiah who would save and transform the world. Many called him Christ—the Lord's Anointed, the Messiah.

While Jesus' ideas resembled those of some of his contemporaries, the totality of his message was strikingly new and changed the course of Western civilization. For about three years, Jesus preached in Judea and Galilee, drawing huge crowds to listen to his message of peace, love, and care for the poor and suffering. He was accompanied by a small group of devoted followers—the apostles—who carried on his message after his death. Many people also believed that he performed miracles and cures. His growing popularity alarmed both Jewish leaders and Roman authorities, who constantly watched for uprisings in Judea. In about 29 C.E., the Roman governor, Pontius Pilate, sentenced Jesus to crucifixion, the cruel death reserved for many of Rome's enemies. The Romans nailed a sign on Jesus' cross identifying him as the "king of the Jews," perhaps mistranslating the powerful notion of Messiah as king, and certainly underestimating the nature and appeal of Jesus and his message.

Jesus' brief, three-year ministry had come to an end. However, three days later, Jesus' followers believed they saw him risen from the dead and subsequently taken into heaven. They believed this proof of Jesus' divinity promised a resurrection for his followers, and the apostles wanted to spread this good news to other Jews.

A small group of Jesus' followers led by the apostles Peter and James formed a Jewish sect that modern historians call the Jesus movement to identify the period when followers of Jesus continued to identify themselves as Jews. The apostles appealed to other Jews by preaching and praying at the Temple and at small gatherings of the Jewish faithful. The earliest history of this Jesus movement is recorded in Acts in what Christians call the New Testament of the Bible. Like others throughout the Roman world, these Jews believed that prophecy and miracles marked the presence of the divine. Thus, the apostles, the followers who had known Jesus personally, began traveling to bring his message to others. They spoke in prophetic tongues and appeared to work miracles. They also began preaching in Jewish communities around the Mediterranean world.

The early Jesus movement could have taken various different directions. Would Jesus' followers withdraw from society like the Essenes and John the Baptist had done? The apostle James moved to Jerusalem and centered his leadership of the church there, thus choosing not to lead a sect in the wilderness. A more thorny issue was the question of accepting Gentiles—non-Jews—into the new religion. James took a position of conservative Judaism, insisting that Christianity required its adherents to follow the circumcision and strict dietary laws that had marked the Jewish people. The apostle Peter seems to have been more willing to preach to Gentiles, particularly "God-fearing" Greeks who were interested in the ethical monotheism of the Jews. Peter believed they would not have to be circumcised or keep all the Jewish festivals, but they would have to follow the dietary restrictions.

However, the man who would be remembered as the Apostle to the Gentiles had not known Jesus before his crucifixion. Saul of Tarsus (ca. 5–64 C.E.), whom we remember by the name of Paul, was a Hellenized Jew and a Roman citizen who had at first harassed Christians. After he experienced a vision of the risen Jesus, he converted and took up the mission of bringing the Christian message beyond the particularity of the Jewish communities to the wider world of the Roman Empire and beyond. He moved beyond Peter by eliminating all dietary restrictions on Christians, and he traveled widely through the eastern portion of the empire establishing new Christian communities. **Map 5.6** shows where Paul journeyed and how the Christian message slowly spread throughout the Roman world. Paul's influence on the young church was immense, and his letters became part of the Christian Scriptures.

Religious tensions between Jews and Roman authorities in Palestine culminated shortly after the deaths of Peter and Paul. Rome finally decided to take strong action against those in Judea, including Zealots, who were rebelling against Roman rule. In the course of the suppression, the Essene community at Qumran was destroyed (but not before they had buried their precious scrolls, which we call the Dead Sea Scrolls), and then the armies proceeded against Jerusalem. In 70 C.E., the son of Emperor Vespasian, Titus (who later became emperor in his own right), led Roman legions into Jerusalem, burned the city, and destroyed the Second Temple. All that seems to have remained of Herod's great

---

All dates are C.E.

THE ROMAN EMPIRE

14	Augustus dies
ca. 29	Jesus is crucified
64	Nero persecutes Christians
70	Titus destroys Jerusalem
193	Septimius Severus establishes military monarchy
ca. 285	Diocletian establishes tetrarchy
313	Constantine issues decree of toleration of Christians
ca. 385	Theodosius makes Christianity official religion
410	Visigoths sack Rome
ca. 420	Augustine writes *City of God*

KEY DATES

The destruction of the Temple inadvertently resolved the tensions within Judaism. The Saducees, Essenes, and Zealots were all destroyed, and the Pharisees made peace with the Romans and recentered Judaism on synagogue worship. An emphasis on prayer and the law replaced sacrifices at the Temple. After 70 C.E., the Hebrew canon of scriptures came to be closed and the Hebrew Bible—what the Christians would call the Old Testament—was completed. Followers of the great teacher Hillel reached a compromise with the authority of Rome that let Jews maintain an identity within the empire, and future rabbis would study scripture and interpret the ways Jews should act while living among Gentiles.

Dispersion of Jews

The conquest of Jerusalem also settled any question about whether Christianity was to be centered in Jerusalem. Early Christianity, like Diaspora Judaism, was to be a religion that was not bound to one city, and it began to claim universality. The Jesus movement within Judaism was transformed and was now more accurately called the early Christian church.

Early Christian Communities

The spread of Christianity was slow. Small groups of converts in the major cities of the empire gathered in one another's houses because there were no designated churches for the new movement. When members of the small communities met together at least once a week, people took turns reading scripture, praying, and offering other forms of worship. As Paul wrote: "When you come together, each one has a hymn, a lesson, a revelation, a tongue, or an interpretation" (1 Cor. 14:26). "Tongue" and "interpretation" refer to speaking prophetically, which people in the communities believed proved the presence of God in their midst. The culmination of the service was the Eucharist—the commemoration of Jesus' last supper—in which the faithful shared cups of wine and pieces of bread. Members then offered prayers of thanksgiving for Christ's sacrifice and death, which the faithful believed offered them salvation and eternal life.

The relatively small numbers of Christians grew consistently throughout the first few centuries after the death of Jesus. Some estimates suggest that the total number of Christians at the beginning of the third century C.E. was about 200,000, or less than 0.5 percent of the total population. Although this is a small percentage, the actual number is significant—Christians were slowly becoming more visible. The church father Tertullian (ca. 160–ca. 217) wrote that there were thousands of Christians in Carthage in about 200, and he was probably accurate—a few thousand Christians in a population of about 500,000. This small but growing number would periodically come into conflict with the power of Rome.

FIGURE 5.11 Western Wall, ca. 19 B.C.E. When the Romans destroyed the Jewish Temple in Jerusalem, all that was left standing was the western wall. This architectural remnant was called the Wailing Wall for centuries as Jews visited the site and lamented the loss of the Temple. Now people often refer to it simply as the Wall.

temple was the western wall. **Figure 5.11** shows this location, which has become an important symbol of Jewish faith and a location for prayer. For many years it was called the Wailing Wall, so designated to mark it as a mourning space for the destruction of the Temple. In the twenty-first century, it is more often called the Western Wall, and in Hebrew, it is simply called the Wall. (See Document 5.3.)

Titus returned to Rome in a triumphal procession and built a great arch celebrating his accomplishment. **Figure 5.12** shows a marble relief from that arch, in which Titus's troops return victorious from Jerusalem clutching spoils from the Temple. This figure shows soldiers carrying an important symbol of Judaism, the great menorah—a candelabra that held seven candles—which had been sacked from the holy place. The Temple was never rebuilt. Many Jews were scattered from Judea all over the Mediterranean after this devastation, and with them traveled numerous followers of the Jesus movement.

FIGURE 5.12 Marble Relief Depicting the Sack of Jerusalem, ca. 81 C.E. The Romans erected a triumphal arch to commemorate Emperor Titus's victory in Jerusalem. The scenes depict the treasures—which the Romans described as a "river of gold and silver"—that flowed from their conquest. They were most impressed, however, by the huge golden menorah from the Temple, shown prominently in this detail from the arch.

FROM CHRISTIAN PERSECUTION TO THE CITY OF GOD, 64–410 C.E.

Conservative Romans looked askance at any innovations, particularly religious novelties. It was one thing for Christians to worship someone who had died within living memory as a divinity, but it was quite another for them to reject the traditional Roman assortment of gods. Furthermore, early Christians seemed to violate the traditional Roman social order by including the poor, slaves, and women as equals in their congregations.

Christians, who gathered unobtrusively in communities, differed significantly from Pagan Romans in their views of what happened after the faithful died. They expected their bodies to be resurrected after death. This new attitude toward the dead transformed traditional Roman attitudes and practices toward corpses. Roman graves were considered polluting and were dug outside the walls of the city. We have seen (Chapter 4) that the bodies of the poor received little respect as they were buried shallowly by garbage. Christians wanted to keep their dead close to the community, and the **catacombs** dug under the city in about the second century to bury the Christian dead are one of the visible reminders of this dramatic change. **Figure 5.13** shows the burial spaces in a catacomb. Here, rich and poor alike were interred to await resurrection together.

Looking for Christian Scapegoats

To quell accusations that he was responsible for a devastating fire in Rome, Emperor Nero looked for scapegoats and implemented the first large-scale persecution of Christians in Rome in 64 C.E. He executed hundreds of Roman Christians, possibly including the apostles Peter and Paul, and set a precedent that would be repeated periodically over the next two centuries. During the contentious years, provincial officials played a leading role in the persecutions. Some of these authorities chose to harass Christians; others ignored the new religion. Whatever their policy, however, the texts make it clear that when Christian men and women were brought to the arena, many died so bravely that some Roman spectators promptly converted.

During the third century when the empire confronted many internal and external problems, its policy toward Christians grew harsher. Under Emperor Decius (r. 249–251) and then again under Emperor Diocletian (r. 285–305), all imperial residents were to sacrifice to the emperor and receive a document recording their compliance. Diocletian, the autocratic emperor who legislated wages, prices, and military matters, thought he could decree religious beliefs as

thinking about DOCUMENTS

DOCUMENT 5.3

Titus Destroys Jerusalem

In the first century C.E., the Jewish historian Josephus wrote a history of the Jews in which he described the violent destruction of Jerusalem in 70 C.E. by Titus. Josephus was an eyewitness who first fought against the Romans, then fled to the Roman camp and flourished in Rome after the war. In this excerpt, Josephus describes first the internal dissensions among the Jews (whom he calls the "seditious") and then relates the destruction that burnt the Second Temple.

The legions had orders to encamp at the distance of six furlongs from Jerusalem, at the mount called the Mount of Olives, which lies over against the city on the east side, and is parted from it by a deep valley, interposed between them, which is named Cedron.

Now, when hitherto the several parties in the city had been dashing one against another perpetually, this foreign war, now suddenly come upon them after a violent manner, put the first stop to their contentions one against another; and as the seditious now saw with astonishment the Romans pitching three several camps, they began to think of an awkward sort of concord, and said one to another: "What do we here, and what do we mean, when we suffer three fortified walls to be built to coop us in, that we shall not be able to breathe freely? While the enemy is securely building a kind of city in opposition to us, and while we sit still within our own walls and become spectators only of what they are doing, with our hands idle, and our armor laid by, as if they were about somewhat that was for our good and advantage. We are, it seems (so did they cry out), only courageous against ourselves [in mutual argument], while the Romans are likely to gain the city without bloodshed by our sedition." Thus did they encourage one another when they were gotten together and took their armor immediately and ran out upon the Tenth legion and fell upon the Romans with great eagerness, and with a prodigious shout, as they were fortifying their camp.... [After a long and bloody siege, the Romans finally entered the city.]

Now the number of those that were carried captive during this whole war was collected to be ninety-seven thousand; as was the number of those that perished during the whole siege eleven hundred thousand, the greater part of whom was indeed of the same nation [with the citizens of Jerusalem], but not belonging to the city itself....

Now this vast multitude is indeed collected out of remote places, but the entire nation was now shut up by fate as in prison, and the Roman army encompassed the city when it was crowded with inhabitants. Accordingly the multitude of those that therein perished exceeded all the destructions that either men or God ever brought upon the world; for, to speak only of what was publicly known, the Romans slew some of them, some they carried captives, and others they made a search for underground, and when they found where they were they broke up the ground and slew all they met with. There were also found slain there above two thousand persons, partly by their own hands and partly by one another, but chiefly destroyed by the famine.... And now the Romans set fire to the extreme parts of the city, and burned them down, and entirely demolished its walls.

SOURCE: Josephus, *The Jewish Wars*, in *The Great Events by Famous Historians*, vol. III, ed. Rossiter Johnson (The National Alumni, 1905), pp. 151, 205–206.

Analyze the Document

1. How do the Jews' internal problems impede their defense of Jerusalem?
2. Why does Titus so thoroughly destroy the city?
3. How do you think the dissension among the Jews might have affected them after their dispersion?

---

well. But this wide-scale demand for conformity only provoked many more Christians to die for their beliefs. **Map 5.6** reflects the extent of Christian strength after the persecutions of Diocletian had ended.

Constantine: The Tolerant Emperor

In the long tradition of Roman emperors, Constantine looked for supernatural help in his wars with his rivals. According to the Greek historian Eusebius (ca. 260–ca. 340), as Constantine prepared for a crucial battle he saw in the sky a vision of a cross with Greek writing reading, "In this sign, conquer." That night he had a prophetic dream explaining that soldiers would triumph only if they fought under Christian symbols. He obeyed the dream and won a decisive victory. To the Romans, dreams and omens carried crucial religious messages, and Constantine's nighttime message convinced him of the power of the Christian God. In 313, he issued a decree of toleration (the Edict of Milan) for all the religions of the empire, including Christianity, and the martyrdoms ended.

Constantine did more than simply tolerate Christians. He actively supported the church. He returned property to Christians who had been persecuted, gave tax advantages to Christian priests, and let Christian advisors play a role in his court's inner circle. Constantine's support of Christians probably derived in part from his military victory under

> Constantine supports church

FIGURE 5.13 Christian Catacombs, ca. second century C.E. Unlike pagan Romans, who buried their dead outside the city, Christians longed to keep their "holy dead" close to the worship sites of the living. These catacombs were underground burial spaces for early Christians in Rome.

the sign of the cross. The women in his family exerted a strong influence on him as well. His half-sister Constantia and his mother, Helena, were both Christians. Whatever religious motives Constantine had for his support of Christianity, the emperor remained a shrewd politician. In fact, his support of the new religion included a practical political basis. For one thing, there were so many Christians in the empire that it would have been unwise to continue to marginalize them. Furthermore, Constantine's withdrawal of support for traditional pagan shrines permitted him to confiscate their gold to help standardize his currency.

Under Constantine's patronage, the Christian movement grew rich and powerful, and the emperor built beautiful churches in support of the religion. As part of the emperor's respect for Christianity, he decided to restore the Holy Places at Jerusalem and Palestine to Christian worship. Helena toured the region to identify the sacred spaces, but this was quite a feat, for since the destruction of the Temple, Jerusalem had become a Roman city that had lost all identification with its Jewish past. Nevertheless, Helena located what she believed were key sites in the life of Jesus, building great churches where he was born and where he died. With the backing of Constantine and his family, Jerusalem was revived as a holy place, and Christians began to make pilgrimages there. These journeys began a tradition of Christian claim on that land that would continue throughout the Middle Ages.

Constantine's support of Christianity throughout his life established a relationship between church and state that moved Christianity in a new direction: It would continue to flourish and grow in the shadow of the imperial throne. It seems that the emperor finally committed to the new religion on his deathbed; he was baptized a Christian. His delay, however, has provoked much historical speculation. Had Constantine judged it politically unwise to become a Christian as he ruled, or had he not yet made up his mind? We do not know for sure, but we do know that subsequent emperors expanded his policies, moving from toleration toward a commitment to sole Christian worship.

The Empire Adopts Christianity

Theodosius I (r. 379–395) put the final cap on the movement toward Christianity by forbidding the public worship of the old Roman cults. With this mandate, Christianity became the official religion of the Roman Empire. Of course, everyone did not immediately convert to Christianity; Judaism remained strong, and those who clung to traditional Roman religious beliefs came to be called pagans. This word came from *pagani*, a derogatory term for backward peasants, and its etymology shows how Christianity spread first from urban centers.

This merging of a political and Christian empire irrevocably changed both Rome and Christianity. After the fourth century, Christian communities looked very different from those of two centuries earlier. Instead of gathering secretly in one another's homes, Christians met publicly in churches that boasted the trappings of astounding wealth. Indeed, where once people converted to Christianity in spite of the danger of persecution, the influential church father Augustine (354–430) complained, some people now converted only to impress the rich and powerful.

Figures 5.14 and **5.15** illustrate this shift in the status of Christianity. In **Figure 5.14,** a second-century statue of Christ depicts him as the Good Shepherd. He appears as an unpretentious peasant, wearing the typical shepherd costume of the day. The Good Shepherd was the most popular portrayal of Christ in the early, simple centuries of Christianity. **Figure 5.15** shows a very different Good Shepherd. In this fifth-century mosaic, Christ wears the royal purple cloth of emperors. Now the Lord, he watches over his flock rather than working to convert nonbelievers. The gold in the mosaic demonstrates the new wealth of

> Christianity changes

thinking about GEOGRAPHY

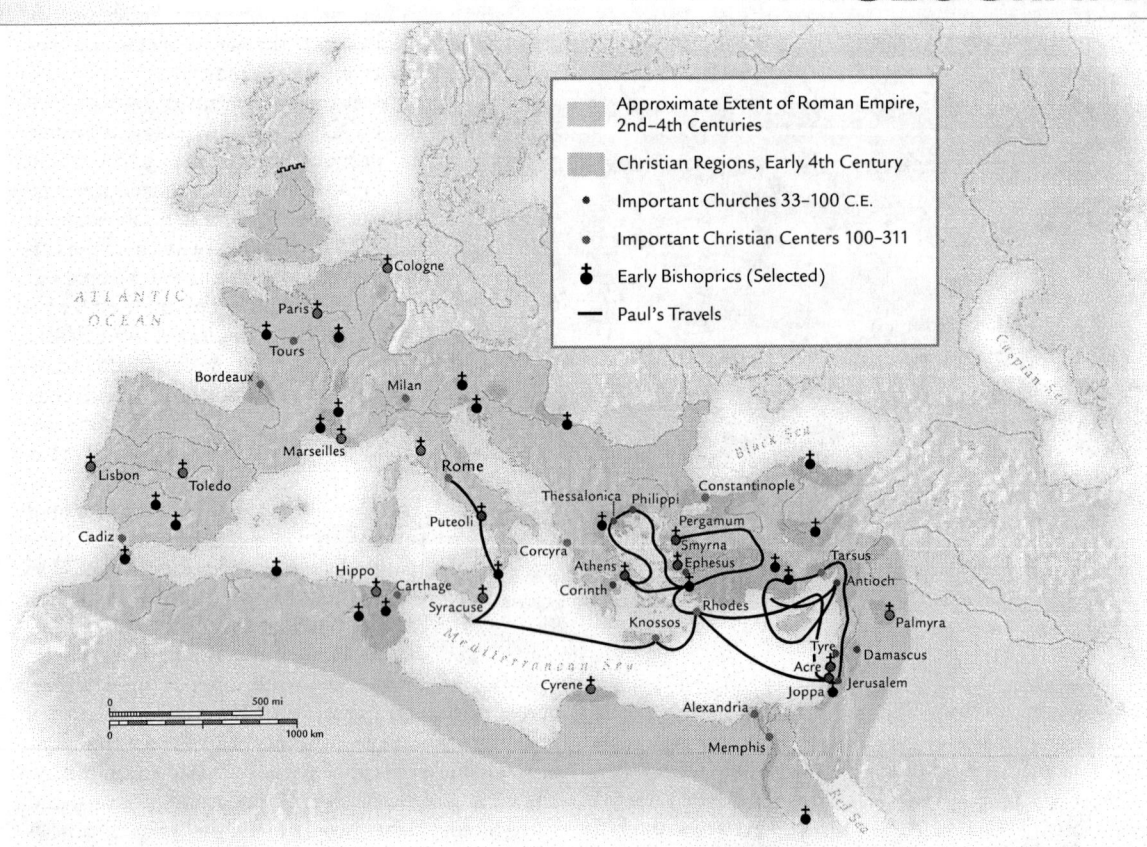

MAP 5.6

The Spread of Christianity to 311 C.E.

This map shows the areas of Christian strength by the fourth century and traces Paul's journey as he conducted his missionary work.

Explore the Map

1. Where were the areas of greatest Christian concentration? What might this clustering reveal about how influential Greek and Eastern thought was for the future development of the church?
2. Why did many of the Christian locations coincide with regions of commerce?
3. Why did Christianity spread mostly within the borders of the Roman Empire?

---

the church, as the image of Christ is transformed from that of a simple man to Lord of the universe.

As the empire embraced Christianity, the organization of the church began to duplicate the civil order of Rome. The emperor Diocletian had clustered provinces into larger units, called dioceses, for ease of administration. The church retained these divisions and placed bishops in charge of the major communities. Bishops were in charge of all aspects of church life, from finances to spiritual guidance, and as early as the third century in most regions they were paid by a church depending increasingly on

Christian organization

their administrative skills. For example, by 245 C.E. the province of North Africa had 90 bishops, and each was served by a well-developed hierarchy of priests and deacons. The ecclesiastical structure of the dioceses was divided into parishes, presided over by priests who reported to the bishops.

With Constantine's support, the church had become powerful. In the political world, power meant the ability to impose a uniformity of practice and even belief. Emperor Constantine tried to guide the church toward this kind of unity, and the church fathers began looking to authority figures to help them resolve differences. Prophecy—so important to the

FIGURE 5.14 Christ as the Good Shepherd, second century C.E. The earliest centuries of Christianity were marked by slow missionary work to gather new converts. The predominant image for this time and initiative was that of Christ the Good Shepherd gathering his flock.

early church—became suspect, replaced by obedience to authority. As leaders began to look to a hierarchical organization for guidance in religious matters, it was perhaps inevitable that questions would arise over who should lead—religious or secular leaders. Ambrose (r. 374–397), the bishop of Milan in Italy, was one of the earliest bishops to challenge the power of the emperors and set a precedent for later bishops. In 390, Ambrose reprimanded Emperor Theodosius for massacring some rebellious citizens: The bishop excommunicated the emperor, forbidding him to participate in church services until he repented. Theodosius acceded to the bishop's demands, and later bishops of Rome (who came to be called popes) looked to this example of the church leading the state.

In the eastern part of the empire, the relationship between bishops and emperor took a different turn. Beginning with Constantine, emperors in the East had involved themselves directly in religious disputes. Since the early third century, for example, Christians had quarreled over the nature of Christ. "Had he always existed," they asked themselves, "or did God bring him forth at a particular time?" In about 320, Arius, bishop of Alexandria, raised a furor when he argued that Jesus had been created by God. Arius's teachings polarized believers all over the empire, and Constantine did not want such a dispute raging in his lands. Therefore, he called a meeting that was the first "ecumenical" council—purportedly with representatives of the whole inhabited world. In 325, Constantine vigorously presided over the bishops he had summoned to the Council of Nicaea to resolve Arius's dispute over the nature of Christ. With the formulation of the Nicene Creed, which stated that Christ had always existed, Constantine and his bishops hoped to put that controversy to rest. However, as we shall see in Chapter 6, Arius's beliefs had already spread, and the church would have to face the problem of **Arianism** again. The council also set the precedent that orthodox Christians could exert their authority over those who believed otherwise.

Religious disagreements

Similarly in North Africa, Christians split over what to do about bishops and others who had "lapsed" during the years of persecution. This controversy was called the Donatist heresy, named after one of the protesting bishops. Church leaders believed it was essential to protect the notion that sacraments—like baptism and the Eucharist—were valid regardless of the behavior of the presiding priest, so they declared that bishops who had proven weak when threatened by torture could continue to hold their offices. The Donatists disagreed, saying that lapsed priests could *not* conduct the sacraments. Yet, passions had run so high over this issue that Donatists separated and tried to start a new church. The dispute catalyzed much violence in North Africa for centuries until the barbarian invasions created enough turmoil to move this issue to the background.

These and many other religious quarrels that spilled into secular politics raised the question of the relationship between church and state. In the early church, the relationship had been simple—Christianity focused on the next world while enduring an antagonistic earthly relationship with an unsympathetic state. Now, with church and state combined, the situation had become exceedingly complex. Many Christians felt ill at ease with all the resulting uncertainty. In his influential work *City of God* (413–427), Augustine tried to address these very complexities. Writing after the Visigoths had sacked Rome and terrified Romans had fled the city in waves, he explained that Christians

City of God

FIGURE 5.15 Christ as the Good Shepherd, ca. 450 C.E. After the Roman Empire became Christian, artists began to portray Christ with more imperial majesty. Here, Christ the Good Shepherd is shown clothed in gold and royal purple and presiding over his flock rather than working with his hands.

should not look at the current disasters with despair, nor see in them divine punishment. Instead, the church father drew from his strong background in Neoplatonism to explain worldly pain much as Plato had (described in Chapter 2), but with a Christian understanding. Augustine claimed that the world—and worldly cities—were made up of individuals who were constantly in struggle between their spiritual and earthly selves. Those people in whom the spiritual dominated belonged to a City of God, and those in whom the earthly dominated belonged to an earthly city. The perfect community of the faithful—the City of God—could exist only outside this world and would dominate at the end of time. In the meantime, all communities were mixed with members of both cities. Therefore, people ought to obey the political order and focus on the worthiness of their own souls rather than the purity of the reigning political institutions. They need not worry even when the city of Rome was sacked.

For Augustine and other religious thinkers, church and state were not incompatible. In fact, these men believed that the state should play an active role in ensuring the health of the church. In the early centuries of Christianity, **heresy** (expressing opinions that differed from official church doctrine) could be considered treason punishable by civil sanctions. Augustine, for example, suggested confiscating the property of the Donatists to persuade them to conform. However, in the late fourth century, a Christian heretic (Priscillian) was sentenced to death. As the ultimate power of the empire was brought to issues of conscience in these ways, church members learned that the path to salvation lay in obedience. Inevitably, there were Christians who objected to this direction, but the majority saw in this Christian order a fulfillment of God's plan—a victory for the earthly church.

The New Roman

Like political institutions and the church itself, everyday Roman life was also transformed with the burgeoning strength of Christianity. As church fathers in many regions of the empire wrote on matters of religion, they also addressed the larger question of how the new Christian Roman was to behave. In some areas of life it was easy simply to prohibit certain behaviors. For example, the church fathers wrote that Christians should not attend gladiator shows or arena games. Over time, the great amphitheaters fell out of use. Instead, Christian Romans satisfied their appetite for spectacle with chariot races, which remained hugely popular for centuries. In other areas, religious leaders and the populace reached a compromise—Christians could read the beloved traditional literature, such as Virgil or Homer (even though it praised pagan gods and suspect morality), but they were to try to extract a Christian message from it. (This is a major reason why such literature has survived.)

Christians also reshaped the social fabric of Roman life. For example, they did not believe in exposing unwanted children. Indeed, through the early centuries, they actively rescued foundling infants and raised them as Christian. Furthermore, they placed enormous priority on caring for the poor and needy. By the middle of the third century, church records show, in Rome alone the bishop provided charity for more than 1,500 widows and others in need.

Views on sexuality also shifted with the influence of the church fathers. As we have seen, although the Romans showed a certain cautiousness in their sexual lives, they also passionately believed that people had a duty to marry and procreate. Some Christian leaders, on the contrary, strongly advocated celibacy as the ideal life. Numerous Roman men complied with this recommendation, and many women used Christian celibacy as a way to free themselves from the expectations that they would marry and bear children. The influential church father Jerome (ca. 348–420) surrounded himself with chaste women who studied and traveled with him and founded monasteries. The Biography featuring Melania the Younger tells of one such fourth-century woman who was famous and admired during her lifetime and who spent her vast wealth establishing enduring religious institutions.

|Christian sexuality|

The most influential writer on sexuality was Augustine. In his widely read work *The Confessions*, he described his inability to give up his mistress and his "habit" of lust. As he explained, only with God's help was he able to summon the resolve to renounce these vices. This experience convinced Augustine that human beings were born with original sin and that this sin was passed to subsequent generations through semen during sexual intercourse. Because of original sin, Augustine concluded, people had to keep constant vigil against the force of lust—even marital intercourse was somewhat suspect. Through this kind of thinking, religious leaders involved themselves in people's private lives, and this watchfulness continued for centuries through a growing body of church law. Hardly any aspect of Roman life was left untouched by the Christianization of the empire.

THE HOLY LIFE

For early Christians, the path to God came through community; congregations of the faithful gathered together to help each other withstand the pressure of a hostile society. By the fourth century, some Christians were choosing another path to spiritual perfection. Men and women by the thousands left society to live alone in the deserts of Egypt and Syria, and their experiences profoundly influenced Christian life and thought.

Some Christians fled into the desert to escape the persecutions and chaos of the mid-third century. Others left during the fourth and fifth centuries because they objected to the union of church and state that developed after Constantine's rule. Still others fled the tax collectors. Whatever the reasons, the popularity of this movement reached enormous proportions. Historians estimate that by 325, as many as 5,000 men and women lived as hermits along the banks of the Nile, each in his or her own small cell. The fame of these holy people spread. Jerome advocated an ascetic life even for urban people and persuaded numerous wealthy Roman women to join him. Romans were scandalized when one of Jerome's young charges starved herself to death in her zeal for asceticism, but such was the passion for what many perceived was a holy life.

|Flight to the desert|

Many of these holy men and women survived extraordinary feats of self-denial—enduring lack of food, sleep, and other basic necessities. Some people insisted on living for decades on platforms perched high on poles. Women in particular sealed themselves into tombs that had only a tiny opening through which they could receive a small loaf of bread, and they eked out their lives in cramped, filthy solitude. These people's contemporaries found their behaviors so unusual that they concluded that to endure such hardships, the holy men and women must be recipients of God's power.

Of course, the extreme deprivation of heroic abstinence was not for everyone. Some people wanted simply to withdraw from the distractions of the world so as to worship God without enduring the rigors of the desert hermits. Communal monasticism developed as a parallel movement to the hermit life and offered an appealing alternative to life in the thick of Roman society. Discipline was strict in these pious oases, but participants had contact with other people, and conditions were not as harsh as those in the desert. In time, communal monasteries were brought into the overall structure of the church. Monks and nuns took vows of obedience to the monastery head (the abbot or abbess), and the monastic leader answered to the local bishop.

|Monastic communities|

The Influence of Holy People

The earliest holy people had been the Christian martyrs. Faithful observers witnessing their brave deaths concluded that God had invested their

BIOGRAPHY

Melania the Younger
(385–ca. 439)

A Model of Holiness

Melania was born in 385, the daughter of a rich Roman patrician. By the time of her birth, Christianity was the official religion of the empire, and as a young girl she experienced the conflict of values that confronted so many Christian Roman families. Starting in her youth, Melania longed to follow a life of ascetic chastity like that of earlier holy women. As a daughter of Rome, however, she was expected to marry and bear children. As was the custom in a society in which women married young, when Melania was 14 years old her family arranged for her to marry Pinian.

The young bride begged her new husband to live chastely with her so they could better worship God. Pinian wanted first to ensure the worldly succession of his family, so he told Melania she must bear two children before he would consider her request. A daughter was born to the young couple. Melania became pregnant again, but during this pregnancy she practiced many austerities in her search for a holy life. For example, she repeatedly prayed on her knees all night against the advice of her physician and the pleas of her mother. Furthermore, as a symbol of her commitment, she began to wear rough wool under the smooth silk clothing of the upper class. It is ironic that this return to republican simplicity was seen as rebellion by her family.

Melania's father tried to exert his paternal authority and make her care for herself and her unborn child in the traditional ways, but Christian beliefs introduced competing loyalties into family life. The young woman disobeyed her father, and her son was born prematurely. The infant boy died shortly after being baptized. Melania and Pinian's daughter died soon after that. Like so many Roman families, this young couple was unable to produce heirs. They saw the will of God in their children's deaths, however, and at age 20, Melania persuaded Pinian to join her in a vow of chastity.

As her first demonstration of religious commitment, she sought to liquidate her property. Her biographer's description of the problems involved in this task suggest the scale of wealth that many imperial Roman families had accumulated. For example, Melania owned thousands of slaves that she could not free without contributing adversely to Rome's unemployment problem. Furthermore, her house was so expensive even the emperor could not afford to buy it. However, the turmoil of the times helped resolve the difficulties of disposing of her property. The Visigoths who sacked Rome burned Melania's home, and she was able to sell the ruined property easily. As she and Pinian fled to Africa in the wake of the invasion, Melania used her money to ransom captives and buy islands for fellow ascetics to use as holy retreats.

After liquidating most of her wealth, Melania escalated her personal renunciations. She began to fast regularly, eating only some moldy bread twice a week. Beyond that, she spent her days reading and writing. She knew both Latin and Greek and studied the scriptures and the writings of church leaders. As her reputation for holiness grew, people began to come to her to listen to her teach.

Melania and Pinian then traveled from North Africa to Jerusalem to tour the holy places that Constantine had identified. From there, they visited the holy men and women living in the deserts of Egypt. Finally, Melania decided to found monasteries in Jerusalem, where she and Pinian could embark on a communal life dedicated to spirituality. Joined by 90 virgins and some reformed prostitutes, Melania spent the rest of her life studying, teaching, and traveling to holy sites. Shortly after her death, the faithful began to venerate her burial place, where miracles reputedly took place.

Melania's life exemplifies the Roman world transformed. She began as a well-off young girl, wearing silk and expecting to carry on the traditions of an upper-class Roman. After the disastrous barbarian invasions, she settled in the Holy Land, wearing rough wool and embodying the new values of the Christian world.

FIGURE 5.16 Melania the Younger Icon.

Connecting People & Society

1. How does Melania's life reveal the conflict of values between pagan and Christian Rome?
2. How did the Visigoths' invasions affect Melania and her family?
3. Where did Melania settle, and what did she do? How might she have served as a model for others?

bodies with the power to withstand torture. People believed that martyrs' remains contained sacred power and saved and venerated their bones, or **relics**. One woman in North Africa was reprimanded by her bishop for bringing a sacred bone to church and kissing it repeatedly. This kind of veneration strengthened the notion of resurrection of the flesh, in which the tortured flesh itself would receive its reward. Christianity thus became a religion that accepted the body. Believers wanted the holy dead to be buried near them, and by the fourth century, most altars included relics. In a very short time, the faithful and the enterprising began to engage in a brisk trade in relics that would be lucrative and influential throughout the Middle Ages. Historians have uncovered letters in which people solicit relics to help increase the power of their churches, and some of the correspondence is quite poignant. Bishop Braulio in seventh-century Spain responded to one such request, writing that he had many valuable relics, but all the labels had been lost. He could no longer identify the bones, but asked if the correspondent wanted them anyway.

Relics were preserved, treasured, and displayed in reliquaries—containers, often covered in precious metals and jewels, that displayed the precious bones that lay within. These reliquaries spread all over Europe and became a visible feature of the growing religion. Exquisite jeweled containers were supposed to express both the power of the relic and the incorruptibility of heaven, where people believed the saint dwelled.

> Saints' cults

The desert fathers and mothers eventually supplanted the martyrs. They, too, seemed to embody holiness physically, and their *Sayings* reinforced the idea that people could not find spirituality without somehow sanctifying the flesh itself. Ironically, these holy people had traveled to the desert to find God and instead discovered their own humanity. They learned about the hunger that could drive one mad and about sexual urges that could relentlessly haunt their dreams. They even discussed nocturnal emissions and reflected on how to overcome boredom. The thinking of these spiritual people gave Christianity a profoundly human touch.

Like the martyrs, many of these holy people became venerated upon their deaths. The cult of saints became a strong part of Christian faith. Just as people believed that martyrs could intercede for them with God, so they felt convinced that prayer to a holy man or woman might also help them attain their desires. Holy men and women who had learned so much about their humanity by transcending it seemed accessible even to the most ordinary of people. Saints gained reputations for doing everything from raising the dead and healing the sick to extending a too-short wooden beam so an overworked carpenter would not have to cut another. The conversion of the northern European countryside was inspired largely by living and dead holy people who had brought God's power down to the community.

> Ascetic influence

The ascetic practices of the monasteries also shaped the lives of everyday Christians. Even for people who did not adhere to the strict rules of the monasteries, the luxuries of the Roman world seemed shameful when compared with the purity of the monasteries. Over time, people concluded that the ideal Christian life should be simple, and some Christians looked with disdain at those who surrounded themselves with comfort and pleasure. This tendency of monastic rigor to influence Christian life continued throughout the Middle Ages.

Monasteries always served both as havens during stormy political times and as outlets for those who sought a highly spiritual life. For centuries, these communities rejuvenated the Christian world and helped the church meet people's changing spiritual needs. Men and women in search of personal spiritual perfection would ultimately become powerful social forces for the medieval world.

LOOKING BACK & MOVING FORWARD

Summary   The conservative Romans who mourned the death of Julius Caesar and celebrated the victory of his young nephew Octavian (Augustus) would hardly have recognized the world of Augustine or of the late-fourth-century emperor Theodosius. The great territorial empire governed four hundred years earlier by Augustus and his successors in the name of the Senate and the people of Rome was still impressive. However, it was now a Christian empire ruled from Constantinople by an emperor who governed in the name of God and was advised by bishops.

KEY TERMS

Pax Romana,   p. 138
principate,   p. 139
praetorian guard,   p. 139
tetrarchy,   p. 153
Neoplatonism,   p. 157
Sadducees,   p. 159
Pharisees,   p. 159

The huge borders of the "civilized" world were still guarded by Roman legions, but by the fourth century these borders had become porous. The guarding legions more often than not wore the trousers of the Germanic peoples and rode horses instead of marching in the disciplined ranks of the tunic-clad Romans.

Sadly for Rome, the centrifugal forces pulling this radically transformed empire apart would prevail. As we will see in Chapter 6, the Roman Empire eventually split into three parts: Byzantium in the east, the Muslim world in the south, and the Germanic kingdoms in the west. However, the glory and accomplishments of Rome would remain in the West's memory and periodically inspire people to try reviving its greatness.

Zealots, p. 160
Essenes, p. 160
catacombs, p. 163
Arianism, p. 167
heresy, p. 168
relics, p. 171

REVIEW, ANALYZE, & CONNECT TO TODAY

REVIEW THE PREVIOUS CHAPTER

Chapter 4—"Pride in Family and City"—described the rise and fall of the Roman Republic and the way expansion changed Roman life and values.

1. Review the "twilight of the Republic" that led to the civil wars and the murder of Julius Caesar. How did Augustus avoid the fate of Julius Caesar? What reforms did Augustus make to help the new empire endure?

2. Review the strengths and virtues that made the early Roman Republic so successful. Which of those were lost through the fourth-century reforms of Diocletian and Constantine? To what degree did these reforms contribute both to the decline of the empire and to its preservation?

ANALYZE THIS CHAPTER

Chapter 5—"Territorial and Christian Empires"—continues the story of the Roman Empire as it dominated the Mediterranean region for hundreds of years. The empire survived many crises and in turn was dramatically transformed by Christianity.

1. Consider the economic advantages of the great territorial empire of the Romans. Who benefited most from the Mediterranean trade? Who benefited least? What central weakness did the economy have during the empire?

2. What was the Silk Road? What goods traveled along it, and why was it so important to both the Roman and Han empires?

3. Describe the social, cultural, and medical ideas that contributed to Rome's declining population.

4. Review the situation in Judea and the various ideas within Judaism during the time of Jesus. How did the political and cultural environment in Judea affect the growth of Christianity?

5. Review the relationship between the early Christians and the Roman authorities. How did Christianity move from a persecuted sect to the religion of the Roman Empire?

6. The adoption of Christianity by the Roman Empire created profound transformations in both the early Christian church and the empire itself. Review these changes and consider which might have the longest-standing impact on the future of Western culture.

CONNECT TO TODAY

Think about the impact of the imperial Romans in establishing a multicultural empire, long-distance trade, and a revolution in religious life.

1. What similar issues is U.S. society struggling with today? In what ways might the study of the Roman Empire help citizens of the twenty-first century sort out and address public issues? In other words, what can we learn from the past?

2. What places in the world today are wrestling with changes in religion and with questions about the church-state relationship such as those that marked the late Roman Empire? How might people of opposing religious views avoid the violent religious struggles experienced by imperial Romans?

BEYOND THE CLASSROOM

**THE *PAX ROMANA*,
27 B.C.E.–180 C.E.**

Eck, Werner, et al. *The Age of Augustus*, 2nd ed. Cambridge, MA: Blackwell, 2007. A concise biography using varied sources to explain this revolution in the structure of Rome.

LeBohec, Yann. *The Imperial Roman Army*. New York: Hippocrene Books, 1994. A good description of the all-important Roman military.

LIFE DURING THE PEACE OF ROME

August, Roland. *Cruelty and Civilization: The Roman Games.* New York: Routledge, 1994. An exciting history of gladiators, chariot racing, and other games that offers an explanation of their appeal and function within society.

Dupont, Florence. *Daily Life in Ancient Rome.* Oxford: Blackwell, 1993. An informative interpretation of ancient Rome that describes and analyzes the everyday experiences of the Romans.

Jackson, Ralph. *Doctors and Diseases in the Roman Empire.* Norman: University of Oklahoma Press, 1988. A broad and concise account of classical medicine as it culminated in the Roman Empire.

Weidmann, Thomas. *Adults and Children in the Roman Empire.* New Haven, CT: Yale University Press, 1989. An interpretative analysis that traces changes in adult attitudes toward childhood.

CRISIS AND TRANSFORMATION, 192–ca. 400 C.E.

Gamsey, Peter D. *Famine and Food Supply in the Graeco-Roman World: Response to Risk and Crisis.* New York: Cambridge University Press, 1988. A study of the concerns and responses of both urban and rural dwellers to food crises, actual or anticipated.

Jones, A.H.M. *The Later Roman Empire, 284–602,* 2 vols. London: Blackwell, 1964. The most comprehensive classic study on the subject by a master historian.

Williams, S. *Diocletian and the Roman Recovery.* New York: Routledge, 1996. A vivid work that brings the emperor and his times to life and clearly explains Diocletian's military and civil reforms.

THE LONGING FOR RELIGIOUS FULFILLMENT

Riches, John. *The World of Jesus: First-Century Judaism in Crisis.* New York: Cambridge University Press, 1990. An examination of the ways in which Jewish figures and groups of the first century—including Jesus—reacted to the basic social, economic, and political realities of the time.

Turcan, Robert. *The Cults of the Roman Empire.* Cambridge, MA: Blackwell, 1996. A sound study of the cults during the Roman period.

FROM CHRISTIAN PERSECUTION TO THE CITY OF GOD, 64–410 C.E.

Brown, Peter. *Power and Persuasion in Late Antiquity: Toward a Christian Empire.* Madison: University of Wisconsin Press, 1992. Reopens the question of how the empire's transformation from paganism to Christianity affected its civic culture.

Carroll, James. *Constantine's Sword: The Church and the Jews.* Boston: Houghton Mifflin, 2002. An award-winning book that explores the relationship between Constantine's conversion, the adoption of the cross as a Christian symbol, and growing anti-Semitism. Provocative and fascinating reading.

Ehrman, Bart D. *Lost Christianities: The Battles for Scripture and the Faiths We Never Knew.* New York: Oxford University Press, 2003. A well-researched and clearly written look at the various early forms of Christianity that shows how they came to be suppressed or forgotten.

Frend, W.H.C. *The Rise of Christianity.* Philadelphia: Fortress Press, 1984. A comprehensive summary of the growth of Christianity, which includes the major figures and controversies of the movement.

Pagels, Elaine. *Beyond Belief: The Secret Gospel of Thomas.* New York: Vintage, 2004. An award-winning scholar of Gnosticism shows the diversity of the beliefs circulating in the early Christian communities.

Salisbury, J.E. *The Blood of Martyrs: Unintended Consequences of Ancient Violence.* New York: Routledge, 2004. A book that explores the ancient Christian martyrdoms that transformed many modern Western ideas, including images of the body, sacrifice, anti-Semitism, motherhood, suicide, and others.

Salisbury, J.E. *Perpetua's Passion: The Death and Memory of a Young Roman Woman.* New York: Routledge, 1997. A description of the cultural, social, and religious environment of early-third-century Carthage told through the story of a young martyr.

Stark, Rodney. *The Rise of Christianity: A Sociologist Reconsiders History.* Princeton, NJ: Princeton University Press, 1996. A controversial but influential analysis of how Christianity spread.

THE HOLY LIFE

Brown, Peter R.L. *The Body and Society: Men, Women, and Sexual Renunciation in Early Christianity.* New York: Columbia University Press, 1988. A classic study of the ascetic movements and their impact by the major scholar of late antiquity.

Bynum, Caroline Walker. *The Resurrection of the Body in Western Christianity, 200–1336.* New York: Columbia University Press, 1995. A fascinating look at the impact of martyrs and saints on ideas of the body and the afterlife.

GLOBAL CONNECTIONS

Wood, Frances. *The Silk Road: Two Thousand Years in the Heart of Asia.* Berkeley: University of California Press, 2004. A comprehensive and beautifully illustrated account that demonstrates the tremendous impact of the Silk Road in spite of relatively light traffic.

THE WORLD & THE WEST

Looking Ahead to the Middle Ages, 400–1400

The breakup of the Roman Empire did not come easily. Warrior bands and official armies alike inflicted destruction and suffering on many throughout the old Roman Empire. From this violence arose what historians have come to call the Middle Ages (or medieval period), which extended from about 400 to about 1400. During that millennium, bloodshed intensified as three distinct cultural identities emerged in the Mediterranean basin and vied with one another for land, power, and affirmation of their faith. In the seventh century, the Prophet Muhammad and his followers established a new religion—Islam—that extended from the old Persian Empire in the east through North Africa and into Spain in the west. Byzantium—the eastern, Greek-speaking portion of the old Roman Empire—also developed its own language, religion, and politics, each of which distinguished it from the other two areas.

Meanwhile, the region in the northwestern portion of the old Roman Empire divided into disparate kingdoms that also boasted a unique culture. People living in these western realms called their region Christendom. Sometimes, but not always, they included the Christian Byzantine Empire in this designation. Byzantines, for their part, preferred to distance themselves from these "barbaric" westerners. Later historians (and geographers) would call the western region of Christendom Europe and Western civilization. However, just as in the ancient world, the West during the Middle Ages developed its distinctive character through interaction with the rest of the world.

But before the tenth century, Europeans' contact with other peoples diminished, as the disruptive violence caused them to withdraw from the great trade nexus that had marked antiquity. While the peoples of Islam and Byzantium maintained their cross-cultural contacts, western Christendom's inhabitants looked inward.

In the meantime, other parts of the world prospered. In the late sixth century, an ambitious ruler in northern China—Yang Jian—reunited China under centralized control after the centuries of fragmentation that followed the Han dynasty's collapse. The resulting succeeding dynasties—the Sui, Tang, and Song—organized Chinese society so efficiently that China became a leader in agricultural and industrial production.

These changes in China had a dramatic effect on the West after the eleventh century. Chinese inventions and innovations (from wheelbarrows to gunpowder) found their way west and transformed life in Christendom. In some cases, we can identify the agents of this transmission; for example, monks smuggled Chinese silkworms to Byzantium in order to implement a new cloth industry. In other cases, we cannot, though new ideas and inventions likely spread slowly from neighbor to neighbor across the Eurasian continent. Chinese technologies moved throughout east Asia as well, altering people's way of life in Korea, Vietnam, and Japan.

Even though India remained politically disunited during the early Middle Ages, the huge subcontinent molded cultures in south and southeast Asia. Over time, Islam attracted a popular following in India. Indeed, the new faith joined Hinduism and Buddhism as one of the major religions of the region. The connections between India and Islam remained strong through trade in the Indian Ocean, as Muslim merchants set up operations in all the major coastal cities in India. These mercantile centers remained fruitful sources of cultural exchange between Indians and Muslims in other lands, including Africa. Silk and porcelain from China; spices from southeast Asia; and pepper, precious gems, cotton, and many other goods from India swept through the Indian Ocean basin. All these goods—as well as exciting new ideas—eventually found their way to Europe, transforming Christendom through commercial activity and the social interaction that often comes with it. Perhaps one of the most influential exports from India was "Arabic numerals," which probably originated in India and acquired the "Arabic" appellation later. These numbers, which we use today, replaced Roman numerals and facilitated advanced mathematical calculations.

Between about 1000 and 1450, many other peoples also established vast empires and huge trading networks. For example, Mongols, nomadic peoples from central Asia, created a great empire based in China that facilitated trade across Asia. Powerful states and empires emerged in Africa as well. In the kingdom of Kongo, for example, rulers built a strong central government. During these same centuries, the arrival of Islam in Africa transformed cultures there. Muslims from North Africa capitalized on the profitable trade across the Sahara Desert and down the African coasts. As they traded, they attracted Africans to their faith. By the tenth century, the kings of Ghana had converted to Islam, and other peoples followed. Over the next two centuries, tremendous wealth accumulated along coastal east Africa. Evidence indicates that a rich tradition of Muslim scholarship also arose in these cities.

Far across the oceans, peoples living in the Americas and Oceania were changing as well. In Central and South America, the Maya, Toltecs, Aztecs, and Incas all built impressive societies, with large populations, social hierarchies, and magnificent architectural structures. Through eastern North America, large populations of healthy communities built large earthen mounds in many places. One near the Mississippi River was a four-level mound bigger than the Great Pyramid at Giza. Pueblo and Navajo peoples practiced irrigation and skillfully constructed complex adobe and stone buildings that still

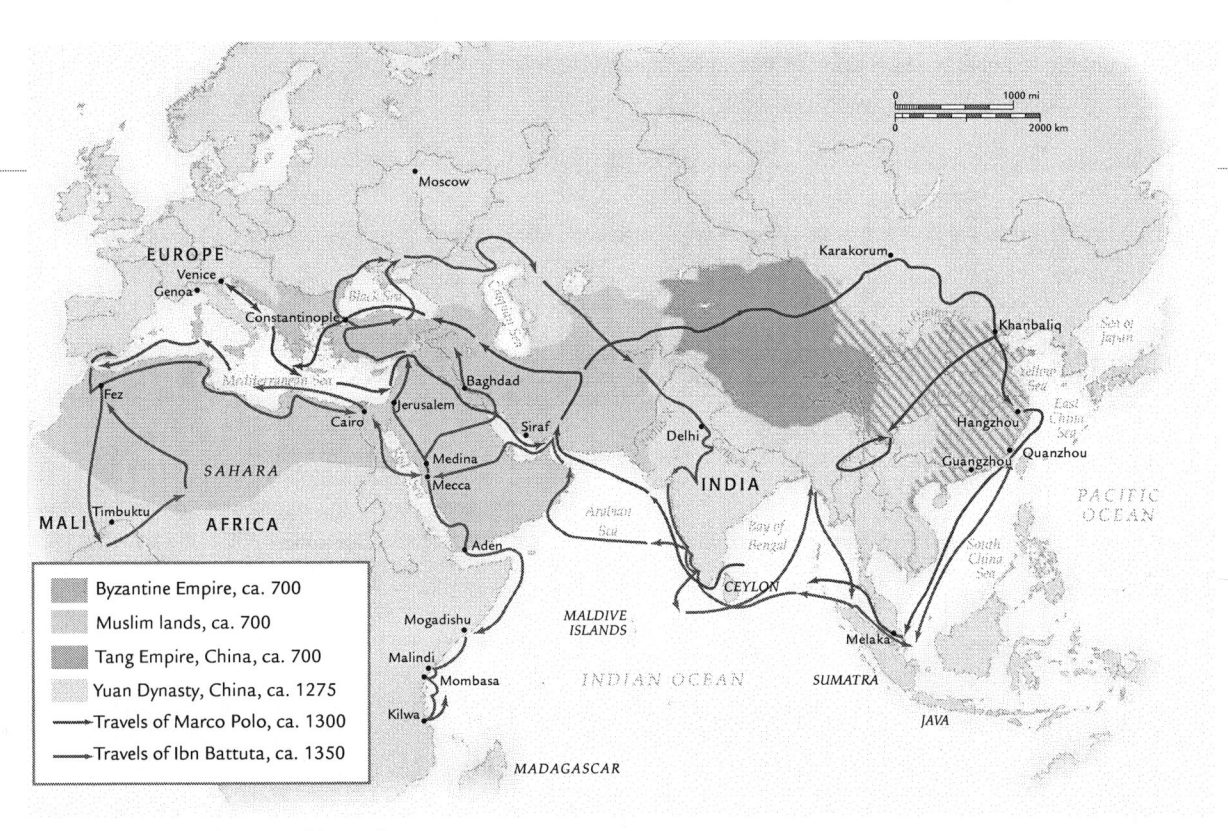

Medieval Empires and Two World Travelers

impress visitors. Modern scientists have reconsidered the view that the Americas were sparsely settled outside the regions of the empires of Mesoamerica; indeed, Amerindians settled throughout North and South America in large numbers. Perhaps even 40,000,000 people might have lived here before the diseases of Eurasia decimated the populations.

By 1000, a brisk trade had emerged among the islands in the south Pacific, testifying to the skill of navigators who could traverse the large spans of the Pacific. By 1100, even the more distant Hawai'ins and Tahitians had forged commercial ties.

What of the West in the face of such dynamic global developments? By 1000, Europeans were once again venturing out and interacting with others around the world. Scandinavian Vikings traveled overland, establishing settlements in eastern Europe and buying and selling goods all the way to China. They also journeyed west into Iceland, Greenland, and North America, where they both traded and fought with indigenous peoples.

By the twelfth century, interactions between Christendom and Islam exerted a particularly powerful impact on both cultures. Crusading Christian armies confronted Muslims on the battlefields of the eastern Mediterranean and North Africa. However, more fruitful exchanges took place in Sicily and Spain, where Muslims and Christians lived side by side in relative harmony. In these places, Christian scholars studied Muslim learning, and Christian artisans and farmers adopted and benefited from Muslim innovations, like improved irrigation techniques. Merchants in the Italian city-states also profited from extensive trade with Muslims all over the Mediterranean.

As the thirteenth century dawned, Europeans began making contact with peoples even farther from their borders. Merchants and others on the move began to roam across the Eurasian continent. Marco Polo, a Venetian merchant, worked at the Chinese court. Ibn Battuta, a Muslim judge, traveled from Mali (in Africa) to Spain, and across eastern Europe to China. These are only the most prominent examples of people who forged global connections during the Middle Ages. In spite of staggering distances and slow travel, the world seemed to be shrinking. It would appear to compress even further in the fifteenth century as Europeans ventured across the oceans.

Thinking Globally

As the center of Western civilization shifts north, how might this affect life in the West?

1. Refer to the map above. What do you notice about trade throughout the Eurasian landmass?

2. What might have been the advantages and disadvantages of travel by land or sea?

3. Notice the location of the large empires. How might these political units have facilitated trade and other interactions?

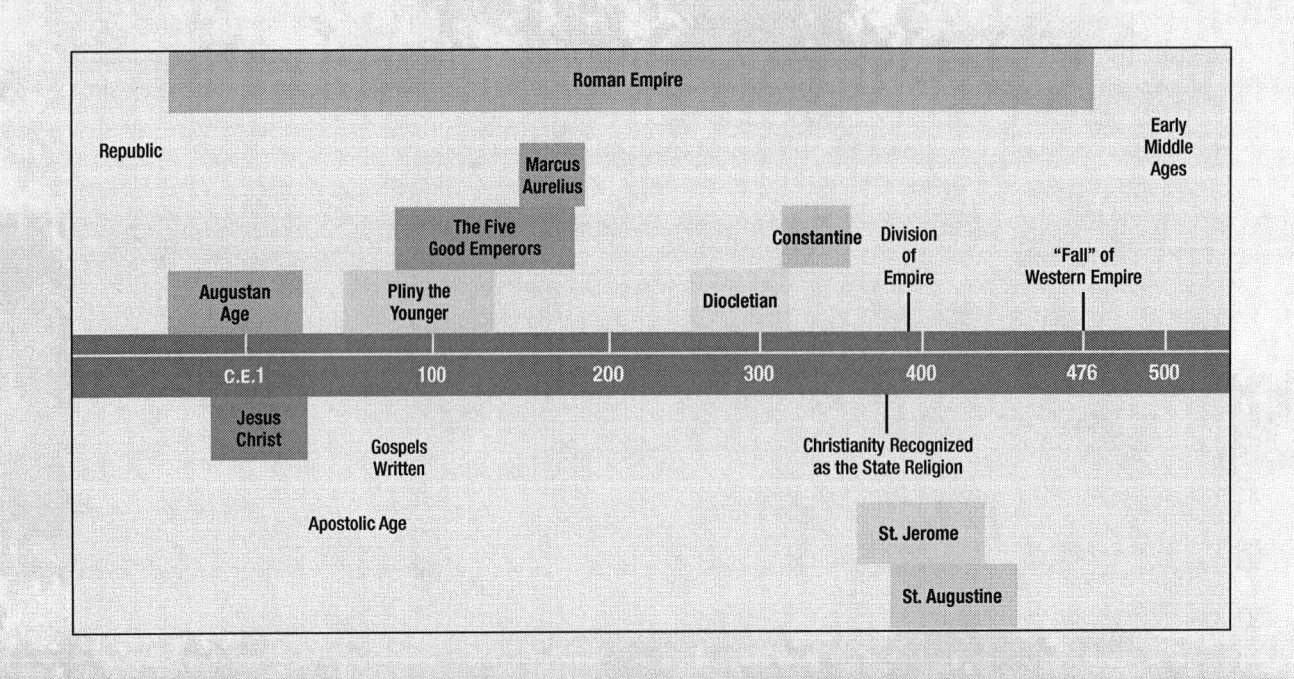

5 The Roman Empire and the Rise of Christianity

With control in the hands of Augustus by 27 B.C.E., the Augustan Age began. A variety of reforms transformed the Republic into the Empire. Rome entered a period of expansion, prosperity, cultural vigor, and relative political stability that would last until the end of the second century. This was particularly so under the long rule of Augustus (27 B.C.E.–C.E. 14) and the five "good emperors" (C.E. 96–180).

During this same period Christianity arose. Initially, it seemed only one of many religious sects and was perceived as a version of Judaism. But through the missionary work of Paul and the internal organization of the Church, Christianity spread and became institutionalized. During the fourth century it was recognized as the state religion within the Roman Empire.

By then enormous difficulties had been experienced within the Empire. Economic, political, and military problems were so great in the third century that the Empire shrank and nearly collapsed. A revival under the strong leadership of Diocletian and Constantine during the late third and early fourth centuries proved only temporary. By the end of the fourth century, the Empire was split into a Western and an Eastern half. The West was increasingly rural, subject to invasion, and generally in decline; the East evolved into the long-lasting Byzantine Empire. By the end of the fifth century, a unified, effective Western Empire was little more than a memory.

The selections in this chapter deal with three topics. The first concerns the general nature of the Empire at its height. During this time, those who predominated were the politically active Roman "gentlemen." What was their lifestyle? What were their interests? How did they relate to Classical culture? These same questions apply to some of the Roman emperors, like Marcus Aurelius, a Stoic philosopher. The documents also deal with broader questions. How was the transition from the Republic to the Empire made and what role did Augustus play in this transition? What were the connections between Roman society, culture, and religion?

The second topic is Christianity. Why was Christianity so appealing, particularly to Roman women? What explains the success of this religious movement? How did Christianity relate to Roman civilization? How did Christian theology relate to Classical philosophy?

The third topic is the decline and fall of Rome, a problem of continuing interest to historians. Some of the primary documents explore reactions to the fall. The secondary documents offer interpretations of the fall. Here the need to distinguish the Western from the Eastern Roman Empire during the decline and fall is stressed. This topic will take us up to the rise of new civilizations in lands once controlled by Rome; this will be covered in the next chapter.

For Classroom Discussion

Why did the Roman Empire "fall?" What insights into this are provided by A.H.M. Jones, the letters of St. Jerome, and Marcellinus' description of the Alani?

Primary Sources

Letters: The Daily Life of a Roman Governor

Pliny the Younger

For a cultured, well-to-do Roman gentleman, the period between C.E. 96 and 180, when the Empire was at its height, was a good time to live. This is reflected in the letters of Pliny the Younger (c. 62–c. 113), a lawyer who rose to the position of governor of Bithynia in Asia Minor. In the following letter he describes a typical day while vacationing at one of his Italian villas.

CONSIDER: *The kinds of activities most important to Pliny, at least during his stay at the villa; Pliny's view of his life and of people around him.*

TO FUSCUS

You desire to know in what manner I dispose of my day in summer-time at my Tuscan villa.

I rise just when I find myself in the humour, though generally with the sun; often indeed sooner, but seldom later. When I am up, I continue to keep the shutters of my chamber-windows closed. For under the influence of darkness and silence, I find myself wonderfully free and abstracted from those outward objects which dissipate attention, and left to my own thoughts; nor do I suffer my mind to wander with my eyes, but keep my eyes in subjection to my mind, which in the absence of external objects, see those which are present to the mental vision. If I have any composition upon my hands, this is the time I choose to consider it, not only with respect to the general plan, but even the style and expression, which I settle and correct as if I were actually writing. In this manner I compose more or less as the subject is more or less difficult, and I find myself able to retain it. Then I call my secretary, and, opening the shutters, I dictate to him what I have composed, after which I dismiss him for a little while, and then call him in again and again dismiss him.

About ten or eleven of the clock (for I do not observe one fixed hour), according as the weather recommends, I betake myself either to the terrace, or the covered portico, and there I meditate and dictate what remains upon the subject in which I am engaged. From thence I get into my chariot, where I employ myself as before, when I was walking or in my study; and find this changing of the scene preserves and enlivens my attention. At my return home I repose myself a while; then I take a walk; and after that, read aloud and with emphasis some Greek or Latin oration, not so much for the sake of strengthening my elocution as my digestion; though indeed the voice at the same time finds its account in this practice. Then I walk again, am anointed, take my exercises, and go into the bath. At supper, if I have only my wife, or a few friends with me, some author is read to us; and after supper we are entertained either with music, or an interlude. When that is finished, I take my walk with my domestics, in the number of which I am not without some persons of literature. Thus we pass our evenings in various conversation; and the day, even when it is at the longest, is quickly spent.

Upon some occasions, I change the order in certain of the articles above mentioned. For instance, if I have lain longer or walked more than usual, after my second sleep and reading aloud, instead of using my chariot I get on horseback; by which means I take as much exercise and lose less time. The visits of my friends from the neighbouring towns claim some part of the day; and sometimes

---

SOURCE: Pliny, *Letters*, trans. by William Melmoth, rev. by W. M. L. Hutchinson, in vol. II of the Loeb Classical Library (Cambridge, MA.: Harvard University Press, 1924), pp. 259–263.

by a seasonable interruption, they relieve me, when I am fatigued. I now and then amuse myself with sporting, but always take my tablets into the field, that though I should catch nothing, I may at least bring home something. Part of my time, too (though not so much as they desire), is allotted to my tenants: and I find their rustic complaints give a zest to my studies and engagements of the politer kind. Farewell.

Meditations: Ideals of an Emperor and Stoic Philosopher

Marcus Aurelius

Emperor Marcus Aurelius (161–180), of great significance for what he did as well as for what he symbolized, was the last of the five "good emperors" who ruled during the relatively stable and prosperous period from the end of the first century through most of the second century. He was also an important Stoic philosopher and in his meditations captured much of the essence of the popular Hellenistic philosophy. Marcus Aurelius approached the Platonic ideal of a philosopher-king and symbolized much of what was best about Roman civilization. The following are selections from his Meditations, *written in the form of a diary toward the end of his life.*

CONSIDER: *Aurelius' standards of conduct; his attitude toward death; how he compares himself to most of those around him; the similarities between Marcus Aurelius and Pliny the Younger.*

Do not despise death, but be well content with it, since this too is one of those things which nature wills. For such as it is to be young and to grow old, and to increase and to reach maturity, and to have teeth and beard and grey hairs, and to beget, and to be pregnant and to bring forth, and all the other natural operations which the seasons of thy life bring, such also is dissolution. This, then, is consistent with the character of a reflecting man, to be neither careless nor impatient nor contemptuous with respect to death, but to wait for it as one of the operations of nature. As thou now waitest for the time when the child shall come out of thy wife's womb, so be ready for the time when thy soul shall fall out of this envelope. But if thou requirest also a vulgar kind of comfort which shall reach thy heart, thou wilt be made best reconciled to death by observing the objects from which thou art going to be removed, and the morals of those with whom thy soul will no longer be mingled. For it is no way right to be offended with men, but it is thy duty to care for them and to bear with them gently; and yet to remember that thy departure will be not from men who have the same principles as thyself. For this is the only thing, if there be any, which could draw us the contrary way and attach us to life, to be permitted to live with those who have the same principles as ourselves. But now thou seest how great is the trouble arising from the discordance of those who live together, so that thou mayest say, Come quick, O death, lest perchance I, too, should forget myself.

He who does wrong does wrong against himself. He who acts unjustly acts unjustly to himself, because he makes himself bad.

He often acts unjustly who does not do a certain thing; not only he who does a certain thing.

Thy present opinion founded on understanding, and thy present conduct directed to social good, and thy present disposition of contentment with everything which happens—that is enough.

Wipe out imagination: check desire: extinguish appetite: keep the ruling faculty in its own power. . . .

How does the ruling faculty make use of itself? For all lies in this. But everything else, whether it is in the power of thy will or not, is only lifeless ashes and smoke. . . .

Man, thou hast been a citizen in this great state (the world): what difference does it make to thee whether for five years (or three)? For that which is conformable to the laws is just for all. Where is the hardship then, if no tyrant nor yet an unjust judge sends thee away from the state, but nature who brought thee into it? The same as if a praetor who has employed an actor dismisses him from the stage.—"But I have not finished the five acts, but only three of them."—Thou sayest well, but in life the three acts are the whole drama; for what shall be a complete drama is determined by him who was once the cause of its composition, and now of its dissolution: but thou art the cause of neither. Depart then satisfied, for he also who releases thee is satisfied.

Rome and the Early Christians

Pliny the Younger and Trajan

After the death of Christ, Christianity began to spread. Centuries would pass before it would become the major religion in the Roman world, but, by the beginning of the second century, it was a well-recognized sect to be contended with,

SOURCE: Marcus Aurelius, "Meditations," trans. G. Long in Whitney J. Oates, ed., *The Stoic and Epicurean Philosophers* (New York: Random House, 1940), pp. 554, 584–585. Copyright © 1940. Reprinted by permission.

SOURCE: From Dana Munro and Edith Bramhall, eds., "The Early Christian Persecutions," in Department of History of the University of Pennsylvania, ed., *Translations and Reprints from the Original Sources of European History,* vol. IV, no. 1 (Philadelphia: University of Pennsylvania Press, 1898), pp. 8–10.

particularly in the Eastern provinces. The more Christianity spread, the more government officials were faced with the issue of how to deal with it. Generally, various religious sects and beliefs were tolerated as long as their adherents were willing to participate in official pagan rituals, which were of a combined religious and political significance. But Christian beliefs demanded exclusivity and thus prevented acceptance of official rituals; to many this constituted both religious and political subversion. This problem and a common official response to it are revealed in the following correspondence in the year 112 between Pliny the Younger, then governor of Bithynia, and the enlightened emperor Trajan.

CONSIDER: *The circumstances under which Pliny became involved in prosecutions of Christians; what evidence this document provides about the general Roman policy toward the Christians; Roman legal practices and institutions revealed in this document; how Christians might have avoided prosecution or persecution.*

It is my custom, my Lord, to refer to you all things concerning which I am in doubt. For who can better guide my indecision or enlighten my ignorance?

I have never taken part in the trials of Christians: hence I do not know for what crime nor to what extent it is customary to punish or investigate. I have been in no little doubt as to whether any discrimination is made for age, or whether the treatment of the weakest does not differ from that of the stronger; whether pardon is granted in case of repentance, or whether he who has ever been a Christian gains nothing by having ceased to be one; whether the *name* itself without the proof of crimes, or the crimes, inseparably connected with the *name*, are punished. Meanwhile, I have followed this procedure in the case of those who have been brought before me as Christians. I asked them whether they were Christians a second and a third time and with threats of punishment; I questioned those who confessed; I ordered those who were obstinate to be executed. For I did not doubt that, whatever it was that they confessed, their stubbornness and inflexible obstinacy ought certainly to be punished. There were others of similar madness, who because they were Roman citizens, I have noted for sending to the City. Soon, the crime spreading, as is usual when attention is called to it, more cases arose. An anonymous accusation containing many names was presented. Those who denied that they were or had been Christians, ought, I thought, to be dismissed since they repeated after me a prayer to the gods and made supplication with incense and wine to your image, which I had ordered to be brought for the purpose together with the statues of the gods, and since besides they cursed Christ, not one of which things they say, those who are really Christians can be compelled to do. Others, accused by the informer, said that they were Christians and afterwards denied it; in fact they had been but had ceased to be, some many years ago, some even twenty years before. All both worshipped your image and the statues of the gods, and cursed Christ. They continued to maintain that this was the amount of their fault or error, that on a fixed day they were accustomed to come together before daylight and to sing by turns a hymn to Christ as a god, and that they bound themselves by oath, not for some crime but that they would not commit robbery, theft, or adultery, that they would not betray a trust nor deny a deposit when called upon. After this it was their custom to disperse and to come together again to partake of food, of an ordinary and harmless kind, however; even this they had ceased to do after the publication of my edict in which according to your command I had forbidden associations. Hence I believed it the more necessary to examine two female slaves, who were called deaconesses, in order to find out what was true, and to do it by torture. I found nothing but a vicious, extravagant superstition. Consequently I have postponed the examination and make haste to consult you. For it seemed to me that the subject would justify consultation, especially on account of the number of those in peril. For many of all ages, of every rank, and even of both sexes are and will be called into danger. The infection of this superstition has not only spread to the cities but even to the villages and country districts. It seems possible to stay it and bring about a reform. It is plain enough that the temples, which had been almost deserted, have begun to be frequented again, that the sacred rites, which had been neglected for a long time, have begun to be restored, and that fodder for victims, for which till now there was scarcely a purchaser, is sold. From which one may readily judge what a number of men can be reclaimed if repentance is permitted.

TRAJAN'S REPLY

You have followed the correct procedure, my Secundus, in conducting the cases of those who were accused before you as Christians, for no general rule can be laid down as a set form. They ought not to be sought out; if they are brought before you and convicted they ought to be punished; provided that he who denies that he is a Christian, and proves this by making supplication to our gods, however much he may have been under suspicion in the past, shall secure pardon on repentance. In the case of no crime should attention be paid to anonymous charges, for they afford a bad precedent and are not worthy of our age.

The Gospel According to St. Matthew

During the first and second centuries Christianity was one of many competing sects in the Empire. But by the fourth century it had become the most influential one and was finally adopted as the official faith of the Roman Empire. From a historical point of view, a crucial problem is to explain the success of Christianity. Part of the explanation comes from an analysis of the basic teachings of Christianity. One of the most useful texts for this purpose is found in the Gospel according to St. Matthew, written toward the end of the first century, about sixty years after the recorded occurrences. The rules for conduct and the general ethical message of Christianity are revealed in the following sermon of Jesus.

CONSIDER: *To whom this message was directed; the appeal of this message to people of those times; the differences in tone and content between these selections and the selections from the Old Testament in Chapter 1.*

5: Now when he saw the crowds, he went up on a mountainside and sat down. His disciples came to him and he began to teach them, saying:

"Blessed are the poor in spirit, for theirs is the kingdom of heaven.
Blessed are those who mourn, for they will be comforted.
Blessed are the meek, for they will inherit the earth.
Blessed are those who hunger and thirst for righteousness, for they will be filled.
Blessed are the merciful, for they will be shown mercy.
Blessed are the pure in heart, for they will see God.
Blessed are the peacemakers, for they will be called sons of God.
Blessed are those who are persecuted because of righteousness, for theirs is the kingdom of heaven.
Blessed are you when people insult you, persecute you and falsely say all kinds of evil against you because of me. Rejoice and be glad, because great is your reward in heaven, for in the same way they persecuted the prophets who were before you.

"You have heard that it was said, 'Do not commit adultery.' But I tell you that anyone who looks at a woman lustfully has already committed adultery with her in his heart. If your right eye causes you to sin, gouge it out and throw it away. It is better for you to lose one part of your body than for your whole body to be thrown into hell. And if your right hand causes you to sin, cut it off and throw it away. It is better for you to lose one part of your body than for your whole body to go into hell.

"It has been said, 'Anyone who divorces his wife must give her a certificate of divorce.' But I tell you that anyone who divorces his wife, except for marital unfaithfulness, causes her to become an adulteress, and anyone who marries the divorced woman commits adultery. . . .

"You have heard that it was said, 'Eye for eye, and tooth for tooth.' But I tell you, Do not resist an evil person. If someone strikes you on the right cheek, turn to him the other also. And if someone wants to sue you and take your tunic, let him have your cloak as well. If someone forces you to go one mile, go with him two miles. Give to the one who asks you, and do not turn away from the one who wants to borrow from you.

"You have heard that it was said, 'Love your neighbor and hate your enemy.' But I tell you: Love your enemies and pray for those who persecute you, that you may be sons of your Father in heaven. He causes his sun to rise on the evil and the good, and sends rain on the righteous and the unrighteous. If you love those who love you, what reward will you get? Are not even the tax collectors doing that? And if you greet only your brothers, what are you doing more than others? Do not even pagans do that? Be perfect, therefore, as your heavenly Father is perfect.

"Watch out for false prophets. They come to you in sheep's clothing, but inwardly they are ferocious wolves. By their fruit you will recognize them. Do people pick grapes from thornbushes, or figs from thistles? Likewise every good tree bears good fruit, but a bad tree bears bad fruit. A good tree cannot bear bad fruit, and a bad tree cannot bear good fruit. Every tree that does not bear good fruit is cut down and thrown into the fire. Thus, by their fruit you will recognize them.

"Not everyone who says to me, 'Lord, Lord,' will enter the kingdom of heaven, but only he who does the will of my Father who is in heaven. Many will say to me on that day, 'Lord, Lord, did we not prophesy in your name, and in your name drive out demons and perform many miracles?' Then I will tell them plainly, 'I never knew you. Away from me, you evil-doers!'

"Therefore everyone who hears these words of mine and puts them into practice is like a wise man who built his house on the rock. The rain came down, the streams rose, and the winds blew and beat against that house; yet it did not fall, because it had its foundation on the rock. But everyone who hears these words of mine and does not put them into practice is like a foolish man who built

SOURCE: *The Holy Bible, New International Version* (Colorado: International Bible Society, 1983), pp. 886–889 as excerpted.

his house on sand. The rain came down, the streams rose, and the winds blew and beat against that house, and it fell with a great crash."

When Jesus had finished saying these things, the crowds were amazed at his teaching, because he taught as one who had authority, and not as their teachers of the law.

Epistle to the Romans
St. Paul

Christianity owes its historical success not only to the content of its message but also to the organizing work of its early missionaries. St. Paul was the most important of these missionaries, traveling from the Near East to Greece and Rome with his message and organizing Christian groups during the decades after the death of Jesus. Paul's Epistle to the Romans *was written during the middle of the first century. It had a strong influence on Christian theology. The following selection focuses on the relation of Christianity to law and authority.*

CONSIDER: *The ways Paul has presented Christianity to meet the concerns of the Romans; how Christianity can be seen as compatible with Roman rule; connections between this message and the message in the Gospel according to St. Matthew.*

[21]But now, quite independently of law, God's justice has been brought to light. [22]The Law and the prophets both bear witness to it: it is God's way of righting wrong, effective through faith in Christ for all who have such faith—all, without distinction. [23]For all alike have sinned, and are deprived of the divine splendour, [24]and all are justified by God's free grace alone, through his act of liberation in the person of Christ Jesus. [25]For God designed him to be the means of expiating sin by his sacrificial death, effective through faith. God meant by this to demonstrate his justice, [26]because in his forbearance he had overlooked the sins of the past—to demonstrate his justice now in the present, showing that he is himself just and also justifies any man who puts his faith in Jesus.

[27]What room then is left for human pride? It is excluded. And on what principle? The keeping of the law would not exclude it, but faith does. [28]For our argument is that a man is justified by faith quite apart from success in keeping the law.

[29]Do you suppose God is the God of the Jews alone? Is he not the God of Gentiles also? [30]Certainly, of Gentiles also, if it be true that God is one. And he will therefore justify both the circumcised in virtue of their faith, and the uncircumcised through their faith. [31]Does this mean that we are using faith to undermine law? By no means: we are placing law itself on a firmer footing.

[6]The gifts we possess differ as they are allotted to us by God's grace, and must be exercised accordingly: the gift of inspired utterance, for example, [7]in proportion to a man's faith; or the gift of administration, in administration. [8]A teacher should employ his gift in teaching, and one who has the gift of stirring speech should use it to stir his hearers. If you give to charity, give with all your heart; if you are a leader, exert yourself to lead; if you are helping others in distress, do it cheerfully.

[1]Every person must submit to the supreme authorities. There is no authority but by act of God, and the existing authorities are instituted by him; [2]consequently anyone who rebels against authority is resisting a divine institution, and those who so resist have themselves to thank for the punishment they will receive. [3]For government, a terror to crime, has no terrors for good behaviour. You wish to have no fear of the authorities? [4]Then continue to do right and you will have their approval, for they are God's agents working for your good. But if you are doing wrong, then you will have cause to fear them; it is not for nothing that they hold the power of the sword, for they are God's agents of punishment, for retribution on the offender. [5]That is why you are obliged to submit. It is an obligation imposed not merely by fear of retribution but by conscience. [6]That is also why you pay taxes. The authorities are in God's service and to these duties they devote their energies.

[7]Discharge your obligations to all men; pay tax and toll, reverence and respect, to those to whom they are due. [8]Leave no claim outstanding against you, except that of mutual love. He who loves his neighbour has satisfied every claim of the law. [9]For the commandments, "Thou shalt not commit adultery, thou shalt not kill, thou shalt not steal, thou shalt not covet," and any other commandment there may be, are all summed up in the one rule, "Love your neighbour as yourself." [10]Love cannot wrong a neighbour; therefore the whole law is summed up in love.

[11]In all this, remember how critical the moment is. It is time for you to wake out of sleep, for deliverance is nearer to us now than it was when first we believed. It is far on in the night; day is near. [12]Let us therefore throw off the deeds of darkness and put on our armour as soldiers of the light. [13]Let us behave with decency as befits the day: no revelling or drunkenness, no debauchery or vice, no quarrels or jealousies! [14]Let Christ Jesus himself be the armour that you wear; give no more thought to satisfying the bodily appetites.

SOURCE: The Epistle of Paul to the Romans (III: 21–31; XII: 6–8; XIII: 1–14), *The New English Bible*. Copyright, The Delegates of the Oxford University Press and the Syndics of the Cambridge University Press, 1961, 1970, pp. 194, 204–205. Reprinted by permission.

The City of God
St. Augustine

Christianity grew in the pagan Greco-Roman world and flourished during the ensuing Middle Ages. Christianity's ability to survive and grow amid paganism is reflected in The City of God. Written by St. Augustine (354–430) in response to accusations that the sack of Rome by the Visigoths in 410 was caused by the pagan gods' anger at being displaced by the ascendant Christianity, this is one of the great works of Christian philosophy. St. Augustine, after studying Classical literature, becoming a professor of rhetoric, and being attracted to various philosophies and religious sects, was baptized in 387 and quickly rose to the post of Bishop of Hippo in his native Africa. He gained a reputation through his writings and became a very influential father of the Christian Church. Augustine argued that there were two cities, an eternal City of God awaiting the faithful and a worldly, sinful City of Men. The Christian Church more closely embodied the City of God and was preordained to replace Rome. The sack of Rome was thus part of God's divine plan and in no way tarnished the promise of the eternal city.

CONSIDER: *The differences between the "heavenly" and "earthly" cities; the "proper" relationship between the two cities; ways this philosophy was conducive to the spread of Christianity within a well-ordered empire and ways this same philosophy enabled Christianity to thrive despite the decline of that empire.*

But the families which do not live by faith seek their peace in the earthly advantages of this life; while the families which live by faith look for those eternal blessings which are promised, and use as pilgrims such advantages of time and of earth as do not fascinate and divert them from God, but rather aid them to endure with greater ease, and to keep down the number of those burdens of the corruptible body which weigh upon the soul. Thus the things necessary for this mortal life are used by both kinds of men and families alike, but each has its own peculiar and widely different aim in using them. The earthly city, which does not live by faith, seeks an earthly peace, and the end it proposes, in the well-ordered concord of civic obedience and rule, is the combination of men's wills to attain the things which are helpful to this life. The heavenly city, or rather the part of it which sojourns on earth and lives by faith, makes use of this peace only because it must, until this mortal condition which necessitates it shall pass away. Consequently, so long as it lives like a captive and a stranger in the earthly city, though it has already received the promise of redemption, and the gift of the Spirit as the earnest of it, it makes no scruple to obey the laws of the earthly city, whereby the things necessary for the maintenance of this mortal life are administered; and thus, as this life is common to both cities, so there is a harmony between them in regard to what belongs to it. But, as the earthly city has had some philosophers whose doctrine is condemned by the divine teaching, and who, being deceived either by their own conjectures or by demons, supposed that many gods must be invited to take an interest in human affairs, and assigned to each a separate function and a separate department,—to one the body, to another the soul; and in the body itself, to one the head, to another the neck, and each of the other members to one of the gods; and in like manner, in the soul, to one god the natural capacity was assigned, to another education, to another anger, to another lust; and so the various affairs of life were assigned,—cattle to one, corn to another, wine to another, oil to another, the woods to another, money to another, navigation to another, wars and victories to another, marriages to another, births and fecundity to another, and other things to other gods: and as the celestial city, on the other hand, knew that one God only was to be worshipped, and that to Him alone was due that service which the Greeks call λατρεία, and which can be given only to a god, it has come to pass that the two cities could not have common laws of religion, and that the heavenly city has been compelled in this matter to dissent, and to become obnoxious to those who think differently, and to stand the brunt of their anger and hatred and persecutions, except in so far as the minds of their enemies have been alarmed by the multitude of the Christians and quelled by the manifest protection of God accorded to them. This heavenly city, then, while it sojourns on earth, calls citizens out of all nations, and gathers together a society of pilgrims of all languages, not scrupling about diversities in the manners, laws, and institutions whereby earthly peace is secured and maintained, but recognising that, however various these are, they all tend to one and the same end of earthly peace. It therefore is so far from rescinding and abolishing these diversities, that it even preserves and adopts them, so long only as no hindrance to the worship of the one supreme and true God is thus introduced. Even the heavenly city, therefore, while in its state of pilgrimage, avails itself of the peace of earth, and, so far as it can without injuring faith and godliness, desires and maintains a common agreement among men regarding the acquisition of the necessaries

SOURCE: Marcus Dods, ed., *The Works of Aurelius Augustine, Bishop of Hippo*, vol. II (Edinburgh, Scotland: T. and T. Clark, 1881), pp. 326–328.

of life, and makes this earthly peace bear upon the peace of heaven; for this alone can be truly called and esteemed the peace of the reasonable creatures, consisting as it does in the perfectly ordered and harmonious enjoyment of God and of one another in God. When we shall have reached that peace, this mortal life shall give place to one that is eternal, and our body shall be no more this animal body which by its corruption weighs down the soul, but a spiritual body feeling no want, and in all its members subjected to the will. In its pilgrim state the heavenly city possesses this peace by faith; and by this faith it lives righteously when it refers to the attainment of that peace every good action towards God and man; for the life of the city is a social life.

The Nomadic Tribes

Ammianus Marcellinus

For much of Roman history, "barbarians"—most of whom were tribes from the north and east—threatened the empire's borders. These pressures increased in the third and fourth centuries as Rome weakened and various tribes, led by warrior kings, pressed against Rome's frontiers. In the following selection, the Roman soldier and historian Ammianus Marcellinus (c. 330–395) describes one of these tribes, the Alans.

CONSIDER: *The characteristics of the Alans' nomadic life; why, according to Marcellinus, the Alans were such fierce fighters; how the Alans' daily life and culture differed from that of the Romans.*

Thus the Alans, whose various tribes there is no point in enumerating, extend over both parts of the earth [*Europe and Asia*]. But, although they are widely separated and wander in their nomadic way over immense areas, they have in course of time come to be known by one name and are all compendiously called Alans, because their character, their wild way of life, and their weapons are the same everywhere. They have no huts and make no use of the plough, but live upon meat and plenty of milk. They use wagons covered with a curved canopy of bark, and move in these over the endless desert. When they come to a grassy place they arrange their carts in a circle and feed like wild animals; then, having exhausted the forage available, they again settle what one might call their mobile towns upon their vehicles, and move on. In these wagons the males couple with the women and their children are born and reared; in fact, these wagons are their permanent dwellings and, wherever they go, they look upon them as their ancestral home.

They drive their cattle before them and pasture them with their flocks, and they pay particular attention to the breeding of horses. The plains there are always green and there are occasional patches of fruit-trees, so that, wherever they go, they never lack food and fodder. This is because the soil is damp and there are numerous rivers. Those whose age or sex makes them unfit to fight stay by the wagons and occupy themselves in light work, but the younger men, who are inured to riding from earliest boyhood, think it beneath their dignity to walk and are all trained in a variety of ways to be skilful warriors. This is why the Persians too, who are of Scythian origin, are such expert fighters.

Almost all Alans are tall and handsome, with yellowish hair and frighteningly fierce eyes. They are active and nimble in the use of arms and in every way a match for the Huns, but less savage in their habits and way of life. Their raiding and hunting expeditions take them as far as the Sea of Azov and the Crimea, and also to Armenia and Media. They take as much delight in the dangers of war as quiet and peaceful folk in ease and leisure. They regard it as the height of good fortune to lose one's life in battle; those who grow old and die a natural death are bitterly reviled as degenerate cowards. Their proudest boast is to have killed a man, no matter whom, and their most coveted trophy is to use the flayed skins of their decapitated foes as trappings for their horses.

No temple or shrine is to be found among them, not so much as a hut thatched with straw, but their savage custom is to stick a naked sword in the earth and worship it as the god of war, the presiding deity of the regions over which they range. They have a wonderful way of foretelling the future. They collect straight twigs of osier, and at an appointed time sort them out uttering a magic formula, and in this way they obtain clear knowledge of what is to come. They are all free from birth, and slavery is unknown among them. To this day they choose as their leaders men who have proved their worth by long experience in war. Now I must return to what remains of my main theme.

The Fall of Rome

St. Jerome

The fall of the Roman Empire, though occurring over a long period of time, was experienced as a profound shock. Even those who were not part of the Roman power structure saw the invasions and decomposition of Rome as a catastrophe. This

---

SOURCE: Ammianus Marcellinus, *The Later Roman Empire*, ed. and trans. by Walter Hamilton (New York: Penguin Books, 1986), pp. 412–414.

SOURCE: From James Harvey Robinson, ed., *Readings in European History*, vol. I (New York: Ginn and Co., 1904), pp. 44–45.

reaction can be found in the letters of St. Jerome (c. 340–420), who lived through much of the decline. St. Jerome, an ascetic for part of his life and a great doctor of the Church, spent most of his life in Jerusalem and is known for his translation of the Bible into Latin.

CONSIDER: Why Jerome was so shocked and overwhelmed by what was happening; any evidence in these letters of an incompatibility between Christianity and the Roman Empire; the methods apparently used in an effort to avoid destruction by invaders.

Nations innumerable and most savage have invaded all Gaul. The whole region between the Alps and the Pyrenees, the ocean and the Rhine, has been devastated by the Quadi, the Vandals, the Sarmati, the Alani, the Gepidae, the hostile Heruli, the Saxons, the Burgundians, the Alemanni and the Pannonians. O wretched Empire! Mayence, formerly so noble a city, has been taken and ruined, and in the church many thousands of men have been massacred. Worms has been destroyed after a long siege. Rheims, that powerful city, Amiens, Arras, Speyer, Strasberg,—all have seen their citizens led away captive into Germany. Aquitaine and the provinces of Lyons and Narbonne, all save a few towns, have been depopulated; and these the sword threatens without, while hunger ravages within. I cannot speak without tears of Toulouse, which the merits of the holy Bishop Exuperius have prevailed so far to save from destruction. Spain, even, is in daily terror lest it perish, remembering the invasion of the Cimbri; and whatsoever the other provinces have suffered once, they continue to suffer in their fear.

I will keep silence concerning the rest, lest I seem to despair of the mercy of God. For a long time, from the Black Sea to the Julian Alps, those things which are ours have not been ours; and for thirty years, since the Danube boundary was broken, war has been waged in the very midst of the Roman Empire. Our tears are dried by old age. Except a few old men, all were born in captivity and siege, and do not desire the liberty they never knew. Who could believe this? How could the whole tale be worthily told? How Rome has fought within her own bosom not for glory, but for preservation—nay, how she has not even fought, but with gold and all her precious things has ransomed her life. . . .

Who could believe [Jerome exclaims in another passage] that Rome, built upon the conquest of the whole world, would fall to the ground? that the mother herself would become the tomb of her peoples? that all the regions of the East, of Africa and Egypt, once ruled by the queenly city, would be filled with troops of slaves and handmaidens? that to-day holy Bethlehem should shelter men and women of noble birth, who once abounded in wealth and are now beggars?

Visual Sources

Carved Gemstone: Augustus and the Empire Transformed

This onyx gemstone with a carved relief scene, known as the Gemma Augustrea (figure 5.1), portrays both a specific event and a general set of views during the early Roman Empire. Made between C.E. 10 and 20, it appears to commemorate a victory by the Romans over the Pannonians and Germans in C.E. 12. In the lower half, moving from right to left, a man and a woman are being dragged by auxiliary soldiers (probably Macedonian allies of the Romans). On the left four Roman soldiers raise a trophy; another barbarian couple will be tied to it. In the upper half, moving from left to right, Tiberius, who led the victorious Roman troops, descends from a chariot held by Victory. The youth in armor is probably his nephew Germanicus. In the center sit the goddess Roma and Augustus, between them the sign of Capricorn

FIGURE 5.1   (© Erich Lessing/Art Resource, NY)

(the month of his conception) and below them an eagle (the bird of the god Jupiter) and armor of the defeated. Augustus is being crowned as ruler of the civilized world by Oikoumene, while on the far right the bearded Ocean and the Earth with one of her children look on.

This scene is particularly revealing of political and religious information. It shows the transformation from the Republic to the Empire under a deified emperor in the making, for Augustus is being transformed into an equivalent of Jupiter and is clearly accepted by the rest of the gods. Moreover, his successor, Tiberius, appears to be in line for a similar fate. It also indicates the growing reach of the Roman Empire and the Romans' use of subordinate allies—the Macedonians—to exert their control. The religious figures and symbols, while Roman, also reveal affinities with Greek religious figures and symbols; artistically, the scene has a Hellenistic flavor. This is evidence for a merging of Roman and Greek cultures. Note also the balance between idealized form and realistic representation: The bodies are somewhat stylized, particularly Augustus' heroic body, but at the same time the individuals are clearly distinguished; these individuals were meant to be recognizable to the viewer.

FIGURE 5.2 (© Scala/Art Resource, NY)

CONSIDER: *The political implications of this scene and of the coin of some 150 years earlier shown in Chapter 4; how contemporaries might have understood the message of this scene.*

Tomb Decoration: Death and Roman Culture

The tomb decoration in figure 5.2, known as the Sarcophagus from Acilia, dates from the mid–third century. Here, a boy, perhaps the young Emperor Gordian III, is standing next to a number of other figures. To his right are perhaps his parents, and to his left important government officials (perhaps senators) as suggested by their costumes. The bundle of scrolls at the feet of the boy and the stance of the figures indicate a dedication to Classical philosophy or scholarship. Indeed, in this period, there were many tombs with scenes representing a commitment to or glorification of pagan culture—a wish by individuals to be remembered as devotees of philosophy or literature.

This commitment to pagan culture is revealed both in what this tomb decoration shows and in what it does not show. Rather than showing mythical scenes, pagan gods, or Christian beliefs, it shows secular figures glorifying literature and philosophy. It is thus evidence for the continued strength of Classical pagan culture, at least among the elite, even during a period of decline for Rome. The style also indicates a continuing Classical balance between idealized forms and realistic representation: While the robes, the bearing, and the figures are stylized, there are clear individual differences, particularly in the head of the boy and in the balding individual to his left.

CONSIDER: *How this tomb decoration compares with the Tomb of Menna (Chapter 1), the thoughts of Marcus Aurelius, and Christian beliefs.*

A Roman Sarcophagus: Picturing the Bible

This sculpted decoration on a late fourth-century Roman sarcophagus (stone coffin) depicts biblical scenes and reveals attitudes of Christians within the Roman Empire. Christ stands in the center facing the viewer, his right hand open. In his left hand he holds an open scroll. To the right, Peter approaches, bearing a cross and looking up to Christ. To the left stands Paul, holding a book roll. The scene to the far left shows Christ washing the feet of Peter. On the far right, Christ—presented as a simple man in plain dress—confronts Pilate, whose outfit suggests the worldly power of a Roman emperor.

CONSIDER: *In what ways this sculpted decoration emphasizes Christ's humanity; how contemporary viewers might understand these scenes.*

SOURCE: Musée de l'Arles et de la Provence antiques.

Secondary Sources

The Roman Empire: The Place of Augustus

Chester G. Starr

With the rise of power of Augustus, the Republic came to an end and the Empire began. Under the long rule of Augustus, patterns were established that would endure well beyond his death in C.E. 14. During his own time Augustus was a controversial person, and ever since scholars have tried to evaluate the man and his rule. In the following selection, Chester Starr, a historian at the University of Michigan, analyzes some of the controversies over the place of Augustus in Roman history, here emphasizing his successes in the political and military fields.

CONSIDER: *The ways in which Augustus might be considered a success; how other writers and scholars might disagree with this evaluation.*

The failure of Augustus' social reforms throws into more vivid light his remarkable success in the political and military fields. Working patiently decade after decade Augustus gave the Roman world a sense of internal security based on a consciously elaborated pattern of government which embodied two principles. First came his own preeminence, and as we have seen in regard to coinage and architecture he was not bashful in stressing his own merits and achievements; no less than 150 statues and busts of the first emperor also survive. The second was his emphasis on outward cooperation with the Roman aristocracy, clothed in old constitutional forms; one may also add that on the local level Augustus, to ensure urban peace, favored the dominance of the rich and wellborn as against democracy. In sum, Augustus' reforms were essentially conservative in character....

Modern historians have evaluated Augustus in many divers ways, but until recently have tended to treat him with respect, partly because of the great triumphs of literature in the "Augustan Age." Of late, however, scholars affected by the overtly arbitrary character of government in some contemporary states have approached Augustus, as the founder of a covertly arbitrary system, with little admiration....

Certainly he was revered with great and genuine enthusiasm by his contemporaries both in Rome and in

SOURCE: Excerpted from *The Roman Empire, 27 B.C.E.–C.E. 476: A Study in Survival* by Chester G. Starr. Copyright © 1982 by Oxford University Press, Inc. Reprinted by permission.

the provinces. In rising to the foreground as a single, unique figure Augustus had concentrated upon himself the yearnings of men for order. To this leader, more as symbol than as living creature, the subjects turned for assurance and prosperity in the material world, for a sense of security and purpose on the spiritual level....

In sum Augustus steered the Empire along lines which it was to follow for centuries to come, both in its strengths and in its weaknesses; the latter often the consequence of artful compromise with the Republican past. When men of later generations looked back on Augustus, they tended to have mixed emotions. His memory among common folk stood high, and the great events of his reign were long commemorated by coins, calendars, and both public and court rites and festivals. Writers of aristocratic stamp from Seneca the Elder on accepted him as inevitable and necessary to stop the Roman revolution; yet these writers rejected almost unanimously his claim that he had restored the Republic. To them the Empire was an autocratic system, and Augustus was the first autocrat. If Augustus could have heard the voices of future generations as he lay on his deathbed and begged for the applause of the bystanders, his self-satisfaction might have been diminished.

Pagan and Christian: The Appeal of Christianity

E. R. Dodds

The beginnings of Christianity coincided with the establishment of the Empire under Augustus and the early emperors who succeeded him. Numerous attempts have been made to analyze Jesus and the rise of Christianity. In the following selection E. R. Dodds views early Christianity from a historical perspective. He focuses on the appeal of Christianity and how it compares with other religions of that period.

CONSIDER: *Typical traits of mystery religions and how Christianity differed from other mystery religions; other factors that might help explain the rise of Christianity in this early period.*

In the first place, its very exclusiveness, its refusal to concede any value to alternative forms of worship, which nowadays is often felt to be a weakness, was in the circumstances of the time a source of strength. The religious tolerance which was the normal Greek and Roman practice had resulted by accumulation in a bewildering mass of alternatives. There were too many cults, too many mysteries, too many philosophies of life to choose from: you could pile one religious insurance on another, yet not feel safe. Christianity made a clean sweep. It lifted the burden of freedom from the shoulders of the individual: one choice, one irrevocable choice, and the road to salvation was clear....

Secondly, Christianity was open to all. In principle, it made no social distinctions; it accepted the manual worker, the slave, the outcast, the ex-criminal; and though in the course of our period it developed a strong hierarchic structure, its hierarchy offered an open career to talent. Above all, it did not, like Neoplatonism, demand education....

Thirdly, in a period when earthly life was increasingly devalued and guilt-feelings were widely prevalent, Christianity held out to the disinherited the conditional promise of a better inheritance in another world. So did several of its pagan rivals. But Christianity wielded both a bigger stick and a juicier carrot. It was accused of being a religion of fear, and such it no doubt was in the hands of the rigorists. But it was also a religion of lively hope....

But lastly, the benefits of becoming a Christian were not confined to the next world. A Christian congregation was from the first a community in a much fuller sense than any corresponding group of Isiac or Mithraist devotees. Its members were bound together not only by common rites but by a common way of life and, as Celsus shrewdly perceived, by their common danger. Their promptitude in bringing material help to brethren in captivity or other distress is attested not only by Christian writers but by Lucian, a far from sympathetic witness. Love of one's neighbour is not an exclusively Christian virtue, but in our period the Christians appear to have practised it much more effectively than any other group. The Church provided the essentials of social security: it cared for widows and orphans, the old, the unemployed, and the disabled; it provided a burial fund for the poor and a nursing service in time of plague. But even more important, I suspect, than these material benefits was the sense of belonging which the Christian community could give. Modern social studies have brought home to us the universality of the "need to belong" and the unexpected ways in which it can influence human behaviour, particularly among the rootless inhabitants of great cities. I see no reason to think that it was otherwise in antiquity: Epictetus has described for us the dreadful loneliness that can beset a man in the midst of his fellows. Such loneliness must have been felt by millions—the urbanised tribesman, the peasant come to town in search of work, the demobilised soldier, the rentier ruined by inflation, and the manumitted slave. For people in that situation membership of a Christian community might be the only way of maintaining their self-respect and giving their life some semblance of meaning. Within the community

SOURCE: From E. R. Dodds, *Pagan and Christian in an Age of Anxiety*, pp. 133–134, 136–138, copyright 1965. Reprinted with the permission of Cambridge University Press.

there was human warmth: some one was interested in them, both here and hereafter. It is therefore not surprising that the earliest and the most striking advances of Christianity were made in the great cities—in Antioch, in Rome, in Alexandria. Christians were in a more than formal sense "members one of another": I think that was a major cause, perhaps the strongest single cause, of the spread of Christianity.

Women of the Roman Empire
Jo Ann McNamara

Roman women, like Greek women, were usually in a subordinate position to men. Rome was and would remain a patriarchy. However, during the Empire and particularly as Christianity grew in importance, women's roles evolved. In the following selection, Jo Ann McNamara stresses how women were able to use their family roles and religion to gain new power and choices.

CONSIDER: *Why Christianity may have been so attractive to women; how Christianity played a role in improving women's power and status.*

The Roman Republic was a patriarchy in the strictest sense of the word. Private life rested upon *patria potestas*, paternal power over the subordinate women, children, slaves, and clients who formed the Roman *familia*. The Roman matron was highly respected within limits established by a strong gender system that defined her role as the supporter of the patriarch's power. Public life was conducted in the name of the Senate and People of Rome, institutionally defined as exclusively male. In the last days of the Republic, the power of these institutions was destroyed by civil war at the same time that the army, led by its emperors (originally only a military title), carried the standards of Rome to victory over the many civilizations of the Mediterranean world and ultimately took power over the city of Rome itself.

Under the Empire, the boundaries between public and private lives became porous and women began to use their familial roles as instruments of public power. Religion, in particular, offered women a bridge across class and gender differences, from private to public life. Roman women experimented widely with a variety of pagan cults, but increasingly Christianity attracted women with a vision of a community where in Christ "There is neither Jew nor Greek, . . . neither bond nor free, . . . neither male nor female." (Galatians 3:28)

Christianity was founded at about the same time as the Roman Empire was established, and for the next three centuries the imperial government and the Christian religion developed on separate but converging tracks. As an outlawed sect, the new religion was peculiarly susceptible to the influence of wealthy and noble women. Their participation was so energetic and prominent that critics often labeled Christianity a religion of women and slaves. In the fourth and fifth centuries, when the Empire had become Christian, it consolidated new political and religious hierarchies which reinforced one another. The synthesis was basically a restructured patriarchy with Christian men firmly in control of both government and church. But Roman Law and Roman Christianity contained a wider range of choices for women regarding marriage and property which passed into the hands of Rome's European successors.

The Later Roman Empire
A. H. M. Jones

Most historians who interpret the decline and fall of the Roman Empire focus on the Western half of the Empire. In fact, the Eastern half did not fall and would not, despite some ups and downs, for another thousand years. A. H. M. Jones, a distinguished British scholar of Greece and Rome, has emphasized the significance of the Eastern Empire's different fate for analyzing the decline and fall of the Western Empire. In the following selection Jones compares conditions in the two halves of the Empire, criticizing those who have theorized that the fall in the West stemmed from long-term internal weaknesses.

CONSIDER: *The primary cause for the collapse in the West according to Jones; other possible causes for the collapse in the West.*

All the historians who have discussed the decline and fall of the Roman empire have been Westerners. Their eyes have been fixed on the collapse of Roman authority in the Western parts and the evolution of the medieval Western European world. They have tended to forget, or to brush aside, one very important fact, that the Roman empire, though it may have declined, did not fall in the fifth century nor indeed for another thousand years. During the fifth century, while the Western parts were being parcelled out into a group of barbarian kingdoms, the empire of the East stood its

SOURCE: Jo Ann McNamara, "Matres Patriae/Matres Ecclesiae: Women of the Roman Empire," in Renate Bridenthal, Claudia Koonz, and Susan Stuard, eds., *Becoming Visible: Women in European History*, 2d ed. (Boston: Houghton Mifflin, 1987), p. 108.

SOURCE: A. H. M. Jones, *The Later Roman Empire*, vol. II (Oxford, England: Basil Blackwell, 1964), pp. 1026–1027, 1062–1064, 1066–1067. By permission of Basil Blackwell, Oxford.

ground. In the sixth it counter-attacked and reconquered Africa from the Vandals and Italy from the Ostrogoths, and part of Spain from the Visigoths. Before the end of the century, it is true, much of Italy and Spain had succumbed to renewed barbarian attacks, and in the seventh the onslaught of the Arabs robbed the empire of Syria, Egypt, and Africa, and the Slavs overran the Balkans. But in Asia Minor the empire lived on, and later, recovering its strength, reconquered much territory that it had lost in the dark days of the seventh century.

These facts are important, for they demonstrate that the empire did not, as some modern historians have suggested, totter into its grave from senile decay, impelled by a gentle push from the barbarians. Most of the internal weaknesses which these historians stress were common to both halves of the empire. The East was even more Christian than the West, its theological disputes far more embittered. The East, like the West, was administered by a corrupt and extortionate bureaucracy. The Eastern government strove as hard to enforce a rigid caste system, tying the *curiales* to their cities and the *coloni* to the soil. Land fell out of cultivation and was deserted in the East as well as in the West. It may be that some of these weaknesses were more accentuated in the West than in the East, but this is a question which needs investigation. It may be also that the initial strength of the Eastern empire in wealth and population was greater, and that it could afford more wastage; but this again must be demonstrated....

The East then probably possessed greater economic resources, and could thus support with less strain a larger number of idle mouths. A smaller part of its resources went, it would seem, to maintain its aristocracy, and more was thus available for the army and other essential services. It also was probably more populous, and since the economic pressure on the peasantry was perhaps less severe, may have suffered less from population decline. If there is any substance in these arguments, the Eastern government should have been able to raise a larger revenue without overstraining its resources, and to levy more troops without depleting its labour force....

The Western empire was poorer and less populous, and its social and economic structure more unhealthy. It was thus less able to withstand the tremendous strains imposed by its defense effort, and the internal weaknesses which it developed undoubtedly contributed to its final collapse in the fifth century. But the major cause of its fall was that it was more exposed to barbarian onslaughts which in persistence and sheer weight of numbers far exceeded anything which the empire had previously had to face. The Eastern empire, owing to its greater wealth and population and sounder economy, was better able to carry the burden of defence, but its resources were overstrained and it developed the same weaknesses as the West, if perhaps in a less acute form. Despite these weaknesses it managed in the sixth century not only to hold its own against the Persians in the East but to reconquer parts of the West, and even when, in the seventh century, it was overrun by the onslaughts of the Persians and the Arabs and the Slavs, it succeeded despite heavy territorial losses in rallying and holding its own. The internal weaknesses of the empire cannot have been a major factor in its decline.

CHAPTER QUESTIONS

1. What are the similarities and differences between Roman and Christian rules of conduct and ethics?
2. What traits of Classical culture and civilization do you find most admirable? Are these also traits of Christianity?
3. In what ways were conditions of Roman civilization conducive to the growth of Christianity? In what ways was Christianity nevertheless contradictory to Roman civilization?
4. How might the very success of the Roman Empire be related to its decline?

GLOSSARY

Note to users: Terms that are foreign or difficult to pronounce are transcribed in parentheses directly after the term itself. The transcriptions are based on the rules of English spelling; that is, they are similar to the transcriptions employed in the *Webster* dictionaries. Each word's most heavily stressed syllable is marked by an acute accent.

A

Absolute monarch (máh-nark) A seventeenth- or eighteenth-century European monarch claiming complete political authority.

Absolutism (áb-suh-loo-tism) (Royal) A government in which all power is vested in the ruler.

Abstract expressionism (ex-présh-un-ism) A twentieth-century painting style infusing nonrepresentational art with strong personal feelings.

Acropolis (uh-króp-uh-liss) The hill at the center of Athens on which the magnificent temples—including the Parthenon—that made the architecture of ancient Athens famous are built.

Act of Union Formal unification of England and Scotland in 1707.

Afrikaners Afrikaans-speaking South Africans of Dutch and other European ancestry.

Age of Reason The eighteenth-century Enlightenment; sometimes includes seventeenth-century science and philosophy.

Agora In ancient Greece, the marketplace or place of public assembly.

Agricultural revolution Neolithic discovery of agriculture; agricultural transformations that began in eighteenth-century western Europe.

Ahura Mazda In Zoroastrianism, the beneficial god of light.

Ahriman In Zoroastrianism, the evil god of darkness.

Akkadian (uh-káy-dee-un) A Semitic language of a region of ancient Mesopotamia.

Albigensians (al-buh-jén-see-unz) A medieval French heretical sect that believed in two gods—an evil and a good principle—that was destroyed in a crusade in the thirteenth century; also called Cathars.

Alchemy (ál-kuh-mee) The medieval study and practice of chemistry, primarily concerned with changing metals into gold and finding a universal remedy for diseases. It was much practiced from the thirteenth to the seventeenth century.

Allies (ál-eyes) The two alliances against Germany and its partners in World War I and World War II.

Al-Qaeda A global terrorist network headed by Osama bin Laden.

Anarchists (ánn-ar-kissts) Those advocating or promoting anarchy, or an absence of government. In the late nineteenth and early twentieth centuries, anarchism arose as an ideology and movement against all governmental authority and private property.

Ancien régime (áwn-syáwn ráy-zhéem) The traditional political and social order in Europe before the French Revolution.

Antigonids (ann-tíg-un-idz) Hellenistic dynasty that ruled in Macedonia from about 300 B.C.E. to about 150 B.C.E.

Anti-Semitism (ann-tye-sém-i-tism) Prejudice against Jews.

Apartheid "Separation" in the Afrikaans language. A policy to rigidly segregate people by color in South Africa, 1948–1989.

Appeasement Attempting to satisfy potential aggressors in order to avoid war.

Aramaic (air-uh-máy-ik) A northwest Semitic language that spread throughout the region. It was the language that Jesus spoke.

Archon (áhr-kahn) A chief magistrate in ancient Athens.

Areopagus (air-ee-áh-pa-gus) A prestigious governing council of ancient Athens.

Arête (ah-ray-táy) Greek term for the valued virtues of manliness, courage, and excellence.

Arianism (áir-ee-un-ism) A fourth-century Christian heresy that taught that Jesus was not of the same substance as God the father, and thus had been created.

Assemblies, Roman Institutions in the Roman Republic that functioned as the legislative branch of government.

Assignats (ah-seen-yáh) Paper money issued in the National Assembly during the French Revolution.

Astrolabe (áss-tro-leyb) Medieval instrument used to determine the altitudes of celestial bodies.

Augury (áh-gur-ee) The art or practice of foretelling events though signs or omens.

Autocracy (au-tóc-ra-cee) Government under the rule of an authoritarian ruler.

Autocrat (áuto-crat) An authoritarian ruler.

Axis World War II alliance whose main members were Germany, Italy, and Japan.

B

Baby boom The increase in births following World War II.

Babylonian Captivity Period during the fourteenth century in which seven popes chose to reside in Avignon instead of Rome. Critics called this period the "Babylonian Captivity" of the papacy.

Bailiffs Medieval French salaried officials hired by the king to collect taxes and represent his interests.

Balance of power Distribution of power among states, or the policy of creating alliances to control powerful states.

Balkans States in the Balkan Peninsula, including Albania, Bulgaria, Greece, Romania, and Yugoslavia.

Baroque (ba-róak) An artistic style of the sixteenth and seventeenth centuries stressing rich ornamentation and dynamic movement; in music, a style marked by strict forms and elaborate ornamentation.

Bastard feudalism (feúd-a-lism) Late medieval corruption of the feudal system replacing feudal loyalty with cash payments.

Bastille (bas-téel) The royal prison symbolizing the old regime that was destroyed in the French Revolution.

Bauhaus (bóugh-house) An influential school of art emphasizing clean, functional lines founded in Germany by the architect Walter Gropius just after World War I.

Bedouin (béd-oh-in) An Arab of any of the nomadic tribes of the deserts of North Africa, Arabia, and Syria.

Berlin airlift The airborne military operation organized to supply Berlin's Western-occupied sectors during the Soviet Union's 1948 Berlin blockage.

Berlin Wall The wall erected in 1961 to divide East and West Berlin.

Bessemer (béss-uh-mer) **process** A method for removing impurities from molten iron.

Black Death Name given the epidemic that swept Europe beginning in 1348. Most historians agree that the main disease was bubonic plague, but the Black Death may have incorporated many other diseases.

Blackshirts Mussolini's black-uniformed Fascist paramilitary forces in the 1920s and 1930s.

Blitzkrieg (blíts-kreeg) "Lightning war," a rapid air and land military assault used by the Germans in World War II.

Boers (boars) Dutch settlers in south Africa.

Bolshevik (bówl-shuh-vick) "Majority faction," the Leninist wing of the Russian Marxist Party; after 1917, the Communist Party.

Bourgeoisie (boor-zhwa-zée) The middle class.

Boxers A nineteenth-century Chinese secret society that believed in the spiritual power of the martial arts and fought against Chinese Christians and foreigners in China.

Boyar A Russian noble.

Brezhnev (bréhzh-nyeff) **Doctrine** Policy that justified Soviet intervention in order to ensure the survival of socialism in another state, initiated by USSR leader Brezhnev in 1968.

Brownshirts Hitler's brown-uniformed paramilitary force in the 1920s and 1930s.

Burschenschaften (bóor-shen-sháhf-ten) Liberal nationalist German student unions during the early nineteenth century.

C

Cabinet system Government by a prime minister and heads of governmental bureaus developed by Britain during the eighteenth century.

Caesaropapism (see-zer-oh-pápe-ism) The practice of having the same person rule both the state and the church.

Cahiers (kye-yéah) Lists of public grievances sent to the French Estates General in 1789.

Caliph (káy-liff) A title meaning "successor to the Prophet" given to Muslim rulers who combined political authority with religious power.

Capitalists Those promoting an economic system characterized by freedom of the market with private and corporate ownership of the means of production and distribution that are operated for profit.

Capitularies (ka-pít-chew-làir-eez) Royal laws issued by Charlemagne and the Carolingians.

Caravel (care-uh-véll) A small, light sailing ship of the kind used by the Spanish and Portuguese in the fifteenth and sixteenth centuries.

Carbonari (car-bun-áh-ree) A secret society of revolutionaries in nineteenth-century Italy.

Cartel (car-téll) An alliance of corporations designed to control the marketplace.

Cartesian (car-tée-zhen) **dualism** A philosophy developed by René Descartes in the seventeenth century that defines two kinds of reality: the mind, or subjective thinking, and the body, or objective physical matter.

Catacombs Underground burial places. The term originally referred to the early Christian burial locations in Rome and elsewhere.

Cathars (cáth-arz) A medieval French dualist heretical sect; also called Albigensians.

Central Powers World War I alliance, primarily of Germany, Austria, and the Ottoman Empire.

Centuriate (sen-chúr-ee-ate) **Assembly** An aristocratic ruling body in ancient Rome that made the laws.

Chancellor A high-ranking official—in Germany, the prime minister.

Chartists English reformers of the 1830s and 1840s who demanded political and social rights for the lower classes.

Checks and balances A balanced division of governmental power among different institutions.

Chivalry (shív-el-ree) Code of performance and ethics for medieval knights. It can also refer to the demonstration of knightly virtues.

Christian humanists During the fifteenth and sixteenth centuries, experts in Greek, Latin, and Hebrew who studied the Bible and other Christian writings in order to understand the correct meaning of early Christian texts.

Civil Constitution of the Clergy New rules nationalizing and governing the clergy enacted during the French Revolution.

Civic humanists Those practicing a branch of humanism that promoted the value of responsible citizenship in which people work to improve their city-states.

Classical style A seventeenth- and eighteenth-century cultural style emphasizing restraint and balance, and following models from ancient Greece and Rome.

Cold War The global struggle between alliances headed by the United States and the Soviet Union during the second half of the twentieth century.

Collectivization The Soviet policy of taking agricultural lands and decisions away from individual owners and placing them in the hands of elected managers and party officials.

Comecon (cómm-ee-con) The economic organization of communist eastern European states during the Cold War.

Committee of Public Safety Ruling committee of twelve leaders during the French Revolutionary period of the Terror.

Common law Laws that arise from customary use rather than from legislation.

Common market The European Economic Community, a union of Western European nations initiated in 1957 to promote common economic policies.

Commonwealth of Independent States A loose confederation of several former republics of the disintegrated Soviet Union founded in 1991.

Commune (cómm-yune) A medieval or early modern town; a semi-independent city government or socialistic community in the nineteenth and twentieth centuries.

Communist Manifesto A short, popular treatise written by Karl Marx and Friedrich Engels in 1848 that contained the fundamentals of their "scientific socialism."

Complutensian Polyglot (comm-plue-tén-see-an pólly-glàht) **Bible** An edition of the Bible written in 1520 that had three columns that compared the Hebrew, Greek, and Latin versions.

Compurgation (comm-pur-gáy-shun) A Germanic legal oath taken by twelve men testifying to the character of the accused.

Concert of Europe The alliance of powers after 1815 created to maintain the status quo and coordinate international relations.

Conciliar (conn-síll-ee-ar) **movement** The belief that the Catholic Church should be led by councils of cardinals rather than popes.

Concordat (conn-córe-dat) A formal agreement, especially between the pope and a government, for the regulation of church affairs.

condottieri (conn-duh-tyáy-ree) From the fourteenth to the sixteenth century, captains of bands of mercenary soldiers, influential in Renaissance Italy.

Congress of Vienna The peace conference held between 1814 and 1815 in Vienna after the defeat of Napoleon.

Conquistadors (conn-kéy-stah-doors) Spanish adventurers in the sixteenth century who went to South and Central America to conquer indigenous peoples and claim their lands.

Conservatism An ideology stressing order and traditional values.

Constitutionalism The idea that political authority rests in written law, not in the person of an absolute monarch.

Constitutional monarchy Government in which the monarch's powers are limited by a set of fundamental laws.

Consuls (cónn-sul) The appointed chief executive officers of the Roman Republic.

Containment The Cold War strategy of the United States to limit the expansion and influence of the Soviet Union.

Continental System Napoleon's policy of preventing trade between continental Europe and Great Britain.

Contra posto (cón-tra páh-sto) A stance of the human body in which one leg bears weight, while the other is relaxed. Also known as counterpoise, it was popular in Renaissance sculpture.

Copernican (co-pér-nick-an) **revolution** The change from an earth-centered to a sun-centered universe initiated by Copernicus in the sixteenth century.

Corinthian order One of three architectural systems developed by the Greeks to decorate their buildings. The Corinthian order is marked by the capitals of columns decorated with acanthus leaves.

Corn Laws British laws that imposed tariffs on grain imports.

Corporate state Mussolini's economic and political machinery to manage the Italian economy and settle issues between labor and management.

Corsair A swift pirate ship.

Cossacks The "free warriors" of southern Russia, noted as cavalrymen.

Cottage industry Handicraft manufacturing usually organized by merchants and performed by rural people in their cottages.

Coup d'état (coo-day-táh) A sudden taking of power that violates constitutional forms by a group of persons in authority.

Creoles (crée-ohlz) People of European descent born in the West Indies or Spanish America, often of mixed ancestry.

Crusades From the late eleventh century through the thirteenth century, Europeans sent a number of military operations to take the Holy Land (Jerusalem and its surrounding territory) from the Muslims. These military ventures in the name of Christendom are collectively called the Crusades.

Cult of sensibility The eighteenth-century emphasis on emotion and nature forwarded by several European artists and authors.

Cuneiform (cue-née-uh-form) A writing system using wedge-shaped characters developed in ancient Mesopotamia.

Curia Regis (kóo-ree-uh régg-ees) A medieval king's advisory body made up of his major vassals.

Cynicism (sín-uh-sism) A Hellenistic philosophy that locates the search for virtue in an utter indifference to worldly needs.

Cyrillic (suh-ríll-ik) **alphabet** An old Slavic alphabet presently used in modified form for Russian and other languages.

D

Dada (dáh-dah) An early twentieth-century artistic movement that attacked traditional cultural styles and stressed the absence of purpose in life.

Dauphin (dough-fán) Heir to the French throne. The title was used from 1349 to 1830.

D-Day The day of the Allied invasion of Normandy in World War II—June 6, 1944.

Decembrists (dee-sém-brists) Russian army officers who briefly rebelled against Tsar Nicholas I in December 1925.

Decolonization The loss of colonies by imperial powers during the years following World War II.

Declaration of the Rights of Man and Citizen France's revolutionary 1789 declaration of rights stressing liberty, equality, and fraternity.

Deductive reasoning Deriving conclusions that logically flow from a premise, reasoning from basic or known truths.

Deism (dée-iz-um) Belief in a God who created the universe and its natural laws but does not intervene further; gained popularity during the Enlightenment.

Demotic A form of ancient Egyptian writing used for ordinary life. A simplified form of hieratic script.

Détente (day-táhnt) The period of relative cooperation between Cold War adversaries during the 1960s and 1970s.

Devotio moderno (day-vóh-tee-oh moh-dáir-noh) A medieval religious movement that emphasized internal spirituality over ritual practices.

Diaspora The dispersion of the Jews after the Babylonian conquest in the sixth century B.C.E. The term comes from the Greek word meaning "to scatter."

Diet The general legislative assembly of certain countries, such as Poland.

Directory The relatively conservative government during the last years of the French Revolution before Napoleon gained power.

Division of labor The division of work in the modern process of industrial production into separate tasks.

Doge (dóhj) The chief magistrate of the Republic of Venice during the Middle Ages and Renaissance.

Domesday (dóomz-day) **Book** A record of all the property and holdings in England, commissioned by William the Conqueror in 1066 so that he could determine the extent of his lands and wealth.

Doric order One of three architectural systems developed by the Greeks to decorate their buildings. The Doric order may be recognized by its columns, which include a wide shaft with a plain capital on the top.

Drachma (dróck-mah) Hellenistic coin containing either 4.3 grams (Alexander's) or 3.5 grams (Egypt's) of silver.

Dreyfus (dry'-fuss) **affair** The political upheaval in France accompanying the unjust 1894 conviction of Jewish army officer Alfred Dreyfus as a German spy that marked the importance of anti-Semitism in France.

Dual Monarchy The Austro-Hungarian Empire; the Habsburg monarchy after the 1867 reform that granted Hungary equality with Austria.

Il Duce (ill dóoch-ay) "The Leader," Mussolini's title as head of the Italian Fascist Party.

Duma Russia's legislative assembly in the years prior to 1917.

E

Ecclesia (ek-cláy-zee-uh) The popular assembly in ancient Athens made up of all male citizens over 18.

Edict of Nantes (náwnt) Edict issued by French king Henry IV in 1598 granting rights to Protestants, later revoked by Louis XIV.

Émigrés (em-ee-gráy) People, mostly aristocrats, who fled France during the French Revolution.

Emir (em-éar) A Muslim ruler, prince, or military commander.

Empirical method The use of observation and experiments based on sensory evidence to come to ideas or conclusions about nature.

Ems (Em's) **Dispatch** Telegram from Prussia's head of state to the French government, edited by Bismarck to look like an insult, that helped cause the Franco-Prussian War.

Enclosure Combining separate parcels of farmland and enclosing them with fences and walls to create large farms or pastures that produced for commerce.

encomienda (en-koh-mee-én-da) A form of economic and social organization established in sixteenth-century Spanish settlements in South and Central America. The encomienda system consisted of a royal grant that allowed Spanish settlers to compel indigenous peoples to work for them. In return, Spanish overseers were to look after their workers' welfare and encourage their conversion to Christianity. In reality, it was a brutal system of enforced labor.

Enlightened absolutism (áb-suh-loo-tism) Rule by a strong, "enlightened" ruler applying Enlightenment ideas to government.

Enlightenment An eighteenth-century cultural movement based on the ideas of the Scientific Revolution and that supported the notion that human reason should determine understanding of the world and the rules of social life.

Entente Cordiale (on-táhnt core-dee-áhl) The series of understandings, or agreements, between France and Britain that led to their alliance in World War I.

Entrepreneur (on-truh-pren-óor) A person who organizes and operates business ventures, especially in commerce and industry.

Epic (épp-ik) A long narrative poem celebrating episodes of a people's heroic tradition.

Epicureanism (epp-uh-cúre-ee-an-ism) A Hellenistic philosophy that held that the goal of life should be to live a life of pleasure regulated by moderation.

Equestrians (ee-quést-ree-ans) A social class in ancient Rome who had enough money to begin to challenge the power of the patricians.

Essenes (Ess-éenz) Members of a Jewish sect of ascetics from the second century B.C.E. to the second century C.E.

Estates Representative assemblies, typically made up of either the clergy, the nobility, the commoners, or all three meeting separately.

Estates General The legislature of France from the Middle Ages to 1789. Each of the three Estates—clergy, nobility, and bourgeoisie—sent representatives.

Ethnic cleansing The policy of brutally driving an ethnic group from their homes and from a certain territory, particularly prominent during the civil wars in the Balkans during the 1990s.

Eugenics (you-génn-iks) The study of hereditary improvement.

Euro (yóu-roe) The common currency of many European states, established in 1999.

Eurocommunism The policy of Western European Communist parties of supporting moderate policies and cooperating with other Leftist parties during the 1970s and 1980s.

European Economic Community The E.E.C., or Common Market, founded in 1957 to eliminate tariff barriers and begin to integrate the economies of western European nations.

European Union (EU) The community of European nations that continued to take steps toward the full economic union of much of Europe during the late twentieth century.

Evolution Darwin's theory of biological development through adaptation.

Existentialism (ekk-siss-ténn-sha-lism) A twentieth-century philosophy asserting that individuals are responsible for their own values and meanings in an indifferent universe.

Expressionism A late-nineteenth- and early-twentieth-century artistic style that emphasized the objective expression of inner experience through the use of conventional characters and symbols.

F

Fabian (fáy-bee-an) **Society** A late-nineteenth-century group of British intellectuals that advocated the adoption of socialist policies through politics rather than revolution.

Factory system Many workers producing goods in a repetitive series of steps and specialized tasks using powerful machines.

Falange (fa-láhn-hey) A Spanish fascist party that supported Francisco Franco during the Spanish civil war.

Fascism (fáh-shism) A philosophy or system of government that advocates a dictatorship of the extreme right together with an ideology of belligerent nationalism.

Fealty (fée-al-tee) In the feudal system, a promise made by vassals and lords to do no harm to each other.

Federates In the late Roman Empire, treaties established with many Gothic tribes allowed these tribes to settle within the Empire. The tribes then became "federates," or allies of Rome.

Fibula (pl. fibulae) An ornamented clasp or brooch, favored by the ancient Germanic tribes to hold their great cloaks closed.

Fief (feef) In the feudal system, the portion—usually land—given by lords to vassals to provide for their maintenance in return for their service.

Five-Year Plan The rapid, massive industrialization of the nation under the direction of the state initiated in the Soviet Union in the late 1920s.

Forum The central public place in ancient Rome which served as a meeting place, marketplace, law court, and political arena.

Fourteen Points U.S. President Wilson's plan to settle World War I and guarantee the peace.

Frankfurt Assembly Convention of liberals and nationalists from several German states that met in 1848 to try to form a unified government for Germany.

Free companies Mercenary soldiers in the Middle Ages and Renaissance who would fight for whoever paid them. They were called "free" to distinguish them from warriors who were bound by feudal ties to a lord.

Free Corps (core) Post–World War I German right-wing paramilitary groups made up mostly of veterans.

Free trade International trade of goods without tariffs, or customs duties.

Fresco A technique of painting on the plaster surface of a wall or ceiling while it is still damp so that the colors become fused with the plaster as it dries, making the image part of the building's surface.

Fronde (frawnd) Mid-seventeenth-century upheavals in France that threatened the royal government.

Fundamentalists Those who believe in an extremely conservative interpretation of a religion.

G

Galley A large medieval ship propelled by sails and oars.

General will Rousseau's notion that rules governing society should be based on the best conscience of the people.

Gentry People of "good birth" and superior social position.

Geocentric Earth-centered.

Gerousia (gay-róo-see-uh) Ruling body in ancient Sparta made up of male citizens over age 60.

Gestapo (guh-stóp-po) Nazi secret police in Hitler's Germany.

Girondins (zhee-roan-dán) Moderate political faction among leaders of the French Revolution.

Glasnost (gláz-nost) Soviet leader Gorbachev's policy of political and cultural openness in the 1980s.

Globalization Twentieth-century tendency for cultural and historical development to become increasingly worldwide in scope.

Global warming The heating of the earth's atmosphere in recent decades, caused in part by the buildup of carbon dioxide and other "greenhouse gases" produced by burning fossil fuels.

Glorious Revolution In 1688, English Parliament offered the crown of England to the Protestant William of Orange and his wife Mary, replacing James II. This change in rule was accomplished peacefully and clarified the precedent that England was a constitutional monarchy with power resting in Parliament.

Gosplan The Soviet State Planning Commission, charged with achieving ambitious economic goals.

Gothic (góth-ik) A style of architecture, usually associated with churches, that originated in France and flourished from the twelfth to the sixteenth century. Gothic architecture is identified by pointed arches, ribbed vaults, stained-glass windows, and flying buttresses.

Grand tour An educational travel taken by the wealthy to certain cities and sites, particularly during the seventeenth and eighteenth centuries.

Great Chain of Being A traditional Western-Christian vision of the hierarchical order of the universe.

Great Depression The global economic depression of the 1930s.

Great fear Panic caused by rumors that bands of brigands were on the loose in the French countryside during the summer of 1789.

Great Purges The long period of Communist Party purges in the Soviet Union during the 1930s, marked by terror, house arrests, show-trials, torture, imprisonments, and executions.

Great Reforms Reforms instituted by Russia's tsar Alexander II in 1861 that included freeing Russia's serfs.

Great Schism (skíz-um) Period in the late Middle Ages from 1378 to 1417 when there were two (and at times three) rival popes.

Greek fire A Byzantine naval weapon made of combustible oil that was launched with a catapult or pumped through tubes to set fire to enemy ships.

Guild An association of persons of the same trade united for the furtherance of some purpose.

Guillotine (ghée-oh-teen) A device for executing the condemned used during the French Revolution.

H

Hacienda (ha-see-én-da) Large landed estates in Spanish America that replaced encomiendas as the dominant economic and social structure.

Haj (hodge) The Muslim annual pilgrimage to Mecca, Medina, and other holy sites.

Hasidim (hah-see-déem) Sect of Jewish mystics founded in Poland in the eighteenth century in opposition to the formalistic Judaism and ritual laxity of the period.

Heliocentric (hee-lee-oh-sén-trick) Pertaining to the theory that the sun is the center of the universe.

Hellenes (Héll-eenz) The name ancient Greeks assigned to themselves, based on their belief that they were descended from a mythical King Hellen.

Hellenistic Of or related to the period between the fourth century B.C.E. and the first century B.C.E.

Helot (héll-ots) A serf in ancient Sparta.

Heresy A religious belief that is considered wrong by orthodox church leaders.

Hermetic doctrine Notion popular in the sixteenth and seventeenth centuries that all matter contains the divine spirit.

Hieratic (high-rát-ick) A form of ancient Egyptian writing consisting of abridged forms of hieroglyphics, used by the priests in keeping records.

Hieroglyph (hígh-roe-gliff) A picture or symbol used in the ancient Egyptian writing system—means "sacred writing."

Hijra (hídge-rah) (also *Hegira*) Muhammad's flight from Mecca to Medina in 622 B.C.E.

Holocaust (hóll-o-cost) The extermination of some six million Jews by the Nazis during World War II.

Holy Alliance Alliance of Russia, Austria, and Prussia to safeguard the principles of Christianity and maintain the international status quo after the Napoleonic Wars.

Homeopathy (home-ee-áh-pa-thee) Medical treatment emphasizing the use of herbal drugs and natural remedies.

Hoplites (hóp-lights) Ancient Greek infantrymen equipped with large round shields and long thrusting spears.

Hubris Excessive pride, which for the ancient Greeks brought punishment from the gods.

Huguenots (húgh-guh-nots) French Protestants of the sixteenth, seventeenth, and eighteenth centuries.

Humanists Students of an intellectual movement based on a deep study of classical culture and an emphasis on the humanities (literature, history, and philosophy) as a means for self-improvement.

Hundred Years' War A series of wars between England and France from 1337 to 1453. France won and England lost its lands in France, thus centralizing and solidifying French power.

I

Icon (éye-con) A sacred image of Jesus, Mary, or the saints that early Christians believed contained religious power.

Iconoclasm (eye-cónn-o-claz-um) A term literally meaning "icon breaking" that refers to an eighth-century religious controversy in Byzantium that argued that people should not venerate icons.

Ideogram (eye-dée-o-gram) A hieroglyph symbol expressing an abstract idea associated with the object it portrays.

Ideograph A written symbol that represents an idea instead of expressing the sound of a word.

Ideology (eye-dee-áh-lo-gee) A set of beliefs about the world and how it should be, often formalized into a political, social, or cultural theory.

Imam Muslim spiritual leader, believed by Shi'ites to be a spiritual descendant of Muhammad who should also be a temporal leader.

Imperialism The policy of extending a nation's authority by territorial acquisition or by the establishment of economic and political control over other nations or peoples.

Impressionism A nineteenth-century school of painting originating in France that emphasized capturing on canvas light as the eye sees it.

Indo-European Belonging to or constituting a family of languages that includes the Germanic, Celtic, Italic, Baltic, Slavic, Greek, Armenian, Iranian, and Indic groups.

Inductive reasoning Drawing general conclusions from particular concrete observations.

Indulgence A certificate issued by the papacy that gave people atonement for their sins and reduced their time in purgatory. Usually indulgences were issued for performing a pious act, but during the Reformation, critics accused the popes of selling indulgences to raise money.

Industrial revolution The rapid emergence of modern industrial production during the late eighteenth and nineteenth centuries.

Information revolution A rapid increase in the ability to store and manipulate information accompanying the development of computers during the second half of the twentieth century.

Inquisition A religious court established in the thirteenth century designed to root out heresy by questioning and torture.

Intendant (ann-tawn-dáunt) A French official sent by the royal government to assert the will of the monarch.

Internationalism The principle of cooperation among nations for their common good.

Ionia (eye-ówn-ee-uh) Ancient district in what is now Turkey that comprised the central portion of the west coast of Asia Minor, together with the adjacent islands.

Ionic order One of three architectural systems developed by the Greeks to decorate their buildings. The Ionic order may be recognized by its columns, which are taller and thinner than the Doric columns and capped with scroll-shaped capitals.

Iron Curtain The dividing line between Eastern and Western Europe during the Cold War.

Islamic fundamentalism A movement within Islam calling for a return to traditional ways and a rejection of alien ideologies that gained strength during the second half of the twentieth century.

J

Jacobins (jáck-o-bins) A radical political organization or club during the French Revolution.

Jacquerie (zhak-rée) The name given to the peasant revolt in France during the fourteenth century.

Jansenism A religious movement among French Catholics stressing the emotional experience of religious belief.

Jesuits (jéh-zu-it) Members of the Catholic religious order the Society of Jesus, founded by Ignatius Loyola in 1534.

Jihad (jée-hod) Islamic holy war in which believers feel they have the authority to fight to defend the faith.

Joint-stock company A business firm that is owned by stockholders who may sell or transfer their shares individually.

Journeyman A worker in a craft who has served his or her apprenticeship.

Joust A medieval contest in which two mounted knights combat with lances.

Junkers (yóong-kers) Prussian aristocracy.

Justification by faith The belief that faith alone—not good works—is needed for salvation. This belief lies at the heart of Protestantism.

K

Kamikaze (kah-mih-káh-zee) Usually refers to suicidal attacks on Allied ships by Japanese pilots during World War II.

Kore (kóh-ray) (pl. *korai*) Greek word for maiden that refers to an ancient Greek statue of a standing female, usually clothed.

Kouros (kóo-ross) (pl. *kouroi*) Greek word for a young man that refers to an ancient Greek statue of a standing nude young man.

Kristallnacht (kriss-táhl-nahkt) The "night of the broken glass"—a Nazi attack on German Jewish homes and businesses in 1938.

Kulak (kóo-lock) A relatively wealthy Russian peasant labeled by Stalin during the period of collectivization as a "class enemy."

Kulturkampf (kool-tóur-kahmpf) Bismarck's fight against the Catholic Church in Germany during the 1870s.

L

Laissez-faire (léss-say-fair) "Hands-off." An economic doctrine opposing governmental regulation of most economic affairs.

Laudanum (láud-a-numb) Opium dissolved in alcohol, used as a medicine in the eighteenth and nineteenth centuries.

League of Nations A post–World War I association of countries to deal with international tensions and conflicts.

Lebensraum (láy-benz-rowm) "Living space." Hitler's policy of expanding his empire to the east to gain more land for Germans.

Legume (lég-yoom) A pod, such as that of a pea or bean, used as food.

Levée en masse (le-váy awn máhss) General call-up of all men, women, and children to serve the nation during the French Revolution.

Levellers Revolutionaries who tried to "level" the social hierarchy during the English civil war.

Liberalism A nineteenth- and twentieth-century ideology supporting individualism, political freedom, constitutional government, and (in the nineteenth century) laissez-faire economic policies.

Liege (léezh) **lord** In the feudal system, a lord who has many vassals, but owes allegiance to no one.

Linear perspective An artistic technique used to represent three-dimensional space convincingly on a flat surface.

Lollards Followers of the English church reformer John Wycliffe who were found heretical.

Long March An arduous Chinese communist retreat from south China to north China in 1934 and 1935.

Luddism The smashing of machines that took jobs away from workers in the first half of the nineteenth century.

M

Ma'at (máh-aht) An Egyptian spiritual precept that conveyed the idea of truth and justice, or, as the Egyptians put it, right order and harmony.

Maccabean (mack-uh-bée-en) **Revolt** Successful Jewish revolt led by Judas Maccabeus in the mid-second century B.C.E. against Hellenistic Seleucid rulers.

Madrigal Musical composition set to a short poem usually about love, written for several voices. Common in Renaissance music.

Magi (máyj-eye) Ancient Persian astrologers or "wise men."

Maginot (máh-zhin-oh) **Line** A string of defensive fortresses on the French/German border that France began building in the late 1920s.

Magna Carta The Great Charter that English barons forced King John of England to sign in 1215 that guaranteed certain rights to the English people. Seen as one of the bases for constitutional law.

Marshall Plan A package of massive economic aid to European nations offered in 1947 to strengthen them and tie them to American influence.

Marxism A variety of socialism propounded by Karl Marx stressing economic determinism and class struggle—"scientific socialism."

Megalith An archaeological term for a stone of great size used in ancient monuments.

Meiji (máy-jee) **Restoration** The reorganizing of Japanese society along modern Western lines; initiated in 1868.

Mendicant orders Members of a religious order, such as the Dominicans or Franciscans, who wandered from city to city begging for alms rather than residing in a monastery.

Mercantilism (mírr-kan-till-ism) Early modern governmental economic policies seeking to control and develop the national economy and bring wealth into the national treasury.

Mercator projection (mer-káy-ter) A method of making maps in which the earth's surface is shown as a rectangle with Europe at the center, causing distortion toward the poles.

Mesolithic Of or pertaining to the period of human culture from about 15,000 years ago to about 7000 B.C.E. characterized by complex stone tools and greater social organization. "Middle Stone Age."

Methodism A Protestant sect founded in the eighteenth century that emphasized piety and emotional worship.

Metics (métt-iks) Foreign residents of Athens.

Miasma (my-ázz-ma) Fumes from waste and marshes blamed for carrying diseases during the eighteenth and the first half of the nineteenth centuries.

Middle Passage The long sea voyage between the African coast and the Americas endured by newly captured slaves.

Minoan (mínn-oh-an) A civilization that lived on the island of Crete from 2800 to 1450 B.C.E.

Mir (mere) Russian village commune.

Missi dominici (mée-see do-min-ée-kee) Royal officials under Charlemagne who traveled around the country to enforce the king's laws.

Mithraism (míth-ra-ism) A Hellenistic mystery religion that appealed to soldiers and involved the worship of the god Mithra.

Mughals (móe-gulls) Islamic rulers of much of India in the sixteenth, seventeenth, and eighteenth centuries.

Munich Conference The 1938 conference where Britain and France attempted to appease Hitler by allowing him to dismantle Czechoslovakia.

Mycenean (my-sen-ée-an) A civilization on the Greek peninsula that reached its high point between 1400 and 1200 B.C.E.

Mystery religions Ancient religions that encouraged believers to cultivate a deep connection with their deity. Initiates swore not to reveal the insights they had gained during rites and ceremonies; the shroud of secrecy resulted in the name "mystery" religions.

N

Napoleonic (na-po-lee-ón-ik) **Code** The legal code introduced in France by Napoleon Bonaparte.

Nationalism A nineteenth- and twentieth-century ideology stressing the importance of national identity and the nation-state.

Natural law Understandable, rational laws of nature that apply to the physical and human world.

Nazi Party Hitler's German National Socialist Party.

Neolithic (nee-oh-líth-ik) Of or denoting a period of human culture beginning around 7000 B.C.E. in the Middle East and later elsewhere, characterized by the invention of farming and the making of technically advanced stone implements. "New Stone Age."

Neoplatonism (nee-oh-pláy-ton-ism) Views based on the ideas of Plato that one should search beyond appearances for true knowledge; stressed abstract reasoning.

New Economic Policy (NEP) Lenin's compromise economic and social policy for the USSR during the 1920s.

New imperialism The second wave of Western imperialism, particularly between 1880 and 1914.

Night of August 4 Surrender of most privileges by the French aristocracy at a meeting held on August 1, 1789.

Nominalism (nóm-in-al-ism) A popular late medieval philosophy based on the doctrine that the universal, or general, has no objective existence or validity, being merely a name expressing the qualities of various objects resembling one another in certain respects. Also called New Nominalism.

North American Free Trade Agreement (NAFTA) The 1994 agreement between the United States, Mexico, and Canada to create a free trade zone.

North Atlantic Treaty Organization (NATO) A military alliance against the Soviet Union initiated in 1949.

Nuremberg Laws Hitler's anti-Jewish laws of 1935.

O

Ockham's razor A principle that states that between alternative explanations for the same phenomenon, the simplest is always to be preferred.

October Revolution The 1917 Bolshevik revolt and seizure of power in Russia.

Old Regime (re-zhéem) European society before the French Revolution.

Oligarchy (áh-luh-gar-kee) Rule by a small group or by a particular social class—often wealthy middle classes, as in ancient Greek or medieval European cities.

Operation Barbarossa (bar-bar-óh-ssa) The German invasion of the USSR during World War II.

Optimates (ahp-tuh-máht-ays) The nobility of the Roman Empire. Also refers to the political party that supported the nobility. Contrast with the *populares*.

Ordeal An ancient form of trial in which the accused was exposed to physical dangers that were presumed to be harmless if the accused was innocent. Ordeals might include grasping hot pokers, trial by battle, immersion in water, and other similar challenges.

Organization of Petroleum Exporting Countries (OPEC) An Arab-dominated organization of Middle Eastern oil-producing states that became effective during and after the 1970s.

Ostracism (áhs-tra-sism) A political technique of ancient Greece by which people believed to be threats to the city-state were chosen for exile by popular vote.

P

Paleolithic (pay-lee-oh-líth-ik) Of or pertaining to the period of human culture beginning with the earliest chipped stone tools, about 750,000 years ago, until the beginning of the Mesolithic, about 15,000 years ago. "Old Stone Age."

Pantheon (pán-thee-on) A great temple in Rome built in 27 B.C.E. and dedicated to all the gods. In 609 C.E., it was rededicated as a Christian church called Santa Maria Rotunda.

Paris Commune The revolutionary government of the city of Paris, first in the 1790s and then in 1871.

Parlement (parl-máwn) A French court of law during the Old Regime.

Parliament Britain's legislature, including the House of Commons and House of Lords.

Parthenon (párth-uh-non) A famous Doric temple of Athena on the Acropolis in ancient Athens.

Patricians The ancient Roman aristocracy who populated the Senate and were particularly powerful during the Republic.

Pax Romana ("pocks" or "packs" row-máhn-ah) Literally, "Roman Peace." Two hundred years of relative, internal peace within the Roman Empire beginning with the rule of Caesar Augustus.

Peace of Paris The 1919 peace settlement after World War I.

Peers Members of the House of Lords in England.

Perestroika (pair-ess-trói-ka) Gorbachev's policy of "restructuring" the Soviet economy during the 1980s.

Petrine (pée-tryn) **doctrine** The belief that the popes, bishops of Rome, should lead the church because they are the successors of Peter, who many claim was the first bishop of Rome.

Phalanstery (fa-láns-ter-ee) The model commune envisioned by the French utopian socialist Fourier.

Phalanx (fáy-langks) An ancient Greek formation of foot soldiers carrying overlapping shields and long spears.

Pharaoh The title of the rulers of ancient Egypt. Also refers to the household and administration of the rulers.

Pharisees (fáir-uh-sees) Members of an ancient Jewish sect that rigidly observed purity laws, including dietary rules. They also believed in the resurrection of the just and the existence of angels.

Philosophes (fee-low-zóff) Leading French intellectuals of the Enlightenment.

Phonogram A character or symbol used to represent a speech sound used in ancient writing.

Physiocrats (físz-ee-oh-crats) Eighteenth-century French economic thinkers who stressed the importance of agriculture and favored free trade.

Pictogram A picture representing an idea used in ancient writing.

Pietism (píe-uh-tism) An eighteenth-century Protestant movement stressing an emotional commitment to religion.

Plebeians (pleb-ée-an) The members of the urban lower classes in ancient Rome.

Plebiscite (pléb-uh-sight) A direct vote that allows the people to either accept or reject a proposed measure.

Pogrom ('puh-grúhm'; also 'póe-grom') An organized persecution or massacre of Jews, especially in eastern Europe.

Polis (póe-liss) (pl. *poleis* [póe-lease]) An ancient Greek city-state.

Poor Laws Eighteenth- and nineteenth-century British laws enacted to deal with the poor.

Populares (pop-you-lahr-ays) In Roman history, the political party of the common people. Also refers to the people themselves. Contrast with the *optimates*.

Popular Front The political partnership of parties of the Left, particularly in France and Spain, during the 1930s.

positivism A mid-nineteenth-century theory of sociology holding that scientific investigation could discover useful fundamental truths about humans and their societies.

Postindustrial societies Late-twentieth-century societies that moved from manufacturing to services led by professionals, managers, and financiers.

Postmodernism A late-twentieth-century approach to the arts stressing relativism and multiple interpretations.

Pragmatic Sanction The international agreement secured by the Habsburg emperor in the 1730s to ensure that his daughter would succeed him without question.

Prague Spring The brief period of democratic reforms and cultural freedom in Czechoslovakia during 1968.

Predestination Doctrine claiming that since God is all-knowing and all-powerful, he must know in advance who is saved or damned. Therefore, the salvation of any individual is predetermined. This doctrine is emphasized by Calvinists.

Preemptive War War initiated by one side on the justification that another side was on the verge of attack.

Prefect Powerful agents of the central government stationed in France's departments.

Preventive war War initiated by one side on the justification that another side might attack sometime in the future.

Principate (prínce-a-pate) The governmental system of the Roman Empire founded by Octavian (also known as Caesar Augustus).

Privateer An armed private vessel commissioned by a government to attack enemy ships.

Protestant Of or pertaining to any branch of the Christian church excluding Roman Catholicism and Eastern Orthodox.

Psychoanalysis Pioneered by Sigmund Freud, a method of investigating human psychological development and treating emotional disorders.

Ptolemaic (ptah-luh-máy-ik) **system** The traditional medieval earth-centered universe and system of planetary movements.

Ptolemies (ptáh-luh-meez) Hellenistic dynasty that ruled in Egypt from about 300 B.C.E. to about 30 B.C.E.

Purgatory In Roman Catholic theology, a state or place in which those who have died in the grace of God expiate their sins by suffering before they can enter heaven.

Purge Expelling or executing political party members suspected of inefficiency or opposition to party policy.

Puritans In the sixteenth and seventeenth centuries, those who wanted to reform the Church of England by removing all elaborate ceremonies and forms. Many Puritans faced persecution and were forced to flee to the American colonies.

Q

Quadrant An instrument for taking altitude of heavenly bodies.

Quadrivium (quad-rív-ee-um) The medieval school curriculum that studied arithmetic, music, geometry, and astronomy after completion of the trivium.

Quadruple (quad-róo-pull) **Alliance** Alliance of Austria, Prussia, Russia, and France in the years after the Napoleonic Wars to maintain the status quo.

Quietism (quíet-ism) A movement among seventeenth-century Spanish Catholics that emphasized the emotional experience of religious belief.

Qur'an (also Koran) The Muslim holy book recorded in the early seventh century by the prophet Muhammad.

R

Racism Belief that racial differences are important and that some races are superior to others.

Raison d'état (ráy-zawn day-táh) "Reason of state." An eighteenth- and nineteenth-century principle justifying arbitrary or aggressive international behavior.

Rationalism The belief that, through reason, humans can understand the world and solve problems.

Realism A medieval Platonist philosophy that believed that the individual objects we perceive are not real, but merely reflections of universal ideas existing in the mind of God. In the nineteenth century, this referred to a cultural style rejecting romanticism and attempting to examine society as it is.

Realpolitik (ray-áhl-po-lee-teek) The pragmatic politics of power; often a self-interested foreign policy associated with Bismarck.

Redshirts Garibaldi's troops used in the unification of Italy.

Reform Bill of 1832 English electoral reform extending the vote to the middle classes of the new industrial cities.

Reichstag (ríkes-tahg) German legislative assembly.

Reign of Terror The violent period of the French Revolution between 1792 and 1794.

Relativity Einstein's theory that all aspects of the physical universe must be defined in relative terms.

Relics In the Roman Catholic and Greek Orthodox churches, valued remnants of saints or other religious figures. Relics usually are parts of bodies but may also include objects that had touched sacred bodies or that were associated with Jesus or Mary, such as remnants of the True Cross.

Renaissance Literally, "rebirth." The term was coined in Italy in the early fourteenth century to refer to the rebirth of the appreciation of classical (Greek and Roman) literature and values. It also refers to the culture that was born in Italy during that century that ultimately spread throughout Europe.

Resistance movements Underground opposition to occupation forces, especially to German troops in conquered European countries during World War II.

Restoration The conservative regimes in power after the defeat of Napoleon in 1815 that hoped to hold back the forces of change or even turn back the clock to prerevolutionary days.

Risorgimento (ree-sor-jee-mén-toe) A nineteenth-century Italian unification movement.

Rococo (roe-coe-cóe) A style of art developed from the baroque that originated in France during the eighteenth century that emphasized elaborate designs to produce a delicate effect.

Romanesque (Roman-ésk) A style of architecture usually associated with churches built in the eleventh and twelfth centuries and that was inspired by Roman architectural features. Romanesque buildings were massive, with round arches, barrel vaulted ceilings, and dark interiors.

Romanticism A cultural ideology during the first half of the nineteenth century stressing feeling over reason.

Rosetta Stone A tablet of black basalt found in 1799 at Rosetta, Egypt, that contains parallel inscriptions in Greek, ancient Egyptian demotic script, and hieroglyphic characters. The stone provided the key to deciphering ancient Egyptian writing.

Rostra The speaker's platform in the Forum of ancient Rome.

Roundheads Members or supporters of the Parliamentary or Puritan party in England during the English civil war (1642).

Royal absolutism The seventeenth- and eighteenth-century system of elevated royal authority.

S

Sacraments In Christianity, rites that were to bring the individual grace or closeness to God. In Roman Catholicism and Greek Orthodoxy there are seven sacraments: baptism, confirmation, the Eucharist, penance, extreme unction, holy orders, and matrimony. Protestants in general acknowledge only two sacraments: baptism and the Lord's Supper.

Sadducees (sád-juh-sees) Members of an ancient Jewish sect that emphasized worship at the Temple in Jerusalem. They rejected new ideas such as resurrection, insisting on only those ideas that could be found in the Torah.

Saga A medieval Scandinavian story of battles, customs, and legends, narrated in prose and generally telling the traditional history of an important Norse family.

Salon (suh-láhn) Seventeenth- and eighteenth-century social and cultural gatherings of members of the upper and middle classes.

Sans-culottes (sawn-key-lóht) Working-class people of Paris during the French Revolution.

Sarcophagus (sar-kóff-a-gus) A stone coffin.

Satellite states Eastern European states under the control of the Soviet Union during the Cold War.

Satrap (sát-trap) An ancient Persian governor in charge of provinces called "satrapies."

Schlieffen (shléaf-en) **Plan** German military strategy in World War I that called for a holding action against Russia while German forces moved through Belgium to knock out France.

Scholasticism The dominant medieval philosophical and theological movement that applied logic from Aristotle to help understand God's plan. It also refers to the desire to join faith with reason.

Scientific Revolution The new sixteenth- and seventeenth-century methods of investigation and discoveries about nature based on observation and reason rather than tradition and authority.

Scutage (skyóot-ij) Medieval payment in lieu of military service.

Seleucids (se-lóo-sids) Hellenistic dynasty that ruled in Asia from about 300 B.C.E. to about 64 B.C.E.

Semitic (sem-ít-ik) Of or pertaining to any of a group of Caucasoid peoples, chiefly Jews and Arabs, of the eastern Mediterranean area.

Senate, Roman The deliberative body and influential governing council of Rome during the Republic and Empire. Composed of ex-magistrates with lifetime membership, the Senate did not legislate, but conducted foreign policy and warfare and authorized public expenditures.

Septuagint (sep-tu-eh-jint) A Greek translation of the Hebrew scriptures (the Old Testament), so named because it was said to be the work of 72 Palestinian Jews in the third century B.C.E., who completed the work in seventy days.

Serfs Medieval peasants who were personally free, but bound to the land. They owed labor obligations as well as fees.

Shi'ite (shée-ite) **Muslims** Those who accepted only the descendants of 'Ali, Muhammad's son-in-law, as the true rulers. It was not the majority party in Islam but did prevail in some of the Muslim countries.

Shire An English county.

Sinn Fein (shín féign) "Ourselves Alone." An extremist twentieth-century Irish nationalist organization.

Skepticism (skép-ti-cism) The systematic doubting of accepted authorities—especially religious authorities.

Second Reich (rike) German regime founded in 1871 and lasting until the end of World War I.

Sepoy (sée-poy) **Mutiny** The 1857 uprising of Indians against British rule.

Social Darwinism The effort to apply Darwin's biological ideas to social ideas stressing competition and "survival of the fittest."

Socialists Those promoting or practicing the nineteenth- and twentieth-century ideology of socialism, stressing cooperation, community, and public ownership of the means of production.

Socratic method The method of arriving at truth by questioning and disputation.

Solidarity A Polish noncommunist union that became the core of resistance to the communist regime during the 1980s.

Sophists (sóff-ists) Fifth-century B.C.E. Greek philosophers who were condemned for using tricky logic to prove that all things are relative and success alone is important.

Sovereignty (sóv-rin-tee) The source of authority exercised by a state; complete independence and self-government.

Soviet A workers' council during the 1905 and 1917 Russian revolutions and part of the structure of government in the Soviet Union.

SS The Schutzstaffel, Hitler's elite party troops of the 1930s and 1940s.

Stadholder (stáhd-holder) A governor of provinces in the Dutch United Provinces.

Statutory law Laws established by a king or legislative body. Contrast with common law.

Stoicism (stów-i-cism) A Hellenistic philosophy that advocated detachment from the material world and an indifference to pain.

Strategoi (stra-táy-goy) Generals in ancient Athens who eventually took a great deal of political power.

Struggle of the Orders The political strife between patrician and plebeian Romans beginning in the fifth century B.C.E. The plebeians gradually won political rights as a result of the struggle.

Sturm und drang (shtúrm unt dráhng) "Storm and stress." A literary movement in late eighteenth-century Germany.

Sumptuary (súmp-chew-air-ee) **laws** Laws restricting or regulating extravagance (for example, in food or dress), often used to maintain separation of social classes.

Sunna (sóon-a) A collection of sayings and traditions of the prophet Muhammad that delineates the customs adhered to by Muslims.

Supply and demand Adam Smith's liberal economic doctrine that demand for goods and services will stimulate production (supply) in a free-market system.

Surrealism (sur-rée-a-lism) A twentieth-century literary and artistic style stressing images from the unconscious mind.

Symphony A long sonata for orchestra.

Syncretism (sín-cre-tism) The attempt or tendency to combine or reconcile differing beliefs, as in philosophy or religion.

Syndicalism (sín-di-cal-ism) A late-nineteenth-century anarchist ideology envisioning labor unions as the center of a free and just society.

T

Taliban The strict, fundamentalist Islamic regime that ruled most of Afghanistan from 1996 to 2001.

Tennis Court Oath Oath taken by members of the French Estates General not to dissolve until they had created a constitution for France.

Tetradrachma (tet-ra-drák-ma) Hellenistic coin worth four drachmas.

Tetrarchy (tét-rar-key) The governmental system of the Roman Empire founded by Diocletian that divided the empire into four administrative units.

Theocracy (thee-áh-kruh-see) Government by priests claiming to rule by divine authority.

Theme A division for the purpose of provincial administration in the Byzantine Empire.

Thermidorian (ther-mi-dór-ee-an) **Reaction** The overthrow of Robespierre and the radicals in July 1794, during the French Revolution.

Third Estate Commoners, or all people except the nobility and clergy, in early modern European society.

Third French Republic The republican government established in 1871 and lasting until Germany's defeat of France in 1940.

Torah (tór-uh) The first five books of the Jewish sacred scriptures, comprising Genesis, Exodus, Leviticus, Numbers, and Deuteronomy.

Tories A conservative British political party during the eighteenth and nineteenth centuries.

Totalitarianism A twentieth-century form of authoritarian government using force, technology, and bureaucracy to effect rule by a single party and controlling most aspects of the lives of the population.

Total war A form of warfare in which all the forces and segments of society are mobilized for a long, all-out struggle.

Transubstantiation (trán-sub-stan-chee-áy-shun) In the Roman Catholic and Greek Orthodox churches, the belief that the bread and wine of the Eucharist were transformed into the actual body and blood of Christ.

Trench warfare An almost stagnant form of defensive warfare fought from trenches.

Triangular trade Trade pattern between European nations and their colonies by which European manufactured goods were traded for raw materials (such as agricultural products) from the Americas or slaves from Africa.

Tribune An official of ancient Rome chosen by the common people to protect their rights.

Triple Alliance Alliance of Germany, Austria-Hungary, and Italy in the years before World War I.

Triumvirate (try-úm-vir-ate) A group of three men sharing civil authority, as in ancient Rome.

Trivium (trív-ee-um) The basic medieval curriculum that studied grammar, rhetoric, and logic; after completion, students could proceed to the quadrivium.

Troubadour (tróo-buh-door) Poets from the late twelfth and early thirteenth centuries who wrote love poems, meant to be sung to music, that reflected the new sensibility of courtly love, which claimed that lovers were ennobled.

Truman Doctrine U.S. policy initiated in 1947 that offered military and economic aid to countries threatened by a communist takeover with the intention of creating a military ring of containment around the Soviet Union and its satellite states.

Tsar The emperor of Russia.

Twelve Tables According to ancient Roman tradition, popular pressure in the fifth century B.C.E. led to the writing down of traditional laws to put an end to patrician monopoly of the laws. The resulting compilation—the Twelve Tables—was seen as the starting point for the tradition of Roman law.

U

Ultra-royalism The nineteenth-century belief in rule by a monarch and that everything about the French Revolution and Enlightenment was contrary to religion, order, and civilization.

Unconscious According to Freud, that part of the mind of which we are not aware; home of basic drives.

Unilateralism Actions or policies taken by one nation in its own interests regardless of the views and interests of its allies.

United Nations (UN) An international organization founded in 1945 to promote peace and cooperation.

Universal A metaphysical entity that does not change, but that describes particular things on earth—for example, "justice" or "beauty." Explained by the ancient Greeks and examined by subsequent philosophers. (Also called "forms" or "ideas.")

Utilitarianism (you-till-a-táre-ee-an-ism) A nineteenth-century liberal philosophy that evaluated institutions on the basis of social usefulness to achieve "the greatest happiness of the greatest number."

Utopian (you-tópe-ee-an) **socialism** A form of early nineteenth-century socialism urging cooperation and communes rather than competition and individualism.

V

Vassal In the feudal system, a noble who binds himself to his lord in return for maintenance.

Versailles (ver-sígh) **treaty** Peace treaty between the Allies and Germany following World War I.

Victorian Referring to the period of Queen Victoria's reign in Britain, 1837–1901.

Vulgate (vúll-gate) A version of the Latin Bible, primarily translated from Hebrew and Greek by Jerome.

W

Wahhabism (wuh-háh-biz-uhm) An Islamic reform movement founded in the eighteenth century that stressed a strict, literal interpretation of the Qur'an.

War guilt clause Article 231 of the Treaty of Versailles that places all blame on Germany for causing World War I.

Warsaw Pact A military alliance in Eastern Europe controlled by the Soviet Union and initiated in 1955.

Waterloo Site in Belgium of a decisive defeat of Napoleon in 1815.

Weimar (wy'e-mar) **Republic** The liberal German government established at the end of World War I and destroyed by Hitler in the 1930s.

Welfare state Governmental programs to protect citizens from severe economic hardships and to provide basic social needs.

Wergeld (véhr-gelt) In Germanic law, the relative price of individuals that established the fee for compensation in case of injury.

Whigs A British political party during the eighteenth and nineteenth centuries.

Witan The ancient Anglo-Saxon men who participated in the Witenagemot.

Witenagemot (wí-ten-uh-guh-mote) Ancient Anglo-Saxon assembly of nobles.

Z

Zealots (zéll-ets) An ancient Jewish sect arising in Palestine in about 6 C.E. that militantly opposed Roman rule and desired to establish an independent Jewish state. The sect was wiped out when the Romans destroyed Jerusalem in 70 C.E.

Zemstva (zémst-fah) Municipal councils established in Russia in the second half of the nineteenth century.

Ziggurat (zíg-gur-raht) A pyramid-shaped Mesopotamian temple.

Zionism A late-nineteenth- and twentieth-century Jewish nationalist movement to create an independent state for Jews in Palestine.

Zollverein (tsóll-ver-rhine) Nineteenth-century German customs union headed by Prussia.

Zoroastrianism (zorro-áss-tree-an-ism) An ancient Persian religion that had a belief in two gods: a god of light named Ahura Mazda and an evil god named Ahriman.